THE NORTH AFRICAN CAMPAIGN
1940-1943

P. C. BHARUCHA
MAJOR

Published by

The Naval & Military Press Ltd
Unit 5 Riverside, Brambleside
Bellbrook Industrial Estate
Uckfield, East Sussex
TN22 1QQ England

Tel: +44 (0)1825 749494

www.naval-military-press.com
www.nmarchive.com

In reprinting in facsimile from the original, any imperfections are inevitably reproduced and the quality may fall short of modern type and cartographic standards.

OFFICIAL HISTORY OF THE INDIAN ARMED FORCES
IN THE SECOND WORLD WAR
1939-45

Campaigns in the Western Theatre

**THE NORTH AFRICAN CAMPAIGN
1940-43**

The Naval & Military Press Ltd

TO ALL WHO SERVED

ADVISORY COMMITTEE

Chairman
SECRETARY, MINISTRY OF DEFENCE, INDIA

Members
DR TARA CHAND
DR S. N. SEN
PROF K. A. NILAKANTA SASTRI
PROF MOHAMMAD HABIB
DR R. C. MAJUMDAR
LIEUT.-GEN. SIR DUDLEY RUSSELL
LIEUT.-GEN. K. S. THIMAYYA
LIEUT.-GEN. S. P. P. THORAT
MILITARY ADVISER TO THE HIGH COMMISSIONER FOR PAKISTAN IN INDIA

Secretary
DR BISHESHWAR PRASAD

CAMPAIGNS IN THE WESTERN THEATRE

    North African Campaign 1940-43

    East African Campaign

    Iraq and Syria

    Iran and Paiforce

    Campaigns in Italy

    Operations in Greece

PREFACE

Two volumes of the Official History of the Indian Armed Forces in the Second World War have appeared earlier. Both the volumes related to the campaigns in Burma, and narrated the fighting on the eastern border of India. In the present volume the scene shifts to the northern coast of Africa and the desert land to the west of Egypt, where the Commonwealth forces were locked in a grim struggle with the Axis forces for the security of the Mediterranean and the Middle East. India was saddled with the responsibility for the defence of Egypt and, when the Second World War began, land forces to the strength of a brigade were sent to the Nile delta. With the commencement of Italian offensive in the Western Desert, more Indian troops were sent to fight the Axis, so that not less than two Indian divisions were constantly involved in the fighting in Africa. This volume narrates the story of the successive campaigns in the region spreading from Egypt to Tunis, where the Italian armies suffered their doom and the German Panzer divisions failed to break the British will to fight. It is a story of three years of war, 1940 to 1943, in which Italy was knocked out of the ring and Germany had her first reverses which paved the way for the ultimate disaster of Hitler's schemes. In these campaigns, the Indian forces, being part of the Middle East forces and the Eighth Army, played their part creditably and gained experience of immense value in desert warfare.

The Government of India had set up an organisation before the conclusion of the Second World War to collect and collate material for the writing of the history of operations in which Indian forces had participated. This organisation grew into the War Department Historical Section, which, on the partition of India, was renamed the Combined Inter-Services Historical Section, India and Pakistan, and both the governments agreed to continue it as their joint venture. This Section was commissioned to produce a history of military operations and organisational activities relating to war, which was to serve as an authoritative reference work for the students of military history and a written monument to the achievements of the Indian forces who served in the last war.

This history has been planned to appear in about twenty volumes divided into three series, viz., the campaigns in the western theatre; the campaigns in the eastern theatre; and the activities pertaining to organisation and administration. The volumes in the first series depict the story of war in North Africa and the Western Desert, East Africa, Iraq and Syria, Iran, Italy and Greece. In the series relating to the eastern theatre are included the volumes dealing with the campaigns in Hong Kong, Malaya, Burma and the Netherlands East Indies. In all these volumes operations have been studied from the inter-service aspect, and every endeavour has been made to bring into full relief the strategic picture and tactical details.

The Historical Section has in its possession an almost complete set of War Diaries and despatches and reports of the commanders in the field. We have been allowed full access to the government records in India, and had the privilege of getting information relating to the campaigns from the War Office in London. But the Government of India was not responsible for the general policy or higher strategy; hence our sources of information for these aspects of the North African campaign have been pre-eminently secondary. We have, however, had the advantage of the comments of the Cabinet Historical Section and the Historical Divisions of New Zealand and Australia, which have helped to eliminate divergences as to facts. Mainly we have depended on the records in our possession, and this history is based on them.

A word may be added here about our view-point. As I had mentioned in the preface of an earlier volume, our endeavour has been to present an accurate narrative of events in the background of the factors and influences which have produced them. These have been viewed objectively, and while at times emphasising the glorious achievements of our troops we have tried to reconstruct the situations in which they fought alongside the British and other Commonwealth forces, whose part has found adequate mention.

This volume has been written by Major P. C. Bharucha, who worked as a Narrator in the Historical Section for nearly seven years. I am indebted to him for his earnest devotion to duty and sincere endeavour to give of his best to a work of this nature. I am also thankful to Mr. P. N. Khera, Narrator, for seeing the book through the press, and to Mr. T. D. Sharma, Cartographer, for preparing the maps and providing illustrations.

This narrative has been shown to some of the commanders who were responsible for the campaigns in North Africa. I am particularly grateful to Field Marshal Viscount Alexander, K.G., G.C.B., G.C.M.G., C.S.I., D.S.O., M.C.; Field Marshal Viscount Montgomery, K.G., G.C.B., D.S.O.; Field Marshal Sir Claude J. E. Auchinleck, G.C.B., G.C.I.E., C.S.I., D.S.O., O.B.E., A.D.C.; General Sir Neil Ritchie; General Sir Frank Messervy, K.C.S.I., K.B.E., C.B., D.S.O.,; Lt.-General Sir Noel Beresford-Peirse, K.B.E., C.B., D.S.O.; Lt.-General Sir Philip Neame, V.C., K.B.E., C.B., D.S.O.; Lt.-General Sir Alan

Cunningham, G.C.M.G., K.C.B., D.S.O., M.C.; Lt.-General Sir Harold Briggs; and Brigadier E. W. D. Vaughan, for their comments which have been extremely helpful in clearing many obscure points and resolving doubts. I am also indebted to Brigadier H. B. Latham of the Cabinet Historical Section for reading the script and making suggestions for its improvement. The volume has also been examined by Lt.-General Sir Dudley Russell, K.B.E., C.B., D.S.O., M.C. and Prof. K. A. Nilakanta Sastri, members of the Advisory Committee. This volume has also been examined by a committee appointed by the Pakistan Government and their comments have been very valuable.

In conclusion I must acknowledge the encouragement and co-operation which I have received from the Ministries of Defence of India and Pakistan.

BISHESHWAR PRASAD

December 1955

CONTENTS

	Page
INTRODUCTION	xxiii

CHAPTER

		Page
I.	NORTH AFRICA	1
II.	HISTORICAL AND POLITICAL BACKGROUND	14
III.	STRATEGIC BACKGROUND	22
IV.	INDIAN TROOPS IN NORTH AFRICA	30
V.	WAR APPROACHES MIDDLE EAST	40
VI.	ITALY DECLARES WAR	49
VII.	INVASION OF EGYPT	65
VIII.	PLANNING FOR ATTACK	74
IX.	BATTLE OF SIDI BARRANI	87
X.	ADVANCE INTO CYRENAICA	101
XI.	PURSUIT BY THE XIII CORPS	115
XII.	ALLIED RETREAT BEGINS	123
XIII.	THE AXIS STAGE A RETURN	131
XIV.	ADVANCE OF AFRIKA KORPS	144
XV.	APPRECIATION OF THE MEKILI STAND	156
XVI.	END OF THE ALLIED RETREAT	165
XVII.	THE JUNE-OFFENSIVE: OPERATION 'BATTLEAXE'	175
XVIII.	PERIOD OF CONSOLIDATION	189
XIX.	THE PERIOD OF REORGANISATION	199
XX.	OPERATION 'CRUSADER'	210
XXI.	'CRUSADER' BEGINS	221
XXII.	'CRUSADER' IN PROGRESS	236
XXIII.	SUCCESS OF 'CRUSADER'	253
XXIV.	PURSUIT OF THE AFRIKA KORPS	267
XXV.	PURSUIT TO BENGHAZI	278
XXVI.	END OF THE ALLIED ADVANCE	291
XXVII.	ALLIED RETREAT BEGINS	300
XXVIII.	EVACUATION OF BENGHAZI	311
XXIX.	BREAK-THROUGH OF THE 7TH BRIGADE	324
XXX.	WITHDRAWAL TO GAZALA	337
XXXI.	THE STAND AT GAZALA	350
XXXII.	AXIS ATTACK ON THE GAZALA LINE	363
XXXIII.	BATTLE OF BRIDGEHEADS AND 'CAULDRON' OFFENSIVE	374
XXXIV.	BATTLE OF GAZALA LINE	388
XXXV.	ATTACK ON TOBRUK	401
XXXVI.	WITHDRAWAL TO EL ALAMEIN	410

Chapter		Page
XXXVII.	The Battle of Alam El Halfa	429
XXXVIII.	Preparations for Counter-Offensive	443
XXXIX.	The Battle of El Alamein	453
XL.	Pursuit of Axis Forces	464
XLI.	Operations in Tripoli	474
XLII.	The Mareth Line	489
XLIII.	Fall of Tunis	506
Appendices		516
Bibliography		556
Index		558

APPENDICES

APPENDIX A

ORDER OF BATTLE—FORCE 'HERON' (EGYPT) AUGUST 1939.
ORDER OF BATTLE—FORCE 'HAWK' (ADEN).

APPENDIX B

INFANTRY BATTALIONS IN MIDDLE EAST COMMAND ON 3 SEPTEMBER 1939.

APPENDIX C

ARMY COUNCIL INSTRUCTIONS TO THE GENERAL OFFICER COMMANDING-IN-CHIEF IN THE MIDDLE EAST.

APPENDIX D

ITALIAN MEDIUM TANK M 11/39 (11 TONNER).
SPECIFICATIONS OF THE ITALIAN LIGHT TANK L 33/35 (CARRO VELOCE 3 TONNER—C.V. 3.).

APPENDIX E

SOME AXIS BOMBS.

APPENDIX F

ORDER OF BATTLE—TENTH ITALIAN ARMY—SEPTEMBER 1940.

APPENDIX G

ITALIAN DISPOSITIONS WITH LOCATIONS AS KNOWN BY HQ WDF BEFORE OPERATIONS BEGAN.

APPENDIX H

ADVANCE TO EL AGHEILA (FEBRUARY 1941).

APPENDIX J

ORDER OF BATTLE—'CYRCOM' (31 March 1941).

APPENDIX K

ORDER OF BATTLE—FORCE 'ASSURANCE'.

APPENDIX L

DIAGRAM OF FORMATION OF THE ADVANCE OF ESCARPMENT FORCE FROM SOFAFI TO ALAM BATTUMA, (14/15 June 1941).

APPENDIX M

THE FOURTEEN ALLIED LANDING GROUNDS IN CHARGE OF 4 IND. DIV. (April-May 1941).

APPENDIX N

ORDER OF BATTLE AND ORGANISATION OF THE ESCARPMENT & COAST FORCES.

APPENDIX P

LOCATION OF PRINCIPAL UNITS IN THE BAQQUSH BOX (18-30 June 1941).

APPENDIX Q

4TH INDIAN DIVISION—ORDER OF BATTLE AND GROUPING—18 November 1941.

APPENDIX R

SUMMARY OF CASUALTIES IN THE 4TH INDIAN DIVISION (November—December 1941).

APPENDIX S

SUMMARY OF TOTAL CASUALTIES OF THE 4TH INDIAN DIVISION (18 November 1941—28 February 1942).

APPENDIX T

THE 18TH INDIAN INFANTRY BRIGADE AT DEIR EL SHEIN (28 June 1942—2 July 1942).

APPENDIX U

5TH INDIAN DIVISION AT RUWEISAT RIDGE (18 July 1942).

APPENDIX V

ALLIED AND AXIS FORCES—August 1942.

MAPS

	Page
Example of a desert formation for an Infantry Brigade	11
Example of a desert formation for an Infantry Battalion	13
Mena-Garawla-Naghamish Area. Move of the 4th Indian Division, 19-21 August 1940	50
Movement of the 4th Indian Division from Mena to Naghamish, 19-21 August 1940	53
Egypt-Libya. The Egyptian frontier showing the Italian wire fence.	57
Italian positions, August 1940	61
Sidi Barrani	75
Dumping Area, 10 November 1940	78
The Bardia Perimeter, August/September 1940, showing Italian fortifications	103
Allied attack on Bardia, 3-5 January 1941	105
Giarabub, Siwa and Kufra Oases	127
Area of Allied retreat, 31 March to 8 April 1941 (Benghazi—Tobruk)	139
3rd Indian Motor Brigade's action at Mekili on 8 April 1941	145
Mekili Area, showing junction of desert tracks	149
Egypt and Cyrenaica (Tobruk area) showing coastal and desert communications	249
Jebel Akhdar	279
Axis offensive, January 1942, converging moves on Benghazi	312
Egypt and Cyrenaica (ZT Msus area) showing desert communications	314
Egypt and Cyrenaica (Antelat area) showing desert communications	315
Africa (Benghazi—Augila Area)	321
Egypt and Cyrenaica (Gazala area) showing coastal and desert communications	336
Southern end of the Gazala Line, 26-27 May 1942	376
18th Indian Infantry Brigade at Deir el Shein	419
Benghazi-Tobruk Area	465
Misurata Area	476
Tripoli Area	480
Gabes Area	490
Tunis Area	507
Operational Area (Alam Halfa)	553

	Facing Page
The Mediterranean with Europe, Middle East and North Africa	21
The alternative route to Egypt via the Persian Gulf and Palestine	29
Battle of Sidi Barrani, 9-11 December 1940	87
Attack on Tobruk, 19-21 January 1941	101
Withdrawal of 4 Ind. Div. through the 10 Defensive Lines, January 1942	339
Tobruk: Axis Assault, 20-21 June 1942 (Sketch 1)	393
Tobruk: Axis Assault, 20-21 June 1942 (Sketch 2)	397
Tobruk: Axis Assault, 20-21 June 1942 (Sketch 3)	401
Africa (Alexandria—Tobruk Area) Communications—Coastal and Interior	405
Tobruk: Axis Assault, 20-21 June 1942 (Sketch 4)	409
Eye Sketch of 29th Ind. Inf. Bde. position at Fuka	415
5th Indian Division at Ruweisat Ridge, 18 July 1942	421
Dispositions on El Alamein front, 9 September 1942	425
North Africa (General Map)	*At the end*

ILLUSTRATIONS

	Facing Page
Dashing forward	116
Bulldozer at work	116
Indian troops in trenches	117
A machine-gun post	117
Major (later General) Maharaj Shri Rajendrasinhji	154
Major General Sir Frank W. Messervy	154
Major-General N. M. de la P. Beresford Peirse	155
Lt. General A. G. O. M. Mayne	155
General Sir Archibald P. Wavell	204
General Sir Claude J. Auchinleck	204
Indian Sappers and Miners building bridge in Nile Delta, October 1941	205
Oasis of Siwa	205
To the battle of Jalo	212
Derna in ruins—Captured, December 1941	212
Benghazi captured, February 1942	213
After the capture of Benghazi	213
Indian Truck drivers studying maps—Western Desert	224
In trenches—Western Desert, November 1941	224
Indians guarding an aerodrome, Western Desert, September 1941	225
Italians and Germans taken prisoners, November 1941	225
The Halfaya Pass, Egypt, February 1942	346
The 4th Indian Division's troops in Western Desert	346
Subedar (Later Sub-Major) Lalbahadur Thapa of 1/2nd Gurkha Rifles, VC	347
Laying the railway track in the desert, March 1942	347
Company Havildar-Major Chhelu Ram of 4/6th Rajputana Rifles, VC	352
Moving through the Desert, 4th Indian Division	352
The 4th Indian Division in action, March 1942	353
Indian troops advancing—Western Desert	353
Around El Alamein	412
Attacking in the desert, July 1942	412
Indian Light Armoured Squadron patrolling the desert, July 1942	413
General Alexander inspecting Indian troops in Egypt, September 1942	413

	Facing Page
General Sir Harold Alexander	430
Major-General F. I. S. Tuker	430
On Ruweisat Ridge	431
Indian troops re-enter Mersa Matruh	431
Field Marshal Viscount Montgomery	468
"We enter Benghazi again"	468
The 4th Indian Division moving into Mersa Matruh	469
Berta-Cyrenaica, March 1943	469
Jawans of the 16th Punjab Regiment during the battle of Wadi Akarit, April 1943	504
Indian troops attacking Wadi Akarit area, April 1943	504
The 4th Indian Division advancing through a Tunisian town, April 1943	505
Indian Sappers clearing mines in Tunisia, May 1943	505
The battle of Enfidaville, 4th Indian Division, May 1943	512
Benghazi	512
The King Emperor with Indian troops in Tunisia, 1943	513
Capture of General von Arnim, Tunisia, May 1943	513

Abbreviations

AA	Anti-Aircraft.
ACV	Armoured Command Vehicle.
AFVs	Armoured Fighting Vehicles.
Armd.	Armoured.
BORs	British Other Ranks.
BTE	British Troops in Egypt.
CCNN	Camicie Nere or Italian Blackshirt.
CHM	Company Havildar-Major.
CIH	Central India Horse.
CO	Commanding Officer.
CRE	Commander Royal Engineers.
CYRCOM	Cyrenaica Command.
D DAY	The day on which an operation is planned to begin. Subsequent days are referred to as D plus 1, D plus 2, *et seq.*
FF	Frontier Force.
HE	High Explosive.
HQ	Headquarters.
IAOC	Indian Army Ordnance Corps.
IE	Indian Engineers.
IORs	Indian Other Ranks.
KEO	King Edward's Own.
LAD	Light Aid Detachment.
LMG	Light Machine Gun.
L of C	Line of Communication.
MT	Mechanical Transport.
NCE	Non-Combatant Enrolled.
NZ	New Zealand.
OETA	Occupied Enemy Territory Administration.
PAVO	Prince Albert Victor's Own.
RA	Royal Artillery.
RAF	Royal Air Force.
RASC	Royal Army Service Corps.
RHA (AT)	Royal Horse Artillery (Animal Transport).
RIASC	Royal Indian Army Service Corps.
RTR	Royal Tank Regiment.
SM	Sappers & Miners
VCOs	Viceroy's Commissioned Officers.
WD	War Diary.
W/T	Wireless Telegraphy.

INTRODUCTION

The Second World War excited little concern in its early months in Western Europe, but before the spring of 1940 was over, German forces had overrun the lands to the west of the Rhine and had almost reached the Atlantic coast. Holland, Belgium and France were knocked out, one by one, in quick succession, and the British Expeditionary Force was compelled to beat a hasty retreat to the British Isles. Dunkirk struck a severe blow to the prestige of England, no less than to her armed strength. The sacrifice was costly, but that fortified the resolve of the British people to fight the Nazi arms, and not only make their land safe from German encroachment but also to liberate Europe from under the heels of the Dictator. The retirement of France from the conflict became final when the Vichy Government was formed. Hitler's plans were next directed to the elimination of England from the war, either by peaceful approach or, on its failure, by an all-out invasion of the island kingdom which might otherwise operate as a base for Anglo-American opposition to his control of Europe. Hitler was fully aware of the dubious attitude of Soviet Russia, as also of the benign goodwill of the United States for the British. He was naturally keen to avoid war on two fronts; and while, initially, he had contrived to keep Russia out of the war, in 1940 he strove to exclude the United Kingdom from the European conflict. Determined British resistance in the Battle of Britain, however, frustrated his plans in the west. He had also failed to bring Japan into the fight, which was an essential plank of his diplomacy to keep the United States out of the war and force Soviet Russia to fight on two fronts. But all this time the spectre of Russian hostility was growing, and Hitler was being led willy nilly into the inevitable fight on the two fronts. The United States also was increasing her material assistance to the United Kingdom and the day was not far when any incident might induce her to enter the lists against the Axis Powers.

While Hitler was anxious to limit the zone of war, his ally and confederate Mussolini found in France's defeat an opportunity to extend his African empire and make himself the sole master of the southern Mediterranean coast, as well as to hold the Suez Canal and the Red Sea area. The prize was too alluring to be missed, particularly when there was the prospect of repeating the achievements of the ancient Roman Emperors. Originally Mussolini had kept out of the war, but when France was defeated he declared war on England, and hoped to exploit Britain's predicament at home to end her empire abroad and dispel her political influence from Somaliland, Kenya and Egypt. The paucity of British forces in the Middle East and the difficulties in their early reinforcement encouraged the Italian Dictator to launch an attack against Egypt, which he expected to conquer ere long. The Italian forces in North Africa, in sheer weight of numbers, were stupendous and were commanded by Marshal Graziani. But the dilatoriness of the move to the Egyptian frontier and long delays on the border itself before embarking on the attack, afforded a respite to the British Middle East Command who received some reinforcements. The disparity between the opposing forces, though great in numbers, was, nevertheless, counter-balanced by the dash and initiative of the British troops which were in sharp contrast to the complete apathy of the Italian soldier and his alacrity to seek riddance from war by mass surrenders.

It may be pertinent here to examine the place of this Italian adventure in North Africa in the Axis strategy and assess its value for Hitler in the realisation of his grand objects. It is clear from Hitler's moves in 1940 that he was keen to limit the zone of war and deal with his enemies one by one. Though not very prominent, his intention to fight Russia is dimly outlined, but, at this stage, in his order of priority the elimination of the British from the lists was number one. Not till the western enemy had been knocked out, did he wish to invite the eastern adversary to a challenge of arms. Therefore he wished to avoid any complications in the Balkans which might afford Russia an excuse for hostility. Italian ambitions knew no limit, and as the sequence clearly showed, Mussolini was eager to extend his empire over Greece and its neighbourhood. Hitler's strategy at this time embraced involving Spain in the war which might be practicable only by giving Franco a portion of the French African empire. But the agreement with the Vichy Government and Italian aggressiveness in North Africa prevented the fruition of that policy. Moreover, at a moment when a few divisions might turn the balance, Hitler needed not only all his forces in the west but also Italian armies to defeat the British in their island. Mussolini's adventure, therefore, not merely deprived Hitler of the much needed Italian forces but had the effect later of diverting his own best divisions to the North African plains, for fighting in Italy when the fullest concentration of forces was necessary to fight Russia or push back the Anglo-American invasion of the European mainland.

This result followed from the weakness of Italy and the half-hearted fighting put up by her armed forces. But if the Italian adventure had succeeded, the advantages to Axis strategy might have been immense. The Mediterranean would have been completely barred out to the British, their support to the anti-Axis

Balkan states would have been frustrated, and Turkey might have been compelled to fall into the Axis camp. In consequence, Germany would have been enabled to strike against the Middle East, dominate Iraq and Iran, control Egypt and Palestine, and thereby be in a position to attack Russia in the under-belly, and also invade India by way of Iran. The advantage to the Axis was great, as also the corresponding danger to the British Empire. The possibilities inherent in the loss of Egypt to the Axis, which were so evident to the British Prime Minister, led Mr. Churchill to spare forces and equipment for the African war, even at a time when Britain herself was face to face with serious invasion threats, or when later the American and Russian opinion was emphatically for opening a Second Front in western Europe and concentrating all war effort in that theatre. To the British, the loss of Egypt or defeat in North Africa would be a serious blow to their world position; hence they were keen to maintain their grip on the Mediterranean, and keep the Suez Canal open.

The British had envisaged the possibility of Italian entry into the war, but not before the French collapse did they realise that they would be compelled to fight the enemy in Africa single-handed. The task was immense and the resources initially were not large. It was not the defence of Egypt alone but with it was involved the defence of Malta, Cyprus, British Somaliland, Kenya and Palestine and the Near East. Britain was unable to spare enough forces for such a huge undertaking; but fortunately, communications with the east held out and reinforcements in men and supplies poured forth from India, Australia and New Zealand. It was also possible occasionally to break through the blockade in the Mediterranean and bring much needed equipment to Egypt. American supplies were also coming in, in an unending stream, by way of the east. By all these means, the problem of building up a force in North Africa to counteract the Axis aggression was gradually solved. And in the last stages when American forces had also landed on the western coast of Africa, the Allied forces had considerable numerical superiority, which enabled them to expel the hostile forces from Africa and launch the invasion of Europe by way of the Italian peninsula.

The campaign in North Africa had three well marked phases, each associated with a separate Commander-in-Chief. In the first stage General Wavell, as the Commander-in-Chief of the Middle East Command, found himself surrounded by overwhelming Italian forces both to the west of Egypt and in East Africa, at a time when the build up of his forces was not complete and the United Kingdom was unable, owing to the Blitzkrieg, to spare either men or equipment. The strategic importance of Egypt with the Suez Canal called for determined effort to save this land from falling under

Italian subjection. And that General Wavell achieved. The Italian forces were held back in the Western Desert and even compelled to beat a retreat into Cyrenaica with heavy losses. But the most remarkable achievement came in East Africa, where within a few months the two Indian divisions, 4th and 5th, had routed the Italian forces, cleared Eritrea of them and occupied the famous fortress of Keren. In the east the danger had now disappeared and the Red Sea and the shores of the Arabian Sea were free from Italian incubus. The long streams of Italian prisoners of war, so evident both in West and East Africa, and the routing of armies exhibited the decaying morale of the Italians and gave promise of ultimate security of the Allied forces in that region. General Wavell had, however, failed to push forth his advantage in the west, as the diversion in Greece dissipated his meagre forces, but his success brought the German Afrika Korps, under General Rommel, into the balance which soon tilted against him. The German General counter-attacked two months earlier than anticipated and, before April 1941 was out, he was on the borders of Egypt. A new element had entered the stage, and henceforth in Africa it was no longer the problem of fighting the effete Italian fascists, but fighting the Germans—a phase of global war.

Two Indian divisions were actively associated with the fighting in this first phase. But largely their field of action was in East Africa, though some brigades had been involved in the push westwards and retreat from Cyrenaica. The spirit displayed by the 3rd Indian Motor Brigade in making its gallant stand at Mekili and refusing to surrender infused the other troops with the resolve to fight and beat the 'invincible' German.

The second phase found General Auchinleck as the Commander-in-Chief and saw some of the hardest and most desperate fighting. A counter-offensive was planned (Operation 'Crusader') in which the 4th Indian Division, fresh from its laurels in East Africa, participated. The fighting at Sidi Rezegh was a battle of armour on either side, in which Rommel had the advantage. He tried to disrupt the rear of the British Eighth Army and his tanks were only 50 miles from the Allied railhead in Egypt. But that was the end of the German advance, for immediately after Tobruk was relieved, the Axis forces were pushed back and pursued westwards up to El Agheila. However, General Auchinleck's offensive lost force and General Rommel retaliated by forcing the Eighth Army to retreat to the Egyptian frontier. The Indian division was involved in some heavy fighting. The Allies came as far back as Alamein where they dug themselves in. Thus ended the second phase of the campaign which had assumed the form of a swing, either party reaching a point and then going back to the base.

The third phase commenced with the opening of the battle of Alamein on 23 October 1942. The Eighth Army was now fighting in a new mood, and the whole atmosphere was surcharged with the magnetic personality of the new commander, General Montgomery. There was also the new confidence of superiority in arms and the round of successes elsewhere. The Middle East Command was no longer the Cinderella of the Allied war effort but was receiving "mountains of everything"—guns, tanks and divisions. The new American tank was in quality superior to the panzer. All this gave a new confidence and the prospects of superiority over the German Afrika Korps, which was unable to get adequate reinforcements or supplies. General Rommel had been unable to convince his High Command that one more Panzer division in North Africa would turn the scales of war, and in view of the pressing claims of Russia, he failed to get the much needed division in time to enable him to push east of Alamein. Support came to him but only when it was too late to avert the disaster. Alamein was the last stand for the Eighth Army and the instructions were to fight to the last man and the last tank. It was this grim resolve and General Montgomery's skilful tactical deployment, particularly his garrisoning of the Alam el Halfa Ridge, which broke the poignancy of the Axis attack and compelled General Rommel to retreat, leaving his tanks and thousands of men on the battlefield.

The battle of Alamein was the beginning of the end of the North African campaign, for the Afrika Korps, licking the wounds, retreated to Bardia and beyond hotly pursued by the Eighth Army, in which the Indian division took a prominent share. Rommel, then Field Marshal, and reinforced considerably, decided to make a last stand on the Mareth Line, though fully conscious of the impossibility of averting the disaster; but before the final showdown came he had left for Europe and the First Army from the United States had landed in Western Africa. The danger of the Axis forces being sandwiched between the two Allied armies, from the east and the west, had materialised. The Mareth Line was the last battle after which North Africa was freed from the Italo-German military hold, and on its part had become the jumping-off ground for the invasion of Italy and the final liberation of Europe from beneath the iron-heels of the two Dictators.

The North African campaign from the first defeat of the Italians at Sidi Barrani, in their aggressive dash to the Nile Delta, to the final Axis disaster at the Mareth Line, had an important bearing on the fortunes of the Second World War. This campaign lasted over two years and was contemporaneous with the war in Russia, Japanese successes in South-East Asia, the anticipatory campaign in Western Asia—Iraq, Syria and Iran, the Balkan fighting, and the Battle of Britain. It had been commenced by Italy with the object of dissolving the British Empire in Africa and acquiring imperial hold over the Mediterranean coasts. Hitler, against his will and perhaps better judgment, had to intervene when Italian reverses prognosticated the exit of the southern Axis partner from the war; and the Fuhrer had to strengthen the Axis resistance in North Africa by the despatch of Rommel and two Panzer divisions to arrest the progress of the British arms westwards. German entry was for strategic, political and psychological reasons. But the early limited object of saving Cyrenaica and keeping Italy into the war, was soon magnified into a desire to hold the Suez Canal, and that, too, again for strategic reasons. German war plans had embraced the project of a two-pronged move into West Asia, from Egypt in the west and Trans-Caucasia in the east, and then, by exploiting their success in Iraq, moving eastward to India and joining the Japanese forces there. Thus Rommel's success at Alamein would have meant grave embarrassment to the Allied war effort in the east, and might have led to the disruption of the American line of supply to Russia, the establishment of German influence over Iraq and Iran, the control of the Persian Gulf and ultimately the invasion of India. General Auchinleck had well appreciated this danger, and had strengthened British hold over Iraq and Syria; and in Egypt he established the last defensive line at Alamein. Thus what was fought at Alamein was a struggle for world supremacy, on the one side, and security of the British Empire, on the other. North Africa had, therefore, great importance for the United Kingdom and that would explain the obstinate insistence of Mr. Churchill to keep the Middle East Command well stocked with supplies and reinforcement, soon after the initial weaknesses had been revealed and Germany had interposed herself in that continent.

The North African campaign was pre-eminently a campaign of the British Commonwealth; and the British, Indian, Australian, New Zealand and South African forces all joined to form the Eighth Army. India had two divisions, the 4th and 5th Indian Infantry Divisions, besides the 3rd Indian Motor Brigade. In the last stages the 10th Indian Division was also involved in the fight. Numerically, therefore, the Indian share would not be great; but the 4th and 5th Indian Divisions, soon after their victorious exploits in East Africa, joined the Western Desert Force, and at every stage, and perhaps in every major battle, whether in fight or pursuit of the hostile forces, were conspicuously employed, and many of their brigades came under the hottest fire to show their mettle. Their contribution to victory in Africa was great; and as in the security of Egypt lay the safety of India, the part which they played had the effect of keeping the danger away from the borders of India.

The North African campaign was an object lesson in desert warfare as the Burma campaign was in jungle warfare. The technique of war in the desert was peculiar in so far as the battle was one of armour and the strategy that of manoeuvre and hurling of a mass of men and steel at one point. In North Africa, the campaign was confined to the long sector along the coast-line which alone provided good-going where the flanks were covered by the deep sea on one side, and dry desert on the other. The route was along a high escarpment, and all important towns were along the sea. The campaign, therefore, developed into a chase for mastery over this road, and the two opposing forces were playing the game of seesaw, one chasing east up to its eastern edge at Alamein and the other chasing westward up to Tunis. Tanks were the main armour employed and superiority in these gave chances of success. And for that reason petrol and water were the most important items of supply. Artillery, particularly anti-tank guns, came in for good display. Movement determined the fate of engagements. And because of the nature of terrain, the war in Africa was three dimensional in so far as the Navy and Air Force co-operated fully with the Army, in lending greater fire power and bringing supplies. Control over the Mediterranean sea passage determined the fate of the struggle; and as the Germans failed to occupy Malta or use their air power to cripple the Royal Navy, the British forces had ultimate success.

In this campaign was developed the technique of Commandos, Long Range Desert Groups and encirclement, for the vast expanses of the desert provided ample opportunity for the employment of these tactics without being detected. General Auchinleck also developed the system of defended localities, on the model of medieval fortifications, which were sited to hold the hostile forces and prevent their uninterrupted march to the base-line. These defended localities or "boxes" were later adopted in the defence plans of Iraq and India also. Mines and wire provided the fortification wall, and artillery and air force the defensive fire. No hostile force, howsoever mighty, could neglect to leave such positions in its rear or on its sides, and while it was so engaged in clearing these pockets, the other force had the time to tackle it on its own chosen ground.

The African disasters paved the way for the ultimate knock-out of Italy from the war, and provided a base from where the Anglo-American forces might encircle their German enemy and bring about his collapse. The end of European war was thus prepared in the deserts of Egypt, Cyrenaica and Libya. And by liberating the Indian and British forces from the Middle East, the success of the Eighth Army provided means for the defeat of Japan in Burma and the deliverance of India from the eastern invader, as it had prevented the German invasion from the west. Russia also profited by the North African campaign, for as long as Egypt remained with the British the German hordes could not attack her from the south.

CHAPTER I

North Africa

North Africa was an important theatre of operations during the Second World War, where the Indian troops were called upon to fight alongside the Commonwealth forces. The struggle lasted nearly three years, covered an area of over two million square miles and took the form of a series of large-scale offensives which, collectively, have come to be known as the North African campaign. Since the main theatres of fighting in North Africa were Libya and Tunisia, it is also customary to speak of operations in those theatres, separately, as the Libyan and the Tunisian campaigns.

North Africa has never been a political or geographical unit. That name itself is of comparatively recent origin and has not yet attained a standard definition. It is therefore necessary to define the area both geographically and politically and to describe its boundaries.

Geographically, North Africa can be said to be that part of the continent of Africa which lies between the Mediterranean Sea and the 20th parallel north of the Equator. Politically, it is that continuous area of land which contains the political units now known as Egypt, Libya, Tunisia, Algeria and the French and Spanish Moroccos. Accordingly, the boundaries of North Africa would be, on the north the Mediterranean Sea, on the east the Suez Canal and the Red Sea, on the south the Anglo-Egyptian Sudan and French West Africa, and on the west the North Atlantic Ocean.

Military campaigns on land are strictly conditioned by the topography of the country in which they are fought. This is so because it is not always possible to overcome an adversary without first overcoming the physical obstacles that shield or protect him. Thus battles tend to become a struggle against the physical features of a country as much as against the personnel of an adversary's army, and cannot therefore be explained or understood except in the context of those environments. A reference here is, thus, necessary to the physical setting in which were fought the major battles of the North African campaign.

The North African campaign covered the whole of North Africa as defined above, but the participation of the Indian forces was limited only to Egypt, Libya and Tunisia. These countries alone have been dealt with in the geographical description that follows, to which a historical background is added to complete the information. The Anglo-Egyptian Sudan has been omitted as forming a part of the East African campaign; and Algeria and Morocco have been left out as no Indian troops were employed in those countries, whether operationally or otherwise.

Egypt

The greater part of Egypt is a desert. Of its total area of 383,000 square miles, only 13,600 are cultivated wherein live most of the inhabitants. The population is approximately 17,000,000.[1] About two-thirds of these are *fellaheen*—small peasant proprietors or those working as tenant-farmers—while the remainder are mostly town dwellers, living in Alexandria, Cairo and the Canal towns. The most densely populated part of Egypt is the delta of the river Nile, often referred to merely as the Delta. It is the triangular area between Cairo, Alexandria and Port Said and the density of population there is more than a thousand to a square mile—greater than that of Bengal. Cairo is the capital of Egypt, and Alexandria its chief port.

It is usual to speak of Egypt as Upper or Lower Egypt, according to the situation on the upper or lower Nile of the part of the country referred to. Broadly speaking, Lower Egypt is the area of the Delta and Upper Egypt that of the river valley further south. A more precise geographical demarcation is the 30th parallel which passes just south of Cairo. Upper Egypt, lying to the south of this line, is almost entirely in East Africa and is therefore outside the purview of the North African campaign.

As to Lower Egypt, it was never a theatre of active operations. The area of actual fighting in Egypt was that which lay further to the west, in what has come to be known as the Western Desert. During the earlier stages of the North African campaign, Egypt became militarily divided into two parts, one lying to the east of Alexandria and the other to the west. For all practical purposes, the eastern portion, namely Lower Egypt, became the base and line of communications area, and the western portion (the Western Desert) the operational area. In military communications, Lower Egypt used always to be referred to as the Delta.

The most easily noticeable physical feature of Egypt, to the west of Alexandria, is the Libyan Plateau. It is a tableland varying in height from 600 to 1600 feet, to the south-east of which is another tableland of the same height. Between these two heights is a feature of immense military importance which has played a decisive role in the North African campaign. It is known as the Qattara

---

[1] *British Survey*, Vol. VII, No. 8, *Egypt*. The 1950 edition of the *Imperial Military Geography* (D. H. Cole) places the figure at 19,000,000, evidently a post-war estimate.

Depression, a vast area of low-lying ground, consisting almost entirely of earth-and-salt marshes over which no vehicular movement is possible except on the smallest and the most insignificant scale.

Next in importance to the Qattara Depression, and belonging to the same class of obstacles militarily, is another prominent feature of Egypt, the Libyan Sand Sea. It is an enormous expanse of sandy desert, which sprawls east and west over Egypt and Libya, covering most of the hinterland of these two countries. In Egypt, it joins the Qattara Depression on its southern flank. Being as impenetrable and untraversable as the Depression itself, it gives to the latter a depth, which makes the Qattara Depression a vaster obstacle than it might otherwise have been.

The rest of the land in Egypt varies in altitude from sea-level to over 600 feet, which is the general surface level for most of the country including the coastal area.

Libya

The next region to the west of Egypt is Libya. It is a vast country, about a thousand miles long and 750 miles wide on an average, and was the most hotly contested field of operations in the North African campaign. Both historically and administratively, it falls into two divisions. The eastern part is known as Cyrenaica and the western as Tripolitania. The two territories together form a single geographical block which is roughly quadrilateral and contains an area of more than half a million square miles. The greater part of Libya, however, is a sheer desert, relieved occasionally by patches of steppes and oases and by small towns along the coast.[2] The south-western corner of this desert is known as the Fezzan, which, after Cyrenaica and Tripolitania, ranks as the third important division of Libya for purposes of civil and military administration. Its military value, however, is negligible, as it is too far inland to affect military operations, which, in North Africa, took place as near the coast as possible to avoid difficulties of supply and maintenance. Libya flanks the Mediterranean for 1000 miles, from Tunisia to Egypt, but its low coast-line, though rugged and hilly in parts, has few good harbours. The most important towns on the coast having good harbours are Tobruk and Benghazi in Cyrenaica and Tripoli in Tripolitania.

The most prominent elevation of Cyrenaica is the Barka Plateau in the north. It has the same altitude as the Libyan Plateau, except that a portion of it, roughly in the centre, rises to a height of over 2600 feet, culminating in the mountain known as the Jebel Akhdar. Other physical features of Cyrenaica are a continuation

---

[2] *British Survey*, Vol. VII, No. 14, *Italian North Africa*.

of those in Egypt, namely the Libyan Plateau, the Libyan Sand Sea and groups of heights of no particular importance in military operations. It is worth noting that the bulk of what is known as the Libyan Plateau lies outside Libya, in Egypt, and only a slight extension of it appears in the eastern corner of Cyrenaica. The Sand Sea, too, lies almost wholly in Egypt, being therefore also known as the Egyptian Sand Sea. The rest of the country, like Egypt, varies in altitude from the sea-level to over 600 feet.

The physical features of Tripolitania, unlike those of Egypt or Cyrenaica, are marked by a general absence of tablelands or high land-masses. The southern part of the province is an exception to this rule but it is operationally unimportant. The country, however, has a large number of isolated hills or high features, as distinct from the tablelands, some of which rise to 2000 feet or even more. The land is generally undulating and varies from the sea-level to over 600 feet.

Tunisia

The third unit of the North African theatre is Tunisia, which lies west of Libya and differs from it in that it is not a country of dry and arid deserts. Its southern end extends into the world-famous desert of Sahara, but the rest of the land is green and fertile and consists of rich agricultural areas. The country is roughly 300 miles long and 150 wide and has an area of about 48,000 square miles. Among its chief towns, having operational importance, are Tunis, Bizerta, Sfax and Gabes.[3]

In its physical features, Tunisia more or less resembles Tripolitania, except that its isolated heights are closer, more numerous and of greater altitude. Almost the only other important physical feature in Tunisia is a projection of the Algerian highlands into its south-west corner, a feature, the military importance of which was recognised as much by the Romans who built a wall across the Tebaga Gap as by the Germans who defended it against the Eighth Army.

North Africa, a strategic unit

Taken as a whole, North Africa is a compact strategic unit. It has a continuous territory, an integrated system of communications and a uniformity of environments. There are so many characteristics common to the whole of North Africa that it will be well to treat them all together. They are, for instance, the hydrography, the typical desert conditions, the coast-line and communications and other points common to all the North African countries.

[3] Whitaker's *Almanac*, 1945; *Enc. Brit.* Vol. XXVII; and Statesman's *Year Book*, 1946.

The total area of the North African theatre of war was over two million square miles. The area of operations in which Indian troops played their part approximated to 1,090,858 square miles, roughly as follows:—

  Egypt   363,200 sq. miles.
  Libya   679,358 sq. miles.
  Tunisia ...   ... 48,300 sq. miles.

The mean length of the whole theatre of fighting was about 2,500 miles and the mean breadth 1200 miles.[4]

Climate

The climate of Africa may be said to be uniformly warm or hot all the year round. Exceptions are the higher regions, some of which may even have snow. Otherwise the temperature is never very low. In the coldest month, the mean temperature at sea-level is never under 55°F, while over most of the continent it is more than 70°F. In the extreme north, the climate is more temperate due to the nearness of the sea.[5]

The atmosphere in this region is dry because of the prevailing moistureless winds. These winds, blowing from the desert towards the sea, lose most of their moisture in their passage over the dry plains of the Sahara, and their dryness causes so much evaporation that often the temperature drops precipitately, thus giving an impression that the dry winds are not hot. These winds also carry fine particles of sand and sometimes work themselves up into suffocating sand-storms, which are typical of the desert and are known by the various names of Khamsin, Sirocco, Harmattan, etc.

Taking by countries, the mean temperature in Egypt is between 54°F in January and 84°F in July. January is the coldest month. Mean maximum temperatures for Alexandria and Cairo are 99°F and 110°F respectively. In the open desert, the temperature may sink to 32°F in January. The same of course applies to the desert region of Libya where, however, more moderate conditions may be met with in the area of Jebel Akhdar. Tripoli has an average temperature of 68°F on the coast while that of Tunisia would be about 10° higher.

As to rainfall, there is very little of it in North Africa. Rain seldom falls in Upper Egypt, and in Lower Egypt it falls only irregularly. The annual average for Cairo is 1.2 inches and that for Alexandria 8 inches. Rain is by no means unknown in the open desert. Although it falls there at long intervals, it comes in sudden bursts of storms which in a short while flood the narrow ravines or

---

[4] *Statesman's Year Book*, 1946.
[5] *A Handbook of Geography*, Vol. II, Herbertson; *Enc. Brit.* Vols. I, VII, IX and XXVII; *Africa* by Walter Fitzgerald; *Statesman's Year Book*, 1946.

turn the desert into a sea of quagmire and morasses. Desert rains have often influenced military operations in a decisive manner. More plentiful rain is met with in the Jebel Akhdar, though one year in five, there too, is expected to be droughty. Tripolitania has 5 to 15 inches in a year; and Tunisia 17 to 22 inches, in unequal distribution.[6]

Population

North Africa has a population of over thirty-three million inhabitants. In round figures, the distribution is: Egypt 16 millions, Libya 1 million, Tunisia 2.6 millions, Algeria 7.3 millions and Morocco a little over 6.2 millions.[7] Estimates of population in Africa vary considerably due to lack of established statistics and must therefore be taken guardedly. Roughly it can be stated that the population of the area over which Indian forces carried their arms totalled about twenty millions, including Egypt.

From the point of view of religious distribution, about nine-tenths of the people of Egypt are Muslims. Racially, they are composed of three elements, Hemito-Semites, Bedouin Arabs and negroid Nubians. Of these, the Hemito-Semites are the ones who constitute the bulk of the population of Egypt and are known in rural districts as *Fellaheen* (Fellah-ploughman). They are Muslims by faith except for a few hundred thousand Coptic Christians in towns and villages. The Bedouin Arabs, who are nomads of Libyan and Arabian deserts, are also Muslims. Only about a seventh of them, however, are truly nomadic, the rest being semi-static tent-dwellers living on the outskirts of cultivated areas. The Nubian negroid population is a community of mixed Arab and negro blood and like the Bedouins entirely Muslim. Foreigners, who number about a quarter million, are British, French, Greeks, Italians and Tunisians.

The population of Libya is by no means so uniform as that of Egypt. The Libyans are fundamentally a Mediterranean people being Berbers or Caucasians, the dark-white race[8]. To this stock there were additions from time to time, chief among whom were the Arabs. Arab blood, language and culture reached Libya in the seventh century as a result of the Arab conquest of North Africa, since when Libya has gradually become an Arab land. In spite of this pressure, the Berbers have to this day preserved their separate identity in a small measure, and even their language can still be found in various parts of Libya, e.g. in western Tripolitania. Other additions from

---

[6] *A Handbook of Geography*, Vol. II; Fitzgerald, *Africa*.
[7] Whitaker's *Almanac* 1945; Herbertson's *Geography*, Vol. II, p. 291; and *British Survey*, Vol. VII.
[8] *British Survey*, Vol. VII, No. 14.

outside were the Greeks on the coast, Arabic-speaking Jews in Tripolitania, and Turks and Maltese scattered all over, not to mention the Italians. On the whole it can be said that the Libyans are either Berbers or Berber-Arabs, the former predominating in Tripolitania and the latter in Cyrenaica. The population of Tunisia is not very different in composition from that of Libya. About one-third are Berbers, more or less a pure race, and one-third Berber-Arabs. The rest comprise Arabs, Arab "Moors", Sudanese negroes, Turks, Tunisian Jews and European Christians.

Typical desert conditions

The greater part of North Africa is one vast desert. West of the Nile, it extends over many hundred miles without a natural barrier and it has become customary to speak of it as the Western Desert. The geographical name for it, however, is the Libyan Desert, while further to its west lies the Sahara Desert.[9]

All conditions popularly associated with a desert are of course to be found in the deserts of Egypt and Libya, for example the sandy surface, the barren soil, lack of water and a general absence of animal and vegetable life. But in addition the North African deserts have other characteristics also. Chief among them may be said to be the sand dunes, a rocky soil producing a hummocky surface, and marshy lands alternating with deeply cut ravines called "wadis". All these, together with the normal desert conditions, greatly influenced the fighting in North Africa and gave to it a special character which is best expressed by the term "desert warfare".

The typical desert surface met with in North Africa, is the result of ceaseless erosion by natural agencies such as heat, wind and rain. Rapid heating and cooling of rocks, due to variations in the day and night temperatures, cause them to expand and contract endlessly, as a consequence of which particles of rock detach themselves from surface layers and become sand. Aided by wind and rain, and working on softer soil for centuries, these forces have produced plateaus, escarpments, sand-hills, water-channels and other features that go to make up the scenery of an African desert. Thus, in the Western Desert one comes across large accumulations of sand, called the sand dunes. These are low sand-hills which can sometimes be seen as a series of apparently endless ranges, lying in the direction of the prevalent winds. In certain parts, they lie parallel to one another, about half a mile apart, covering vast areas and rendering them untraversable except in a direction parallel to the lines themselves. Such areas are to be found to the west and south-west of the oases of Farafra and Dakhla. East of these oases is another remarkable line of sand dunes, rarely more than three miles wide but having

[9] Herbertson's *Geography*, Vol. II; *Enc. Brit.* Vol. IX, p. 23, and Vol. XXVI.

an average length of about 500 miles. In the northern part of the desert, the dunes lie roughly north-west to south-east.

Nearer the coast, about thirty miles inland, the desert is characterised by a comparative absence of sand. This is so because for several centuries strong wind, blowing seaward, has carried off the top soil into the Mediterranean. As a result the ground is now flat and stony with barely a covering of dust hiding the rocky subsoil. In some parts even this covering is gone and the solid rocks can be seen and felt radiating the fierce heat of a blazing sun. Except on the coastal margin, vegetation is scarce and the inhabitants of this region, the Bedouin Arabs, live a difficult existence, wandering from one water-point to another and carrying on a slender trade with the settlers on the coast.[10]

Barring the Nile, North Africa has no river of any size or importance. Its substitute for rivers is what are known as "wadis" These are channels or water-courses, some of which have high and sometimes very steep banks. Most of them are merely storm-water drains, dry for the best part of the year. But there are others which may flow with stream-water for long periods during certain seasons. As a rule, however, wadis are just dried up beds of water-channels or of intermittently flowing rivulets. A good number of them are deep and wide enough to affect military operations in about the same way as a river.

Next to the wadis in hydrographic importance come the water-wells and cisterns. Most of them are too small to sustain large numbers of men, but they were nevertheless useful sources of water for troops garrisoned or operating in an otherwise waterless area. These water-points are to be found along desert tracks or at track-junctions. They are encountered roughly at intervals of 25 miles, except in the trackless areas where none might be seen for hundreds of miles. The difference between the wells and cisterns is that whereas wells are dug in the earth's surface, cisterns are tanks hewn out of rocks, measuring about three feet square. Originally, they had been made by the Romans to collect and store surface water and, while most of them have silted up, there are still many in use to-day.[11]

Wells or cisterns that have water in them may either have small habitations surrounding them or they may be only halting and watering stations for the desert travellers. They generally have a mound of earth about ten feet high near their site, in order to make them conspicuous in an otherwise featureless desert. Names of most of them begin with the Arabic word Bir (plural Abiar or Abar), meaning a well, for example Bir Sofafi, Bir el Gubi, Bir Hakeim, etc. These "birs" or wells have had an importance of their own in the

[10] *Tiger Strikes*, p. 11.
[11] *Ibid*.

North African campaign. Besides being the coveted sources of water supply, they were practically the only landmarks in a desert void of other distinguishing features. They were in a way desert sign-posts to guide the troops in their operational movements, and were practically the only means of naming objectives and explaining operational tasks to the unit commanders and their men. As a result they soon became prominent place-names on maps and in newspaper columns of the world, and in the eyes of the common man acquired an importance out of all proportion to their size or civic value. As some of them were situated at junctions of imporant desert-tracks, their possession sometimes became an object of large-scale military operations and, thus, some of those minute specks in the desert became well known throughout the world. The bigger ones among the Birs, having a sizable population, are to be found only at the oases, chief among which are the Siwa and the Kufra Oases.

Of the larger oases, there are six in the Western Desert, namely Siwa, Kufra, Bahariya, Farafra, Dakhla and the Kharga or the Great Oasis. Of these Kufra is situated in Libya while all others lie in the Egyptian territory. All of them are fertile areas, their fertility resulting from a plentiful supply of water from a sand-stone bed, 300 to 500 feet below surface, whence the water rises up through natural fissures or artificial boreholes.[12] The Oasis of Siwa is about 150 miles south of the Gulf of Sollum and 300 miles west of the Nile. The other four oases lie parallel to, and 100 to 150 miles west of, the Nile, between 25° and 27°N, Bahariya being the most northerly and Kharga the most southerly.

Finally, one more typical feature of the Western Desert must be mentioned, namely the marshes. These are either swampy areas or tracts of salt-earth regions known as Sabakha. In either case the soil is too soft to sustain the weight of vehicles and desert marshes are, therefore, obstacles to wheeled traffic. When they cover large areas or are in great concentration, as at the Qattara Depression, they become important factors in military operations.

Communications

The roads of North Africa fall somewhat sharply into three conventional divisions, namely the main roads, the secondary roads and the foot-tracks. The main roads are generally fit for heavy motor traffic and are either macadamised or pucka-built. The secondary roads are narrow and unmetalled and incapable of taking heavy or two-way motor traffic, besides often being in a state of disrepair ; while the foot-tracks are good enough only for foot or animal traffic, although some of them can, in an emergency, be quickly enlarged into secondary roads.

[12] *Enc. Brit.* Vol. IX, p. 23.

Of the main roads, North Africa has very few, the outstanding being the coastal road, 1800 miles long from Alexandria to Tunis. It runs roughly parallel to the coast, occasionally swerving inland to touch bigger towns. It starts near Alexandria and runs unbroken up to Tunis, except for a 20-mile stretch of a secondary road on the Libya—Tunisia boundary line. Among the towns or other localities, which stand on or near this main road, the more important ones militarily are: El Daba, Fuka, Matruh, Sidi Barrani, Sollum, Tobruk, Gazala, Benghazi, Agedabia, El Agheila, Tripoli, Medenine, Enfidaville and Tunis.

As the main road enters Tunisia, it begins to branch out into offshoots which increase in number further up and reach out to the borders of Algeria and beyond. Otherwise, up to Tunisia the main road has very few ramifications. They either branch out southward or run parallel to the road for a short distance. Chief among these are branches linking El Daba to the Qattara Depression, Bu Amad to El Adem, El Gubba to Barce and the west of El Agheila to the desert tracks.

Of the secondary roads, there are several in North Africa. In Egypt and Libya, secondary roads serve as links between the desert tracks and the main roads. The principal ones radiate from the road-junctions at the Gufra and the Dakhla Oases. In Tunisia, the secondary roads are more numerous but not so important from the point of view of this narrative.

As to the desert tracks or foot-tracks, there are more of them in Egypt and Libya than in Tunisia. As they are too numerous to be described and do not lend themselves to a systematic grouping, they will be dealt with in their proper places.

In the rest of the trackless desert specially in the parts where there are no obstacles, movement of vehicles is free and unfettered. There being no need to keep within the width of a normal road, as in the case of road-bound vehicles, vast numbers of tanks, trucks and artillery vehicles may be seen moving all abreast, in the wide spaces of the interior of the desert, sometimes on a front of three to five miles, in what has now come to be known as "desert formation".[13]

The railways of North Africa are a necessary, though at best a poor, adjunct to the road communications. From the point of view of military operations they were very inadequate and unsatisfactory. At the commencement of the war there was just one line along the coast, skirting the northern edge of the Western Desert. It proceeded westwards from Alexandria. From time to time that line was extended to satisfy the operational needs of the North African campaign until the Western Desert railway finally reached Tobruk. Apart from this main line, which in its last stage of extension was

---

[13] *See* sketches on pp. 11 and 13.

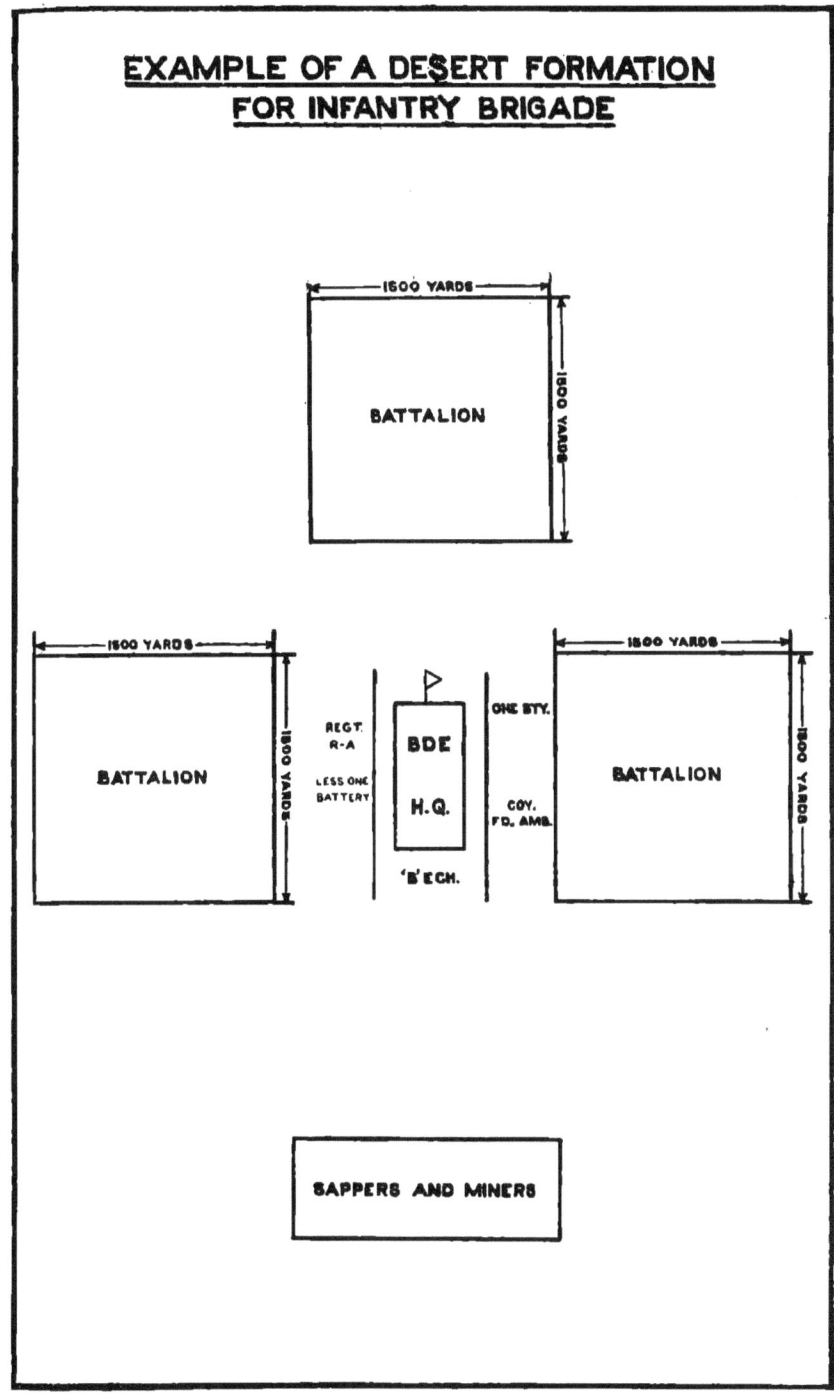

about 400 miles long, there were other railway tracks in Egypt, which served the base and lines of communication areas and were linked to the desert railway. Besides the main line from the Delta to the Egyptian border, there were two more separate stretches of railway lines in Libya: one between Barce and Benghazi which extended south-east to Soluk, and the other between Tripoli and Zuara. A narrow-gauge branch of the latter went southwards.

Tunisia is not so deficient in railway communications as Egypt or Libya. It has a network of railway lines most of which are in the north. Of these, the track along the coast is a narrow-gauge system which runs from Gabes to Sfax, thence inland to Sousse. From Sousse, it edges the coast again up to Hammamet, whence it crosses the neck of the peninsula of Cape Bon to reach Tunis. The remaining railway tracks in Tunisia link up with one another and finally converge on Tunis.

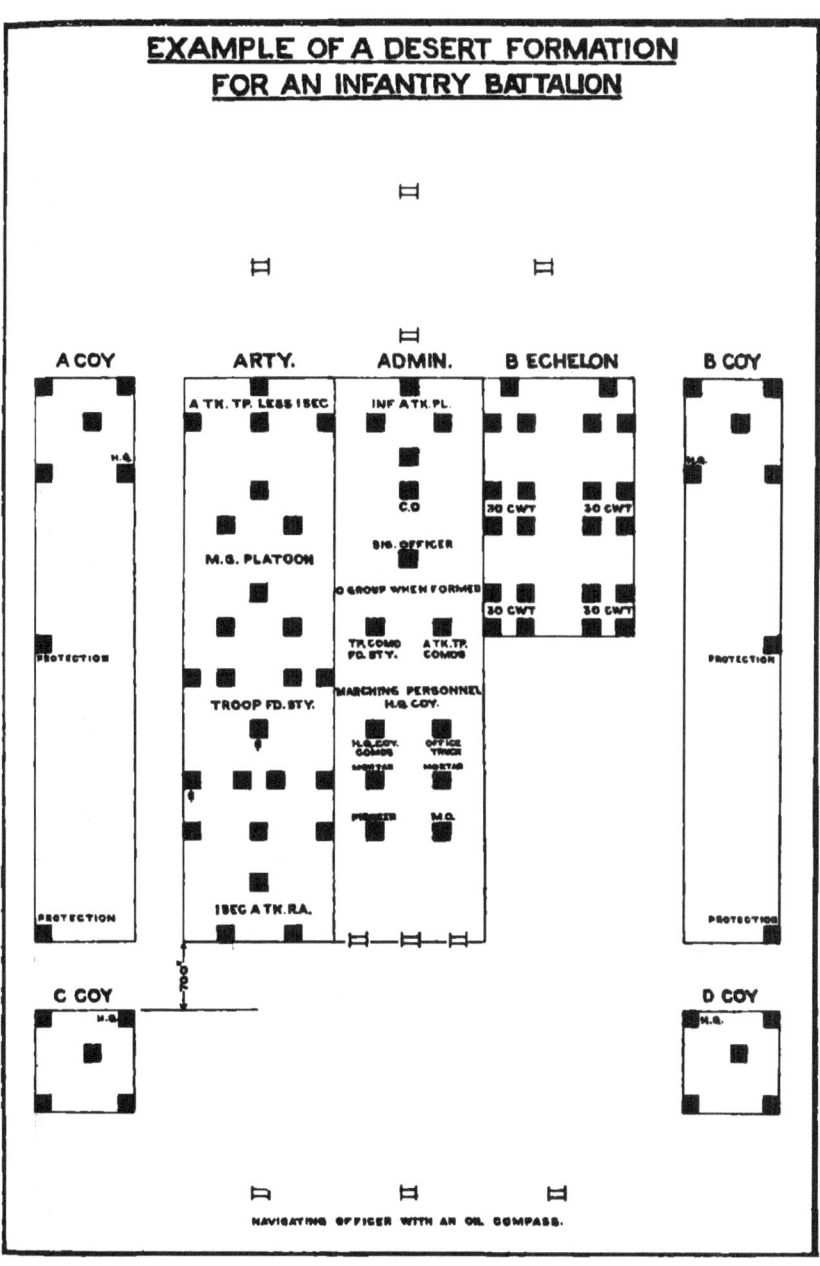

CHAPTER II

Historical and Political Background

North Africa has never been under a single rule at any time. Its different parts have always been under the domination of different rulers, who had little or no contact with one another in the distant past. For that reason it is not possible to discuss the history of North Africa as a unit. It must therefore be treated separately as the history of each of its component parts like Egypt, Libya or Tunisia.

Egypt

The earliest known history of Egypt dates back to the Pharaonic age. Precise chronology of that epoch not being available, historians have divided the period into thirty-one dynasties which they use as units for measuring time. The dynasties are again grouped into longer periods, which go under such self-explanatory names as the Old Kingdom, Pyramid Period, Middle Kingdom, the New Empire and the Deltaic Dynasties.[1] Towards the end of the Deltaic period Egypt was dominated by the Persians who ruled the land from Dynasties XXVI to XXXI. In 332 B.C. Alexander conquered Egypt from the Persians and founded Alexandria. Thus started the Hellenistic period. Nine years later Alexander died and when his domains were divided, Egypt went to Ptolemy (son of Lagus) who founded the Ptolemaic Dynasty. The Ptolemaic rulers were finally defeated by Augustus of Rome in 30 B.C., who initiated the Roman Period. Egypt remained under the Romans for more than 500 years and became a stronghold of Christianity. Later, religious differences developed and culminated in a schism which ultimately led to a civil war. Internal strife so weakened Egypt that it fell without a conflict when the Persians attacked it again in A.D. 616. The Persians were however ejected by the Romans within ten years and the latter returned to rule. But Egypt never recovered its original strength. The way had been paved for the Arab (Muslim) conquest.[2] Muslims invaded that land in A.D. 639 and completed its conquest within the next two years. Thereafter Egypt became a province of the Eastern Caliphate and remained so from 641 to 968. The Caliphs ruled through their governors who later established semi-independent dynasties and became virtual rulers of their respective provinces.

[1] *Enc. Brit.* Vol. IX, p. 80 et seq.
[2] *Ibid.*

In 1463, there began a struggle between the Egyptian and Ottoman (Turkish) Sultanates which led to an open war between the two. The war ended in Egypt becoming a part of the Ottoman Empire and thus began the Turkish period of Egyptian history. The Turks appointed Mamelukes, who were the defeated rulers of Egypt, to administer the country as their governors, and the Turkish rule continued undisturbed until the emergence of Napoleon Bonaparte on the scene.

Napoleon gained control of Egypt in 1799 and appointed his own governors in Cairo, Alexandria and Upper Egypt. But he was forced to leave that country in 1801 after a combined attack by Britain and Turkey. Thereafter, for some years, Egypt became a scene of internal strife between its own rival factions, and finally the control of the government passed into the hands of Muhammed Ali, an Albanian, who ruled for forty years under the nominal suzerainty of the Turkish Sultans.

Suez Canal

One of Muhammed Ali's successors was Ismail, the first Khedive, who was much taken up with the idea of modernising Egypt. He gave his country such public amenities and social services as railways, telegraphs, post offices, harbours and above all the Suez Canal, but not without drawing heavily on foreign credit. By 1870 the effort had so impoverished him that he was willing to sell the greater bulk of his Suez Canal shares to obtain financial relief. These shares were eventually bought by Great Britain who thus acquired a substantial interest in the ownership of the Canal. One far-reaching consequence of that transaction was that Egypt gradually became a "sphere of influence" of the British.

The opening of the Suez Canal at once "put Egypt upon the chess-board of international politics."[3] Britain's large share in the control over the Suez Canal aroused the jealousy of France and other European powers and led to much diplomatic wrangling. The matter was finally settled by the signing of the Suez Canal Convention which laid down that the Canal would always be "free and open in time of war as in time of peace, to every vessel of commerce or of war, without distinction of flag."

Modernisation brought to Egypt a political awakening and an intensely national spirit. In 1882, a section of the Egyptian army began to agitate against what it called preferences shown to the officers of Turkish orign. The agiation expanded into a country-wide movement against all foreigners, and later against all Christians whether foreign or native. If finally became a national rising which the government of the day was too weak to suppress. Great Britain

---

[3] *British Survey*, Vol. VII, No. 8.

and France grew alarmed at this turn of events and stepped in to prevent the government from being overthrown. Accordingly, in May 1882, the British and French fleets appeared off Alexandria to take necessary action and, on 11 July 1882, the British fleet bombarded Alexandria. Later, British troops landed at Ismailia and the Battle of Tel el Kebir was fought on 13 September 1882. The revolt was suppressed. The Khedive who had fled was induced to return to Cairo, a ministry was formed with British approval and for all practical purposes Egypt passed under the tutelage of Great Britain. The Sudan was excluded at first as it was in a state of rebellion and the British did not want additional responsibility. But in 1898 that part of Egypt, too, was brought under British control and an Anglo-Egyptian Condominium established over it.[4]

From 1900 onwards Egypt began to take shape as a fairly advanced state. Its progress was accompanied by a growing national upsurge which culminated in a movement for getting rid of the British domination. This nationalist movement assumed a grave aspect and was sometimes accompanied by serious disorders. At last, in 1922, Great Britain decided to put an end to it by making the maximum concessions possible to the Egyptian demand for independence. Accordingly, in February, she made a declaration granting independence to Egypt subject to certain reservations concerning defence of the country, security of the imperial communications and the Condominium over the Sudan. This gesture failed to satisfy Egypt's aspirations. However, in 1936, spurred by dangers arising from the Italian conquest of Ethiopia, both the United Kingdom and Egypt made fresh efforts to come to an agreement. The result was the Anglo-Egyptian Treaty of 1936 which continued to govern their relations during the war years. This treaty provided for a military alliance between the two countries, as also for the withdrawal of British forces from Cairo and Alexandria and their being stationed in certain limited and defined areas of the Canal Zone. By the same treaty, all other British restrictions on Egyptian sovereignty were to be withdrawn, except in the matter of the Anglo-Egyptian Condominium over the Sudan.[5] Withdrawal of the British troops from Alexandria was to be completed within eight years ; and that from Cairo, it was hoped, would be achieved within four years. The number of British personnel in the Canal Zone was not to exceed 10,000 land forces and 400 pilots ; and they were to stay there for a period of 20 years in the first instance, after which there were to be fresh negotiations in the matter.

At first the treaty was hailed as the fulfilment of Egypt's ambition to become the mistress in her own house. But the enthusiasm

[4] *Enc. Brit.* Vol. IX, p. 114.
[5] *Brit. Survey*, Vol. VII, No. 8.

wanted later, due to several reasons. One important reason was perhaps the slowness of the Egyptian Government itself in carrying out the terms of the treaty. By the provisions of the treaty, Egypt had undertaken to build barracks for British troops in the Canal Zone and to improve the country's internal communications, so as to prepare the way for the withdrawal of the British troops from Cairo and Alexandria. The progress in the execution of these works, on the Egyptian side, was rather slow. At the same time the international situation was worsening rapidly and the United Kingdom too could hardly have thought the time suitable for relaxing her hold on that strategic area. Thus, when World War II broke out in 1939, British forces had evacuated neither Cairo nor Alexandria. In fact, the tide had turned and more British troops came in to defend Egypt and the Middle East against threats of aggression from Italy and Germany.

Libya

The history of Libya is that of its two divisions, Cyrenaica and Tripolitania. Cyrenaica was first colonised by the Greeks and later it came under the sway of the Ptolemies. From them it passed to the Romans. Tripolitania, on the other hand, was originally a Phoenician colony. Later it became a dependency of Carthage and followed the vicissitudes of its fortunes. The province got its name from the Romans. Both Tripolitania and Cyrenaica were conquered by the Vandals in the 5th century A.D. The Vandals were suppressed in the following century by a Byzantine general and presumably Tripoli passed under Byzantine rule. Christianity seems to have entered Tripoli sometime before.[6] In the middle of the 7th century, the whole of Libya was overrun by the Arabs and Christianity gave place to Islam. For some time Cyrenaica thrived in trade and art and enjoyed a measure of prosperity.[7]

During the same period, however, Tripoli was having a chequered if not a hectic existence. This was so because it was being constantly attacked and harassed by the neighbouring countries. First it was occupied by the rulers of Tunisia; then it was pillaged by the Normans of Sicily. Later, from 1320 to 1400, it was ruled by an independent dynasty at the end of which it again fell to the Tunisians. In 1510 it was conquered by Ferdinand the Catholic of Spain, who handed it over to the Knights of St. John. The Knights were expelled in 1553 by the Turkish Corsairs, the famous pirate rulers of the Mediterranean. The Corsairs ruled the shores of the whole of Libya and rapidly expanded their piratical activities. Their power grew until their name became a terror in the Mediterranean

---

[6] *Enc. Brit.* Vol. XXVII, p. 290.
[7] *Enc. Brit.* Vol. VII, p. 702.

and they fought the fleets of half of Europe. In course of time they got themselves recognised by the Turkish Sultan as his representatives for governing Libya. Thus, in the latter half of the 16th century, Libya became a part of the Ottoman Empire.[8]

In 1714, the then governor of Libya, Ahmad Pasha Caramanli, shook off the Ottoman yoke, achieved practical independence, founded his own dynasty under the nominal suzerainty of the Turks and gave to his territory a semblance of order and good government. He might have succeeded better but there was a fatal weakness in his regime. His power was resting on no better foundation than the pursuit of piracy and on the revenues collected from an organised blackmail in the Mediterranean Sea. This method of obtaining his revenues brought him into sharp conflict with other powers, particularly with the United States of America between the years 1803 and 1805 and with Great Britain in 1816.[9]

As time passed, the Caramanli dynasty found it more and more difficult to pursue its traditional trade of piracy. It was meeting with increasing resistance from the European powers whose navies were growing and who sought freedom of movement in the Mediterranean for developing their trade and colonies abroad. By 1835 the Caramanli dynasty seems to have run its natural course. Its trade had all but vanished and it was in great financial difficulty. The ruling family was also torn by internal factions and had grown too weak to rule. Thereupon Turkey started administering Libya directly by sending its own governors. The system lasted until 1911 when the Young Turks came to power in Turkey and made a bid, among other things, to modernise Libya. But the enthusiastic Young Turks had little chance. Within a year, in 1912, Italy declared war on Turkey and landed troops at several points on the Libyan coast. Turkish resistance was feeble and poorly organised and Italy had her own way. In the following year the Turks accepted defeat and agreed to transfer Libya to Italy by a negotiated treaty.

The people of Libya, however, did not like the change. They were not prepared to accept an Italian rule and started resistance to the foreign regime. Before the Italians could overcome the opposition or placate the Libyans, however, there broke out World War I in 1914, during which Germans and Turks sent officers and arms to Libya to help the anti-Italian agitation. The principal opponents of the Italian rule in Libya were the leaders of a tribe called the Senussis. It was a religious sect, members of which lived in monastic settlements and, at that time, controlled a great part of the hinterland of Libya including the Oases of Giarabub and Kufra.

[8] *Enc. Brit.* Vol. VII, p. 702 ; *Brit. Survey*, Vol. VII, No. 14.
[9] *Ibid.*

After World War I, Italy decided to re-establish her authority in Libya by liquidating or otherwise overcoming all opposition to her rule. At first progress was slow but the tempo increased after the Fascists came to power. A number of Senussi settlements were wiped out or suppressed and many brutalities were perpetrated in a bitter struggle which lasted several years. By 1931, all tribal opposition had been crushed and the Italians were somewhat in control of the country. But before modernisation of Libya or her economic exploitation could proceed further, there commenced the Second World War in 1939.[10]

Tunisia

The history of Tunisia, like that of Tripoli, begins with the establishment of the Phoenician colonies. The Punic settlers semitized the coast but left the Berbers of the interior almost untouched. Later, when the Romans succeeded the Carthaginians, Tunisia was latinised and began to be called "Africa", apparently from a latinisation of the Berber term "Ifriqe" or "Ifrigia", which was perhaps the name of the largest or the most important Berber tribe. In 439 Rome lost Tunisia to the Vandals but recovered it a century later and retained it until the Arab invasions of 648 to 669. Thenceforth Tunisia was ruled by the dynasties of Muslim Berbers until the beginning of the sixteenth century.[11]

At about this time, the Turks who had already conquered Algeria began to feel interested in the adjoining Tunisia. A disputed succession led them to occupy Tunisia, which was done in 1525 by Khairad-din Barbarossa in the name of the Sultan of Constantinople. Thereupon, the superseded ruler of Tunisia appealed to Spain for help, and for many decades thereafter his country was the object of conflict between Turkey and Spain, in which Charles V and Don Juan played principal roles. The Spaniards at last gave up the struggle in the beginning of the 17th century and Tunisia passed under the rule of the Beys owing allegiance to Turkey. Originally the Beys were high officers whose function was to manage the tribes and collect the tributes. In the seventeenth century, however, they rose to be the rulers of the country under the suzerainty of Turkey.

The main source of revenue of the Beys, as in the case of Tripolitania, was piracy on the Mediterranean Sea, and their power depended on its continuance. But times had changed, and in 1819 piracy finally came to an end when the then ruling Bey was confronted with a collective ultimatum from the European powers, assembled at that time at Aix-la-Chapelle. This placed the Tunisian Government into great financial difficulties, which increased with the

[10] *Enc. Brit.* Vol. VII, p. 702, and Vol. XXVII, p. 290; *Brit. Survey*, Vol. VII, No. 14.
[11] *Enc. Brit.* Vol. XXVII, p. 398.

passage of time. Finally, Great Britain came to the rescue of the hard-pressed Bey who was willing to accept British advice and protection along with financial assistance, and Tunisia thus became a virtual protectorate of the British. That state of affairs lasted until 1878 when Great Britain acquired Cyprus as a new base in the Mediterranean and decided to placate France by releasing her hold on Tunisia. Accordingly, in that year, an arrangement was arrived at between the two powers by which Great Britain agreed to allow France "a free hand" in Tunisia if, in return, France agreed to acquiesce in the British base in Cyprus. Three years later, a French force attacked Tunisia and compelled the Bey to acknowledge a French protectorate. Great Britain recognised the French supremacy over Tunisia in 1883, and other powers, except Turkey, followed suit later, Turkey continuing to insist that Tunisia was a part of the Ottoman Empire. With the passage of time, however, Turkey gave up pressing her claim seriously and, at the outbreak of the Second World War, Tunisia was a thriving protectorate of France.

Political Status

At the beginning of the Second World War, the countries of North Africa were in various stages of political development. None of them was completely independent or democratically governed and every one of them was under the political domination of one or the other European power.

Egypt

In 1939 Egypt was a constitutional hereditary monarchy. The reigning monarch was King Farouk I who had come to the throne in April 1936. The constitution then in force had been enacted in December 1935 and provided for a Parliament composed of a Senate and a Chamber of Deputies. Two-fifths of the Senate members were appointed by the King and the remaining elected for ten years. Freedom of the Egyptian Parliament and the King to enact laws and ordinances was naturally subject to restrictions inherent in the Anglo-Egyptian Treaty of 1936. The British forces of occupation were still in Egypt in 1939 and the independence and sovereignty of that country were to that extent limited.[12]

Libya

Libya, also known as the Italian North Africa, was, in 1939, an Italian colony. For administrative as well as military reasons, the Italians had divided it into four provinces or prefectures, namely Tripoli, Misurata, Benghazi and Derna. The first named two pro-

[12] Statesman's *Year Book*, 1939.

vinces formed the division of Tripolitania and the other two of Cyrenaica. The hinterland of all the four provinces was grouped into a separate unit and called the "military territory", which had its capital at Hun. Later, by a decree promulgated in October 1938, the four provinces were incorporated into the national territory of Italy, the region of Libyan Sahara alone being excluded. Administration of the whole of Libya was entrusted to a Governor-General who had his headquarters in Tripolitania.[13]

Tunisia

Tunisia was a protectorate of France in 1939. The reigning king was Mohamed el Habib Bey, who had succeeded to the throne in 1929, the country being administered by a Resident-General under the direction of the French Foreign Office. The Resident-General, who was a French Minister, was helped by a council of eleven other ministers, three of whom were Tunisian and the rest French. The country was divided by the French, for administrative and military convenience, into nineteen districts and six military circles. The heads of these were all French, subordinate officials being mostly Tunisians. Justice between the Europeans and the Tunisians was administered by French courts; between the Tunisians themselves by their own courts.[14]

---

[13] *Ibid.*
[14] *Ibid.*

CHAPTER III

Strategic Background

It would be axiomatic to say that whereas a war is waged for political, economic, ideological or other reasons, a campaign is fought only for strategic reasons. The campaign in North Africa bears this out fully. It was begun by Italy and continued by Germany for strategic reasons, and was resisted and carried to its final conclusion by the Allies for the same reasons. It will therefore be proper here to make a rapid survey of the strategic picture of the globe, and determine the place of North Africa in it.

Roots of British Imperial Strategy

Great Britain is a highly industrialised country but, at the same time, insular as to its geographical location. Its access to the other countries, for trade, can therefore be only across the seas. It has an abundance of certain minerals, such as coal and iron, but not enough of raw materials, agricultural products, foodstuffs, etc. To make up this deficiency, it is obliged to carry on a vast overseas trade, exchanging manufactured goods for some of these products. In the matter of foodstuffs, for instance, it is only 50% self-supporting. Of certain essential items of food such as meat, wheat, sugar and fats, it must import from 60 to 90% of its normal requirements. It must also import large quantities of cotton, jute and rubber. And as to its needs of petrol, oil, etc. for its industries and services, it must depend on the Middle East and other countries for more than 95% of its requirements. It also lacks certain metals, and metal ores, necessary for its heavy industries and for the manufacture of armaments. In short, like many other countries, it is not self-sufficient economically, and must carry on trade with distant parts of the world for its very survival.[1]

The necessity for trading had, in the past, led Britain to establish trading posts in different parts of the world, which were linked to the British Isles by certain sea routes along which trade and commerce used to flow to and fro. In course of time these trading posts and the sea routes became so important that they had to be protected by the use of military force. This eventually led to the establishment of defensive positions at vital strategic points along the sea routes and at the trading terminals. It even led to wars overseas, with their inevitable sequels of conquests of territories, treaties,

[1] Brig. Cole, *Imp. Mil. Geog.*, 10th ed., p. 34.

alliances, territorial possessions and more defensive positions to protect them. Thus, out of Great Britain's insularity and economic insufficiency, there was gradually growing up a vast maritime empire. Other political and historical forces, not connected with trade, such as emigration and colonisation, a spirit of enterprise and adventure, religious dissensions, an urge to expand, etc. were no doubt also adding to this gradual imperial growth. As a result, at the end of World War I, Great Britain had what has been aptly described as a "far-flung Empire", with countries and nations in varying degrees of political dependence on it and at varying stages of political and intellectual growth.

Defensive and offensive strategy

It should be clear from this that the sea and air routes connecting the British Isles to their far-flung sources of food, raw materials, etc. are vital for the very existence of the United Kingdom; and it should therefore be natural for that country to take steps to protect or defend them. But the very means of ensuring this defence, namely manpower and certain raw materials needed for fighting a war, themselves lie in these distant parts, the loss of any of which would lead to a corresponding diminution of her power to win the war. The defensive strategy of Great Britain, in any big war, would therefore be shaped by her need as much of defending her widely spreadout imperial possessions, as of securing the sea and air routes leading to them. Correspondingly, the offensive strategy of any power at war with the United Kingdom would be the reverse, namely, to sever the links between the British Isles and the imperial posts, either by seizing the latter or cutting the sea and air communications. A war against the British Empire would therefore tend to be fought along its sea and air routes (as in North Africa), or at their terminals (as in Malaya), or in territories controlling or giving access to these (as in Europe). A brief survey, therefore, of Great Britain's imperial possessions, and of the network of her lines of communication, is essential to understand the strategic reasons underlying the prolonged and costly campaign in North Africa.

Imperial communications

To put it very broadly, Great Britain at the outbreak of World War II had links with the outside world across the Atlantic, the Pacific and the Indian Oceans. The Atlantic connects the British Isles on the one hand to Europe and, on the other, to the North and South Americas, and to British possessions on or near the American continent. One branch of these latter routes goes to the Panama Canal and enters the Pacific, thus providing a shorter route to the western sea-board of the American continent. Another branch goes further south, that is round South America, via Cape Horn, and ultimately connects up with Australia and New Zealand. A third branch, which runs along the west coast of the continent of Africa, links Britain to South and West Africa, circles the Cape of Good Hope and enters the Indian Ocean to link up finally with India, Ceylon and other Indian Ocean countries. While the fourth branch enters the Mediterranean Sea via the Strait of Gibraltar and emerges into the Indian Ocean through the Red Sea. This, too, like the longer Cape route, connects the British Isles to India, Ceylon and the countries of the Far East.[2]

In the Pacific, the important sea routes are those which connect the ports and naval bases of Australia to Singapore and Hong Kong. But in the Indian Ocean they lead from India and Ceylon to Burma and the Malay Straits on the one hand, and to Aden, East Africa and the Persian Gulf countries on the other. These are the main lines of communication by sea, which bind the distant part of the British Empire together, and which have been, without exaggeration, called the life-lines of the British Empire. By severing any of these vital arteries, a powerful foe would isolate Great Britain from the distant parts of her Empire and reduce her power to fight; and by doing so on a large scale, it might even annihilate the power. It is for this reason that a war undertaken by the United Kingdom in Europe does not remain confined to that continent, but spreads out to all parts of the globe wherever important British possessions and lines of communications may be; and it is for the same reason that the United Kingdom has taken care to secure her highways by establishing on them a series of defended ports, fortified islands, land garrisons and air and naval bases. Other powers, such as the United States, France and Italy, too, have similar bases, outposts, garrisons, etc., which all, considered together, form what may be called the strategic picture of the globe. For determining the place of North Africa in that picture, however, it is not necessary to describe all of them, but only those located in the Mediterranean Sea and on the coasts of the Mediterranean countries.[3]

The Mediterranean Chess-board

The Mediterranean Sea is 2000 miles long from Gibraltar to Port Said and has an average width of about 400 miles.[4] It has three bottle-necks, one at the Strait of Gibraltar, the other at Port Said commanding the entrance to the Suez Canal, and the third roughly in the centre, between Sicily and Cape Bon. It is flanked on its north

[2] Brig. Cole, *Imp. Mil. Geog.*, 10th ed., pp. 56-61.
[3] For similar reasons, it is not necessary to describe the air and cable communications of the British Empire either.
[4] Brig. Cole, *Imp. Mil. Geog.*, 10th ed., p. 76 et seq.

by Spain, France, Italy, Yugoslavia, Greece and Turkey or what are known as the European Mediterranean countries; and on the south by Morocco, Algeria, Tunis, Libya and Egypt or what is known as North Africa. At its eastern limit are the Arab countries of Syria, Lebanon, Palestine and Transjordan, while at its western tip is situated the international port of Tangier. In the sea itself are a number of fortified or defended islands. They are the Balearic Isles (Spanish); Corsica (French); Sardinia, Sicily and the Dodecanese Islands (Italian); Crete and the Ionian Islands (Greek); and Cyprus and Malta (British).[5] Of the North African countries, it need hardly be repeated here that on the eve of the Second World War, Morocco was partly French and partly Spanish, Algeria and Tunis were wholly French possessions, Libya was in the hands of Italy and Egypt was a 'sphere of influence' of the British. Similarly, on the east coast of the Mediterranean, Palestine and Transjordan were held by the British, and Syria and Lebanon by the French, under several mandates from the League of Nations.

At the outbreak of World War II, the whole of the Mediterranean was ringed round by a series of naval bases, situated on its surrounding coasts. Thus Spain had Cartagena on her mainland, the defended port of Mahon on the Balearic islands and the military harbour of Ceuta in the Spanish Morocco. France had the naval bases and defended harbours at Oran, Algiers, Philipville, Bona and Bizerta, in addition to Toulon on its mainland. Italy had Spezia, Taranto and Brindisi, all on her mainland, in addition to Cagliari in South Sardinia, Tripoli in Africa, and the naval stations of Pola, Trieste, Saseno and Leros in the Adriatic and the Aegean Seas.[6] Greece had a naval anchorage at Corfu and a deep-water harbour at Salonika. Lastly, Britain had Gibraltar, the base of her Home Fleet; Malta, the base of her Mediterranean Fleet; Haifa, on the coast of Palestine; and Alexandria, belonging to Egypt but in use by the British throughout the war.

Importance of the Mediterranean

By its very geography, the Mediterranean Sea is fated to play an important part in the affairs of the three continents bordering on it—Europe, Asia and Africa. Always important to the Western Powers as the shortest route to North Africa and the Middle East, it has acquired an additional value for them since the opening of the Suez Canal and discovery of oil in the Middle East. These last two factors need a careful consideration, as without them the Mediterranean would not have half the strategic value that it possesses to-day.

[5] *Ibid.*
[6] After World War II Italy was dispossessed of these Adriatic and Aegean possessions. Pola was handed to Yugoslavia, Saseno to Albania and Leros to Greece, while Trieste remained to be settled.

The Suez Canal, built between 1860 and 1869, is owned by a French Company registered in Egypt, of which the British Government is one of the largest shareholders. It is managed by a Board of 32 Directors of whom 10 are British, 18 French, 2 Egyptian,[7] 1 Dutch, 1 American and 7 representing the ship-owning interests. Its value to Great Britain, it need hardly be said, lies in the shorter route it offers to India and the Far East, the alternative being the longer route round the Cape of Good Hope which increases the time of journey by approximately two-thirds more. Thus, for example, a voyage from Plymouth to Bombay would take 35 days by the Cape route but 21 by the Suez. Similarly a voyage from the same port to Sydney and Hong Kong would take 41 and 43 days respectively, as compared to 28 and 32 days by the Suez route. The advantage of shorter route need no emphasizing. It means economy in time and shipping tonnage and therefore less pressure on shipping space, a benefit which cannot be lightly thrown away during a war.

The other factor enhancing the value of the Mediterranean, as already mentioned, is the oil of the Middle East. This oil is essential to the British Navy which depends on it for its very mobility. Of the world's total resources, worked and unworked, 45% are located in North and South America and the Caribbean, 41% in the Middle East, 12% in Europe, mainly in the Russian territories, and 2% in the Far East. In the matter of actual production, the Middle East stands third after America and the Caribbean area ; and since the domestic needs of the United States are so great as to require practically all the oil produced by it for internal consumption, the Middle East oil is the only source on which Great Britain, Western Europe and practically the whole of Asia and Africa must depend for satisfying the bulk of their needs.

The oilfields of the Middle East are scattered all over the Arab countries. They are to be found in Iran, Iraq, Egypt, Saudi Arabia and in the Persian Gulf area, The more important ones are in the south-west of Iran, controlled by the Anglo-Iranian Oil Company which holds concessions for oil rights over an area of about 100,000 square miles. Here they are in the interior, in four groups, at Agha Jari, Masjid-i-Sulaiman, Haft Khel and Gach Saran, where crude oil is produced and pipelined to a refinery and storage area at Abadan on the coast, about 130 miles away. For export, this oil is shipped from the nearby Iranian port of Khurramshahr (Mohammerah). The annual production, two years before the outbreak of the war, was 10 million tons, which went on increasing during the war years.

The next important source of the Middle East oil is Iraq. The

---

[7] Later proposed to be raised to seven.
[8] Brig. Cole, *Imp. Mil. Geog.*, 10th ed., pp. 101-3.

annual production here, before the war, was only 5 million tons, but it was far easier of access than the Iranian oil, in that it had an outlet in the Mediterranean Sea. The oil producing agency here is the Iraq Petroleum Company in which the British, French and Americans have about equal shares. The area of the oilfields is around Kirkuk, in the north, from where oil is carried by two pipelines to Haditha, where they bifurcate, one branch going across Syria and ending at the Mediterranean port of Tripoli, on the coast of Lebanon ; and the other going through Transjordan and terminating at Haifa, on the coast of Palestine.

The third important oil region consists of the Persian Gulf and Saudi Arabia. The production here is entirely an American enterprise, except at Kuwait, where the capital is American and British in equal proportions. The Kuwait oilfields had just started operating before the commencement of World War II, but made a very rapid progress during the war years ; while Bahrein and the oilfields in Saudi Arabia had a production of about 10 million tons a year.

The fourth, a small but promising source of oil supply, is Egypt. The small oilfields there are worked by the Anglo-Egyptian Oilfields Ltd., which have a total production of a little over a million tons.

To sum up, the military value of the Mediterranean is, therefore, in a very large measure, due to the oil countries of the Middle East, namely Egypt, Syria, Iraq, Iran and Saudi Arabia which, together, not only form a land-bridge between Europe and Asia, but also stand in a commanding position at the eastern gateway of Suez, with one flank on the Mediterranean Sea and another on the Indian Ocean.

Strategic importance of North Africa

It should be clear from the above, that the strategic value of North Africa is due to the fact that it constitutes the southern shore of the Mediterranean, which provides the shortest and easiest route from every shore of Europe to the Black Sea and the Suez Canal. The Black Sea (via Dardanelles) gives access to Russia, and the Suez Canal to India and the Far East ; and, therefore, to control the Mediterranean sea route is to dominate a wide field of the global strategy. To achieve such domination, however, it is essential to hold certain points on the North African coast, particularly the coast opposite Sardinia, Sicily, Malta, Crete and Cyprus. But such points cannot be held by isolated garrisons and, therefore, any power wishing to hold them must be prepared to occupy the whole of North Africa. It was this attempt—to gain mastery of the whole of North Africa—on the part of several European powers that led to the North African campaign of the Second World War.

At the outbreak of the war, the powers most interested in the

Mediterranean were Great Britain, France and Italy. All were equally keen for the reasons of general strategy described above, as also for reasons peculiar to the circumstances of each one of them. Thus, for instance, the United Kingdom had a stake in India and therefore in the Suez Canal. She was interested in the oil of Persia and Iraq and therefore in the eastern Mediterranean and the Persian Gulf. For the sake of all these, she had to safeguard Egypt against an invasion from Libya, which naturally led her to take an interest in that part of North Africa.

The interests of France were almost identical. She was interested in the oil pipeline passing through Syria and Lebanon and terminating in the eastern Mediterranean. For maintaining contact with these territories, the Mediterranean was her only route, which also gave her an easy access to her dependencies of Tunisia and Algeria and a shorter route to Indo-China. She had a share in the ownership of the Suez Canal and was not prepared to see Egypt dominated by a power hostile to her.

As to Italy, she had several reasons for being interested in the Mediterranean and North Africa. In the first place she had a direct stake in Libya with which her communication was through the Mediterranean. Due to the proximity of North Africa to her coasts, she could not allow African shores opposite to be controlled by unfriendly powers. After the advent of the Fascists, Italy was planning to revive the grandeur of the old Roman Empire, and to further that project she wanted to acquire Corsica, Tunis, Malta, Suez and Aden. But it was not easy to realise this ambition as long as the British and the French retained their hold on the Mediterranean; and to oust them it was necessary for her to possess herself of all North Africa from Tunis to Port Said.

The powers vitally interested in North Africa in 1939 were thus the United Kingdom, France and Italy. There were other powers also who evinced a certain amount of concern—Spain, for instance, because of her possession of Spanish Morocco and her share in the international control of Tangier; Turkey and the Arab States because of the Muslim population inhabiting the whole of North Africa; and Russia and the United States because of their yet nascent international rivalries. After the start of World War II, Germany also became interested, though only for the strategic reason of prosecuting her war to victory.[9]

How North Africa was drawn into war

Until 1940, the main balancing factor in North Africa, strategically, was France, with her vast territorial possessions and a powerful fleet in the Mediterranean. In June of that year, however,

[9] *War in Outline, 1939-44,* (U.S.A.'s Fighting Forces Series).

France suffered a defeat at the hands of Germany and Italy and most of her overseas possessions passed under the control of her conquerors. That upset the political equilibrium in North Africa, and on new adjustments the balance was found to have altered in favour of Italy.

Hitherto Italy had three frontiers to guard in North Africa. Two of them were against France, in the west and south; and one against Great Britain—in the east. In addition, she had to protect the north coast against the British and French Mediterranean Fleets. After the fall of France, however, the situation altered radically. The German and Italian Armistice Commission took over the French military resources in Africa and Syria, thus releasing the Italians from the necessity of guarding the western and southern frontiers. This enabled the Italians to concentrate their forces against Egypt. The French Mediterranean Fleet, too, had disappeared, having been first immobilised at Toulon and then demilitarised at Alexandria. Later it was attacked and destroyed by the British Fleet at Oran and Dakar to prevent its falling into hostile hands.

Thus Italy had only one frontier left to defend in North Africa. Britain, on the other hand, had to guard two frontiers and watch the back door in Syria. She was also known to be militarily unprepared for a war in Africa. France was out of the picture and Germany's star was in the ascendant. Italy's Dictator, Mussolini, saw in this state of affairs an opportunity to invade Egypt and ordered the commencement of the war in Africa.[10]

---

[10] *War in Outline, 1939-44.*

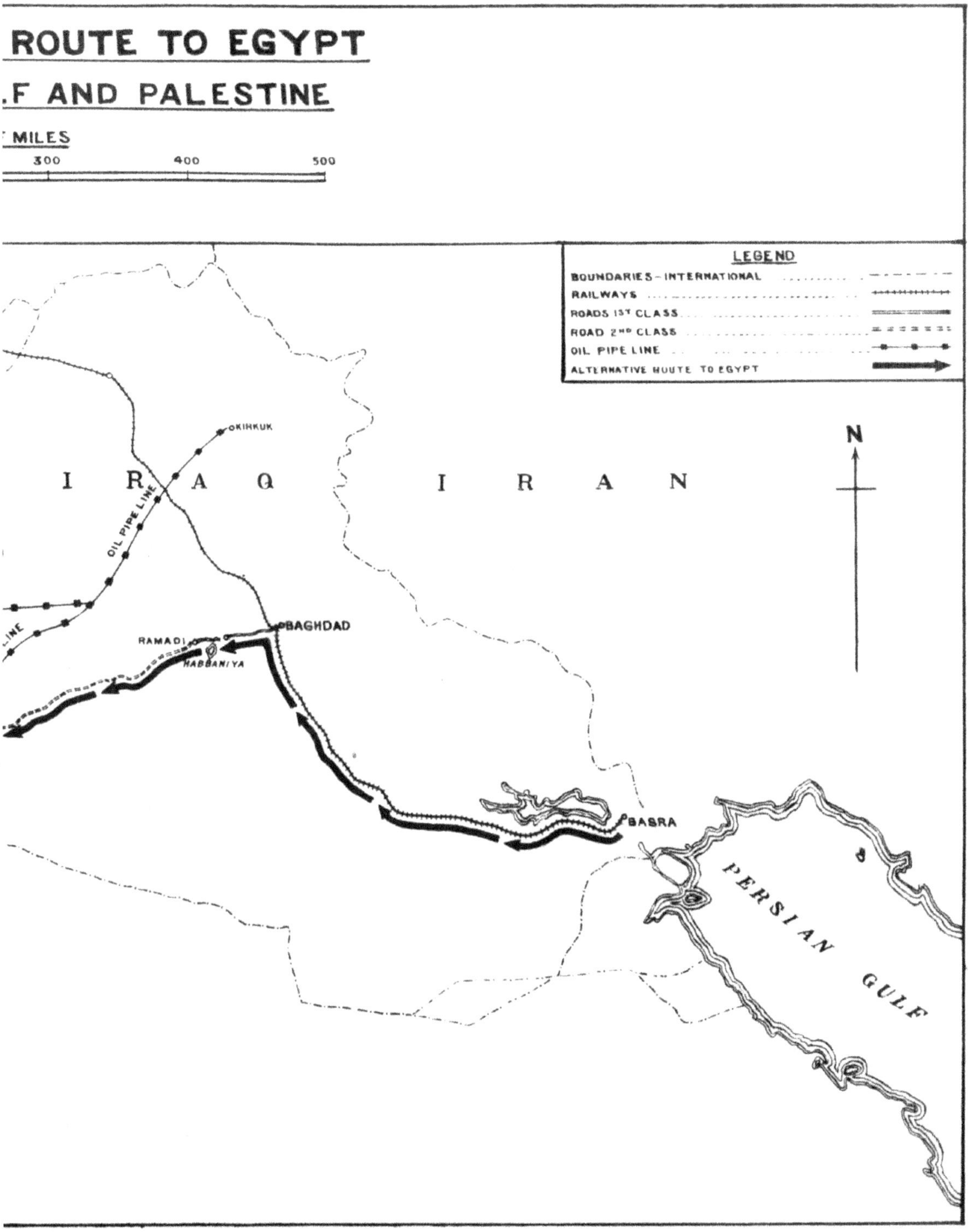

ROUTE TO EGYPT
...F AND PALESTINE

MILES 300 400 500

LEGEND
BOUNDARIES — INTERNATIONAL
RAILWAYS
ROADS 1ST CLASS
ROAD 2ND CLASS
OIL PIPE LINE
ALTERNATIVE ROUTE TO EGYPT

N

IRAQ   IRAN

KIRKUK
OIL PIPE LINE
RAMADI BAGHDAD
HABBANIYA
BASRA

PERSIAN GULF

CHAPTER IV

Indian Troops in North Africa

India and the Commonwealth

Military defence of every part of the British Empire had always been the sole responsibility of the government of the United Kingdom. But on many occasions when an imperial interest nearer India was threatened, India was called upon to send troops and participate in the defence of that part of the British Empire. This involved constant preparedness on the part of the Army in India, who had always to be ready with previously worked out plans for despatching troops abroad. Such plans were generally drawn up in advance, on an advice from the India Office, whenever the international situation appeared threatening.

One such crisis occurred in 1935 when Italy invaded Ethiopia. This led to considerable planning in India and a comprehensive project for sending troops overseas was produced, which may be called the 1935-plan. From 1935 onwards, until the outbreak of the Second World War, the international situation was never easy. Incidents like the German occupation of the Rhineland, the civil war in Spain, the German annexations of Austria and Sudetenland and the "Munich Crisis" had never permitted any relaxation of military preparedness in India.

Planning in India[1]

The 1935-plan remained in abeyance until brought into execution in 1939, although some modifications and additions were made to it during the intervening years. In 1937, that plan consisted of four schemes under which troops were to be sent out of India. They were Scheme M for Singapore, Scheme R for Burma, Scheme P for Iran and Scheme E for Egypt. Scheme E also included Scheme A for Aden.

In the 1935-plan, Scheme E was given the last place in the order of importance. That plan was altered, in July 1939, to give it the top priority due to the increasing hostility of Italy. The force under that scheme was to be ready to move at 24 days' notice and was to consist of (a) one mixed infantry brigade, out of which one battalion was earmarked for Aden, (b) one field brigade i.e. a regiment of Royal Artillery, mechanised, (c) one field company, Sappers

---

[1] For detailed discussion see volume, *'Defence of India : Policy and Planning.'*

and Miners, and (d) one field ambulance and an Indian General Hospital. This force was to be employed in Egypt and Palestine; in Palestine on internal security duty and in Egypt on miscellaneous tasks such as the defence of the Western Desert and the Suez Canal and the garrisoning of Alexandria and Cairo.

India having agreed to provide the above forces, the Army Headquarters proceeded to allocate the necessary troops. Thus to Scheme E was assigned the 11th Indian Infantry Brigade and to Scheme A the 5th Battalion of the 11th Sikh Regiment. Preparations were taken in hand to get these troops into a maximum state of readiness, though without exceeding the normal peacetime expenditure laid down for the establishments concerned.

Schemes Heron and Hawk

As the preparations went forward, the need for secrecy and security measures became increasingly evident. As a result some slight changes were introduced in the 1935-plan. Thus, at one stage in 1938, the very obvious and transparent name Scheme E for Egypt was changed into the code-name Heron as a security precaution. For the same reason Scheme A (Aden), which was to be a part of Heron, was renamed Scheme Hawk.

A few months later, in September when the German Reich Chancellor, Herr Hitler, made his demands on Czechoslovakia and a war seemed imminent, the tempo of planning and preparations in India quickened considerably. At the same time, the Secretary of State for India requested the Viceroy, in a telegram, that the Force Heron be doubled and given a divisional headquarters, thus converting it into a two-brigade division, evidently to meet the needs of the anticipated emergency. The Army Headquarters (India) accordingly prepared a second contingent of Force Heron, which later came to be known as Heron II or Herontwo, the first being renamed Heron I or Heronone. Herontwo was to consist of:

HQ 4th Indian Infantry Division
10th Indian Infantry Brigade
6th Medium Regiment
4th Field Regiment
44th Divisional Headquarters Company Sappers and Miners
24th Field Company Sappers and Miners
One Company 3rd Divisional Signals
One Indian General Hospital (200 Beds)
and other ancillary units.

A few days later, on 29 September 1938, came the "Munich Crisis" when Mr. Neville Chamberlain and M. Daladier met Herr Hitler and Sgr. Mussolini in a conference at Munich to settle the fate of Sudetenland. The international situation was then extremely grave and the Secretary of State for India signalled to the Government of India requesting that Scheme Heron be implemented forthwith. On the same day, the Army Headquarters (India) fixed the following day, 1 October, as the Z-day and ordered that Heron and Hawk be put into operation as from that date. Meanwhile, however, at 2230 hours on 30 September, news was received by the Government of India that a settlement had been reached at Munich and the crisis was over. The Secretary of State for India confirmed that information shortly after and requested the cancellation of Heron which was done at 2355 hours on 3 October 1938. The attempted implementation of Heron and Hawk, nevertheless, proved a good rehearsal and led to several defects being discovered and remedied. The headquarters of Force Heron at that time was in the Deccan District.

Schemes Emu and Wren

It has been explained that at some stage in 1938, the code-names Heron and Hawk were adopted to disguise the titles for Schemes E and A. For the same reason some more code-names were coined in the same year for the other schemes also. Thus Schemes M (Singapore), R (Burma) and P (Iran) were respectively renamed Emu, Wren and Sparrow. Emu was allotted the 12th Indian Infantry Brigade and 1 Mountain Regiment RA, Wren was given the 9th Indian Infantry Brigade, and Sparrow was put down as an alternative to Wren. At about the same time the 5th Battalion of the Sikh Regiment, in Scheme Hawk, was replaced by the 4/16th Punjab Regiment.

Modernisation Committee and the Chatfield Report

While the above schemes were being planned and perfected, other military problems connected with them were also receiving careful consideration, both in the United Kingdom and in India. In India, such consideration was influenced by two facts of major importance. Firstly, for the Indian Army to be useful in any European war, it would have to be modernised. Secondly, the extent of burden to be shouldered by India would have to be clearly defined. Steps were taken during 1938 to meet both these requirements, which was done in the following three stages:

(i) In the summer of 1938, the Commander-in-Chief in India. appointed a Modernisation Committee to go into the question of re-equipping and reorganising the Army in India, in order to bring it up to modern standards. The Committee issued its report in October 1938.

(ii) At about the same time a deputation was sent out from India to London to collaborate with the Pownall Committee of the United Kingdom on the question of determining the total forces required for the external defence of India.

(iii) As a result of the two above, the British Government sent the Chatfield Committee to India in October 1938, to consider, among other things, (a) the re-grouping of the Indian forces, (b) the organisation of the external defence of India, and (c) the sharing of the defence responsibilities between Great Britain and India. That Committee produced its report in February 1939.

In that report the Chatfield Committee accepted practically all the recommendations of the Modernisation Committee and added its own as regards the reorganisation of the Indian Army and the extent of its responsibilities. It particularly recommended that the Army in India be re-grouped so as to allot separate forces for (a) the Frontier Defence, (b) the Internal Security, (c) the Coastal Defence, and (d) the Air Defence. The rest of the troops, not coming under any of those heads, were classified as General Reserve. A portion of that Reserve was to be especially organised for overseas service and was to be known as the External Defence Troops. Its strength was fixed at one division and that division, instead of having its normal three brigades, was to have three self-contained brigade groups, which were to be so organised as to be able to act as independent brigades or be capable of being combined under a Force Headquarters, according to the varying exigencies. Finally, the principle was accepted that external security of India was the joint responsibility of both the Government of India as well as Great Britain.

Radley Report

Some months before the Chatfield Committee had completed its work, the Army Headquarters (India) had been considering the question of despatching troops overseas under the schemes Heron, Hawk, etc. One aspect of it concerned the route to be followed by reinforcements moving from India to the Middle East. The obvious route for such reinforcemens was via the Red Sea. But owing to the possibility of air attacks from Italian East Africa, in case of a breach of peace with Italy, it was thought wiser to explore and chalk out in advance an alternative route from Basra to Palestine via Iraq and Transjordan. The effect of such a change-over would be to transfer India's sea route to Egypt from the Red Sea to the Persian Gulf. The War Office was in agreement with India on the advisability of taking such a precaution and undertook to bear the expenses if India would send out a military officer to explore the route. The officer selected for the purpose was Lieut.-Colonel H.P. Radley of the 2nd Punjab Regiment, who was to go to Basra, "travelling in plain clothes as on a private visit", leaving Karachi on 6 March 1938, and arriving at Basra four days later.[2] His task was to examine the overland route from Basra to Egypt, via Habbaniya and Palestine, with a view to finding out whether it would serve as an alternative route for sending a brigade group in an emergency and also as a line of communication thereafter.

Col. Radley studied the proposed route in great detail and issued his report in May 1938. The route examined by him was the one which ran via Basra—Habbaniya—Ramadi—Rutba—Pipeline to Mafraq—Haifa (or Lydda)—Egypt. There was a railway along this route from Basra to Baghdad (that is, 53 miles short of Habbaniya) and again from Haifa to the Egyptian border. The rest of the journey would have to be performed by road. Some of the roads were indifferent, particularly the stretches along the Transjordan, and water was scarce in most of the places. However, Col. Radley reached the conclusion that the despatch of a force equal to a brigade over this route was not an impracticable proposition, provided certain requirements were fulfilled. These were: (1) the Iraqi Government should be willing to allow the British the use of its railways, rivers, ports, aerodromes and other means of communication, which it was under an obligation to do by the terms of the Anglo-Iraqi Treaty of Alliance ; (2) there should be no serious opposition from the Euphrates tribes ; (3) the road across Transjordan should be improved ; (4) enough road-transport should be available ; (5) sufficient water-receptacles should be prepared in advance to enable water being dumped between Habbaniya and Rutba ; and (6) a bridge be constructed over Wadi Harun as also an all-weather road round Lake Habbaniya, to avoid traffic interruptions during the seasonal floods from April to July every year.

The Army Headquarters (India) considered these demands too onerous to justify the use of this overland route in any but the most pressing circumstances. It therefore ignored the Radley report and in revising Force Heron (which it was then doing in anticipation of its possible future move to the Middle East at a short notice) it allowed Heronone to remain on its former basis of the move being via the Red Sea instead of the Persian Gulf. Explaining this to the War Office, it pointed out that lack of transport and the difficulty of maintaining a permanent line of communication from Basra to Egypt had influenced its decision. At the same time, however, it expressed the opinion that a restricted use of the proposed route was possible provided the forces using it could be maintained from Egypt instead of India. This was in December 1938.

Next month, however, the Army Headquarters sent out another

[2] "Commitments of the Army in India, West of India", Historical Section file No. 7422.

military officer, Lieut.-Colonel Key of the Sikh Regiment, to re-examine the same route. The officer in question reported that although the political situation in Iraq was somewhat unstable, a brigade could be got through according to the programme, if sufficient transport were made available by Palestine. He, however, recommended that, since it would be a peace move, tactical considerations ought to be subordinated to administrative conveniences, in order to make the movement easy and rapid. No steps were taken on this report, and for the next six months Heron remained in India, it being doubtful whether it would make use of the overland route at all.

Despatch of Indian troops to Egypt

War clouds darkened the international horizon once again in July 1939 and, on the 22nd of that month, the Secretary of State for India passed to the Viceroy a request from the British Government that the scheme Heronone be implemented at once. Accordingly, warning orders were sent out by Army Headquarters (India), fixing 26 July as the Z-day and 3 August as the date of embarkation.

The troops that thus embarked on the scheduled date, consisted of the 11th Infantry Brigade and the 4th Field Regiment RA. The former sailed from Bombay and the latter from Karachi, each in a convoy consisting of three vessels. The two convoys then joined up at sea on 6 August 1939, and the whole force proceeded to Suez where it disembarked between 15 and 17 August 1939. From there, the 4th Field Regiment was sent to Mena and the 11th Indian Brigade to Fayid. The Brigade, which was then commanded by Brigadier A. B. McPherson, consisted of the 2nd Battalion the Cameron Highlanders, 1st Battalion the 6th Rajputana Rifles and the 4th Battalion the 7th Rajput Regiment.[3] The force numbered a little over 5000 men, consisting of 1,300 BORs (British other ranks), 2,800 IORs (Indian other ranks), 775 NCsE (Non-combatants enrolled) and nearly 400 other personnel including officers and VCOs (Viceroy's Commissioned Officers).

Forces R and K4

Hardly had Heronone been despatched when Army Headquarters (India) began to take steps to get Herontwo into a state of readiness. However, during that process, it informed the War Office on 4 August 1939, that the movement of Heronone had compromised the secrecy of Herontwo and that, therefore, it proposed to change the code-name Herontwo into Force R. Herontwo was tactically so organised that it could be employed either in Singapore,

---

[3] A fuller Order of Battle of Force Heron is given in Appendix A.

Burma, Iran, Egypt or elsewhere as might be required. For each of these roles the Army Headquarters proposed to give the force a slightly varying code-name, as follows:—

R1-Singapore
R2-Burma
R3-Iran
R4-Egypt
R5-Elsewhere.

However, the War Office intimated that a Force "R" was already figuring in its own planning. To avoid confusion, India was requested to select some other letter. The letter K was chosen to replace R and Force R4 (Egypt) accordingly became Force K4. To Force K was allotted the 9th (Jhansi) Brigade which was later renamed the 5th Indian Infantry Brigade.

As August 1939 advanced, the rumbles of the coming war began to grow louder and India accelerated her pace of preparations. Some of these were aimed at sending Force K4 to Egypt by the Persian Gulf route, via Iraq, Transjordan and Palestine. Army Headquarters calculated that the move would require 35 cars for officers, 255 20-seater buses for men, and 410 lorries for carrying personal kit and equipment of troops. In addition, it was thought likely that about 1,000 lorries would be necessary to carry reserve rations for 150 days for the British troops and 135 days for the Indian troops. To obviate this last onerous demand on transport, it was decided to send the reserve supplies in advance by the Red Sea.

All these arrangements, however, proved unnecessary when the time came for taking action. For, when the war broke out on 3 September 1939, and the Scheme K4 had to be implemented at once, it was found that the Red Sea had by no means become immediately unsafe. The Germans were too occupied in Poland, and Italy was neutral, and neither of them seemed to have any definite plan for blocking the Red Sea. On the other hand, the Persian Gulf route was still causing anxiety as to the availability of adequate transport.

Accordingly, on 9 September 1939, Army Headquarters asked the War Office if it might despatch Force K4 to Egypt by the Red Sea route. The War Office had no hesitation in agreeing to the request and confirmation reached India the same day. 15 September 1939 was fixed as the Z-day and 23 September as the date of sailing. The embarkation proceeded smoothly as the units had been warned of the contemplated move, as early as 8 September, and had had enough time to give final touches to their preparations. Like Heronone, Force K4, too, embarked in two batches, at Bombay and Karachi. It set sail according to schedule on 23 September and disembarked at Suez on 3 and 4 October 1939. It consisted of:—

Force Headquarters (formerly HQ Deccan District)
One Company 3rd Divisional Signals
12 Field Company Queen Victoria's Own Madras Sappers and Miners
14th Field Ambulance
HQ 5th Indian Infantry Brigade with under command 1st Battalion Royal Fusiliers
3rd Battalion, 1st Punjab Regiment
4th Battalion, Rajputana Rifles, and the
1st Field Regiment RA.

Fourth Indian Division

On disembarkation, the 5th Indian Brigade was sent to Beni Yusef and the Force Headquarters to Mena. Next day, 5 October 1939, the Force Headquarters was reorganised and named Headquarters 4th Indian Division. Thus was the 4th Indian Division born in the surroundings of the pyramids of Egypt. It came into existence as a result of the merging of the two forces—Heronone and K4—under one Headquarters. Major-General P. G. Scarlet, commander of Force K4, became its first commander.

From that day this new formation, which was still incomplete in several respects, began to develop into a full-fledged division by receiving more units and equipment from time to time. At the start, the division consisted of only two brigades, the 11th (Heronone) and the 5th (K4) Indian Infantry Brigades. Several months elapsed before it received its normal complement of the third brigade and a divisional cavalry regiment.

The troops forming the 4th Indian Division were not only without proper equipment but also lacked training. Neither officers nor men had ever handled an anti-tank rifle or a mortar. They had no motor vehicles or trained drivers. Although the reorganisation of the Indian Army—from an animal to a mechanical transport basis—had been sanctioned some time ago, the new equipment had not reached India by then.

Middle East Command

On arrival in Egypt, the troops of the 4th Indian Division came under the Middle East Command. It would, therefore, be appropriate here to review briefly the extent and nature of this command which was responsible for the entire conduct of the military operations in North Africa.[4]

The Middle East Command was formed at the beginning of August 1939. It started with five officers who constituted the

[4] General Wavell's *Despatch* on Operations in the Middle East from August 39 to November 40,

planning staff. It came into existence at the behest of the Army Council which issued instructions on 24 July 1939 to General Sir Archibald P. Wavell KCB, CMG, MC. General Wavell was then General Officer Commanding-in-Chief, British troops in Egypt and under the instructions became the General Officer Commanding-in-Chief in the Middle East. According to those instructions the area of the Middle East Command, in peace-time, comprised Egypt, the Sudan, Palestine, Transjordan and Cyprus.[5] In case of an outbreak of war, it was to be extended further by including all military forces in British Somaliland, Aden, Iraq and on the shores of the Persian Gulf (with the exception of such forces as were then already under the control of the Royal Air Force). The Headquarters of the Middle East Command was to be located in Cairo.[6]

Among the tasks assigned to the General Officer Commanding-in-Chief, Middle East, the principal one required him to review and co-ordinate war plans in consultation with the local air and naval commanders. In the event of an actual outbreak of war, he was to be responsible for co-ordinating the action of all land forces under the various Allied commanders. In carrying out his various tasks, General Wavell was to be assisted by a Joint Planning Staff, a Middle East Intelligence Centre and a General Headquarters. His immediate subordinate officers were to be the General Officer Commanding-in-Chief in Egypt and the General Officer Commanding-in-Chief of the British troops in Egypt. As to high policies, he was to be guided by the War Office from time to time.[7]

A week before the United Kingdom and France declared war against Germany, there occurred a slight change in the Allied commands of the Middle East theatre. The French government appointed General Weygand to be Commander-in-Chief of the French forces in the East Mediterranean, so that General Wavell now had a distinguished colleague of great military experience with whom he could hold consultations from time to time and co-ordinate the Allied planning. General Weygand assumed command on 2 September 1939 and immediately plunged into talks with Turkey over the possibility of utilising the Turkish naval base of Smyrna or any other suitable base in case of emergency. The conversations began on the same day as that on which the United Kingdom and France declared themselves as being at war with Germany.

British strength in North Africa

At the commencement of the war, the fighting forces at the

[5] *Ibid.*
[6] Details of the charter i.e. instructions establishing the Middle East Command will be found in Appendix C.
[7] General Wavell's *Despatch* on Operations in the Middle East from August 39 to November 40.

disposal of General Wavell consisted of garrisons in Egypt, Palestine, the Sudan, Cyprus and British Somaliland, which were distributed as follows:

A. *Egypt*
  (i) 7th Armoured Divisions[8]—Two Armoured Brigades (each of two regiments only), one Armoured Car Regiment, one Motor Battalion.
  (ii) 4th Indian Division—4th Field Regiment RA, 11th Indian Infantry Brigade.
  (iii) RA Group—3rd Regiment RHA (AT), 4th Regiment RHA, 31st Field Regiment RA, 7th Medium Regiment RA.
  (iv) Eight British Infantry Battalions.[9]

B. *Palestine*
  (i) 8th (British) Division—Two Brigades, each of three British Battalions, no artillery.
  (ii) Two British Cavalry Regiments.
  (iii) Four additional British battalions (less one Company of one battalion in Cyprus).

C. *Sudan*
  (i) Three British Battalions.
  (ii) The Sudan Defence Force consisting of twenty Companies in all, of which the greater part were employed on internal security over the vast area of the Sudan.

D. *Cyprus*
   One Company British Battalion.

E. *British Somaliland*
   Headquarters and three Companies of Camel Corps.

It will be seen from the above that the troops in the Middle East Command included no complete formation of any kind. There were in all 26 battalions of infantry but only 64 field guns. Of the other artillery, there were only 48 anti-tank guns and 12 anti-aircraft guns. In addition to these forces, there was the Egyptian army which was in many respects better equipped than most of the British units. But as Egypt did not declare war on Germany and as it was not likely to do so in the near future, support of the Egyptian army had to be discounted for all practical purposes except in matters of passive defence and internal security.[10]

[8] The proper title of this formation at this date was "Armoured Division (Egypt)." It was not till 16 Feb. 1940 that it received the title "7th Armoured Division".
[9] For a fuller Order of Battle showing details of infantry battalions see Appendix B.
[10] General Wavell's *Despatch* on Operations in the Middle East, from August 1939 to November 1940.

CHAPTER V

War Approaches Middle East

World War II which started in Europe did not spread to the Middle East all at once. It took ten months to move to Africa and a further period of ten months to reach the Middle East proper. No danger, therefore, threatened General Wavell's command immediately on the outbreak of the war. Germany was fully occupied in Poland and Italy was neutral. There was, however, a vast Italian army in Libya which was a potential threat to Tunisia on the one hand, and to Egypt on the other. In consequence, both the United Kingdom and France decided to adopt measures for strengthening their respective positions in the Mediterranean and particularly in Turkey, Syria, Iraq, Palestine, Transjordan and Egypt.

One of these measures was to secure the co-operation of Turkey. This was accomplished in October 1939 when a tripartite treaty was concluded between Great Britain, France and Turkey. Great Britain and France promised by that treaty to render assistance to Turkey if she was assailed by a European power or got involved in a war through an act of aggression in the Mediterranean. Turkey agreed in return to assist Great Britain and France if they got engaged in hostilities on account of their guarantees to Rumania and Greece. An important stipulation was that nothing in the treaty was to be construed as compelling Turkey to go to war with Russia.

At this time, the Turkish army had a peace-scale strength of about 175,000 men (with an air-arm of about 400 aeroplanes) and was capable of eventually putting a million men into the field, though not necessarily well equipped.

But it was strategically, more than militarily, that Turkey was a bastion of strength to the Allies. On the one hand she could admit Allied naval units into the Dardanelles, and thereby prevent the supply of Russian and Rumanian oil across the sea to Germany, and for that matter also to Italy, and, on the other, she could protect the northern flank of the Middle East countries and prevent any army, advancing through Syria, from capturing the oilfields of Mosul. Her position as a Muslim power of importance was also useful to the Allies in securing support of Muslim countries to the south and east of the Mediterranean Sea.

Next to Turkey, the areas most vital for defence in the Middle East were Syria, Iraq, Palestine and Egypt. In Syria, which was her mandated territory, France began to assemble her colonial troops in anticipation of trouble. She hoped to raise their strength to 120,000 men eventually. Syria's strategic importance lay in the fact that on the one hand she could help to buttress Turkey's morale by protecting its southern flank, and on the other she could deny to the Axis Powers the easiest routes available for their eastward thrust.

In Iraq and Palestine, which were both important to the United Kingdom because of the Kirkuk—Haifa oil pipeline running across those countries, Great Britain had hardly any means of resisting aggression other than her friendship with those countries. Iraq agreed to implement her treaty with Great Britain, closed down the German legation and permitted the British air force all facilities agreed to under the treaty, although later she changed her attitude. In Palestine, both the Arabs and the Jews decided to call a halt to their internal quarrels and bury the hatchet for the duration of the war. In Transjordan, Emir Abdulla continued to be loyal and co-operative with the British. Egypt alone remained a doubtful factor.

Although Egypt stood by her treaty with the United Kingdom, she still hoped to be able to keep out of the war. She, however, helped in all passive preparations for her own defence, which included improvement of strategic roads and communications and creation of an excellent naval base at Alexandria.

On the sea, the combined British and French fleets had the complete command of the Mediterranean. In the air too, the position was fairly satisfactory. The French had a powerful air force based on Rayat, in the Lebanon while the British air force, though widely dispersed through Iraq, Aden, Palestine, and Egypt, was yet capable of being concentrated at any threatened point within a reasonably short time. On land, the British Army was being continually reinforced by arrival of troops from India, Australia and New Zealand. Such was the situation as the general result of the Anglo-French collaboration in the Middle East during the first half of 1940.

Collapse of France

Italy entered war as Germany's ally on 11 June 1940 and attacked France. On 25 June, France capitulated to Germany. This development had far-reaching and dangerous effects in the Middle East which may be briefly summed up as follows:—

    (a) The British domination of the Mediterranean Sea, which was based largely on the support of the French fleet, became a thing of the past. The Italian fleet became temporarily supreme. The flow of British reinforcements and supplies to the Middle East, via the Mediterranean Sea, became paralysed if not impossible.

(b) The Allies lost support of the French air squadrons in Syria and North Africa which greatly altered the balance of power in the air. The *Regia Aeronautica* then became free to concentrate all its strength in the central and eastern Mediterranean. Based on Sardinia, southern Italy, Sicily, the Libyan coast or the Dodecanese islands, it could strike at will, and without serious opposition, at the Suez Canal and the naval base at Alexandria, or at oil refineries and the harbour installations of Haifa, or at the oil tankers and naval craft in its vicinity. On the other hand, there was hardly any important and accessible target in Italy, or Italian Africa, on which the British aircraft could concentrate with immediate benefit.

(c) The exit of France deprived British aircraft of stepping-stones through that country, along which they could otherwise hop up to Egypt. Thereafter, most of the British aircraft had to travel at a snail's space on shipboard, packed in crates. Worse still, the advantage of the stepping-stones was now transferred to the Germans who could, if they wished, assist an Italian invasion of Egypt with dive-bombers and air-borne troops.

(d) On land, the defection of France left huge gaps west of Libya and east of Palestine. Sgr. Mussolini was now able to ignore the Tunisian front and turn towards Egypt. Syria became a potential threat in the rear of the Allied army in the Middle East. Collaboration with Turkey became more difficult and she seeing the support on her southern flank disappear, began to waver in her friendship for the Allies.

(e) Finally, with the elimination of the French strength on sea, the Italian East Africa came into its own. From the lately modernised ports of Massawa and Assab, Italy could now harass shipping in the Red Sea; and from the port of Mogadishu, she could even threaten the longer route round the Cape of Good Hope to India. The Allies, however, had one great asset in that Italy's land communications with her East African Empire were definitely cut after her entry into the war, and she could not reinforce that part, except by air.

Allied preparations in Africa

It has been mentioned that on assuming command of the Middle East, General Wavell set about organising its defences. The only likely aggressor in the Middle East at the time was Italy, and General Wavell's preparations were accordingly directed against that single power. Some years before the outbreak of the Second World War, Germany and Italy had established a close identity of political interests and ideologies, and they were pursuing these jointly in an alliance which came to be popularly known as the Axis.[1] It was therefore to be expected that, in case of a war, the two countries would be found fighting side by side and Italy would be attacking British and French possessions in Africa. However, Italy did not enter the war immediately on its outbreak, nor for many months later. This gave General Wavell some more time for strengthening his command and making general preparations against an almost certain eventuality.

The preparations were, however, greatly impeded by the desire of the British Government to do nothing that might precipitate Italy's entry into the war or impair the existing relations between the United Kingdom and Italy. General Wavell was not even permitted to set up a proper intelligence service inside the Italian territory; much less was he allowed to get into touch with the patriot chiefs of Abyssinia.[2] In the circumstances, he concentrated upon training, equipping and reinforcing his troops and establishing good relations with the military commanders of the countries bordering on his own Command. Accordingly, during the first few months of the war, he improved his relations with the military authorities of Syria, French North Africa, French Somaliland, Turkey, Iraq and the Sudan. In December 1939, he paid a short visit to England to discuss problems of the Middle East with the Chief of the Imperial General Staff. During that visit he also attended an Inter-Allied Conference on the Middle East problems, which was held in Paris and at which General Weygand from Syria was also present. On returning to the Middle East, he took over operational control from the East Africa Command, which was until then (3 February 1940) directly under the War Office.

Inside his own Command, General Wavell established several training centres and brought about a close co-ordination between the operational and administrative sides of the Command. This was achieved by his gradually taking over all administrative responsibilities. He thus accomplished a complete fusion between the operational and the administrative wings of the Middle East Command before June 1940. During that period (September 1939—June 1940) he also received the following reinforcements:

5th Indian Infantry Brigade from India,
2nd Battalion Durham Light Infantry from China,

---

[1] Formation of the Rome-Berlin Axis was announced on 24 Oct. 1936, (*War in Outline*, American Publication).
[2] Gen. Wavell's *Despatch*, Aug. 39-Nov. 40.

1st Cavalry Division (Horsed), incomplete in training and equipment,

16th Australian Infantry Brigade, and a portion of divisional troops of the 6th Australian Division, from Australia, and

4th New Zealand Infantry Brigade, with some divisional troops of a New Zealand Division.

Besides the above reinforcements, small contingents of officers and men were also received from Southern Rhodesia, Malta, Cyprus, Mauritius and Palestine. There was also an infantry brigade and an air force contingent garrisoning Kenya, at the southern frontier of the Italian East Africa, which had been received from South Africa for that express purpose.

Military situation on Italy's entry into war

Briefly, the general situation in North and East Africa at the time of Italy's entry into war was as follows:—

Egypt had a frontier of over 650 miles with Libya, while the frontiers of the Sudan, Kenya and British Somaliland, each bordering on Italian East Africa, were about 1,000 and 700 and 600 miles respectively.

The Italian troops in North and East Africa, in June 1940, were estimated by General Wavell to be over 215,000 men in Libya and over 200,000 in Italian East Africa; as against which the Commonwealth and Allied[3] Garrisons in the Middle East Command totalled a little over 85,000 men, roughly distributed as follows:

Egypt

(a) 7th Armoured Division comprising:
    4th Armoured Brigade (of two regiments)
    7th Armoured Brigade (only partly equipped)
  Support Group (two battalions):
    3rd RHA (Anti-tank Regiment), and
    4th RHA

(b) 4th Indian Division comprising:
    Two Field Regiments RA
    Two Indian Infantry Brigades (5th and 11th)

(c) Part of New Zealand Division comprising:
    One Cavalry Regiment (less one squadron)
    One Field Regiment New Zealand artillery
    Three Infantry battalions
    One Machine Gun battalion (incomplete in training and equipment)

(d) Fourteen British infantry battalions

---

[3] The term "Allied" is used here to include the 'partisan' troops i.e. nationals of France, Poland, Czechoslovakia etc. while "Commonwealth" includes also the Crown Colonies and other British Imperial possessions.

(e) 7th Medium Regiment RA
     31st Field Regiment RA
                                    Total about 36,000.

Sudan

(with 1,000 miles of frontier with Italian East Africa).
Three British battalions and
Sudan Defence Force
                                    Total about 9,000.

Kenya

(with over 700 miles of frontier with Italian East Africa)
Two East African Brigades
Two Light Batteries
                                    Total about 8,500.
(Two brigades from West Africa had been ordered to Kenya and arrived during July)

British Somaliland

Headquarters and five companies Somaliland
    Camel Corps
One King's African Rifles Battalion
                                    Total about 1,475.

Palestine

1st Cavalry Division (incomplete in training
    and equipment)
Two British Cavalry Regiments
One Brigade of three British
    infantry battalions
Two British battalions
6th Australian Division comprising:
    Two Brigades
    Two Artillery Regiments
    Divisional Recce Unit (incomplete
    in training and equipment)
                                    Total about 27,500.

Aden

Two Indian battalions
                                    Total about 2,500.

Cyprus

One British battalion
                                    Total about 800.

Thus the respective strengths of the Commonwealth and Italian troops stood in the proportion of 85,000 to 415,000 or roughly 1 against 5. But that was not all. The state of Allied preparedness was none too satisfactory. Not a single unit or formation of the above garrisons was fully equipped due to very little equipment having been received in the Middle East. There was specially a serious shortage of anti-aircraft and anti-tank guns and other artillery.

In the air, the Italians had a very considerable numerical advantage over the combined strength of the Royal Air Force and the South African Air Force, although, in the judgment of General Wavell, that handicap was adequately balanced by the superior qualities of the British machines and pilots. On the sea, the shortest route by which the Middle East could be reinforced, namely the Mediterranean, became extremely precarious, due to the ease with which the Suez Canal might be blocked by Italy, should she enter the war; and even the longer route via the Cape of Good Hope was not entirely free from the danger of attack by Italian naval and air forces. On land, the position was even worse. The frontier between Egypt and Libya was only thinly guarded by a very small force. A larger force could not be placed there on account of the supply and maintenance difficulties, as the frontier harbour of Sollum was very small and there was a shortage of water. To add to the difficulties, there was no good road for the last 50 miles to the frontier, that is from Sidi Barrani onwards.

In this state of general unpreparedness and lack of fighting men and material, there was of course no question of opposing an Italian invasion with an equal number of troops, should the Italians choose to attack. The problem was one of making a successful stand without being involved in a disastrous clash, which could be best done by withdrawing to a defendable position and offering resistance there. Such a position was being built at Matruh, a locality well within the Egyptian border—about half-way between Alexandria and the frontier—and destined to be the scene of many a later conflict. In the circumstances, the defensive tactics adopted by General Wavell was to permit the Italians to advance on the defences of Matruh, by a gradual and orderly withdrawal, before meeting them in any strength. His idea was to draw the Italians as far away as possible from their supply base and, at the same time, to conserve his fighting strength until the last moment. With that aim in view, he had instructed the small force guarding the frontier to start harassing the Italian border posts from the date of the declaration of war; but to withdraw, fighting delaying actions, if attacked in large numbers.

Similar orders were also given to the troops occupying principal places on the Sudan frontier who were just small mobile forces. The long vulnerable 1000-mile boundary line between the Sudan and

East Africa was not covered by these small bodies to any adequate degree. They were therefore instructed to hold the frontier only so long as they were left in peace. If attacked by a superior force, they were to withdraw fighting a delaying action. A similar policy of holding the frontier posts, as long as possible, was also adopted for Kenya.

In addition, steps had been taken to organise internal resistance in Italian East Africa should Italy enter the war. Such preparations as were possible, had been made to assist the patriotic leaders in Abyssinia to organise an armed rebellion or guerilla warfare against the Italians. A quantity of arms had been collected and a Mission was formed to get into touch with the patriots as soon as possible after the start of the war. Arrangements were also made for accommodating Haile Selassie, the Emperor of Abyssinia, in Khartoum, until it should be found possible for him to enter Abyssinia to be restored to his throne.

Partisan troops in the Middle East

A peculiar feature of the Middle East Command was that some of its fighting troops were nationals belonging to the Axis-occupied countries. These were either refugees or escapees from those countries, or individuals already residing in Allied territories at the time of the outbreak of the war who had banded themselves together to fight for the Allied cause. The more important amongst them were the French, Poles, Czechs and Belgians. A considerable number of the nationals of these countries were in Syria when France signed an armistice with Germany and, being dissatisfied, had crossed into Palestine to join the Allied forces. The French, amongst these, consisted of a number of sub-units and individual soldiers besides a large part of a French colonial battalion then stationed at Cyprus. The Polish contingent consisted of the whole of the Polish Carpathian Brigade—about 4000 strong—which had been serving with the French in Syria; while the rest comprised a large party of Czechs who had been awaiting onward passage to France, and a few Spanish and Belgian volunteers. All of these were accepted for service into the Allied army. The French, Poles and Czechs were formed into separate contingents, the Spanish volunteers were drafted into British commando units, and the Belgians were either placed in the British Arab Force or sent to the United Kingdom.

Thus, from the time the Middle East Command was formed until the declaration of war by Italy, the main activities of the Middle East forces were the establishment of closer relations with the neighbouring military commanders, training and equipping, receiving reinforcements and building up supplies, and planning and preparing defences against a possible attack by Italy.

It remains to take note of one more point. Soon after the Germans attacked France, General Weygand, the Commander-in-Chief of the French forces in the Middle East, was recalled to Paris for more important duties, and his place was taken by General Massiet, the Commander of the French Mobile Forces in the Levant. This left General Wavell with a greater burden than hitherto in his capacity as the Commander-in-Chief of the land forces in North and East Africa and Palestine.

CHAPTER VI

Italy Declares War

News of Italy's entry into the war reached the 4th Indian Division at 2000 hours on 10 June 1940. The rest of Egypt received it almost simultaneously, which produced a flurry of activities as precautions began to be taken against the possibility of instantaneous attacks from air, sea or land. Italy had declared that she would be at war against Great Britain and France as from the first minute of 11 June 1940. Headquarters British troops in Egypt, therefore, issued orders putting all units on four hours' notice to move. At the same time Egyptian authorities arrested such of the Italians residing in Egypt as were considered capable of indulging in fifth column activities.

Italian aircraft raided Allied forward positions in the Western Desert on the same day. No raid, however, occurred over Cairo or its neighbourhood, although alarms were sounded several times. Nothing more spectacular happened for another six weeks, as neither the Italians nor the Allies made any substantial move in North Africa. The 4th Indian Division, which was then at Mena, under Major-General Neame, continued to train, reinforce and equip itself, waiting at the same time for further orders.[1] One of its brigades—the 5th—was then at El Daba.

A few weeks later, the division received its cavalry regiment from India. It was the Central India Horse, which arrived at Mena on 6 August 1940. As it happened, there was a change in the divisional command on the same day, General Neame handing over to Major-General Beresford-Peirse[2] and leaving to fill another appointment. The arrival of the Central India Horse had not only strengthened the division but had made it fit for the first time to enter the forward area. Soon after, the division was warned to be ready for a move to a forward position in the Western Desert, which meant that it was now about to begin the long record of its fighting experiences. The divisional commander, Maj.-General Beresford—Peirse, accompanied by his staff, carried out a preliminary reconnaissance to that end on 13 August, and the expected orders arrived the next day, directing that the move should commence from 19 August. The destination named was Naghamish and the area of concentration was the Naghamish Nulla.[3]

[1] W/D 4 Div., June 1940.
[2] Major-General N. M. de la P. Beresford-Peirse, CB, DSO.
[3] W/D 4 Div., Aug. 1940.

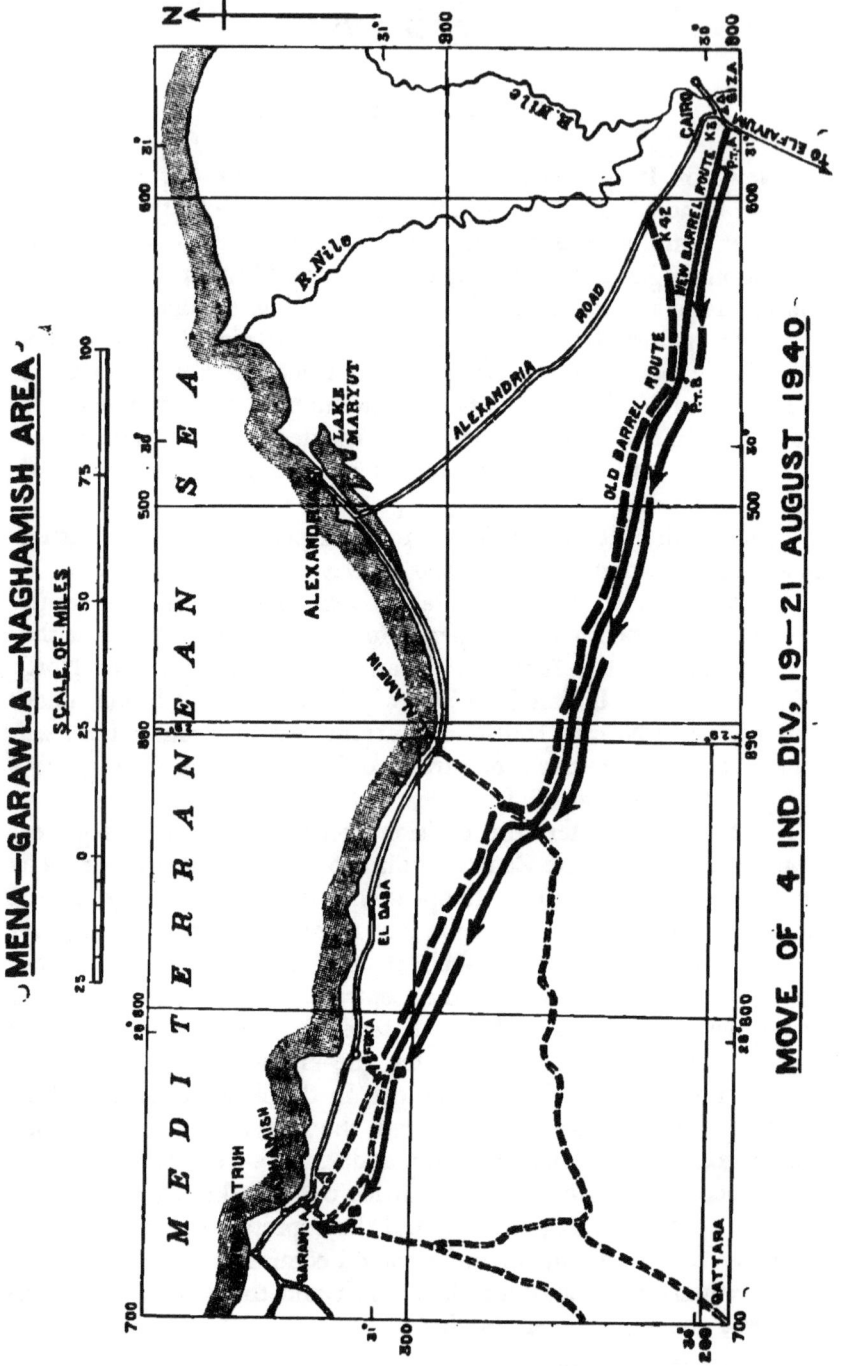

Move to Western Desert

The move commenced as scheduled. It was carried out in three groups, each of which proceeded separately. One of the groups went through the desert, another by road and the third by rail. The desert group consisted of what were classed as desert-worthy vehicles, that is, transport capable of enduring the strain of a cross-desert journey. Incidentally, not more than one per cent of the vehicles broke down during that hard test. The road group contained the second best vehicles; while the rest, chiefly tracked transport and motor cycles, formed the rail group.[4]

The Barrel Routes

For the move of the desert group, a route was marked out by placing empty tar-barrels at intervals. Such a method of identifying a road or laying out a new one was necessary in the desert, since in the absence of easily recognisable landmarks it was possible for vehicles and convoys to go astray or get lost.[5]

One such track, which later came to be known as the Old Barrel Route, was already in existence. It started from Kilometre 42, on the road Mena—Alexandria and, proceeding west, north-west and then north, it finally ended at Fuka. The route marked out for the move of the desert group was similar in character. It was called the New Tar Barrel Route in order to distinguish it from the old one. It started from Kilometre 3 instead of Kilometre 42, and did not end at Fuka but in the proximity of Garawla. It lay to the south of the Old Barrel Route and roughly parallel to it. The distance between the parallel routes was about 25 kilometres at first, which narrowed down gradually until the two roads were no more than a hundred yards apart.[6]

Starting from Mena, the New Barrel Route proceeded north-west towards the Old Barrel Route, which it reached near Gabr Abu Milha, approximately 55 miles west-north-west of Cairo. Thence it ran roughly parallel to the Old Barrel Route, until it arrived at a place 15 miles south of Fuka. There it branched into two tracks, each of which joined the track Garawla—Bir Khalda. The Bir Khalda track then proceeded to the Garawla—Naghamish area, the destination of the 4th Indian Division. This was a locality situated along the Alexandria—Mersa Matruh road, between Kilometres 16 and 26.[7]

The total cross-desert distance involved in the march was 290 miles. Approximately 1000 vehicles traversed that distance and the

---

[4] W/D 4 Div. and Ops. Inst. Aug. 1940.
[5] *Tiger Strikes*, p. 12.
[6] Report on Western Desert Move of 4 Ind. Div., W/D 4 Div., p. 72 et seq.
[7] *Ibid*, and W/D 4 Div., Sep. 1940, p. 91.

time taken was 2½ days. The column was divided into three groups, the 5th Indian Infantry Brigade, the Divisional Headquarters and the 1st Field Regiment RA. The Brigade Group went first and was followed by the Divisional Headquarters, distance between the two being about two hours' journey. About half an hour's journey in the rear of the latter, again, was the Field Regiment group. The Divisional Headquarters was exactly twenty hours on the move, excluding two night halts and the halts for rest during the day, thus doing 14½ miles per hour on an average while on the move, and 5·7 miles on the whole.[8]

Experiences during the move

The nature of the area which the desert group crossed can be vividly visualised from an official report of the move. Throughout the march conditions were such as to demand a high standard of driving. In places the earth was too soft for heavy vehicles or for artillery without tractors. In other places soft patches of ground were concealed by hard surface-crusts which broke under the weight of the vehicles and caused them to sink into sand. There were also stretches of ground where the surface consisted either of a flat, stony area or of small stones and patches of slab rock. For the most of the way, however, movement in desert formation was possible. Even defiles, where met, were crossed by several parallel columns abreast.[9]

No cover from air observation was available. Aircraft of the Royal Air Forces, which offered overhead protection to the column during the move, reported that the column was liable to be detected easily from the air, since dust thrown up by the vehicles was visible for miles back. That disadvantage was, however, balanced by the fact that a convoy moving in desert formation offered poor targets to the hostile aircraft, on account of its wide dispersal.

Owing to the ruggedness of the ground, frequent light repairs to vehicles were necessary on the way, for which ample Light Aid Detachment (LAD) arrangements were needed. Light Aid Detachments were also useful for towing the vehicles which broke down completely, as also for assisting the convoy to keep such breakdowns to a minimum. It was also clear that in case of a withdrawal over the same ground, even more thorough and energetic LAD precautions would be necessary. In addition, orders would have to be issued in advance and requisite arrangements made for the destruction of vehicles which might have to be abandoned. A generous proportion of spare vehicles would also have to be maintained as against the possibility of hostile interference on the way, so as to be

---

[8] Report on Western Desert Move of 4 Ind. Div., War Diary 4 Div., p. 72.
[9] *Ibid.*

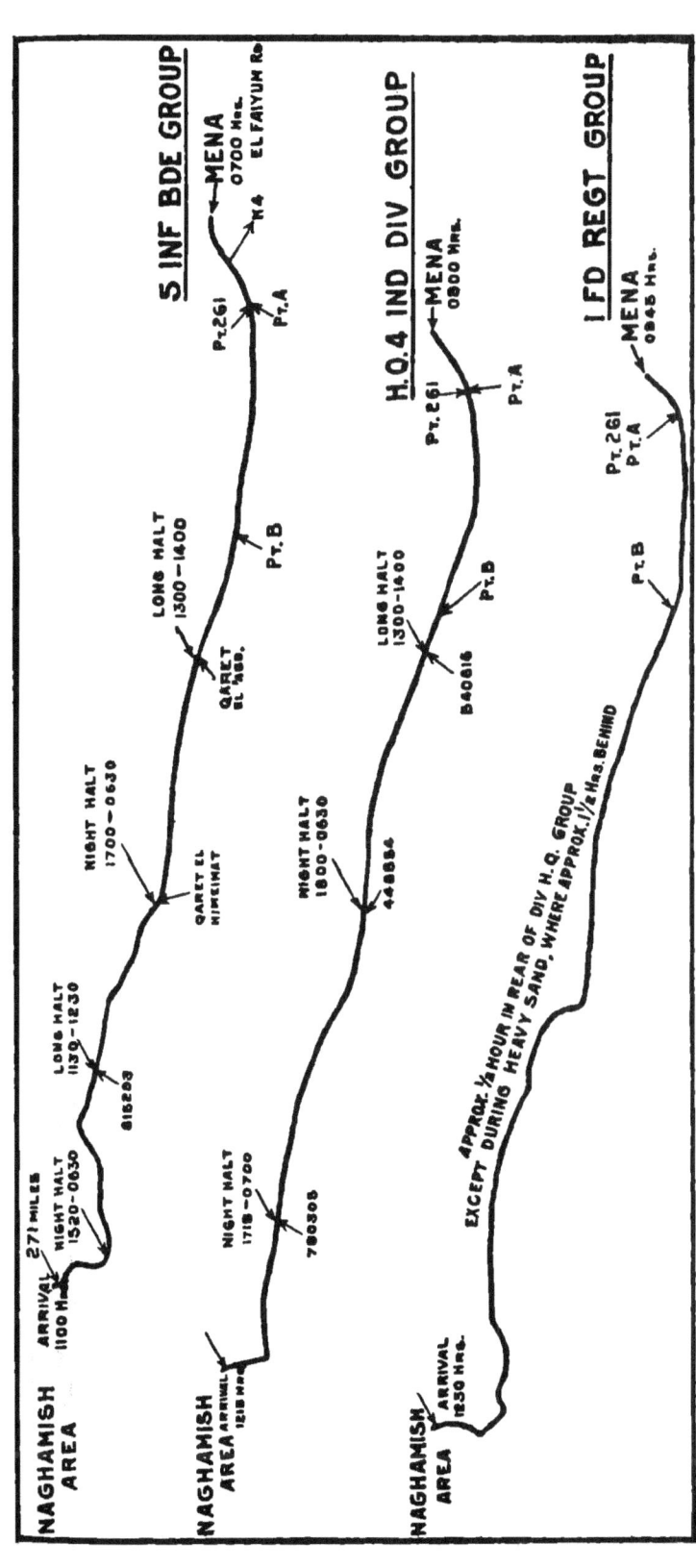

MOVEMENT OF 4 IND DIV FROM MENA TO NAGHAMISH, 19-21 AUGUST 1940

sure of being able to ferry the stranded personnel and rescue stores from the disabled or destroyed vehicles.

As it was, the 4th Indian Division took with it only 4 per cent spare 2nd-line vehicles. No spares of the 1st-line vehicles existed. The Division had to leave on the way only about one per cent of the vehicles for subsequent recovery. Another two per cent were repaired by the LAD or the drivers, and taken along *en route*. All vehicle casualties were entirely from mechanical defects, the move having taken place without opposition.

The desert route, it was found, was not suitable for very heavy vehicles such as the workshop type or the six-wheelers or even for light vehicles which had not been made fully desert-worthy. Field artillery could only be taken if good tractors in a sound state of repair were available and then at a greatly reduced speed. The average pace would be 4 m.i.h. (miles-in-the-hour) over large stretches of soft sand or over thin surface-crusts with soft sand underneath. Over the harder ground speed would be restricted by large stones.

Communication from the tail to the head of the convoy was always a slow affair whenever wireless silence was ordered. It could be done only by vehicles having messages overtaking the other vehicles. Owing to the nature of the ground, however, that was not easy. It took over three hours to overtake about half the length of the Divisional Headquarters column; and it was found that improvement was effected only by limiting the pace of the column or by moving in shorter bounds. The best means of course was the wireless.[10]

Strict march discipline was found to be absolutely essential in the desert to prevent vehicles wandering away from the column and getting lost. Trying short-cuts and inattention to rules of driving and maintenance would lead to heavy casualties in men and vehicles. That point was brought home to the division by a Cypriot Company of the RASC which accompanied it. It was said to have caused the column "considerable delay, anxiety and sweat" due to lack of training and military discipline on the part of the drivers.

As to the rate of petrol consumption, the expenditure was somewhat heavy, mostly owing to the greater use of the low gear on the way. On the 4th Indian Division's track, the consumption was 35 per cent more than it would be on an average metalled road. Similarly, consumption of water for the radiators was very high whenever there was a hot wind following the convoy. Although the 4th Indian Division did not experience that kind of difficulty, it was reported that a New Zealand convoy, with a hot wind following it all the way, needed approximately 10 gallons per vehicle for a forty-mile journey.

[10] War Diary 4 Div.

All water, whether for radiators or for drinking and washing, had to be carried along, as there was none on the way except for the last 50 miles of the journey. In addition to carrying that normal requirement, each vehicle had also to provide itself with an extra supply of drinking water if there was a risk of hostile action, so that the personnel may be able to tide over the period of being stranded in case the vehicle became a casualty. Although there was some water in the desert wells, in the area west of Fuka, a report of the quantity available and its fitness for drinking was lacking.

Finally, this move once again brought out the point that is often overlooked. In fixing a day for the commencement of a move involving a long absence from the place of departure, it is desirable to choose a day other than a Sunday or a Monday. This move commenced on a Monday and, as a result, several individuals who, for reasons of security, could not be notified earlier, were unable to attend to their personal affairs of banking, shopping, etc. At the same time, the official work too could not be got through satisfactorily, as various depots, establishments and Headquarters Staff Officers were in the practice of working with reduced staffs during a week-end.[11]

Arrival in the Western Desert

On their arrival in the Naghamish area, all vehicles, except those required forward, went into what were designated the "waggon line" areas. These were vehicle parks, kept well to the rear of the defensive position in order not to give away the defensive layout.[12]

Simultaneously with the desert column, the rail and road columns were also heading for the Naghamish area. The rail parties arrived partly on 21 and partly on 22 August. They were carrying 50 per cent of the Bren guns of all infantry battalions of the division as mobile anti-aircraft protection to the trains. The other 50 per cent were with the desert column, the road party having only 3 anti-aircraft light machine-guns. Aircraft of the Royal Air Force were held in readiness to provide protection to the detraining parties in case Italians bombed the detraining station. No air attack however took place either during the march or at the destination.[13]

The road convoy, which was composed of heavy and slow-moving vehicles, as well as other vehicles not considered desert-worthy, started on 20 August and reached the concentration area on the following day. Starting from Mena, it went along the Mena-Alexandria road to Amiriya. Then, turning off the road at Bahig, it made a slight detour and moved to El Daba, via Burg el

---

[11] War Diary 4 Div.
[12] *Ibid*, p. 60, Aug. 1940.
[13] *Ibid*.

Arab. Thence it proceeded to the concentration area approximately 63 miles away.[14]

The total distance travelled by the road column was 258 miles, speed being regulated at 15 m.i.h. (miles-in-the-hour) and density to 15 v.t.m. (vehicles-to-the-mile). Night journeys were not performed in order to avoid showing lights after dark. Throughout the move special attention was paid to dispersion and anti-craft defence. Co-ordination during the move was ensured by ordering that a representative from each serial (i.e., vehicles bearing the same unit marks and numbers) should 'liaise' with the serial which preceded as well as that which followed his own. The units composing the road convoy were the 1st and 31st Field Regiments RA, Divisional Signals, Ordnance Workshops, 14th Field Ambulance, 15th Field Hygiene Section, 17th Field Post Office, 18th Field Company and 232nd Field Company RASC.[15]

Defensive Positions

On arrival in the respective areas allotted to them, all units of the 4th Indian Division started digging themselves in. The place was very dusty and washing was difficult owing to the shortage of water which was rationed at 2 gallons a day per man. That included water for drinking, ablutions and washing. Both the advance and the rear headquarters of the division took up their camping sites in the "waggon line" area, immediately on arrival.[16] On 24 August, however, the Advanced Headquarters moved into another location, nearer to its proposed battle ground.

On the same day, the Divisional Commander directed the Commander Royal Engineers (CRE) to start work on establishing pill-boxes and sangars in the forward area. The CRE was also directed to make arrangements, as from 27 August, for water-storage and for supply of water, by pipe and rail, to the extent of 640 tanks per day, some tanks having 200-gallon capacity. The pill-boxes were to be designed in consultation with the infantry brigades to resist field artillery shell-fire. Three unseasoned pill-boxes were to be got ready within the first three weeks, and thereafter at three per week, as it required a minimum of one month for the concrete to harden. It was decided to enrol civilian labour from amongst the Bedouins and Cypriots to assist the Sappers, commencing with about 250 Bedouins at once.[17]

The work of preparing the defensive positions continued until the end of the month. By that time the division was further strengthened by the arrival, in the concentration area, of several

[14] W/D 4 Div., Aug. 1940, p. 66.
[15] *Ibid*, p. 67.
[16] *Ibid*, p. 60.
[17] *Ibid*.

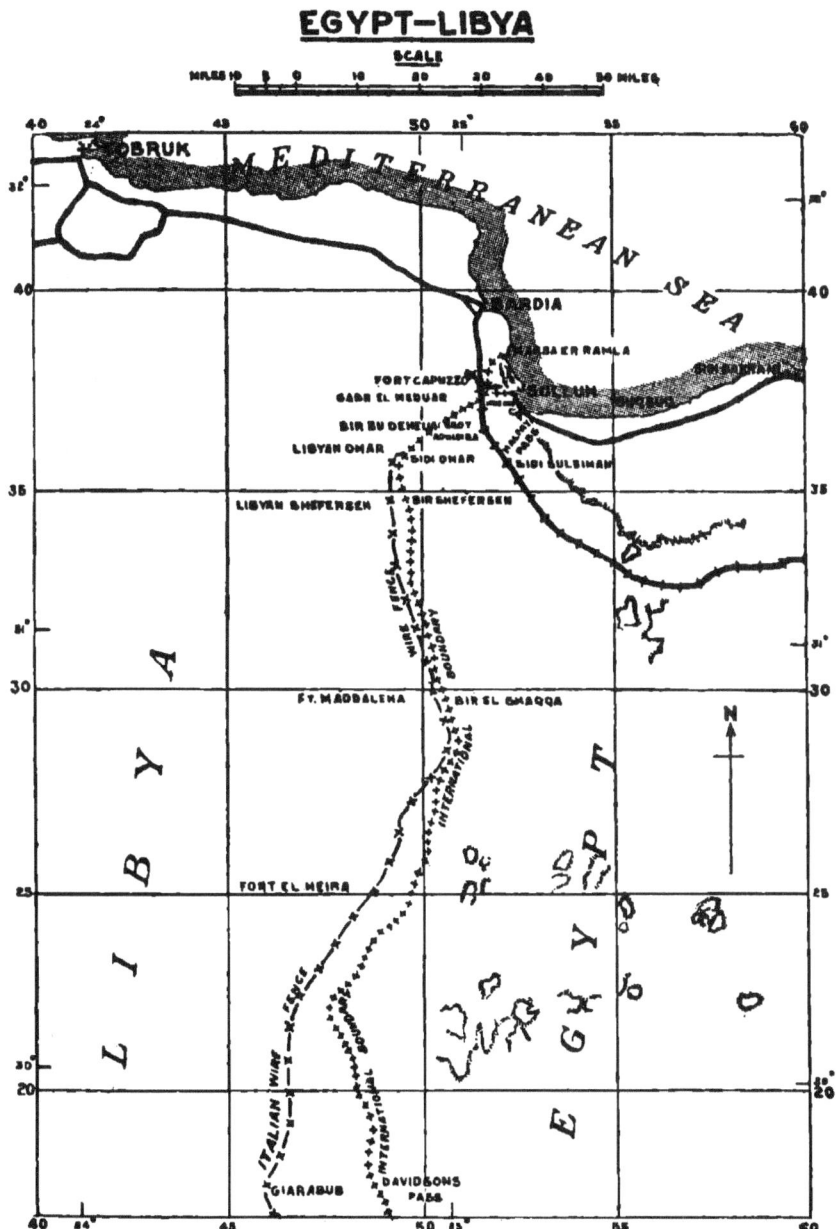

THE EGYPTIAN FRONTIER SHOWING THE ITALIAN WIRE FENCE
(FROM SOLLUM TO GIARABUB)

units amongst which were the 7th Medium Regiment RA, Headquarters 11th Indian Infantry Brigade, 2 Camerons, 1 Rajputana Rifles, one company 4 Rajput Regiment, 1 Northumberland Fusiliers and Headquarters Royal Engineers. There was no fighting in the area immediately ahead of the 4th Indian Division. Yet the situation was by no means very easy as can be ascertained from the division's intelligence summaries and operational instructions issued during the last week of August 1940.[18]

It was then believed that the Italians would launch their attack at no distant date. That possibility appears to have caused a certain degree of nervousness even at the Headquarters of the 4th Indian Division at Naghamish, which was really a great distance behind the frontier. For, on 25 August, the Divisional Commander ordered the backloading of such extra kit, tents, baggage, etc. as might have been brought up by the troops in the belief "that there might be ample time justifying our having such kit". Simultaneously, defensive preparations were ordered to be accelerated. Anti-tank mines were ordered to be drawn as rapidly as possible from the CRE, and stored under brigade arrangements in the forward area. A demand for 20,000 mines had been already placed on the BTE (British troops in Egypt) and efforts were made to procure more.[19]

The Egyptian Frontier

While the 4th Indian Division was digging in at Naghamish, the western frontier of Egypt, about 150 miles away, was being guarded by the 7th (British) Armoured Brigade and certain other tank and artillery units. That force was operating at a disadvantage as to its supplies, since it was 120 miles away from the rail terminus at Matruh. Its main task was to patrol the frontier and harass the Italians by attacking their outposts, convoys and patrols.

But such activities were causing no small wear and tear to the armoured vehicles. There was a general lack of spare parts to replace those worn out and the distance from the front to the railhead made deliveries slow and difficult. As a result, a rapidly mounting deterioration had set in and tanks were finding their way to workshops in increasing numbers. Thus, at the end of July 1940, there were no more than 200 tanks in action, out of a total of 306, the rest being under repairs. General Wavell saw that, if that state of affairs was allowed to persist, most of his tanks would be out of action just when the Italians would be advancing, and took steps to avoid such a situation. The remedy applied was to change the composition of the force guarding the Egyptian frontier so as to

---

[18] *Ibid* and W/D 4 Div., p. 83, Aug. 1940.
[19] W/D 4 Div. pp. 80-87, Aug. 1940.

conserve the armour.[20] Accordingly in the last week of July he issued instructions that all tracked vehicles were to be withdrawn from the frontier for overhaul and refit. The area was thereafter to be held with a skilful use of dummy tanks and a small force commanded by the Support Group of the 7th (British) Armoured Division.

This new force which was then distributed over a front of some 60 miles, from Sollum to Fort Maddalena, continued the same policy of active patrolling and harassment. But opportunities for such tactics were now diminishing. The Italian forces were growing in numbers and their artillery was more active than before. In spite of that, six more weeks elapsed before the Italians made their first major move which started the fighting in North Africa.

In that fighting the 4th Indian Division had its own part to play. Since the war in Europe had inevitable repurcussions on the situation in Africa, it is necessary to digress here a little and take note of the earlier happenings in Europe and of their influence on the situation in the Middle East Command, before returning to the activities of the 4th Indian Division at Naghamish.[21]

Fall of France and its sequel

Heavy fighting had been going on in France during the first half of June 1940. The Germans had entered Paris on the 14th of that month and the French Government had moved its seat to Vichy. On 17 June the Vichy Government asked for armistice terms, which it accepted on the 22nd. That situation faced the colonies and overseas possessions of France with the delicate questions of whether or not to continue the struggle against Germany. Each colony took its own decision according to the circumstances with which it was confronted. In North Africa the French Commander, General Nogues, after a little hesitation, decided to obey orders of the Vichy Government to capitulate. His example was followed shortly afterwards by General Mittelhauser, the commander in Syria. In French Somaliland, General Legentilhomme held out for a month but finally gave up on failing to induce the colony to continue the resistance. He was superseded by General Germain.

All this, among other things, meant a total collapse of the French resistance on the continent of Africa. The resultant situation emboldened the Italian forces in East Africa to start operations on the borders of the Sudan, Kenya and British Somaliland. They crossed the Sudan frontier early in July 1940 and captured Kassala, Gallabat and Kurmuk. On 15 July, they occupied Moyale in Kenya. On 4 August, they invaded British Somaliland and forced

[20] Gen. Wavell's *Despatch* August 39 to Nov. 40.
[21] *Ibid*.

its evacuation by the British and Indian garrisons. Simultaneously on the Egyptian frontier, the Italian North African army grew more aggressive and menacing.

Hitherto the Allied and Italian forces on the Egyptian frontier had been engaged in nothing more than patrol skirmishes, artillery duels and reciprocal air attacks. Serious fighting had not yet begun. The Italians were still busy constructing defences on their side of the border as if anticipating an Allied attack. Those defences were known to be located at Capuzzo, Bardia and Gabr Saleh.[22]

Italian Defences

Capuzzo was an old desert fort, with a water pipeline and an airfield in the neighbourhood. It was a focal point for several roads and tracks converging on it from all points of the compass. Some of them were only 3 to 6 metres wide whilst others were fit for use by wheeled traffic. The airfield stood to the north-west of the fort about half a kilometre away. The water pipeline, which came from Bardia, lay along the north and east of the fort. Along it, in the same two directions, ran the main tarmac road to Bardia, closely skirting the fort on its northern side.[23]

Unlike Capuzzo, Bardia had neither a fort nor an aerodrome, nor was it a junction of many roads. Its importance lay in the fact that it was the first port and town just outside the Egyptian frontier, 8 miles from the border and 20 miles from Sollum. Both the port and the town were of small size but had been carefully developed by the Italians to serve as an advanced base for an invasion of Egypt. The port, which was inland, was joined to the open sea by a narrow channel bordered by steep and rocky cliffs and permitting the passage of vessels up to 4,000 tons. The town itself was sited 350 feet above sea level on the high ground to the north of the harbour. The Italians had fortified the whole area round the town to a depth of seven to eight miles, with wires, minefields, tanktraps, machine-gun posts, gun-emplacements and the rest.[24]

Some 45 miles to the south-west of Bardia, and 25 miles from the frontier, was situated the third Italian defensive position, Gabr Saleh. It was merely a camp and a defence post for the protection of some Italian dumps.[25] The post however stood on the line of any possible Allied advance on Capuzzo through a very vital point known as Bir el Gubi.[26]

[22] W/D 4 Div., p. 83.
[23] Map, Sheet 40A, 1/100,000, Cyrenaica.
[24] *Conquest of North Africa*, p. 15, Burke Publishing Co. Ltd.; and *Middle East Training Pamphlet No. 10*, p. 17.
[25] W/D 4 Div., p. 85, Aug., 1940, and pp. 85-89 and Map Sheet 40A, 1/100,000 Cyrenaica.
[26] In 1940, such an advance would not be considered easy or even practicable as it would involve a very wide turning movement.

ITALIAN POSITIONS AUGUST 1940

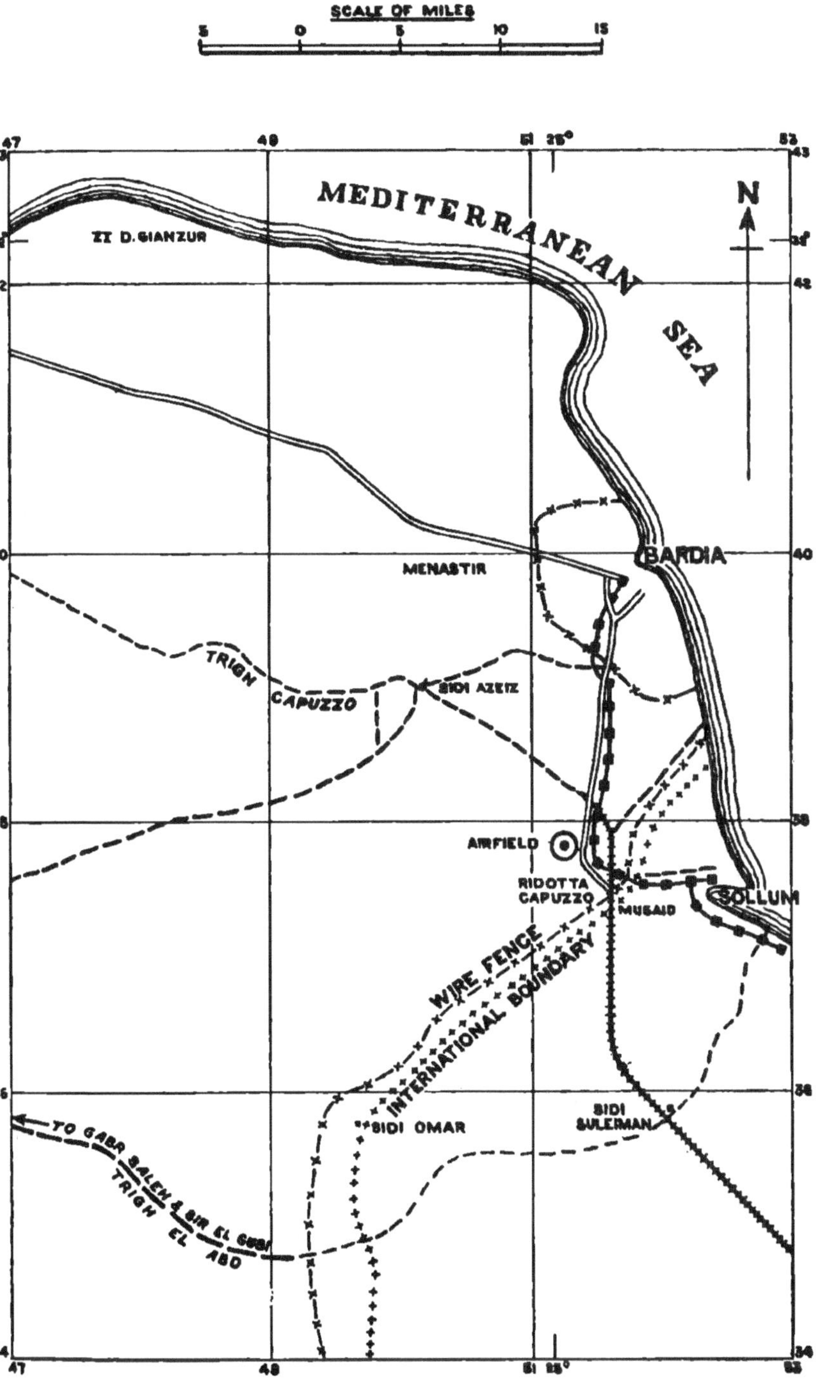

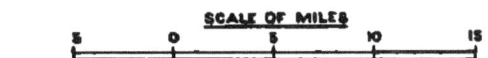

In all these three localities—Capuzzo, Bardia and Gabr Saleh—the defences were built on more or less the same pattern and were all designed to withstand tank and infantry attacks. At Capuzzo, defences took the form of an outer and an inner line of trenches and dugouts, the outer line being at a distance of 500 yards and the inner about 300 yards from the fort. This double line was protected by another line of anti-tank mines and ditches. Gaps were, however, left in the western face of this defensive system, somewhere in the centre of the aerodrome, to enable aircraft to land and take off. The dugouts were mostly small, with a capacity for one or two men and were possibly used also to store ammunition and provisions. They were interspersed with gun-emplacements for anti-tank, anti-aircraft and machine-guns and were connected together with communicating trenches. The defences were strongest in the north-east, that is, opposite to the line of the Allied artillery fire.[27]

The Bardia defences consisted of a fortified perimeter, about 17 miles in circumference. The perimeter was made of a chain of concrete posts standing at intervals of 700 yards from one another. Each post was designed to hold two or more medium machine-guns and one or more anti-tank guns. Every post was surrounded by a circular, concreted, anti-tank ditch and a wire obstacle. In addition, the perimeter as a whole was protected by a continuous wire-fencing and a number of anti-tank trenches, reinforced at weaker spots by mined patches. The forward posts were supported by another line of posts, 500 yards in the rear, unprotected by wire or anti-tank obstacles.[28]

The perimeter defences of the camp at Gabr Saleh were constructed in exactly the same way as those at Capuzzo. Towards the end of August 1940, a new camp with a landing ground made a sudden appearance some two miles south-west of Gabr Saleh, apparently made by the Italians in a great hurry.

An outstanding feature of all the Italian defences in the area Capuzzo—Bardia—Gabr Saleh was that they were constructed in great haste or rather with remarkable speed. A force getting ready to invade a territory does not spend its time in digging in, in that elaborate manner. As to why the Italians spent so much time and energy in building those hurried defences, when they were due to advance shortly afterwards, it is not easy to judge. Perhaps at that time no invasion was contemplated. At any rate it led the Allied high command to infer that the Italian commanders did not intend to advance on Sollum in the immediate future and that far from having offensive intentions themselves, they were fearing the same from the Allied side.

[27] W/D 4 Div., pp. 85-89; Map Sheet 40A, Cyrenaica.
[28] W/D 4 Div., p. 89; *Middle East Training Pamphlet No. 10*, p. 17.

Thus, for a time, there was a comparative quiet on the frontier, as well as in the area of the 4th Indian Division, except for air reconnaissances and mutual bombing of positions from the air. In particular, the Italian aircraft concentrated their bombing attacks on Matruh, paying occasional visits to the 4th Indian Division locations; while the Allied aircraft carried out strategic reconnaissance of the area Bir Hakeim—Bir el Gubi—Gabr Saleh—Maddalena—Giarabub. The object of these reconnoitring flights was to find out whether new lines of communication were coming into existence in that area, indicating a possible Italian advance from any of those places. None were discernible.

Italian Tactics and Weapons

It might be appropriate here to comment briefly on the kinds of aircraft and tanks used by the Italians at this period, and the manner of their employment. The aircraft which bombed Matruh were Savoia 79s. In the first raid, 19 of them came in three waves of 13, 5 and 1 and dropped 35 bombs in all, causing a few casualties and a little damage. In the second raid, which came two hours later, 25 Savoia 79s came up in four waves of 15, 5, 4 and 1, flying at a height of about 16000 feet, and dropped 85 HE (high explosive) bombs. Again, some damage and a few casualties were caused. At about the same time, some new types of Italian planes came to the notice of Allied observers. They were seen from the air, for the first time, on the landing ground at Derna and were probably S. 82s. They were reported to be very large bomber-transports, capable of carrying up to 50 lightly equipped men.

As to tanks, the Italian medium tanks of that time, (August 1940), were believed to be not very effective. They were considered very blind, in so far as the vision of the crew was greatly restricted by the nature of their construction. They were also somewhat clumsy in their movement and had no wireless aerials. They were more heavily armoured in the front than at the sides and were therefore constantly obliged to turn so as to present the front to any gun that opened fire on them. Even this front armour was not sufficiently thick and could be penetrated by the British anti-tank guns and Bofors from a distance of about 400 yards. As to the Italian light tanks, they had difficulty in firing on the move and were therefore obliged to halt in order to aim, thus either themselves becoming easy targets or, as sometimes happened, creating the impression of being "dead" and luring an unwary opponent on to their firing range. Stones of more than nine inches' diameter constituted a partial obstacle for any Italian tank. If stones or boulders of that size, or larger, were scattered about at intervals of approximately six feet, the tanks automatically slowed down in an effort to avoid the obstacles. Artificial fields of stones were thus found very useful for side-tracking Italian armoured vehicles and tanks and diverting them on to anti-tank positions.[29]

In respect of the other items of Italian armament, one point of interest might be mentioned. The Italians were then reported to have used a particular kind of missile which at that time used to be referred to as the "flaming onions". These first came to notice when they were fired against a patrol of the 3rd Coldstream Guards on the night of 2/3 September. They were luminous, spherical objects in red, green and white colours. They travelled at a comparatively slower speed and appeared to cause no damage. When first seen their effect was unnerving but soon they came to be regarded as harmless objects which were being used by the Italians for some yet unknown purpose.[30]

---

[29] W/D 4 Div., Aug. 1940, p. 108—For specifications of Italian Light and Medium Tanks see Appendix D.
[30] W/D 4 Div., p. 117, Aug.-Sep. 1940.

CHAPTER VII

Invasion of Egypt

Early in September 1940, the 4th Indian Division was still busy digging defences in the Naghamish position. That work, however, received a sudden set-back when, on 11 September, the division received orders to quit Naghamish and withdraw to Baqqush. The order was contained in a divisional operational instruction of the same date which explained that the withdrawal was a practice move, to be rehearsed in conditions closely approximating to those which might occur in actual operations. In order that the work on the Naghamish defences might be interrupted as little as possible, some units were left behind to continue the job. They were the Central India Horse, the 2nd Battalion Camerons, the 4th Battalion Rajput Regiment, the 4th and 18th Field Companies of Sappers and Miners, and Headquarters and Detachments of the 1st Northumberland Fusiliers. These units too were withdrawn soon after.[1]

Whether the withdrawal of the 4th Indian Division to Baqqush was really intended as a practice move or whether it was merely disguised as such, it is not very clear. A significant point is that the order for that withdrawal was issued on 11 September, the day on which the Italian forces in Libya made their first move towards invading Egypt. In that case it is possible that the division's withdrawal was something more than a mere practice move and might have been intended to vacate positions for the forward Allied[2] troops to fall back upon. Or it may be that the intention was to put the division on a job of preparing and holding a rear position. Whatever the motive, the next few days witnessed two principal troop movements in Libya and Egypt: the forward move of Italy's North African Army, better known as the Italian Tenth Army, towards Sidi Barrani, and the rearward move of the 4th Indian Division towards Baqqush.

Italian advance

As to the Italian advance, the Allied intelligence service does not appear to have succeeded in foreseeing or forecasting it. This is the conclusion one is led to on reading the day-to-day intelligence

---

[1] W/D 4 Div., p. 95, Sep. 1940.
[2] If the term "Allied" has been used at times hereafter in preference to "Commonwealth" or "Imperial" troops, it is because there were also troops of other nationalities such as Free French, Poles etc.

reports received by the 4th Indian Division. These reports were the carefully compiled summaries of facts relating to Italian positions, movements and other activities, as observed by forward troops or as gathered from air and ground reconnaissances. Most of them were no doubt accurate. But to have accurate facts is one matter, to interpret them correctly quite another. And it was here that the Allied intelligence service seems to have gone wrong. It appears that the one clue most sought after by the intelligence experts was movement of large masses of mechanical transport as a signal indicating that the invasion of Egypt had commenced. They seem to have overlooked the possibility that Italian formations might not be fully motorised, except some specially constituted mobile colunms. In that event the quantity of transport on the move might not be a proper gauge for measuring the strength of the forces in question. There would always be too few vehicles giving an impression of small units or columns moving, when, as a matter of fact, one or more divisions might be involved.

Thus, while the Italians were making a major move in force towards Sidi Barrani, the Allied intelligence experts persisted in believing that those were small, local movements. It was only some days after the invaders had crossed the borders of Egypt and settled down in Sidi Barrani that it became apparent to the Allied observers that the Italians were advancing in considerable strength and that the number of their vehicles was no proper indication of the size of their force. This is clear from a paragraph in the 4th Indian Division's intelligence summary of 20 September 1940, which frankly admits its previous error. "It appears," says the report, "that the present enemy thrust is a serious effort at invasion and is not a local operation. Five Divisions (of 2 Brigades each) and a tank group are taking part. Sufficient mechanical transport has not been seen to account for a force of this strength. Possibly the Divisions are not fully motorised; some of the Libyan troops are reported to be on foot. Possibly only a proportion of each Division has gone forward, leaving the remainder in reserve in the area Capuzzo—Bardia—Azeiz; this does not sound a very reasonable plan. But if the force is well dispersed behind the advanced guard at Barrani, it would be very difficult to spot it and estimate its strength.".[3]

Divisional intelligence reports for September 1940 are full of such speculations. All conjectures have as their basis, movements of Italian transport as seen from air or reported by ground troops. Indeed, intelligence summaries received by the 4th Indian Division from higher level and re-issued by it to its lower formations, at that period, are full of day-to-day figures of quantities of transports observed, and directions in which they were found heading. It must

[3] W/D 4 Div., p. 136, Sep. 1940.

be admitted, however, that those records were not quite useless and did provide a fairly good picture of the activities and possible intentions of the Italians. But on the whole the picture was inadequate and led to an underestimate of the opponent's strength. It might have placed the Allied troops into serious difficulties had they decided to give battle to the advancing force, basing their calculation on figures produced by their intelligence experts; and if such a result did not ensue, it was mainly because the Allied plan was different. That plan was to fall back fighting a delaying action, since, as stated earlier, there was no question of offering a battle or launching out on an offensive. Consequently, it was not very material whether the strength of the advancing force was correctly estimated or not at this particular juncture. Further, at that time, much detailed and unnecessary "intelligence" was being issued by the 4th Indian Division, mainly in order to accustom the troops to a war outlook and to train the intelligence personnel in their duties. That fact must have been known to the commanders of the various formations, who would not thus be acting without using their own judgment in the matter.

Manner of Italian advance

In any case the manner in which the advance of the Italian Tenth Army began and developed later is worth noting. At first there was a stepping up of mutual air attacks. The Italian air force intensified its bombing of the Allied rail terminus at Matruh, while the Royal Air Force struck harder at the Italian aerodromes and their seaplane bases. The aim of each side seemed to be to attack the supply bases and communications of the other. Thus, during the first half of September 1940, the Allied air activity was directed towards bombing the Italian aerodromes at Tmimi, Tobruk and Derna and the seaplane bases at Bomba and Gazala, the raids being carried out by squadrons of No. 202 Group RAF. In addition, strategic reconnaissance flights were undertaken to keep a watch on concentrations and movements of Italian troops and vehicles. One important object of those flights was to discover whether the Italian Tenth Army was making any move southwards to capture the Siwa Oasis—a position of tactical importance on the southern flank of any advance along the coast.[4]

The Italian air activity on the other hand was confined to bombing attacks on Matruh, evidently with a view to damaging the railhead. All attacks were, more or less, on the same pattern as described before, the bombers, Savoia 79s, coming in waves at an elevation of about 16,000 feet and causing some casualties and damage. More than a dozen such raids were made on Matruh

[4] W/D 4 Div., p. 105, Sep. 1940.

during the first half of September, while a few were also directed against Baqqush, Sidi Omar, Sidi Barrani and smaller tactical positions. The bombs dropped included incendiary and what came to be known as the Thermos bombs. The latter were obviously so named because of their resemblance in shape to a thermos flask.[5]

The Thermos bombs were small, of delayed action type, and so designed that they would not explode on impact with ground but would go off if moved.[6] Thus they would lie scattered after a raid until moved or touched when they would blow up with fatal results. Their range of blast was not more than a hundred yards but they had a considerable nuisance value. They could be destroyed from a distance by rifle fire or by dragging over them a rake improvised out of strings and stones. They however ceased to cause worry to the troops after their nature and method of destruction were fully understood.[7]

The invasion

In addition to the bombing, the Italians resorted to a persistent shelling of the Allied positions on the frontier. The fire used to be directed from Capuzzo and Ramla at the Allied barracks and dumps in Sollum and Musaid, and the weapons used were "Pompoms" and 105 and 152-mm guns.[8] The tempo of their artillery increased after 4 September 1940 and, as it turned out later, was a prelude to their move to invade Egypt.

The first sign of this move appeared on 10 September 1940, when, after one of their usual shellings, a large number of Italian vehicles started moving south towards Capuzzo. Since Capuzzo was on the Italian side of the frontier, this forward movement was most likely an approach march to a concentration area prior to the invasion. A little later, another group of about 500 vehicles (possibly the same ones) was spotted heading for the frontier, and there were also other activities. Some transport movements were taking place south and west of Sidi Azeiz and between Azeiz and Capuzzo, while about a thousand infantrymen were reported to be on the march in the same area. All this puzzled the Allied observers as far as can be gathered from the intelligence records of the 4th Indian Division; nor was the object of those movements clear even to the forward troops who were watching them. A conjecture was, however, made that "it may be intended to reoccupy the frontier line Sidi Omar—Bir Shefersen, possibly as a preliminary to a further advance."

Next day, 11 September, the picture became slightly clearer. A

---

[5] W/D 4 Div., p. 125, Sep. 1940.
[6] W/D 4 Div., p. 138, Sep.-Oct., 1940.
[7] Some more information on the characteristics and mechanism of a Thermos bomb will be found in Appendix E.
[8] W/D 4 Div., p. 115 *et seq.*

column of approximately 350 Italian vehicles had touched the frontier wire at Sidi Omar; and the rest of the invading force was ranged all along the Egyptian frontier in a north-south line running from Sidi Azeiz to Bir Shefersen. On the following day, some advanced elements of the Italian Tenth Army crossed the border, at least at one point in the north, somewhere near Nazarain, and entered the Egyptian territory.[9]

Allied opposition

The Allied opposition to this drift was not appreciable. It consisted of offensive patrols by 3 Coldstream Guards and 2 Rifle Brigade and a harassing fire by a unit of the Royal Horse Artillery, in addition to the bombing of troop concentrations at Sidi Omar on 10 and 13 September by the Royal Air Force. At the same time the Allied troops evacuated Musaid and Sollum which were not intended to be defended and were therefore being held only by light forces; and these were immediately occupied by the Italians, being the first Egyptian towns to be captured by them.[10]

On 14 September 1940, the Allied intelligence section was of opinion that any further hostile advance was unlikely, although the Italian troops would, no doubt, make minor moves to consolidate their gains. No particular significance was attached to their crossing the frontier, and it was surmised that this advance was only a propaganda stunt, so that an Italian success might be publicised simultaneously with the then impending German attack on England.

That reasoning did not, however, hold the ground for very long. The onward movement of the Tenth Italian Army continued. The 7th (British) Armoured Division, which was making an orderly withdrawal before it, succeeded in inflicting some losses on the advancing troops but was unable to halt or delay the advance. At the same time, roads were blocked and destroyed or mined by units of the 4th Indian Division's Royal Engineers; and water wells *en route* were salted to accentuate the already prevailing water scarcity.[11] It was now more or less clear that a regular Italian offensive was on.

On 15 September, the Italian troops were seen advancing in two columns along the main road on the coast. Next day they reached a point three miles west of Buq Buq, a small locality that had already been vacated by the Allied troops, who had begun a withdrawal towards Sidi Barrani. Occupying Buq Buq, the Italian columns continued their move towards Sidi Barrani, meeting with no more resistance than artillery fire from a Battery of the Royal

---

[9] W/D 4 Div., Sep. 1940, p. 115 *et seq.*
[10] W/D 4 Div., Sep. 1940, p. 123.
[11] W/D 4 Div., 123 *et seq.* Also *Conquest of North Africa* (Burke Publishing Company Ltd.), p. 12.

Horse Artillery and some bombing of their troop concentrations by the aircraft of 202 Group RAF. The Allied troops, at the same time, were withdrawing towards Matruh.

By 17 September, the Italian force had reached and occupied Sidi Barrani, a small fishing village on the coast, which also had an airfield. The force had advanced approximately 60 miles in four days. The speed of advance, hardly perceptible at first, had increased considerably during the closing stages of the move. The troops seemed to be well equipped with tanks, both light and medium, and were making a liberal use of artillery. For instance, the barrage put down on Sollum Barracks and Musaid, immediately prior to the invasion, was one of the most impressive yet seen. Unlike the creeping barrage which moves by bounds, the fire in that case was seen to advance like a solid curtain. The transport columns, too, whether on the move or stationary, were well protected by small field guns and anti-tank guns.[12]

Italian convoys

This 60-mile advance revealed that the Italians had their own method of moving in a formation and defending their convoys. The method had its advantages as well as weakness and is therefore worth describing. During the later stages of their advance on Sidi Barrani, from 14 to 16 September, the Italian troops made their lorries move in groups of 50 each. Each group comprised ten rows of five vehicles abreast, and was led by a staff car 300 yards ahead. Screens of similar armed vehicles were used to provide flank protection up to 400 yards on each side. Not infrequently the groups became separated from one another during the march, and so, at intervals, a group that was very much ahead had to wait for the next following one to join up before moving on again, the process being repeated throughout the column. This had the effect of reducing the speed at times to as little as 600 yards an hour, even with the comparatively smaller number of vehicles involved in the move. The accompanying tanks, which were normally carried in tank transporters, came to the ground whenever opposition was encountered. Each column was self-contained as to defence, being equipped with guns from 105-mm downwards. In one case, heavy anti-aircraft guns were also found to be accompanying the column. Air protection by fighters was almost continuous during the move.

The weakness of this formation was that it presented an easy target for machine-gun and artillery fire. Thus, during the move on Sidi Barrani, about 10 per cent of the advancing vehicles were put out of action by Allied gunners and rather heavy casualties inflicted on the infantry in the lorries. Unlike the British practice,

[12] W/D 4 Div., Sep. 1940, pp. 123, 127, 129 *et seq.*

the Italians would not use their armoured cars away from the columns but preferred to use them as close escorts. All vehicles in their convoys appeared to be desert-worthy. During the night-halts, these used to be protected against the danger of raids by being kept in a close leaguer, with tanks along the perimeter. Efficient vehicle evacuation was one of the strong points of the Italian leaguers.

Composition of the Italian Tenth Army[13]

The forces taking part in this advance were:
HQ XXI Corps
    62nd Metropolitan Division
    63rd Metropolitan Division
    1st Blackshirt Division
    1st Libyan Division   } One Group
    2nd Libyan Division
    Maletti Mobile Group   One Group
HQ XXII Corps
    4th Blackshirt Division } Guarding the line of
    Cantanzaro Division   } Communication

The XXI Corps was a Metropolitan Corps and consisted of the above-mentioned 62nd and 63rd Divisions which were all-white and motorised.

The composition of a Metropolitan Division was a headquarters with signals etc., two infantry regiments of three battalions each, a medium machine-gun battalion, a divisional artillery regiment (about 48 guns), an engineer battalion, a light tank battalion, a mechanical transport company, an anti-tank company and some other minor units. The establishment of each division totalled about 13,000 personnel.

The Blackshirts, sometimes referred to by the abbreviation CCNN,[14] were organised on much the same lines as the Metropolitan Divisions, but did not have a divisional light tank battalion. They were a little inferior in equipment and training to the regular formations. Each Blackshirt Division had an establishment of about 8,000 all-white personnel, recruited mostly from amongst the Italian colonists in Libya on a political and voluntary basis, as distinct from the conscript-basis of the Metropolitan Divisions. The infantry part of a Balckshirt Division consisted of two Legions of three battalions each. Its artillery regiment had 36 guns.

The Libyan Divisions were composed each of two infantry regiments of three battalions, plus artillery, engineer and other

---

[13] It appears, at some stage, there had been a change in numbers, as XXI Corps has been referred to by Marshal Graziani in his books *"Africa Settentrimale"* 1940-41 as XXIII Corps. For a fuller Order of Battle see Appendix F.

[14] The Italian equivalent for "Blackshirts" was "Camicie Nere"; hence the abbreviation CCNN.

supporting units. The battalions were organised on the basis of a headquarters and three companies of four platoons each. Of these, the headquarters platoon had three heavy machine-guns and a total strength of 43 other ranks. Of the remaining three platoons, one was a patrolling unit with two light machine-guns (11 other ranks); and the other two were rifle-units with one non-commissioned officer and 16 other ranks each. As a rule, one battalion had between 700 and 800 men. A Libyan Division had an establishment of 900 white and 6,500 non-white troops.

The Maletti Mobile Group, which was a mobile column named after its commander, General Pietro Maletti, consisted of tanks and artillery manned by the Blackshirts and the Libyans. Its task seems to have been to protect the Italian flank on the south of its advance.

The Metropolitan, the Blackshirt and the Libyan formations described above constituted the force that invaded Egypt. This force comprised in fact the whole of the Italian Tenth Army, less one Blackshirt Division which (together with Cantanzaro Division) was on the L of C duties under XXIII corps. Broadly speaking, the Italian forces in Libya consisted of two armies, the Fifth and the Tenth. The former had three corps under it, X, XV and XXIII, and the latter two, XXI and XXII.[15] The XXI Corps consisted only of the Metropolitan Divisions and the XXII of the Blackshirt Divisions. The Libyan Divisions did not form a corps but were given the status of a Group commanded by an air-army-corps general. The commander of the Fifth Army was General Garibaldi and that of the Tenth, General Guidi, while the Supreme Commander of all Italian forces in North Africa was Marshal Graziani.

Withdrawal to Baqqush

As stated before, almost simultaneously with the advance of the Italian Tenth Army to Sidi Barrani, the 4th Indian Division was to make a practice withdrawal to Baqqush, commencing on 14 September 1940. The move began at 1130 hours and continued throughout that day and the whole of the following night. It was carried out according to plan, except for some delay when it was found that Italian aircraft had littered the Baqqush area with Thermos bombs. Unlike the earlier move from the Nile Delta to Naghamish, the return move to Baqqush was neither planned elaborately nor hedged in with many precautions. Experience seemed to show that they were unnecessary. The only precautions taken therefore were a blackout of vehicle headlights during the night march, and a certain amount of dispersal during the day. It was decided that the move of the 5th and 11th Indian Infantry Brigades should be carried out

[15] See footnote 13 on p. 71.

during the hours of darkness, and of troops other than those of the brigades, at dusk, while only a limited amount of transport consisting mainly of the Echelon vehicles and the Field Ambulance cars was to be allowed to proceed during the daylight. Accordingly, no unusual movement was permitted within the Naghamish position after 1600 hours on the evening of withdrawal. The "thinning out" by the two Infantry Brigades commenced at 2000 hours; the front line was completely evacuated by 2100 hours and the whole of the Naghamish area by 2400 hours. During all this time, the Central India Horse held the area where the main road, named Road to Rome, descended from the escarpment to the coastal plain. At the same time the 11th Indian Infantry Brigade guarded the south flank until the 5th Brigade had cleared the road, after which it was withdrawn on foot.[16]

The work of constructing defences at Baqqush commenced immediately on the completion of the move. All troops in the Baqqush area, among whom were a New Zealand Brigade Group and the 16th (British) Infantry Brigade, came under the command of the 4th Indian Division. The Italian aircraft kept track of the division and paid it occasional night-visits with the Thermos and the High Explosive bombs. The total casualties from these, however, were only one officer and about four other ranks of the division, all killed through picking up the Thermos bombs.[17]

Simultaneously with the digging of the defences, the division began to take steps to make its position tank-proof. It was feared that in case of an attack by the Italians, some at least of their tanks might succeed in penetrating the easily accessible area to its rear. But the division lacked trained anti-tank personnel and advantage was therefore taken of the presence of the New Zealand troops who gave an impressive tank hunting demonstration to the representatives from all arms of the 4th Indian Division. Men from the 5th and 11th Indian Infantry Brigades were already being trained at Maadi, by a New Zealand Anti-tank Battery, with a view to raising an Indian Infantry Anti-tank group, and the proposed establishment had been submitted to the Western Desert Force for approval. The requisite sanction was received on 2 October 1940. As a result two Indian Anti-tank Companies, probably the first Indian-manned anti-tank units of the war, came into being, one for the 5th and the other for the 11th Indian Infantry Brigade.[18]

---

[16] W/D 4 Div., p. 133.
[17] W/D 4 Div., pp. 91 & 94.
[18] W/D 4 Div., Sep. 1940, p. 158.

CHAPTER VIII

Planning for Attack

The manner of Italian advance left no doubt that, after occupying Sidi Barrani, the Italians would continue to push towards Matruh and beyond. It was clear that if the advance was to be checked, the Allies would have to take a firm stand somewhere between Sidi Barrani and Alexandria, and a plan for making such a stand was then undoubtedly under active consideration, if not ready. In the meanwhile, General Wavell wished his forward troops to fall back fighting a delaying action, until the advancing force was drawn to an area favourable for attack. It was then to be engaged in a battle and destroyed or defeated on the spot.[1]

Such a spot might have been Matruh, Naghamish or Baqqush; or any place further east, had the Italians continued their advance. But contrary to expectations the Italians did not do so. Marshal Graziani decided to make a long halt at Sidi Barrani where he busied himself with constructing defence fortifications, as if he was working on a plan of consolidating the conquered territory at each bound with a view to using it as a spring-board for the next. As a result what might have been a battle of Naghamish or Baqqush ultimately became the battle of Sidi Barrani. In any case, just at that time there was no indication of what the Italians intended to do; and so the 4th Indian Division, then digging defences at Baqqush, speeded up its work, expecting the Italians to reach that position in the next few days. But the Italians failed to arrive and the hurry and bustle subsided a few days later.

The occupation of Sidi Barrani by the Italians was not necessarily a military achievement of great significance. But to realise its full implication it must be viewed against the general military situation in the other theatres of the war. With the collapse of France, Europe had become more or less an Axis-dominated continent. England herself was facing a threat of invasion by Germany. On 7 September, four days before General Graziani commenced his move towards Egypt, the Germans had opened the "Blitz" on London, and, so critical was the situation that on the same day, the General Headquarters Home Forces felt compelled to issue the code-word "Cromwell" (invasion imminent) to the London formations and the Southern and Eastern Commands. A few days after

---

[1] *Conquest of North Africa* (HMS pamphlet), p. 12; W/D 4 Div., Oct. 1940, p. 158.

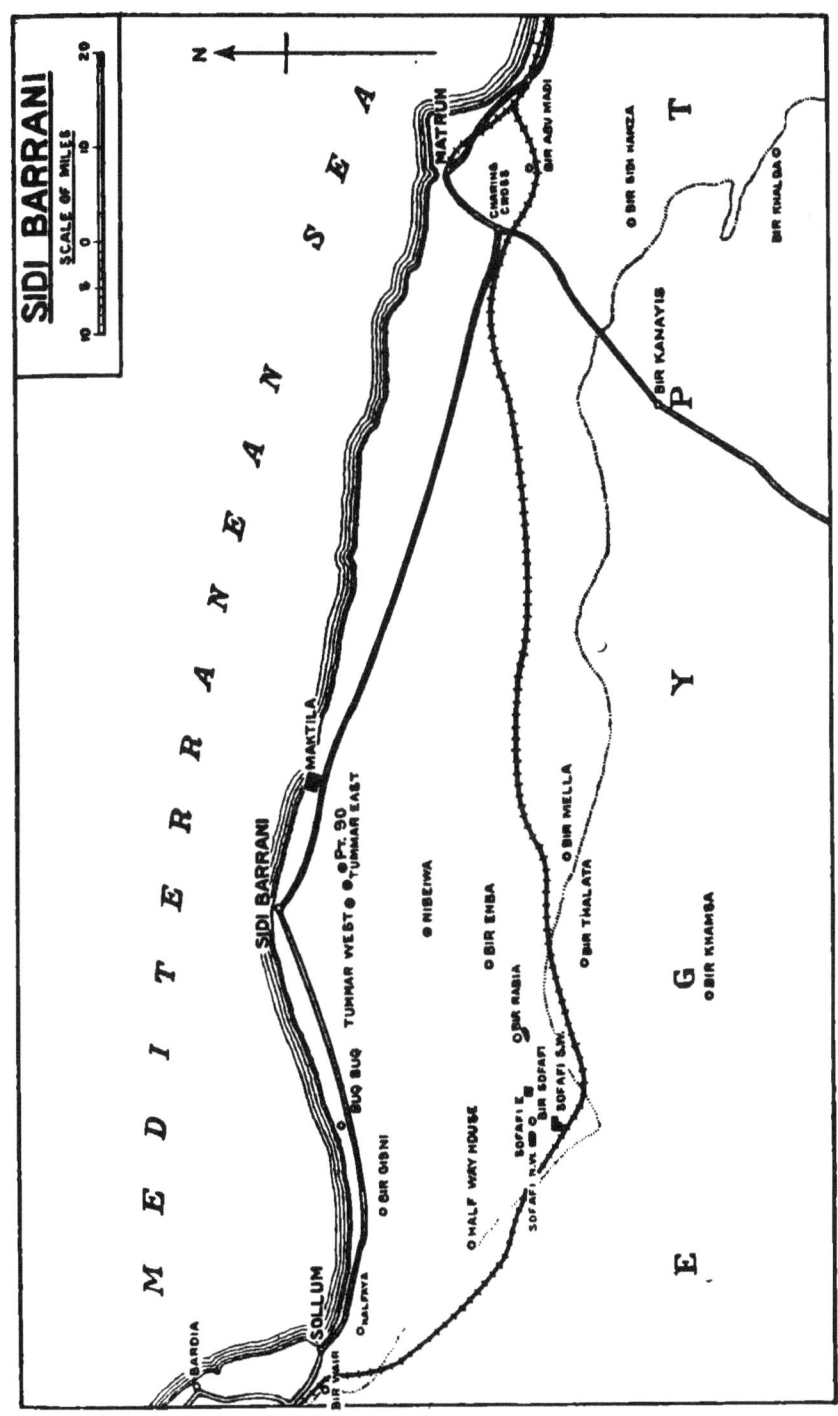

the occupation of Sidi Barrani by the Italians, Germany, Italy and Japan were to sign a ten-year pact in Berlin, confirming the Rome-Berlin-Tokyo Axis, and pledging themselves to the "New Order" and to a common war against any intervening power. No country in Europe, except Russia, was in a position to oppose the combined strength of Germany and Italy, and even Russia, after her pact of non-aggression with Germany, seemed to have lined up with the Axis. Outside Europe, the United States was still neutral; a relentless submarine war was going on in the Atlantic; the Mediterranean had been blockaded; the Middle East was in a state of uncertainty; India was in a great political ferment; and Britain's capacity to win the war was being doubted on all sides.[2]

Once again to Naghamish

It was against this background that the 4th Indian Division, which, as we have seen, had moved from Mena to Naghamish and thence to Baqqush, now received orders from the Western Desert Force to return once again to Naghamish. The divisional orders were issued accordingly and the Division's Headquarters moved back to its former position in the Naghamish area on 10 October 1940. This time the area was put on a sounder defensive footing. It was divided into two holding sections, namely the right and the left sectors. The 5th Indian Infantry Brigade was to defend the former and the 11th Indian Infantry Brigade the latter. Once again this move was officially dubbed a practice move. But it is possible that it constituted an actual advance, inspired by the calculation that the Italian force had definitely stopped at Sidi Barrani and that there was no risk of an attack in the immediate future. For the next ten days, until 20 October, the division, in its new position, had no activity other than reconnaissances, practice moves over short distances, training and digging in. During that time there were three insignificant air raids over the divisional area. The general routine was at one time enlivened, on 21 October 1940, by a visit to the division from Mr. Anthony Eden, the then Secretary of State for War in the United Kingdom.

On the same day, a unit of the 4th Indian Division embarked on a venture which might be rightly described as the first operation in Cyrenaica in which the troops of the division were used. The operation consisted of a raid on an Italian camp. It was undertaken by 2 Camerons of the 11th Indian Infantry Brigade, under orders from the 7th (British) Armoured Division. The raiding party, which included a detachment of 'J' Battery 3rd Royal Horse Artillery, set out on the 21st in transports provided by the 4th

[2] *Chronology of the Second World War*, Royal Institute of International Affairs, pp. 30-36.

Indian Division, and returned on 24 October. Its achievement consisted of eight Italian vehicles destroyed at a loss of 2 Camerons killed, 3 wounded and 3 missing. This was the first encounter of a unit of this division with the Italian troops on land.[3]

Before long, however, the division witnessed the first clash in the air also. It happened on 31 October, when about 15 Italian aircraft bombed the divisional area of Naghamish, on their way to Matruh. They were at once engaged by the Royal Air Force fighters and there ensued the first aerial combat over the Divisional Headquarters resulting in a loss to the Italian air force of nine aircraft and to the Royal Air Force of four. This bombing raid was the first serious notice taken by the Italians of the existence of the 4th Indian Division.

Henceforth the 4th Indian Division appears to have been marked off for some definite operational undertaking. However, for reasons of security, neither officers nor men were allowed to know, or even to have a hint of the time, place or nature of such an operation. Orders were issued in the last week of October that the digging in on defensive positions at Naghamish was to cease at once, except by the Sapper units. The fighting troops were switched from digging to active training. Among other things the new training seems to have had one aim in view, namely to get both the Allied and the Italian troops so used to seeing training manoeuvres that, when necessary, it would be possible to use training moves as a mask to conceal actual dispositions of the troops for battle. With that aim the training was made to approximate more closely than ever before to the actual fighting conditions. Realism was increased by occasional heavy dust storms which accompanied all practice moves.[4]

Further forward move

While practice rehearsals were thus going on, plans were set on foot for moving the 4th Indian Division further forward towards the frontier. The object in view was that the division should relieve the Support Group of the 7th (British) Armoured Division, which had long been in contact with the Italians and needed a breathing time to enable it to rest and refit. The Indian Division was to take over from the Support Group at no distant date. Its task was to be to hold the front at Sidi Barrani and maintain contact with the Italian forward troops. A warning order to that effect was received by the division from the Western Desert Force on 8 November 1940.

The first unit to move forward was the divisional cavalry, the Central India Horse. It moved out of the Naghamish position on 10 November and passed under the command of the 7th (British)

[3] W/D 4 Div., Oct. 1940.
[4] *Ibid.*

Armoured Division, so that it might acquire the knowledge and training necessary for maintaining a harassing contact with the Italians.[5] On the following day, another divisional unit, the 4th Battalion Rajputana Rifles, also moved out of Naghamish to establish dumps in the forward area, in anticipation of the forward move

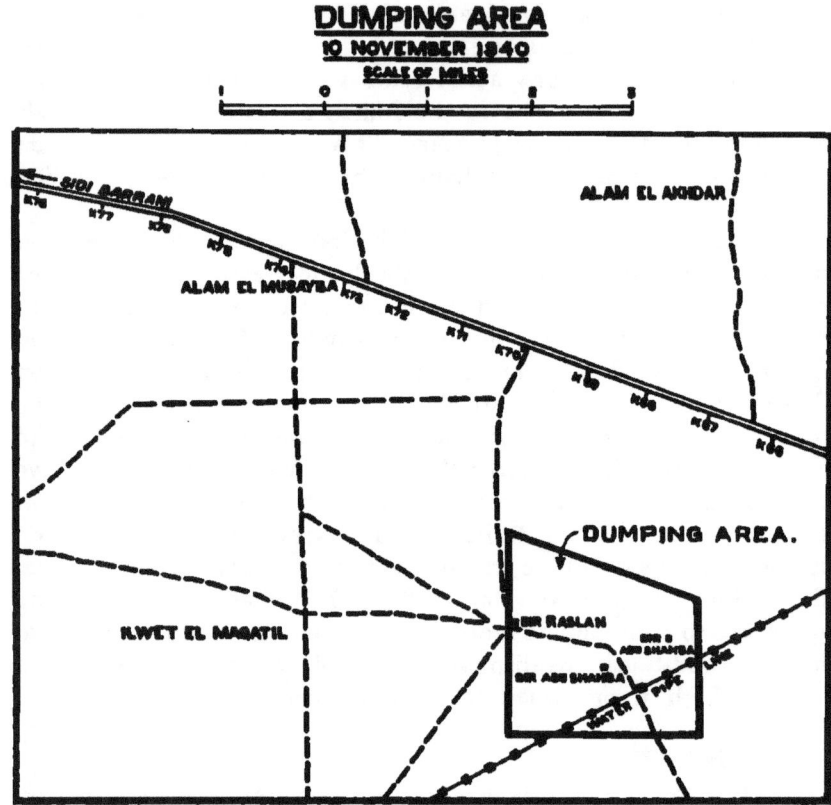

of the whole division. Dumping began on 12 November. The dumps, which included water storage also, were formed in the general area 660353-663352-663350-660350. This area was a quadrilateral, roughly four kilometres on each side, and was situated to the south of the main Sidi Barrani road along the stretch from Kilometres 66 to 70, being about a mile away from the main road and some 40 miles behind the front.[6]

The dumping party, which was under the command of the 4th Battalion Rajputana Rifles, included one troop 'P' Battery Royal Horse Artillery, one section 18 Field Company Sappers and Miners, and a detachment of the Divisional Signals. Instructions to the

[5] W/D 4 Div., November 1940.
[6] Map 1/100,000 Egypt, Western Desert, Sheet 3 W, Matruh West.

commander of this force enjoined that the move to the dumping area was to be concealed from the Italian air reconnaissance and, therefore, a distance of not less than 400 yards was to be maintained between the vehicles during the move. The move took place along the existing routes by sub-units and companies, the latter following one another at half-hourly intervals. Forty troop-carrying lorries were involved in the move.[7] The duty of the dumping force was to provide labour for the formation of the dumps and to protect them from the air and ground action of the Italians. The sappers had the special assignment of storing water and were not to be employed on other duties. The dumps were to be carefully camouflaged and, with a view to further deceiving the Italians, it was proposed to send out another battalion to create dummy dumps in the neighbourhood. The intention does not, however, appear to have been put into practice.

In case of an Italian advance in strength, the Force Commander was authorised to destroy the dumps and retire. Otherwise, he was to reconnoitre the country and the tracks in the surrounding area and send back topographical information to the Divisional Headquarters. Petrol, ammunition and food supplies were to be drawn from points which were to be opened at Bir el Afarit (690348), about twenty miles behind the dumping position.[8] Water, which was allowed at half a gallon per man and one gallon per vehicle per day, was to be drawn from a still more distant point, somewhere near Matruh. Forty troops-carrying lorries were to be used for drawing those supplies. Communication with the Divisional Headquarters was to be through a despatch rider and a liaison officer. Although strict wireless silence had been imposed on the force, it was allotted one No. 9 W/T set for listening purposes.[9]

Hardly had this force been a few days on the job when it was relieved by the 4th Battalion Rajput Regiment on 16 November 1940. That unit in turn was relieved by the 3rd Battalion 1st Punjab Regiment on 21 November, which again was replaced by another force, the 1st Battalion Rajputana Rifles on 28 November 1940. This rapid rotation of reliefs was presumably designed to give practice to the units concerned as well as to accustom the Allied and Italian troops to regard those ceaseless movements as local adjustments having no particular significance.[10]

Practice manoeuvres

On 25 and 26 November 1940, the 4th Indian Division took part in a particularly big practice manoeuvre staged by the Western

[7] W/D 4 Div., November 1940.
[8] Map 1/100,000 Egypt, Western Desert, Sheet 3 W. Matruh West.
[9] W/D 4 Div., November 1940.
[10] *Ibid.*

Desert Force. It was called Exercise No. 1. Except for that, and the severe intermittent dust storms, nothing eventful happened in the divisional area during the last few days of November 1940.[11]

The Italian Tenth Army's offensive in Cyrenaica was, as we have seen, launched on 10 September 1940, resulting in the establishment of its forces in and around Sidi Barrani, inside the Egyptian border. The Western Desert Force, not being strong enough to check that advance, had retired slowly fighting a delaying action, the withdrawal being only a temporary measure and in fact a part of General Wavell's plan to have the Tenth Army at a disadvantage before starting a counter-offensive. General Wavell had decided to catch the Italian force on the prepared positions at Matruh and then deal with it at an advantage. The backward move of the Western Desert Force was, therefore, contrary to what was then largely believed, a genuine tactical withdrawal made necessary by the numerical superiority of the Tenth Army. But Marshal Graziani, it would appear, had his own plans, so that instead of rushing headlong in the wake of the retiring Allied troops, he halted some fifteen miles east of Sidi Barrani and refused to move forward. Whatever might be his own reasons for doing so, the effect was to frustrate the carefully laid out plan of General Wavell. Expressing that frustration Lieutenant-General Sir Arthur Smith (in an official version of an account given by the then Commander of the Western Desert Force, Lieutenant-General Sir Richard O'Connor) says: "No further advance, however, took place which was a real disappointment at the time, as complete plans had been prepared to destroy his (Graziani's) whole force had he made the attempt".[12]

Planning for attack

As the Italian force thus refused to advance, it became apparent to the Allied High Command that fresh plans would have to be made to strike at it in its existing position. It was fully realised that the Italians had the advantage of superiority in numbers both on the ground and in the air, and there was, in addition, the supreme difficulty of maintaining a fighting force so far forward from the railhead at Matruh. But it was hoped that these disadvantages would be overcome by the superior training, equipment and mobility of the Allied troops, and on that assumption it was decided to plan for attacking the Italians at Sidi Barrani as soon as possible.

Thus, on 22 October 1940, the Headquarters Western Desert Force received instructions to investigate the possibility of an early attack on the Italian positions at Sidi Barrani. The investigations were to be based on a proposed plan that the 7th (British) Armoured

---

[11] *Ibid.*
[12] W/D 4 Div., Nov. 1940 and *Middle East Training Pamphlet No. 10*, pp. 1-5.

Division, the 4th Indian Division and the 7th Royal Tank Regiment would undertake a four- or five-day operation, involving an approach march on the first day, an attack on the second, and a withdrawal on the third or fourth day. To minimise maintenance difficulties, troops were to be prepared to live on limited quantities of food and water and undergo considerable hardships. The investigations were to be conducted in absolute secrecy.

At this stage, the knowledge, that offensive operations were contemplated, was restricted only to the Commanders of the 7th Armoured and the 4th Indian Divisions. Later, on 6 November, more officers were taken into confidence, when a conference was held for finalising the plan that had, by then, reached an advanced stage of discussion. At that conference the Royal Air Force Commander, all infantry brigadiers, the chief Staff Officers of the two divisions and the Assistant Quarter-Master-General of the Western Desert Force were the only privileged individuals admitted to the secret. The plan was finalised but nothing was put into writing and it was decided to restrict the knowledge of it to the smallest number of officers until a much later date.

As to the date of launching the attack, it was felt that a period of moonlight nights was necessary, since the final advance to the forming-up positions could not safely be undertaken by day. The latest date in November on which there was just sufficient moonlight was the 22nd. But that was considered too early, since neither reinforcements nor artillery would have arrived by then. General O'Connor recommended, therefore, that the most suitable period would be between 8 and 10 December 1940.

The plan of attack that finally emerged from those discussions was somewhat complicated. It relied for its success on precise timing and good training, and could not be satisfactorily carried out without at least some practice and a test-trial. It was therefore decided to have a rehearsal, with an approximate facsimile of Italian camps and defences marked out on the ground. Live ammunition was to be used during the practice.[13]

Once again, in order to maintain secrecy, the rehearsal was dubbed a training exercise, since several had already taken place without arousing any suspicion. It was accordingly announced that in the near future the Western Desert Force would carry out two training exercises, to be called Exercise No. 1 and Exercise No. 2. But it was a secret known only to the select few, that whereas Exercise No. 1 was to be the rehearsal for the attack, Exercise No. 2 was to be the attack itself, This deception worked well. The rehearsal (Exercise I) took place on 26-27 November 1940. Everything was

---

[13] *Middle East Training Pamphlet No. 10*, pp. 1-5; W/D 4 Div., Nov. 1940.

made to look as much like the actual battle as possible. Both the artillery and the machine-guns used live ammunition. Very few officers were aware of the real object of the rehearsal. The exercise brought to the surface some of the defects of the plan. As a result some tactical alterations were made which later proved to be a great improvement. A training memorandum was then issued suggesting that those alterations would be carried out "in future exercises".

Four days before the actual attack, on 5 December, the principal infantry commanders and senior staff officers met in a final conference at Baqqush to give finishing touches to the overall plan. Heads of services and representatives of the Navy and Royal Air Force, who were present at the conference, confirmed the actions to be taken by their respective branches. After that the next step was to translate the plan into action and it was only then that written orders were permitted to be issued, the issue being restricted, even at that stage, to the next junior commanders and staff officers. The masking device of calling the actual attack Exercise No. 2 was, so far as the other ranks were concerned, adhered to till the last minute.[14]

The efforts to preserve secrecy to such an extent imposed no small strain on the senior commanders and officers who had to work out all the details personally and possibly had to invent excuses to justify some of their activities. Thus, for example, the formation of dumps in the forward area and the movements of certain units had to be put down to defensive measures against a possible Italian attack on Matruh; whereas in actual fact they were a part of the offensive preparations.

Italian defences

In order to follow the fortunes of the Allied offensive against the Italians, which commenced in a matter of days after this final conference, it is necessary to understand the general plan of the offensive. That plan was naturally founded on the data then available as to the defences, dispositions, strength, etc., of the Italian forces. The information on which the plan was based can be summarised as follows.

The Italian force due to be attacked consisted, as already stated, among other units, of two Metropolitan Divisions, two Libyan Divisions, one Blackshirt Division and a Mobile Group of tanks and armoured vehicles under General Maletti. This was the bulk of the Tenth Italian Army of Marshal Graziani. It was disposed in a series of fortified positions which made a defensive ring covering its line of communication. The ring extended from the coast to the

---

[14] According to some other sources, all ranks were for the first time taken into confidence on 7 December, two days before the attack. This was possibly true of the 7th Armoured Division only.

rear areas and was made up of eight strongly defended positions, which were:
- (1) Maktila
- (2) Sidi Barrani
- (3) Tummar West
- (4) Tummar East
- (5) Point 90
- (6) Nibeiwa
- (7) Sofafi *and*
- (8) Rabia.

Of these, Maktila and Sidi Barrani were on the coast; the Tummars and Point 90 were to the south of Sidi Barrani; Nibeiwa was to the south of the Tummars; and Sofafi and Rabia to the south-west of Nibeiwa. At some distance from Rabia and to its south-east was the minute landmark of Bir Enba and the locality around it was known as the Bir Enba gap, from the fact that it constituted an undefended gap to the south of the Italian defences, through which the attacking troops would draw nearer to the first objective to be attacked.[15] Of these defences, the most important and relevant from the point of view of the operations that followed were Nibeiwa, Tummar West and Sidi Barrani.[16]

Nibeiwa was a fortified camp, roughly rectangular in shape, and was believed to contain the majority of General Maletti's mobile force. It was situated on a spur and astride the track Sidi Barrani—Bir Enba. It measured 2400 yards by 1800 yards in area, the longer sides facing east and west respectively. By virtue of its location athwart the track Sidi Barrani—Enba, it blocked the passage from Bir Enba to the coast and vice versa. It had a perimeter, and certain anti-tank obstacles outside it, which constituted its defences. The perimeter consisted of a wall and sangars and was complete the whole way round, except for a small gap in the rear, that is on the west side. Outside the perimeter and 150 yards away were two anti-tank obstacles, one to its north-east and the other on the south-east. Each of those obstacles consisted of a stone-and-mud bank and a shallow ditch just in front. The bank was made by filling the space between two parallel stone walls with sand from the ditch. Along the line of the perimeter, and spaced according to the tactical necessity, were the machine-gun emplacements.

Nibeiwa contained more machine-gun emplacements around its perimeter than any other Italian camp in the Sidi Barrani group. The main strength of the Nibeiwa camp lay in its eastern and south-eastern faces. Its weakest points were in the north-west, where the Italian supply vehicles entered and left. The layout of the camp

---

[15] For further details of Italian dispositions see Appendix G.
[16] *Middle East Training Pamphlet No. 10*, pp. 1-5 and 71.

left no doubt that the Italian commander concerned expected an attack from the east, that is a frontal attack, not one from the rear which faced west, nor from the flanks which faced north and south.

The camp at Tummar West was in many ways similar to that at Nibeiwa in the layout of its defences. The points of difference were that the Tummar camp was triangular in shape and, except for two gaps in the north, an anti-tank trench encircled the whole perimeter at an average distance of 50 yards from it. Further, this particular camp and the one at Sidi Barrani were the only positions round which the Italians had constructed wire defences. But the wires at this time were by no means complete.

Allied plan of attack

It was this layout of the defences that had to be attacked and the Italian forces therein captured or destroyed. The overall Allied plan was to make the attack in three phases. The first phase was to consist of operations against Nibeiwa, the second against Tummar West, and the third was to be the exploitation. In the last stage, the advance was to be directed towards Sidi Barrani with the object of cutting the Italian line of communication to the east, and much depended upon the success of this vital phase. If the situation was favourable the operation was to be extended to raiding the administrative installations of the Italians in the Buq Buq or the Sofafi areas, as might appear feasible.[17] The formations to be employed were the 7th (British) Armoured Division, the 4th Indian Infantry Division, the 7th Royal Tank Regiment (with "I" tanks), and Selby Force, a mixed column under Brigadier Selby. The 4th Indian Division was to have under its command, the 7th Royal Tank Regiment as well as one Medium and three Field regiments of artillery and three troop-carrying mechanised transport companies. In addition all the three infantry brigades of the division were fully mobile.[18]

Each of the above formations was assigned a definite role in the offensive operations. The role of the 4th Indian Division and the "I" tanks was to capture the camps of Nibeiwa, Tummar West, Tummar East and Point 90, in that order. The role of the 7th Armoured Division was to protect the desert flank of the Indian Division and particularly to defend it against a possible flank attack from Sofafi, exploiting later towards Buq Buq, should the tactical situation permit. The task of the Selby Force, which was based on Matruh, was to help the 4th Indian Division by attacking Maktila and keeping that position engaged, so that its garrison might not rush to the

[17] *Middle East Training Pamphlet No. 10*; W/D 4 Div.
[18] W/D 4 Div.

assistance of the Tummar garrison. In return, the 4th Indian Division, after capturing all its objectives, was to exploit northwards to the sea, and prevent the Maktila and Sidi Barrani garrisons from withdrawing westwards.[19]

In executing their various parts, the ground formations were to receive assistance both from sea and air. The Royal Navy was to assist the project by bombarding the Maktila and Sidi Barrani camps on the coast, which would also help the Selby Force. If feasible, the Navy was also to exploit its success by bombarding the Italian communications all along the coast between Sollum and Sidi Barrani.[20]

The Royal Air Force was to co-operate in the battles with a force of nine squadrons and one flight, six of the squadrons being bombers and the rest fighters. The role of the bombers was to attack the Italian communications and aerodromes and that of the fighters to strafe Italian transports and protect Allied ground troops against dive-bombing attacks. In addition to the nine squadrons, there were two more squadrons from the Army Co-operation Group which were placed directly under Headquarters Western Desert Force. One of them, composed of Hurricanes and Lysanders, was available for tactical reconnaissance; and the other, of Gladiators, for ground strafing of opportunity targets.[21]

A careful analysis of the roles assigned to various fighting formations and services will make it clear that the general plan aimed at closing all avenues of escape to the Italian force, and then attacking it within an enclosed area. It was thought that, placed in that predicament, the Italian troops would react in any one or more of the ways which could be anticipated beforehand and provided against. Thus, barring a successful stand, they would try to retreat; or alternatively they would make efforts to get reinforcements and supplies; and if any one of the camps was attacked, the other camps would endeavour to give it artillery or infantry support. All these possibilities had been taken into account in the Allied plans.

For retreating, or receiving reinforcements, the Italian force would need to have its line of communication with Buq Buq intact. The Allied plan, therefore, provided for that line to be cut by naval and air bombardments and subsequently by the action of the 4th Indian Division, in the last stage of its offensive. As to the mutual support from the adjacent camps, the Italian dispositions were such that the camps fell into three groups: the northern or the Maktila group, the southern or the Sofafi group, and the central or the Tummar group. The Allied plan for the offensive envisaged an

[19] *Ibid.*
[20] *Ibid.*
[21] *Ibid.*

initial attack on the central group. One effect of such a move would be that the northern and the southern groups would, clearly enough, be in a position to give support to the central group, by rushing reinforcements. These possibilities, as has been stated before, were neutralised by placing the Selby Force and the 7th Armoured Division in the north and south respectively, with orders to counter such moves on the part of the Maktila and Sofafi garrisons.

Thus, so far as the Western Desert Force was concerned, the stage had been set for an offensive to capture or destroy the major part of the Italian Tenth Army garrisoning the area Maktila—Sofafi—Buq Buq. The Allied formations taking part in the offensive had been assigned their specific roles and they, in their turn, had worked out the details of the task, and had assigned duties to their own units and sub-units. It is necessary to see how this was done in order to be able to follow the planning and the moves leading to the battle of Sidi Barrani.

CHAPTER IX

Battle of Sidi Barrani

Allied and Italian strength

The planning stage of the contemplated Allied offensive was nearing its end in the first week of December 1940, and arrangements were in progress for launching the actual attack, the immediate aim of the offensive being to drive out the Italian force which had invaded Egypt and which was then on the Egyptian soil, disposed in the triangle Maktila—Sofafi—Buq Buq. In broad outline, the Allied plan of attack, as mentioned in the preceding chapter, consisted of a thrust at the centre of the Italian defences and a simultaneous neutralisation of the northern and southern group of camps. The final plan naturally had to take into consideration the exact dispositions of the Italian troops.[1] On 6 December 1940, three days before the launching of the attack, they were known to be as follows:—

Location	Formation/Unit	Approximate Strength
Maktila	1st Libyan Division	5000 Libyans
Sidi Barrani	4th CCNN Division	15000 Libyans
Tummar West Tummar East	2nd Libyan Division	6000 Libyans
Point 90	Part of the 1st Libyan Division	1000 Libyans
Nibeiwa	Maletti Group	2500 Libyans
Sofafi	Part of 63rd Division	1 Infantry Regiment 3000 Italians (approx.)
Rabia		7000 Italians
Along the Coast, Sidi Barrani to Buq Buq.	Blackshirt Division	10,000 men
Along Escarpment	62nd Division	10,000 men (approx.)

Thus about 60,000 Italian and Libyan troops were ranged against the Western Desert Force which, besides other arms of service, comprised the following formations of armour and infantry:—

    7th (British) Armoured Division
        7th Armoured Brigade
        4th Armoured Brigade
        Support Group

---

[1] *Middle East Training Pamphlet No. 10*, p. 71. W/Ds 4 Div., 5 Bde., 11 Bde.

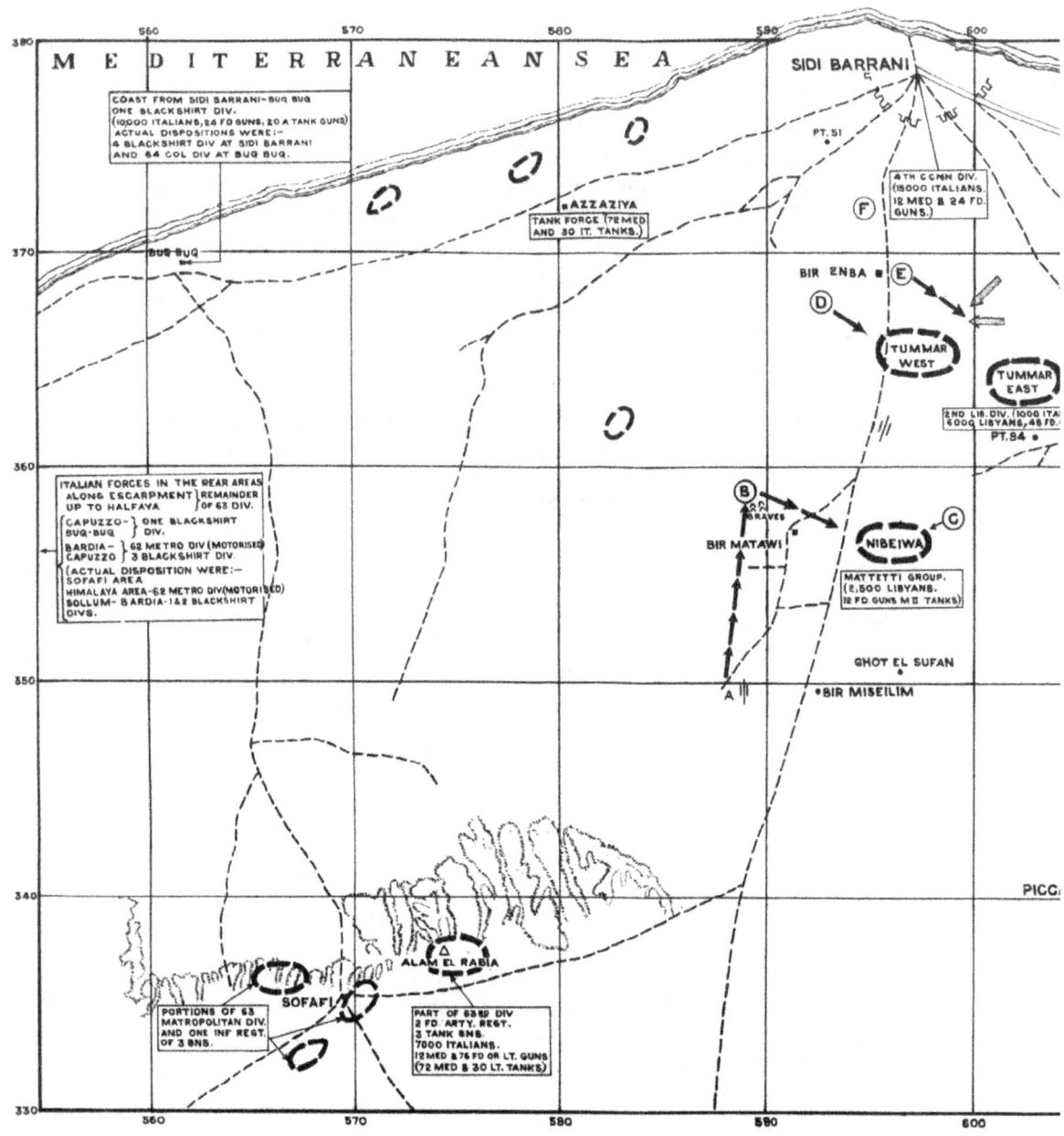

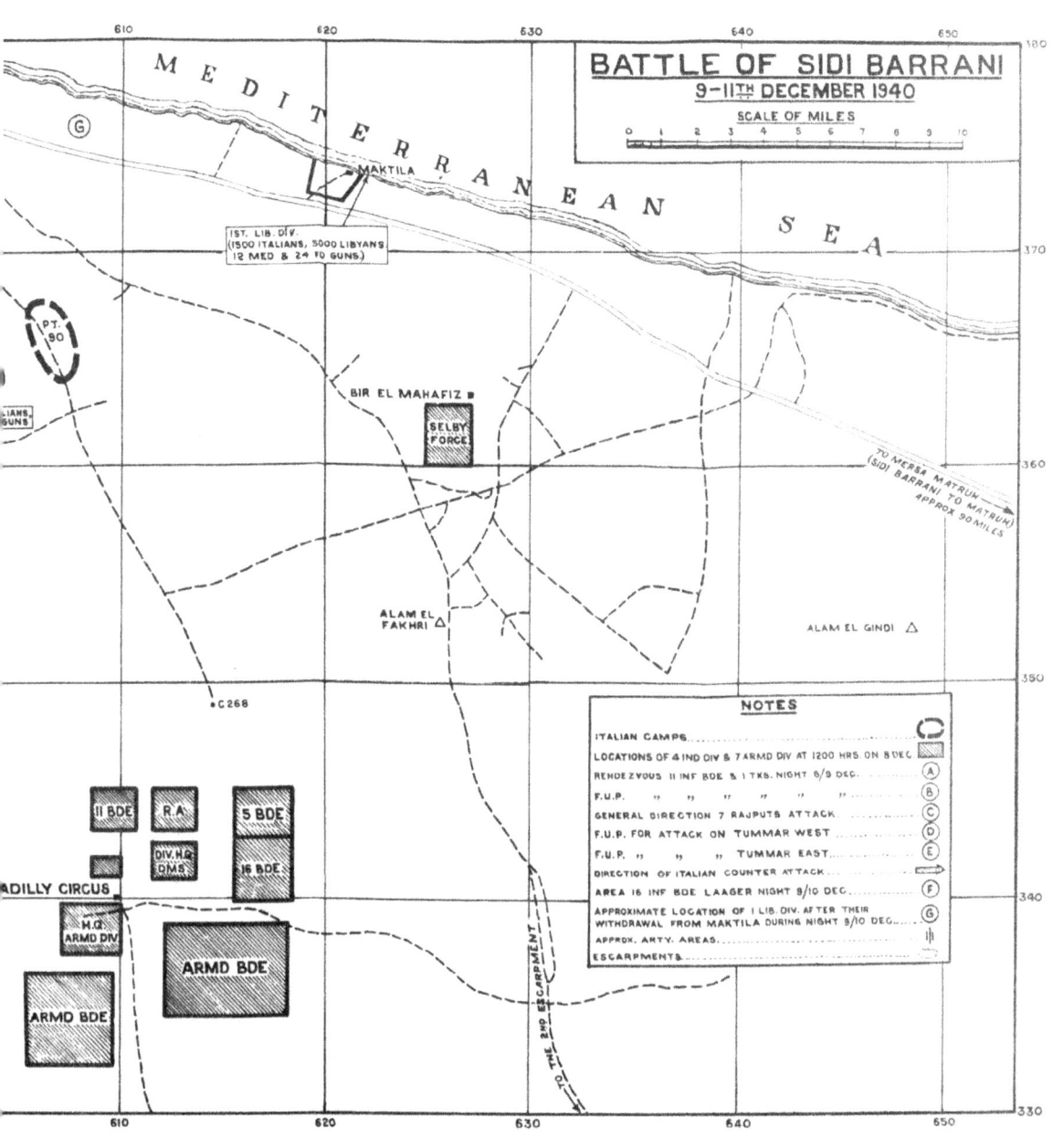

4th Indian Infantry Division
    5th Indian Infantry Brigade
        1st Battalion Royal Fusiliers
        3rd Battalion 1st Punjab Regiment
        4th Battalion 6th Rajputana Rifles
    11th Indian Infantry Brigade
        2nd Battalion QO Cameron Highlanders
        1st Battalion 6th Rajputana Rifles
        4th Battalion 7th Rajput Regiment
    16th (British) Infantry Brigade
        2nd Battalion Queens
        2nd Battalion Leicesters
        1st Battalion Argyll & Sutherland Highlanders
7th Royal Tank Regiment, *and*
Selby Force (composed of detachments from the garrison of Mersa Matruh).

To the above force must be added the 7th Indian Infantry Brigade which had arrived at Baqqush a month earlier and which, during the operations, was employed to protect the forward supply dumps between Matruh and Nibeiwa and also as a Western Desert Force reserve. Later it replaced the 16th (British) Brigade as the third brigade of the 4th Indian Division.

It was decided that the operations of the 4th Indian Division should be conducted west of a north-west line passing through the centre of the Nibeiwa and Tummar camps. That area was selected with a view to avoiding air action. The Italian bombers over that location were likely to find it difficult to distinguish between friend and foe and would, it was hoped, refrain from bombing through fear of hitting their own troops.[2]

The main striking arm for the attack on Nibeiwa was the 7th Royal Tank Regiment. It was to be assisted by a brief artillery bombardment on the defences concerned. The 11th Indian Infantry Brigade was to be the mopping-up infantry behind the tanks and, after completing the mopping operations, was to remain in Nibeiwa as its garrison.

The attack on Tummar West was to be on the same pattern as that on Nibeiwa. The 7th Royal Tank Regiment was once again to be the main striking force, supported as before by an artillery bombardment. But this time it was to be followed by the 5th Indian Infantry Brigade as its mopping-up infantry. Other formations of the Western Desert Force, assisting this operation, were the Support Group, the 4th Armoured Brigade of the 7th Armoured Division and the Selby Force. The Support Group was to prevent any

---

[2] *Middle East Training Pamphlet No. 10*, p. 5. W/D 4 Div.

interference from Sofafi; the 4th Armoured Brigade was to protect the desert flank; and the Selby Force was to prevent any hostile interference from Maktila, at the same time creating a diversion from the main attack. The 7th Armoured and the 16th Infantry Brigades were to remain as divisional reserve.

Disposing the formations and units mentioned above, for the battle, was no easy task. Units had to be transported to the battle area and placed within striking distance of their objectives. Before that stage could be reached they had to be concentrated in an assembly area. The approach march to the assembly point was approximately sixty miles, of which the last fifteen had to be covered in the moonlight; and the whole move had to be held back to the last possible moment so as to maintain secrecy and produce surprise.

Only one line of advance was available for the move to the battle area, that immediately south of the main escarpment. There being no road as such, the force had to be moved over the open desert. The paucity of roads increased the risk of detection from air, as thousands of vehicles, moving in a desert formation, would be cramming the same route during a period of 48 hours. Further, the layout of the assembly area had to be based on the intended tactical dispositions for the attack. For, a few factors are so essential to the success of an attack as a correct layout in the area of assembly, corresponding as nearly as possible to the actual deployment for the battle. These and similar considerations made it imperative that the date and time of the start of various units be so related to their varying rates of travelling speeds that they would all arrive in the assembly area almost simultaneously. From there the infantry was to be transported to within an attacking distance, that is about 1000 yards from the perimeter of its objective, after which the assaulting troops would have to follow the 'I' tanks on foot.

Making all these arrangements called for a high degree of administrative co-ordination and precision in timing, and imposed no small strain on the staff cocerned. Anxiety was felt lest the approach march should be detected from the air. It was by no means allayed when, on the first day of the march, an Italian reconnaissance aircraft appeared overhead. But the weather was hazy and although something unusual was suspected by the Italian intelligence staff, as later reports showed, the imminent possibility of a large-scale offensive was not even remotely considered by them. The approach march, it can be said, went very much according to the plan, due in a large measure to the close co-operation between the 7th Armoured and the 4th Indian Divisions and the 7th Royal Tank Regiment. All troops arrived at their allotted positions without any untoward incident, and were well in their positions before midnight. Nearly all men were by now aware that they were poised for real fighting, since the camouflage of 'exercise' no longer shrouded the true intentions and the 'secret' had been allowed to trickle down to the other ranks as from 7 December. The period of waiting, before the launching of an attack, is always an anxious time for the troops and their commanders. However, so careful was the planning and so well had the smallest detail been worked out that a virtual certainty of success filled the air and imparted confidence to the troops awaiting the signal for the assault. On few occasions, it has been said, could an attack have been undertaken with such self-assurance as on this occasion.[3]

Topography of the battle area

The action that followed, like most military operations, assumed its outline from the contour of the ground and the nature of the surroundings in which it was fought. It is necessary therefore to digress a little to take a bird's-eye view of the country from Sollum to Baqqush.

A very prominent feature in the physical relief of Egypt, as stated earlier, is the Libyan Plateau, which stands as a solid mass between Sollum and Matruh. The elevation of that plateau is 650 to 750 feet above the sea-level. But near the coast the height is between 30 and 175 feet only. This lesser height, facing the coastline, has however a very steep gradient. It thus presents to the sea a somewhat precipitate wall which is a complete barrier to mechanical transport proceeding from the coast to the interior of the desert, except at certain gaps or passes. This edge of the plateau which walls off the coast from the hinterland, over a long distance, is known as the escarpment. There are three escarpments between Sollum and Fuka, or, to be precise, three prominent divisions in the same landscape of escarpments. The first, or as it is often called the main escarpment, runs south-eastwards from Sollum Bay for about 35 miles to Sofafi, whence it continues in a general easterly direction for about 50 miles more. The second, which starts about 25 miles south of Sidi Barrani, and which lies north of the first escarpment in that area, continues eastward till it passes beyond Matruh, some 25 miles to its south; while the third, from west of Matruh to south of Fuka, hardly an escarpment in the real sense of the term, ends beyond Fuka through varying degrees of abruptness. In addition to these three escarpments there are also some other smaller ones further inland.[4] All escarpments are more or less bare, rugged rocks. Their top surfaces are cut and channelled by water-

[3] *Middle East Training Pamphlet No. 10*; W/D 4 Div.; W/D 11 Bde.; W/D 5 Bde.
[4] The description of escarpments is simplified to the maximum by leaving out the various unnecessary details. The escarpment that mattered for the battle was only the first escarpment.

courses (called wadis), which are dry for the most part of the year. There is no obstacle in the desert except for these canals and some rocky cliffs; and vehicles can therefore drive anywhere, not being bound to keep a particular track or road. It is from this characteristic feature that there arose the practice for convoys to move in what has come to be known as "desert formation", in which masses of tanks, trucks and cars can all move abreast simultaneously on a wide front of four or five miles instead of being obliged to keep within the narrow width of a normal road. Between the escarpments and the sea was the coastal strip, that is, the narrow and low-lying coastland, overlooked by the escarpments. All Italian defensive positions round Sidi Barrani were on this coastal strip, except the Sofafi—Rabia group of camps which was on the first escarpment. The Bir Enba gap referred to earlier—the gap in the Italian line of defended localities—lay between the first and the second escarpment.

The 4th Indian Infantry and the 7th Armoured Divisions were on the coast below this second escarpment, which they climbed at Bir Sidi Hamza and Bir Kanayis respectively for opening the offensive. Arriving at a point fifteen miles to the south-west of Nibeiwa, the Indian Division dropped its 5th Indian and the 16th British Infantry Brigades to await the time when they should be going into action in the later stages of the operation. Proceeding onwards with the 11th Indian Infantry Brigade and the four artillery regiments as well as the tanks of the 7th Royal Tank Regiment, it again detached the 4th Battalion 7th Rajput Regiment, before reaching its battle position. This battalion was to "demonstrate' with a feint attack from the east while the real attack would be going in from the west. The demonstration was to commence at 0300 hours on the morning of the attack; and taking advantage of the noise and distractions created by it, the other two battalions (with 72 guns and 44 tanks) were to get into their positions for opening the offensive, which was to commence four hours later and was to pass through three phases.[5]

PHASE I: ATTACK ON NIBEIWA

The first objective in the offensive was Nibeiwa, to be attacked from the west by the 7th Royal Tank Regiment and the 11th Indian Infantry Brigade. Allied guns began registering their targets at 0700 hours on 9 December and followed it up at 0715 hours with a heavy artillery bombardment of the defences. Meanwhile the "I"

---

[5] For the operations in this chapter the main sources are: *Middle East Training Pamphlet No. 10*; War Diaries of 4 Div. and of its Brigades and Battalions and notes by Major-General Beresford-Peirse.

tanks moved forward to their objective, from the north-west, while the infantry was carried round in motor transport on much the same axis as the tanks. At 0735 hours, the "I" tanks reached the Nibeiwa perimeter and surprised the Italian M. II tanks, which, no doubt, due to the secrecy with which the various moves had been conducted, were caught in the open, unmanned and formed up in close order on what was evidently their parade ground. All these were quickly destroyed, including the few which were obviously manned in a hurry and made some ineffective attempts at resistance. The "I" tanks then continued their advance towards the interior of the camp and for the first time met with a resistance from the Italian weapons which were of all description—artillery, machine-guns, anti-tank guns, rifles and hand grenades—and which were concentrated against them both with energy and determination. But none of the Italian weapons was able to produce any appreciable impression on their armour, and it soon became evident that the Italians had no missile capable of piercing the extra-thick armour plates of these British tanks. In fact, on finding the tanks impervious to their fire, the Italian and Libyan infantry became somewhat bewildered and lost their morale, and as a result the tanks were able to range freely. Moving methodically, they cleared up the areas allotted to their various sub-units.

At that stage, the leading infantry battalion, the 2nd Battalion Queen's Own Cameron Highlanders, which was a part of the 11th Indian Infantry Brigade, took over and began the mopping-up operation. The Camerons had advanced behind the tanks in their transport to within 700 yards of the perimeter. Doing this last lap of distance on foot, under the cover of the tanks, they commenced taking prisoners of which there were several hundreds. Here and there a few stubborn posts continued to resist but they were ultimately overcome and virtually the whole of the Niebiwa camp gave in before 0830 hours, that is within an hour of the commencement of the action, after which it was garrisoned by the 11th Indian Infantry Brigade, according to a previously arranged plan. The first phase of the offensive was thus over in about an hour and a quarter and the second began at once.

PHASE II: ATTACK ON THE TUMMAR CAMPS

The objective in this case was Tummar West. The striking arm was the same, the Royal Tank Regiment. The infantry following was the 5th Indian Infantry Brigade. It had been decided to attack this objective from the rear, that is from the west of the Tummar camps; and so immediately after the success at Nibeiwa, at 0830 hours, the Commander of the 4th Indian Division called up the 5th

Indian Infantry Brigade and ordered it to get to its position to the west of Tummar. The brigade, transported mechanically, moved northward and then to the west. In the meanwhile, the 16th (British) Infantry Brigade, which was in the divisional reserve, was also moved up to a point just west of Nibeiwa. The artillery, already warned to be ready for the opening of the second phase of the offensive, was ordered to take up its prearranged positions to the north of Nibeiwa, while the "I" tanks which were refilling at Nibeiwa in preparation for their next job, drove up to a position north-west of their objective. All these arrangements took $4\frac{3}{4}$ hours after the completion of the first phase, so that everything was ready for an attack on Tummar West by 1315 hours on 9 December 1940.

The artillery concentration against the Tummar defences began at 1335 hours; and at 1350 hours, the "I" tanks, about twenty-two in number, penetrated the camp from the north. The leading infantry, in this case the 1st Battalion Royal Fusiliers of the 5th Indian Infantry Brigade, followed up in their transport within 500 yards of the camp, reaching there about 20 minutes after the tanks. The sequence of events at Tummar West was much the same as at Nibeiwa, except that hardly any Italian tank was met with in the latter area. The progress of the "I" tanks towards the interior of the camp was once again resisted by the Italian artillery with a heavy fire. But once again were the Italian and Libyan troops horrified and demoralised to find the British tanks immune to all attacks from the best of their weapons. As a result, the tanks careered on, as at Nibeiwa, shooting down the gunners or overrunning gun positions, whilst the Royal Fusiliers, following behind, quickly mopped up the remaining points of resistance.

The success of the attack on Tummar West was considered by the Commander of the 4th Indian Division to justify his extending Phase II of the operation to include also the Tummar East. He, therefore, ordered an immediate attack on that encampment. The artillery, which was still in the same position as for the Tummar West operation, was asked not to move but to put down a concentration against Tummar East from the same positions. The "I" tanks which had just rallied after their previous attack, were again moved round and made to enter Tummar East from the north. The infantry following the tanks in this case was the 4th Battalion Rajputana Rifles of the 5th Indian Infantry Brigade. It happened that as the attack was going in, the Italian garrison of Tummar East was, by a mere chance, launching a counter-attack towards Tummar West, in which act it was caught up rather badly by the joint machine-guns of the 4th Battalion Rajputana Rifles and the 1st Battalion Royal Northumberland Fusiliers. Some 400 casualties were sustained by the Italian force in that action lasting barely ten minutes, while the counter-attack it was attempting to launch failed completely. The Rajputana Rifles then resumed mopping up their own sector and by dark were in a partial occupation of Tummar East. The rest of the mopping up proceeded according to the plan.

PHASE III: EXPLOITATION

Meanwhile, at 1615 hours, the Commander of the 4th Indian Division had already ordered the commencement of Phase III, namely exploitation. It comprised cutting the road Sidi Barrani—Buq Buq so that the garrisons of Sidi Barrani and Maktila might not escape towards Buq Buq or receive reinforcements. This task was assigned to the 16th (British) Infantry Brigade which was allotted two regiments of artillery for the night of 9/10 December, for carrying out that operation. The 'I' tanks were to join the fighting after a hurried process of refitting just enough to be able to go through the battle before dark.

It must be recalled here that, in the general plan, the 4th Armoured Brigade was also allotted the task of cutting the Sidi Barrani—Buq Buq road, which it had done as early as 1000 hours on the morning of the offensive, by penetrating behind, that is, to the west of the Tummar and Nibeiwa camps, and getting astride the road of retreat. But it is not possible for an armoured brigade to hold such a position indefinitely and infantry was needed to consolidate the gains. That task particularly was the assignment of the 4th Indian Division to be carried out in its exploitation phase. Hence the order of the divisional commander at 1600 hours for the commencement of Phase III.

However, it was not until the first light on 10 December that Phase III could make any headway. The advance of the 16th (British) Infantry Brigade began at 0555 hours and by 0700 hours the Brigade was 2000 yards further north from its bivouac area of the preceding night. At 0730 hours, one of its battalions, the 2nd Battalion Leicestershire Regiment, got involved in a fierce clash with an Italian defended camp. But after a brisk fight it forced the camp to surrender, capturing 2000 prisoners of the 4th Blackshirt Division. The remainder of the 16th Brigade, in the meanwhile, was continuing its northward advance to cut the road Sidi Barrani—Buq Buq, in the course of which it was overtaken by a violent dust storm which reduced visibility, at times to 150 yards, and made progress difficult. To this was added the heavy and accurate fire of the Italians which caused not a few casualties in men and transport. In spite of these difficulties, however, the 16th Infantry Brigade managed to keep moving, being materially aided, at this juncture, by the arrival of some ten "I" tanks, which overran the Italian gun positions and opened the way for the final stage of its advance. Thus, by 1330 hours, one of the battalions, the 1st Battalion Argyll and Sutherland Highlanders, had reached its objective and was astride the southern of the two roads leading from Sidi Barrani to Buq Buq, the northern road at the same time being cut by the 2nd Battalion Queen's Royal Regiment (West Surrey). The result of these moves was to isolate Sidi Barrani from its western flank by severing its link with Buq Buq.

While the 16th Brigade was thus blocking the western exits from Sidi Barrani, the 11th Indian Infantry Brigade had been moved up to guard the exits on the south and south-west. The combined effect of these two moves was to encircle Sidi Barrani completely, by closing all avenues of escape to its garrison. Hardly had the encirclement been thus completed, which happened at 1330 hours with the Argylls reaching their objectives west of Sidi Barrani, when the Commander of the 4th Indian Division decided to attack the camp and reduce it before the daylight should fail. The fighting that followed resulted in the capture of the village of Sidi Barrani itself and was virtually the climax as well as the end of this thirty-six hours' battle, fought in the three phases described above, and known collectively as the Battle of Sidi Barrani.

Capture of Sidi Barrani

The task of capturing Sidi Barrani was assigned to the 16th (British) Infantry Brigade. But since two of its battalions had already had hard fighting that day and were in need of reorganisation, it was given two more battalions from the 4th Indian Division. These were the 2nd Battalion Queen's Own Cameron Highlander and the 4th Battalion Rajputana Rifles, both of which had been previously withdrawn from their respective brigades to form a divisional reserve. In addition, the 16th Brigade was also given all the remaining "I" tanks, which now numbered ten. Its northern flank was to be protected by 2 Royal Tanks (of the 4th Armoured Brigade), while unforeseen contingencies were provided for by the maintenance of a close liaison between the 7th (British) Armoured and the 4th Indian Infantry Divisions. The liaison was to be maintained through radio-telegraphy which worked satisfactorily, the arrangement being that the GSOI of the 7th Armoured Division was to be located at the same place as the Commander of the 4th Indian Division, and was to have efficient communications to his own Headquarters. There was no concern felt for the success of this operation, since the garrison of Sidi Barrani, now isolated from all sides, was not expected to offer much resistance and the 4th Blackshirt Division was not in the village itself but further away to the east.

The attack on Sidi Barrani commenced at 1615 hours with the usual artillery support, the objective being the road Sidi Barrani-Matruh, which was to be cut just east of the former. Assisted by some cruisers of the Royal Tanks, the 2nd Battalion Queen's Own Cameron Highlanders attacked from the north and the 2nd Queen's Royal Regiment from the south. The combined support of the 'I' tanks, cruisers and artillery proved well co-ordinated and efficient, and the infantry had little difficulty in reaching the objective or in capturing the village which surrendered before dark, with a large number of prisoners, guns and other equipment.

Selby Force

It will be recalled that, according to the original plan of operations, while the central group of Italian camps was being attacked by the 4th Indian Division, the southern group was to be isolated by the 7th Armoured Division, and the northern, that is the Maktila garrison, was to be contained by Selby force. It is necessary here to see how much Selby Force was able to achieve and with what results. It had begun its move on 8 December and after an uneventful approach march had established itself at a point approximately two miles east of Maktila with its headquarters at Bir el Mahafiz (628364). Maktila was then garrisoned by the 1st Libyan Division, and the role assigned to Selby Force was to prevent this formation from withdrawing to the west or reinforcing the Tummar and the Sidi Barrani camps. As to harassing or attacking that Libyan formation, Selby Force was not to make an initial move in that direction, except after receiving the information that the 4th Indian Division was successful in its attack on the Tummar camps and the 7th Armoured Division in getting astride the road Sidi Barrani—Buq Buq. Thus, throughout the night of 8/9 December, the Force remained on the east of Maktila, waiting for the news that should enable it to make the initial move. Nothing happened in that sector for the greater part of the night, except that the naval bombardment of Maktila was carried out according to the plan.

Towards the morning, however, the 1st Libyan Division, having grown wise to the threat of Selby Force in front of it, had started shelling it. The shelling commenced at 0530 hours and continued spasmodically for the rest of the morning. In the meantime, the 4th Indian Division had begun its attack on the Nibeiwa camp which surrendered during the next hour. The second phase of attack on the Tummar Camps then began at 1330 hours and lasted till the night, after which only was Selby Force to commence its own move as laid down in the plan. But at 1430 hours the Force Commander received a situation report giving information about the capture of Nibeiwa and about the cutting of the road Buq Buq—

Sidi Barrani by the 7th Armoured Division. Although no mention was made therein of the Tummar camps having fallen, the Commander of the Force came to the conclusion that in view of the high probability that the Libyan Division might withdraw from Maktila during the night, it was his duty to take steps to prevent its escape. He therefore ordered his force to move westward towards Sidi Barrani and block the western exits of Maktila before midnight.

Accordingly, the 3rd Battalion Coldstream Guards commenced its move westwards. But it was heavily shelled during its progress towards the road which it was to cut, and darkness having fallen early, it failed to reach its objective as intended. Meanwhile, the Maktila garrison had started withdrawing and, when the Coldstream Guards reached the outskirts of that area early in the morning, they learned that the Libyan Division had vacated Maktila. That news reached the Force Headquarters at 0700 hours on 10 December, and was confirmed at 1000 hours. The Commander of the 4th Indian Division was paying a visit to Selby Force just at this hour and, after whatever exchange of information and consultations there might have been during that time, the Force Commander issued orders that the withdrawing Libyan Division be pursued with all possible speed.

Situation on 10 December 1940

While this pursuit was in progress, the general situation was far from reassuring or stable. Sidi Barrani had fallen but a large part of the 4th Blackshirt Division was still holding out in an area to its east and could not be ignored. The 1st Libyan Division was in full retreat but had not yet lost its fighting value. The Italian camp at Point 90 was still intact, as the Commander of the 4th Indian Division had decided that it could be dealt with later, after the more important camps had been liquidated. The Sofafi—Rabia group of camps had been isolated and contained so far, but had not been reduced; and the garrisons therein could be expected any moment to attempt a break-through or a withdrawal. Finally, there were some Italian forces, retreating or otherwise, on the coastal road between Sidi Barrani and Buq Buq, who might rally and counter-attack. Yet, despite these uncertainties, it was evident that the back of the Italian resistance had been broken and that another successful day might see the whole situation completely cleared up.

Consequently, the Commander of the West Desert Force paid a visit that afternoon to the Headquarters 7th (British) Armoured Division and, after a review of the situation, passed orders to the effect that the 7th Armoured Division was to send out forces in two directions; to the Sofafi camps to prevent an Italian withdrawal along the escarpment and towards Buq Buq to cut it off along the coast. In the event of the Italians continuing their withdrawal beyond Buq Buq, a further force was to be despatched over the escarpment, towards Halfaya and Sollum, to stop their westward moves.

Next morning, 11 December, at 1030 hours, the Commander of the Western Desert Force paid a similar visit to the Headquarters of the 4th Indian Division, which was then at Point 51 (593376). While he was there the news was received that all resistance in the north had practically ceased, the only opposition left being that to the east of Sidi Barrani. At 0900 hours in the morning that day, it had been discovered that the Sofafi—Rabia group of Italian camps was empty. The garrisons were withdrawing along the escarpment and the Allied air reconnaissance had already reported having seen about 200 vehicles and 500 men, strung out in a line, five miles west-north-west of the Sofafi camps. As to the situation to the east of Sidi Barrani, the Italian and Libyan troops in the Sidi Barrani and the Maktila areas, finding themselves cut off from escape to the west by the Indian and Armoured Divisions, had started moving eastwards in an endeavour to find a way out from that side. At the same time Selby Force had begun moving west in pursuit of the Libyan Division, which it contacted at 0845 hours and attacked in the area Sq. 626372. By 0955 hours, two of the Libyan battalions had surrendered, after which there remained only the remnants of the Libyan and the Blackshirt Divisions to be dealt with to clear up the whole area. Both were to the east of Sidi Barrani.

The completion of this task was the assignment of Selby Force which it carried out by dividing itself into two columns. One column which, a little earlier, had played a part in capturing the two battalions of the Libyan Division, continued its westward advance to Sidi Barrani in spite of a heavy sand-storm and eventually forced the remainder of the Libyan Division to surrender. This task was completed by 1300 hours, after which it contacted the Blackshirt Division which was then still holding out. Meanwhile the second Selby Column, consisting of the 1st Battalion South Staffords, who had been marching independently, it is said, towards the sound of the guns rather than towards a clearly defined objective, came up on the right of the Blackshirt Division and attacked it at once. Threatened by the two columns from two sides, that Italian formation, the last to surrender, capitulated at 1700 hours on 11 December. This final attack is sometimes called the second battle of Sidi Barrani, the first being the main attack of the 4th Indian Infantry Division already described. While these events were taking place, the 7th Armoured Brigade had, in an engagement lasting from afternoon to dusk, captured two strong points in the sand dunes in the area 553368—558368 which were a menace to the Allied movements.

Late that evening, Selby Force made contact with the Indian Division after its very successful action. Last of all to commence fighting, it was the last in finishing it too. It had captured some 8,500 prisoners, Italian and Libyan, and a quantity of guns and other material for about 50 casualties suffered by it.

This episode marked the victorious end of the first major offensive in Africa. The invasion of Egypt had been repulsed and the Italian aggression in Africa and elsewhere received a set-back from which it never really recovered. The success of the Allied arms had exceeded the highest hopes of General Wavell. Such Italian troops as were inside the Egyptian border were completely defeated and the capture of the war material was immense. General Wavell's plan of liquidating that part of the Italian Tenth Army which had established itself in the triangle Maktila—Sofafi—Buq Buq had been carried out almost to the letter. And yet there was scope for more successes if the westward advance could proceed further on the same momentum, which in fact it did.

It must be mentioned at this stage that soon after the victory at Sidi Barrani an important change took place in the composition of the Western Desert Force. The 4th Indian Infantry Division was needed in East Africa, where an Allied offensive was about to commence, and was therefore ordered out to the Sudan. Its place was allotted to the 6th Australian Division which had already begun moving westward. "It was at 1630 hours on 10 December," says General Beresford-Peirse, "just as I was watching the 2 Queens moving off from their starting line to take the Barrani village that a liaison officer arrived from Cairo in a car, with orders that the 4th Indian Division was to be relieved by the 6th Australian Division as soon as possible and to move to the Sudan. This was at that moment a singularly unpalatable order for the Indian Division, involved as they were in winning the first big success of the war." He did not pass on that order till the final success had been achieved on 11 December.

Liberation of Egypt

By 12 December, all Italian positions in Egypt were in Allied hands, except Sollum, Sidi Omar and Musaid. But for these three localities, the whole of the Egyptian territory had been cleared of Marshal Graziani's defeated army. Only a few groups and parties lingered on. Some of these were round the area 517366, approximately six miles south-west of the Sollum harbour; while others were retreating from Musaid towards Capuzzo or from Halfaya towards Sollum. The general trend was a withdrawal towards Sollum, Capuzzo and Bardia.

The Italians held the triangle Bardia—Capuzzo—Sollum for two more days. But on 14 December, they voluntarily withdrew from Capuzzo, and also vacated the neighbouring high ground that was overlooking Sollum. This last move was particularly an indiscreet step, as it at once opened the way for the 7th Armoured Division to contact the south-west defence of Bardia and to close the road Bardia—Tobruk. It also solved General Wavell's problem of a rapidly extending line of communication, since part of the supplies could thereafter be received through the small but serviceable beachhead of Sollum.

The last of the fighting on the Egyptian soil took place on 16 December. On that day the 4th Armoured Brigade captured Sidi Omar with 700 prisoners, itself suffering no casualty, while the Support Group of the 7th Armoured Division occupied Sollum and Musaid. After that there were no Italian troops left on the Egyptian soil. What remained of them were now in Cyrenaica and these were less than half of the force originally assembled for the invasion of Egypt. From the opening of the offensive up to date, the Western Desert Force had taken over 38,000 Italian and Libyan prisoners, together with large quantities of tanks, lorries, guns, ammunition and stores.[8] Its casualties were less than a thousand men, majority of whom were only wounded.

It is worth noting here that the reverses suffered by the Italians in Egypt had not materially altered their fighting strength in North Africa. The force that was routed was only the army assembled for the invasion of Egypt. Marshall Graziani still had at his disposal about 200,000 troops in Libya, and enough war material, to return to the attack, given sufficient time to reorganise. To deny him just that time, was the Allied plan. It was therefore decided to pursue the retreating Italian Tenth army with vigour and to give it no chance to reorganise.

---

[8] To put it numerically, captured stores and equipment consisted of 237 guns, 73 light and medium tanks and over 1000 vehicles.

CHAPTER X

Advance into Cyrenaica

Advance to Bardia and Tobruk

With his decision to pursue the retreating Italians, General Wavell's offensive against the Tenth Army entered a new phase. Hitherto the operations had consisted of an attack on static defences. But now a new period was about to begin involving a more dynamic and mobile warfare and a continuous advance. The original offensive, due to its great success, had outgrown all planning and had rather unexpectedly turned into a regular campaign. But, since such a campaign had not been anticipated and provided for beforehand, everything had to be extemporised to meet the unexpected situation. Problems of supplies and maintenance became particularly difficult and imposed a great strain on the administrative units which, nevertheless, managed to keep pace with the developments.

The pursuit was primarily the task of the 7th (British) Armoured Division, for which job it had been split into two main groups. One of these was the 4th Armoured Brigade with detachments from 2 Royal Tanks, the Royal Air Force Armoured Cars, 11th Hussars and the Royal Horse Artillery, while the other group consisted only of the 7th Armoured Brigade. The retreating Italians at this juncture were falling back on Bardia which was their next defensive position. The Allied plan was to attack Bardia on the one hand, and to sit astride the road Bardia—Tobruk on the other, so as to cut off Bardia's communications during the attack.[1]

The 4th Indian Division had already left for the Sudan.[2] Consequently, there were no Indian troops in the operations from that point onward. Yet it is necessary to record these operations in some detail, since they provide a necessary background to the later ones in which Indian formations took active part, and bring out many lessons of military value which the Indian forces employed in their subsequent battles in the same theatre of war. This record will also serve to link the period of fighting in Cyrenaica with that in which the 4th Indian Division returned to North Africa to resume the struggle it had left incomplete.

The general situation on the first day of the pursuit, 17

---

[1] General Wavell's *Despatch*, p. 3264; Lt. Gen. Martel: *Our Armoured Forces*, pp. 87-88.
[2] W/D 4 Ind. Div.

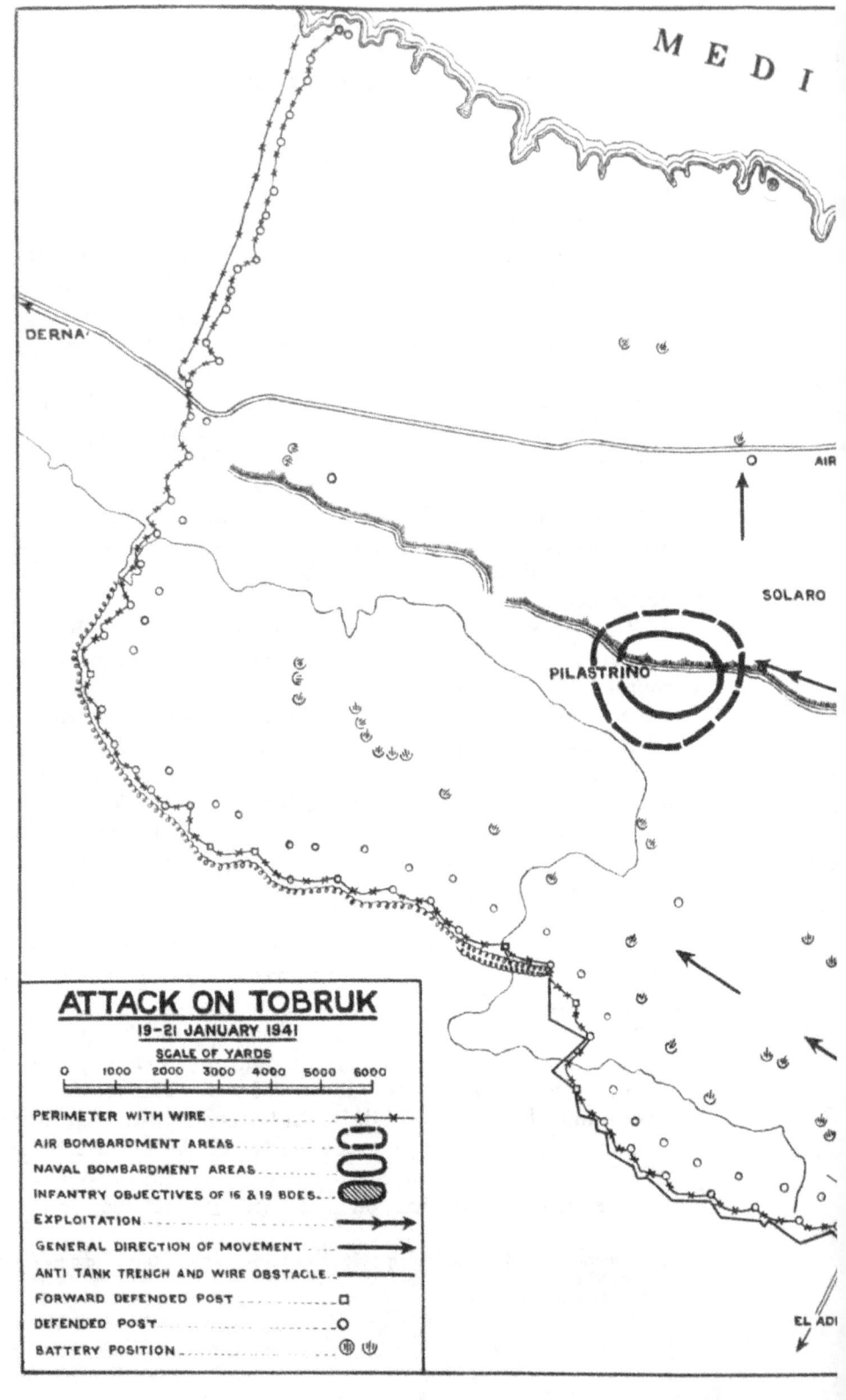

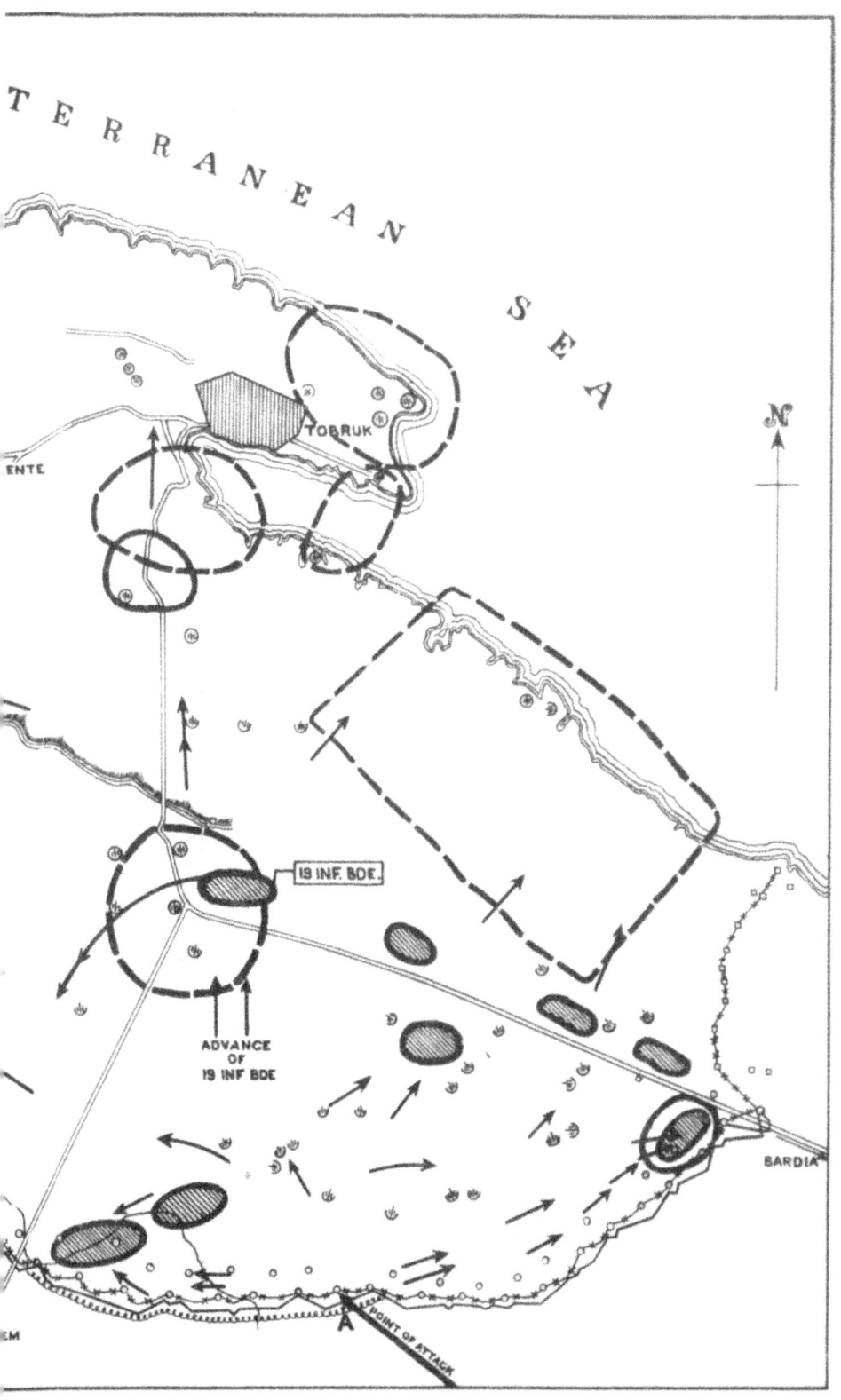

December, was as satisfactory as might be expected. The 4th Armoured Brigade was astride the road Bardia—Tobruk, thus severing communications between these two garrisoned localities. The 7th Armoured Brigade was containing the Bardia defences on the north-west. The 16th (British) Infantry Brigade had placed itself opposite the south-east face of the Bardia perimeter, which had also enabled it to cover the use of the Sollum harbour. The greater part of the Italian army in Cyrenaica had voluntarily withdrawn into that virtually besieged perimeter and had, by that unaccountable move, only succeeded in restricting its own freedom of action, while creating for the Western Desert Force an administrative situation favourable for an offensive against Bardia.

The fighting that followed was the first of the struggles for the mastery of Cyrenaica and divides itself into four main stages, namely, operations (*a*) at Bardia (*b*) at Tobruk (*c*) on the line Derna—Mekili and (*d*) on the north of Agedabia. The events of that campaign would be best dealt with in that sequence.

STAGE I: BARDIA

Bardia, as described earlier, is a small port about eight miles from the Egyptian border and twenty miles beyond Sollum. The harbour is joined to the open sea by a narrow ravine which permits the passage of vessels up to 400 tons. Both, the port and the town, had been developed by Italians as an advanced base for the invasion of Egypt. The town, which is small, stands at a height of 350 feet above sea level, at the head of a cove on the south side of the Gulf of Sollum. It is perched on one of the cliffs overlooking the sea, the cliffs themselves forming the edge of an escarpment. This escarpment, which slopes towards the beach, is the northwestern extremity of the Libyan Plateau, large areas of which are level plain. On a part of that plain, to the south-west of the escarpment, there stood the ring of Italian defences circling the town and port of Bardia and intended to protect the latter against an Allied attack.

The Bardia fortifications

The stronghold of Bardia was in existence even before the war and comprised coastal, anti-aircraft and land defences. The last named were contained in a fortified horse-shoe perimeter measuring $10\frac{1}{2}$ miles long, $4\frac{1}{2}$ miles deep and 17 miles along the periphery. The outermost ring of the perimeter consisted of an arc of anti-tank trenches, which were reinforced by mines wherever the trenches were not considered sufficiently good obstacles. Behind the trenches and inside the ring was a continuous all-round wire obstacle.

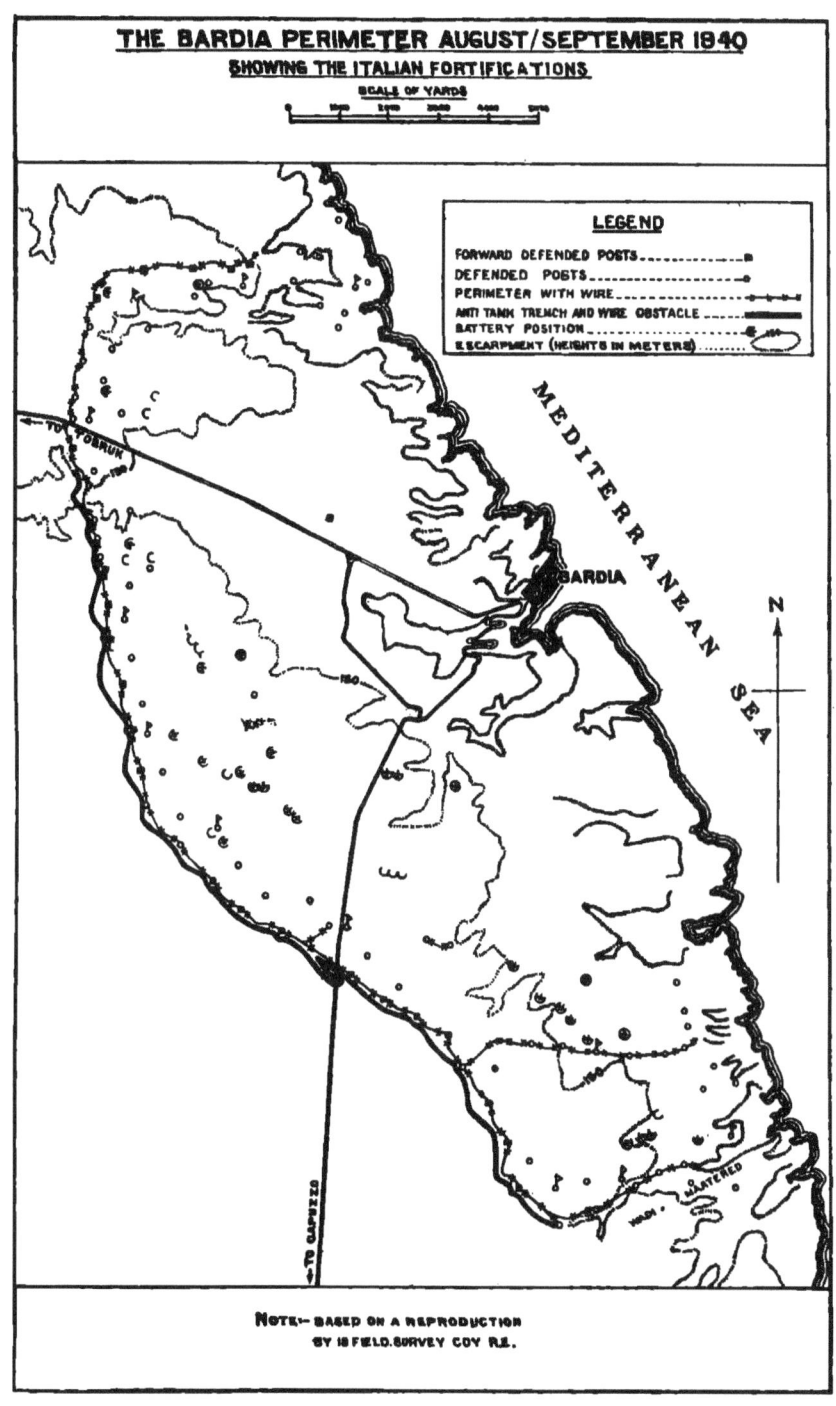

Within this second ring was a chain of concrete defence-posts, which were the forward posts, some 700 yards apart, each containing two or more medium machine-guns. Each post was surrounded by a circular, concrete, anti-tanks ditch and a wire obstacle. Behind the forward posts, about 500 yards in the rear, was the fourth ring, that of supporting posts, which were similar to the forward posts in design and fighting power, except that they were not protected by ani-tank or wire obstacles. After the ring of the supporting posts came a chain of battery positions and then the infantry dugouts. In the heart of these roughly concentric rings of defences was the town and port of Bardia, strengthened towards the sea with coastal guns and batteries and against overhead attacks by anti-aircraft defences.[3]

The concentric rings of defences were neither regular nor symmetrical since their layout had naturally to conform to the configuration of the land. That was specially the case in the south-east corner of the perimeter where a naturally strong position was provided by Wadi Maatered. Here advantage was taken to provide an additional line of defensive posts to serve as a "switch-line", 3000 to 4000 yards to the north of the wadi.

Weakness in the layout of Italian defences

Invulnerable as the Bardia defences might seem on a casual review, they had three main weaknesses in their design and layout. Firstly, the gun emplacements and their connecting trenches for the crew were unequally protected. That is, while the weapons in the emplacements were open and exposed to bombardment, the concrete trenches for the guncrew were extraordinarily safe and cosy, being deep and narrow, and roofed against the weather. As a result, during heavy bombardments, such as normally precedes an assault, the crew preferred to remain underground rather than come out and perform the superhuman task of manning the unprotected guns. Thus, much of the Italian artillery power was often wasted and that, too, at critical times.

The second fault in the layout of the Bardia defences was the great distance between the anti-tank trenches and the wire surrounding the perimeter. The trenches were outside the wire, had no depth and, at places, were as much as 300 yards ahead of the forward posts. Nor were they guarded at night. It was thus possible for the Allied artillery to bombard the forward posts while the trenches were being bridged for the tanks to pass, since the distance between them and the forward posts made it easy for the

---

[3] *Middle East Training Pamphlet No. 10*, pp. 17 and 50.
Our Armoured Forces, p. 88.
General Wavell's *Despatch*, p. 3264.

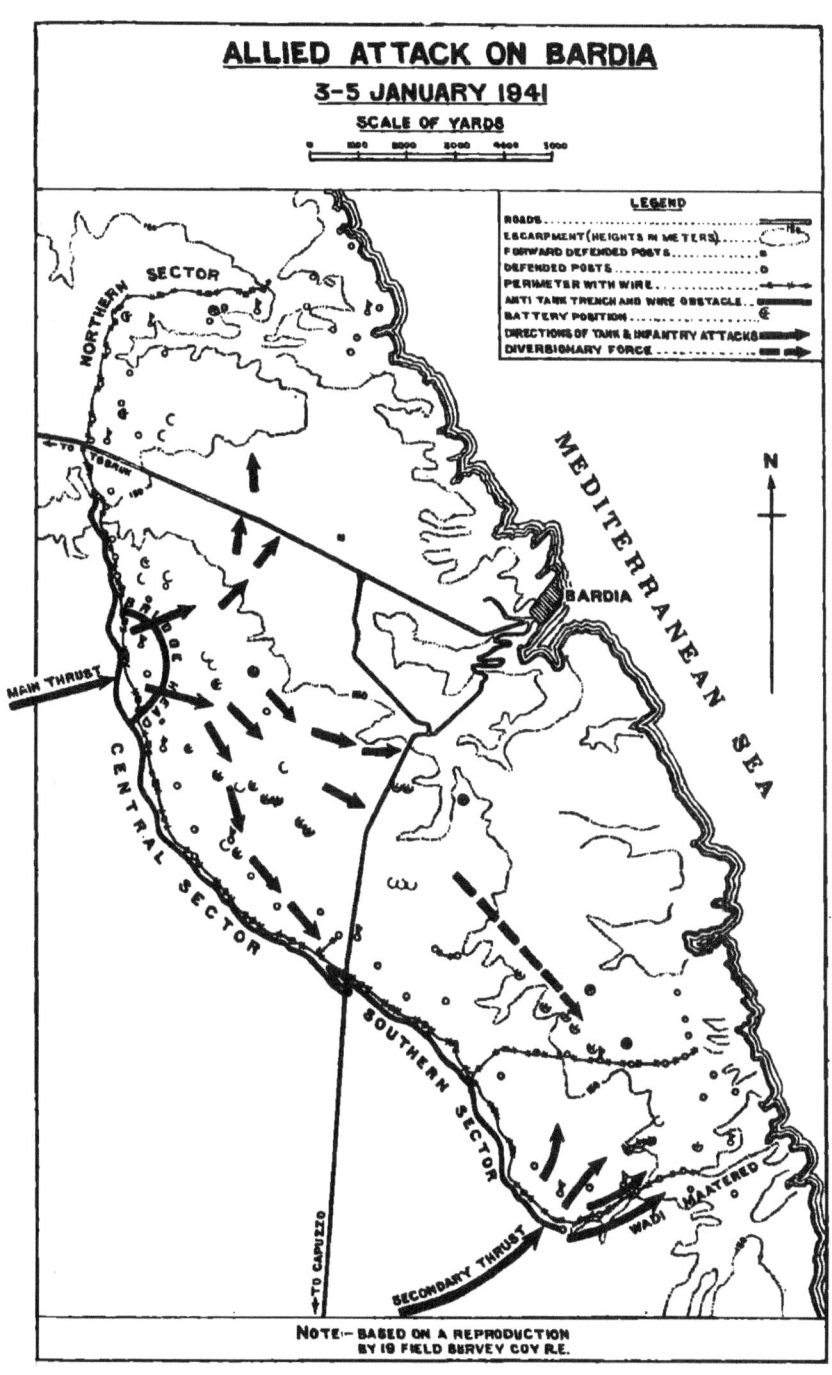

artillery to shoot over the heads of the sappers bridging the trenches. Had the anti-tank obstacles been close enough to the forward posts, such artillery support would have been difficult to give, if not impossible. Again, as the anti-tank trenches were not guarded at night they were a gift to any adventurous night patrol, more certainly so during or before an assault.

The third weakness of the defensive system of Bardia was the wide interval between the adjacent forward posts, so that a very effective kind of mutual support or cross-fire was not possible, and gaps between the posts were, therefore, not impenetrable.

In fact, the defences of Bardia were hardly capable of resisting a determined attack by a field army, well equipped with artillery and tanks; though perhaps they were adequate for repulsing raids by a small mobile force.

Decision to attack Bardia

After the fall of Sidi Barrani, the Middle East Command had to decide whether to stand fast on the frontier of Egypt or to continue to attack and pursue. Assuming that the air and naval situation was favourable for a continued offensive on land, any decision as to future operations had to take the administrative aspect into consideration. The Allied fighting forces were already 140 miles beyond the nearest railhead, which was then at Mersa Matruh, and there was no third-line transport. However, it was felt that, since Sollum was in Allied hands and the Italian forces had withdrawn from the high ground overlooking the harbour, the pursuit of the retreating Italian force could, at least temporarily, be maintained without much risk.

Accordingly, on 16 December 1940, the decision was taken to attack Bardia at an early date. Some delay was, however, inevitable since supplies and ammunition had to be brought from Matruh over a distance of 140 miles. Thus, although the infantry was in contact with the Bardia defences from 17 December 1940, the attack did not commence until 3 January 1941. By 27 December, two infantry brigades of the 6th Australian Division, the 16th and 17th Australian Infantry Brigades, had got into the line and were facing the south-eastern defences of Bardia. The third Australian Brigade, the 19th, reached the area on 1 January 1941.

At about this time, the designation Western Desert Force was dropped and Headquarters Western Desert Force became Headquarters XIII Corps.[4] The forces at the disposal of the XIII Corps for the attack on Bardia consisted of the 7th (British) Armoured Division, the 6th Australian Infantry Division, the 7th Battalion Royal Tank Regiment (about 26 tanks only), four Field Regiments,

[4] *M. E. Training Pamphlet No. 10*, p. 18.

one Medium Artillery Regiment, one Machine-gun Battalion and any additional artillery that could be spared by the 7th Armoured Division.

The composition of this force, however, was not well suited to the task of attacking Bardia. The proportion of the infantry tanks was not adequate for the level, open ground inside the perimeter which called for infantry tanks as the main assaulting arm. The other alternative was to employ more than the normal complement of infantry, both for the assault and the exploitation stages. But the slow-moving and unprotected infantry, advancing over open ground, required a greater quantity of artillery ammunition for its protection than would be required to protect the tanks. Hence the long pause before the attack, which was necessary for the purpose of accumulating large dumps of ammunition, at a rate of some 300 rounds per gun.

For the purpose of attack, the perimeter around Bardia was divided into three parts, which may be called the northern, central and the southern sectors. The northern sector was the area to the north of the road Bardia—Tobruk, the southern was that to the east of the road Bardia—Capuzzo while the central was the area between the two.

Plan of attack

The plan of attack was to cover the entire northern sector with naval and air bombardment, and penetrate the central and southern sectors with tank and infantry attacks. At the same time two diversionary attacks or demonstrations were to be made, one in the North by the 7th (British) Armoured Division and another in the south-east by the 17th Australian Infantry Brigade. It was exepected that the naval and air bombardment of the northern sector would make the left flank of the central sector safe during the initial break-through. This safety would be further ensured by the diversionary demonstration of the 7th (British) Armoured Division in the north-west corner of the perimeter, for it would be natural for the Italians to conclude, from the heavy bombardment in the northern sector and the presence of an Armoured Division on its outskirts, that the attack was about to be launched against that particular sector, and thus be led into adopting a false line of defence. Whereas, in fact, while the Italian command would thus be on the wrong scent, it was planned to make two tank-cum-infantry thrusts against the perimeter in the central and the southern sector respectively. The former was to be the main and initial attack and the latter a secondary one. The main thrust, after breaking through, was to split itself into two groups; one group was to advance northward and the other eastward. The objective of the former, designated the first objective, was to be the edge of the escarpment; while that of the latter, termed the general objective was the road Bardia—Capuzzo. On the first objective being reached, the move was to convert itself into exploitation towards the road Bardia—Tobruk and the high ground overlooking Bardia from the south-west. The exploitation was to come to a halt after the general objective had been attained.[5]

By the time the main thrust came to a halt, the secondary thrust was to have breached the perimeter in the southern sector and be ready to continue, from that stage on, the eastward advance of the main thrust. The secondary thrust also, like the main thrust, had to split itself into two groups. The objective of group one was the escarpment and the high ground above Bardia. That was designated the second objective, and the exploitation thereafter was towards the south of Bardia. The objective of group two was Wadi Maatared. That group, in its eastward sweep, was intended to come upon the Italian gun and infantry positions in the south-eastern lobe of the perimeter, from the rear and flanks. Thus, that doubly fortified area, with a secondary "switch-line", would be subjected to an attack from the rear and flanks, while at the same time a diversionary force would be engaging it in the front.

It remains now to describe how the main and the secondary thrusts were actually carried out. In each case a point of penetration was selected as the first step. In the case of the main thrust it was a gap between two forward posts. The forward and supporting posts were numbered serially for the purposes of identification and reference. The gap selected was between posts 45 and 47. The initial thrust therefore resolved itself into an effort to capture a series of five posts, two forward and three in support, namely posts 45-44-47-46-49. That aim was achieved by an infantry assault, covered by the heaviest possible artillery concentration.

The assault force consisted of one infantry battalion, which assembled at its starting point during darkness and delivered the attack at first light. A dark night was especially required to avoid being caught by the Italian artillery in a long approach march on open ground in broad daylight. While the assault was progressing, the anti-tank ditches were filled in at five points for the tanks to pass, and the wire was cut by Bangalore torpedoes in several places. The Allied artillery was able to neutralize the small-arms fire of the Italian troops without endangering their own men on account of the long distance between the dugouts and the outskirt of the perimeter—a serious mistake, as already pointed out, in the layout of the Italian defences.

[5] *M. E. Training Pamphlet No. 10*, p. 19.

Having reduced the five selected posts, the infantry turned that area into a bridgehead and held it until the tanks were able to cross through. Thereafter, the tanks and infantry, preceded by a series of artillery concentrations, moved towards their objectives as described above in the plan of attack. The secondary thrust was more or less on the same pattern as the main one and, therefore, has not been described in detail.

Fall of Bardia

The attack on the Bardia perimeter began at 0530 hours on 3 January 1941. The first day's objective was the bridgehead, which was formed by the 2/1st Australian Infantry Battalion after the capture of the five posts in the central sector. Next day, the 16th and 17th Australian Brigades began their thrusts against the central and southern sectors, and, by 1745 hours, their tanks and infantry had reached and entered the town of Bardia. After that there remained only the troops in the south-east corner of the perimeter, the better fortified and the more resolute among the defenders of Bardia, who held out for a day longer. During the fighting and at the end of the battle for Bardia, the Allied troops collected some 45,000 prisoners, with 462 guns including 262 field pieces, 129 tanks consisting of 12 medium and the rest light.

STAGE II: TOBRUK

The next defensive position available to the Italians after Bardia was Tobruk and, as expected, they decided to make a stand at that point. Tobruk is only 76 miles from Bardia and 100 miles from Sollum, and so a move towards it could not gravely complicate the line of communication problem for the Allies which, on the other hand, would become greatly simplified if that excellent harbour could be captured. Therefore an advance towards Tobruk seemed justified to the Commander XIII Corps, both on operational as well as administrative grounds. In fact, even while the battle for Bardia was still in progress, he had issued instructions for the necessary preparations to be made for a rapid investment and reduction of Tobruk as soon as possible after the fall of Bardia. It is therefore not surprising that, on 6 January 1941, the very next day after the fall of Bardia, the 7th (British) Armoured Division had already cut the routes westward to Tobruk, and on the following day, the 19th Australian Infantry Brigade was closing upon the eastern face of its perimeter; while the rest of the 6th Australian Division, with the 7th Royal Tanks, had also begun moving in the same direction.

Tobruk fortifications

Tobruk is a town of considerable size. Like Bardia, it is situated on cliffs overlooking the sea but, unlike Bardia, it is something of a natural fortress too. Possessing a good though small harbour, it was Italy's principal naval base on the Libyan coast, and later became her main base for the land and air forces in Cyrenaica. An important point about Tobruk was that it possessed an adequate water supply.

The defensive ring surrounding Tobruk was similar in layout to that of Bardia. Like the latter, it was well provided with seaward and anti-aircraft defences, while on the land side it was protected by a fortified preimeter some 16 miles long, 10 miles deep and 29½ miles along the periphery. The perimeter was obviously more extensive than that of Bardia, and therefore it was not easy to surround it with anti-tank ditches on an elaborate scale. In many places, therefore, the ditches were barely two feet deep. They were not guarded by men but were protected by anti-tank mines and booby-traps, both of which could be, and were, removed by Allied patrols without any hostile interference.

Although, in general the problem presented by the Tobruk defences was similar to that which had been so successfully solved at Bardia, there were still some points of difference which required corresponding modifications in the plan of attack. Firstly, the greater extent of the Tobruk defensive system enabled the Royal Navy, and the Royal Air Force to have a larger variety of targets. Next, the harbour was an effective outlet, enabling the Italian troops to escape or receive reinforcements, and would have to be blocked by a naval force ; and finally, the open country outside the perimeter called for a relatively long approach march, while, within the perimeter itself, it called for a bigger force of tanks. On the other hand, in relation to the area to be defended, the Italian garrison was not adequate, and it was therefore to be expected that, once the perimeter was broken through, events would develop very swiftly.

Other points to be taken into consideration were that the larger area within the perimeter would offer a greater scope to the Italian garrison for counter-attacks and, consequently, any deep penetration would have to be given secure flanks. Further, since the town of Tobruk lay some 9 miles from the edge of the perimeter where the attack would begin, it was doubtful whether the advance, if resisted with determination, would be quick enough to prevent any effective demolitions in the harbour. These were some of the factors that actually influenced the operations which began a few days later.

The ground over which the attack was to be made was, for the most part, level, open country, terminating towards the sea into escarpments which overlooked Tobruk. Towards the land was the semicircular ring of defended localities, constituting the perimeter, from the south-east corner of which proceeded two roads: the roads Bardia—Tobruk and El Adem—Tobruk. These met in a junction at Sidi Mahmoud, from where a single road proceeded northwards to Tobruk and joined the road Tobruk—Derna. Thus, the communications of the Tobruk garrison with the areas outside the perimeter were to the east towards Bardia, to the south with El Adem and to the west with Derna. The important features on the ground were the heights of Pilastrino and Solaro, roughly in the centre of the perimeter. These stood on the edges of the escarpments and overlooked Tobruk. Almost the only other important feature was the road-fork in the area Sidi Mahmoud. All those points, except Solaro, and several other road-junctions and vital spots were selected as targets for air and naval bombardment, while the area chosen for the infantry attack was the ground enclosed by the above mentioned road-fork and the south-eastern part of the perimeter.

Allied and Italian Forces

The attacking force, which was under the command of Headquarters 6th Australian Division, was much the same as at Bardia, with certain additions. The additional units were a second machine-gun battalion (1st Battalion Cheshire Regiment), one field artillery regiment and one medium battery. A great deficiency, however, was the armour, since the most important unit, the 7th Royal Tank Regiment, had no more than 16 tanks left in fighting trim. As a compensating factor, on the other hand, the 6th Australian Division had succeeded in expanding its divisional cavalry from one squadron to three, by utilising the captured arms and by repairing old carriers and weapons. One of these squadrons was made up wholly from the captured Italian tanks, while the other two consisted of the Bren and machine-gun carriers.

The force thus composed was hardly suited to the task of attacking and capturing Tobruk. The nature of the ground and the extensive area of the defences called for a large-scale all-armoured attack. But armour was the main deficiency. The opponents to be tackled were two Italian infantry divisions, the 61st and the 60th, the only ones remaining in Cyrenaica. The former was in Tobruk and the latter further west. In addition there were the Headquarters and Corps troops of the XXII (Italian) Corps; while somewhere near Mekili was the nucleus of an armoured formation yet in the process of being assembled.

The plan for the attack on Tobruk had to take into account the lessons learned at Bardia. One of the lessons was that the Italian forward and supporting posts were easily neutralised because of their distances from the anti-tank and wire obstacles and from one another. Another was that the Italian artillery, if left unengaged, was capable of causing very great damage. The first point was provided for in the artillery plan by ensuring a liberal quantity of supporting fire to the attacking troops; the second was met by allotting far more guns to the counter-battery tasks than was done during the attack on Bardia.

Allied plan

The role of the infantry and tanks in the attack was to effect a breach in the wire covering the forward posts 55 and 57. Thereafter their task was to clear the ground enclosed by the road-fork El Adem—Sidi Mahmoud—Bardia and the south-eastern part of the perimeter. That involved reducing eight miles of defended posts and silencing some twelve battery positions. The striking arm was the 16th Australian Infantry Brigade which, after entering the perimeter, was to split itself into three columns. Two of these columns were to fan out east and west and reduce the forward posts on each side. The objective of the third was the line of batteries which occupied the centre of the road-fork. As the battalions of the 16th Australian Infantry Brigade would ultimately become widely separated, it was arranged that the battery area, after its capture, should be looked after by a mixed force to be kept ready. The force was formed with the 1st Battalion Royal Northumberland Fusiliers and certain troops of the Australian Divisional Cavalry Regiment.

From the captured battery area onward, the attack was to be carried forward by the 19th Australian Infantry Brigade, until the junction of the road-fork was reached. After that the Brigade was to clear the ground on the south-west and exploit northward and westward according to the circumstances. This attack had to be undertaken without the assistance of tanks, as none were available. In the meanwhile, units of the 17th Australian Infantry Brigade were to take control of the ground overlooking the seaward wadis, between the road-junction and the perimeter, thus releasing the 16th Australian Brigade to concentrate towards the road Tobruk—El Adem.

It was not possible, however, to put the above plan into operation immediately the defences of Tobruk had been contacted. Time was necessary for collecting ammunition. As stated earlier, due to the paucity of tanks, a heavy burden fell upon the artillery which had to afford protection to the very vulnerable infantry moving across an open ground. The artillery needed a few days for dumping the required quantities of ammunition for that difficult task. Actually an interval of no less than 13 days thus elapsed between the first contact and the final assault.

That period of waiting was, however, made use of in several ways by improving the ground for the impending assault. Batteries were moved into position and observation posts were established. Detailed reconnaissance of the Italian forward posts, wires and anti-tank obstacles was carried out from day to day. Aggressive patrolling against widely separated parts of those defences was undertaken and continued to the last day. Italian observation posts and working parties were attacked and harried daily, and at least two Bangalore torpedoes were exploded every night in the wire obstacles, though always far away from the selected point of attack so as not to betray the intended location.

Fall of Tobruk

The D-day was 20 January 1941. But it had to be put off by 24 hours because of severe sand-storms. The air bombardment started three days before the D-day and prearranged targets were covered by the Royal Air Force for a few hours every day and every night. The most bombed of the targets were the harbour and the roads leading to it from the east and south. Other targets were the points of escarpments overlooking the harbour and the road-fork in the Sidi Mahmoud area. Two days before the D-Day the Royal Navy also started shelling its own pre-assigned targets. Two of them were again the points of escarpments overlooking the harbour and these, to some extent, overlapped the aerial targets. The remaining targets to come under the air-navy shelling were those that had been specially selected with a view to weakening the defences on the west of the perimeter and those which had the object of cutting the road Tobruk—Derna.

The infantry assault commenced on the morning of 21 January. By noon, the 16th and the 19th Australian Infantry Brigades had captured their objectives, suffering only small losses. The Italian artillery was unable to do much damage because of the accurate counter-battery work by the Allied guns. The hostile airforce took no part in the battle, presumably because of the heavy loss suffered by it at Bardia. It was, therefore, possible to begin the stage of exploitation almost at once and, during the afternoon, the 19th Australian Infantry Brigade exploited towards Solaro and Pilastrino. By nightfall the eastern half of the perimeter too was in Allied hands, and satisfactory advance was being made also westward and northward towards Tobruk.[6]

That night, 21/22 January, there were fires and explosions in the Tobruk harbour. Some Free French infantry, which was then under the 7th Armoured Division, penetrated the perimeter near the sea to the west of Tobruk. The fighting came to an end soon after;

[6] General Wavell's *Despatch*, p. 3266.

and the Allies entered Tobruk the next morning without opposition. As anticipated, the harbour could not be reached in time to save it from large-scale demolitions, due to lack of tanks. The Italian garrison was therefore able to destroy some installations and large quantities of useful stores. The number of prisoners taken, though less than that at Sidi Barrani and Bardia, amounted to 30,000 personnel, about half of whom were the corps and the line of communication troops, including specialists of the various branches.

CHAPTER XI

Pursuit by the XIII Corps

Advance to El Agheila

The capture of Tobruk gave the Allies a good harbour, about 100 miles nearer the front than Sollum. It shortened the line of communication and eased the supply and transport position. It also brought about an increase in the Allied vehicles and fuel by the addition of captured vehicles and petrol dumps abandoned by the Italian troops. Italian forces, on the other hand, had suffered such losses in men and material that the Italian Tenth Army in Cyrenaica was now no longer superior to the XIII Corps, whether in numbers, mobility or offensive power. Therefore, further pursuit, and the resultant dispersal, were not considered unsafe either by General Wavell or by General O'Connor, Commander XIII Corps.[1] In fact, the latter had issued the necessary instructions for extending the pursuit towards Benghazi even before the fall of Tobruk.

STAGE III: DERNA—MEKILI

It is not clear what the Italian High Command's intentions were after the loss of Tobruk. All that can be said with certainty is that the Italian force, now remaining in Cyrenaica, had taken up new positions so as to block the main approaches to Benghazi. There were two principal routes by which Benghazi could be approached. One was the coastal road through Derna and Barce; and the other, the desert road through Mekili and Got Derva. The former, the northern line of advance, was covered by the 60th Italian Division, less one infantry brigade group. The latter, the southern line, was blocked by a composite force of infantry and tanks under General Babini. The Babini Force, which included a Brigade Group of the 60th Division, was disposed in and around Mekili; while the rest of the 60th Division was just east of Derna. Together the two forces held the line Derna—Mekili, on the tableland of the Jebel Akhdar, blocking the Allied advance towards Benghazi.

The two places, Derna and Mekili, are about fifty miles apart. Derna is a junction of two main tracks and several desert tracks. Both the places had to be held simultaneously or not at all. Holding just one of them would not suffice either to block the Allied advance to Benghazi or to prevent the encirclement of the holding

[1] General Wavell's *Despatch*, p. 3267.

force from the rear. The Allied plan was to exploit this difficulty of the Italian Command and their tactics were framed accordingly.

It was decided that pressure must be brought on the Derna force to prevent its disengagement or withdrawal; while, at the same time, the Mekili force must be attacked and destroyed or captured. The bulk of the Italian armour in Cyrenaica, which included 160 tanks of different marks, formed a part of the Mekili force. If, therefore, the Mekili force was eliminated, a rapid advance to Benghazi, by the desert route, would be possible. That would also result in all Italian forces in the Jebel area, including the Derna force, being cut off.

Accordingly, an infantry brigade group of the 6th Australian Division was marked out to advance on Derna in mechanical transport, as soon as Tobruk was taken; and at the same time the 7th Armoured Division was ordered to be ready to send a strong force towards Mekili. This double advance began on 21 January 1941 and, by the 26th, a portion of the 7th Armoured Division was in contact with the Italian troops to the north of Mekili, while the Australian brigade had gained contact with the force at Derna. The stage had thus been set for the attack which was about to commence when an unexpected move by the Babini Force made the projected operation unnecessary.

The Babini Force, it appears, suddenly abandoned Mekili and withdrew to Slonta, north-westwards, during the night of 26/27 January. That withdrawal, unexpected as it was, was particularly unwise for the Italians in that it compromised the position of their Derna force and uncovered the most direct route to Benghazi. The withdrawing force was, of course, pursued by the 7th Armoured Division and harassed by the Allied air force. But, despite some losses which it could not avoid, it managed to keep its units practically intact. In fact, if any formation did suffer in this cross-desert dash, it was strangely enough the 7th Armoured Division itself. Owing to the rugged nature of the ground, its units suffered severe mechanical losses during the pursuit which reduced its strength to about 50 cruiser tanks and 95 light tanks. It would hardly have been prudent to engage the Babini Force in this condition, and further action was therefore postponed until 12 February 1941, when a reinforcement of a new cruiser unit was due to reach Mekili, which was all the more necessary since the Babini Force still possessed a strong group of medium tanks.

Preparations for advance on Benghazi

The intervening period of waiting was devoted to preparing for the contemplated advance on Benghazi. The preparations were directed towards a new plan which was a modified version of the

Dashing Forward (*Courtesy Imperial War Museum*)

Bulldozer at work (*Courtesy Imperial War Museum*)

Indian troops in trenches (Courtesy Imperial War Museum)

A machine-gun post (Courtesy Imperial War Museum)

original. It consisted in developing a strong pressure against Derna so as to create the impression that the Allied advance would be along the northern route. To that end the 17th Australian Infantry Brigade Group was to be brought up to join the 19th Australian Brigade Group at Derna. At the same time, the 16th Australian Infantry Brigade was to be moved to Mekili to join the 7th Armoured Division for the real westward drive. That drive which was to be the main advance, was to develop from the south-east of Benghazi in the direction of Agedabia or Benghazi according to the situation at the moment. Ten days' supplies were stored at Mekili and sufficient transport kept ready to provide for the maintenance needs of the advancing force.

But the Italians carried out yet another unexpected move on 30 January 1941.[2] They withdrew from their forward positions east of Derna on to the Wadi Derna itself. Pressure was therefore increased in that area to clear Derna if possible, so as to secure an additional port for expediting supplies. It proved quite effective and by 3 February not only was Derna evacuated but the Italian forces had commenced a general withdrawal as if for evacuating the whole of Cyrenaica. Air reconnaissances reported large columns moving westward and tanks being loaded in ships at Benghazi. The Italian command had evidently realised the grave risk involved in keeping all its infantry and armour confined to the mountain region east of Barce; hence the withdrawal which was clearly in the direction of Benghazi.

PHASE IV: AGEDABIA

A new situation developed as a result of this rather unexpected withdrawal. Lieutenant-General O'Connor, Commanding the XIII Corps, had to solve the riddle of the possible Italian intentions and that too without delay. The withdrawal might portend an outright retreat from Cyrenaica by the coastal road down south; or a halt at Benghazi to defend it; or evacuation through that port. If the destination of the retreat was south of Benghazi then the time during which the Italian force could be intercepted was growing short. The same was true of the possible escape of the retreating troops through the port of Benghazi. Only in the event of the Italians choosing to make a stand at Benghazi was there sufficient time to deal with the situation in the ordinary manner. In the circumstances, General O'Connor decided to adopt the more difficult but surer course of attacking the retreating force at once. He wished particularly to strike at the left flank of the retreating column while it would be moving south from Benghazi towards Agedabia. With that view

[2] General Wavell's *Despatch*, pp. 3267-8.

he called for immediate air action against the railway terminals of Barce and Soluk and the junction at Benghazi. The idea was to arrest the entrainment or move of the Italian tanks so that they might not be available to the retreating force for protecting their desert flank during the southward withdrawal.

At the same time he issued two more orders. He directed the 6th Australian Division to press hard on the Italian rearguards along the coastal road, and the 7th Armoured Division to move across the desert to Msus with all the resources at its command. From Msus the Armoured Division was to operate towards Soluk or Agedabia according to the needs of the situation. The Headquarters XIII Corps was moved to Mekili to be nearer the scene of the operation, and an Advanced Headquarters was set up at Bomba where the greater part of the Corps administrative staff was also stationed.

The Armoured Division (less the 4th Armoured Brigade) began its move south-westward, early in the morning of 4 February 1941. Already reduced in the number of medium and light tanks to the equivalent of an armoured brigade, it was going out on a perilous mission. With just two days' rations and a bare sufficiency of ammunition and fuel, it was expected to move over unreconnoitred country and give battle to the Italian columns without waiting to reorganise. The move proved more than ordinarily difficult. The unreconnoitred desert revealed "a phenomenally rough surface" for over 50 miles of the distance. This slowed down the division's progress and took a heavy toll of vehicles, particularly the light tanks. However, better ground was discovered towards nightfall, west of Bir el Gerrari, and the Divisional Commander, thereupon, decided to continue the move in the moonlight. Msus was reached before moon-set, and before daybreak the bulk of the 7th Armoured Division stood concentrated near Bir el Miluz.

The 7th Armoured Division was to operate from Msus towards Soluk or Agedabia, according to the requirements of the situation. The Divisional Commander decided to send out detachments in both these directions simultaneously and, accordingly, two detachments went out at first light on 5 February 1941, bound on their northerly and southerly courses respectively. The northern column was to try to reach Soluk via Sheleidima, while the southern was to move straight to the coast via Antelat. The southern column consisted of the Force Headquarters, the Rifle Brigade, two squadrons 11th Hussars and two batteries Royal Horse Artillery, the northern comprising the residue of the 7th Armoured Brigade and the Support Group (less the Rifle Brigade). The 4th Armoured Brigade remained behind, ready to move as and where necessary.

The progress of the northern column was interrupted by some resistance near Sheleidima. But the southern column was more fortunate and managed to reach before noon an area of low dunes, some 25 miles west of Antelat. The spot where it stopped proved to be an ideal tactical position for intercepting the Italian columns retreating towards Agedabia. For, along it passed the main road to Tripoli and a lesser track in the same direction, both of which the Italians were expected to use in their retreat. These two roads also came nearest to each other, and to the sea, in the same area, thus forming an easily defendable bottle-neck. Further, the low dunes in the vicinity provided an excellent delaying position in an otherwise flat coastal plain. The southern column, therefore, decided to make a stand there, and took up fighting positions across the route of the Italian withdrawal.

The two roads to Tripoli, which the southern column of the 7th Armoured Division was now preparing to intercept, ran almost due south, through Ghemines and Agedabia. By noon on 5 February, the Rifle Brigade was established astride both of them, blocking the path of the Italian retreat. At the same time armoured cars went out to reconnoitre both towards Ghemines as well as Agedabia. The blocking force astride the roads saw nothing for a few hours except the civilian traffic which, unaware of the 'block', was moving north and south in the normal course. But, towards evening, a large Italian column rolled down the road, struck the block and, being surprised, surrendered. That column consisted mainly of artillery but also yielded some 5000 prisoners.[3] As this surprise victory was being consummated, the 4th Armoured Brigade was moving towards Antelat to be ready at hand for any subsequent move. That night, 5/6 February, Headquarters 7th Armoured Division and the Commander XIII Corps also moved to Antelat, to be prepared for the coming moves.

Battle of Beda Fomm

The main body of the retreating Italian force was, however, still far behind. It was seen the next day, 6 February, at an early hour of the morning, moving south from Ghemines along the motor road north of the block. The 4th Armoured Brigade was at once moved up from Antelat to a place called Beda Fomm, approximately eight miles north-east of the block and about the same distance from the road. The armoured units of the 7th Brigade also took up positions in the same area, so as to be able to attack the eastern flank of the approaching column. As the column came up to the block and clashed with it, a battle developed which is often spoken of as the Battle of Beda Fomm.

The battle raged for a whole day as the blocking force checked and shelled the Italian column. Infantry in lorries, supply vehicles,

[3] General Wavell's *Despatch*, p. 3267.

artillery and tanks, all came under its heavy fire. Simultaneously, the 4th Brigade attacked the eastern flank and forced the Italian artillery and tanks to deploy eastward. The Italian force lost some 60 tanks fighting this two-sided action. This, however, does not appear to have diminished its fighting power, since the damaged tanks were quickly replaced and the fighting continued with unabated fury. For a time the fate of the battle seemed to hang in balance and it appeared to the Divisional Commander[4] that the 4th Armoured Brigade would not by itself suffice to secure a decision. He therefore decided to strengthen it by throwing as much of the 7th Armoured Brigade into the struggle as was available.

It will be recalled that at this time the bulk of the 7th Armoured Brigade was moving from Msus to Soluk. The brigade was ordered to change its direction and move towards Beda Fomm instead. At the same time the Corps Commander, General O'Connor, decided to divert a part of the 6th Australian Division also to the scene of the battle. That formation, which was then moving towards Barce, was directed by wireless to dispatch a force to Ghemines, using divisional resources for transport. The idea was that an infantry force, of the size of a brigade group, should appear on the rear of the Italian column and complete its encirclement.

The situation was still nebulous at nightfall on 6 February, though not without some hopeful prospects. The blocking force remained in its original position, north of Agedabia. Tanks of the 4th Armoured Brigade, in spite of being heavily committed, dominated the open country east of the motor road; while on the road itself stood the Italian column, virtually pinned to it in a long, unmanageable column of vehicles extending twenty miles back. In front of that column was the blocking force; on its east was the 4th Armoured Brigade, on its west the sea; while its rear was threatened by the approach of the Australian Infantry Brigade from Ghemines, which finally completed the encirclement.

Surrounded on all sides, the Italian force tried the only course left to it, namely that of a tank and infantry attack to break through. Accordingly, 30 Italian tanks counter-attacked the blocking force on the night of 6/7 February. The Rifle Brigade came in for considerable rough-handling and for a time a situation was created which threatened to get out of hand. Serious efforts were made by the Italian tanks and infantry to take advantage of the darkness and penetrate along the tracks into the positions held by the Rifle Brigade. The attempt was frustrated by an expert handling of the artillery and anti-tank weapons, and as the morning dawned the Italian counter-attack lost its cohesion and finally came to a halt at

[4] General Michael O'Moore-Creagh.

daybreak. That morning, 7 February 1941, the Italian force commander, General Bergonzoli, offered his unconditional surrender and the fighting ceased, the capitulation more or less marking the end of the Italian Tenth Army, whose commander himself was killed during the action.

Fall of Benghazi

As to Benghazi, it had capitulated in the meanwhile, on 6 February, to the Australian Brigade Group which was on its way to Ghemines.[5] After that began the work of clearing up the rest of Cyrenaica for which the Headquarters 7th Armoured Division directed a detachment of armoured cars and a portion of the Support Group towards Agedabia and El Agheila as soon as the battle of Beda Fomm had ended. That force carried out a rapid mopping-up of those areas, and cleared Cyrenaica of all isolated groups of the Italian Tenth Army as far as the borders of Tripolitania.

It might be noted here that, throughout the critical days of 6 and 7 February, the Italian Air Force gave no support to its land troops fighting for their very existence. The last appearance of the Italian aircraft was on 5 February 1941, over Msus, when they dropped some Thermos bombs in an unsuccessful effort to slow down the Allied movements. After that they were no more in evidence until the Allies reached El Agheila.

End of the advance

The XIII Corps reached El Agheila on 7 February 1941, which was the farthest point touched by it in its advance into Libya. There, at the western border of Cyrenaica, ended the triumphant offensive of General Wavell, during which, commencing from Sidi Barrani, the Allied forces had captured 130,000 personnel, 824 guns and 408 tanks, besides a very great amount of small arms and ammunition.[6]

It was neither necessary, nor intended, that the Allied advance should come to a halt at El Agheila. The XIII Corps was well set for capturing the rest of the Italian North Africa which it would have very likely done had it been vouchsafed a fair chance.[7] But the changing circumstances ruled otherwise and, as a result, not only was the Corps unable to proceed any further but it was not even able to hold on to its gains. In fact, it found itself falling back within a few weeks of reaching El Agheila, at first slowly and

---

[5] General Wavell's *Despatch*, p. 3268.
[6] The figures are approximate. For details see Appendix H.
[7] By "a fair chance" is meant an advance carried on, on its momentum, without the complications of factors arising from German intervention in Africa, Allied intervention in Greece and the consequent delay in the supply of reinforcements and equipment to the African theatre of war.

voluntarily and later precipitately under hostile pressure. With that the period of the Allied advance came to an end and that of their long retreat began. This advance and the retreat, together, are sometimes spoken of as the First Libyan Campaign.

CHAPTER XII

Allied Retreat Begins

It has been observed that directly the tide of the Allied advance had reached its high-water mark at El Agheila, then it began to roll back. The causes of this reverse are worth investigating. Amidst a number of factors, directly or indirectly responsible for the turning of the tide, at least three stand out prominently. They are the German participation in the fighting in Africa; the Allied participation in the fighting in Greece; and a minor miscalculation of the Middle East High Command.

Germans in North Africa

The immediate cause of the set-back was that Germany had decided to take a hand in the fighting in North Africa. In spite of the vigilance of the Royal Navy, two German armoured divisions had been able to cross the Mediterranean and reach Tripolitania. They were the nucleus of what later came to be known as the *Afrika Korps*.

The advance guard of the *Afrika Korps* was already in Western Cyrenaica on 7 February 1941, the day on which the XIII Corps reached the farthest point of its advance. Strengthened by Italian reinforcements, the *Afrika Korps* had taken up positions near El Agheila between the salt marshes and the coast. It was on meeting this obstacle that the Allied advance came to a halt. It may be mentioned here that by this date, the Italian commander, Marshal Graziani, had been relieved of his command in Africa and recalled to Italy. He had been replaced by two commanders: an Italian commander, General Garibaldi, and a German Officer, General Rommel. Hereafter, the opponents of the XIII Corps were not Italians alone but the Axis forces, comprising both the German and the Italian troops.

Rommel appeared on the scene with a different set of tactics and with more powerful armament than Graziani had possessed. Nominally under the command of Garibaldi, who was the supreme commander of the Libyan theatre, he assumed operational command in the forward areas and, as a representative of the more dominant of the two Axis partners, carried out the campaign more or less independently of his Italian chief. He had commanded a German division against France in 1940 and was already looking upon himself as a veteran of tank warfare. He was a believer in bold and audacious moves and in quick tactical manoeuvrings. Most of the time in the front line with his men, he was always quick to seize and exploit the slightest tactical advantage. In short, he was a different type of adversary from Marshal Graziani and more difficult to contend with. Moreover, he had the advantage of stepping into the picture when it had changed favourably for the Axis. The Allied line of communication had become dangerously extended. The nearest railhead was still Mersa Matruh, more than 650 miles away. But most important of all, General Wavell's position had been gravely weakened at this time by his having to send out his tried and experienced troops to other theatres of war.

These were East Africa, Greece, Crete, Iraq, Syria and Persia. Not all of them made demands on his resources at once. But a beginning had been made. Already the 4th Indian Infantry Division had been withdrawn after Sidi Barrani, being needed in East Africa where a general offensive against the Italians was about to be launched. That was early in December 1940. In February 1941, that veteran formation was too deeply committed in the fighting in Eritrea and on the heights of Keren to be recalled without endangering the prospects of victory in East Africa. At that stage, however, there were no other actual demands on General Wavell's resources in men and material. Yet the picture of the Middle East strategy was slowly changing, and General Wavell, who was not unaware of this gradual change, could be presumed to be already taxed with potential demands. The first of these materialised early in March, when a decision was taken to aid Greece against German penetration in the Balkans.[1]

Allied troops in Greece

As has been noticed earlier, Italy invaded Greece in October 1940. Contrary to her calculations she failed to secure a quick and easy victory. The determination and energy with which the Greeks unexpectedly resisted the invasion surprised Italy no less than it did the rest of the world. By February 1941, it had become clear both to Italy and Germany that the prestige of the Axis was at stake in Greece and that single-handed Italy would not be able to save it. A defeat in Greece would also upset the larger Axis plan for the control of the Eastern Mediterranean through the occupation of Greece, Crete and the Greek Islands in the Aegean Sea. Germany therefore decided to intervene in the struggle. Alarmed at this, the Greek Government promptly agreed to the immediate occupation of Crete by British forces so as to prevent its eventual occupation by

---

[1] General Wavell's *Despatch*, pp. 3443 and 3423-27.
W/Ds 4 Div. and 5 Div.

Germany[2]; and later also asked for help in defending the mainland of Greece itself.

The British Government agreed to the demands of Greece and asked General Wavell to proceed to implement them. General Wavell had already divested himself of a considerable portion of his much needed air force to help Greece. Now he proceeded to transfer a further quota of one New Zealand Infantry Division, one Australian Infantry Division, a British Armoured Brigade and several units of Royal Artillery, about 58,000 men in all. This force, together with much valuable equipment, was placed under the command of General Sir Henry Maitland Wilson, Commander of the Allied forces in Greece. The diversion of men and material made in this way, though necessitated by strategic considerations, could not, naturally, take place without an adverse effect on the North African operations and the trend of war in the desert. The situation was further altered by the dramatic appearance there of the *Afrika Korps*, with its highly trained personnel, superior armour, better mobility, new tactics and a formidable commander.

Allied Fighting Strength in Libya

It will be helpful, at this stage, to take stock of the troops available in the Middle East Command in early February 1941 and their state of readiness for battle. The 4th and 5th Indian Divisions were in Eritrea, deeply involved in heavy fighting. The 11th and 12th African Divisions and the 1st South African Division were likewise committed in East Africa. That left in the Western Desert, and in the back areas of Egypt and Palestine, only the following formations:—

Western Desert	7th Armoured Division
	6th Australian Division
Egypt	2nd Armoured Division
	New Zealand Division
	6th British Division
	Polish Brigade Group
Palestine	7th Australian Division
	9th Australian Division

Of the above formations the 7th Armoured Division was no longer in fighting trim. It was in such a state of mechanical exhaustion as to be practically extinct as a fighting unit. Many weeks of repairs and overhaul to its armoured vehicles were necessary before it could be made battleworthy once again. To buttress its

---

[2] Greece consented to the occupation of Crete by Britain not only for the purpose of preventing its eventual occupation by Germany but also because it was needed by Britain as a refuelling station in the Mediterranean.

failing strength it had already been allotted, some months previously, two regiments of the 2nd (British) Armoured Division. Those regiments too had ultimately reached the same state of unfitness as the division to which they were assigned. As a result, not only was the 7th Armoured Division temporarily out of the picture, but the 2nd Armoured Division which stepped in to fill the void was also obliged to start its career with a grave handicap, especially since its resources, inadequate as they were, had to be divided up between the two competing theatres of Cyrenaica and Greece.

It was on 1 January 1941, that this new armoured division had landed in Egypt, having been sent from the United Kingdom as a part of the reinforcements promised to General Wavell. It then consisted of two cruiser and two light tank regiments only, the other two regiments having been already used up as stated above. The divisional commander was Major-General J. C. Tilly who, on arrival in Egypt, gave to General Wavell quite an alarming description of the mechanical unworthiness of his two cruiser regiments. The tracks were fast becoming unserviceable and the engines were nearing their maximum limit of mileage. There was no prospect of either being replaced within reasonable time. It was decided in the circumstances to make the best of the existing assets and leave the rest to chance.

The formations composing the 2nd Armoured Division were the 1st and 3rd Armoured Brigades of two regiments each, assisted by a Support Group. Of these, General Wavell decided to despatch the 1st Armoured Brigade to Greece and the 3rd to Cyrenaica, for which purpose the two formations were reconstituted so that each would have one cruiser and one light tank regiment. The Support Group was also divided for employment with each brigade in Greece and Cyrenaica, respectively.

As to infantry, only the New Zealand Division and the 6th Australian Division were fully trained and equipped. The 6th British Division was still in the process of formation and had no artillery or supporting arms, and was therefore of little value as a fighting formation. The Polish Brigade, though fit for operational duties, was not satisfactorily equipped, while of the two Australian Divisions, the 7th and the 9th, neither was fully trained or equipped and both were new and inexperienced.

There was hardly any hope of receiving immediate reinforcements or supplies, since the European situation was far from reassuring. This was the time when Mr. Churchill had broadcast to the United States: "give us the tools and we will finish the job". On 1 March, Bulgaria officially joined the Axis, thus bringing Germany to the very borders of Greece. The fate of Yugoslavia was hanging in the balance. Spain and Turkey, always uncertain factors, were being subjected to pressures by Germany, and were causing great anxiety to the Allies; while in the Far East, Japan was consolidating her gains in Indo-China and maturing plans for drawing Thailand within its orbit. In other respects, however, the situation had begun to improve for the United Kingdom. On 11 March, the President of the United States signed the Lease-Lend Bill, promising "ships, planes, food and ammunition" to the United Kingdom and, four days later, his war supplies representative, Mr. W. A. Harriman, had arrived in London to implement the pledge. There were also signs of recovery in the British air and sea power. In reply to the German raids on London, the Royal Air Force had begun raiding Cologne and Berlin; while on the sea there was fought the Battle of Matapan on 28 March in which Italy sustained a loss of four cruisers, three destroyers and several battleships damaged. On 30 March, His Majesty the King sent a message to the Viceroy of India, congratulating India on the part played by her armed forces in the capture of Keren in East Africa; and on the following day General Rommel opened a new chapter in the fighting in North Africa by launching his *Afrika Korps*, for the first time, against XIII Corps of General Wavell.[3]

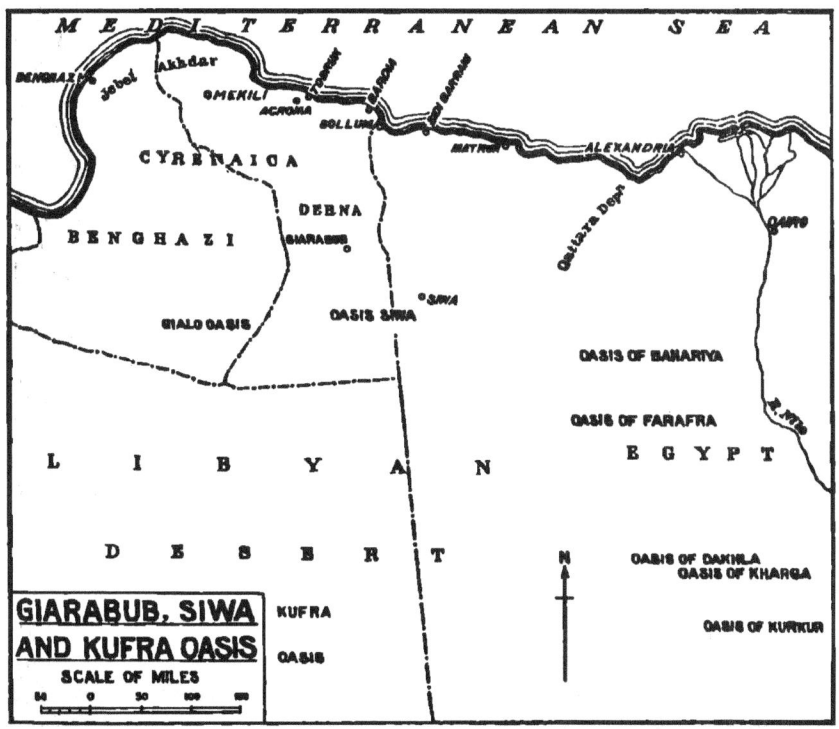

[3] Royal Inst. of International Affairs: *Chronology of the Second World War*, pp. 48-51.

Capture of Giarabub and Kufra Oases

Before the *Afrika Korps* was ready to try conclusions with the greatly depleted XIII Corps, General Wavell was, however, able to register one more victory against the Italians. It resulted out of an isolated operaion in the interior of the desert. It will have been noticed that so far most of the fighting in North Africa had been confined to the coastal area. This was due to the fact that the main road, which offered the easiest line of advance or retreat, lay in the coastal region. However, it is always open to an enterprising opponent to penetrate into the desert along the lesser routes and appear on the flank of a force advancing along the coast. To attack a flank in this way, the adversary would need a tactical position in the interior of the desert, of a sufficient size to be used as a base.[4]

There were two such positions near the Egyptian border. One to the west of it was Giarabub, in the hands of the Italians. The other to the east of the border was Siwa, an oasis in the hands of the Allies. The two positions were 20 miles apart. Hence Giarabub had an additional tactical value in that it could also be used as a jumping-off place by the Italians for an attack on Siwa. On the other hand, the value of the Siwa oasis lay in the fact that it had an ample supply of fresh water. It was therefore necessary to control both Giarabub and Siwa to protect the Allied flank or line of communication during an advance. With that aim in view, General Wavell had, during his advance into Libya, placed a small force opposite to Giarabub to contain the Italian garrison there. When the advance had progressed to some distance, the Giarabub garrison, which consisted of about 1000 Italians and some African troops, was cut off from the rest of the Italian force. It was then attacked and captured without great difficulty by an Australian force on 21 March 1941.

Giarabub has been described in no flattering terms in an intelligence report of the 4th Indian Division. "It is a village," says the report, "in a depression which is a continuation of the Siwa depression. To the south of it is the Sand Sea which is impassable to all forms of MT. The climate is very hot in summer and rather cold in winter. The oasis is completely lacking in fresh water but has an abundance of saline water. This is drunk though not liked by the natives; and Europeans can become used to it. The period of acclimatization is, however, long and painful, as the water has much the same effect as a diet of Epsom Salts. Snakes, scorpions and mosquitoes abound"[5]

While the oasis of Giarabub was being captured by the Australian troops, the Kufra oasis was taken by a unit of Free

[4] W/D 4 Ind. Div., Sep. 40, p. 145.
[5] *Ibid.*

French forces advancing from Lake Chad. These two gains were the last of the unbroken series of General Wavell's victories in Cyrenaica.

General Wavell's achievements

Reviewing General Wavell's offensive from start to finish, one cannot but conclude that his achievements were great and far-reaching in their significance. The magnitude of the disaster sustained by Italy can be judged from the fact that, in a little over two months, the small Allied force in Egypt took about 130,000 Italian prisoners—a number bigger than its own size. There was also a large number of Italian casualties in killed and wounded, and a proportionate loss in equipment, morale and prestige. Sgr. Mussolini himself acknowledged his enormous defeat, when at the end of the campaign he declared that the whole of his Tenth Army had been swept away with almost its entire strength of men and guns, and that the 5th Air Squadron had almost literally been wiped out. His chances of founding a second Roman Empire had indeed received a tremendous set-back.

There can be no doubt that the success of the Libyan Campaign had a profound influence on the course of the rest of the war. One Axis partner was at least temporarily crippled. On the other, therefore, fell the double burden of fighting his own war as well as that of his badly defeated partner. This delayed, and ultimately foiled, the over-all plan of the Axis of seizing Egypt and Iraq and thereby placing themselves in a position for attacking Turkey and Russia from the south, or Persia and India from the west. To that extent, both India and Russia could be said to be owing a debt to the victories of General Wavell; the former for the complete avoidance of a possible attack and the latter for its general deferment.

In spite of this brilliant victory, the military situation in North Africa at this stage was not one which General Wavell could have viewed with any degree of equanimity, had he taken all the factors into consideration. But there was one factor to which he did not give the weight that it deserved, namely the possibility that the Axis might reinforce and be ready to counter-attack before the end of March 1941. This was an error of judgment which he himself publicly acknowledged later. His own estimate of the time by which the Axis would recover was May 1941, at the earliest, and this belief, it seems, was shared at the General Headquarters, Cairo, by all who mattered.[6] Concurrently with it went also the

---

[6] The Defence Committee in England also had not estimated the German threat to be so close. They had calculated on German concentration of effort in the Balkans, particularly Greece. It is also evident from Hitler's communication to Mussolini that the German General Staff had also not hoped for a counter-offensive in North Africa to start before the summer of 1941.

belief that by May the summer heat of the desert would have put an end to the campaigning season in North Africa. The Germans, the new-comers to the desert, it was thought, would not undertake an operation in midsummer against the previously acclimatized Allied troops. They would, it was argued, require time to move their men across the sea to Tripoli, to inure them to desert conditions, to train them in desert warfare, and to acclimatize them to the desert heat. On that calculation the date of the Axis counter-offensive, should one materialise at all, was estimated to be in July 1941. By that time the campaigns in East Africa and Greece were expected to be over; and it was hoped that North Africa would have been well replenished with men and supplies, particularly the tanks. Such were the optimistic calculations of the Middle East High Command which, as the turn of events proved later, were far from accurate and led to the most disappointing results.

CHAPTER XIII

The Axis Stage a Return

Ineffectiveness of naval blockade

It has been observed in the preceding chapter that General Wavell had to reduce his forces in the North African theatre in order to supply the two other theatres—East Africa and Greece. This he did on the assumption that it would take the Axis several months to gather enough manpower and material in North Africa for a counter-offensive. In the meantime his depleted resources would have been adequately replenished for a further drive towards Tripoli. In reaching that conclusion, he was no doubt influenced by the hope that the Royal Navy would prove strong enough to intercept Axis convoys across the Central Mediterranean, or at least to restrict the size of Axis reinforcements reaching Tripoli from Italy; and that in any event it would give a fair warning to the Middle East Command of any serious accession to the Axis strength. In short, he was relying on the sea-blockade to keep the Axis from mounting a quick counter-offensive.[1] He was hoping that the Royal Navy along with the Royal Air Force, would, by such means, aid his land force to hold the Axis at El Agheila, until he could be ready to strike again some time after May or June 1941.

By the time the XIII Corps had reached El Agheila, it had come to the end of its tether. Two months of pursuit of the Italians had left it in an exhausted condition. Its main component, the 7th Armoured Division, was worn out with the breathless chase. Its men were tired, its support was overworked and most of its tanks were past ordinary servicing or first-line repairs. The supply problem, too, had become very acute. The supply line was now 900 miles long, from El Agheila to the Nile Valley.[2] Nor could the port of Benghazi be used to shorten it, since the *Luftwaffe* was operating against that port at full strength from Tripolitania; and the number of aircraft which the Royal Air Force could muster against that force was much too small to keep the harbour open. Finally, even had the supplies been no problem, General Wavell's force which had reached El Agheila was itself too meagre to push forward, consisting as it did of only two battalions of infantry, three batteries of artillery, a regiment of armoured cars and a

---
[1] Chester Wilmot: *Tobruk*, pp. 63-67. Also General Wavell's *Despatch*, pp. 3427-28.
[2] *Ibid.*

squadron of tanks. That was the full Allied strength available in the middle of February 1941 for the defence of the El Agheila—Marsa Brega area, with no prospects of any worthwhile reinforcements to be had either immediately or even during the following month. It was hardly surprising, in the circumstances, that General Wavell should regard the naval blockade as the only practical means of safeguarding the position of the XIII Corps.

But, in the meantime, the German High Command had decided to intervene in Africa. General Rommel had been selected to lead the Axis forces there and he was already putting into shape what was to be the *Afrika Korps*.[2] That task required training his men to fight in conditions ordinarily encountered in a desert. The Allied Commanders always preferred to give such training by first transporting their men to the desert and then practising them behind the lines. That certainly was a sound method though it meant deferment of the training period until the men could be transported to the desert. But General Rommel was not prepared to brook such delays. He decided to train his men in Germany under artificially created desert conditions. A sandy spot in the Baltic area, it is said, had a terrain which closely resembled that in Libya. The climatic conditions of the desert were artificially produced there by heating the barracks. There, General Rommel tried out his desert tactics and studied the maintenance problems. There, the troops were trained in the ways of desert fighting and made to rehearse in artificial sand-storms, with food and water rationed on the desert scale. Thus practised, the troops were intended to go into action almost as soon as they disembarked at Tripoli. Whether sound or not, this "rush" training was one of the main factors that upset General Wavell's calculations.

The other important factor was the inadequacy of the naval blockade. This was by no means due to a want of effort on the part of the Royal Navy. It was rather the result of the Navy being overtaxed with a multiplicity of demands during the vital period from February to May 1941. From January 1941, the German aircraft, operating from Tripoli and Sicily, had intensified their reconnaissance of the Mediterranean. They had spread a protective cover over the Axis convoys crossing the narrow strait between Sicily and Tripoli, and were able to range almost unhindered, since the Royal Air Force could not spare enough aircraft to oppose them. This greatly increased the difficulty of the Navy in enforcing the blockade. For, far from being able to intercept the Axis convoys at will, as it had done in 1940, its ships were now themselves exposed to attacks from the *Luftwaffe*.

[2] D. Young: *Rommel*, p. 86.

The situation became even worse during February and March 1941, when the Royal Navy was too preoccupied in rendering aid to Greece to be able to maintain the close patrolling of the Sicilian and the Tripolitanian coasts. It had, in addition, to perform the other equally important duties of patrolling the seas, watching the Axis ports, chasing and fighting hostile convoys, escorting their own, and so forth. As a result, its resources were stretched to the absolute limit and the Central Mediterranean could not receive adequate attention. Taking advantage of this situation, the Axis ships slipped through the blockade, carrying General Rommel's forces to Africa. In this, the Axis had the clandestine support of the Vichy French inasmuch as Axis vessels, flying French flags, were allowed to sail from the south of France ostensibly for French North Africa, from where they crept eastward to Tripoli, hugging the coast within the three-mile limit. The game was not discovered until it was too late.[4]

Afrika Korps in Cyrenaica

In the circumstances, it is hardly surprising that the Axis ships had managed to transfer to the Italian North Africa, all that General Rommel needed. This was done not only in spite of the blockade but without even the proper knowledge of the Royal Navy. Before the middle of March 1941, General Rommel had thus built up in Tripolitania an Italo-German force of a considerable size and strength. It consisted of the 15th German Armoured Division; the 5th German Light Motorized Division (virtually a light armoured formation); the 132nd Ariete (Italian Armoured) Division; five of the best Italian infantry divisions; considerable German motorized infantry; about 300 German tanks, half of them Mark III (Medium) and Mark IV (Heavy); and a mass of supporting field and anti-tank artillery. In addition, the *Luftwaffe* had transferred to Libya a far greater number of aircraft than the Royal Air Force had in the entire Middle East.

Thus, somewhat earlier than anticipated by General Wavell, the *Afrika Korps* was well established in Libya ready to strike back. The magnitude of this new menace was not sufficiently appreciated either by the General Headquarters at Cairo or by the Headquarters of the Cyrenaica Command until it was too late. The first sign of the gathering storm became evident in the middle of February 1941. German planes began to make their appearance at Benghazi and Marsa Brega, where they more than filled the void created by the disappearance of the Italian air force. Stukas (JU87s) and medium bombers (JU88s) paid so much attention to the Benghazi harbour that even a restricted use of that facility was no longer possible.

[4] Wilmot: *Tobruk*, p. 67.

ME110s strafed and machine-gunned the Benghazi—El Agheila road with such persistency that that stretch of the road came to be nicknamed the "Messerschmidt Alley". The *Luftwaffe* had a fighter superiority of about five to one against a solitary squadron of the Royal Australian Air Force, the Squadron No. 3. The Royal Air Force was unable to spare any aircraft to oppose the raids or what is more likely, the situation was not considered serious enough to justify the diversion of any to a front that was, at least outwardly, quiescent. The result was that a state of affairs was soon reached when the Allied supply columns could not use the roads freely, except during the nights. The real reason for the increased activity of the *Luftwaffe*, namely that it was a preparation for a determined counter-offensive, was, it would appear, not even suspected at the Allied Headquarters.

A second and more definite pointer to the changing situation was provided towards the end of February, when the 17th Australian Infantry Brigade reported the presence of German troops and armoured cars near El Agheila. The evidence was confirmed by the report of the Royal Air Force reconnaissance units, according to which large convoys were seen moving eastwards from Tripoli. Allied intelligence reports from Tunisia and Tripoli provided further corroboration of the rising strength of the Axis forces. But no evidence was strong enough to shake the conviction of the Allied High Command that a regular attack by the Germans before May 1941 was not a military possibility. The subsequent events, however, should have dispelled such a notion. But that did not happen either.

These intelligence reports, according to Mr. Churchill, had begun to cause the Chiefs of Staff some concern, and they sent a "warning telegram" to General Wavell on 27 February stating that, in view of the arrival of German armoured formations and aircraft in Tripolitania, the question of defence commitments in Egypt and Cyrenaica had been considered afresh by them; and that they would be grateful to have a short appreciation from him. But General Wavell did not consider the information to be definite enough to justify an alarm. He had started on the basis that, even after the landing of German troops in Libya, the Axis would not be in a position to start an offensive operation in less than two months and that, owing to the start of the summer in May, a large German operation on the desert flank would not be possible before July. Even in his appreciation of 2 March, when he was aware of "recent reinforcements to Tropolitania" and "considerable increase in mechanical transport on Tripoli—Sirte road," he would not concede the view that Benghazi was threatened or that a large-scale attack could develop before the end of summer. He was by no means self-complacent; but the danger in the Balkans, his preoccupation with Greece, his confidence in the invincibility of the Royal Navy and an inadequate realisation of the resourcefulness of the Germans had made him somewhat inert to the realities.[5]

General Neame, who took over the Cyrenaica Command on 27 February 1941 from Lt.-Gen. Sir H. M. Wilson and held it until his capture on 8 April, also makes references to this vexed question of fixing the probable date of a German counter-offensive, in his notes which he recorded during his captivity while events were still fresh in his mind. It appears that on 8 March he had made personal representations to the General Headquarters at Cairo about the state of his troops and pressed urgently for certain items such as signals, transport, anti-tank guns, mines and workshop facilities, in all of which his command was gravely deficient.[6] Discussing the possibilities of a German attack, he had then expressed the opinion that the Germans had not gone to Libya for nothing and would not long rest content with a defensive role. Considering that only six days earlier General Wavell had telegraphed an appreciation to the War Cabinet in England, fixing May as the probable month, this opinion, rather vaguely expressed and not supported by any particularly convincing evidence, could not have proved very helpful to the Middle East Command. A few days later, during 17 and 18 March, when the Commander-in-Chief and the Chief of the Imperial General Staff visited Cyrenaica, the general situation was discussed again and, according to General Neame, "both now realised that a German attack was probable". But there is no substantial evidence anywhere to show that either they or he had any idea that Rommel's counter-offensive was not only probable but actually impending and likely to burst upon them within a fortnight from that date.

Allied Military Strength in March 41

Early in March 1941, the 6th Australian Division was pulled out of Libya, prior to its being sent to Greece. It was relieved on 8 March by the 9th Australian Division. This new formation was commanded by Major-General L. J. Morshead and comprised the 18th, 20th and 26th Australian Brigades. It was, however, hardly in a fit condition to be sent to a front which, though dormant at that time, might burst into activity any day in the near future. However, so remote was such a possibility believed to be that General Morshead was informed that his division would be required only for garrisoning duties, and further, that enough time would be available for completing its training and equipment. As to the state of the division's

[5] Churchill: *The Second World War*, III, pp. 174-5; Wavell's *Despatch*, p. 3425.
[6] P. Neame: *Playing with Strife*, pp. 266-72.

training, most of its units had hardly cleared the elementary stage. As to its equipment, the division's field regiments had no guns; its cavalry was without carriers; and its infantry units were short in Bren guns, mortars, anti-tank weapons, signal equipment and transport.

Such was the condition of the 9th Australian Division when it arrived in Cyrenaica to relieve the 6th. Almost at once, one of its brigades, the 20th, was moved forward to El Agheila. The task of this latter formation was to support the 3rd Armoured Brigade, a newly arrived British formation which was then guarding the El Agheila bottle-neck. This British brigade was a component of the 2nd Armoured Division which, it will be remembered, was sent to General Wavell as an instalment of the reinforcements promised to him.

The 3rd Armoured Brigade was, however, as weak in tanks as was its supporting infantry, the 20th Australian Brigade, in weapons and artillery. Were a determined counter-offensive to be launched by the Germans, these two formations were likely to prove embarrassments, rather than help, to each other. It was obvious that the Germans were mounting such an attack and that the avalanche would descend on these pitifully weak formations at no distant date. Among the first to appreciate the danger of the situation was, it would seem, Major-General Morshead, commander of the 9th Australian Division. He conveyed his fears in a report to "CYRCOM" (Cyrenaica Command), adding that the Germans would probably open their offensive with a full armoured division and, cutting across the desert to Mekili, would proceed to outflank the Allied forces in Cyrenaica. In conclusion, General Morshead urged that the 20th Australian Brigade be withdrawn from the El Agheila area.

General Neame, who was not unaware of the risks involved in retaining immobile and ill-equipped troops in the front line and within easy reach of the German armour, was also of the same opinion. But the great difficulty was to obtain troops and transport to carry out the relief with. However, the matter seems to have been discussed between him and General Wavell, on 17 March, (even before either of them had seen General Morshead's report which did not reach Cyrcom until the next day) and a decision taken to withdraw the 20th Australian Brigade. This decision was confirmed on the same day at a subsequent meeting at Beda Fomm between General Wavell and General Morshead, when the Chief of the Imperial General Staff was also present. As a result it was finally agreed that the Australian formation in question should be withdrawn to Benghazi and other dispositions readjusted to conform to the altered plan.

The main troops available for readjustment in North Africa on this date were:—[1]

    2nd Armoured Division (British).
       3rd Armoured Brigade.
       3rd Hussars (Light Tank).
       5th Royal Tank Regiment (cruisers).
       6th Royal Tank Regiment (captured Italian tanks),
       1st Regiment Royal Horse Artillery.

    2nd Support Group.
       1st Tower Hamlets.
       104th Royal Horse Artillery (23-pdrs.).
       J. Battery Royal Horse Artillery (anti-tank regiment).
       One Company 1 Royal Northumberland Fusiliers (machine-gun regiment).
       One Company French motor battalion.

    3rd Indian Motor Brigade.
       2nd Royal Lancers.
       11th FF Cavalry (PAVO).
       18th FF Cavalry (KEO).

    9th Australian Division.
       20th Brigade.
       24th Brigade (Training in the area Tobruk—Gazala).
       26th Brigade (two battalions).

In the new arrangement, the 9th Australian Division was to hold a sixty-two mile front, along the line of the escarpment, to the east of Benghazi. That line commenced from Er Regima, 20 miles east of Benghazi town, and ran northwards to Tocra and the coast. Of the division's three brigades, the 20th was assigned positions to the east and north-east of Benghazi. The 24th Brigade was training in the Tobruk—Gazala area; and the 26th had only two battalions, one with the division and the other in the act of arriving in the divisional area. The supporting artillery of the division was only one field regiment, the 51st (British), with sixteen guns.

Ahead of the 9th Australian Division was the 2nd (British) Armoured Division under Major-General Gambier-Parry, guarding the El Agheila front. In actual effect, this division was nothing more than the 3rd Armoured Brigade mentioned above plus a

[1] General Wavell's *Despatch*, pp. 3424-29. W/Ds 3 Ind Mot Bde, 2 RL., 11 Cav., 18 Cav. For a fuller order of battle see Appendix J.

Support Group.¹ The three regiments of the 3rd Brigade were the 3rd Hussars and the 5th and 6th Royal Tank Regiments. One of these regiments was equipped with obsolete tanks, the other had only captured Italian tanks, and the third had worn-out cruisers. With this strength, the 2nd Armoured Division could not be expected to stop the Germans from crossing the desert and reaching Mekili; and the flank of the 9th Australian Division, south of Er Regima, was by no means secure from that point of view. Such was the state of the Allied forces and their dispositions on 23 March 1941.

Allied Withdrawal Begins

By this date, the *Afrika Korps* was ready to commence action, and there was no doubt left that it could drive the advanced Allied elements out of the El Agheila—Marsa Brega area with very little effort. The most forward of these, therefore, withdrew a little distance on 24 March. The danger was now too near to be ignored any more, and there was nothing left for the rest of the Allied force also, but to withdraw to safer positions. The safest position, in the circumstances, might have been Tobruk. But there was no plan for carrying out such a withdrawal, nor was enough transport available for the purpose. More than that, General Wavell was unwilling to give up Benghazi without a struggle. In fact, just as the German—Italian army had begun to close up to the Agheila—Marsa Brega defences and the symptoms pointed to an imminent Axis attack, General Wavell sent a personal signal to General Neame, giving the information that no large reinforcements would be available for the next two months, and stating that the task of General Neame in the circumstances was to delay the Axis advance, over the 150 miles from El Agheila to Benghazi, for an equal period. Thus, when the *Afrika Korps* struck its first blow on 31 March, there had been no deeper withdrawals than that of the armour to the south of Agedabia and of the infantry to the north of Benghazi. The main dispositions of General Neame's forces, on this date, consisted of the elements of the 2nd Armoured Division and the Support Group to the north of El Agheila, the 20th Australian Brigade on the escarpment between Benghazi and Barce, and the 3rd Indian Motor Brigade at Mekili.

The first blow of the *Afrika Korps* fell on the 3rd Armoured Brigade which was then at Marsa Brega and on the 2nd Support Group holding the Marsa Brega defile. Both the formations were badly mauled and lost a proportion of their armour to the speedier

---

¹ The strength of an armoured division's Support Group was normally two battalions motorized infantry, a field regiment, an anti-tank battery and an A/A battery with a Group HQ, Engineers, Signals and Medical personnel.

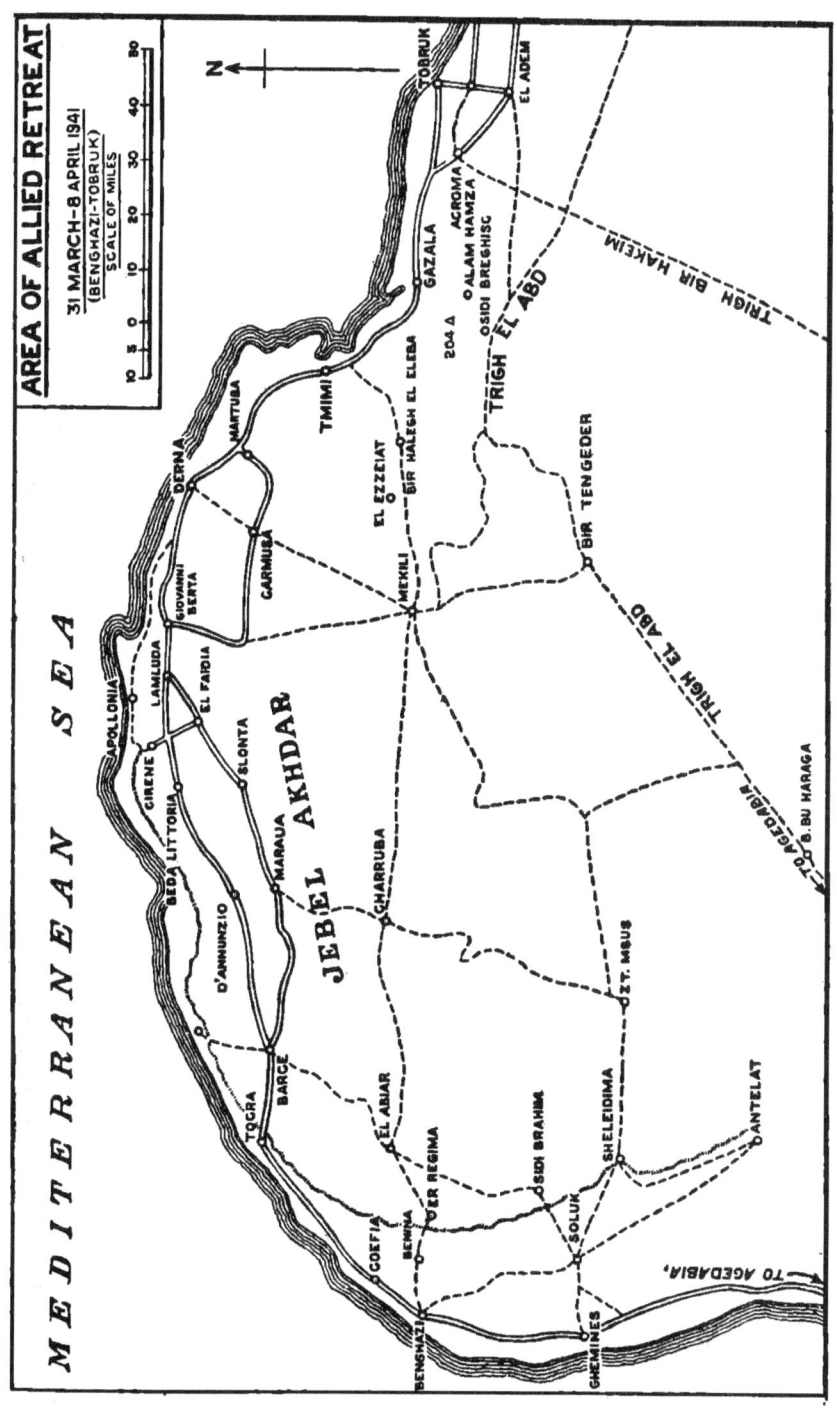

and more heavily gunned tanks of the German armoured division. Then, on 2 April, the 3rd Armoured Brigade was caught again and re-attacked at Agedabia, about 100 miles south of Benghazi. In that engagement it lost still more of its remaining tanks. From that time on, the superiority in armour rested with General Rommel and it became a question as to what he would do with it.

There were two theories as to his possible intentions. The one which found favour with General Wavell and his Headquarters at Cairo, or which at least reflected their hopes and outlook, was that Rommel would not attempt more than the recapture of Benghazi for some time to come yet, as he could not possibly be so foolhardy as to commit his inexperienced and supposedly scanty forces to a cross-desert advance. The other theory was that he would cut across the desert and make for Mekili, thus outflanking the Allied forces on the Er Regima—Tocra line. The latter was the view of the Australian Commander, General Morshead, and it was also the constant anxiety of General Neame. As subsequent events proved, that was the correct view. However, the first theory carried the day, mainly owing to the anxiety of the Middle East Command to keep Rommel out of Benghazi for a period of nearly two months. In keeping with this intention, and under General Wavell's own orders, the immediate defence plan was based on the assumption that Rommel would press his advance along the coastal road.

Accordingly, it was decided that the 9th Australian Division was to stand fast on the line Er Regima—Tocra; while whatever remained of the 3rd Armoured Brigade, could cover the open desert flank. General Neame's plan was to withdraw the 2nd Armoured Division from the Agedabia—Benghazi road to a more easterly location—about Antelat or Msus—from where that formation would be in a position, not only to deny the free use of the desert routes to Rommel but also to cover the open flank of the 9th Australian Division. But General Wavell, less apprehensive of a cross-desert advance by the Axis troops, wished the armour to be employed for blocking the road to Benghazi rather than the desert routes; and this in spite of the fact that the town was of no particular military value and General Neame had already given orders, in anticipation of its evacuation, for certain demolitions to be carried out and everything of any possible use to the Axis to be removed or destroyed. The test of the soundness of this plan came the very next day. German aircraft, strafing the already battered 3rd Armoured Brigade, destroyed or damaged most of the latter's wireless equipment, as a result of which the brigade lost its link of communications with the headquarters. In the meantime, German armoured columns had begun to move across the desert towards Mekili.

On that day of 3 April, General Wavell was at the Headquarters of the Cyrenaica Command, where he had flown for consultation on the afternoon of 2 April. The fact of the Germans having begun their trans-desert move was then not known to him, nor even to the Cyrenaica Command. In fact, due to a breakdown of the wireless communications on that day, the Command was very much out of touch with the happenings on the desert flank. The 2nd Armoured Division, whose task it was to secure that flank, was deficient in trained signallers and wireless equipment from the very start, due to its best units and equipment having been sent away to Greece; and, as it did not have enough anti-aircraft guns to defend itself with, the German dive-bombers took a continuous toll of its signal vehicles, resulting in frequent breakdown of communications over long intervals. It is not surprising, therefore, that on 3 April the Cyrenaica Command was not only unaware of the move of the German armour towards Msus but could not even satisfactorily ascertain the whereabouts of the 3rd Armoured Brigade or the Support Group. It was, however, not completely without a clue. For, on that day, there was an air reconnaissance report that a German armoured column was already in Msus, about 90 miles from Mekili. Though exaggerated, that report was a pointer in the right direction, But, unfortunately, it was soon contradicted by another which gave rise to the belief that the armoured column at Msus was British, not German.

As the intelligence, so the orders. Conflicting instructions were issued, almost simultaneously, by the Headquarters of the Cyrenaica Command and the 2nd Armoured Division. The Command had desired the Armoured Division, in the first instance, to withdraw from Agedabia and move north towards El Abiar and Charruba. The move had already commenced when, at the intervention of General Wavell, the order was changed and the division was instructed to stay on or near the Agedabia—Benghazi road, keeping itself in the Antelat—Sheleidima area, for the dual task of blocking the routes across the desert and threatening Rommel's flank, if he moved towards Benghazi. At about the same time, some orders reached the 3rd Armoured Brigade directing it to move towards Msus. These had been issued by the Divisional Commander on hearing the report of the German move towards Msus, since there was a vital petrol dump at Msus on which depended the mobility of the 2nd Armoured Division and which it was essential should not fall into Rommel's hands intact. The result was that while the Support Group moved north-west towards Benghazi, the 3rd Armoured Brigade moved south-east towards Msus,* which it reached on the night of 3/4 April 1941. Meanwhile Benghazi had been completely evacuated by the Allied forces on 3 April.

* General Wavell's *Despatch*, pp. 3428-29.

To stabilize the rapidly worsening situation, General Wavell summoned Lieut.-General Sir Richard O'Connor to the Headquarters of the Cyrenaica Command. General O'Connor did not assume command but remained at "Cyrcom" as an adviser. On his advice, or in consultation with him, "Cyrcom" decided to withdraw the 3rd Armoured Brigade to Mekili and the 9th Australian Division to Derna. The former was to move across the desert and the latter across the Jebel Akhdar, covered by the 20th Australian Brigade which was to hold the pass at Er Regima. Meanwhile, the Axis forces were pressing forward at an accelerated pace, using three separate routes, two of which lay across the desert and one along the main coast road.

On 4 April, the only force that challenged the Axis advance along the coastal road was one battalion, the 2/13th, of the 20th Australian Brigade. Disposed along a 9-mile front, the task of that battalion, with its three companies, was to deny a passage through the Er Regima pass to the Germans. But that was easier said than done, for the Er Regima Pass was not the only possible entrance to the escarpment from the plains. There were other minor passes to be guarded and at least one flanking wadi to watch. Besides, to meet the German attack, which would be made with tanks, the 2/13th had only four 4.5 inch howitzers and two captured Italian anti-tank guns.

The commander of the Australian battalion was told that the Er Regima Pass would have to be held till 1900 hours that evening (4 April). That hour was fixed not so much by tactical exigencies as by the consideration that the transport necessary for the withdrawal of this unit could not be sent before that hour. In the meantime, more field and anti-tank guns and automatic weapons were ordered to be despatched to that unit with the utmost speed in order to enable it to make a stand till then.

The race between the Germans approaching from the west and the guns arriving from the east was won by the Germans by a few hours. The battle was joined at 1700 hours and the 2/13th was attacked with an overwhelming force by waves of German tanks and lorried infantry. Caught at a tremendous disadvantage, and unable to resist, its forward elements had begun to fall back slowly. The promised reinforcement of artillery had not arrived till then. But just as the German tanks were about to break into its positions, the battalion received four (18-pounder) field guns, which quickly went into action and changed the situation. The onrush of the tanks was halted and after sunset, as darkness came on, the Germans decided to consolidate their positions rather than press forward.

That night, the transport which was to have reached the battalion at 1900 hours arrived at 2300 hours. The 2/13th was thereby enabled to withdraw successfully, after which it joined the fifty-mile-long procession of Allied retreating vehicles winding their way towards Barce and beyond, along the coastal road. The retreating column was the 9th Australian Division and other Allied units. The destination of the Australian Division, in the first instance, was Derna, which was later changed to Tobruk in view of the rapid advance of the Germans.

The stand at Tobruk

All through the night the procession crept on, impeded by its own congestion at a time when speed was a vital necessity. Barce was reached in the early hours of the morning (5 April). But the town was ablaze and was being looted by the Senussi Arabs. For three more days the 9th Australian Division was kept perpetually on the move by the rapidly changing exigencies. At last, on the night of 8/9 April, it withdrew into Tobruk—there to stand and play one of the most famous roles in the history of World War II. That remarkable episode will be dealt with in the subsequent chapters. But before that, it is necessary to recount what was happening on the desert flank of the retreating column as it was withdrawing towards Tobruk. The dominant note of those happenings was confusion and uncertainty among the Allied formations who, nevertheless, fought a determined rearguard action and succeeded in delaying the Axis advance sufficiently to permit the safe withdrawal of the 9th Australian Division. Amongst these was an Indian formation which played a notable part. It was the 3rd Indian Motor Brigade. The action it fought during the vital days, from 4 to 8 April 1941, forms a shining chapter in the annals of desert warfare and must be dealt with first in the succeeding pages.

CHAPTER XIV

Advance of Afrika Korps

On the eve of the Allied retreat from El Agheila, General Wavell had issued instructions to General Neame that, if attacked, he was to withdraw fighting a delaying action. If General Neame considered it necessary he was to yield Benghazi; but in that event he was to hold the high ground above Benghazi as long as possible.[1] At this stage, 26-28 March, General Neame could not possibly have foreseen that in less than a week Benghazi would have been evacuated by the Allies and occupied by the Axis, as he had no firm data pointing to that conclusion. Nor was General Wavell willing to believe that an Axis attack in strength was on the verge of starting, or was actually in progress. The events of the few succeeding days must have convinced both that they had allowed their hopes to sway their calculations.

The events commenced on 31 March 1941, when the *Afrika Korps* opened its counter-attack in Cyrenaica. The attacking force consisted of the 5th German Light Armoured Division and two Italian divisions. Of the latter, one division was motorised and the other armoured. The force and weight of the attack, which was supported by a considerable number of aircraft, made the 2nd Armoured Division withdraw at once.

As instructed, this formation slowly retired northward. The withdrawal continued for the following three days, so that on 2 April 1951, the Armoured Division was north of Agedabia. Here the divisional commander received the intelligence that a large Axis force was approaching Msus, the site of the division's principal petrol dump. Since, in the event of the dump being captured by the Axis force, the Armoured Division would become immobilised and valueless as a fighting formation, the divisional commander detached the 3rd Armoured Brigade and despatched it to Msus for the protection of the petrol dump. That left the 2nd Armoured Division with only the Support Group, which continued to fall back on the left flank of the 9th Australian Division.[2]

The 3rd Armoured Brigade, on arrival at Msus, learned that its mission had been frustrated by an unfortunate occurrence. An Allied detachment, guarding the petrol dump, had destroyed all the petrol in a panicky haste, on hearing that an Axis column was

[1] General Wavell's *Despatch, Feb.-July 1941*, p. 3428.
[2] Ibid.

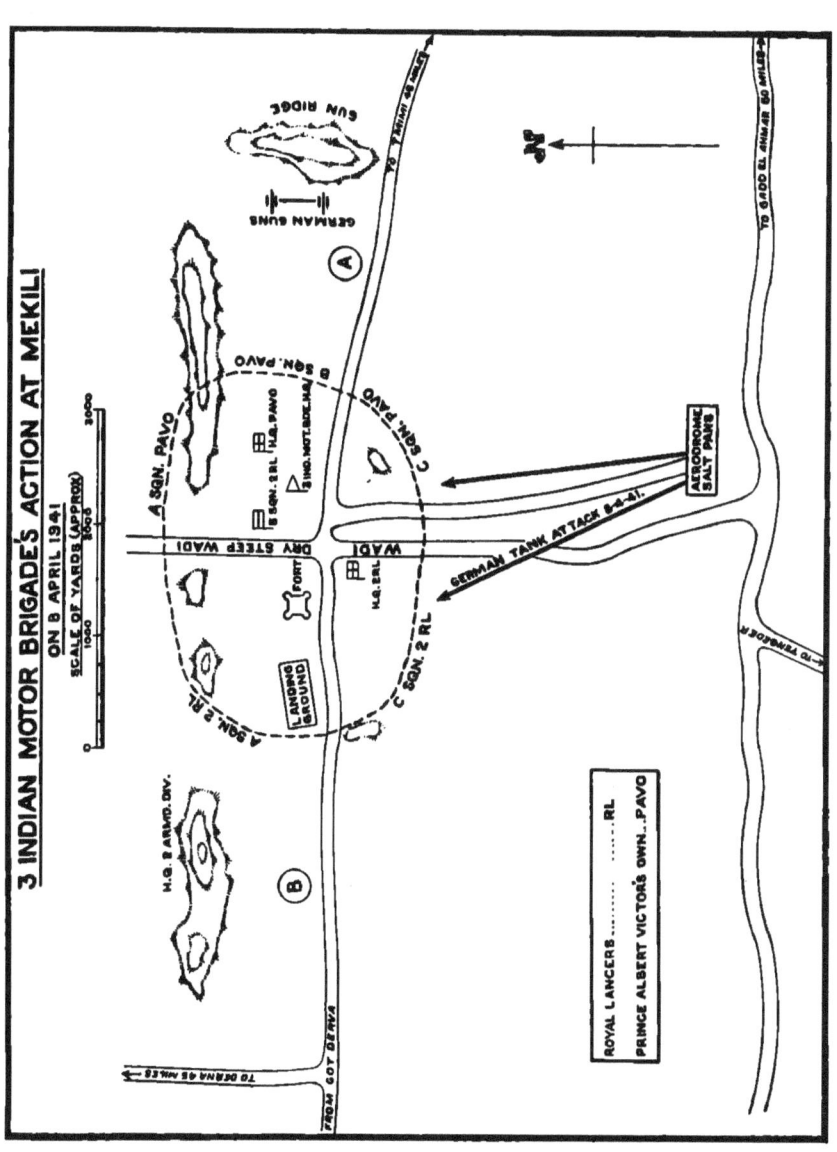

approaching the site of the dump. Thenceforward the movements of that brigade, as well as of its parent formation, the 2nd Armoured Division, were dictated by the quantity of petrol available, which was, of course, very little.

At the Headquarters of General Neame at Barce, there was a general absence of news and some difficulty in issuing orders. The absence of news was due to a breakdown of signals as a result of the Command having become mobile during the retreat. The chief means of signalling at the disposal of the Command were the Italian peace-time overhead lines, to maintain which, use had to be made of the captured Italian and Arab linesmen. The wireless set of the Command itself was too weak and inadequate for the task it had to perform. In consequence, during the hectic days of retreat, General Neame was always at a disadvantage as to his communications.[3] However, on the night of 3/4 April 1941, he issued his orders, principally affecting the movements of two of his most important formations—the 2nd armoured and the 9th Australian Divisions. The former was to withdraw to the line Wadi Derna—Mekili, and the latter, in the same direction, towards Derna. The ultimate 'rendezvous' of both was Mekili, where they were to be joined, on 6 April, by the 3rd Indian Motor Brigade, which was to move up from El Adem for that very purpose.

Role of the 3rd Indian Motor Brigade

The Indian Brigade was expected to reach Mekili on or before 5 April, that is, some days before the arrival of the Australian and the Armoured Divisions. It was, therefore, charged with the task of holding that locality until the arrival of those two formations after which it was to pass under the command of the 2nd Armoured Division.[4] The Headquarters of the 2nd Armoured Division arrived there to schedule on the following day, but there was no news of its principal formation, the 3rd Armoured Brigade. As became known later, it was then still at Msus. The premature destruction of the petrol dump at Msus had practically immobilised the 3rd Armoured Brigade, which, in addition, had been cut off from all communications due to the failure of its wireless and a general breakdown of signals in the Cyrenaica Command. As to the 9th Australian Division, it had not been possible for it either, to reach Mekili according to the programme. Its most active brigade, guarding the Er Regima area on the high ground above Benghazi, had been attacked by the Axis on the afternoon of 4 April, and had received a rather heavy battering from 2000 to 3000 motorized infantry supported by Italian artillery and about fifty

---
[3] P. Neame: *Playing with Strife*, p. 272.
[4] W/D 3 Ind Mot Bde.

German tanks. Although the attack had been repulsed, the Australians had suffered heavy losses, and it was found impossible to hold the Er Regima feature any longer. In the circumstances, the Australian Division was ordered to withdraw to Barce, since, being short of transport, it would not be able to cope with the swift mechanized manoeuvres of the *Afrika Korps*. But these orders had to be changed from time to time, due to the rapid trans-desert move of the Axis troops and the lack of news from the 3rd Armoured Brigade; and so, instead of withdrawing to Mekili via Derna, as originally planned, the 9th Australian Division eventually retired to Tobruk.[5]

The final result of all these changes was that the 3rd Indian Motor Brigade found itself in a very perilous situation, being the only fighting formation at Mekili. Since Mekili was an important junction of desert tracks, directly in the path of the Axis advance across the desert, it stood in imminent danger of being attacked and wiped out in a very unequal battle. The forlornness of the situation, the general lack of communications and petrol, and the necessity of making a solitary stand in the desert, placed a heavy responsibility on Brigadier Vaughan, commanding that Indian formation. Undaunted, he began to organise the defences.

The area to be defended was roughly all ground around the Mekili Fort within a radius of about 2000 yards. This constituted the vital perimeter that had to be defended on all four sides, and accordingly the ground was divided into four sectors. The dividing lines were a north-south wadi and an east-west road, the latter—the Tmimi—Got Derva road—cutting the wadi at right angle, roughly in the centre of the perimeter. As a result, the perimeter had four approximately equal sectors, which may be called the north-left and north-right, and the south-left and south-right sectors.[6] Of the two northern sectors, the left contained Mekili Fort and a landing ground, and the right had headquarters of the brigade and of one of its regiments, the PAVO.[7] The latter also contained B Squadron of the 2nd Royal Lancers which was the brigade reserve under Major M. K. Rajendrasinhji (later General Rajendrasinhji and Commander-in-Chief of the Indian Army). Of the two southern sectors, the one on the left held the headquarters of the 2nd Royal Lancers and that on the right enclosed an unoccupied hill.

Outside these sectors, the northern preiphery was defended by A Squadron 2nd Royal Lancers on the left, and by A and B Squadrons of PAVO on the right. The southern periphery was likewise guarded on the left and right respectively by the C

---

[5] W/Ds 3 Ind Mot Bde, 2 R.L., 11 Cav., 18 Cav.
[6] Brig. E. W. D. Vaughan's *Report*, p. 10.
[7] Prince Albert Victor's Own (11th FF.), briefly 11 Cav.

Squadron of the 2nd Royal Lancers and the PAVO. Some distance away from the outskirts of the perimeter were two hills, one on the east and the other on the north-west. The former was named Gun Ridge and the latter was temporarily the site of the Headquarters 2nd Armoured Division. Other hill features of some importance were a "pimple" in the south-right sector and a portion of a long east-west ridge in the north-right sector. Outside the southern perimeter, about 2500 yards away, were some salt pans and an aerodrome.

Hardly had Brigadier Vaughan made his scant dispositions when the advanced elements of the *Afrika Korps* arrived at Mekili. They reached there on the morning of 6 April and started shelling the south-east face of PAVO at approximately 0900 hours. The shelling continued intermittently till about 1100 hours when some Axis vehicles were noticed debouching from Gun Ridge. The vehicles moved in the direction of B squadron PAVO and assayed an attack but were quickly repulsed. They retired leaving behind 37 prisoners but it was certain that they would attack again. From that point on, the forward elements of the Indian Brigade were continually in contact with the Axis forces on the eastern and south-eastern flanks of the Mekili perimeter.

The stand at Mekili

At about 1800 hours on the same day (6 April) the Brigade Commander was confronted by an unexpected problem of a rare type. An officer of PAVO brought in a German Staff Officer who had crossed the no man's land under a white flag to demand the surrender of Mekili Fort. The latter informed the Brigade Commander that Mekili had been surrounded by German forces and urged an immediate capitulation, after pointing out that further resistance by the garrison would only lead to an unnecessary loss of life. The demand was refused; and the officer, who had not been blindfolded before being brought in, was now ordered to be blindfolded and returned to his line by a devious route.[8]

In about four hours after this incident, at 2200 hours, General Gambier-Parry, Commander of the 2nd Armoured Division, arrived at the Brigade Headquarters with some of his staff. He had with him Advance Divisional Headquarters and 'M' Battery RHA (Anti-tank), which were at that moment on the hill just west of the northern perimeter. It was decided to leave those troops there for the rest of the night and to move them in the morning to a position west of A Squadron 2nd Royal Lancers.

On General Gambier-Parry's arrival at Mekili, the 3rd Indian Motor Brigade passed under the command of the 2nd Armoured

---
[8] Brig. E. W. D. Vaughan's *Report*; W/Ds 3 Ind Mot Bde, 11 Cav.

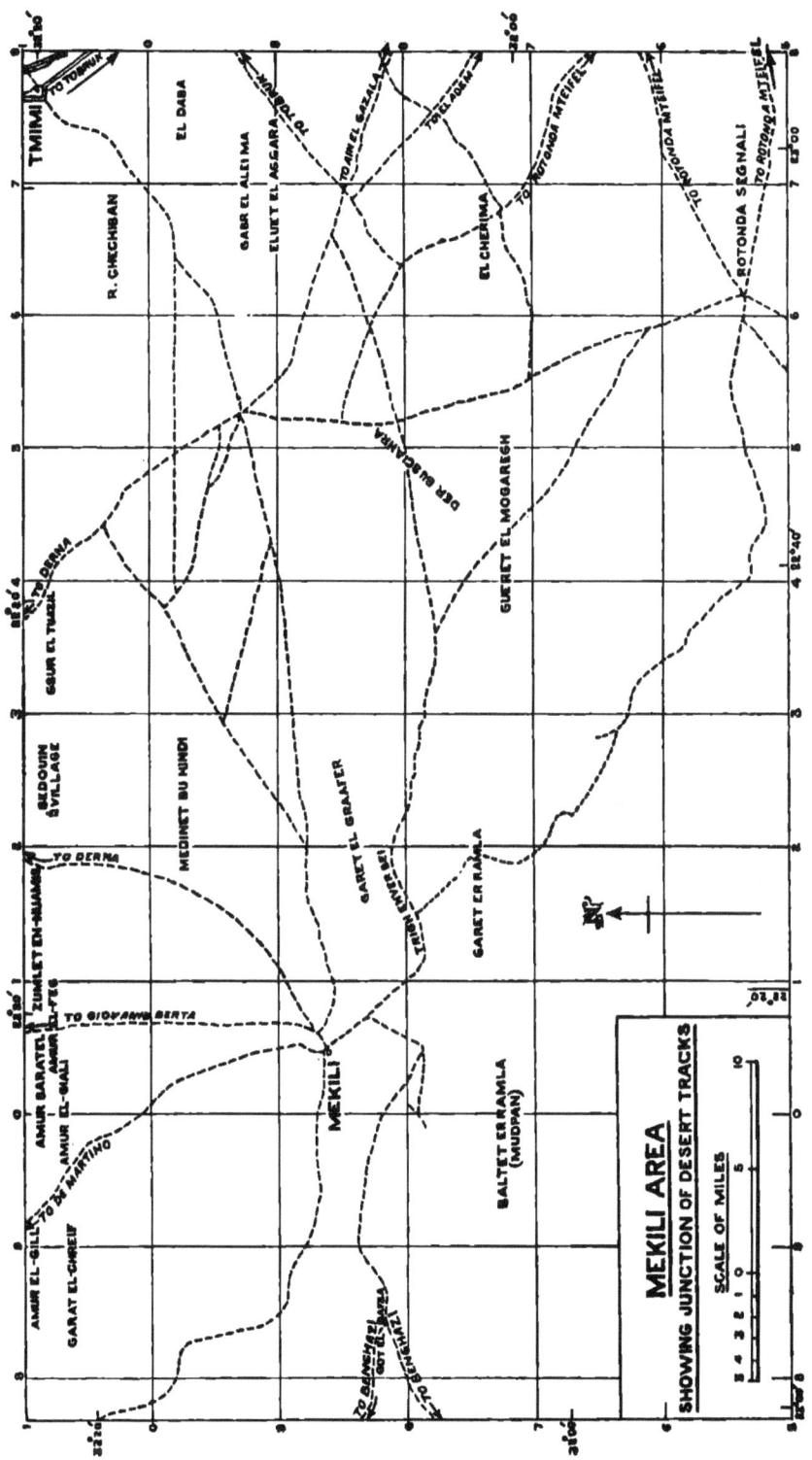

Division. There was no news yet of the whereabouts of the 3rd Armoured Brigade, nor of an expected and much needed reinforcement of guns. The guns failed to reach Mekili and what happened to them remained a mystery for the time being. As to the 3rd Armoured Brigade, it was learnt later that due to lack of petrol it had been directed to Derna. This had placed the 3rd Indian Motor Brigade in a very difficult position, especially after its audacious refusal to surrender.

Meanwhile there were indications that the Axis forces were preparing for an all-out attack on Mekili. Early in the morning of 7 April they moved about 10 guns to the west of Gun Ridge. A sortie by the 2nd Australian Anti-Tank Regiment failed to deal with them and the Australians gave up the counter-attack after having lost one gun and some men. The commander of the 3rd Indian Motor Brigade asked for urgent air action but none materialised. The Axis commander organising the attack could not be unaware of the weakness of the Mekili defences as he must have got an eye-witness report from the German Staff Officer who had, a little earlier, brought the surrender ultimatum to the Brigade Headquarters and who had not been blindfolded when being conducted to the brigade commander. It was therefore to be expected that the attack, when it should come, would be more thorough than it might otherwise have been.

Rommel's personal message to the Indian Motor Brigade

The Germans must have thought it incredible that the Indian Motor Brigade really meant to resist; or, probably they wished to conserve their resources instead of wasting them in overcoming what to them must have looked like a minor point of resistance. In any case, at about midday on 7 April, another German officer appeared at Brigade Headquarters with a second verbal demand for surrender. He, too, was sent back with the same answer as the first one. Meanwhile, the rear Headquarters of the 2nd Armoured Division had arrived at Mekili and joined the Advance Divisional Headquarters. Similarly a little later, one squadron of the 18th Cavalry, which was at Gadd-el-Ahmar, also managed to get into the perimeter. At about 1600 hours on the same day, Axis troops attempted another minor attack on the perimeter when some Italian lorried infantry attacked C Squadron of the 2nd Royal Lancers. On meeting resistance, they gave up the attempt and disengaged, leaving behind a few prisoners.

Thus the Germans who were in a hurry to get to Tobruk were being detained at Mekili by the 3rd Indian Motor Brigade, which would neither heed their ultimatums nor give way to minor attacks. It was therefore not to be doubted that they would be mounting a rather strong attack to reduce this obstacle without delay. Preparations for such an attack had been possibly completed by 1730 hours on 7 April, when still another German messenger with a white flag of truce—the third in 48 hours—arrived at the Brigade Headquarters, carrying a written message signed by General Rommel himself. The message reiterated the demand for surrender but was now accompanied by an offer from the General that the surrendering garrison would be given the honours of war.[9]

Attack on Mekili

The messenger, after delivering his ultimatum, added that his commander was in a hurry to get the reply. The brigade commander's reaction to this was to delay the matters even more than he might have otherwise done. Then, at the end of a considerable interval, he scrawled a curt refusal and returned it to the envoy.

No sooner had the man reached his own lines, near Gun Ridge, than there commenced a bombardment of the Indian brigade's positions. It started on the east face of PAVO, then lifted on to the Brigade Headquarters and finally rested on the Fort area. As an artillery barrage, it was not a very serious affair and lasted only 45 minutes. But it was enough of an ordeal for the young officers who had no previous experience of shell-fire. Shortly after dark that evening, C Squadron 2nd Royal Lancers withdrew from the small ridge near the landing ground in the north-left sector, yielding its possession to some German armoured cars. The latter, however, gave it up of their own accord a little later, when it was reoccupied by the Lancers.

All day on 7 April, there came in reports of dust being visible in the direction of the Salt Pans, indicating a likely approach of the Axis tanks. The dust settled down towards evening and some sixty vehicles could be seen on the Pans. There was no doubt that, if these were tanks, they were intended to close in on Mekili in a very short while. In the meantime, General Neame, aware of the dangers to which the Indian brigade would be exposed, had decided to withdraw it to a safer position.

That night, at about 2130 hours, the commander of the Indian Motor Brigade was summoned to the Headquarters 2nd Armoured Division and informed that orders had been received from "Cyrcom" for a withdrawal to El Adem. The move was to be carried out by the brigade commander who was also instructed to take out the Headquarters 2nd Armoured Division in a "box", at first light the following morning. There was every reason to believe that it would be a fighting withdrawal, full of risks, and defence

[9] Brig. Vaughan's *Report*; W/Ds 3 Ind Mot Bde and 11 Cav.

arrangements had to be made accordingly. The "box" was to be so organised that its southern flank would be stronger than the northern and each flank would have a proportion of anti-tank guns. The plan of withdrawal, which can best be explained diagrammatically, was as follow:—[10]

Rear Guard
2nd Royal Lancers and two
troops Bofors.

Right Flank	*Left Flank*
Two squadrons PAVO	One squadron PAVO
Two troops Bofors.	One troop Bofors.

Main Body
Field squadron and ancillary troops
Services of Brigade HQ
HQ 2nd Armoured Division
HQ 3rd Indian Motor Brigade and one troop Bofors.

Advance Guard
One squadron 18 Cavalry
One Cruiser Tank (Div Comd's escort, being the only tank available).

The entire success of the plan depended on two things. First, that the Axis guns should be struck down before there was enough light for them to function properly; second, that the bulk of the headquarters vehicles of the 2nd Armoured Division should be across the defile of the Fort, ready to move off on a broad front, as soon as the break-through was effected. The withdrawal was to commence at 0615 hours, the starting point being the location of the Brigade Headquarters. The break-through was to be effected by one squadron of the 18th Cavalry, which was to rush the Axis guns, at that hour, firing on the move.

By the time the details of this plan had been worked out, it was midnight; and it is possible that instructions for the move did not reach some of the troops before the morning. If so, that fact partly accounts for the confusion that ensued at the commencement of the withdrawal. It started with the divisional vehicles not being able to adhere to the schedule.

At 0600 hours on the morning of 8 April, the Headquarters of the 3rd Indian Motor Brigade was standing ready for a move-off at the appointed time; and so also the single squadron of the 18th Cavalry which was to spearhead the break-through. The time appointed for the break-through was 0615 hours but, even till

---

[10] Brig. Vaughan's *Report*; W/D 3rd Ind Mot Bde.

0610 hours, there was no sign of the solitary cruiser tank that was to escort the Advance Guard. As a result, after a little more delay, the Advance Guard was despatched without the tank. The tank, however, put in its appearance about forty minutes later and was immediately sent off to assist the break-through squadron of the 18th Cavalry.

While all this was happening there arose an occasion for a further delay: the vehicles of the 2nd Armoured Division which should have been across the defile by then, had not even arrived at the starting point. In fact, there was no sign of them at all. Since further delay might have seriously jeopardised the whole plan, the Brigade Commander decided to act on his own responsibility and started off with his own headquarters but without the divisional vehicles.[11]

The effort to break out

No sooner had the Brigade Headquarters left the starting point than it found itself in great difficulty. An intense artillery and light machine-gun fire broke out from the direction of Gun Ridge. To that was added fire from the south of the ridge, which was further augmented by LMG fire from the right rear. There was a great deal of dust and smoke, obscuring visibility, so that after a brief move the Brigade Headquarters found itself running into the face of an Axis tank, while another tank could be seen heading for it from the north. To oppose those tanks without any means of countering them might have led to a certain disaster, and the Brigade commander therefore decided to withdraw a little distance to be able to reconsider his plans and alter them as might appear necessary.

The alteration that suggested itself to his mind was that he should give up the idea of attempting a break-through along the road Got Derva—Tmimi, and instead make a wide detour to the south and then to the east. At this stage he rang up the Commander 2nd Armoured Division and informed him that the Gun Ridge appeared to have been strengthened by the Axis troops during the night and a break-through was not feasible. He then made his suggestion about the detour and added that he would return to confer with him.

On his way back to the Divisional Headquarters, the Brigade commander saw the rearguard of his column, the 2nd Royal Lancers, being heavily attacked by German tanks. Worse still, he was surprised to find on reaching Mekili that the vehicles of General Gambier-Parry's Headquarters had still not arrived at the appointed starting point. Instead, they were standing to the west

[11] Vaughan's *Report*; W/D 3rd Ind Mot Bde.

of that position pointing in a contrary direction. The Divisional commander himself did not seem to be favouring the idea of a detour to the south but accepted the Brigade commander's alternative suggestion to try a "rush-through" eastwards, taking advantage of the dust and smoke. The two commanders then set off in the Divisional ACV, (Armoured Command Vehicle) heading east. The Headquarters vehicles had been asked to turn round and follow.

The column had hardly gone a little distance when it came under heavy machine-gun fire from a ridge to the north-west of the Fort, and also from another feature in the same direction where a battery of small guns could be easily seen from the ACV. At that point the Divisional commander decided that a withdrawal was not practicable. He put up a white handkerchief out of the roof of the ACV as a mark of his willingness to surrender and, both, the Brigade and the Divisional commanders, became prisoners.[12]

Just previous to the surrender, the solitary cruiser tank had wirelessed to say that it was in amongst the German guns and achieving good results. The tank was, however, destroyed shortly afterwards and the crew killed. As to the break-through squadron of 18 Cav, it remained in action against the Axis guns from the east for some hours and finally succeeded in forcing its way out, suffering about 25 per cent casualties in the attempt. The Rear Guard, the 2nd Royal Lancers, lost one complete squadron which capitulated, but not until some of its troops had finished all their ammunition and had even got ready to attack the German tanks with only the bayonets. The bulk of the headquarters of 2nd Armoured Division, the MT Coy, the Field Squadron, the Headquarters of the 3rd Indian Motor Brigade and other details went into Rommel's bag of prisoners, together with the Brigade and the Divisional commanders. But the majority of men of the PAVO Regiment and certain other detachments escaped capture. So also did portions of the A and B Squadrons of 2nd Royal Lancers, which, under the command of Major M. K. Rajendrasinhji[13], broke across the ground held by Axis forces and successfully reached El Adem, capturing about 300 prisoners on the way—an achievement for which Major Rajendrasinhji received the first Distinguished Service Order ever to be awarded to an Indian officer. No trace of the forces of Eighth Army remained at Mekili after these capitulations and the dashing break-through, and the way was open for Rommel to push on to Tobruk.

[12] Brig. E. W. D. Vaughan's *Report*, pp. 7-8.
[13] Later General Maharaj Rajendrasinhji, DSO, Chief of Army Staff and Commander-in-Chief, Indian Army.

Major (later General) Maharaj Shri Rajendrasinhji

Major-General Sir Frank W. Messervy

Major-General N. M. de la P. Beresford Peirse

Lt. General A.G.O.M. Mayne

An unintended rearguard action

This disaster led to an almost complete disintegration of the 2nd Armoured Division and resulted in a great set-back for the 3rd Indian Motor Brigade. Yet it was all to good purpose. The stubborn refusal of the Indian brigade to surrender had imposed enough delay on General Rommel's advance to enable the 9th Australian Division to withdraw safely into Tobruk. The stabilization of Tobruk was thus made possible, in some measure at least, by its gallant action; and if Tobruk was finally the means of saving Egypt, a part of the credit for it must go to this Indian formation. It was an unintended rearguard action, fought for the benefit of the 9th Australian Division. But it would be a mistake to judge it merely as such; for, it had the far-reaching consequence of contributing towards a major turning-point of the war. It started a chain of events which ended with the Allied victory in Africa and the invasion of Italy. Had not Rommel got involved in a clash with the 3rd Indian Motor Brigade at Mekili he could have moved on fast enough to intercept and attack the 9th Australian Division during its unavoidably slow and processionlike withdrawal towards Tobruk. In that event, Tobruk might never have come into the Allied hands again.

CHAPTER XV

Appreciation of the Mekili Stand

The action fought by the 3rd Indian Motor Brigade in the desert, from 4 to 8 April 1941, appears superficially like a small item in a war of colossal proportions. Yet, when seen in its proper setting of time and place, and examined from the point of view of its influence on subsequent events, it stands out as an episode of far-reaching significance. It was the Indian brigade's first action of the war. It was fought under chaotic conditions produced by the breakdown of communications and utter disorganisation of its parent formation. The duty it was called upon to perform was to stand firm while others were retiring. The result it achieved was to hold up the advance of a strong hostile force while a deteriorating situation was being stabilized and a withdrawal was being converted into a stand that was later to become world-famous under the name "Tobruk".

In a war of speed, small delays inflicted on a powerful opponent often produce far-reaching results. This statement summarizes the achievement of the 3rd Indian Motor Brigade. The little time it gained for the retiring Allied force at a crucial juncture made all the difference to the subsequent happenings. Perhaps it is no exaggeration to say that, but for the action fought by the 3rd Indian Motor Brigade, that tactical marvel known as Tobruk might never have materialised. For there would have been no time to organise Tobruk. Nor perhaps is it altogether idle to speculate as to whether there might have been an "Alamein". For it is conceivable that long before the Alamein Line was constructed or even thought of, Rommel might have seized Egypt and Suez. These statements may seem extravagant claims for an action which, even to the troops fighting it, must have seemed one of the commonplaces of the war. They therefore need careful scrutiny which is one of the objects of what follows.

History of the 3rd Indian Motor Brigade

In order to appreciate this important action of the Brigade in its true perspective, a few preliminary remarks are necessary as to the composition and history of this formation. The Brigade, as a part of the 1st Armoured Division, came into existence in India on 1 July 1940. But that was only on paper. The units composing it had never assembled all in one place while in India.[1] However, these units were: —

    Brigade Headquarters
    Signal Squadron
    2nd Royal Lancers (Gardner's Horse)
    18th Cavalry (King Edward VII's Own)
    11th (F.F.) Cavalry (Prince Albert Victor's Own)
    35th Field Squadron Sappers and Miners
    MT Coy
    13th Workshop Coy
    27th Workshop Coy
    Field Ambulance
    Details.

In October 1940, the Brigade was warned to get ready to proceed overseas. At this date, two of its cavalry regiments, 2nd and 18th, were still in the process of being mechanised. Each of them had been given about twenty-five Morris six-wheelers on which to train and practise for the change-over. Both regiments had given up their horses only two months before the date of mobilising, and their training in mechanisation was hardly six months old. The personnel were therefore by no means well familiar with their new equipment. But even they, such as they were, were not all available for the use of the regiments. For, of those that had finished their training, some had to be sent out to assist in forming new cavalry units as well as to man an Indian cavalry training centre; while some others were required for the Brigade Headquarters and as reinforcements. As to equipment, none of the regiments at that time had either a mechanical transport company or a signal squadron or field ambulance or other details.

What was true of the 2nd and 18th was also true of the Indian Motor Brigade's third regiment, the PAVO (Prince Albert Victor's Own). This last unit was, however, better placed as to training than the other two, having been marked out as an armoured regiment for frontier duties in India, to be equipped with two armoured cars and one light-tank squadron. But even this regiment lost some of its strength before it went overseas. For on the one hand, no armour was allowed to be taken overseas; and on the other, in July 1940, it had to part with one squadron to the Central India Horse; which deficiency was later made up with "mechanically untrained" drafts from other regiments.

This was the state of the 3rd Indian Motor Brigade when it started mobilising on 1 December 1940.[2] The mobilisation was to

[1] Brig. E. W. D. Vaughan's *Report*, p. 2.
[2] *Ibid*, pp. 2-3; W/D 3rd Mot Bde, p. 3; and Scheme "Assurance" File No. F/1002, pp. 1-5.

be completed by 15 January 1941 and the Brigade was to move overseas at any time on receipt of the code signal "Assurance". All the details as to its establishment, equipment and movements, up to the point of disembarkation in Egypt, were embodied in a scheme issued on 23 December 1940 and called scheme "Assurance," the Brigade being known as "Force Assurance".[3]

The Brigade was deficient in many respects on the eve of embarking at the end of January 1941. Men of the Signal Squadron were inexperienced and new. The wireless personnel had too few wireless transmission sets and too little practice in using them. Regiments were about 40% below strength in light machine-guns. They had only one anti-tank rifle each, instead of the full quota of 42 per regiment. None of the men had seen a Bren gun at all and, due to shortage of ammunition, most of them had fired only a few rounds from their weapons before going into action. Above everything else, the Brigade had no armour at all. Thus, judged by ordinary standards, the 3rd Indian Motor Brigade was sadly deficient in training and equipment, and definitely unfitted to oppose any up-to-date armoured formation of its time. General Wavell was well aware of this, for he had at one time warned General Neame, the General Officer Commanding Cyrenaica, of the danger of exposing that frail motorised cavalry to an attack by armoured troops.

The Indian Motor Brigade embarked at Bombay on 22 January 1941 and arrived in Egypt on 6 February. Two days later it moved to El Tahag. It remained there until the end of the month, trying to complete its training and equipment. Early in March it moved to Mersa Matruh, and thence to El Adem a fortnight later. Its arrival at El Adem, as it happened unfortunately, synchronised with the commencement of the withdrawal of the Allied troops from El Agheila and Marsa Brega. Three days later Rommel followed up with his armour like a destructive tornado, and it was in that setting that the Brigade played its vital role of helping to save Egypt. To understand this it is necessary to consider some of the characteristics of desert warfare.[4]

Physical features of Cyrenaica

Certain physical features of Cyrenaica have always dominated and governed military operations in this campaign. Of these features, the main ones have been four: the coastal plain, the escarpment and its passes, the desert plateau and the salt marshes. Each of these had some share in shaping the desert tactics. It is

[3] For details of Force Assurance see Appendix K.
[4] W/D 3rd Ind Mot Bde, pp. 8, 48, 52-4; W/Ds PAVO, pp. 28, 68.

therefore worth considering them in detail here, even at the risk of some repetition.

The Coastal Plain

As has been mentioned earlier, along the coastal plain runs the railway and the only main road of North Africa. The obvious military advantage of controlling the coastal margin is that it includes the possession of the ports and harbours situated therein. Movement of motor transport is difficult off the road as the coastal margin has many patches of soft sand.

Escarpment and its Passes

From the coastal plain rises the escarpment, at places abruptly and at places in several tiers, but always steeply and up to a height of about 600 feet above sea-level. This escarpment presents a dead wall to the passage of any vehicular traffic from the coast, thus shutting off the coast from the desert. Access to the top of the escarpment and to the open desert behind by mechanical transport is gained only along the constructed tracks and roads, which wind up steeply and through certain passes. Hence the tactical necessity of controlling those passes.

The Desert Plateau

The top of the escarpment which stretches back inland constitutes the desert plateau. At the western end of Cyrenaica, this plateau rises into higher hills, known as the Jebel Akhdar where water becomes available from wells, making extensive cultivation possible. These hills rise to a height of over 2500 feet and are not easily negotiable by mechanical transport except along the constructed roads and tracks.

Over the greater part of the desert plateau, that is in the open desert, the ground is hard and strong, enabling movement by tanks and mechanical transport almost anywhere on a wide front. In this respect, the desert can be compared to the sea. It is vast, spacious and featureless; and there is no point where a stand can be made to block the further advance of a hostile force, for it is always open to such a force to by-pass and outflank. Thus, whichever of the two contending sides succeeds in using the desert as a line of advance, has, as against many other handicaps, the supreme advantage of going ahead, evading all points of opposition and accepting battle only when suitable.

Salt Marshes

The simile however ceases here—especially in regard to the Western Desert. For, at either end of the desert, that is, at

El Agheila in the west and El Alamein in the east, there are vast areas of salt marshes. These are barriers to mechanical transport. They lie close to the coast leaving only narrow necks between themselves and the shores. Only across these narrow straits can vehicular traffic pass. To circumvent the marshes by a huge detour would be fruitless toil, if not an impossible task. Therefore any force that sweeps across the desert in either direction can ultimately be held up at the bottle-neck of El Agheila or Alamein. Conversely, the force that launches out of either of those bottle-necks meets little obstacle in the intervening space. This peculiarity in the topographical structure of the desert had imparted to the campaign in Cyrenaica, as will be seen hereafter, its peculiar shape, namely that of a see-saw struggle; or a pendulum oscillating from east to west; or a shuttlecock bandied to and fro between Benghazi and El Alamein; or a spring withdrawing under pressure and rebouncing on being released—and so forth.

Nature of Axis Advance

The break-through of the *Afrika Korps* from El Agheila on 31 March 1941, mentioned before, was just one of those oscillatory swings. But it could not be then seen in its proper perspective as it can be seen at this distance of time. As a result, there was needless confusion and panic in meeting the situation. Had the Allied commanders then known, as we can easily see now, that this advance, if left to exhaust itself, would peter out as an oscillation that must return to its starting point under a compelling law of nature, they would have spared themselves much vain anxiety and effort. They would have contented themselves with holding the vital ports and harbours and leaving the desert free to the opponents in which to let them squander their strength and resources; and in which the opponents might be obliged to stretch their communications and lines of supply to the breaking point. When thus weakened, the adversary could be dealt with, with greater ease and economy of effort.

But neither of the contending sides was aware that that was the pattern on which the campaign was being fought; that the pattern was the result of an invisible force which was directing the campaign independently of the generals; and that that force was simply the dead weight of the peculiar physical structure of an immense battle-ground.

Even in the internal combustion age, in which the Second World War was being fought, there are rigid limits up to which a line of communication may stretch with impunity. These limits are more pronounced in a desert. They are not incapable of being reduced to a mathematical formula, so that one may say "thus far—

for so many hundred and odd miles only—can the opponent's line of communication stretch; at the end of the distance there will be no strength left in him; beyond it he can no more extend than can a pendulum overreach the farthest point of its swing; at that point he can no more tarry than can the pendulum at an extreme of its arc. Both have only one recourse—to fall back to the original position". On such a calculation, the question of meeting the advance of the *Afrika Korps* would have resolved itself into finding a point beyond the eastern extreme of the swing and retiring to it. Such a point was El Alamein. It was ultimately discovered empirically. But, at the commencement of the Axis advance in March 1941, its existence was neither known nor suspected in such a context.

Nature of Allied Retreat

The method adopted by General Wavell, therefore, for stopping the Axis advance was the common-sense method of trying to halt it as quickly and as far from its objective as possible. The advance, however, could not be halted by presenting to it a frontal opposition, since General Wavell had neither the required strength in men and material nor a line of natural obstacle on which to make a stand. In the circumstances, the tide of the Axis advance might have rolled on until the whole of Egypt had been deluged as far as Alexandria or Cairo. Such indeed seemed to be the prospects. But at this critical juncture the military acumen of General Wavell prevailed and he took a decision that altered the situation radically. He decided that this meagre force should continue to retire before the irresistible advance of the *Afrika Korps*, abandoning everything except Tobruk. Tobruk, however, was to be garrisoned and retained as a sort of a fortified island surrounded, as it would be, on three sides by hostile forces and on the fourth by the sea. It was to be fed and maintained from the sea. On the land-side it would inevitably face the flank of the Axis advance and operate against it, producing in General Rommel an apprehension as to what might happen to his flank if he ignored Tobruk and went ahead without stopping to clear it. As events turned out, Rommel could neither reduce Tobruk nor continue his advance without doing so.

Tactical Effectiveness of Tobruk

If such was the intention of General Wavell it was fulfilled admirably. Tobruk became such a serious menace to the left flank of General Rommel that he decided not to proceed further until that threat had first been eliminated. Accordingly he made a number of assaults on that stronghold all of which however failed. Each time he failed, he became more obsessed than before by the desire to remove the deadly peril from his flank. But Tobruk stood there stable and unshaken, challenging him to proceed onward if he dared. In course of time the world found itself witnessing a tactical miracle. A formidable force which could not be stopped frontally by any means had been brought to a standstill by a threat on the flank. Tobruk became world-famous. It had saved Egypt and Suez; and therefore temporarily at least was the only means the Allies had of holding the Middle East and India. Had Tobruk not come into existence so opportunely, it is possible that the Allied force would have been driven out of North Africa in a matter of weeks, and the chances of Allied victory in World War II would have been jeopardised to that extent.

Who made Tobruk possible?

But who made Tobruk possible? The conclusion is inescapable that, more than any other Allied unit or formation, it was the 3rd Indian Motor Brigade that made this miracle possible. When General Wavell decided to garrison Tobruk the situation was that the Germans were making a cross-desert dash towards it, and the chances were that they would reach and seize Tobruk before the Allied garrison could get into it in sufficient strength to fortify it. However, the Germans failed to arrive there in time because the *Afrika Korps* was delayed at Mekili for nearly two days by the 3rd Indian Motor Brigade which would not yield the way to proceed. It was during this precious interval that the 9th Australian Division which was withdrawing from Benghazi was able to garrison and fortify Tobruk. Had not the Indian Motor Brigade intervened to detain Rommel at Mekili, not only would the Germans have occupied Tobruk with ease, but they might have also intercepted the 9th Australian Division, which was on its way to that place, and destroyed it without much difficulty. This becomes clear on a careful examination of the chronological sequence in which events occurred between 2 and 8 April 1941.

The Scrutiny

The advance of the Axis and the simultaneous Allied retreat had commenced on 31 March 1941. On 2 April, the 2nd Armoured Division was in the vicinity of Agedabia in the course of its withdrawal. There it received the news that an Axis force was approaching Msus. This was the first indication that Rommel was intending to cut across the desert and reach Tobruk or Gazala before the withdrawing Allied force could get there in strength. Such a cross-desert advance would require him to proceed from Msus to Mekili. No news of the Axis move across the desert had however reached the headquarters of "Cyrcom", where plans were being formulated in complete ignorance of the enveloping threat which the move presented.[5]

Accordingly, "Cyrcom" ordered the 9th Australian and the 2nd Armoured Divisions to proceed through Derna to Mekili. The orders were issued on the night of 3/4 April 1941. The two formations were to be joined at Mekili, on 6 April, by the 3rd Indian Motor Brigade which was to proceed there from El Adem. All moves were carried out as ordered, except that the 9th Australian Division did not move as intended, as a result of unexpected developments and the conflicting orders it received from General Neame and General O'Connor. At first General Neame ordered it to move to Wadi Derna during the night of 5/6 April. Later, somehow, his Headquarters ordered the Australian division to stand fast in its positions on the Barce escarpment. As the movement to Derna had already started, the troops were with difficulty stopped and brought back to Barce. Next day, 6 April, General O'Connor countermanded this arrangement and ordered the division to withdraw to Gazala area with all possible speed as the Axis forces were reported to be shelling Mekili and were apparently advancing by the desert route.

In the ordinary course the Axis forces should have reached Gazala, or further east, ahead of the 9th Australian Division, which was therefore in grave danger of envelopment. But, as narrated earlier, General Rommel could not get clear of the 3rd Indian Motor Brigade at Mekili until the morning of 8 April. This gave a chance to the Australian Division to garrison Tobruk. Once Tobruk was garrisoned, the Germans could do nothing. Having lost the race to get there, they failed to get Tobruk. Having lost Tobruk, they lost Egypt and North Africa, and for that matter even Sicily and Italy, in an inexorable chain of sequences, thus finally turning the tide of war in the direction of Allied victory. It is not claimed that events could not have shaped themselves in other ways than they did. But it stands to reason that if the march of events during the fateful days between 4 and 8 April 1941 had not been interrupted or deflected by the 3rd Indian Motor Brigade, the Axis had a fair chance of reaching Alexandria before Alamein was even thought of. It will always remain a matter of speculation and opinion as to how far this frail, poorly-equipped unit of the

---

[5] Australian account of 'Operations in Cyrenaica'.

Indian cavalry was responsible for turning the current of human history into a different direction from that which it was about to take.⁶

---

⁶ It has been argued that, apart from the resistance offered by the 3rd Indian Motor Brigade, there were other factors which might have imposed an equal delay on Rommel's advance to Tobruk. The factors named are: (1) resistance by other troops, (2) time Rommel would need for a build-up before attacking Tobruk, (3) his administrative difficulties and (4) that the Tobruk perimeter could not have been fortified in 3 or 4 days. The facts are, however, that (1) there were actually no other troops on Rommel's way to Tobruk which he could not have outflanked, (2) no build-up would be necessary for attacking Tobruk before the Australians had got in; in fact the few troops in it would have had to be pulled out hurriedly, (3) it is unlikely that the comparatively slow-moving armour could not have been overtaken by the supply vehicles and (4) the time of a few days was enough to seal the gaps in the perimeter with mines. Fortification of Tobruk had been actually taken in hand three weeks before, at the instance of General Neame (vide *Playing with Strife*, p. 280) and it was therefore easy to hurry the process.

A point has also been made about the "pendulum theory" enunciated above, namely that if one just held the ports and the bottle-necks (Agheila or Alamein) at either end of the Cyrenaica desert and left the opponent to advance unopposed, he could do so, deliberately, by bounds, building his communications and advancing from firm base to firm base, till he should have sufficient strength to overwhelm each port in turn and finally the strong position at the end. This would be true, if the garrisons of the ports remained passive and purely on the defensive. But such is not the implication of the theory. The garrisons, on the contrary, would have to be very active and parts of them would have to move out at intervals and destroy the adversary's build-up and communications. It is not unlikely that any campaigning in North Africa in future, should there be one at all, will be on this new pattern.

CHAPTER XVI

End of the Allied Retreat

After the disaster suffered by the 2nd Armoured Division and the 3rd Indian Motor Brigade, the situation sorted itself out slowly. Survivors of the 2nd Royal Lancers, who had managed to fight their way through the German ring round Mekili, reached El Adem on or about 10 April 1941. There they passed under the command of the remnants of the 11th PAVO Cavalry who were holding a position below the escarpment. The two battered units then combined together to form one squadron.

On 11 April, the PAVO, under the command of the Support Group, withdrew to Sollum, and the next day to Matruh. Here the men were given duties of "wide" patrolling until 20 April, on which day they moved to the command of the 6th Australian Division. As a part of that division, they withdrew to Baqqush and later to Sidi Haneish. At that stage, the 5th Indian Infantry Brigade took this wandering unit under its charge and employed the men as dismounted local reserve.

This unit, which still consisted of the remnants of the 2nd Royal Lancers and PAVO, at last found itself at El Daba on 27 April 1941. A few days later, its personnel were placed under the command of the 'B' echelon of the 7th Armoured Brigade as protective detachments. The men of the 2nd Royal Lancers were here detached from the PAVO group and sent from camp to camp until they joined the 4th Indian Division at Sidi Barrani on 6 June 1941. From there, by easy stages, they were sent to Mena, just outside Cairo, for a well deserved rest. As to PAVO, they found themselves, at the end of May 1941, under the direct command of the Headquarters 4th Indian Division.[1]

The third regiment of the Indian Motor Brigade, the 18th KEO Cavalry,[2] had, on the other hand, better luck than its two sister regiments. When the brigade was ordered to Mekili, this regiment (less one squadron) was dismounted and left in Tobruk, along with two immobile Australian infantry battalions, to garrison that port. The dismounting was done to make its vehicles available to the other units of the Cyrenaica Command which were gravely deficient in transport. The third squadron of the regiment went with the brigade to Mekili; and, after the short-lived defence of

[1] W/Ds 2 RL, 11 PAVO, 5 Ind Inf Bde.
[2] 18th King Edward VII's Own Cavalry.

that place, such of its personnel as had succeeded in extricating themselves withdrew eastwards and linked up with the 9th Australian Division just outside Tobruk. There they passed under the command of the Australian division on 8 April 1941, and went with it on the following night into the shortly-to-be-besieged Toburk, where they rejoined their regiment as a part of the defending garrison. When the siege of Tobruk began, on the evening of 11 April 1941, the 18th KEO Cavalry consisted of a headquarter squadron and three other squadrons of Jats, Kaim Khanis and Rajputs respectively. It was equipped with 15-cwt trucks and armed with rifles, Bren guns and anti-tank rifles but had no armour. From that date on, the history of the operations of the 18th Cavalry becomes entwined with that of the historic defence of Tobruk. As such it will be the subject of a separate treatment. Meanwhile it is necessary to digress in order to follow the activities of other units and formations during the Allied withdrawal and their subsequent return to the offensive.

Return of the 4th Indian Division to North Africa

It will be recalled that at the time General Rommel opened his counter-offensive in Cyrenaica, on 31 March 1941, the 4th Indian Division was engaged in a victorious campaign in East Africa against the Italians. By the middle of April 1941 it had come to the end of its successful labours and, on 23 April, it sailed from Port Sudan to return to its original battlefield in North Africa. Arriving at Suez, complete with its three brigades, the 5th, 7th and 11th, it was ordered to move with all possible speed to Baqqush to relieve the 6th Australian Division. This it did on 1 May 1941.[3]

A few days before the arrival of the 4th Indian Division at Baqqush there was a change in the divisional command. The Divisional Commander, Mojor-General Beresford-Peirse, was promoted Lieut-General Commanding Western Desert Force.[4] He was succeeded in command of the 4th Indian Division by Major-General F. W. Messervy, until then Commander of the 9th Indian Infantry Brigade.

The background of events, against which the 4th Indian Division had to find its bearings afresh in its former theatre of war, was something like the following: Tobruk was besieged. Axis troops had captured Bardia as early as 13 April and had reached the Egyptian frontier at Sollum. The Allied forces in Greece had begun evacuation of that country on 24 April and part of that

---

[3] W/Ds 4 Div, 5 Bde, 7 Bde, 11 Bde.
[4] Although, earlier, the title Western Desert Force had been changed to XIII Corps, the old designation, it appears, crept into use again and continued to be used till September 1941.

force was returning to the Western Desert, while General Rommel had launched a second and more serious attack on Tobruk which had petered out by 3 May 1941.

The 4th Indian Division itself was stretched over a distance of 130 miles from Sidi Barrani to El Daba. It was obliged to place itself in this extended formation as its duties entailed protection of as many as fourteen Allied landing grounds lying dispersed over a vast area[2]. It had at the same time to train and practise for coming to grips with the *Afrika Korps* in no distant future. At the end of May 1941, it was joined by a new brigade, the 23rd (Composite) Brigade, which arrived from Egypt and consisted of:

    1 Buffs
    4 Border Regiment
    No. 1 Czecho-Slovak Force.

In the meanwhile, in the first week of May, Allied forces in the Western Desert received a welcome accession of strength in the shape of fifty 'I' tanks and cruisers which arrived most unexpectedly from the United Kingdom. They had been intended for use in Greece but, as that campaign was over by then, they were diverted to Egypt. During the same week there also took place an incident which clarified the general situation and provided an indication of the likely Axis moves in the near future. The General Headquarters at Cairo had succeeded in intercepting a German cipher message addressed to General Rommel from the Mediterranean High Command. The message contained the High Command's disapproval of Rommel's expensive way of conducting his campaign, and chid him for what his superiors regarded as a reckless wastage of his resources. It was dated the 3rd May and seemed to refer to Rommel's attack on Tobruk on 14 April 1941, but was perhaps more directly inspired by the still poorer results of his second attack during the period 30 April—3 May 1941. The message also ordered him not to attack Tobruk again, nor to advance into Egypt except for purposes of reconnaissance. In brief, he was to conserve his resources and undertake no further offensive operations.

Preparations for a counter-offensive

As to the Allied position, the withdrawal from Benghazi having been successfully completed and the situation stabilized, it was a question of opening a counter-offensive as soon as possible; pending that the Axis forces were to be given no respite. In pursuance of that policy, a rather severe air and ground assault was delivered on 12 May 1941, on the most forward of the Axis troops who were then at Sofafi. To the surprise of all concerned the troops withdrew somewhat precipitately to Capuzzo. The withdrawal

---
[2] For a complete list of the landing grounds see Appendix M.

could not be due merely to the assault and might have resulted from General Rommel's desire to fall in with the wishes of the German Mediterranean Command and economise on his resources. Whatever the reason, the unexpected success proved a good morale-raiser and was the beginning of a long series of minor and major offensives, the first of which took place on 15 May 1941.

General Beresford-Peirse decided that in view of the German High Command having urged Rommel to go slow, it was the most proper time to press the Axis back. He drew up a plan accordingly to drive the Axis out from Halfaya and Sollum. The plan turned on making a strong show of force so as to induce the Axis to withdraw voluntarily to the west of Tobruk. To that end the Tobruk garrison was to stage a formidable demonstration of its own. The main striking force in the action was to make a direct thrust at its obectives, while the 4th Indian Division was to play the dual role of being a reserve mobile striking column and preventing groups of Axis forces from by-passing any thrust made by the main striking force. Actually, as it turned out, the 4th Indian Division found itself compelled to do nothing more difficult than passing prisoners of war and the wounded to the back area.[6]

The action took place according to the plan and was successful as anticipated. The Axis abandoned Halfaya and Sollum which were duly occupied. Capuzzo could not be reached since the Axis troops counter-attacked in the afternoon of 15 May, and checked any exploitation beyond those two objectives.

The May-offensive

On the following day, the Allied forces were in possession of Sollum, Musaid, Bir Wair, Sidi Suleiman and Halfaya. But as stated earlier, the Allied attack was more in the nature of a demonstration than an offensive and no arrangements had therefore been made for holding those places against continuous Axis pressure. Accordingly, the next day, the units occupying Sollum, Musaid and Bir Wair withdrew to the area Halfaya—Sidi Suleiman. The last-named two places were then counter-attacked by two Axis columns on 18 May. The attackers used about 75 tanks but failed to secure their flank from the south. The tanks were driven back by units of the 7th (British) Armoured Division who operated against the Axis flanks and broke up the counter-attack.

The small action described above, now spoken of as the May-offensive, turned out to be a kind of "prodding attack" causing General Rommel to react in a way so as to disclose his real strength. The results achieved seemed to justify the mounting of a second offensive in which the 4th Indian Division was to play a more

[6] W/D 4 Div.

important role. It is now known as the June-offensive. In anticipation of that, the Indian division was asked to move forward to Sidi Barrani. Accordingly it handed over to the 23rd (Composite) Brigade the permanent protection of the fourteen landing grounds on 4 June 1941, and moved to its new location where it began to make active preparations for the impending operations planned to take place between 15 and 18 June 1941.

The June-offensive

The object of these operations was to clear the frontier area of all Axis forces, and to push General Rommel back to the west of Tobruk. If possible, the success was to be exploited further westwards up to the line Derna—Mekili. The operations were to be carried out in two or, if necessary, more stages. Stage I was to be the destruction of all Axis troops within the area Bardia—Sollum—Halfaya—Sidi Omar—Sidi Azeiz. On the occupation of Sollum, that port was to be reopened in readiness for further operations. A secure line of communication was to be established across Sollum and Halfaya with advanced maintenance installations in that area.

The operations were to be carried out jointly by the 7th Armoured and 4th Indian Divisions, the garrison of Tobruk assisting at a later stage. The role of the 4th Indian Division was to capture the area Bardia—Sollum—Halfaya—Capuzzo and to liquidate all resistance therein. After that it was to consolidate the road defiles of Sollum and Halfaya so as to enable the line of communications to be established for facilitating further advance. In the intervening stages, it was to mask the Axis forces within Bardia, if necessary, so as to deny them the observation of subsequent moves of the Allied armour and infantry. The role of the 7th Armoured Division was to protect the desert flank of the 4th Indian Division. In addition it was to bring the Axis armour to a battle and defeat it decisively. It was hoped that thereby the road would be opened for a free onward move of the Allied force towards Tobruk.[7] In the later stages of the operations, the 4th Indian Division was to clear up the area Bardia—Menastir and protect the third-line convoys serving the 7th Armoured Division. It was also to remain prepared for a move forward to El Adem if required.

The Coast Force and the Escarpment Force: their roles

In the main outline, the plan of the operation of the June-offensive was similar in tactics to that which had proved so successful a month before. Practically the only difference was that now there were six times as many 'I' tanks as in the previous operation and

[7] *Report* by Comd. 4 Ind. Div. on Operations in Western Desert, 15-18 June 1941, pp. 1-2. W/D HQ 4 Div.

double the number of infantry. Information as to terrain over which operations were to be conducted being scanty, the plan was based on such knowledge of the country as could be gleaned from maps and a remote reconnaissance of the area of immediate action. The force available for the operation was divided into two parts. One part was named the Coast Force and the other the Escarpment Force.[8] There was also to be a smaller supplementary force, named the Halfaya Group. It was specially intended to help in the capture of the Halfaya Pass.

The Coast Force was to consist of:—
    11th Indian Infantry Brigade.
    Central India Horse.
    Two troops 4 R Tanks (6 tanks).
    2 Camerons (after zero hour).
    25 Field Regiment (16 guns).
    One medium battery (eight 6"-hows) and ancillary units.

The Escarpment Force comprised:—
    4th Armoured Brigade (less detachments).
    Advanced Headquarters 4th Indian Division.
    22 Guards Brigade.
    2 Camerons (up to zero hour only).
    Artillery group (Field Medium and Anti-tank guns).

The Halfaya Group was composed of:—
    One squadron 4 RTR (15 'I' tanks).
    2 Camerons.
    One platoon Anti-tank.[9]

The role of the Coast Force was to advance along the coast and capture and hold the Halfaya position. Thereafter it was to clear the area of the wadis, between Halfaya and Sollum. In the meanwhile the Escarpment Force was to capture and hold the triangle Sollum Barracks 524375—Bir Wair 517373—Capuzzo. The Halfaya Group was to move with the Escarpment Force and attack the Halfaya position from the top, after which it was to pass to the command of the Coast Force. D-day was fixed to fall on 15 June 1941. But the fact was not allowed to be known to the troops until the 13th. Even the Brigade Commanders and staff officers concerned were not permitted to know the secret until 3 June 1941, that is one day before the commencement of the preliminary moves for the grouping for operations.

However, as the above plans were being given the last touches, there arose a need for their modification. That was due to the last-minute receipt of air-photos on 11 June. The photographs revealed a series of anti-tank obstacles running south of the coast road, from

[8] *Ibid.*
[9] For details see Appendix N.

Musaid to the escarpment, just west of Sollum. At first there was considerable doubt and speculation as to the nature of those obstacles. But the point was soon settled when a Royal Air Force officer (who had gallantly volunteered to fly over them at a height of 50 feet to inspect them optically) reported that they consisted of concrete slabs. As such, the obstacles were not considered a serious hindrance to the contemplated operations; but they were an unmistakable indication of the fact that the Axis commanders had learned the lesson of the May-offensive, and that their new defensive plans were obviously framed to deal with a second attack on similar lines, namely a frontal attack.

It became necessary, therefore, to introduce modifications in the original plan. The altered plan was aimed at simulating the old line of attack up to the last possible moment and then abruptly changing directions. That was to be achieved by advancing as far as possible along the edge of the escarpment and then swinging westward. It was hoped such tactics would upset the anti-tank plans of the Axis which were obviously based on defeating a direct attack from the south.

The basis of the modified plan was a wider sweep to the west. Thus, instead of attacking the objectives from the south, it was now decided to attack the triangle Sollum—Bir Wair—Capuzzo from the west and south-west of Capuzzo. This outflanking movement had one advantage. It would bring, during action, the 4th and 7th Armoured Brigades within supporting distance of each other. When necessary, therefore, they could be united as one armoured force, should a major tank battle develop in that area. Such a contingency was not unlikely since the Axis armoured force would feel compelled to turn west and north-west of Capuzzo in order to meet a threat in that area of comparatively weaker defences. As the 4th Armoured Brigade had 'I' tanks and the 7th had 'cruisers', the combination would be invaluable for defeating the Axis armour and thereby opening the road for an onward sweep towards Tobruk. Almost the only other modification in the altered plan was that the Halfaya Group, instead of passing after the zero hour from the command of the Escarpment Force to that of the Coast Force, was to be with the Coast Force from the very beginning.[10]

The general method of attack as visualised in the plan was for the 'I' tanks to go for the objectives with the close support of artillery. The infantry was in the meantime to follow in mechanical transport and wait at about ten minutes' distance—approximately 500 yards. At a given signal from the tanks, indicating that the area was sufficiently under control, the infantry was to move in and take over the objective.

[10] *Report* by Comd., 4 Ind. Div., W/D HQ 4 Div.

In its final form, the altered plan of attack stood as follows. Halfaya was to be attacked by the Coast Force including the Halfaya Group. The triangle Sollum—Bir Wair—Capuzzo was to be taken by the Escarpment Force including the Guards Brigade. The way for the latter was to be paved by the 7th Armoured Brigade crossing the frontier wire and securing the frontier post of Bir Hafid.

For the attack on Halfaya, the Coast Force and the Halfaya Group were to be stationed on the D-day at or near Bir Nuh (527360), a few miles from the objective. There, at 0515 hours, the Halfaya Group was to pass under the command of the Coast Force, and the two forces were immediately to move to the attack in their prearranged separate directions. The attack was expcted to take place at 0600 hours.

Similarly, for the capture of the triangle Sollum—Bir Wair—Capuzzo, the Escarpment Force was to be in the area, Qaret Abu Faris (514356), on the D-day. The action was to commence at 0915 hours the same morning, when the 7th Armoured Brigade was to start from the same area and cross the frontier wire to capture the border post of Bir Hafid. Thereafter, the Escarpment Force was to follow across the frontier wire, by 1115 hours, at a point south-west of Capuzzo, near the Boundary Post 42, (508367). Its first action would be to capture a stretch of the frontier extending from the Boundary Post 38 (513371), to Point 206 (514368). Next would come the "mopping up" of the areas Musaid (519375), Bir Musaid (521375) and Sollum Barracks (524375).[11]

The approach-march

All details as to plans and preliminary preparations having been settled, it was now a question of arranging a satisfactory approach-march. This was a difficult problem since the approach had to be such as to take the Axis forces unawares as to the direction from which the main attack was likely to be made. The movements of the Coast Force and the Escarpment Force were therefore arranged to take place separately and on different dates. Prior to the commencement of the approach-march, units of each of the two forces had first to assemble at Sidi Barrani and then move forward to their dispersal areas; and thence to their respective areas of attack. The area of dispersal for the Coast Force was Ilwet et Naas (553363)—Alam el Idris (553360); its area of attack being Halfaya. For the Escarpment Force the dispersal area was Abar Abu Safafi (562336); Capuzzo being its area of attack. The initial moves to Sidi Barrani were managed without difficulty. The 11th Indian Infantry Brigade simply marched from Matruh to Sidi Barrani, a distance of about 80 miles.

[11] W/Ds HQ 4 Div, & 11 Bde. June 1941,

By 8 June, the 11th Brigade was bivouacked some ten miles east of Sidi Barrani. From there its two battalions, the 2nd Mahrattas and the 1st Rajputana Rifles, proceeded forward again on 10 June. The third battalion, the 2nd Camerons, remained behind to move with the Escarpment Force. The marching troops dribbled forward across the sand dunes in open desert formation by day; whilst the transport moved up at dusk, and convoys of food, water and other requirements were moved only after dark. This arrangement was adhered to throughout the march, although the procedure was slow and the brigade was on the move for four days. At last, however, on the evening of 13 June, the two battalions reached their dispersal area—the line Ilwet el Naas—Alam el Idris. They rested there for twenty-four hours before moving to the attack. Owing to this careful method of approach, the Axis forces, it appears, were not aware till the last moment of the menace that was approaching them from this unsuspected direction.[12]

But the problem of an unobserved approach-march was not so simple for the Escarpment Force, which had to move forward a considerable amount of artillery, armour and vehicles. The distance to be covered was about 50 miles, from Abar Abu Safafi to Capuzzo by the projected route; and the move had to take place under cover of darkness. The Artillery Group, being the slowest moving, was given an early start. It set off from Sidi Barrani at 1900 hours on 13 June. It bivouacked when it got dark and moved again when the moon had risen at about 0200 hours. The remainder of the Escarpment Force left Sidi Barrani at 0200 hours the next day, there being sufficient moonlight for the movement. But the march could not be completed before sunrise and the dispersal area was not reached till 1000 hours in the morning. During the hours of light, therefore, from dawn till 1000 hours, fighter protection was provided over the area of movement, and one Axis bomber was shot down in the course of the march.

The onward move to the battle area was resumed the same day at 1645 hours. Leaving the Guards Brigade behind to move independently, the rest of the Escarpment Force proceeded, in a desert formation, over the escarpment. The destination was Halfway House (542346), some 16 miles from the dispersal area. It was reached without incident. The Force then went into "leaguer" at dusk, in a close formation of three columns in which form the further move of that night was planned to take place. At about 2000 hours, that same night, an Axis aircraft flew over the area, rather low, and must have seen something but, all vehicles then being at a standstill, did not possibly suspect that a move in strength was then under progress.

[12] W/Ds 4 Div., 11 Bde, 1 Raj Rif., 2 Mahrattas.

The march was resumed at 0200 hours, 15 June, as the moon arose. Moving north-west, parallel to the escarpment, the Force finally reached an area just south of Alam Battuma, 10 miles from Halfway House. Here a halt was called till dawn. But the Halfaya Group, consisting of the 2nd Camerons and one squadron 4th Royal Tank Regiment, detached itself and pushed on slowly towards its objective—the top of the Halfaya Pass—with one battery of the 31st Field Regiment, Royal Artillery, for support. The battery was to give a five minutes' intense fire on the objectives to help the tanks in; after which it was to remain another twenty-five minutes in support during the battle.[13]

The desert formation in which the Escarpment Force advanced from Sofafi to Alam Battuma was approximately 3 miles wide and 5 miles long. The order of march was: Headquarters, 4th Armoured Brigade, 4th Royal Tanks, 31st Field Regiment, a detachment of carriers of the 7th Indian Infantry Brigade (supplied to the 11th Indian Infantry Brigade), detachment of the Royal Engineers, the Artillery Group, and advanced Headquarters of the 4th Indian Division. On the right of the Armoured Brigade, about 1500 yards away, went one squadron 4th Royal Tanks; while the left and right flanks of the carrier-detachment of the 7th Indian Infantry Brigade were protected by the 7th Royal Tanks and the 2nd Camerons respectively.[14]

All was ready for the opening of the June-offensive by the break of dawn. Units that were to initiate the action had taken up their allotted positions and were waiting for the signal to start. From all signs in front of them it appeared that the Axis troops were unaware of the impending danger and would be taken by surprise.

---

[13] *Ibid.*
[14] For a diagram showing the formation as it moved during the day see Appendix L.

CHAPTER XVII

The June-Offensive : Operation "Battleaxe"

The June-offensive lasted from 15 to 18 June 1941, and consisted of operations by the Eescarpment Force, the Halfaya Group, the Coast Force and the 7th Armoured Division. The Armoured Division was to begin the offensive by opening a gap in the frontier wire through which the Escarpment Force was to move west to attack the area Musaid—Bir Wair—Capuzzo from the side. The 7th Armoured Brigade was first to do this particular task, after which it was to try and take the Hafid Ridge, an important feature dominating the area of the operations.

Operations of the Escarpment Force

The attack started at daybreak on 15 June 1941. The first objective to be captured was Point 207 (518364) which was taken by the 7th Armoured Brigade early that morning. Later in the morning, at 0715 hours, the Brigade was relieved by a squadron of the 4th Royal Tank Regiment and was thus enabled to move north to its next bound, the frontier wire. Forcing a gap through the wire, somewhere near Boundary post 42, it proceeded towards its main objective—the Hafid Ridge, west of Capuzzo.[1] In the meanwhile another armoured formation was preparing to follow the 7th Armoured Brigade through the gap. It was the 4th Armoured Brigade, which formed a part of the Escarpment Force. It consisted of the 7th RTR[2] and the 4th RTR and was then located at Qaret Abu Faris. It began to move at 0815 hours in the direction of the gap at Boundary Post 42, on arriving where it split itself into two groups ; the 7th RTR proceeded to the area Nezuet Ghirba (507368) to be ready for the attack on Capuzzo, while the 4th RTR (less two squadrons) moved north-east to clear up the area Boundary Post 38—Point 206.

Although the direction of the attack was very much different from what the Axis commanders might have expected, it turned out that in this direction too the Axis forces were well entrenched and in a position to offer stiff resistance. The resistance increased after the first hour of the surprise for the Axis was over, and hard fighting followed. This lasted till 1100 hours, by which time the outline of the battle had become sufficiently distinct to enable the Divisional

[1] *Report* by Comd. 4 Ind. Div. on Ops. in Western Desert 15-18 June 41, pp. 11-14
[2] Royal Tank Regiment.

Commander to reassess the situation. The general trend of the events, at that hour, showed that the Allied successes so far had been only partial and insignificant. The attack by the 4th RTR on Boundary Post 38—Point 206 was under progress and Boundary Post 38 had been captured, but Point 206 was offering stubborn resistance. The 7th Armoured Brigade had reached Hafid Ridge as planned, but had been shelled off that position immediately and was engaged in a tank battle somewhere in the same area. Capuzzo had not been attacked, but the 7th RTR had reached the area Nezuet Ghirba in readiness for the task. The Guards Brigade was also in the process of moving up to the same place; while the Advance Divisional Headquarters and the Headquarters 4th Armoured Brigade were already concentrated there to assist in the attack on Capuzzo which was due to commence within a few hours.

There were, however, two outstanding obstacles which needed to be reduced before an attack on Capuzzo could get under way. They were Point 206 and the Hafid Ridge. The 7th Armoured Brigade was ordered to continue its efforts to take the Hafid Ridge. But as to Point 206, it was obviousy necessary to reinforce the 4th RTR. This was done by restoring to that unit one of its squadrons which, at the commencement of the operation, had been placed on Point 207. That squadron, which was still there, was now ordered to clear up the Point 206 area instead. After that it was to hand it over to a company of 2 Scots Guards (Guards Brigade) and return to its original task.

It was thus not until 1130 hours that morning that steps could be taken to fix the zero hour for the attack on Capuzzo. In doing so, consideration had to be given to the time that the artillery would need to get ready for the action. It was obvious that the maximum artillery support would be necessary if the attack was to have a fair chance of success, for the morning's experience had shown that the defences of the Axis, even on their vulnerable flank, were by no means weak or scanty. The zero hour was therefore fixed for 1300 hours to allow the Artillery Group to move into position for support. It was later postponed to 1330 hours at the request of the Commander, Royal Artillery. However, at 1315 hours, a new situation arose which called for a further extension of the time. A report had just then come in that about 20 Axis tanks were heavily counter-attacking Boundary Post 38. In order to allow this unexpected threat to be dealt with first, it was decided to further postpone the zero hour. But, as communication to the 7th RTR failed at this critical juncture, the zero hour continued to remain at 1300 hours.

Attack on Capuzzo

Accordingly, the attack on the Capuzzo area started exactly as scheduled. For two succeeding hours, the tanks of the 7th RTR (less one squadron) battled to overcome the Axis defences, and at last managed to gain control of the area Capuzzo—Bir Wair, at about 1530 hours. The next step, as prearranged, was for two battalions of the Guards Brigade Group, with one squadron of the 7th RTR in close support, to go in and take over the area. But there was a breakdown of the wireless as the infantry got on the move; and a tank-battle was still in progress a little ahead. It was, therefore, not possible for the two battalions, namely 3 Coldstream Guards and 1 Royal Buffs, to push ahead as planned. They, thus, could not reach the area until 1730 hours, which was long after the scheduled hour. But they lost no time in consolidating the position, the task being carried out by 65 Anti-tank Regiment with 31 Field Regiment Royal Artillery in close support. Support was also available, if required, from the 7th Royal Tank Regiment which, on being relieved, had just then rallied further forward. The action ended with tanks and infantry having taken 150 Axis prisoners of war. Capuzzo had thus been taken more or less according to the plan.

The next step according to the plan was the clearing up of the positions round Musaid, Bir Musaid and the Sollum Barracks. An attack on Musaid area was therefore arranged to go in at 2000 hours with tank and artillery support, and was to be carried out by the remaining battalion of the Guards Brigade, namely the 2nd Scots Guards. But just at that hour a report was received at Force Headquarters that about one hundred Axis tanks were counter-attacking Capuzzo from the north. This upset all calculations about securing Musaid, since all available tanks were now required to meet the counter-attack and no tank support could be given to Scots Guards. The 2nd Scots Guards was therefore ordered to postpone the action and the commander was asked, instead, to secure that objective by a silent night attack in his own time, if possible.[3]

Fighting at Hafid Ridge and Point 206

Meanwhile, fighting was in progress in the other parts of the battle area also, particularly at Hafid Ridge and Point 206. Hafid Ridge was still holding out in spite of ceaseless efforts of the 7th Armoured Brigade to take it. But Point 206 had capitulated that evening, yielding 200 Axis prisoners and four guns. Amongst other actions of that evening were a few attacks by Axis bombers on the Divisional Headquarters and some desultory tank fights on the left flank of the Escarpment Force.

On the night of 15 June, the battle situation was what might be well described as unstable or fluid. At 2000 hours commanders of the 7th Armoured and 4th Indian Divisions met together to review

[3] W/D, 4 Div.

the situation and recast their plans, if necessary. They decided that the 4th Indian Division should concentrate on clearing the Musaid—Sollum Barracks area while the 7th Armoured Division would clear the Hafid Ridge. Just at that stage it became known from air reports that three Axis columns were moving on Sidi Azeiz, some ten miles north-west of Capuzzo. They were estimated to reach the battle area by the morning and their approach presaged a tank attack on the Capuzzo area. To meet that threat, it was essential to know the Axis tank dispositions; and detailed tactical reconnaissance reports were therefore asked for to be got ready before the morning. In the meantime, the Advance Headquarters of the 4th Indian Division, and the Headquarters of Guards Brigade, moved east of the frontier wire for safety, where they spent the night in the vicinity of Boundary Post 39, waiting for the daylight.

Thus ended a whole day of fighting for the Escarpment Force and the 7th Armoured Division. It may be recalled that simultaneously with the Escarpment Force, two other forces had gone into action on the same day. They were the Coast Force and the Halfaya Group. It is now necessary to review the activities of those two forces on that vital day, so as to complete the picture of the operations on the whole front during 15 June, the first day of the June-offensive.

Operations of the Halfaya Group

The Halfaya Group had passed under the command of the Coast Force at 0515 hours on the morning of 15 June. The infantry part of the Coast Force consisted of the 11th Indian Infantry Brigade, with its two battalions (2 Mahrattas and 1 Raj Rif); while the third battalion of that brigade, the 2 Camerons, along with a squadron of the 4th RTR and a platoon of anti-tank guns, constituted the Halfaya Group. The specific task of the Halfaya Group was to attack Halfaya Pass in conjunction with the rest of the Coast Force.

Operations of the Coast Force

The Coast Force moved forward at 0515 hours on 15 June to attack Halfaya according to the plan. It had been arranged that while it would be attacking the Pass from below the escarpment, the Halfaya Group would be doing so from the top.

The action on the top of the escarpment commenced at first light but did not go as planned. Camerons moved forward in motor transport behind a squadron of the 4th RTR. This squadron consisted of 12 'I' Tanks and went a little distance ahead of the infantry, the whole force heading straight for the Halfaya Pass. At first all seemed to go well and the tanks had practically reached their objective. But, before the infantry could follow up, an unforeseen development intervened to upset all calculations. Contrary to expectations the tanks met a very heavy fire from some unsuspected Axis guns sited on the top of the Pass. The fire was so close that all tanks but one were put out of action. It appeared to proceed from two 88-mm anti-aircraft guns (or possibly 6-inch naval guns) which must have been mounted on concrete emplacements. The guns had held their fire until the tanks were well within their range and had then opened up suddenly. The surprise was complete, as also the disaster to the unfortunate squadron of the 4th RTR. The tank support of 2 Camerons was thus wiped out at one blow.[4]

Deprived of their armour the Camerons tried to make progress on their own. This was especially difficult as the ground was flat and offered little cover and the day was breaking. Nevertheless, one company managed to reach its objective. The remaining two companies tried to follow up and were making good progress until attacked on the way by armoured fighting vehicles. As a result one company was lost, but the other got away and joined the first company on the objective.

Having reached the vicinity of the Halfaya pass, with all these losses, the commander of 2 Camerons discovered that he was not in a particularly happy position. His battalion was now in the open with only one 'I' tank and two anti-tank guns for warding off a counter-attack that must come sooner or later. His wireless communications with 25 Field Regiment in the coastal plain had also broken down. He was therefore without any artillery support and in no condition to hold on to his gains. In the circumstances he decided to withdraw to more suitable positions at the head of the wadis, which was done at 1125 hours.

While the Halfaya Group was contending against these difficulties, the Coast Force was trying to capture Halfaya from below the escarpment. It had advanced along the slopes of the escarpment, clearing wadis and broken ground *en route*. The Mahrattas were leading and two troops (six tanks) of the 4th RTR were advancing in the plain in close co-operation. The tanks, however, ran into a minefield and four out of the six were immediately put out of action. As this was happening, the leading infantry, 2 Mahrattas, came under a heavy artillery and machine-gun fire and suffered many casualties. This severely handicapped its efforts for a further progress and the prospects of the Coast Force reaching its objective were thereafter far from hopeful.

It was now obvious to the Force commander that the nature of the operation had changed completely. From being primarily a tank attack supported by infantry and artillery in a weakly defended direction, it had become an unaided infantry attack against a

[4] W/Ds 4 Div., 11 Bde., CIH, 1 Raj Rif, 2 Mahrattas.

position clearly held in some strength. Further, owing to the difficulties of signal communication—a handicap inherent in the conditions of desert warfare—it was not possible to build up and co-ordinate another attack to suit the changed conditions without some intervening delay. The position therefore remained unaltered for the rest of the night.

On the night of 15 June, the general situation was as follows:—The area Capuzzo—Bir Wair had been captured by the Escarpment Force and was being consolidated in spite of heavy counter-attacks. The 7th Armoured Division had been unable to take Hafid Ridge and was still continuing its efforts. The expected tank battle had not matured at the appointed time, but there were indications that the Axis tanks were coming out of Tobruk to offer a battle. The attempt to seize Halfaya had definitely failed and a fresh effort was necessary. A deliberate infantry attack, that is, without the support of tanks, was therefore to be attempted the following morning. A night advance was under preparation to clear the Musaid area.[5]

Operations on 16 June

The first action of the succeeding morning, 16 June, was the attack on Musaid by the Escarpment Force. It was carried out by 2 Scots Guards with bayonets at 0440 hours and was eminently successful. By 0515 hours the objective had been captured and the Scots Guards had taken 92 prisoners, with 18 killed, at a cost to themselves of 7 other ranks wounded.

With Musaid under control, the battalion commander felt confident of successfully taking the Sollum Barracks also, which were on the top of the escarpment. The attack commenced at 1130 hours that morning, supported by 212 Medium Battery and one battery 31 Field Regiment RA. The attacking troops motored up to within 600 yards of the objective under cover of an artillery bombardment and then went in with bayonets. Once again the bayonet attack proved immensely successful. The Sollum Barracks area was cleared up satisfactorily. Scots Guards took 220 prisoners and inflicted further casualties amounting to 30 killed and wounded, their own losses being two killed and six wounded.

Thus the day, 16 June, had opened somewhat satisfactorily for the Allied troops. But it was a short-lived satisfaction; for almost simultaneously a new menace was coming into existence in that rather large numbers of Axis tanks had arrived on the scene and were evidently preparing for a big attack. This was not wholly unexpected since in the over-all Allied plan of the June-offensive

[5] *Report* by Comd. 4 Ind. Div. on Ops. in Western Desert, 15-18 June, 41, pp. 16-18.

a tank battle had not only been visualised but had actually been planned for. The plan had been based on the expectation that the Allied operations in the Capuzzo and Musaid areas would succeed in drawing the Axis armour into action and that it would be possible for the 7th Armoured Division to defeat it decisively in that area so as to open up the road to Tobruk. But the anticipated tank battle had not materialised so far. However, the moment had now come. Axis tanks from Tobruk, which were earlier known to be heading for the battle area, had at last arrived there and on the morning of the 16th were in the vicinity of Capuzzo, which was then being held by 1 Buffs of the Guards Brigade.

The area held by 1 Buffs was shelled heavily that morning. The battalion sustained a few casualties, its commanding officer being mortally wounded, after which, for the rest of the day, it was harassed and attacked by Axis tanks almost continuously. All through that day the various positions occupied by its units and sections were approached by groups of those tanks which at one time numbered eighty; and three definite counter-attacks developed, each with a force estimated at forty armoured fighting vehicles. But on each occasion the attacking or approaching tanks were driven back by Allied tanks supported by 31 Field Regiment RA. The anti-tank guns were, as a rule, unable to get into action, since Axis tanks kept themselves well beyond their range. Only on one occasion did the latter venture within their ranging distance, when they offered good targets to 257 Battery of 65 Anti-tank Regiment which disabled no less than sixteen medium tanks.

The Axis tank attacks were not supported by artillery or from the air, though there were instances of some desultory bombing and shelling in their behalf. Their aircraft, for example, bombed forward positions of the Escarpment Force and those of the Brigade and Advance Divisional Headquarters in the afternoon, causing a few casualties. Three of them were shot down by the 9th Australian Light Anti-aircraft Battery and one ME110 by the 4th Light Anti-aircraft Battery. Then once again there was a heavy shelling of the area of 1 Buffs towards the close of the day.

Thus the second day of the June-offensive (16 June) was marked by tank skirmishes which in one case flared up into a regular battle. The tank attacks of the Axis on that day were directed simultaneously against two objectives—the Capuzzo area, already dealt with, and the frontier-wire area from Boundary Post 45 to Sidi Omar; and it was in the latter area that the early skirmishes led, at last, to the first big battle between Allied cruisers and the Axis armour. The cruisers eventually succeeded in beating back all attacks. But they were themselves counter-attacked later in the day while they were waiting to refill, and had to withdraw approximately 5000 yards east of the frontier wire.⁶

A little later, at about 1800 hours, 1 Buffs reported another large concentration of Axis armoured vehicles moving west across their front. At dusk, the Advance Divisional Headquarters, by way of precaution against further air and ground attacks, moved about a mile to the south so as to get protection of a troop of PAVO (11 Cav, 3rd Ind Mot Bde) who were then holding a position thereabout. As the evening light began to fade the Divisional Headquarters was able to see another tank battle in progress in an area to its south. Small parties of Axis troops had, by that time, succeeded in crossing the frontier wire at about Boundary Post 45 and entering the Egyptian territory.

Further efforts to take Halfaya

While the tank battles were in progress, the Escarpment Force was consolidating its gains in the Capuzzo, Musaid and Sollum areas; and the Coast Force was making determined efforts to seize the Halfaya Pass. The Allies, it will be remembered, had attacked the Halfaya position on the preceding day with tanks. But the attempt had failed and it had been decided to make a deliberate infantry attack on it the following morning without the support of tanks. That attack went in at 0730 hours. The attacking battalions were, as before, 2 Mahrattas and 1 Rajputana Rifles, with 2 Camerons in reserve. The action commenced with the Mahrattas operating along the lower slopes of the escarpment and the Rajputana Rifles moving along the top. The objective of the Rajputana Rifles, who were moving parallel to and on the left of the Mahrattas, was the top of the Halfaya Pass. The attack from below the escarpment was to be made by the Mahrattas themselves.⁷

The two battalions met with resistance from the very start, but with great perseverance managed to cover about one thousand yards of the most exposed ground, before being held up just short of their objectives. Further progress was not possible owing to the increasing intensity of the opposition. When held up, the forward elements of 1 Raj Rif were only about 500 yards from the road which went through the Halfaya Pass; and to help it over that short distance, the battalion commander decided to call out 2 Camerons from the reserve. The Camerons were ordered to secure the left and rear of 1 Raj Rif, after which the latter were to attempt a move-on again. But it took some time to complete the new dispositions, so that it was not until 1930 hours that the Rajputana Rifles were ready to make a second attack. This they did on a front of

⁶ *Report* by Comd. 4 Ind. Div.
⁷ W/Ds. 4 Div., 11 Bde., 1 Raj Rif, 2 Mahrattas.

some 800 yards, behind a barrage of all obtainable artillery. Their commanding officer was unfortunately killed just before the action commenced when his presence was most essential. The attack progressed about 500 yards more, but was finally held up in the plain, between the two wadi-heads. In achieving even that little progress the battalion sustained such heavy casualties that it became necessary to reorganise it into two companies. The position it had arrived in was also not safe; and it was therefore withdrawn during the night to the cover of the wadi-heads to carry out the reorganisation.[8]

The second attempt to take the Halfaya position had thus ended in a failure like the first one. It was now decided to rest the troops during the night and make yet another effort the next day. The first attempt had been a tank attack supported by artillery and infantry; the second was a purely infantry attack; now the third was to be an infiltrating attack. Infantry were to infiltrate forward taking each Axis post in turn by concentrating all available artillery on it.

At this stage, 2100 hours on the night of 16 June, the general battle situation was neither very satisfactory nor the reverse. In the Capuzzo area, the Sollum Barracks and Musaid had been cleared. Forward elements of the Guards Brigade had reached the top of the escarpment and were overlooking Sollum, although the escarpment road to Sollum was still not in their hands. All Axis counter-attacks against Capuzzo had been successfully dealt with. The 7th Armoured Division had scored initial successes against the Axis armour but was now being pressed back by superior numbers. In the frontier area, forward Axis elements had already crossed into the Egyptian territory between Boundary Post 45 and Sidi Omar. In the Halfaya sector two attempts to take that position had failed; a third was to be made the following morning.

The Tank Battle

That attempt, however, was not made. For in the few hours before the morning, the situation had changed so radically that it was not considered safe to carry out that plan. This was due to the increasing threat from the Axis tanks. The first intimation of the adverse change reached the Force Headquarters just after midnight when an urgent message was received from the commander of the 7th Armoured Division, requesting that the 4th Armoured Brigade and the 8th Field Regiment RA be made available to him by 0600 hours in the area Bir Nuh, as he feared that Axis tanks would make a dash for Halfaya, from the west, early in the morning. If they got through the Pass in sufficient strength, there was a

[8] *Ibid.*

danger of the Allied forces to the west of Sollum—Halfaya line being cut off completely. Such a contingency, in his opinion, could be best forestalled by intercepting Axis tanks on their way to Halfaya and destroying as much armour as possible. He had accordingly asked for the additional armoured brigade and field artillery to be transferred to Bir Nuh, from where they would be in a position to support the 7th Armoured Brigade and be available, at the same time, to counter-attack Axis tanks trying to reach Halfaya.[9]

In any case, the situation was no longer one in which the Allied forces could continue to remain on the offensive. It had changed overnight and now demanded immediate defensive measures for averting what might well turn out to be a disaster. The request for reinforcements from the 7th Armoured Division was reasonable in that context. But it was not easy to accede to it in its entirety, as there was a great deficiency of tanks in the 4th Armoured Brigade which at that time consisted of only two regiments, the 4th and 7th RTRs. The number of "I" tanks which could then be regarded as operational runners in the 4th RTR was only fifteen, and in the 7th RTR it was no more than five, although the latter was expecting a reinforcement of sixteen more by the next evening. Further, it was essential that some at least of these few tanks remained in support of the Guards Brigade in the triangle Capuzzo—Sollum—Halfaya which was now becoming more exposed. In the circumstances it was decided that, instead of sending the whole of the 4th Armoured Brigade to Bir Nuh, only the 4th RTR be sent with 8 Field Regiment RA in support. The 7th RTR was to remain in the Capuzzo area as a support to the Guards Brigade.

Accordingly, the 4th RTR left its location, Boundary Post 39, at 0600 hours in the morning and made for Bir Nuh. Almost immediately thereafter twelve Axis medium tanks came out of the area Boundary Posts 38—39 and attacked the Headquarters of the Guards Brigade and the Advance Headquarters of the Division. Among the medium tanks were Mark IVs which fired a sort of thin, moving barrage of 75-mm shells as they came on. It was quite a spectacular performance and the attack, though not wholly unexpected, succeeded in taking the two headquarters by surprise. Both the headquarters beat a hasty retreat and, after performing what the commander of the 4th Indian Division afterwards characterised as a "record withdrawal", managed to get under the cover of the 4th RTR which had then reached Point 207 on its way to Bir Nuh.

Surveying the situation from there, the two headquarters noticed that the Guards Brigade was in the imminent danger of being isolated. It had only a four-mile-wide escarpment route left as its

[9] *Report* by Comd. 4 Ind. Div. on Ops. in Western Desert, 15-18 June 41, pp. 20-22.

life-line for food and water which any further easterly advance of the Axis tanks might well have succeeded in cutting off completely. Moreover, the south-west flank of this brigade was also open and vulnerable, and there was a danger of its being attacked and over-run from that direction as well. To obviate this last possibility especially, the commander of the 4th Armoured Brigade was asked to counter-attack with the 4th RTR, back on to the positions at Boundary Posts 38 and 39, so as to remove the threat to that flank of the Guards Brigade. The operation was carried out successfully and the threat was at least temporarily averted.

But now the much desired tank battle had burst out in all its fury. The Allied commanders who had originally planned to draw the Axis armour into action found that their prayer had been granted with a vengeance. Not only did the Axis armoured forces come out into the open but they did so with such superiority of armour and at so awkward a place and time that there was nothing left for the Allied force but to withdraw as hurriedly as possible. The armoured battle was already on since the early morning of 17 June and Axis tanks were rapidly gaining the upper hand.

Thus at 0915 hours on the morning of that day, the 7th Armoured Division reported that it was falling back in face of heavy odds. One of its cruiser regiments, according to the report, was being heavily engaged by Axis tanks near about Sidi Suleiman and another had withdrawn to Bir el Khireigat. It had therefore no option but to effect a general withdrawal.[19]

Allied Withdrawal

On receipt of that report, the Force Commander asked the Brigade Commander and the Commander Royal Artillery to be prepared for a possible withdrawal, which might take place either by day or by night and would have to be via the Halfway House where a bridgehead would be formed. But that was at 0930 hours. At 1000 hours, however, came the news that the 4th RTR, which had earlier that morning saved a situation by counter-attacking at Boundary Posts 38-39, had been itself attacked heavily from the direction of Boundary Post 40 and was withdrawing troop by troop. This was a major disaster. It was now clear to all concerned that the situation was very grave and that unless the Guards Brigade Group was immediately withdrawn the whole of it might well be lost. Commander 22nd Guards Brigade was therefore ordered at 1030 hours to put his plans for withdrawal into immediate effect. The orders were conveyed by wireless as well as through liaison officers to leave no room for doubt. The withdrawal was to be initiated by 1 Buffs

[19] *Ibid.*

from Capuzzo at 1100 hours and the remaining battalions were to follow at half-hourly intervals.

It was essential for a successful withdrawal that the four-mile-wide gap on the escarpment be kept open for the brigade to pass through. This burden fell on the 4th Armoured Brigade which was to prevent Axis forces from closing the corridor. An air cover over the withdrawing troops was also arranged. There were two principal areas from which troops were to be extricated, Capuzzo and Point 207. In the former were three battalions of Guards Brigade and in the latter the two headquarters and some infantry. On reaching Halfway House, 1 Buffs were to form a bridgehead on the other side of the narrow valley through which the retiring forces were to pass to the back areas of comparative safety.

The Buffs led the withdrawal as planned, starting at 1100 hours. The other two battalions followed in the wake, moving off respectively at 1130 and 1200 hours. A small party of tanks of the 4th Armoured Brigade protected the west flank of the withdrawal and also engaged the Axis forces in the area of Point 207 so as to prevent their closing the gap. The last retiring battalion slipped out between two columns of Axis armoured fighting vehicles approaching from opposite directions (north and south) to close the gap. The tail of the withdrawal was shelled heavily by the Axis as those last vehicles were leaving the area, while a battery of 31 Field Regiment RA also received a similar treatment on its way back. Except for these minor incidents the Guards Brigade completed its withdrawal without much trouble. As to the headquarters and infantry on Pt. 207, they were also retiring simultaneously. The withdrawal of the headquarters, which were then being shelled, began at 1045 hours. But the infantry did not get on the move until 1115 hours. However, by 1215 hours, the last batch was out of the reach of the Axis.

By 1530 hours on 17 June, the Guards Brigade Group had reached Halfway House without the loss of a single man or gun. The 1 Buffs then formed a bridgehead there and the remaining battalions moved down to positions in the coastal sector. An effective fighter screen covered the troops all the time, watching their passage through the narrow valley. At the same time, the remnants of the 4th Armoured Brigade put up an extremely gallant fight all day long, near Pt. 207 and Bir Nuh, to stop Axis armoured vehicles from getting in and creating havoc amidst the mass of transport and guns withdrawing down the narrow corridor. Late that evening, however, Axis bombers made an appearance, putting in a heavy dive-bombing attack which fell entirely on 8 Field Regiment RA then in support of the 4th Armoured Brigade. Three guns were knocked out and some seventy casualties sustained, including three officers killed, during the brief space of that attack.

In spite of this the withdrawal continued steadily, and the rear elements of the main withdrawing force cleared the other end of the Halfway House corridor just before nightfall. Work was then begun at 2200 hours for demolishing the track behind the force leading down the escarpment. The withdrawal finally came to an end late in the night (17/18 June) when Guards Brigade reached its destination in the back area. A little later its three battalions took up their new positions respectively at Buq Buq, Alam Hamid (582375) and Sidi Barrani.

End of the June-Offensive

The withdrawal thus completed was that of the Escarpment Force, which had failed in its role of capturing the triangle Sollum—Bir Wair—Capuzzo and had been obliged to vacate positions already occupied. The 7th Armoured Division had similarly failed in its purpose of defeating and eliminating the Axis armour and, as we shall see presently, the Coast Force too had fared no better. The whole of the June-offensive was thus a big failure.

The first intimation that the Coast Force had of the grave danger it was in, came at 1000 hours on the morning of 17 June, when it received the information that a large force of Axis armoured vehicles was heading for Halfaya. At that moment the Coast Force was in the area Sidi Suleiman (518356) and was composed of the 11th Indian Infantry Brigade, the Central India Horse, an anti-tank company, two tanks, two artillery regiments and a medium battery. This was hardly the right composition for resisting tank attacks and, for that as well as other reasons, it was decided to withdraw it to safer positions.

Orders for withdrawal which were sent out through a liaison officer reached the 11th Brigade at 1430 hours. The brigade was to withdraw that night to the area Ilwet el Naas (552363), the infantry marching on foot. The Brigade Commander issued instructions to his forward battalions to start thinning out at 2100 hours and be clear of their respective areas by 2200 hours. Meanwhile, they were to strengthen and prepare rear positions to which they were to retire. Later, however, the plan of withdrawal to Ilwet el Naas was altered on more transport becoming available, when Western Desert Force ordered that the marching infantry should, as soon as clear of the Axis forces, embus in the additional transport then available and move back direct to Buq Buq.

But it had not been easy to get clear of the Axis troops. For, at 2015 hours, a little before the time fixed for the withdrawal, some Axis armoured vehicles and lorried infantry had appeared on the scene and begun attacking the forward troops, while their medium artillery put down a heavy concentration on the Brigade Headquarters and on the guns of the 25th Field Regiment RA. This artillery attack did not, however, deter the Field Regiment from engaging the Axis tanks and armoured vehicles which had, in the meanwhile, closed up to the positions of the 11th Brigade. A close-range duel followed and the hostile tanks were prevented from penetrating the infantry positions. The Axis infantry, too, was not quick in following up and so, taking advantage of that and of the gradually increasing darkness, the 11th Indian Infantry Brigade broke off the engagement and withdrew to schedule with surprisingly few casualties. The 25th Field Regiment also succeeded in getting all its guns away which was a remarkable achievement in the existing conditions. The infantry embussed as arranged, and the whole Brigade Group, less Central India Horse, then moved during the night back to Baqqush, the Central India Horse taking up a covering position in the coastal plain.[11]

At 0600 hours the next morning, 18 June, when the withdrawal was nearing completion, the situation was as follows:—The 11th Indian Infantry Brigade was still moving towards Baqqush. The Central India Horse was in contact with Axis patrols and had been reinforced by PAVO (less one squadron). The 22 Guards Brigade was disposed in the areas Buq Buq, Alam Hamid and Sidi Barrani with the 31st Field Regiment RA in support of the forward troops. The Axis forces had not followed up the withdrawal, presumably because of the losses suffered during the preceding engagements. Possibly due to a similar reason, the Axis aircraft were also unusually inactive. Headquarters 4th Indian Division was at Sidi Barrani and the 7th Armoured Division in the coastal sector.

The rest of that day (18 June) was spent in reorganising and redisposing the troops withdrawn. The 7th Armoured Division took over the command of the whole forward area and 22 Guards Brigade of the coastal sector, while the Headquarters 4th Indian Division moved down to Baqqush.

Thus ended "Battleaxe", an ambitious and well-planned operation, the object of which was to drive the Axis beyond Tobruk. The object had not been attained and the operation had failed signally. Among other reasons the failure was no doubt due to an underestimation of General Rommel's armoured strength. But like all failures this one had its redeeming features. For one thing, General Rommel had been obliged to disclose the quality and strength of his armour; for another, much experience had been gained and several important lessons learnt which proved useful in subsequent operations.

[11] W/Ds, 11 Bde., CIH.

CHAPTER XVIII

Period of Consolidation

The Buq Buq—Sofafi Line

As has been seen in the preceding chapter, the operations between 15 and 18 June had failed. The Allied forces had withdrawn almost back to the area from which they had started for action. Had General Rommel cared to pursue, it is problematic as to what he might not have achieved. A second impact from his powerful armoured columns might well have sent the Western Desert Force reeling back to Alamein or Alexandria.

But as things turned out General Rommel did not proceed to exploit his success. For one thing, he was unable to get past Tobruk. For another, he was probably still being restrained by the German Mediterranean Command who had earlier admonished him on his wasteful ways of conducting the campaign. Or, it is possible, that he had sustained such severe losses in trying to push back the June-offensive that he had no strength left to carry out the pursuit. It is also possible that Germany having invaded Russia at about this time (22 June), the German High Command did not want any additional entanglements in North Africa. Whatever the reason or reasons, the inability or reluctance of General Rommel to follow up the Allied withdrawal gave the Western Desert Force an opportunity to halt, to reorganise and to form a stable line of defence.

The line so formed extended from Buq Buq to Sofafi. It was hardly a proper line, being no more than a row of weakly defended localities, but so long as Rommel was not going to subject it to a test, it was good enough as a defensive system that could be later improved, strengthened and made the starting place for a fresh offensive.[1]

The Buq Buq—Sofafi line was the most advanced of the Allied defensive screens. While it was being held, efforts were made to construct further lines behind it so as to give it a depth. Thus there sprang up three defensive areas behind the Buq Buq—Sofafi line during the period July—October 1941. They were one behind the other, and from the areas of their location came to be known as the Matruh defences, the Baqqush Box and the Alamein Box.

Change in tactics

While the defences were being thus strengthened, the forward

[1] W/D. 4 Ind. Div., June-July 41.

area was being held by small columns of mobile infantry and artillery. The 7th Armoured Division which had been badly mauled in its AFVs was withdrawn to Matruh to refit and replace its losses. The policy of the Allied Desert Force which so far was offensive was hereafter changed into what its Operation Instruction of 23 June described as an "offensive-defensive attitude". The immediate tactical objects of the Force were also changed so as to correspond with the change in the policy. They were now defined as follows: (a) to harass the Axis force so as to cause the maximum interference with their preparations for an advance; (b) to resist such an advance as far as practicable, otherwise to effect a fighting withdrawal in which harassing operations were to continue : (c) if forced to fight, to try and bring the Axis troops to battle in an area considered suitable for developing the maximum fighting strength of the Desert Force.

Such an area was Mersa Matruh—Minqar Qaim (720310)—Minqar Sidi Hamza el Gharbi (710320), where the 7th Armoured Division and the Matruh garrison could fight in conjunction, while the Baqqush garrison gave depth to the defence in the rear.[2]

The Baqqush Box

The locality in which the Baqqush garrison was camped constituted the main defensive area of the Western Desert Force. Because of the enclosed, boxlike structure of its defensive system, it came to be spoken of as the Baqqush Box. The function of the Box was to enclose and secure the water sources of that particular area and give depth to the Matruh defences. It was also to form a strongly defended perimeter to which the forward troops could fall back if forced to do so. The garrison of the Box consisted of the 4th Indian Division (less the 5th Indian Infantry Brigade), and the Polish Brigade. The 22nd Guards Brigade, which was then in the Matruh area, was also to move into the Box, less the 2nd Scots Guards and 1st Buffs who were to remain outside until pushed into it by the pressure of an Axis advance.

The Matruh Defences

The area immediately in front of the Baqqush Box, comprising the Matruh defences, was the responsibility of the 7th Armoured Division. In that task it was to be assisted by the 2nd Scots Guards, 1st Buffs and some units of the 4th Indian Division. Other fighting units, required for guarding the area outside the Box, were found by reorganising the Coastal and Escarpment Forces and from the Support Group of the 7th Armoured Division. Out of these units was also formed a special force called the Landing Ground Group.[3]

[2] W/Ds. 4 Div., 7 Bde., 11 Bde.
[3] Ibid.

The Landing Ground Group was charged with the protection of the Sidi Barrani airfields against airborne or parachute landings. The airfields to be thus protected were 0.2 (599379), 0.3 (599376) and 0.5 (604372). The protecting force comprised one battalion of the 22nd Guards Brigade with the troop-carrying transport, one battery 31st Field Regiment (6 guns), one battery 65th Anti-Tank Regiment, 9th Australian Light Anti-Aircraft Battery, and ancillary units from the 4th Indian Division. It was to guard the landing grounds only so long as the RAF fighter aircraft could use them to operate over Tobruk in defence of the besieged garrison. Should that become impossible through hostile action, it was to be withdrawn into the Baqqush Box under orders of the 7th Armoured Division.

The garrisoning and defending forces inside the Baqqush Box were, as already stated, the 4th Indian Division and the 22nd Guards Brigade. The former had only two brigades with itself, the 7th and 11th Indian Infantry Brigades, and the latter only one battalion, the 3rd Coldstream Guards. The units under the 7th Brigade were 1 Royal Sussex, 4 Sikh and 4/16 Punjab. Those under the 11th Bdigade were 2 Camerons, 2 Mahrattas and 1 Raj Rif. To the 7th Brigade was assigned the task of guarding the south face of the Box and to the 11th the east face. West face was the responsibility of the Guards Brigade whilst the north face was open to the sea and therefore under protection of the Royal Navy. As to the absent brigade of the 4th Indian Division, namely the 5th Indian Infantry Brigade, it was then away in Syria; while the two absent battalions of the Guards Brigade were, as already mentioned, outside the Baqqush Box guarding the forward area.[4]

It was in this way that the Western Desert Force tried to stabilise a position immediately after its withdrawal, that is, by hastily organising defences at Matruh and Baqqush. The next step was to consolidate that position in anticipation of General Rommel's further advance. From all intelligence then available it appeared that the advance would not be long delayed. At the end of June 1941, the *Afrika Korps* was reported to be reinforcing feverishly. Therefore, an attack in full strength could be expected to mature at any time in July 1941.

Further construction of defences

Thus it was essential for General Wavell's Desert Force to get ready for a defensive battle as speedily as possible. To that end tasks were assigned to the 4th Indian, the 7th Armoured and the 1st South African Divisions to be carried out in their respective sectors. The 4th Indian Division was to construct two defended

---

[4] Precise locations of units inside the Baqqush Box are given in Appendix P.

localities in its area, at about re-entrants 71303336 and 70683213.⁵ The 7th Armoured Division was to repair its mechanical defects with all possible speed and, in the meanwhile, obtain identifications of Axis units by sending out strong patrols. The task of the 1st South African Division was to prepare a one-infantry-brigade position, with its forward defended localities resting on a general line along 712 northing.⁶ This last position was to extend from the coast to the northern end of Wadi Majid; thence along the Wadi's eastern edge to its head; thence south of Charing Cross to Abar Ailet Idris (714327).⁷

The object of that one-brigade defence position was to deny to the Axis troops such observation of the Matruh defences as could be obtained from the Matruh escarpment. On the other hand the aim of the two defended localities to be constructed by the 4th Indian Division was more complex. It was to build and man defences with an eye to the operational necessities of the 7th Armoured Division. These were three: firstly, a pivot was required round which the 'I' tanks of the Armoured Division could operate; secondly, the Axis armoured forces had to be driven into an open area where the Allied tanks could easily get at them; and finally, a gap had to be kept open in the escarpment, so that the Armoured Division's 'I' tanks would be able to pass southwards if required to operate there. The 4th Indian Division was to site its defended localities in such a way as to ensure these facilities to the 7th Armoured Division. The gap was to be across the major escarpment at Minqar Sidi Hamza el Gharbi (710320). The open ground towards which the Axis tanks were to be manoeuvred for a battle was an area to the south of the minor escarpment, stretching southeast to north-west at an approximate distance of 4 miles from Abar Ailet Idris; and the pivot was to be a well-defended post to which the 'I' tanks could rally after every engagement, for petrol, stores and maintenance.⁸

Each of the defended localities to be built by the 4th Indian Division was to be designed to hold one infantry company, one troop of field guns, (either 18-pounders or 25-pounders), and seven days' food and water. It had been made clear to the Commander 4th Indian Division by the higher command that the situation was considered "desperate" in view of the overwhelming armoured strength at General Rommel's disposal. The degree of resistance to be offered by those posts was therefore to be "the last man and the last round", and to that end the posts were to be

---

⁵ The references are to the GSGS map, Western Desert, 1/100,000, Matruh East.
⁶ Ibid.
⁷ Ibid.
⁸ W/D HQ, 4 Ind. Div. June-July 41.

designed to function as "independent commands". Once a battle was joined, each "post-command" was to become a defended island, enclosed by minefields, and be solely responsible for the conduct of its own defence. Before the battle, however, and otherwise as far as the tactical situation would permit, it could depend on the 7th Armoured Division for its information and on the 4th Indian Division for its administration.

Between the two defended localities described above, there was a featureless area devoid of any tank obstacle. In that area, the 4th Indian Division was called upon by sheer tactical necessity to lay out a third post similar to the other two. Since there was no landmark in that area, the siting of the third post was to be governed by purely arithmetical factors, the absence of obstacles being compensated for by minefields and that of natural cover by camouflage.

Thus, it was with a hastily extemporised defence structure of this nature that the Desert Force of General Wavell hoped to stave off the threatened advance of the *Afrika Korps*. But the *Afrika Korps* failed to arrive as expected. For, instead of advancing towards Egypt, as he might have then done with profit, General Rommel preferred to stay put at Capuzzo and Halfaya. He actually went a step further and applied himself to strengthening his Bardia and Halfaya positions, as if he himself feared an Allied counter-attack. June 1941 passed into July, and July into August but still there was no sign of the avalanche of tanks that he was expected to unleash against the shaky Allied defences. It is true that Germany was then too preoccupied with the war against Russia to take enough interest in North Africa. But complacency was at a discount at the Allied headquarters after General Rommel had falsified their erstwhile predictions by launching his offensive two months earlier than they had prophesied. Speculation at the Allied headquarters therefore put down the delay to Rommel's not having finished with reinforcing the men, armour and armament necessary for a big and final drive. Were that process to take time, there was still a chance for the Allied High Command to build a more permanent line of defences behind the comparatively fragile screen of the Baqqush Box.

Beginnings of the Alamein Line

The rudiments of such a line were already existing. They consisted of a narrow strip of desert land, with the El Alamein railway station at one end and the Qattara Depression at the other. The station area had already been converted into a fortified box which was then being held by the 1st South African Division. The Qattara Depression was an impassable obstacle in itself, being too soft and marshy to be crossed by vehicles and too widespread for them to go round. The strip of desert land thus became a bottle-neck between the fortified box and the Qattara Depression. Were strong defensive positions to be built across that strip, the whole of it would then become a line of defence capable of holding up an Axis advance of fairly great strength. Such a line did ultimately come into being. It turned out to be the last-ditch Allied stand for saving Egypt and, indeed, the whole of the Middle East and India. It subsequently became known all over the world as the famous Alamein Line and proved to be one of the major turning points of World War II. However, at this stage, its potentialities were known to none and only sheer necessity dictated that the work of building it be taken into hand.

Accordingly, the work of bringing into existence the earliest semblance of the Alamein Line formed a part of the Allied defence programme from July to October 1941. It happened that at this time the 5th Indian Division had just returned to Egypt having finished its operations in East Africa. It had arrived at Port Suez on 29 June. By mid-July its rear parties had followed up completing its three brigades—the 9th, 10th and 29th. It was then in the back area being spread out in a series of tented camps from El Tahag to Quassasin, not far from Alamein; and a decision was now taken to put this division on the job of constructing the proposed line of defence at El Alamein.[9]

The 5th Indian Division starts work on Alamein Line

The Commander of the 5th Indian Division held a divisional conference at Quassasin on 3 August 1941, and explained the contemplated plan to his formation and unit commanders. The plan envisaged that the strip of desert land between El Alamein and the Qattara Depression be secured by building three main fortresses. Fortress 'A' was to be positioned in an area at the junction of Barrel Route and the Alamein track; 'B' in the area Jebel Kalakh; and 'C' in the area Naqb Abu Dweiss. They were to be ready for occupation by 1 October 1941.

In conformity with that plan, the 5th Indian Division carried out preliminary surveys of the three fortress positions and made arrangements for moving up to the Alamein position. Just then it received orders, emanating from the Commander-in-Chief Middle East Forces, requiring the division, less the 29th Brigade, to proceed to Kirkuk, in northern Iraq, for protecting the oil installations of the Iraq Petroleum Co. Quitting its unfinished work on the Alamein Line, the division left for Kirkuk on 31 August 1941.

[9] W/Ds. HQ, 5 Div., 9 Bde., 10 Bde., 29 Bde.

Its 29th Brigade moved to Baqqush in relief of the 161st Indian Infantry Brigade.

The Tobruk and the Siwa Defences

Construction of the Alamein Line was only one item in the Allied defence programme from July to October 1941. Other items related to Tobruk and the oasis of Siwa. Tobruk, it may be recalled, had been besieged by the Axis since April 1941. It was being held by a garrison composed of the 9th Australian Division and other Allied units. The besieged garrison was entrenched behind a semi-circular ring of defences, some ten miles in diameter, surrounding the Tobruk harbour. It had been already attacked twice by General Rommel who was beaten off on both the occasions. The Axis forces had, however, succeeded in May 1941 in pushing a salient into the western section of the defence at Meduar. But, by July 1941, the Tobruk garrison had regained most of the sailent and was defying the *Afrika Korps* with impunity.

It was essential that Tobruk be actively assisted and sustained so as to enable it to perform its function properly. That function was to harass the Axis flank by continual raids and patrols and by a display of aggressive intentions. There was no doubt that the task was being carried out with great daring and was succeeding in its aim. General Rommel was being kept perpetually nervous as to his flank facing Tobruk and seemed reluctant to advance until it had been got rid of first. To keep that threat alive it was necessary to give protection to Tobruk from air and sea.

The Oasis of Siwa

As to the Oasis of Siwa, it formed an important item of the Allied defence scheme because of its tactical value. In addition to being important for defence it was also a position of value for any Allied offensive that would have to be undertaken to push the Axis back beyond the Egyptian border.

To understand the tactical importance of Siwa it is necessary to glance at the layout of the boundary line separating Egypt from the Italian territory. The line was built by the Italians and consisted of about 200 miles of barbed wire fencing running north and south. One end of the fence rested on the sea, near about Sollum; the other end on an oasis known as the Oasis of Giarabub, or thereabouts. To the south of Giarabub was the Great Sand Sea, a vast area of trackless desert impassable to any type of mechanical vehicles. It was, therefore, not necessary to extend the barbed wire fencing beyond Giarabub. It was, however, necessary to maintain a strong military garrison there which the Italians had done.

What the Oasis of Giarabub was to the Italians, the Oasis of Siwa was to the Allies, namely a tactical desert post. Siwa stood on the Allied side of the border line, almost opposite to Giarabub and about 80 miles to its east. The two oases were connected together by a road which ran across the boundary, passing through a minor locality known as Ain Melfa. Giarabub, Melfa and Siwa were all situated in a depression which was an extension of the Qattara Depression, and between Giarabub and Siwa were a series of salt-water lakes. The importance of Melfa lay in the fact that only through it was an entrance possible to the escarpment for the traffic approaching from the west. In the earlier stages of the war, Giarabub and Melfa were Italian possessions while Siwa was British. If the Axis forces decided to turn Giarabub into a strong tactical position they could always deploy, through Melfa, on to the escarpment which was the general battle ground. Thereby they would place themselves in a position to attack the desert flank of any Allied force whether retreating or advancing across the escarpment. They could do that all the better if they seized Siwa and turned it also into a strong tactical base, since it was more spacious and better in climate and water supply than Giarabub.

This menace to the outpost of Siwa, as well as to the Allied flank, had been taken full notice of by General Wavell early in March 1941. It will be remembered that during his advance across Cyrenaica he had placed a force opposite to Giarabub to contain its Italian garrison of about 1000 men. Later, when General Wavell's advance had progressed deep into Cyrenaica, the Italian garrison found itself cut off and was easily attacked and captured by an Australian force on 21 March 1941. General Rommel made no effort thereafter to recapture Giarabub, presumably because he could not spare ground forces for its continued occupation. He therefore contented himself by occasional bombing from the air to prevent any serious construction of fortifications in either of these two areas. However, at a time when the Allied forces were being driven to bay and the Axis had supremacy, at least in tanks, it was mere common prudence to strengthen the oases garrisons. Such a step was taken in August 1941 when the 7th Indian Infantry Brigade was despatched to garrison Giarabub and Siwa. Prior to that, Giarabub was being held by detachments of the 4th Indian Division, and Siwa by those of the 1st South African Division.[10]

The Oases Force

Thus on 13 August 1941, the 7th Indian Infantry Brigade was ordered to proceed to Siwa. On reaching there it was to assume

[10] W/Ds. HQ, 4 Div., 7 Bde., 4 Sikh, 4/16 Punjab.

command of the detachments at both the oases. Its main task was to patrol the approaches to Giarabub, Siwa and Melfa and defend the oases against any form of attack. If overwhelmed, it was to retire after carrying out a scheme of demolitions. If the Axis tried to advance eastward from Siwa, it was to impose delay on its pace by fighting a harassing rearward action. The three battalions constituting the 7th Brigade were, 1 Royal Sussex, 4/11 Sikh and 4/16 Punjab. Of these, 4/11 Sikh had been despatched to Siwa a week before the whole brigade was ordered to proceed there. Accordingly the Sikh battalion was in its position at Giarabub on 6 August. The remainder of the brigade reached Siwa on 15 August. Later, that is on 2 September, the 7th Brigade transferred its headquarters to Giarabub. There, during the period 30 September to 3 October 1941, it was relieved by a formation of the 5th Indian Division, namely the 29th Indian Infantry Brigade, which, with other units under its command, came to be known as the Oases Group or the Oases Force.[11]

Aim of Allied defences

The ultimate aim of the Allied defence scheme, from June to October 1941, was the protection of the Nile Delta. This was sought to be achieved by covering the Delta with a protective screen consisting of the Matruh defences, the Baqqush Box and the proposed Alamein line. The Oases Force and the Tobruk garrison were additional buttresses on either flanks. All these defences were essentially static in nature. The mobile part was limited to short, sharp, intermittent clashes on the Matruh and Tobruk fronts and occasional air raids on all fronts. This state of affairs lasted from June to November 1941. In the meanwhile the most important question of mounting an offensive to regain the lost ground was being studied and considered at various levels. On the Axis side, too, it was the same. General Rommel had fortified Bardia and Halfaya to make them unapproachable from sea and impregnable from land. His mobile troops and tanks ranged in periodical clashes with the Allied tanks and patrols and he, too, was busy preparing for an offensive.

A race for supplies

In fact, it was a race between the Axis and the Allied high commands as to which of the two would be able to launch the attack first. Both sides were training vigorously. Both were building themselves up in men, armour and equipment; and both were straining every nerve to pull in as much supply and reinforcement as could be got across the seas.

[11] W/Ds. 7 Bde., 29 Bde.

The battle of supply raged incessantly from the end of June to the end of October 1941.

Changes in Middle East Command

To all outward appearances, the period June to October 1941 was a period of calm. But behind that facade were going on vigorous defensive and offensive preparations on both sides, accompanied by the usual patrol activity and continual fight for information concerning each other's dispositions. The beginning of this period, July 1941, was marked by an important event. There took place a change of higher commands both in the Allied and the Axis camps. Until the end of June 1941, General Sir A. P. Wavell was the Commander-in-Chief of the Allied forces in the Middle East. He was transferred to India as the Commander-in-Chief India Command and his place in the Middle East was taken by General Sir Claude J. Auchinleck who relieved him on 5 July 1941. At about the same time two other appointments were made. General Sir Alan Cunningham was appointed commander of the XIII Corps, the former Western Desert Force, and General Sir Henry Maitland Wilson became commander of the newly formed army of the Middle East, of which more later. On the Axis side General Garibaldi, who was the Supreme Commander of the Axis forces in Libya, gave place to General Ettore Bastico on 19 July 1941.

CHAPTER XIX

The Period of Reorganisation

General Auchinleck assumes command

General Auchinleck assumed command of the Middle East on 5 July 1941. The situation he inherited from his predecessor may be summed up as follows:—The June offensive in North Africa had failed but General Rommel had been halted. The withdrawal to Matruh and Baqqush had been completed. Work on the Matruh defences was nearly finished but the Baqqush Box was still incomplete. Construction of the Alamein Line had not been taken in hand and the Oasis Group had not been formed. But Tobruk had been stabilised and was functioning satisfactorily. Outside North Africa, Eritrea and Abyssinia had been practically subjugated though not fully. The Axis-inspired revolt in Iraq had been suppressed. The Allied invasion of Syria was progressing well and was drawing to a close. Cyprus was more or less out of the danger zone because of Germany's failure in Syria. Iran was about to be invaded by the Allies. Above all, Germany had attacked Russia and was too heavily engaged there to cause any immediate trouble in the Middle East.

On assuming command General Auchinleck discovered that in the Middle East there existed an efficient machinery for settling matters expeditiously and ensuring close co-operation among the three services—the army, navy and air. It may be of interest here to review it briefly. First, on the highest level stood the Middle East War Council, which was presided over by the Minister of State and concerned itself chiefly with political matters.[1] Military matters not having a political side were not its primary concern. Next below was the Middle East Defence Committee, which was composed of the Commanders-in-Chief of the three services with the Minister of State as the Chairman. This body dealt with major operations and plans and disposed of military matters on the highest level in the Middle East Command. Below that came the Commanders-in-Chief's own Committee which normally met once a week and was attended by Senior Staff Officers. The main task of this body was to settle all important operational and administrative questions arising from time to time. Finally, there were the several daily Staff Conferences at the General Headquarters to provide for daily inter-services liaison. Thus, a suitable organisation was already

[1] Churchill: *The Second World War*, Vol. III, p. 314.

in existence for co-ordinating the efforts of the three services when General Auchinleck took over from General Wavell.[2]

The Reorganisation

However, it was the army itself that was in a state of extreme disorganisation. That was not surprising considering the burdens that the army had been lately called upon to shoulder. General Wavell's campaigns in Libya, Eritrea, Abyssinia, Greece, Crete, Iraq and Syria had followed one another with such bewildering rapidity, and had been conducted with such inadequate resources, that a certain amount of disorganisation in the army was quite inevitable. Brigades had, by exigencies of circumstances, become separated from their divisions, and units from their brigades. Some units and formations had practically ceased to exist whilst others had been broken up and dispersed. All this called for a comprehensive programme of reorganisation. Troops had to be sorted out, posted to their proper units and re-equipped and trained.

The System of Allied Defences

While this work was in progress the needs of immediate defence could not be ignored. The most vital theatre of war in the Middle East was undoubtedly the Western Desert. Here it was necessary to have a clear-cut plan and a dependable system of defence. Three of the areas essential to the system already existed, namely Tobruk, Matruh and Baqqush; and work had just been started on preparing a fourth, namely the Alamein—Qattara area.[3]

As to the plan of defence it was necessarily dependent on several factors. One of them was the available intelligence appreciation indicating that General Rommel was not likely to be ready to attack until September 1941, especially with the Delta as his objective. Another factor for consideration was the superiority of the Axis in armour; and a third was the possibility that by September the Allied inferiority in armour might have been remedied or considerably alleviated. Finally, although Rommel was not expected to make a dash for the Delta until then, there was, nevertheless, the possibility that he would in the meanwhile try to register a series of small advances by seizing limited objectives. It was necessary to guard against such an eventuality; and to that end General Auchinleck issued instructions on 21 July 1941 to Lt.-Gen. Beresford-Peirse, who was then commanding the Western Desert Force.

---

[2] Gen. Auchinleck's *Despatch* in Supplement to the *London Gazette* of 21 Aug. 46, pp. 4215-16.

[3] Preparation of the Alamein-Qattara defensive area was by no means the same thing as construction of the Alamein line proper. Alamein line, popularly known as such, did not come into existence until much later.

Briefly, the instructions were that in the event of the Axis trying to advance further, its armour should be brought to battle in the area south of Matruh. A maximum of Allied armour was therefore to be kept concentrated in the proximity of that area and, to enable that to be done, no serviceable cruiser or "I" tank was to be located in the "boxes" at Matruh or Baqqush. The tank battle was to be fought by the 7th (British) Armoured Division, and effective infantry support was to be given to the tanks; for which, positions were to be prepared to the west and south of Matruh for occupation by not more than two infantry brigades.

A few days later, on 30 July, General Auchinleck issued further instructions elaborating his policy for the defence of Egypt. These related to the actions to be taken respectively by the X Corps, the Western Desert Force and the BTE (British Troops in Egypt), in the event of a forced withdrawal from Matruh, necessitating the 'last-ditch' defence of Egypt. At this date the Allied army in Egypt consisted broadly of two principal groups—the Western Desert Force for the forward area, and the British Troops in Egypt for the line of communications area, the boundary between the two being the line Daba—Bab el Qaud—Longitude 28° to Qaret Agnes—Sitra —Siwa—Jalo. The X Corps formed a part of the Western Desert Force and comprised the 5th Indian Division and the 2nd South African Division. General Auchinleck's orders to these troops were that in the event of a forced withdrawal from Matruh, the X Corps was to try and hold a position near El Alamein with the help of a small armoured force. But should the required armour be not available, it was to fall back further and hold a sector of the Delta defences. Should the Western Desert Force be unable to stop the advance of the Axis by any means, it could also retire as a whole towards El Alamein or the Delta, but less the Matruh and Baqqush Boxes which were to be left behind intact. The troops so withdrawn were in that case to pass under the command of the General Officer Commanding-in-Chief British Troops in Egypt, and the Matruh and Baqqush Boxes were thereafter to be under the direct command of the General Headquarters.

The Long-range Plan

It will be seen from the above that General Auchinleck's plan was, in the first instance, to try and defeat the German tanks by engaging them in a battle south of Matruh. If that did not succeed, a final stand was to be made at El Alamein or further east to defend the Delta, during which time the Matruh and Baqqush Boxes were to function as self-defending islands on the flank of the Axis in much the same way as Tobruk had been doing for some time past. This was essentially a short-term plan pending the completion of the

Alamein Line and the arrival of the expected reinforcements and equipment. There was also a long-range plan. It envisaged an early resumption of a full-scale offensive for driving the Axis out of Libya.

In fact, one of the chief preoccupations of General Auchinleck was the mounting of such an offensive. He was keen on taking advantage of the favourable conditions created by the Russian campaign. To consider the same matter he was summoned to London by the Prime Minister of the United Kingdom where, at a joint meeting of the War Cabinet and the Defence Committee, he explained the situation and the various problems involved. Briefly, he is said to have summed up the situation as follows. The Axis had superiority in armour, the Allies in air. Both were fairly even on land. Outside North Africa, there was not much fighting except in Syria. Provided the state of affairs remained unaltered, he could retake Cyrenaica, given two armoured divisions, preferably three. If that was not possible he could undertake a limited offensive to relieve Tobruk with one armoured division plus an armoured brigade and one army tank brigade. He did not think either offensive was possible in September. The first of November was the earliest date by which he could get ready; but only if the necessary equipment, especially tanks, reached him in sufficient time.[4] From the thorough and lengthy discussions that took place at those meetings, there emerged the final decision of the British Government to take offensive in North Africa at the earliest opportunity or at the latest in November, after which the British Prime Minister set himself the task of assisting in making this possible.[5]

Preparations for the offensive

On his return from London, General Auchinleck commenced making preparations for the proposed offensive in Libya. Unlike the earlier campaign of General Wavell, this one was not intended to stop after driving the Axis beyond Cyrenaica but was aimed at clearing the whole of Libya, that is Tripolitania as well as Cyrenaica, in one non-stop sweep. The idea was to leave no foothold to the Axis whence it could revive the threat to Egypt. Whilst details of such a plan were being worked out at various command and staff levels, General Auchinleck addressed himself to the task of putting the Middle East Command on a sounder footing. There were several problems that demanded his urgent attention, and these had to be resolved before the commencement of the campaign lest they

---

[4] Gen. Auchinleck's *Despatch* in Supplement to the *London Gazette* dated 15-1-48. p. 311.
[5] Churchill: *The Second World War*, Vol. III, p. 361.

should interfere with it later. Most of them were administrative, whilst others related to training, reorganisation, re-equipment, internal security, external relations etc. It is necessary here to take note of a few of them. The Allied operations in Greece, Crete, Iraq, Syria, Persia and East Africa having come to an end, vast masses of fighting men had been released from operational duties. The majority of them had come to be concentrated in Egypt, Syria and Palestine by September 1941, and had to be appropriately re-grouped for the coming offensive.

The Eighth and the Ninth Armies

It was clear that from this point of time, the strength of the fighting forces would be better reckoned in terms of armies and corps rather than in those of divisions and brigades as heretofore. The existing operational headquarters were obviously too small and inadequate for these greatly enhanced numbers and the widened scope of work and responsibilities. General Auchinleck, therefore, decided to alter the basic organisation so as to bring it in harmony with the changed situation. This he did by dividing his command into two main operational theatres, giving to each theatre a separate army with its own army headquarters and an independent base and line of communications area. The two armies were to be called respectively, the Eighth and Ninth Army. Western Desert was marked out as the operational theatre of the Eighth Army; and Syria and Palestine as that of the Ninth Army. The Base and Line of Communication area of each Army was to be directly administered by the General Headquarters at Cairo. Thereby the two Armies, it was hoped, would be relieved of much of their administrative work and be able to confine their attention to the operational tasks almost exclusively.

Accordingly, the Headquarters of the Eighth Army, commanded by Lieutenant-General Sir Alan Cunningham, came into existence on 26 September 1941. All Western Desert troops, forward of Bahig, passed under his command, except those in Tobruk which were not taken over until 30 October. As a result, Headquarters British Troops in Egypt became in effect a large Base and Line of Communications command. Administratively, it was responsible for the upkeep of the Eighth Army, and operationally for internal security and anti-aircraft defence of the Egyptian base. The Western Desert Force, as such, disappeared finally and Headquarters Western Desert Force became HQ XIII Corps for the second and the last time. As to the Ninth Army, it was commanded by General Sir Henry Maitland Wilson with Palestine and Transjordan as its Base and Line of Communication area. To cope with the increased administrative work at his General Headquarters in Cairo, General

Auchinleck procured sanction for the appointment of a Lieutenant-General (Administration) as his principal administrative staff-officer.

Administrative reorganisation

As the proposed reinforcements began to arrive in the Middle East, it became necessary to increase the capacity of docks and to provide additional means of transport and communications to cope with the growing volume of traffic. Work was taken in hand to meet those demands and, as one of the important measures, the Western Desert Railway was extended by a further 75 miles from its railhead at Matruh, the new railhead now being at Bir Misheifa, south of Sidi Barrani. The railway track between Suez and Ismailia was likewise doubled and more tracks were laid elsewhere in Egypt, Palestine and Syria. A swing bridge was constructed over the Suez Canal; a mammoth depot was established at Kantara East; deep water quays were ordered to be built at Suez and Safaga, and about one mile of wharfage was added to the existing wharfs in the same area. In directions other than communications, too, there were similar improvements. An oil pipeline was laid from Suez to Port Said with a carrying capacity of one thousand tons of oil per day. The existing desert water pipeline was extended beyond Matruh. Wells were bored throughout the Middle East and hundreds of miles of distribution pipes were laid to tap them. The road mileage was increased. Aerodromes and landing grounds were constructed with the forthcoming operations in view. New hospitals were established and more camps were laid out. The supply system was overhauled, local production was co-ordinated and stimulated; civilian labour, to supplement the uniformed labour, was augmented and various other steps were taken to bring up the Middle East Command to a general state of readiness for the offensive planned to take place in November.[6]

Training and Equipment

As to training, every aspect of it received the closest attention, although in the earlier stages the scope was limited by deficiencies in equipment. Emphasis was specially laid on desert movements of mechanised columns by day and night; and one full brigade of the 5th Indian Division was given a complete course at the Combined Training Centre at Kabrit. The Middle East Officers' Cadet Training Unit was reorganised and expanded, while, to speed up the training, the specialist wings were abolished and a new system evolved of giving the same eight weeks' basic course to all cadets, after which the would-be specialists were passed on to the school of

---

[6] Gen. Auchinleck's *Despatch* in Supplement to the *London Gazette*, p. 4224.

General Sir Archibald P. Wavell

General Sir Claude J. Auchinleck

Indian Sappers and Miners building bridge in Nile Delta, October 1941

Oasis of Siwa

the arm concerned. The annual training capacity was thus increased from 1300 to 2040 cadets. Care was also taken to maintain special courses and centres for imparting training in parachuting, anti-aircraft work, coast defence, ordnance service, infantry regimental specialists' work, camouflage and other similar arms of the services.

The re-equipping of units was carried out on a fairly elaborate scale, and with no less speed, as large consignments of war material of every description began to flow into the Middle East. Vehicles of all types arrived in a steady stream from Great Britain, Canada, Australia and South Africa and from July onwards tanks and trucks from the United States also began to come in increasing numbers. Thus, between 1 July and 31 October, the Middle East had received about 34,000 trucks, 2100 armoured vehicles, 600 field guns, 200 anti-tank guns, 240 anti-aircraft guns, 3,700 Bren guns, 900 mortars, 80,000 rifles and vast quantities of ammunition and other equipment. Large as these consignments were, they were not enough to carry out a full-scale equipment of the troops and were necessarily limited in quantity by the amount of shipping space available. Lack of shipping space was also reflected in the shortage of personnel and administrative units but had to be accepted as inevitable. The shortage extended to every arm of the service, the rearward units suffering the most. In many cases, even units actually in contact with the Axis forces could not be brought up to their full establishment. This state of affairs lasted till the very end, so that just before the opening of the main offensive the over-all deficit in personnel was a little above sixteen per cent.

Nevertheless, the personnel and equipment already received, as also the later arrivals, were disposed to the best advantage possible and deficiences were thereby compensated for to a degree. As a result there was an all-round improvement, of which the most striking example was offered by the armoured formations. Thus, for instance, at the beginning of July, it was not possible to put into the field anything more than a poorly equipped and undersized 7th Armoured Division, and two armoured car regiments in no better conditions. Yet, by the end of October, through re-equipment and additions, this force had been brought up to requirement and further strengthened by the addition of the 2nd Armoured Brigade, the 1st Army Tank Brigade, the 32nd Army Tank Brigade (less one battalion) and three armoured car regiments. Similar improvements took place in the condition of the other formations also. The worn-out or unsuitable transport of the 1st South African Division, for example, was replaced by some 1300 new vehicles. The transport of the 4th Indian Division, which was below establishment, was also completed in a similar way; while the New Zealand

Division, whose transport had been lost in Greece, was allotted enough of it to bring it up to its full establishment.

There was also a similar improvement in the state of artillery, both field and anti-aircraft. Especially was there an increase in the number of 2-pounder guns though there was a deficiency of personnel to man them; and, although there were not enough of the larger guns to bring all regiments to the full scale of 48 guns, it was yet found possible to equip at least four artillery regiments on the newly-decided scale of 64 guns per regiment, by giving 16 eight-pounder guns to each as a part of its standard requirements.

The situation was even better in the anti-aircraft section. Arrivals of new anti-aircraft artillery had increased the fire-power of the heavy artillery by 40% and of the light by 75%. This particularly enabled the carrying out of a new plan for forming divisional anti-aircraft regiments which had been non-existent so far. This was done by giving to each division a full light anti-aircraft regiment to be controlled and disposed by it independently for its own defence. It was possible to form several such regiments on a 36-gun basis, of which five were assigned to the Eighth Army and two to the 1st Australian Corps in the Ninth Army. A corresponding improvement was also brought about in the anti-tank section. The total absence of anti-tank regiments in all infantry divisions was remedied by converting the 149th Field and 73rd Medium Regiments into anti-tank artillery.

Likewise, the Royal Engineers and Signals units also benefited from the arrivals of stores and supplies between July and October 1941. American bridging equipment with its own special carriers came in, in sufficient numbers; and it was also possible to satisfy scale requirement of most of the Royal Engineer units in respect of all other important items. But there was always a chronic shortage of personnel, which continued to the last in spite of the receipt of several complete engineering units from the United Kingdom and South and East Africa.

As to the Corps of Signals, although its needs always outstripped the supplies, it was yet possible to put the forward areas immediately on a satisfactory basis. But this could not be done for the line of communication area in the rear which always suffered from a shortage of permanent line equipments, like the telephones, switchboards, etc. The wireless equipment also fell short of the normal demand. But the acutest shortage felt by the Signals was in the matter of personnel, since, in spite of the arrival of two corps-signal units, there still remained an over-all deficiency of about 6000 men, which could not be remedied before the opening of the November offensive.

Reorganisation of the other Arms

Reorganisation in the other arms of the service kept pace with that in the infantry and the supporting arms. The Royal Army Service Corps improved its shortage and distribution facilities for petrol, oil and lubricants as more stores reached the field. It was also able to reduce its own deficiencies in vehicles and manpower, so that at the end of October 1941, it had 75% of the authorised strength in vehicles and 85% in manpower. But it was not possible for it for a long time thereafter to have a satisfactory reserve of vehicles.

In the same way, the Royal Army Ordnance Corps too was able, to a large extent, to remedy its shortage of vehicles and equipment. But it always suffered from a serious lack of machine tools and essential units, which could not be remedied before the commencement of the offensive. However, much was accomplished by a complete reorganisation of the repairs and spare-parts section of this service. In a war of swift movements and long communications, it had to cater for the speedy repairing of vehicles and quick delivery of spare parts and fighting stores wherever required. To make that possible two innovations were effected. Firstly, a system was evolved whereby repairs were cancelled out by "assembly exchanges" and the scale of second-line workshop repairs was thereby reduced; and secondly, special units were formed to deliver stores and accessories by air as well as by road.

Like other services, the medical service also received its share of replenishment in personnel, stores and transport from the incoming supply convoys, so that by the end of October 1941, the Royal Army Medical Corps in the Middle East had been almost completely equipped. Still, its transport resources always seemed to be lagging behind its minimum needs because the authorised scale was itself too inadequate to meet the highly mobile conditions involved in desert warfare. Previous experience had emphasised the necessity for a larger proportion of motor ambulance convoys; and also for the mobile type of casualty clearing stations and surgical units instead of the static ones. Motor ambulances, however, arrived very slowly and were not enough even when the main offensive opened. But it was possible to organise mobile casualty clearing stations by providing some three units with enough transport for carrying one light section and about half of heavy section in a single shift. Mobile surgical teams were also similarly formed and provided with their own transport, so that major surgery could be performed as far forward as the main dressing stations. Finally, efforts were made to increase the number of hospital beds which were considerably short and also to bring up the number of the field hygiene sections, which always remained too few for the needs of the forces.

Need to relieve Australian troops

Thus, as a necessary prelude to the Allied offensive scheduled to take place in November 1941, the whole of the Middle East had been reorganised and put in a condition to take the strain of the forthcoming campaign. Within the space of four months, from 1 July to 31 October 1941, a force of practically two Armies had been re-equipped and provided with bases, supply depots, training centres, reinforcement camps and establishments. It had not been an easy task. Units had to be restored to their parent formations. Reinforcements had to be found in their proper places. Detachments and drafts had to be distributed to the best advantage of the service concerned. Equipment had to be utilised in such a way as to meet all operational needs and yet permit a maximum of training to be carried out. At the same time Cyprus had to be reinforced and garrisoned; surplus units from Syria and East Africa had to be withdrawn; and concentration of troops had to be begun for the forthcoming offensive. In the midst of all these varied activities, a major relief move had to be undertaken, *i.e.* the Australian forces garrisoning Tobruk had to be relieved in response to a pressing representation received from the Australian Government.

As early as 18 July 1941, General Auchinleck had received a letter from Lieutenant-General Sir Thomas Blamey, commanding the Australian Imperial Forces, on the subject of Tobruk. General Blamey urged that immediate consideration be given to the question of relieving the garrison of Tobruk on the ground of great deterioration having taken place in the health of his men. The letter was written at the instance of the Australian Government and General Blamey further represented that, should it be found impracticable to relieve the garrison in its entirety, the relief of at least the Australian portion of the garrison should be considered as being very desirable in view of a growing feeling in his country that all Australian forces should be concentrated under one command and be made to serve as one force. The British Government had been committed to such a policy by an earlier agreement with the Australian Government, and now there was a popular demand for its fulfilment which was not without some justification. War Office, therefore, backed up the request of Lieutenant-General Blamey and urged the Middle East Command to try and give full effect to the Australian Government's desire.[7]

General Auchinleck agreed with the request in principle but was doubtful whether such an undertaking would be at all practicable. He felt that the moment was not opportune, and that the urgency was not so great as to justify subjecting the Mediterranean

---

[7] Winston S. Churchill: *The Second World War*, Vol. III, pp. 367-72.

naval units to the triple strain of evacuating the garrison, replacing it by a new one and protecting the shores of North Africa. However, in deference to the wishes of the Australian Government, a plan was drawn up for bringing the Australian forces out of Tobruk, bit by bit, over a stretch of successive periods of moonless nights. It was also decided to bring out the 18th (Indian) KEO Cavalry along with the Australians. Thus, according to the final plan of relief, the 18th Australian Infantry Brigade, and the 18th KEO Cavalry, were to be relieved by the Polish Independent Brigade ; and the rest of the 9th Australian Division by the 70th (British) Division. The moonless periods chosen were, in the first instance, 19-29 August, 18-28 September and 12-26 October. The first relief was carried out with complete success but subsequent reliefs proved somewhat difficult. These too were, however, eventually successful and, by 26 October 1941, all Australian troops were out of Tobruk except the 2/13th Battalion which remained there until the siege was finally raised.

Change in Tobruk Command

The exit of the Australian Division from Tobruk automatically led to a change in that command after which the new incumbent was Major-General R. Mack. Scobie, commanding the 70th Division, who took over from the Australian commander, Major-General Morshead, on 22 October 1941.

CHAPTER XX

Operation 'Crusader'

The November-offensive

As narrated in the preceding account, July to October 1941 was a period of intensive preparations throughout the Middle East Command. The Middle East war machine was being geared to the opening of the November-offensive during that period, and even while that process was yet half complete General Auchinleck had issued instructions to Lieutenant-General Sir Alan Cunningham, commander-designate of the Eighth Army, to prepare the necessary plans for launching the offensive. The instructions were contained in a personal letter, dated 2 September 1941, which set out the decision of General Auchinleck to drive the Axis out of North Africa and gave several details as to how he proposed to carry out that task. General Cunningham was to be ready with his plans, or alternative recommendations, by 1 October 1941.[1]

The plan was to be based on the assumption that the whole of Libya, that is Tripolitania as well as Cyrenaica, was to be cleared in one non-stop sweep. The idea was to leave no foothold to the Axis in North Africa and, at the same time, to secure Tripoli as a possible base for launching a future offensive against Italy in case it was decided to do so subsequently. The attack was to take place early in November 1941 and was to be called operation 'Crusader'. By then, the necessary forces were expected to be trained and concentrated and the requisite maintenance arrangements completed for a prolonged offensive.

General Auchinleck proposed to carry out this offensive in two successive phases. The aim of the first phase was the capture of Cyrenaica, that of the second Tripolitania. An immediate object, however, which was also an important part of the first phase, was to destroy the Axis armoured force at the earliest opportunity.

Two courses seemed possible for carrying out the first phase of the offensive. One was to advance through the desert and the other to do so along the coast. In the former case, the main striking force would have to be based on Giarabub, and it would have to move through Jalo, keeping all the time to the interior of the desert. Its object in that case would be to take the Axis forces in the rear and to capture Benghazi. Such a move, though evidently not along

---

[1] Gen. Auchinleck's *Despatch* in Supplement to *London Gazette*, p. 331.

the coast, would yet necessitate the placing of an additional smaller force in the coastal sector to block the path of the Axis troops towards Alexandria, and to tie up a proportion of their forces in that part of the front. In the other case, viz. a primary advance along the coast, the main striking force would have to make a direct attack towards Tobruk; while some other columns would have to simulate an advance across the desert by making a feint from the centre and the south so as to cause a dispersal of the Axis strength. General Cunningham was instructed to prepare detailed plans for both these courses of action. The plans had to be flexible and capable of being rapidly modified, lest the Axis commander change his own dispositions and tactics at the last minute, which he would certainly do if he came to know of the Allied intentions. For that reason, as well as to misguide the Axis about the true direction of the main blow, the preliminary deployment was to be on a wide front extending from Giarabub to the coast.

The forces placed at General Cunningham's disposal, for the first phase of the offensive, were two corps headquarters, one armoured division, one armoured brigade group, four infantry divisions, two infantry brigades and an army tank brigade. In addition, at a particular stage of the operations, the Tobruk garrison was to join up and assist in the campaign. That would mean an addition of four infantry brigade groups, about one hundred tanks and considerable artillery. Finally, if General Cunningham so wished, an endeavour would be made to land a brigade group behind the Axis front from the sea. But success or failure of the whole offensive was not to be made to depend on that part of the operation.

General Cunningham's plan

General Cunningham submitted his appreciation of the situation and plan to General Auchinleck on 29 September 1941. Of the two courses suggested to him, he preferred that of an attack from the centre along the coast. He rejected the other course, that is an advance through the desert, for several reasons. One of them was that the lines of communication for an attack across the desert would be long, difficult and vulnerable. Another was that such an advance would cause the Allied air and armoured forces to be split, thereby bringing about a diminution in their efficiency. Above all, the capture of Benghazi, in the rear of the Axis forces, was not likely to ensure the immediate surrender of the Axis in Eastern Cyrenaica, since the latter had built up enough reserves there to enable their troops to subsist over quite a long stretch of time. For these and other reasons General Cunningham recommended a direct attack towards Tobruk in preference to one towards Benghazi. His plan was approved at a conference of the Commanders-in-Chief of the three services on 3 October 1941. The plan, in fact, went no further than the destruction of the Axis armour and the relief of Tobruk. Subsequent actions for capturing Benghazi were to depend upon the degree of success achieved in this part of the operations.

Over-all Plan

The central idea of the plan, as accepted finally, was to draw the Axis armoured forces into a battle away from their supporting fortresses, minefields and infantry-defended localities. That was to be achieved by the Allied armoured forces moving directly on Tobruk. The two Panzer Divisions of the Axis, believed to be lying between Bardia and Tobruk, would thereby feel compelled to leave their own ground to give battle to the Allied armour. In order to make them do so the more thoroughly, it was decided to send the Allied armour along a wide detour, as far away as possible from the prepared defences of the Axis, round Sidi Omar and Capuzzo. It was calculated that the Axis force thus coming out to meet the Allied armour would number about 250 tanks. In addition, there were 138 Italian tanks whose fighting power was not considered to be of great significance and was therefore written down as being equal to about 50 German tanks. Thus a total force of about 300 Axis tanks was to be opposed by about 450 to 500 Allied cruiser and American tanks. Although this calculation proved wrong ultimately, it had seemed reasonable, at the time it was made, to believe that the Allied numerical superiority would suffice to bring about the destruction of the two Panzer Divisions. After that a motorised division, which was to follow the Allied armour, was to force a passage to Tobruk and effect a junction with its garrison. The role of the infantry for the duration of the tank battle was to be restricted merely to containing the Axis forces in the frontier area.

General Preparations

The general over-all plan having been approved, preparations for the offensive were taken in hand at once. They included administrative arrangements, reconnaissance and a preparatory bombardment of the supply lines of the Axis. The administrative arrangements were directed towards solving the two principal difficulties always to be met with in the desert—the transport and the water-supply; and the solution of both these problems seemed to call for an extension of the desert railway to the forward areas. Originally the railhead was at Matruh, about 130 miles from the frontier, the proposed battlefield itself being about 75 miles further ahead. The total distance between the railhead and the front was therefore more than twice of what would normally be considered as

To the battle of Jalo

Derna in ruins—Captured, December 1941

Benghazi captured, February 1942

After the capture of Benghazi

manageable. The forces to be maintained on the front totalled about 118,000 men, for which the average maintenance needs came to about 3,000 tons a day, water being extra. Since water had to be carried by rail and sea from Alexandria to Matruh, and thence by road to field, the carriage of water alone would take up a large proportion of transport which would otherwise be more usefully employed in carrying petrol and stores and building up reserves of ammunition. To alleviate this situation the railhead had been pushed forward 75 miles, as far as Bir Misheifa; and about 145 miles of pipeline had been laid and filled with water, between Alexandria and the forward area. In addition, ten large reservoirs and seven new pumping stations were built and brought into use. Finally, nearly 30,000 tons of munitions, fuel and supplies were stored in the forward area, just enough to sustain the full weight of the attack for about a week.

Reconnaissance of the Axis positions necessarily formed an essential part of the preparations for launching the offensive. For many weeks before the operation, every part of Libya in which Axis troops were quartered was carefully reconnoitred. The work was chiefly carried out by the Royal Air Force, the Long Range Desert Group and the armoured car regiments. As to the reconnaissance from air, the whole of the Axis line of communication, from Tripoli to the front line, was examined by the Royal Air Force and a thorough photographic survey made of all important areas between Gazala and the Egyptian frontier. The photographs thus secured made it possible to "pin-point" practically all the Axis dispositions round Tobruk. No less useful information was obtained from the land reconnaissance which was carried out behind the Axis line by the Long Range Desert Group and in front of it by the armoured car regiments. The former operated over an area approximately 500 miles from north to south and 600 miles from east to west. Its patrols secured much useful topographical information. Small parties of them lay up for long periods, up to 300 miles behind the Axis advanced positions, and took a complete census of the Axis traffic passing along the coastal road between Benghazi and Tripoli. Meanwhile, the armoured car regiments, by their reconnaissance, established the fact that the area vital to the proposed operation—south of Trigh el Abd and west of the frontier—was not being carefully guarded by the Axis troops.

The Royal Navy and the Royal Air Force shared the army's work of preparing the ground for the impending offensive, by bombarding the supply lines of the Axis which, for many weeks, were subjected to constant heavy attacks by sea and air. Many ships carrying reinforcements of men and vehicles were sunk, and many thousands of tons of stores and fuel were destroyed on the ground. The effect of this bombardment on subsequent land operations appears to have been far-reaching and considerable.

Axis forces and dispositions

The greater part of the Axis forces in North Africa, on the eve of "Crusader", was concentrated in Eastern Cyrenaica, and consisted of three armoured, two motorised and five infantry divisions. These were organised into three corps and a frontier group, the three corps being the *Afrika Korps*, the Mobile Corps and the 21st Corps. Of these, the *Afrika Korps* was entirely a German formation and the Mobile Corps a purely Italian one, while the 21st Corps and Frontier Group were Italian formations stiffened by the introduction of German elements. Thus the organisation of the Axis forces towards mid-November 1941 was as follows:—

>Panzer Gruppe, Afrika (General Rommel)
>*Afrika Korps*—
>>15th Panzer Division
>>21st Panzer Division
>>90th Light Division or Afrika Division (special infantry for overseas).
>
>*Mobile Corps*—
>>Ariete Division (Armoured)
>>Trieste Division (Motorised)
>>Trento Division
>
>*21st Corps*—
>>Bologna Division
>>Pavia Division
>>Brescia Division
>
>*Frontier Group*—
>>Savona Division
>>Elements of other divisions, German and Italian.

As regards the disposition of the Axis troops, the 21st Corps was investing Tobruk, where later it was joined by the Trento Division from the Mobile Corps. The Frontier Group was on the Libyan border, where the defences at Halfaya, Sollum and Capuzzo were being manned by some German infantry battalions, and those at Sidi Omar by the Savona Division, Bardia being manned by a mixed garrison of Germans and Italians. The 21st Panzer Division of the *Afrika Korps* was disposed astride Trigh-Capuzzo, some 12 miles south of Gambut, blocking the desert road to Tobruk, while the 15th Panzer Division and the Afrika Division were concentrated round El Adem, Ed Duda and Sidi Rezegh. As to the Italian Mobile Corps, its armoured and motorised divisions, the Ariete and Trieste, were at Bir el Gubi and Bir Hakeim respectively. An important location in the 21st Panzer Division's area, south of Gambut, was the headquarters of General Rommel, commander of the Panzer Gruppe, Afrika.

Allied forces and dispositions

On the Allied side, the forces under the Eighth Army were the XIII and the XXX Corps, the Oases Force, a reserve column and, at a later stage, the Tobruk garrison. They were organised as follows:—

    XIII Corps (Lieutenant-General A. R. Godwin-Austen)
      New Zealand Division
      (Major-General B. Freyberg),
      4th Indian Division
      (Major-General F. W. Messervy),
      1st Army Tank Brigade
      (Brigadier H. R. B. Watkins),
    XXX Corps (Lieutenant-General C. W. M. Norrie)
      7th Armoured Division
      (Major-General W. H. E. Gott),
      4th Armoured Brigade Group
      (Brigadier A. H. Gatehouse),
      1st South African Division (2 Brigades)
      (Major-General G. E. Brink),
      22 Guards (Motor) Brigade
      (Brigadier J. C. O. Marriott).
    Oases Force (Brigadier D. W. Reid)
      6th South African Armoured Car Regiment
      29th Indian Infantry Brigade (one Battalion Group).
    In reserve (Major-General I. P. de Villiers)
      2nd South African Division (2 Brigades).
    Tobruk Garrison (Major-General R. Mack. Scobie)
      70th Division
      (Major-General Scobie),
      32nd Army Tank Brigade
      (Brigadier A. C. Willison),
      Polish Carpathian Infantry Brigade Group
      (Major-General S. Kopanski).

Detailed Plan

It has been mentioned earlier, that the main object of the Eighth Army was to destroy all Axis forces in that part of Cyrenaica which lay to the east of Tobruk. That was to be achieved through a series of separate operations which were: (*a*) to isolate the Axis force on the Egyptian frontier by cutting its communications eastward, southward and at a later stage westward; (b) to further cut the eastward communications of the rest of the Axis force by holding two vital roads south of Tobruk; (c) to destroy the Axis armour; (d) to relieve Tobruk; and finally (e) to deal with the unarmoured Axis infantry, which would be mostly Italian. The Allied flanks and lines of communication were also to be protected at the same time through all those various stages of fighting.

Of the several operations mentioned above, that of isolating the Axis force on the frontier was the task of the XIII Corps. The XXX Corps was assigned the duties of holding the roads south of Tobruk, destroying the Axis armour and relieving Tobruk. The rest of the operations, namely protecting each other's flanks and lines of communication and dealing with the Axis infantry, were to be carried out by both the Corps jointly.

In order to understand how the Axis communications were to be cut, it is necessary to examine the road system in the area of the contemplated operations. In the first place there was the main coastal road. The Axis did not have an absolutely uninterrupted use of that thoroughfare, since it was cut at Tobruk by the besieged Allied garrison. But barring that brief interruption of a few miles, the rest of that road, from Tripoli to Matruh, was under the control of the Axis. However, in actual practice the interruption created no particular difficulty for the Axis, since a little to the west of Tobruk the main road bifurcated into two, and the bifurcating arm, which looped south, by-passed Tobruk and joined the main road again to the east of it. Thus the Tobruk by-pass road provided a link just at the point of interruption and enabled the Axis to have a continuous passage from west to east. A little to the south of the by-pass road, and running parallel to it, was a desert track known as Trigh-Capuzzo. It was in a serviceable condition and could be used as an alternative route.

Both the Trigh-Capuzzo as well as the Tobruk by-pass roads ran across a valley-like area of flat ground flanked by ridges on either side. The two ridges were Ed Duda and Sidi Rezegh which stood about 5,000 yards apart and commanded all the area between them, including the above-said two main lines of communication of the Axis forces. The communications of the Axis eastward of that area could therefore be effectively severed by any force securing the two ridges and cutting the Trigh-Capuzzo and the Tobruk by-pass road.

As for the Allied forces, the Axis-held coast road was obviously of no use to them. They had, however, the unfettered use of practically all the desert roads and tracks to the south of the coast road, the most important among them for the purpose of operation "Crusader" being the desert track, Trigh el Abd. This track had two offshoots, one at Bir Gibni and the other in the proximity of

Bir el Gubi. The Bir Gibni offshoot proceeded westward and joined the Tobruk by-pass road at El Adem, whence three other roads led to the Tobruk harbour. The Bir el Gubi offshoot, on the other hand, proceeded northward and merely joined the Bir Gibni track near Sidi Muftah. Bir el Gubi was a junction of several smaller desert tracks and for all practical purposes the terminal point of Trigh el Abd.

From the above description of the road system, it should be evident that Trigh el Abd would provide a suitable axis of advance for the Allies, at least in the initial stages of their move. It was, therefore, planned that before the commencement of the operations the XXX Corps was to take up positions astride the Trigh el Abd. In that event it would have the Tobruk garrison on its left and the XIII Corps on its right. It would thus be in a position to move to the right or left according to whether the one or the other needed the support of its armour. As will be easy to see from the order of battle on page 215, the bulk of the Allied armour was concentrated under the XXX Corps. Therefore it was of great importance that it should be able to manoeuvre freely, so as to intercept the Axis armour in whatever direction the latter tried to throw its weight. Bir el Gubi was regarded as a suitable pivot for such movements and it was therefore planned to secure that locality during the initial moves for the attack.

Dispositions for "Crusader"

Briefly, the more immediate plan of the Eighth Army was as follows:—The 7th Armoured Division was to be disposed astride the Trigh el Abd. Its formations for securing that track would be the 7th and 22nd Armoured Brigades and the 4th Armoured Brigade Group. Of these, the 7th was to be in the centre, the 4th on its right, and the 22nd on the left. Although the Armoured Division was to be ready to move to the right or the left as need might arise, it was considered more likely that it would be called upon to move to the left. In that event, the 7th and 22nd Brigades were to effect that leftward move, while the 4th Brigade would remain in the same position to accomplish its dual task of protecting the right flank of the other two brigades and the left flank of the XIII Corps.

Simultaneously with the above move, the XIII Corps was to pin down and cut off the Axis troops on the Egyptian frontier. That task was to be achieved chiefly by the 4th Indian Division with its three Indian infantry brigades, the 5th, 7th and 11th. Of these, the 5th Indian Infantry Brigade was to hold a line running south from Buq Buq, from where it was to perform the double function of containing the Axis troops on its front and covering the Allied base and railhead to its south ; the 7th was to get astride the frontier line and mask the Axis positions at Sidi Omar, so as to enable the Allied movements south of Sidi Omar to take place in secrecy or at least without interference ; while the 11th Indian Infantry Brigade was to contain the Axis troops at Sollum from below the escarpment. Thus, the disposition of the three Indian brigades was calculated to isolate the frontier forces of the Axis from the east and south. To complete the isolation it was necessary to intercept them also in the west. That was the task of the New Zealand Division. But no move in that direction was to take place until the Axis armour had been brought to battle by the XXX Corps and the Army Commander considered the situation to be well in hand.[2]

After the XXX and XIII Corps had taken up their dispositions, as stated above, the battle was planned to commence with the XXX Corps engaging the Axis armour. Only in the event of the battle being successful or giving a promise of success were the other subsidiary moves to take place. The principal among them related to raising of the siege of Tobruk. The basis of the plan for relieving Tobruk was the capture of the two ridges, Ed Duda and Sidi Rezegh, mentioned earlier. At a given signal the 1st South African Division was to secure a position about Sidi Rezegh, and from that dominance, to cut the Trigh-Capuzzo and the Tobruk by-pass roads on the one hand, and threaten the rear of the Axis forces investing Tobruk on the other. At the same time a part of the Tobruk garrison was to make a sortie southwards and capture the ridge Ed Duda. Almost simultaneously, if not before, the New Zealand Division from the XIII Corps was to move west and isolate the Axis force on the frontier by cutting its westward communications ; after which, the XXX and XIII Corps were to deal jointly with the Axis infantry—mostly Italian—which by that time would have been deprived of its supporting armour.

Role of the Oases Force

As mentioned earlier, the Allied forces under the Eighth Army were the XIII and XXX Corps, the Oases Force, a reserve column and, at a particular stage, the Tobruk garrison. The dispositions and the intended roles of the two Corps and the Allied troops in Tobruk were as stated above. As to the Oases Force it had a specific assignment of its own in the "Crusader" operation. Its pre-operational task, it may be recalled, was to guard the desert posts of Siwa and Giarabub, but once the operations commenced it was to become more dynamic and fulfil several other functions. One of these, and the primary one, was the protection of a particular Allied landing

[2] W/Ds 4 Div., 5 Bde., 7 Bde., 11 Bde., Nov. 41.

ground in the interior of the desert, and of the air troops in that area.

The landing ground was situated some eighty miles west of Giarabub; and the air force stationed there had been charged with the task of harassing the Axis in the coastal sector south of Benghazi, and striking at any Axis column advancing or retreating past the oasis, whenever an opportunity for doing so offered itself. This desert air-post, therefore, had considerable tactical value but it was also very vulnerable, in that at a little distance to its south-west was the oasis of Jalo, on the Axis side of the battle ground, from where the Axis could neutralise or even completely destroy that air station. To eliminate that danger, the Oases Force was charged with the secondary task of moving against Jalo and capturing that oasis.

Besides this primary task of protecting that air station and the secondary task of capturing Jalo, the Oases Force had some subsidiary tasks also. One of them was the working of a deception scheme to cause diversion of a part of the Axis armour in a false direction; another was to produce confusion and disruption in the rear of the Axis fighting forces; and the last but not the least, to co-operate with the Long Range Desert Group in the best interests of the main offensive. The latter force, it will be remembered, was given the role of observing Axis movement across the desert, including those along the approaches to Jalo from the north.

D-day

While the above plans were receiving the finishing touches, General Auchinleck was considering the question of fixing the most suitable date for opening the offensive. It was known to him that General Rommel was preparing to attack Tobruk, in which event, it would be sound tactics to let him take the initiative in launching the offensive so as to catch him facing the wrong way. General Auchinleck did seriously consider the question from that point of view. But he did not know how much delay that would involve. It was not unlikely that the Axis would not be ready for yet many weeks, and since the Allied offensive could not be deferred indefinitely merely to gain a tactical advantage of this character, General Auchinleck reluctantly fixed 18 November 1941 as the D-day.[3] It is now known that this date forestalled Rommel's move by only a week and that General Rommel had intended to attack Tobruk on 23 November, from the east.

D-day was naturally preceded by movements of troops to the forward area. The concentration of the Eighth Army in the vicinity of its battle positions took a fortnight to complete, the

[3] Gen. Auchinleck's *Despatch* in Supplement to *London Gazette*, pp. 334-35.

greater part of it having been moved up during the first two weeks of November. The movement was conducted in great secrecy with a view to taking the Axis by surprise, but was nevertheless characterized by a continuous flow of vehicles across the desert, which was as unavoidable as it was difficult to conceal. Yet, as was later discovered from the captured intelligence papers, the Axis troops had no knowledge whatsoever of the vitally significant movements that had been going on, on their flanks and rear, for several days together, which was probably due to the high degree of camouflage and dispersion that was practised, and the success of the Royal Air Force in keeping hostile reconnaissance planes out of the skies.

All Allied formations which were due to take part in the opening of the operation 'Crusader' were thus in their places by early night on 17 November, waiting for the signal to advance. There was no moon in the sky and rain was coming down heavily in the coastal area.

CHAPTER XXI

'Crusader' Begins

Eve of the November-offensive

Throughout the night of 17 November 1941, Allied troops waited in their positions for the first glimmer of the dawn. That night was the culmination of a long period of intensive preparations. Within a few hours the much-prepared offensive would be launched and the skill and resources of the two contending sides would be pitted against each other in a remorseless trial of strength. At this moment the Allied forces appeared to be better placed for action than their opponents. They had a fairly accurate idea of the Axis dispositions, but the Axis forces had no notion of how near to them the Allied troops had approached or how soon the blow would fall. All the advantages of surprise, initiative and pre-arranged co-ordination thus rested with the attacking troops. In that confidence the Allied commanders waited for the dawn to break.

The three battle areas

It will be appropriate to review at this stage the Allied and Axis dispositions on the eve of the battle. The battle front lay lengthwise along the coast, from Tobruk to the Egyptian frontier. Broadly, it fell into three battle areas which, for convenience, may be termed the Tobruk area, the frontier area and the in-between gap or the centre area. The Tobruk area included the surroundings of Tobruk. The frontier area comprised Sollum, Halfaya, Capuzzo, Bardia and Sidi Omar and the centre area embraced El Adem, Ed Duda, Sidi Rezegh, Bir el Gubi, Bir Hakeim and part of a desert track known as Trigh-Capuzzo.

Relatively to the above areas, the Allied and Axis troops were ranged opposite to each other as follows: Inside Tobruk was the besieged Allied garrison consisting of the 70th (British) Division and a Polish Infantry Brigade plus artillery and tanks.[1] Opposite to these and investing Tobruk, were four Italian infantry formations, namely the Bologna, Pavia, Brescia and Trento Divisions which had been stiffened in morale by the introduction amongst them of some three German infantry battalions. These opposing forces constituted one infantry block—that in

---

[1] The Tanks were nearly one complete brigade, and the Poles, it would appear, had their own artillery.

the Tobruk area—as distinct from a second infantry block situated on the frontier.

In the frontier area, Sollum, Capuzzo and Halfaya were manned by some German infantry battalions. Bardia was occupied by a mixed garrison of Italians and Germans; and Sidi Omar was being guarded by the Italian Savona Division. Corresponding Allied dispositions in the same area were, the 11th Indian Infantry Brigade on the coast between Sollum and Buq Buq, and the 7th Indian Infantry Brigade near Sidi Omar; the New Zealand Division being somewhere in the vicinity.[2] These Axis and Allied troops waiting for the battle in the frontier area constituted the second infantry block.

In the centre area, between the two infantry blocks, were massed the armoured forces, both Allied and Axis. The German armour, consisting of the 15th Panzer Division and some German infantry of the Afrika Division were concentrated round El Adem, Ed Duda and Sidi Rezegh. Another German armoured formation, the 21st Panzer Division, lay astride Trigh-Capuzzo, some 12 miles south of Gambut, the site of General Rommel's headquarters. The two Italian divisions, the Ariete (armoured) and the Trieste (motorised), lay respectively at Bir el Gubi and Bir Hakeim. Opposing this force was the Allied armour, comprising the 7th Armoured Division, the 4th Armoured Brigade Group and the 22nd Guards (Motor) Brigade. This force had not up to that time taken up its allotted dispositions but was waiting on the frontier to do so before the commencement of the operations. It was to place itself astride the Trigh el Abd so as to have the bulk of the Axis armour on its left and in the front. In that position it would also be able to cut the east-west communication of the Axis troops.

Such was the general disposition of the Allied and Axis forces on the eve of the battle. Briefly, the XXX Corps was to fight in the Tobruk area and the XIII Corps in the frontier area. The centre area was to be the responsibility of the armoured part of the XXX Corps and, at a later stage, of the Infantry of the XIII Corps. The operations were to be started by the XXX Corps, preferably with a tank battle. Next, the Tobruk garrison was to become active and join it after making a sortie, after which the XIII Corps was to swing into action finally and operate westwards, leading to the ultimate linking up of all the three forces.

Battle of Sidi Rezegh

Soon after dawn on 18 November, the 7th Armoured Division crossed the frontier wire-fence near Maddalena with an armoured

---

[2] The 5th Indian Infantry Brigade was then in the back-area, somewhere south west of Matruh, and was not intended to participate directly in the fighting.

car screen thrown on well in front, reaching its battle positions towards evening on the same day. By night practically all formations and units of the XXX Corps were in their appointed places. The same night, vessels of the Royal Navy bombarded the Halfaya fortifications. But neither the bombardment nor the approach of the units of the XXX Corps to their respecive positions appears to have occasioned any stir in the Axis camps. The only reaction was increased shelling in the frontier area. The Axis forces were undoubtedly unaware of the Allied preparations for an attack and apparently suspected nothing. There was, therefore, no move on their part for the whole of the first day and part of the second day, probably in the belief that the Allied movements were merely a reconnaissance in force. General Cunningham, on the other hand, finding the battle front so quiescent, decided to adhere to his plan and ordered a move towards Tobruk, whereupon the Axis armour at last came out to engage the Allied forces, and on the following day, 19 November, there began an armoured battle in the surroundings of Sidi Rezegh, which continued intermittently for several days and which has since come to be known as the Battle of Sidi Rezegh.[3]

Throughout the Battle of Sidi Rezegh, three Allied armoured brigades were confronted by the three Axis armoured divisions—that is, the 4th, 7th and 22nd Armoured Brigades were ranged against the 15th and 21st Panzer Divisions plus the Italian Ariete Division. The battle started on 19 November with practically all these coming into conflict with one another in some location or the other. The 7th Armoured Brigade, stationed on Trigh el Abd, engaged in a skirmish with some German and Italian tanks; while, on its left, the 22nd Armoured Brigade got into conflict with the Ariete Division. At the same time, on its right, the 4th Armoured Brigade found itself involved in a somewhat heavier combat with considerable German armour near Gabr Abu Milha.

Reviewing this situation a little later, the Commander XXX Corps reached the conclusion that the concentration of the Axis armour was much greater in the area to the right of the 7th Armoured Brigade than to its left; and he, therefore, transferred the 22nd Armoured Brigade from the left to the right sector. This left the Ariete Division unopposed, to remedy which he ordered the 1st South African Division to watch the gap thus created. At the same time the 7th Armoured Brigade was ordered to disengage itself from the affray it was having and proceed to Sidi Rezegh, which feature it was to capture jointly with the Support Group of the 7th Armoured Division. Simultaneously, the Tobruk garrison, too, had

[3] Gen. Auchinleck's *Despatch* in Supplement to *London Gazette*, 15 Jan. 1948, p. 336.

been ordered to make its appointed sortie to capture Ed Duda. The sortie was to link up with and be supported by the 5th South African Brigade advancing from the south.

As arranged, the Support Group got into position to launch its attack on Sidi Rezegh on the following morning, 21 November. But it was not able to make an undisturbed attack on that feature, as just half an hour before that time two strong Axis armoured columns were seen to approach Sidi Rezegh from the south-east, thus threatening its left flank. The 7th Armoured Brigade could not obviously turn to meet this new threat; for if it did, then Sidi Rezegh could not be captured at the scheduled hour, which would mean that the Tobruk garrison capturing Ed Duda would find itself in an exposed position. It was too late to cancel the Tobruk sortie and therefore the assault on Sidi Rezegh could not be called off. The other alternative was to split the force and divert a portion of it to meet the new threat while the remaining portion attacked Sidi Rezegh. That was the plan which was ultimately adopted, and two regiments of the 7th Armoured Brigade were sent forward to meet the Axis armoured columns while one remained behind to back up the effort of the Support Group in launching the scheduled attack on Sidi Rezegh.

The attack, aided by this single regiment, went in at 0830 hours and the feature was at last captured after a hard struggle. But the other two regiments were not so successful. They had engaged the Axis armoured columns of the 15th Panzer Division from the south-east and one regiment had suffered very heavily while the other had achieved very little. The action ended when the survivors of both regiments returned to the aerodrome to refuel and refit for engaging in fresh encounters. But hardly had they arrived there when the 21st Panzer Division appeared to the south of Sidi Rezegh and directly attacked the Support Group. Heavy fighting followed again which lasted until the German tanks in their turn had exhausted their fuel and withdrawn to refill.[4]

Meanwhile Sidi Rezegh continued to be dominated by the Support Group and the 7th Armoured Brigade, but it was becoming increasingly clear that the situation would not remain the same for very long; for already there were indications that the 15th and 21st Panzer Divisions had joined their forces together and were forming up for a combined counter-attack on that feature. The Support Group had become considerably weakened from the preceding armoured battles, and the 7th Armoured Brigade was by no means strong enough to withstand a combined attack from the two Panzer divisions. But there was no Allied formation in the vicinity which

---

[4] General Auchinleck's *Despatch* in Supplement to the *London Gazette*, dated 13-1-48, p. 337.

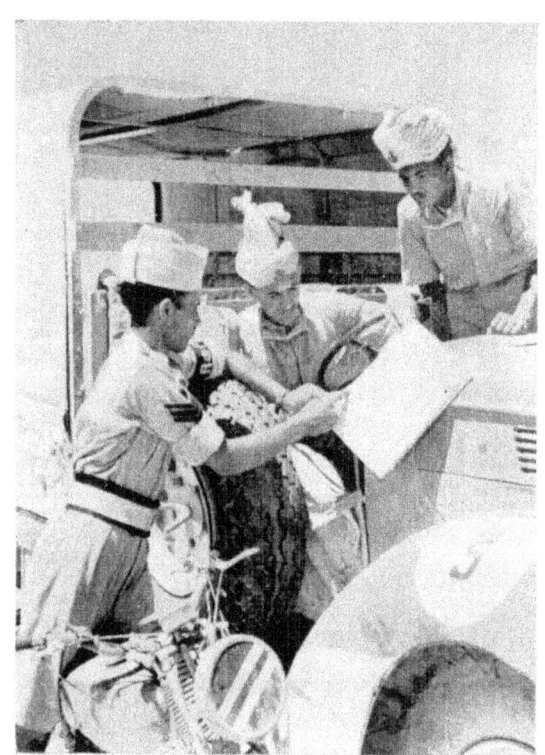

Indian Truck drivers studying maps—Western Desert

In trenches—Western Desert, November 1941

Indians guarding an aerodrome, Western Desert, September 1941

Italians and Germans taken prisoners, November 1941

could possibly be sent to their rescue, except the 5th South African Infantry Brigade and the 4th and 22nd Armoured Brigades. Of these, the South African Brigade had been delayed in its arrival; and as to the two Armoured Brigades, it was evident that some time would necessarily elapse before they could be moved from their positions near Gabr Saleh. In the circumstances, the 7th Armoured Brigade and the Support Group prepared themselves to resist the counter-attack unaided and even succeeded in beating off the first Axis attempt to take the ridge. Meanwhile, the 4th and 22nd Armoured Brigades which had been ordered to their rescue had, at last, started moving towards Sidi Rezegh to engage the Axis armour. This led to some desultory fighting on the morning of 22 November, which developed into a pitched battle towards the afternoon and nearly decided the fate of 'Crusader'.

The battle raged from noon till dark and the fighting was so heavy that the dust and smoke produced by the tanks soon made it impossible to distinguish friend from foe. Towards the conclusion of the combat, the 4th and 22nd Armoured Brigades found themselves being driven off their positions; while the Support Group felt compelled to abandon Sidi Rezegh. The Axis forces lost no time in pressing their advantage and made good their success by striking two crippling blows in quick succession. One was directed against the 5th South African Brigade, while the other fell on the headquarters of the 4th Armoured Brigade. The former was practically wiped out in spite of the intervention of the 22nd Armoured Brigade which found itself greatly outnumbered, while the latter lost most of its wireless links and in consequence was put out of action for a whole day. Seeing this situation, the Commander XXX Corps decided to rally the two armoured brigades in a central position, which formations he placed to the north of Trigh el Abd; while one infantry brigade, the 1st South African, was moved to Taieb el Essom to watch the western flank.

Advance of XIII Corps

Thus, from 18 to 22 November, the XXX Corps had its hands full trying to neutralise the Axis armour. Meanwhile the XIII Corps was standing by, waiting for the orders to commence its initial moves. It will be recalled that according to the general plan the XIII Corps was to make no move at all until the XXX Corps had achieved a substantial success in liquidating the armoured strength of the Axis. But in the course of the battles fought to this purpose, some exaggerated reports had gone out from the field, attributing heavy tank losses to the Axis, which created a false optimism and led to a premature move being made by the XIII Corps. Thus, on 21 November, being led by those optimistic reports to conclude that the Axis armoured forces had been or were being sufficiently neutralised, General Cunningham gave orders for the XIII Corps to begin its intended operations. The aim of these was only to secure the area of the two Omars, that is Omar Nuovo and the Libyan Omar, further advance depending on the way that would be thus laid open. But the operations nevertheless turned out to be very important in that, once begun, they did not stop until Benghazi had been reached by the Eighth Army; and they were also interesting from an Indian point of view in that a preponderant part in them was played by an Indian formation—the 4th Indian Division.

XIII Corps at this time was composed of three formations, the 4th Indian Division, the New Zealand Division and the 1st Army Tank Brigade. The New Zealand Division had three infantry brigades, a machine-gun battalion and the divisional cavalry. The composition of the 4th Indian Division was as follows:[5]

    4th Indian Infantry Division
      Central India Horse
      3 Sqns in trucks
      20 Carriers
      1 Sqn. South African Armoured Cars;
    5th Indian Infantry Brigade Group
      1 Buffs
      3/1 Punjab
      4 Raj Rif
      1 Fd Regt RA;
    7th Indian Infantry Brigade Group
      1 R. Sussex
      4 Sikh
      4/16 Punjab
      25 Fd Regt RA;
    11th Indian Infantry Brigade Group
      2 Camerons
      2 Mahrattas
      1 Raj Rif
      31 Fd Regt RA
      One Bn Army Tps.

The operations that followed and carried the Eighth Army right across Cyrenaica may be conveniently divided into four stages: (1) the capture of Omar Nuovo and Libyan Omar, (2) the operations against the line El Adem—Bir el Gubi, (3) the operations against the Gazala line and (4) pursuit of the Axis forces to Benghazi. In

[5] For a detailed Order of Battle see Appendix Q.

all of these the 4th Indian Division took a prominent part. It need not be repeated that the main object of these operations was to destroy the Axis forces in Libya rather than capture vast territories, since mere acquisition of ground was of little importance except for the moral and political effect it had on the various peoples of the world. In a desert, where only strong positions like Tobruk or Halfaya had any military significance at all, the war had to be concentrated against men, tanks and supplies, but chiefly against the tanks; and at the commencement of these operations the tank strength of General Rommel was 260 German and about 150 Italian tanks, while that of the Allies was 300 cruisers and 150 Army tanks.[6]

However, eliminating the Axis tanks was the business of the XXX Corps, not of the XIII Corps—much less of the 4th Indian Division. The XXX Corps was, so to speak, the mobile corps of the Eighth Army and had all the armour except the Army tanks, while the XIII Corps was preponderatingly the infantry corps. As for the 4th Indian Division, its primary task was to attack the two Omars, Omar Nuovo and the Libyan Omar, and in that task it was to be assisted by a group of 45 Army tanks in the initial stage of the fighting. The attack was to be carried out in two successive sweeps—the first one leading to the capture of Omar Nuovo by 1 Royal Sussex who were to be assisted by 45 Army tanks and 70 guns; and the next one ending with the capture of the Libyan Omar by 4/16 Punjab, with the same supporting arms.

Battle of the Omars

The Omar positions consisted of two main defended areas along the frontier wire, so sited as to enable resistance to be offered to an Allied attack from the south and the south-east. They were, therefore, not protected from the north. The flanks on the south-east and south had been covered by a system of minefields, which was later extended to cover also the north-west corner of the Libyan Omar. According to a subsequent Allied intelligence appreciation, however, there was yet another extension of the same minefields, which aimed at finally sealing up the whole of the northern gap; so that, by 22 November, the entire group of the defended localities of the two Omars had a minefield belt running practically all round. The defences inside this ring seemed to have been carefully dug and as all unnecessary earth had been removed, they were very difficult to locate, the more so because of the general flatness of the ground.

On D-Day, 18 November 1941, the three brigades of the 4th

[6] *War Information Circular No. 26-A.*, p. 3; W/Ds. 4 Div.

Indian Division were rather widely dispersed; and only two of them were definitely intended for operations in the forward area. The 5th Indian Infantry Brigade, which had returned from Syria in October, was still deficient in transport and equipment. In consequence, it was retained in the back area, south-west of Matruh, and was split up on various line of communication and protective tasks, while its remaining transport and equipment had been further drawn on to supplement the deficiencies of the rest of the division. As to the other two brigades, the 11th was placed in a holding role, in a position between the sea and the escarpment, behind a wide minefield. Its task was to prevent any possible Axis movement down the coastal plain. The escarpment in that area was very high and presented an absolute barrier to motor traffic except through the passes at Sollum, Halfaya and Halfway House. It was the task of the brigade to guard these passes.[7]

Now, since the 5th and 11th Brigades were thus tied up in their respective tasks, there remained only the 7th Brigade Group for a mobile, fighting role. In fact, that was the only brigade which had received any form of collective training prior to the operations, and it was the only one that was fully mobile with troop-carrying transport. It was therefore allotted the task of capturing the Axis camps at Omar Nuovo and Libyan Omar. The dispersion of the three brigades of the 4th Indian Division over so wide an area, however expedient, was not without its effect of weakening that formation, and the matter is of some interest in view of the fact that its final concentration, as a full division, had to take place later under conditions of active contact with the hostile forces.

Dispositions of the 4th Indian Division

Although the D-day for the forthcoming offensive was 18 November 1941, the 4th Indian Division can be said to have commenced its operations some days ahead. For, as early as 6 November, the 11th Indian Infantry Brigade had started a deception scheme in the coastal sector, according to a prearranged plan, to make it appear that the main Allied attack was intended to go in from that direction. While this was going on, there were being carried out several reliefs and moves on the escarpment and elsewhere to effect the final concentration for the opening of the offensive. As a result, on 17 November, some of the important dispositions in the frontier area were as follows:—The 7th Indian Infantry Brigade, less 1st Royal Sussex, was in an area just east of Alam el Fakhri (5233),[8] the Royal Sussex being temporarily left

[7] 4 Ind. Div. *Account of Operations in Cyrenaica*, pp. 3 & 4; W/Ds. 4 Div., 5 Bde., 11 Bde. and 7 Bde.
[8] References are to the GSGS Map 1/250,000, Egypt & Cyrenaica, Sheet 3, Sollum—Tobruk.

behind on the escarpment to check a possible Axis move along that side as well as to be available later for an advance to Bir Bu Deheua, whence an attack could be launched on Omar Nuovo. The 5th Brigade, as already mentioned, was south-west of Matruh. The Central India Horse, with one squadron of South African Armoured Cars under command, was watching the Axis line from Halfaya to Sidi Omar. The Advanced Headquarters of the 4th Indian Division had opened at Pt. 203 (5233). The 1st Army Tank Brigade was positioned in an area just south of Qaret el Ruweibat (5234); and the New Zealand Division was concentrated in the vicinity of Qabr Husri (5123). Further south, at Giarabub, was a small force from the 29th Indian Infantry Brigade.

As against these dispositions of the XIII Corps, the Axis dispositions were approximately as follows:—In the frontier area was a line of strong positions from Halfaya to Pt. 207, and thence along the frontier wire to Omar Nuovo and the Libyan Omar. The frontier wire itself was not originally intended as a military obstacle but as a means of preventing the Arabs from wandering backward and forward across the Italo-Egyptian frontier. It was a double apron fence and by now had many gaps in it, but was still an obstacle to be reckoned with, especially in case of a move by mechanical transport on a broad front. North of Halfaya, further Axis troops were in position at Sollum and Bardia.

Advance of the 4th Indian Division

According to the plan 'Crusader' the XIII Corps was not to join battle with the Axis forces until the XXX Corps had succeeded in liquidating the Axis armour, thus making it safe for the infantry of the former to engage the hostile troops on its own front. However, as related earlier, the XIII Corps was led to make that attack prematurely due to the receipt of exaggerated reports of the success of the XXX Corps in the battle of Sidi Rezegh. But even this attack had not commenced until three days after the D-day. Meanwhile it was to be expected that although the XIII Corps would refrain from attacking the Axis troops during the early days of 'Crusader,' the latter might not necessarily remain static or inactive, but might initiate the action themselves, most likely with a tank attack. This, however, did not happen, which must be attributed partly to the preoccupation of the Axis tanks in the battle of Sidi Rezegh, and partly to their being bogged in their own harbours in the coastal sector due to the heavy rains in that area on the night of the D-day. Whatever the reason, it enabled the 4th Indian Division to make its preliminary moves without any undue interference from the Axis. Thus, on the night of 18 November, the 7th Indian Infantry Brigade, less Royal Sussex, moved forward and established itself in the general area Pt. 203(5035)—Bir Shefersen (4934)—Pt. 195(4935). To the west, the brigade's patrols made contact with the XXX Corps about Bir Gibni (4735), where the artillery of both the sides was in action and a little skirmishing was going on between the Allied and the Axis armoured vehicles. Except for this, there was no notable Axis reaction to the move of the 7th Brigade and, in consequence, 1 Royal Sussex were ordered at midday to move forward and to revert to the command of the 7th Brigade. The brigade itself was ordered to despatch a column, the following morning, to Bir Bu Deheua and to occupy it if no serious opposition was encountered, that place being the point from which it was to launch its attack on the Omars.

Capture of Bir Bu Deheua

As ordered, the 7th Brigade despatched the column on the morning of 19 November. This consisted only of the 1st Royal Sussex who were assigned the task of opening the attack on the Omars. The Royal Sussex reached their destination by midday and shortly thereafter occupied Bir Bu Deheua, the jumping-off ground for the proposed attack. The same afternoon the New Zealand Division also moved forward to the line of Trigh el Abd; and the advanced headquarters of the 4th Indian Division crept further west towards the frontier wire, being now located at Pt. 202. Thus everything was ready for the attack on Omar Nuovo, which was to commence on receipt of the news of the success in the tank battles taking place in the XXX Corps area. It will be remembered that two tank battles had occurred in that area during the same day, in one of which the Italian Ariete Division had been engaged at Bir el Gubi (4137), and in the other about a hundred German tanks had been brought to battle in the area Gabr Taieb el Essom (4635). The over-optimistic reports of those battles having produced the impression that the events were moving as planned, the Commander of the 4th Indian Division began to consider attacking Omar Nuovo from the north, that is, by going round from Bir Bu Deheua.[9]

The north flank was chosen as it was the only side with large gaps in the belt of the encircling minefields. This side had been originally left open by the Axis on the assumption that the Allied attack would, in all likelihood, come from the east or the south-east. However, after the launching of the operation 'Crusader' the Axis command became more cautious and began extending the minefields towards the open gaps also. But this had been interfered with by the 4th Indian Division, and the northern gap had in consequence never been fully closed. That was the achievement of

---

[9] 4 Ind. Div. *Operation Account*, pp. 7-8; W/Ds. 4 Div., 7 Bde.

the 7th Indian Brigade which had successfully carried out active patrolling and harassment of the mine-laying squads under the orders of the Divisional Commander. At the same time, to isolate the positions intended to be attacked, the Central India Horse had been ordered to stop all lateral Axis traffic to the Omars, particularly from the Halfaya—Pt. 207 direction. The attack on Omar Nuovo could not, however, be made that day as expected, since in view of the indecisiveness of the tank battles, the Corps Commander was unwilling to commit the 4th Indian Division to a set-piece attack of such importance. Nor, for that reason, could the attack be made on the following day, 20 November; as particularly on that day, more units had to be rushed to the intended battle area due to a number of Axis tanks, guns and infantry having made an unexpected appearanc on the north and north-west of Bir Bu Deheua, thus presenting a menace to the rear and flanks of 1 Royal Sussex, who would be unable to attack Omar Nuovo if interfered with by those units. To obviate such a contingency, the Divisional Commander moved the whole of the 42nd RTR and the 8th Field Regiment to the threatened area to support the Royal Sussex. Except for these movements, nothing noteworthy had happened during the day in the XIII Corps area.

In contrast, however, the XXX Corps area on that day was a scene of intense activity. There were waves of counter-attack by the Axis tanks, which sought to dislodge the 7th Armoured Division from Sidi Rezegh, while a tank battle was being fought out in the Gabr Saleh area. At the same time another Axis tank force of considerable size had begun moving eastward, towards the XIII Corps area, with the object of disrupting the Allied line of communication and creating confusion in the rear of the fighting men. It was the larger part of the main German armoured force, which was then at Sidi Muftah. It advanced in the afternoon, south-eastwards, in a general drive towards the frontier, but met with heavy fighting which effectively put a stop to its further progress.

While the Axis armoured force was thus meeting with frustration in its attacks in the east as well as in the west, the 4th Indian Division was waiting for orders to attack Omar Nuovo. The order came from the XIII Corps on 21 November. The attack was to be carried out on the following day by the 7th Indian Infantry Brigade, commencing at 1200 hours, and preparations were taken in hand accordingly. The New Zealand Division was moved north to the line of Trigh-Capuzzo and the 1st Army Tank Brigade was put under its command, less the 42nd RTR, one squadron of the 44th RTR and a battery of the 8th Field Regiment, all of which remained with the 4th Indian Division. For the rest, the division continued to enjoy immunity from air action due to the superiority of the RAF, while enthusiastic accounts were being received by it of the armoured battles on its west and of the success of the 7th Armoured Division in holding on to Sidi Rezegh as also of the still more successful sortie from Tobruk which by that night was well on its way towards Ed Duda.

As mentioned earlier, the position to be attacked by the 7th Indian Infantry Brigade consisted of the two localities, Omar Nuovo and the Libyan Omar, which in layout and shape had the outline more or less of a dumb-bell, the Libyan Omar forming its western bulge and Omar Nuovo the eastern one. Each of these localities consisted of several defended positions, of which the Libyan Omar had four and Omar Nuovo three. The two groups of defences were separated by a distance of about two miles, the Libyan Omar group being situated to the west-south-west of Omar Nuovo. As explained earlier, both the groups were girdled by a continuous belt of minefields. Some five miles to the north-east of the minefield was the main Axis position of Ghot Adhidiba (5036) for which the Italian name was Cova. Both the Cova and Omar positions were held by the Savona Division which had its headquarters probably at Bir Ghirba. ,

The 1st Royal Sussex were to initiate the operations by attacking Omar Nuovo from the north, which stretch had been searched for minefields during the preceding night by patrols who had found none, although there had been prior indications of these having been laid. The next step, after the capture of Omar Nuovo by the Royal Sussex, was to be the attack on the Libyan Omar from the east by 4/16 Punjab; while 4 Sikh, the brigade's third battalion was to protect the east flank of the other two battalions during the operations, more particularly against any interference from the direction of Ghot Adhidiba and Pt. 207. Smoke was to be used during the attack on Omar Nuovo to prevent any observation from Libyan Omar.

Attack on Omar Nuovo

Zero hour for the attack on the Omar Nuovo position had been originally fixed for 1200 hours, as it was thought that, at that hour, the Italians would be just about ready to retire for their siesta, while the midday haze, which in the desert is very deceptive, would be in favour of the attacking troops. But this programme, however advantageous, could not be adhered to, due to an unexpected delay in locating the minefields, which necessitated the shifting of the scheduled time to 1230 hours. For forty-five minutes before that hour, the Royal Air Force had carried out an intermittent bombing of both the Omars, after which the artillery had put down a heavy concentration on Omar Nuovo lasting twenty minutes, as also a thick smoke screen between the two Omars. The forty-five Army tanks, which were to support the attack of the Royal Sussex, had been scheduled to cross the minefields two minutes after the artillery had ceased its fire. But they did not arrive on the spot till twenty minutes later and so lost much of the benefit of the artillery preparation.[10]

The order of advance for the attack on Omar Nuovo was carriers, tanks, and infantry in lorries. Accordingly, at 1250 hours, two platoons of carriers, the one of Royal Sussex and the other of 4/16 Punjab, went in, trying to pick a way through the minefield for the two squadrons of tanks which were following them. Moving behind the tanks were the men of Royal Sussex, embussed on a two-company front, after which went the third squadron of tanks which was in reserve. The minefield was found to have been hastily laid and was apparently incomplete. Some of the mines, it was afterwards discovered, were not even armed. Both the carrier platoons were, therefore, able to move through without casualties. The left squadron of tanks also got through without harm, and the right squadron had only five tanks immobilised which was by no means excessive.

However, soon after the tanks had passed through the minefield, they came under a heavy anti-tank fire, and the number of casualties began to mount rapidly. Among the anti-tank weapons they had to contend with, were two 88-mm dual-purpose (anti-aircraft plus anti-tank) guns, which proved catastrophic for the two squadrons, and practically held up the advance. Success was finally made possible only through the resolute behaviour of the 1st Royal Sussex who, not to be daunted, debussed on the inner edge of the minefield and, advancing on foot with fixed bayonets, managed to capture the whole of Omar Nuovo by 1350 hours, taking the posts one by one in spite of a heavy fire from the small arms of the Axis troops. An examination of the captured position showed that the three fortified localities of Omar Nuovo were about 200 yards square each, and roughly 500 yards apart from one another. The trenches were flush with the ground, making detection difficult, and there were none of the queer parapets of stone which the Italians had used the year before at Sidi Barrani. As to the 88-mm guns, they had been dug in on slight mounds and were able to command a magnificent all-round field of fire during the advance of the tanks. The smoke screen laid by the Divisional artillery between the two Omars had, however, proved effective in preventing the Libyan Omar from giving any supporting fire to Omar Nuovo in its difficulties.

[10] *War Inf. Circular No. 26-A*, p. 4; W/D. 7 Bde.

Attack on Libyan Omar

Immediately after the capture of Omar Nuovo, the tanks began to rally for the attack on Libyan Omar, in doing which, however, they once again encountered mines, which not only reduced their strength further but also delayed the opening of this second phase of the operation. The zero hour, therefore, had to be moved further back and was finally fixed for 1515 hours, when the artillery once again put down a heavy concentration of fire for twenty minutes in preparation for the attack. The two squadrons of tanks then moved into the attack over ground known to be clear of mines, and no casualties were suffered in consequence. The attack was on a narrower front than the previous one, one squadron of tanks going straight through to the objective and the other following behind accompanied by the infantry of 4/16 Punjab. On approaching the defended positions, the leading squadron found itself under heavy and accurate fire from two more German 88-mm guns and suffered many casualties; while the second squadron, attempting to turn back to avoid the fire, swung north and ran on to a wired minefield, on which several tanks became immobilised, some being later knocked out by the anti-tank guns of the Axis.

This mishap, however, did not stop the Indian troops from pressing home their attack, although once again the full benefit of the artillery preparation was not available to the attacking troops, this time due to some delay caused by the infantry debussing prematurely.[11] Despite this handicap, 4/16 Punjab managed to penetrate a few positions, taking about 1500 prisoners with many guns and other material. But, due to inadequate tank support, resulting from heavy tank casualties, they were unable to clear more than half of the Libyan Omar in a single day, and so, towards dark, when the action had to be deferred for the night, the western half was still in the hands of the Axis, including several strong points with anti-tank guns, which it was hoped to eliminate on the following morning.[12]

But the action was not resumed the next morning and, in fact, the complete capture of Libyan Omar had to be postponed for several days more. This was due to the fact that the western half of Libyan Omar, despite the nest of the anti-tank guns in it, now no longer presented a serious threat to the Allied troops who were firmly established in Omar Nuovo; and, further, since the supplies and water had thus been cut from the Axis garrison, it was considered possible that the isolated troops would yield to mere harassing tactics and surrender within a few days without any actual attack being necessary. As a matter of fact the garrison did

---

[11] Brigadier S. S. Lavender, DSO, who was at the time commanding this battalion, however, refutes the suggestion that the infantry debussed prematurely.
[12] 4 Ind. Div. Acct. of Ops. in Cyrenaica, p. 10; W/D. 4/16 Punjab.

surrender a few days later; but not until a substantial attack had been put in and its German element had escaped during the preceding night in whatever vehicles were mobile and available. A hectic chase was immediately organised and the escaping party was captured just as it was trying to enter Halfaya for which it was apparently headed.[13]

This completed the 7th Indian Brigade's task of capturing the two Omars, Omar Nuovo having been taken by 1 Royal Sussex and Libyan Omar by 4/16 Punjab. Unlike the Royal Sussex, however, 4/16 Punjab had to operate under certain handicaps which made its task more difficult. One of these was that the two supporting squadrons of tanks which were fresh when they were moving in to attack Omar Nuovo, had become considerably depleted in strength by the time they were ready to attack Libyan Omar. This reduction was aggravated by further losses during the advance towards the objective, so that 4/16 Punjab did not have anything like a full complement of the tank support when it was most needed. A second handicap was that, whereas Omar Nuovo had been manned entirely by the Italians, the part of Libyan Omar which had held out in the first instance had comprised a company of German troops also. Libyan Omar, being the main Axis position, was a much harder nut to crack.

While the battle for the Libyan Omar was in progress, 4 Sikh had been demonstrating east of the Omars, and Central India Horse was guarding the lateral route from Halfaya to Pt. 207. Towards the close of the operation, the artillery activity was continuous on the CIH front, and the Advanced Divisional Headquarters of the 4th Indian Division was preparing to move further west towards the frontier wire.

---

[13] According to Brigadier S. S. Lavender, DSO, then commanding the battalion in question, the Germans did not escape in vehicles but on foot and were recaptured long before Halfaya, somewhere near Bir Shefersen.

CHAPTER XXII

'Crusader' in Progress

Operations of XIII Corps

An obvious conclusion from the foregoing account is that the first phase of the battle of Sidi Rezegh had gone in favour of the Axis. The XXX Corps had not been able to carry through its plans to victory in spite of its best efforts. It had rather suffered a serious set-back in is attempt to take and hold Sidi Rezegh, and so great were its tank losses that it had become reduced to less than half its former strength. In fact, to sum up its achievements, all that could be claimed for it was that, after four days of hard fighting, it was just successful in preventing its own extinction and a possible disorganisation of the Eighth Army which could have followed its collapse, although even in the midst of its great reverses it had no doubt struck hard at the Axis armour and taken a heavy toll of the Axis tanks. As to the XIII Corps, it had fared somewhat better. During the time that the XXX Corps had been fighting its armoured battles, it had held the frontier and cut off the Axis communications to the west; and, by its action in capturing the best part of the Omar camps and threatening Bardia and Capuzzo, had proved effective in checking a headlong deterioration. The Omar positions, as related earlier, had been captured by the 4th Indian Division, while the threat to Bardia and Capuzzo was the work of the New Zealand Division.

This Allied Division, it will be recalled, was one of the three formations constituting the XIII Corps, the other two being the 4th Indian Division and the 1st Army Tank Brigade. It received the word to commence operations on 22 November and, moving forward quickly, soon gained control of all country to the west of the line of the Axis fortresses, up to the outskirts of Bardia. While doing this, it was able to help the attack of the 4th Indian Division by demonstrating towards Bir Ghirba and had little difficulty in occupying Capuzzo, Musaid and the Sollum Barracks. But it was unable to occupy Bardia, which its patrols found strongly garrisoned and for attacking which it was not permitted enough time, since it was required to move at once towards Tobruk.

The garrison of Tobruk, that is the 70th (British) Division, having made a sortie according to the plan, was at this stage, (21 Nov.), still far from Ed Duda, the position so far reached being a locality some four miles north-west of Sidi Rezegh and about

[1] On 23rd November alone, the Germans are said to have lost some 70 tanks.

an equal distance from its own perimeter. Having traversed this distance, however, it was now experiencing difficulty in making further progress due to increasing resistance; and being in an exposed position it was also in danger of being attacked and overwhelmed. To obviate this as well as to facilitate its progress, the New Zealand Division was ordered to proceed to its assistance, leaving behind only a small force to guard its recent acquisitions in the frontier area. Accordingly, leaving its 5th Brigade to mask Bardia and Sollum, it pushed on to Tobruk with the 6th New Zealand Brigade as its main formation, occupying Gambut on the way the same evening and capturing the headquarters of the *Afrika Korps*. On the following day (23 Nov.), the 6th Brigade stormed Point 175, some five miles west of Sidi Rezegh, and then tried to make contact with the XXX Corps on its left. The contact could not be established as the XXX Corps had already started withdrawing. But in that effort to link up, one of the New Zealand battalions encountered a group of Axis tanks and got involved in a brief battle. These tanks were a part of about one hundred German armoured vehicles which, a few hours before, had overwhelmed and practically wiped out the 5th South African Brigade in the Tobruk area near about Hareifet en Nibeidat (4339), and, while emerging from a valley after that attack, had chanced upon the battalion. Both sides were equally surprised and unprepared for the meeting, and it was probably for that reason that the engagement was less fierce than it might otherwise have been. The battalion at last managed to free itself of the tanks and returned safely to the brigade, where it learned that the XXX Corps had started retiring eastward.

Situation in the XXX Corps area

The reason for the withdrawal of the XXX Corps was that it had suffered heavily in the recent engagements with the Axis armour. The Germans had made determined attacks on Sidi Rezegh with their main armoured force and recaptured that feature; while, in the fighting that preceded this reoccupation, the Allied armour had received some very hard knocks. As a result, the 4th Armoured Brigade had become very much disorganised, the 22nd Armoured Brigade had only 45 tanks left, and the 7th Armoured Brigade no more than ten.[2] The Germans, on the other hand, had a larger number in running order and could recover others from the battlefield; while their Italian Ariete Division, which had not been seriously engaged since the commencement of the operations, was estimated to have at least about eighty tanks. Viewing this situation in the light of his future needs, General Cunningham came to the

---

[2] Gen. Auchinleck's *Despatch* in Supplement to *London Gazette* of 13 January 1948, pp. 338-339.

conclusion that if he continued to attack the Axis regardless of his own losses, he might soon find himself without any serviceable tank at all; and if the Germans still retained an appreciable number in hand, the consequences could be disastrous. The Axis could, in that case, sweep on almost unopposed to Alexandria or Cairo and the Allies would lose their last foothold in North Africa. On the other hand, a timely withdrawal by the XXX Corps would go a long way towards alleviating the situation. For although the Allied tank superiority had practically vanished, the disadvantage was only temporary. Much could still be done given some time for reorganisation. The 4th Armoured Brigade which had become momentarily disorganised had yet a large number of tanks capable of action; and after its reorganisation, the Eighth Army would still have a total of about one hundred tanks, excluding those of the infantry pattern which were too slow to be sent into battle. The effective Axis tanks, too, did not total up to much more than that number, though about one half of them were German and, as such, superior to the Allied tanks, most of which were of the light American type.

On the whole, the situation was serious enough to fill any commander with anxiety and General Cunningham was by no means self-complacent. He apprised General Auchinleck of the existing state of affairs and did not conceal his misgivings about the future. He had his fears that, taking advantage of his reduced tank strength, the Axis armour might break through in force to his rear and dislocate the line of communication and repairs organisation east of the frontier. To his mind, the withdrawal of the XXX Corps was therefore a correct step and the continuation of the offensive one full of unpredictable hazards. But General Auchinleck could not be made to share this view. He was of the opinion that the Axis resources had been stretched well to their limit and the battle could be won by continuing the offensive a little longer. He, therefore, issued instructions for a fresh counter-attack on Sidi Rezegh, which General Cunningham proceeded to give effect to. But the latter's anxiety was by no means allayed, and, in fact, increased considerably when on the following day some Axis tanks made an eastward dash and his prophecy seemed to be well on the verge of coming true. It will be recalled that on two occasions before this, General Rommel had despatched columns of tanks eastward in the hope of disrupting the Allied line of communication and creating confusion in the rear. He decided to repeat the same tactics for the third time, and so, collecting some thirty tanks and lorried infantry, despatched the column to the frontier on 24 November, which by swift and audacious moves spread considerable havoc in the rearward areas amongst the Allied transport and headquarters.

Axis thrust towards the Allied line of communication

The confusion and consternation caused by this small column makes an instructive story about how fighting units react when communications break down and news or instructions are lacking. Before narrating it, however, it is necessary to survey the situation on the frontier as it existed on 24 November. The 5th New Zealand Brigade, which had been left behind by the New Zealand Division, was disposed in the area Capuzzo—Musaid—Sollum Barracks with its headquarters at Sidi Azeiz (5038).[3] Its divisional cavalry as well as an infantry battalion were at Menastir (5039). The 4th Indian Division had moved its advanced headquarters to Bir Shefersen just east of the frontier wire, while its 7th Brigade was still trying to overcome the Axis resistance in the Libyan Omar. The Indian brigade had been asked to clear that area in its own time without incurring heavy casualties, that is more by starving the garrison out than by active fighting. Accordingly, by 23 November, 4/16 Punjab had begun clearing the area by infiltration, in the course of which that battalion captured a further batch of 1,500 prisoners. But the position proved to be more extensive than was at first thought and the Axis artillery from Ghot Adhidiba was shelling Omar Nuovo heavily. As a result, when night settled on the scene there still remained the west and north-west corners of the position to be overcome.

At the same time, owing to the critical situation prevailing in the XXX Corps area through heavy tank losses in the earlier fighting at Sidi Rezegh, the control of the operations for the relief of Tobruk was transferred to XIII Corps. This Corps was now instructed to move westward, using the main road Bardia—Tobruk as well as the north axis of Trigh-Capuzzo. The move commenced at once, less the 4th Indian Division which was left behind to look after the frontier, with the 5th New Zealand Brigade under its command. The Indian division was to follow the Corps as soon as it could be relieved by the 5th Indian Brigade, which was being brought forward from the rear to fill that gap.[4]

Such was the situation in the area of the 4th Indian Division on the night of 23 November when, unknown to the division, a column of some thirty Axis tanks and lorried infantry was moving east towards the frontier. This was the same column which, as mentioned earlier, General Rommel had decided to send towards the Allied line of communication in an effort to weaken the Eighth Army by creating confusion in its rear. Owing to the lack of information, the

---

[3] The map references are to GSGS maps, 1/250,000 Egypt and Cyrenaica, Sheet 3, Sollum—Tobruk.

[4] 4 Ind. Div.'s. *Account of Operations in Cyrenaica*, pp. 11-12; W/D's. 4 Div., 7 Bde., 4/16 Punjab.

4th Indian Division was unaware of the seriousness of the situation of the XXX Corps area and so unable to appreciate the imminence of this danger. In fact, the first indication that the things were not normal came only on the morning of 24 November, when some survivors of the 5th South African Brigade arrived in the divisional area with news of their disastrous clash with the Axis tanks on the previous day. But even in this, there was no hint of the surprise that was to overtake the Indian division before the end of the day.

The first portents of that surprise made their appearance during the afternoon, when the Divisional Headquarters picked up wireless intercepts from the armoured car patrols of the XXX Corps, indicating that some Axis tanks were making a dash towards Egypt, and that quite a few of them had reached the frontier wire, while a yet larger column was some thirty miles away, advancing eastward. This was confirmed soon afterwards when some XXX Corps vehicles began to pass through the divisional area as if in a hectic rush. The stream of the vehicles, which consisted mostly of "B" echelon and administrative units, presented the appearance of a general move towards the rear area. Their spectacular passage through the divisional area was later described by a G-III on the headquarters of the 4th Indian Division: "We saw," he wrote, "a great column of vehicles of every size and description, which turned out to be most of XXX Corps supply column, with a few other odd detachments which had joined up. The whole column went straight through the Div. HQ at a good speed and in a great cloud of dust. They seemed to be in a hurry if nothing else; so we stopped one or two lorries and asked what it was all about. No one apparently knew what was really happening but the general idea seemed to be that a column of tanks was somewhere behind them and they were getting out of it quick."

The situation was yet too vague to enable any definite defensive arrangements to be taken in hand and remained so till evening, when HQ XXX Corps itself arrived in the divisional area and imparted the information that the German armour was advancing eastward and that their own soft vehicles were withdrawing to avoid being caught up. At this, the divisional commander took immediate steps to protect his own headquarters. Such anti-tank and anti-aircraft guns as were with the divisional headquarters, and one or two available tanks, were moved out to cover gaps in the frontier wire in the vicinity, and information was sent at the same time to some five tanks of the 42nd RTR which were being repaired nearby. This tank detachment, according to later reports, had spent the night in getting the repairs completed, after which, having evacuated its administrative vehicles, it gallantly went into action against the German tanks hovering in the neighbourhood, and destroyed three of them before it was finally overwhelmed.

The work of closing the gaps in the frontier wire continued well into the night. A little before this, however, the Indian division's headquarters had received a message to say that Allied aircraft were about to attack the Axis tanks by ground strafing. The identification strips were duly laid out to mark off the divisional ground and soon the fighters appeared out of the sky flying low and machine-gunning everything. The divisional headquarters was not touched, owing to the precaution taken, but several Allied vehicles were hit and some casualties were caused. This, no doubt, induced the withdrawing transport of the XXX Corps to accelerate their pace, or vary the rate of their movement, and added not a little to the general tendency towards confusion. The consternation increased as the German tanks approached nearer and the growing darkness covered them from view. For a time there was much firing all about the divisional headquarters, but whether from Allied or Axis side, it was impossible to say. Later, at about 2000 hours, when darkness was complete several verey lights were seen going up on all sides. They were the normal recognition signals which the German detachments usually sent up at night and were an indication that several parties of Axis tanks were in close proximity of the Advanced Divisional Headquarters and seemingly on all sides. This proved to be true when it was discovered later that one of the Axis detachments had actually passed not more than a thousand yards to the south, where the main dressing station of the 17th Indian Field ambulance was situated. The dressing station was, of course, captured but was allowed to continue functioning.

The 4th Indian Division moves to safety

With a view to meeting this new danger, and in spite of the general uncertainty as to the whereabouts of the Axis troops, the 4th Indian Division carried out two important moves during that night. In the first place the Central India Horse and the 31st Field Regiment (less one battery) were moved out to clear the area east of the frontier. They were to operate columns against the Axis tanks, and, more especially, prevent their replenishing at the Allied 50th Field Supply Depot which was situated near the wire. Before moving out, the CIH handed over its patrolling task to a squadron of the 6th South African Armoured Car Regiment which was then under its command.

The second move of the Indian division related to its own Advanced Headquarters. It was decided to shift it from its exposed position near the frontier wire into the comparative security of Omar Nuovo. The move was timed to take place at midnight but, as the situation appeared to worsen every few minutes, it was decided to start off at 2230 hours. Actually the move began even earlier, at 2210 hours, such being the eagerness of all concerned to quit that insecure spot.

The headquarters set off in three columns, the 7th Brigade patrolling the south to give it cover. There was no moon and a vehicle in front could hardly be seen as anything better than a rather darker patch in the enveloping darkness. The move was carried out in silence while German verey lights were still going up in all directions. Since the columns of vehicles had to find their way through the minefields surrounding the Libyan Omar, it had been arranged that a guide from the Libyan Omar camp should meet the leading convoy outside the minefield and conduct it into the defended locality through a known gap, showing the way with a lamp. But it happened that due to the haste with which the move was carried out, the convoy reached the spot earlier than the appointed time when the guide had not yet arrived. In moving helter-skelter on the edge of the minefield, trying to look for the guide, the divisional headquarters stumbled upon a part of the XXX Corps headquarters which was also trying to gain shelter in the Omar position. The latter's vehicles had missed the main gap and were already half way into the minefield and an almost certain mishap was averted by the guide turning up at this moment.[5]

Before morning the divisional headquarters was safely inside Omar Nuovo. But, as soon as there was light enough to see the locality in which the headquarters had settled, it was observed that the position was overlooked from Pt. 204 by the Axis artillery, which began shelling the vehicles. Needless to say that this quickened up the dispersion of vehicles then in progress. The shelling went on intermittently for about 20 minutes but caused little damage beyond a few punctures.

Having opened in its new position, the divisional headquarters began to take stock of the situation. There was a certain amount of confusion in the frontier area and the dispositions of the Axis columns were not easy to ascertain. Only one thing was certain, and it was that Axis tank columns were still in the area trying to disrupt the line of communication and scatter the various units composing it, apart from some other groups which had actually crossed the frontier wire at several points and had spread out to the east of it. It was to be expected that some of these roving tanks would attack units of the Indian division sooner or later, and such an attack was not long in coming. It came early on the morning of 25 November, and resulted in a duel between the German tanks

---

[5] War Inf. Cir. No. 26-A, pp. 5-6; W/D. HQ. 4 Div.

and the 4th Indian Division's artillery. The action was remarkable in that it was the first attempt by German tanks to 'take on' artillery.

The tank-artillery duel

The scene of the action was an area to the east of the Omars and the units involved were the 4th Sikh and the 1st Field Regiment RA.* The latter was supporting the 4th Sikh in that area on the morning of 25 November. At 0730 hours a troop of the Field Regiment was fired on by some twenty-five German tanks, which then withdrew to a distance. This was, as it turned out, a prelude to further tank attacks on the artillery. Immediately after that incident, the 1st Field Regiment moved into action to the north-east of Bir el Hurush (5030). There had hardly been time enough to dig gun pits, when at 0840 hours another batch of some twenty-eight German tanks was observed approaching from the south. They were about 3000 yards away when first seen and consisted of Mark IIIs with a proportion of Mark IVs. They were advancing in lines of four or five with intervals of about thirty yards between the tanks and seventy yards between the lines, except for the rear two tanks which remained farther back. They began to fire at about 2000 yards range as they advanced on the east flank of the 1st Field Regiment, towards the positions occupied by the 52nd Field Battery.

As the tanks drew nearer the gun area, their fire became more intense and more accurate. The brunt of the shelling was naturally borne by the 52nd Field Battery, whose guns, however, held their fire until the tanks had come within 800 yards. At this range the 52nd Battery and a troop of the 11th Field Battery opened fire on the advancing tanks which, despite that opposition, continued to move on. They at last halted about 500 yards from the guns when an intense fire-fight occurred. After ten minutes the tanks moved west and continued the fight from a distance of about 400 yards from a hull-down position. The duel lasted another ten minutes after which the tanks decided to proceed again and moved almost head-on towards the 52nd Battery. The guns of the battery opposed this progress with such rapid fire that the tanks gave up the attempt, having made only a short distance. Then after a few minutes they withdrew precipitately, dispersing towards south and south-east. They were pursued by two troops of the 2nd South African Anti-tank Regiment which had just arrived in that area, but the pursuit was inconclusive inasmuch as only one damaged tank was captured. The entire action had cost the Germans seven tanks destroyed and three or four damaged, while to the Allies the cost

* W/D. 4 Sikh.

was 66 casualties, of which 42 were suffered by the 52nd Field Battery alone from its total of 73 men in that position. Five guns had also been damaged but they were soon repaired and put back into action. A further gain to the Allied side, from this action, was that the 4th Sikh Battalion, and a large amount of transport, which might have been easily overrun by the tanks, had been saved, while the British gunners had acquired a new confidence in meeting massed attacks from the German tanks.

The same afternoon, 25 November, there occurred the third and last clash between the German tanks and the British artillery. This time the attack was made by some twenty-eight tanks, from the south-east of the Omars. It was not quite clear why the Germans had chosen that particular direction, since they themselves had laid extensive minefields in that sector. However, the attack did come from that unexpected corner and had to be met. The tanks approached firing and were once again allowed to come to a close range. The 1st Field Regiment then opened fire and five tanks were soon burning. At this, the rest of the machines attempted to move off to the west; but, since that involved going round the gun area and over the exposed ground, they fell an easy prey to the artillery which had them at a disadvantage. All the guns, including the medium, came into action and a further batch of six German tanks was disabled, bringing the artillery's gains for the whole of that day to nineteen tanks destroyed and several others lightly damaged. The action concluded with the withdrawal of the remaining tanks southwards. It was probably in this action, if not in the preceding one, that the German Commander of the 5th German Tank Regiment received the wound, for which he was treated by the 17th Indian Field Ambulance, then captive in the German hands.

Raid on the frontier

The German tanks involved in these duels were only one part of the armoured force sent out by General Rommel to disrupt the Allied line of communication and spread confusion in the rear area. Another part of that force had by that time, 25 November, crossed the frontier wire and reached a point nineteen miles east of Sidi Omar. This column proved even more intractable than the first one. Some of its tanks actually succeeded in threatening the Allied railhead in Egypt, by dashing up to within fifty miles of it, while others, moving south along the frontier wire, caused a stir even in the headquarters of the Eighth Army near Maddalena. More trouble ensued next day, 26 November, when a number of these tanks turned into Halfaya and, after an unsuccessful attack on Capuzzo and Musaid, passed through a gap east of the Sollum barracks and later entered Bardia, where they were joined by other columns from the south-east. Turning Bardia into a base, or rather a pivot, they attacked and captured the headquarters of the 5th New Zealand Infantry Brigade at Sidi Azeiz and, next day, made two more attacks on Capuzzo, one of which was within an ace of succeeding. Just at this juncture they were recalled by the German High Command and they disappeared from the frontier area as quickly as they had come.[7]

Failure of the eastward thrust

The reasons behind the sudden withdrawal of the German tanks from the frontier area provide a noteworthy example of success obtained in one sector by a steady maintenance of an objective in another sector. The objectives persevered in, in this case, were the capture of Sidi Rezegh and the ultimate relief of Tobruk. The New Zealand Division, which had already been despatched westwards from the frontier area a few days earlier, (and which had since then been followed up by the XIII Corps, charged with the operations for the relief of Tobruk), had generated enough pressure in the Tobruk area to oblige the German Command to recall their tanks at once. This it had done by concentrating on its objective and keeping it steadily in view. Had it been, on the other hand, ordered to sacrifice its objective, viz. Sidi Rezegh, and turn about for defence in view of the dislocation in its rear, it is likely that the German tanks would have remained longer in the frontier area and achieved more substantial results.

But now, however, the results achieved must have appeared to General Rommel as falling far short of his expectations, unless from the very start he was looking upon this venture as an experiment or a gamble. For, although his tanks had caused a great deal of commotion in the Allied rear, they had not succeeded in inflicting any serious material damage. What had happened was that, in the face of their lightning advance, the Allied transport and other units had simply dispersed or had become scattered. These reassembled and reorganised themselves soon after the departure of the Axis tanks and the situation returned to normal almost immediately. The staggered communications of the Eighth Army had proved elastic enough to absorb the shock and regain their shape automatically. It was, in fact, the Axis that had lost a great advantage in this audacious push, since the absence of so many of its tanks from the Tobruk area had enabled the New Zealand Division to fight through to Tobruk. In addition, the Axis had lost several tanks in this dubious gamble and spent up much of its strength and other resources which might have proved more useful in the main fighting

[7] Gen. Auchinleck's *Despatch* in Supplement to *London Gazette* of 13 Jan. 48, pp. 338-39.

then in progress in the Sidi Rezegh and Tobruk sectors and at Libyan Omar on the frontier.

Thus ended the strange attempt of General Rommel to defeat the Eighth Army by striking it in the rear and disorganising its supplies and communications. Among the reasons for this failure, three stand out more prominently than others. They are: (1) The occupation of most of the Omar area by the 4th Indian Division which denied the raiding tanks a safe harbour, (2) The success of the New Zealand Division and the garrison of Tobruk in maintaining a steady pressure against Sidi Rezegh and in the Tobruk area generally, and (3) The small size of the raiding armoured force.

Change in the Eighth Army Command

Although the effort of the Axis to disrupt the communications of the XXX Corps had achieved no substantial results, it had nevertheless one major consequence. It led to a change in the Eighth Army's Command. As has already been mentioned, General Cunningham, who was then commanding the Eighth Army, had always felt a great anxiety about the possibility of a serious Axis thrust towards the rear of his Army. When such a thrust did actually materialise—and that at a stage when the tank position of the Eighth Army was at its worst—his anxiety naturally increased and he began to entertain doubts about the advisability of a sustained offensive in the circumstances. At this time General Auchinleck was at the Advanced Headquarters of the Eighth Army, having flown there on 23 November in response to an urgent request from General Cunningham. The critical tank situation as it then prevailed was reviewed and discussed by the two commanders. General Cunningham was particularly frank and unreserved in acquainting General Auchinleck with all relevant details and made no secret about his own misgivings as to the likely outcome. He pointed out that if the offensive were to continue at the then existing rate, there was a risk that almost all the remaining tanks of the Eighth Army would be lost and the safety of Egypt might be ultimately jeopardised. He also expressed concern about the possibility of another Axis thrust to his rear, more powerful than the last one, which could, not unreasonably, be expected to result in a serious breakdown of his supplies and repairs organisation.

The gist of these arguments would seem to point to the conclusion that he was advocating a suspension of the offensive or even its complete abandonment. But that was by no means his intention. He was merely pointing out to the Commander-in-Chief some of the possibilities which were causing him concern and wanted a final decision whether to go on or not. He felt that the Commander-in-Chief with his wider knowledge of the background was in a better position to take such a decision. As far as he was concerned, he was prepared to carry out whatever the orders. But he had no form of defensive plan ready, since he was by no means too eager to switch on to the defensive. In keeping with that attitude, he made no direct recommendation to General Auchinleck either for the abandonment of the offensive or for switching on to the defensive.

In any case, General Auchinleck was not prepared to accept any such counsel, even if tendered. He was rather of the opinion that the Axis resources were probably as overstrained as his own and the continuance of the offensive a little longer might yield the desired result. The crisis in tanks, far from making him cautious or meek, gave a fresh impetus to his aggressive spirit and he decided to go on attacking. Accordingly, he ordered General Cunningham to resume the offensive, and returned to his headquarters at Cairo on 25 November. This bold decision was not only a correct one but, as proved by later events, actually instrumental in saving 'Crusader' from a complete wreckage and giving a new lease of life to the Eighth Army.

Back at his headquarters, General Auchinleck re-examined his decision and, no doubt, confirmed it. But while convinced as to its correctness, he could not but be aware that for the offensive to succeed, it would have to be conducted with a high degree of faith and confidence as to the ultimate results. He was not sure that General Cunningham, in the discussions he had had with him, had given him proof of that necessary measure of faith and confidence in his decision. The impression he got was rather that the Eighth Army Commander had showed an excessive amount of anxiety about his lines of communication and the possibility of a German break-through to his rear; and that, under the stress of his reverses, he had become cautious as well as defensive in his outlook. Considering it all in all, he reached the conclusion that it would not be proper for him to retain in the field a commander who was not able to see eye to eye with him, and in whose method of carrying out his intentions he had not the completest trust. He, therefore, decided to replace General Cunningham and, having selected his Deputy Chief of the General Staff, Major-General N. M. Ritchie, to succeed him, asked for the approval of His Majesty's Government to this momentous change. The approval was immediately given, and General Ritchie assumed command of the Eighth Army on 26 November 1941.[8]

While this change was being effected, fighting was in progress both at Sidi Rezegh in the XXX Corps area, and on the frontier

[8] General Auchinleck's *Despatch* in Supplement to *London Gazette* of 13 Jan. 48, pp. 338-39.

in the XIII Corps area. In the latter area, the 4th Indian Division was just then preparing to take steps to liquidate the remainder of the Libyan Omar. It will be remembered that the attack on this position had commenced on 22 November but the Axis resistance had proved too strong to be overcome in a day. As a result, about one-third of that camp, in the north and west, was still in the hands of the Axis when Axis tanks were making their thrust at the Allied communications. On 27 November, as this thrust was petering out, the Indian battalion, 4/16 Punjab, made a dawn attack on that part of Libyan Omar which was still holding out. The attempt was unsuccessful and it was necessary to wait and make fresh plans for reducing this stronghold. A second attack was not put in until 30 November.

Some minor events

In the meantime, a few minor events were taking place which may be noticed in passing. They are of interest only in so far as they show how communications had become dislocated after the raid by the Axis tanks.[9]

In the first place, the 4th Indian Division was placed under the direct command of the Eighth Army from 1200 hours on 26 November. Changes were accordingly made in the divisional boundary and the new boundary line was made exclusive of Bardia—Sidi Azeiz in the north. This at once produced a minor complication. It meant that a part of the 5th New Zealand Brigade was to be under the XIII Corps and the remainder under the 4th Indian Division. Accordingly, the Brigade Headquarters, the Divisional Cavalry Regiment and one battalion communicated with and received orders from the XIII Corps, while the other two battalions, which were in the area Capuzzo—Sollum Barracks, were expected to receive orders from the 4th Indian Division, with which they did not even have a direct means of communication.

In keeping with this confused state of affairs there had occurred a few more incidents, of which two or three only need be mentioned. At this time the Indian division did not have with itself the 5th Indian Infantry Brigade, as the latter was in the rear area. But it was later decided to bring it forward in order to relieve the 5th New Zealand Brigade mentioned above. Accordingly, on 26 November, the Indian division ordered the 5th Indian Brigade to move forward with all its available resources to Conference Cairn (5233).[10] At the same time, however, the brigade also received direct orders from the Eighth Army requiring it to pass to the

---

[9] 4 Ind. Div's. *Account of Operations in Cyrenaica*, pp. 16-22. W/Ds. 4 Div., 5 Bde.

[10] The map references are GSGS Maps, 1/250,000 Egypt and Cyrenaica series.

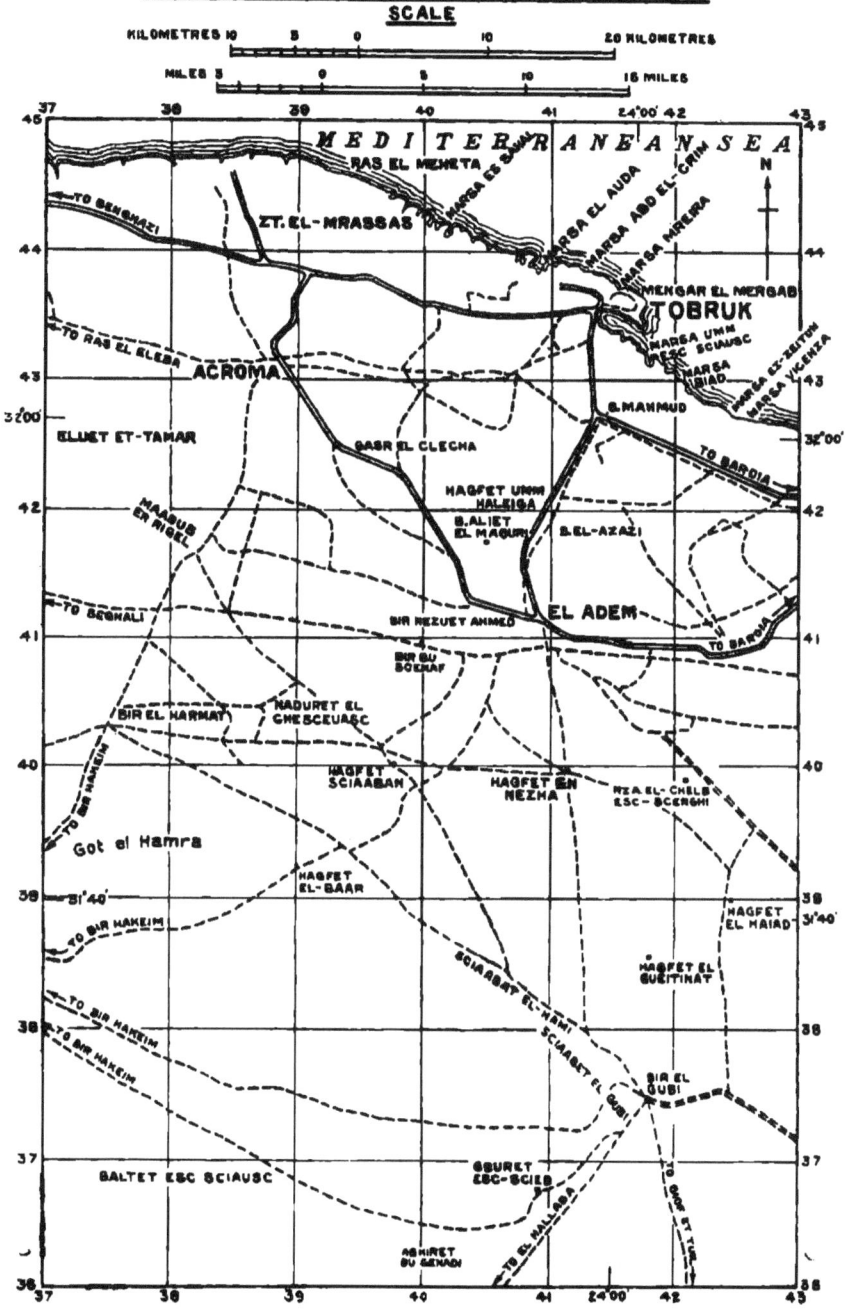

command of the 2nd South African Division. The conflict in orders was eventually resolved by the brigade commander deciding on his own to act on the orders of the 4th Indian Division. The same day the New Zealand Cavalry Regiment, mentioned above, moved of its own accord into the Libyan Omar camp. The explanation of the commander was that he was out of touch with his division and was running short of supplies and petrol. In the tangled state of affairs then prevailing on the battle front he needed instructions. This unit was soon followed into the Omar camp by the 22nd New Zealand Battalion which reported that it was also in a similar plight. It was out of touch with every headquarters and its supplies were running low.

Of a piece with this type of confusion was the fact of the 4th Indian Division being bombed by no other than the Allied planes. On the morning of 26 November some Albacores bombed the Omar camps from 0500 to 0630 hours. The damage done was not much but the units spent the time in cold and uncomfortable slit trenches. Later it was discovered that an air communique had reported this raid as "a successful attack on some 2000 MT."

Operations in the Tobruk area

As days passed the situation became clearer and it became apparent that the weight of fighting had shifted from east to west, that is from the frontier area to the Tobruk area. In the latter place, the New Zealand Division, less its 5th Brigade, had been making steady progress towards Sidi Rezegh and, by 27 November, that division had completed its gallant and determined advance and joined hands with the Tobruk garrison. It had formed a corridor through Sidi Rezegh and Belhamed, and it was this action that had caused the sudden recall of the Axis tanks from the frontier area as narrated earlier. By 27 November those tanks were found to be speeding westwards; and from that time the centre of fighting had moved to the Tobruk area. This was the beginning of the second Battle of Sidi Rezegh and much heavy fighting occurred in that phase, which will be described in the succeeding part of this narrative. Before that, however, it is necessary to survey the frontier area and to see how the Axis resistance in that part was finally overcome.

The 4th Indian clears Libyan Omar

At this time, the XIII Corps being too preoccupied with the battle in front of Tobruk to be able to give sufficient attention to the frontier area, the commander of the 4th Indian Division had assumed control of that area, up to and including Bardia, as from 28 November. The arrangement was confirmed later. But, in the meantime, this division had already started preparations for launching its final assault on the portion of Libyan Omar which was still holding out. Of its formations, the 5th Indian Infantry Brigade had by then arrived in the area and was more or less complete with its battalions and transport. It was to operate in conjunction with the 7th Indian Infantry Brigade, which had already been moved for that purpose to the north of Libyan Omar. But the 11th Indian Infantry Brigade, which was on the coastal sector, and which normally formed a part of the division, was not available for the projected action. It had been replaced by the 2nd South African Brigade and despatched to the frontier wire, where it was placed in the Eighth Army's reserve.

The commander of the 4th Indian Division had long since begun to tidy up his frontier as a preliminary to the final assault on the Libyan Omar. As a result, the 22nd New Zealand Battalion had been ordered to move into Capuzzo and form a new brigade headquarters there to replace the headquarters of the 5th New Zealand Brigade. This headquarters, it may be recalled, had been overrun a little earlier by the German tanks moving towards the Allied rear. Similarly, another New Zealand unit, the New Zealand Divisional Cavalry Regiment, was ordered to move to Menastir to patrol westwards and block the approaches to Bardia. Since the units located at Capuzzo and Menastir were short of supplies, arrangements were made to get the necessary supply convoys through, to both these places, before the commencement of the action. A part of the 5th Indian Brigade was also ordered to move to the Capuzzo area to relieve as much of the 5th New Zealand Brigade as could conveniently be done.

The plan of the attack required that the 5th New Zealand Brigade should move north to Menastir, and thence operate columns to the west with the ultimate object of rejoining its own division in the Sidi Rezegh—Tobruk area. At the same time, one battalion of the 5th Indian Brigade, 3/1 Punjab, was to attempt a surprise night attack on Libyan Omar, with the 31st Field Regiment and Central India Horse under command. The rest of the dispositions were so laid as to isolate the Axis garrison in Bardia from the rest of the Axis troops to its west. The attack on Libyan Omar was to go in from the north on the night of 30 November and it was hoped to clear up that area before the following morning.[11]

The action commenced on 30th November as planned. The 3/1 Punjab carried out a successful night attack from the north in which it not only captured the Omar position against very stiff opposition but held it throughout the night and exploited the success further. At the same time, to complete the task so well begun by this

[11] *Ibid.* W/Ds. 7 Bde., 11 Bde., 3/1 Punjab, 4/16 Punjab.

battalion, the commander of the 4th Indian Division sent a second battalion, the 4/16 Punjab of the 7th Brigade, from the other side, which, during the rest of the day, gradually infiltrated forward and gained entrance into the remaining Axis-held positions. In the afternoon the 4/16 Battalion got a good-sized reinforcement of three tanks, after which it went forward more rapidly, collecting several prisoners on the way. Towards night, all that remained of the opposition was a small pocket of about one hundred Germans. These tried to escape under the cover of darkness but were eventually rounded up by the armoured car patrols. The action ended at first light on 1 December, when, at last, Libyan Omar was declared clear of all Axis troops.

Having reduced the stronghold of Libyan Omar, the 4th Indian Division addressed itself to the task of clearing up the rest of the frontier area and then moving forward westwards. Accordingly, the 5th New Zealand Infantry Brigade was asked to mop up the coastal area, which was practically all that remained of the Axis resistance on the frontier. At the same time columns were sent out to operate westwards along two separate axes. The New Zealand Divisional Cavalry Regiment was made to move out on the axis of the main road Bardia—Tobruk, and the 31st Field Regiment, with the Central India Horse under command, on the axis of the Trigh-Capuzzo. The two columns soon liquidated all resistance along their respective lines of advance, with the result that by the evening of 2 December 1941, there was no Axis resistance left in the frontier, except some isolated pockets in the Bardia and the Halfaya areas, which could be ignored for the time being.

CHAPTER XXIII

Success of 'Crusader'

As narrated earlier, the first phase of the battle of Sidi Rezegh had gone in favour of the Axis. The second phase opened almost directly thereafter. It can be said to have commenced on 25 November, about two days after the conclusion of the first one.

During the intervening gap, however, the Axis had started the raid on the Allied line of communication, as already explained. This had lasted from 24 to 27 November, so that for the period between 25 and 27 November two actions were being fought out simultaneously: one in the XIII Corps area against the raiding tanks, and the other in the XXX Corps area, where the second phase of the battle of Sidi Rezegh had just then begun. Of the two actions, the latter is undoubtedly the more important, not only because it resulted in the German raiding tanks being withdrawn from the frontier as described earlier, but also because it was ultimately responsible for opening the way for the Allied advance to Benghazi. It is necessary therefore to review the fighting in the XXX Corps area as from 23 November, when the Germans had recaptured Sidi Rezegh and the Corps had started withdrawing east, only to be stopped by the personal intervention of General Auchinleck who had flown to General Cunningham's headquarters on 23 November and had soon thereafter ordered the resumption of the offensive against Sidi Rezegh.

At about this time, the garrison of Tobruk, that is the 70th (British) Division, which had made a sortie on 21 November, was on the way to Ed Duda, four miles north-west of Sidi Rezegh. But its pace had slackened since its arrival there due to increasing resistance, and it had been found necessary to relieve the pressure against it to facilitate its progress. The New Zealand Division (from the XIII Corps) had been despatched for the purpose with instructions to attack Sidi Rezegh. Two of its brigades, the 4th and the 6th, had thereafter become engaged in that action; and their base for attack on Sidi Rezegh was Point 175, a ridge about five miles to its west.

This attack was to have been made jointly with the 70th Division. The objectives to be attacked were Sidi Rezegh and Ed Duda—the two points commanding the valley through which ran the Axis lines of communication from east to west. The New Zealand Division was to capture Sidi Rezegh, and the Tobruk garrison Ed Duda, and both were to effect a junction across the valley.

According to this plan, the 4th New Zealand Brigade had struck north from Point 175 and taken Zafraan without great difficulty by dawn on 25 November. The same night it had captured Belhamed by a skilfully planned bayonet attack. It had been previously arranged that while this brigade would keep the Axis forces busy at Belhamed, the 6th New Zealand Brigade would make for Sidi Rezegh. The latter put in the attack as planned and pressed it with great determination. It made satisfactory progress at first but soon came up against stubborn defences on the high ground above the Sidi Rezegh mosque. The progress had however caused the brigade such heavy losses that it became necessary to halt and reorganise before pressing further. By the night of 26 November, the reorganisation had been completed and the operation resumed. Sidi Rezegh fell before the spirited effort of the New Zealand force and the way was thus cleared for a junction with the Tobruk garrison.[1]

The Tobruk Sortie

The Tobruk force opened the final phase of its long-deferred attack at midday on 26 November. It captured Ed Duda within a few hours in spite of severe opposition, and before night was in possession of the greater part of the Ed Duda ridge. There it was to be met by the infantry of the New Zealand Division for a final link-up with the Eighth Army according to the plan. Strenuous attempts were made by the New Zealanders to effect this junction. They were at last successful, when General Freyberg, commanding the New Zealand forces, was able to move his reserve battalion to Duda, by the south of Belhamed. But, although this battalion did succeed in establishing contact with the Tobruk infantry, then engaged in consolidating the Ed Duda ridge, the link was by no means strong enough to withstand heavy counter-attacks from the Axis. Further, the fact of the contact having been established did not necessarily mean that the siege of Tobruk had been raised, or that its relief had been finally effected; since, for this to happen, it was necessary for the Allies to make their precarious footholds on the Sidi Rezegh and Ed Duda ridges more secure and to clear up the valley between them. That work was far from complete and, to add to the difficulties, as soon as the New Zealand battalion had passed through to Ed Duda, the Axis forces in the valley closed in and took up positions with the obvious intention of holding the gap and protecting their communications.

[1] Gen. Auchinleck's *Despatch* in Supplement to the *London Gazette*, 15 Jan. 48, p 340.

The Allied infantry, however, began its scheduled tasks of clearing the valley, undeterred by this new development. Thus, on 28 November, the New Zealand infantry began sweeping the area with the help of tanks and armoured cars. At the same time the 70th Division hunted out and dislodged parties of Axis troops from the edge of the escarpment between Ed Duda and Belhamed. Numerous prisoners and much booty were taken in both those actions, and a corridor was swept clear, making a safe passage to Tobruk. The XIII Corps Headquarters, and the administrative echelons of the New Zealand Division, passed through that lane and entered Tobruk. Two supply convoys were also got through, which were badly needed as the 70th Division had run short of ammunition and other necessaries. These proved useful also for re-equipping the troops against a possible counter-attack on the Tobruk corridor, which was by no means a remote possibility.

The reaction of the Axis High Command to the loss of Belhamed, Sidi Rezegh and Ed Duda was quick and vigorous. Axis wireless messages had been intercepted a day earlier asking their armoured formations which had been then engaged in raiding the frontier to return immediately; and should they succeed in returning, an early and heavy assault on the XIII Corps positions seemed to be a distinct possibility. Efforts were accordingly made to prevent the Axis tanks from returning west. They were several times attacked on the way by the tanks of the 7th Armoured Division whose strength now totalled about one hundred and twenty. But these could not prevail against the better armour and the more powerful guns of the German tanks; and far from deterring the Axis tanks from attacking the XIII Corps, they themselves suffered heavy losses which left them powerless to intervene in the next day's battle.

Allied reverses

The battle began on 29 November with violent assaults on both the flanks of the corridor. Several heavy, though unsuccessful, attacks were made on the Ed Duda ridge, after which the Axis troops at last penetrated the area between Ed Duda and Belhamed and secured a foothold on the crest of a height. They were thrown back from that position by the garrison of Tobruk which made a counter-attack at the break of day on 30 November. But, in the meanwhile, the Axis had captured Point 175 from the New Zealand troops, and during the rest of the day occupied the whole of the Sidi Rezegh ridge. That same afternoon some fifty German tanks together with a large infantry force fell upon the 6th New Zealand Brigade, which then had barely one-third of its fighting strength and not more than two support tanks to meet the attack. As a result it was overwhelmed and after a gallant resistance ceased to exist as a fighting formation.

Two days before the mishap General Ritchie had realised that the New Zealand Division, with its greatly depleted strength and its third brigade away, would need help to meet its heavy commitments. He had, therefore, ordered the 1st South African Infantry Brigade to join the XIII Corps. But that formation was new to the desert and its advance was hampered by the large number of vehicles which it had to marshal and control. It had frequently to halt, change direction and find its way again, which greatly retarded its progress. As a result it was late in reaching its destination, and spent some more time before going into action. It was ordered to attack Point 175 from the east which it did at dawn on 1 December. But it failed to make any impression on that strongly held position. Had this formation arrived well in time when called up, that is on the morning of 29 November, it is possible that its presence might have turned the scale. In such an event, the Allied tanks, which had by then been reinforced and which once again numbered one hundred and twenty, might have been freed to intervene at Sidi Rezegh. However, as things happened, the most important Allied gains, that is those in the Sidi Rezegh area, had been lost and the grip on the other positions had considerably weakened.

One such position was Belhamed. It fell early on 1 December, having been attacked from Sidi Rezegh by a strong force of German tanks and infantry. This led to the retirement of the New Zealand Division from Zafraan, since after that it stood in the danger of being entirely cut off. Then again, the attack on Point 175 by the South African Infantry Brigade had to be abandoned as it was not considered likely to produce any important result. The sum total of all these losses was that the hard-won Tobruk corridor had vanished and Tobruk was once more isolated, now with greater commitments than before and smaller resources to meet them. The length of its perimeter which needed to be manned hereafter had increased by seventeen miles; its garrison had suffered heavy losses and its tank strength was only twenty runners. This was the end of the second battle of Sidi Rezegh. Like the first, it had gone in favour of the Axis.

Abandonment of Sidi Rezegh

At this juncture, General Ritchie made an important tactical discovery which led to the abandonment of all efforts to capture Sidi Rezegh. He saw that there was another area which very much resembled Sidi Rezegh in its tactical layout but which had other advantages also. That was El Adem, a valley under observation from two opposite ridges to the north and the south. The main Axis communications between east and west passed through this valley, which it was possible to cut by securing El Adem. In addition, the position had another advantage in that it could be used to force the Axis tanks to leave the valley between Sidi Rezegh and Belhamed and come out in the open, where it would be possible to deal with them better. As things stood, however, those tanks were protected by a formidable screen of anti-tank guns which had the effect of sealing up the eastern entrance to the valley. To force them to emerge from that seclusion, it was only necessary to dominate the El Adem ridges and simultaneously to isolate Bardia and the Axis supply dumps to its west. In such a case the Axis tanks would have to come out to restore their communications.

That in brief was the new plan of General Ritchie, the main item of which was the capture of El Adem at an early date. To implement this he required fresh reinforcements. General Auchinleck, who had then flown to his headquarters, found some for him from Syria and Cyprus; and it was in these circumstances that some three unbrigaded Indian battalions were combined to form the 38th Indian Infantry Brigade. But these were not enough and in the main General Ritchie was thrown on his own resources for solving the problem. This he did by regrouping his forces so as to release some fresh troops for operational requirements. Among the Indian forces thus released were two brigades of the 4th Indian Division, the 5th and the 7th Indian Infantry Brigades, which were ordered to be relieved by the 2nd South African Division. The 11th Indian Infantry Brigade, which had already been drawn into the army reserve near Maddalena, was also furnished with transport and made ready for the operation. The method of regrouping and reorganising to find fresh troops was also extended likewise to several other formations. From all this reorganisation there emerged a new order of battle of the Eighth Army which was as follows:—

> *XXX Corps.* (Lieutenant-General Norrie)
>   7th Armoured Division
>   4th Armoured Brigade
>   7th Support Group
>   4th Indian Division
>   1st South African Infantry Brigade
>   Five armoured car regiments
> *XIII Corps.* (Lieutenant-General Godwin-Austen)
>   70th Division
>   32nd Army Tank Brigade
>   Polish Carpathian Brigade Group

>   Polish Carpathian Cavalry
>   18th and 19th New Zealand Infantry Battalions
>   2/13th Australian Infantry Battalion
>   11th Czechoslovak Battalion
>   2nd South African Division
>   3rd South African Infantry Brigade Group
>   6th South African Infantry Brigade Group
>   5th New Zealand Infantry Brigade Group (attached)
>   1st Army Tank Brigade Group (attached)
> *Rear Area*
>   New Zealand Division
>   4th NZ Infantry Brigade
>   6th NZ Infantry Brigade
>   38th Indian Infantry Brigade
>   5th South African Infantry Brigade
> *Matruh Fortress*
>   2nd South African Infantry Brigade Group
>   4th South African Infantry Brigade Group

The new plan for the capture of El Adem involved an attack on Bir el Gubi as a preliminary move. El Gubi was the key to the situation in so far as it was one of the two bases or "pivots of manoeuvre" round which the Axis armour and mobile troops revolved. By denying that base it was possible to unhinge the Axis defence in the El Adem region and make El Adem vulnerable to that extent. In pursuance of that plan it was decided to attack Bir el Gubi before every other objective and the task was allotted to the 11th Indian Infantry Brigade which was placed under the 7th (British) Armoured Division for the purpose, the latter then being under the XXX Corps. After the capture of El Gubi, the XXX Corps was to move northwards and secure a ridge to the south of El Adem. Next, it was to attack and capture the western end of the El Adem ridge itself.

While the operation for the capture of Bir el Gubi would be under way, XIII and the XXX Corps were to proceed with their own allotted tasks. The XIII Corps was to move forward from Ed Duda along the El Adem ridge as far as the road Tobruk—El Adem. After that it was to join up with the XXX Corps which would be advancing from the south as mentioned above. Pending those moves, the 7th Armoured Division was to stand off to the east in wait for the Axis tanks which were expected to emerge from the valley to meet the infantry attacks on El Gubi and El Adem. As a diversionary move some Allied armoured cars were to raid the Acroma area, where one such raid had already succeeded in drawing the attention of the Axis aircraft somewhat in excess of the right tactical value of that target.

The last eastward thrust

It was inevitable that all this reorganisation and recasting of plans should take some time. It was also to be expected that during that interval there might be some fresh moves by the Axis, tending to upset that plan. One such move did commence while the Eighth Army was still in the middle of its preparations. It took the shape of an eastward thrust towards the frontier. Once again, and now for the last time, General Rommel resorted to his favourite strategem of trying to weaken the fighting power of the Eighth Army by striking in its rear and disorganising its communications and supplies. It may be recalled that he had tried these tactics on three previous occasions with very little success; and judging from the results he could not possibly have undertaken this move as a serious operation. It must either have been intended to cover an assault on Tobruk which took place on the following day, or it may have been a part of his effort to get supplies from his dumps west of Bardia. It is probable that he intended to accomplish both these results in addition to rescuing, if possible, some of his troops then cut off in Bardia.

Whatever his expectations, they were not fulfilled by the tank columns which set out for the frontier on 3 December. Two strong fighting patrols of the Axis had begun moving towards Bardia on that day. One took the coast road and the other the Trigh-Capuzzo. The coastal column did not succeed in getting beyond Gambut, for, on the north-east of that locality, it came up against the 5th New Zealand Brigade which inflicted a heavy loss on it and successfully cut short its progress. The Trigh-Capuzzo column, too, met with a similar fate at the hands of a strong detachment of the 5th Indian Infantry Brigade near Sidi Azeiz. Meeting the German tanks in that vicinity, the Indian detachment withdrew on Sidi Azeiz in contact with the approaching tanks, and practically lured the latter on to is artillery. Three Axis tanks were then destroyed by the 31st Field Regiment at a range of 400 yards and further losses were inflicted by the infantry of the 5th Indian Brigade. At this, the tanks abandoned the effort to advance and withdrew to safety. But the following morning some fifteen of them, along with infantry, made a second attack in the area of the 31st Field Regiment near Sidi Azeiz. That attack, however, was characterised by a reluctance on their part to come too close to the guns, probably due to the preceding day's experience. In any case the advance was easily halted and the tanks retired after a brief fight, leaving behind a hundred Germans dead and another hundred prisoners.

The frustration of these two columns provoked the Axis into sending out a third and more powerful column on the following day, 4 December. The column emerged from the main Axis leaguer near Sidi Rezegh and set off for Bardia along the track Trigh—Capuzzo. But its progress was impeded from the very start. At first it was bombed on the way by the Allied aircraft and then it was attacked by the Support Group of the 7th Armoured Division. Finally it encountered a strong opposition from the troops of the 2nd South African Division who had just arrived in that area. At this stage, the tanks gave up the attempt to proceed further and returned to the leaguer. That marked the end of the last effort of General Rommel to win an easy and inexpensive victory by merely disorganising the communications and supplies in the rear of his opponent's army.[2]

During this brief period, that is from 3 to 5 December, General Ritchie was making his final adjustments for attacking El Adem. This involved the transfer of the 4th Indian Division from the frontier to the XXX Corps area south of Tobruk. The Indian division, as we have seen, was to be relieved by the 2nd South African Division, and the relief was actually in progress while the German tank columns were making efforts to reach Bardia. Thus, of the three brigades of the 4th Indian Division, the 11th Indian Infantry Brigade had commenced its move towards Bir el Gubi on 3 December; the 5th Brigade followed the next day, and the 7th, which was delayed due to the non-arrival of its troop-carrying transport, at last put in its appearance in the Tobruk area on 6 December. In the meantime, the 11th Indian Infantry Brigade had commenced its operation against Bir el Gubi.

The 11th Indian Brigade's attack on Bir el Gubi

To carry out its assignment of capturing El Gubi, as a prelude to the capture of El Adem, the 11th Brigade set out from its concentration area, near about Bir Duedar (4336),[3] during the day on 3 December. From there it performed a long night march so as to be in a position to attack from the west. The distance of the approach was about thirty miles and the route was entirely unknown and unreconnoitred. The brigade had little or no opportunity for training in desert navigation and it was launched out on its toilsome journey with only forty-five minutes of daylight left for completing its preparations. The march involved a movement of encircling the Axis positions and there was the usual risk of being detected during the move. However, owing to the skill of the navigating officer and the generally high standard of the brigade, the move was completed without any incident in about six hours; and,

---

[2] 4 Ind. Div's. *Account of Ops. in Cyrenaica*, pp. 23-4; W/D. 5 Bde., 11 Bde.
[3] The map references are to GSGS maps, 1/250,000, Egypt and Cyrenaica (Sheet 3).

by 0400 hours on 4 December, the brigade was in position to the west of Bir el Gubi, about three miles from the Axis troops, preparing to attack.[4]

The attack commenced at 0700 hours with two battalions, the 2nd Camerons and the 2nd Mahrattas. At first the battalions met with a certain measure of success but soon came up against an unexpected opposition. Although it had been known that Bir el Gubi was strongly held, and although such an eventuality had been allowed for in the preparations, the stubbornness of the actual defence came as a surprise. The Axis troops were well-entrenched and were supported by field and anti-tank guns as well as tanks. The Italian garrison was full of determination and was hitting out with vigour. In the circumstances, the 11th Brigade failed to register much progress on the first day, but continued the action on the following day, 5 December. All its three battalions had now been committed to action and heavy casualties were being incurred in the fighting that followed. In the evening, the Axis troops counter-attacked the few positions already secured by the brigade, resulting in two companies of the 2nd Mahrattas being overrun completely. Fairly heavy casualties were suffered also by the 2nd Camerons, particularly amongst the officers. Thus at the end of two days of heavy fighting, the 11th Brigade was in no enviable position. It had lost all the positions it had previously captured and also one-third of its fighting strength. It was ordered to withdraw but found it difficult to disengage. Eventually it managed to retire through the Guards Brigade, which had specially taken up a position on its south-west to cover its withdrawal. It was followed up by the Axis troops until it passed through the covering position and rejoined the 4th Indian Division to the south-east of El Gubi.[5]

Axis attack on Tobruk

While the action against El Gubi was in progress, Axis troops were busy delivering a heavy assault against the Tobruk salient. They launched the attack at dawn on 4 December and, before morning, fighting was ranging all along the salient's perimeter. In the afternoon the Allied position deteriorated further when the anti-tank guns of the Axis arrived on the scene and wiped out the few remaining tanks of the 32nd Army Tank Brigade. By the evening, the Axis forces had made fairly deep penetrations into the perimeter and, towards the night, the prospects of the garrison holding out much longer seemed far from hopeful. However, at the critical stage, the tide turned unexpectedly. The garrison

[4] W/Ds. 4 Div., 7 Bde., 5 Bde., 11 Bde.; 4 Ind. Div's. *Account of Ops. in Cyrenaica*, pp. 23-4.
[5] *Ibid.*, W/D. 2/5 Mahrattas.

which was fortifying itself against a possible night assault discovered that the attackers had withdrawn. As far as could be gathered then, the Italian Bologna Division had retired westward under the cover of the day's hard fighting, thus freeing the eastern sector of Tobruk from the siege. Later it transpired that this retirement was part of the plan for a general withdrawal. This was confirmed the next day, 5 December, when the *Afrika Korps* and the Italian Mobile Corps which were then concentrated near Sidi Rezegh also began a systematic withdrawal. Utilising the cover from their artillery, sited on the southern escarpment, they fell back on a new line running from El Adem to Bir el Gubi.[6]

Axis withdrawal begins

This withdrawal naturally came as a surprise to the Allied troops, and what the real reason behind it was, is difficult to say even at this stage. In any case it neither improved the Allied position very much nor did it place the Axis forces at any particular disadvantage. It was as necessary as before to capture Bir el Gubi and take El Adem. The western and south-western sides of the Tobruk perimeter were still dominated by the Axis positions and the failure of the 11th Indian Brigade to take El Gubi had not improved matters. However, the fact remained that the Axis had been pushed back a little; and there were indications that it intended to withdraw still farther. General Ritchie was therefore anxious that the XIII and XXX Corps should be ready to commence their respective operations. The 4th Indian Division, which was then under the XXX Corps, was, on 5 December, still assembling somewhere to the south-east of El Gubi and, to give it time, the Corps Commander, General Norrie, fixed the evening of 6 December as the time for commencing the operations. But a new situation came to light on that day. It was discovered that two German Panzer Divisions were sitting astride the Indian division's line of advance on a patch of rising ground north-west of El Gubi. It therefore became necessary to clear that ground first by bringing the tanks to battle.

Accordingly General Norrie posted the infantry to the south of Bir el Gubi, while the Allied armoured vehicles went out to meet the Axis armour. At first the latter appeared to be evading a fight. But later, in the afternoon, they were detected west of Bir el Gubi, forming up to attack the Guards Brigade. The attack, however, never developed and instead the tanks retired after a short while. Once again it is difficult to assign a reason for this seemingly unnecessary rearward move. It is likely that the Panzer units had

[6] Gen. Auchinleck's *Despatch* in Supplement to the *London Gazette*, pp. 342-3.

orders to avoid any serious engagement with the Allied tank force which was now manifestly superior in numbers. In any case, this led to a daylong affray between the Allied and Axis tanks round Bir el Gubi, which, however, produced no worthwhile results.

Meanwhile, believing that a further Axis withdrawal was imminent, General Ritchie had ordered the XIII Corps to commence its allotted operation against El Adem. On receipt of these instructions, the 23rd (British) Infantry Brigade began its advance on 7 December after dark, along the Ed Duda ridge. By the evening of the following day, the Corps had completely cleared the southeast side of Tobruk and was dominating the Tobruk—El Adem road.

The advance of the XIII Corps was, as events showed, well-timed for taking advantage of a further Axis withdrawal. For, on 8 December, the Axis began a rapid though orderly withdrawal to Gazala, which continued on 9 December. An effort to intercept the withdrawing force was made by a British armoured brigade which advanced to "Knightsbridge" in the hope of coming up on the western flank of the retreating force. But the attempt was only partly successful. Moreover, as the supply system of the XXX Corps had been stretched to the limit, the armoured brigade was unable to follow up the retreating troops effectively. In fact, lack of petrol finally brought it to a complete standstill on 9 December, after which the task of keeping up the momentum of the advance devolved, amongst others, on the 4th Indian Division.[7]

The 4th Indian Division in Pursuit

The 4th Indian Division was now complete with its three brigades, the 11th Brigade having reverted to its command after the El Gubi action. A fourth brigade, the 22nd Guards, also passed under its temporary command. The Central Indian Horse and a battery of the 31st Field Regiment, too, had arrived from the frontier and rejoined the 4th Indian Division, which had thus become a well-integrated formation ready for a major move.

In the course of the night of 8 December, various patrols reported that there were signs of German withdrawal from their part of the front; and the same night the 4th Indian Division received its orders to advance. The divisional plan of advance was to move in a long column of brigade groups, in the order, 7th and 5th Brigades, the Divisional Headquarters and the 11th Brigade. The Central India Horse was to protect the left flank and the 11th Brigade was to constitute the reserve. The axis of advance was to lie west of El Gubi and was directed on to Hagiag er Raml (3841).[8]

[7] W/D. 4 Div.
[8] The map references are to GSGS maps, 1/250,000, Egypt and Cyrenaica (Sheet 3).

From there the 7th Brigade was to wheel right and get on to El Adem. The final objective of the division was Acroma, a nerve-centre of communications, the possession of which by the Allies would deny to the Axis any access to the east of Tobruk and thereby force it to relax its hold on El Adem and El Gubi.

In accordance with the orders received by it, the 4th Indian Division began its advance early on 9 December. The Central India Horse which was protecting its left flank was given the additional assignment of exploiting towards Acroma if possible. The 22nd Guards Brigade was ordered to secure the divisional axis from the south-west, that is from Bir Hakeim, a junction of several desert roads from some of which the Axis troops would be able to approach and harry the left flank of the Indian division's advance. Throughout 9 December, the advance continued without incident, the 7th Indian Infantry Brigade reaching El Adem at 1815 hours where it made contact with the 23rd (British) Infantry Brigade from Tobruk. In the meantime, the 5th Indian Infantry Brigade had been obliged to detach one of its battalions, 3/1 Punjab, to send it to the assistance of the Central India Horse who had come up against strong opposition. The rest of this brigade had moved on during the day and reached Naduret el Chesceuasc (3840). The Advanced Divisional Headquarters with its reserve, the 11th Indian Infantry Brigade, had followed in its wake and stationed itself at Pt. 175 (3939). The Central India Horse had reached the escarpment west of Hagiag er Raml, after which it was unable to advance due to opposition. One of its squadrons on the escarpment, however, came up against parties of Axis troops withdrawing in all possible directions and had a busy time collecting batches of prisoners in large numbers.[9]

Relief of Tobruk

This day of success was followed by another even more successful. The 4th Indian Division's advance continued without interruption. During the morning (10 December) the 7th Indian Infantry Brigade reached Acroma without opposition. At the same time the 5th Indian Infantry Brigade drew forward so as to get level with the 7th, thereby forming an extended line some fifteen miles westward. Still further west, a mixed force of an Indian divisional motorised cavalry and infantry engaged the left flanks of the Axis rearguard resting on Bir el Harmat, and finally secured Hagiag er Raml. On this very day, the Support Group of the 7th Armoured Division moved round by way of Acroma and proceeded further west until it came into contact with the Axis outposts. Here the advance slowed down.

[9] W/D.: HQ 4 Div.; 5, 7, 11 Bdes.; CIH; 3/1 Punjab.

The Axis outposts which the Indian division had come up against were the forward defences of a new Axis line running southward from Gazala which General Rommel had now decided to occupy. The scene of fighting had thus shifted from El Adem—El Gubi line to what may be called the Gazala line. At this stage the Advanced Headquarters of the 4th Indian Division moved forward to Bir ez Zibli (3842), with the 11th Indian Infantry Brigade following. Here the 4th Indian Division reverted to the XIII Corps, the 22nd Guards Brigade passing to the XXX Corps.

While the XXX Corps was thus pursuing the Axis towards the Gazala line, the XIII Corps was systematically clearing the western perimeter of Tobruk. Its method of working was to make an outflanking movement along the ridge and then to clear the positions in the intervening low ground. Repeating this process, it quickly rolled up the Axis opposition in the Tobruk area and was ready by 10 December to make a concerted move, along with the XXX Corps, on to Acroma. But Acroma had only a little before been occupied by the 7th Indian Infantry Brigade, which had taken it on the same day, as stated already. This had removed the last vestige of the Axis domination of the western defence of Tobruk, and the long fight for the relief of that beleaguered fortress was at last at an end. Tobruk was now free. Its relief was complete. Its eight-month old siege had come to an end, and its garrison was released to make fresh contributions to the onward move of the Eighth Army.

It remains only to mention that, of the isolated pockets of Axis troops still holding out in the frontier area, the Cova and Bir Ghirba positions were cleared by the 2nd South African Division, after which only the Bardia and Halfaya pockets remained to be reduced. They could not, however, be dealt with then, as the main concern of the Eighth Army was the pursuit of the retreating Axis force.

XXX Corps reverts to the Frontier

Hitherto the pursuit was being conducted by the XXX Corps, and XIII Corps had just joined it. But the supply system of the Eighth Army was too inadequate to maintain two corps in the forward area. General Ritchie, therefore, decided that the XIII Corps, which was more conveniently placed for the job, should take up the pursuit from this point onwards, and that the XXX Corps should revert to the rear and clear the frontier area of the last lingering remnants of Axis resistance around Bardia and Halfaya. This final elimination of the Axis garrisons was necessary to open up direct road and rail communication with Tobruk and to facilitate future stages of the operations. With the forward troops moving on towards Benghazi, as they were expected to do, the supplies by sea would have to be supplemented with those by road and rail, while the transport now absorbed by the long detour through the desert would be needed for operational duties. Thus the roles of the two corps were rightly made complementary, the XXX Corps improving the supply system and the XIII Corps maintaining the pursuit.

CHAPTER XXIV

Pursuit of the Afrika Korps

Battle of Alam Hamza

The XIII Corps began organising the pursuit as soon as the Army commander had named it as the pursuit force. Its main problem however was administrative, the settlement of which involved a certain amount of delay. As for its operational task, it had under its command the 4th Indian Division, the 7th Armoured Division and the 5th New Zealand Brigade. Its plan of operation was simple. One infantry formation was to hold the Axis force frontally at Gazala, while another was to work its way to the rear of the Axis line and cut off the further retreat of the Axis to the west. The 5th New Zealand Brigade was assigned the former task and the 4th Indian Division the latter.

The operation was to begin with the New Zealand Brigade advancing along the main road, astride the coastal escarpment, and making an effort to contain Gazala. Simultaneously, the 4th Indian Division was to move along an approximate axis of 42 Northing Grid and get behind the Gazala line. This it was to do by bypassing Gazala and securing the objectives Bir Halegh el Eleba (T.49)—Tmimi (P. 70).[1] After that it was to exploit forward towards Derna. The 7th Armoured Division was to protect the southern and eastern flanks of the 4th Indian Division. If possible, it was also to raid Axis communications near Tmimi and patrol towards Mekili. The 70th Division was to be left in Tobruk to mop up Axis troops still lurking in the deep coastal wadis. The operation was timed to start at 1200 hours on 11 December, and 37 Easting Grid was to be the starting line.[2]

The commander of the 4th Indian Division, Major-General Messervy, began to make his own plan as soon as he became aware of the intentions of the XIII Corps. He decided that the administrative difficulties did not permit of a three-brigade advance and so obtained the permission of the Corps to leave the 11th Indian Infantry brigade behind, less the 1st Battalion of Rajputana Rifles. Accordingly, he located the 11th Brigade in the Tobruk area to reorganise and refit, and took the 1st Battalion Rajputana Rifles under him as the divisional reserve. The division, less the 11th

---

[1] The map references are to GSGS maps, 1/100,000, Egypt, Western Desert series.
[2] W/Ds.: HQ 4 Div.; 5, 7, 11 Bdes.; 1 Raj Rif; CIH.

Brigade, was to advance on a two-brigade front, of which the 5th on the right was to be the directing brigade. Each brigade was allotted one squadron of Central India Horse which was to be under its command. The Advanced Divisional Headquarters was to move between the two brigades. It was to be accompanied by the Central India Horse (less two squadrons), the 1st Battalion Rajputana Rifles and a detachment from the 8th Royal Tank Regiment, consisting of twelve Valentine tanks. Such transport as the 11th Brigade would not need in its rear location was used to complete deficiencies of the other two brigades.

The 4th Indian Division on the move

On the morning of 11 December, General Messervy visited the Corps headquarters at Tobruk to discuss and settle the last administrative details relating to his division's advance. The upshot of the discussion was that the starting time, which had been originally fixed at 1200 hours, was now postponed to 1430 hours. Meanwhile the 5th New Zealand Brigade was asked to begin its advance with the objective of reaching Gazala and containing the Axis garrison there. A little later, at 1420 hours, the 4th Indian Division also moved out of its locality and proceeded westward, with a view to taking the Gazala position from the rear. One battalion of the 5th Indian Infantry Brigade, the Buffs, could not accompany the division as it was still in action against the Axis troops somewhere in the vicinity of the feature Pt. 209. It was asked to disengage itself and follow the division's advance. Barring a minor instance of opposition on the 5th Brigade's flank, the move was carried out without incident and by night the Advanced Divisional Headquarters had reached Bir Ucheida (3742).[3]

The next stretch of the move was from Bir Ucheida to the objectives of the 5th and the 7th Indian Infantry Brigades, namely Tmimi and Bir Halegh el Eleba, respectively. It was decided that both the brigades should continue the advance on the 7th Brigade's axis until their arrival at Bir Halegh el Eleba which was to be reached in the evening of 12 December. From there the 5th Brigade would turn north-east during the night and proceed to take its objective, Tmimi. In agreement with this decision, the division resumed its advance from Bir Ucheida at 0500 hours; and moving in the darkness, somewhat faster than its accompanying brigades, found itself at daylight at some point about fourteen miles west of Bir Ucheida and about as much ahead of the brigades. The headquarters therefore remained halted during the day in that position waiting for the brigades to catch up. The 7th Brigade

---

[3] 4 Ind. Div's. *Acct. of Operations in Cyrenaica*, pp. 29-32. W/Ds. *Ibid.*

arrived and resumed its position on the left of the division. The 5th Brigade was delayed owing to the difficulty in arranging the administrative sides of its move. It however reached there before the evening and took up its position on the right of the divisional headquarters.

The Indian Division on the Gazala line

Early next morning, 13 December, the Indian division resumed its advance to cover the final stage of its journey to the rear of the Gazala position. But hardly had it proceeded some distance when it came to a halt, somewhere about Gabr el Abidi (U.96), both its brigades reporting that they had come up against and contacted Axis positions which were no doubt well fortified. It now became clear that the original plan of moving south of Gazala and reaching the rear would not be carried out, for the path of the 4th Indian Division was blocked by what appeared to be a line of strong points and defended localities. The line seemed to stretch from Gazala to Sidi Breghisc (U. 77) via Alam Hamza (U. 97). In actual fact, as was discovered later, it was longer still. It was the prototype of what has since become popularly known as the Gazala line and it ran south-west from the coast in the direction Gazala—Alam Hamza—Sidi Breghisc—Trigh el Abd. It contained three strong points or fortified features. They were Points 205-208 (U. 97) in the vicinity of Alam Hamza, Pt. 201 at Sidi Breghisc and Pt. 204 (U. 87) between Sidi Breghisc and Alam Hamza.

So long as the Gazala line was intact there was no question of the 4th Indian Division reaching its two objectives, Bir Halegh el Eleba and Tmimi, without fighting. It was necessary to force a gap through the Gazala line and the positions to be attacked for the purpose were Pt. 204 and Pts. 205-208. The 5th Brigade was ordered to secure both of these features and the 7th Brigade was asked to conform on the left to its advance so as to be able to attack Sidi Breghisc, should the opportunity occur. In the meanwhile the 5th New Zealand Brigade was to attack the Gazala poisition on the coast.

In conformity with that plan, the 5th Indian Brigade began its attack at 1245 hours, using the 4th Battalion Rajputana Rifles against the Pts. 205-208 feature. That turned out to be a very strong position with carefully concealed trenches, and in consequence the attack came to a halt after a little progress. The left company had suffered particularly heavy casualties and it was necessary to employ a second battalion in the same sector or in the neighbouring one to produce relief. For that reason 1 Buffs were asked to attack Pt. 204. Presumably as a result of the Axis troops having been drawn off to oppose the Rajputana Rifles, the Buffs found Pt. 204

unoccupied and were thus able to establish themselves there without much loss of time. During the afternoon, German tanks and lorried infantry essayed an attack on the area but retired quickly after a brief firefight, having suffered losses both in lorries and tanks.[4]

While the 5th Indian Infantry Brigade was engaging the Axis forces in the area of Pts. 205-208, the 7th Indian Infantry Brigade on its left was to find some means of attacking Sidi Breghisc. It could not however get started at all, as there was difficulty in selecting an objective, the country forward of it being in the form of a deep re-entrant. But it transpired that there were some Axis troops behind it, which were going to be engaged by the Support Group of the 7th Armoured Division from the south. The 7th Indian Infantry Brigade was therefore ordered to turn about and attack the same troops from the north, that is from their rear. Reconnaissance for that attack started in the afternoon. At the same time guns of the 25th Field Regiment, protected by carriers and anti-tank guns, began registering their targets, and the 4th Sikh Battalion embussed to go to the fighting area.[5]

Another tank-artillery duel

Before that attack could go in, however, a new circumstance had developed. Finding that the guns of the 25th Field Regiment were in the act of registering for the attack, some forty Axis tanks advanced against them evidently with a view to putting them out. The tanks were supported by artillery and lorried infantry and were moving forward methodically. The batteries of the 25th Field Regiment, disposed as they then were in inter-supporting positions in echelons, had been ordered to hold their fire until the force had approached within a practicable range. In the meanwhile the 4th Sikh Battalion, which had been waiting embussed in the vicinity, was gradually withdrawn to give the guns a clear field of fire. More anti-tank guns were called up and ten Valentines of the 8th Royal Tank Regiment also arrived on the scene. Without any doubt a fierce clash between the British guns and the Axis tanks was now imminent.

As the force of Axis tanks and lorried infantry drew nearer, there was ample opportunity for observing the German tactics in detail. Their Mark IV tanks and artillery advanced in bounds, firing at fairly long ranges. Under the cover of that fire advanced the Mark IIIs and the transport-borne infantry, obviously heading

---

[4] W/D. 4 Raj Rif 4 Ind. Div's. *Acct. of Ops. in Cyrenaica*, pp. 29-32.
[5] The reason why the 25th Field Regiment was so far forward was that it was being used by the 7th Indian Infantry Brigade as its Advanced Guard to protect its vulnerable lorried infantry against Axis armour.

for the gun positions. The batteries of the 25th Field Regiment, having been ordered to hold fire until the force had come within 1200 yards, stood their ground without replying to the long-range shots from the advancing force. Then, as that force came within the specified range, there started a firefight in which twelve Axis tanks were knocked out and the remainder driven back by the close-range volleys of the 12th Battery. But, by that time, the leading battery had been overrun, having been unable to hold the attack in the initial stages. Seven officers and 58 men fell at their guns in that firefight and several guns were damaged, though most of them were in action the next day. The casualties were evacuated by the gun tractors of the 12th Battery as they occurred. In this action, the crew of the field and anti-tank guns had once again proved that discipline and gallantry were as important as fire-power in a duel between the artillery and tanks, especially if the latter be heavily supported by infantry and field guns.

The 4th Indian Division in the fray

Thus, the entire front of the 4th Indian Division was alive with infantry clashes, tank-vs-artillery battles and air raids on 13 December. The air-attacks were frequent and were made by dive-bombing, Stukas flying in formations. On 12 December, there had been eleven such attacks in the headquarters area alone. There were several more on the following day. The Stukas usually arrived in waves of between twenty and forty, flying comparatively slowly.[8] They were escorted by a dozen or twenty fighters though sometimes they came over unprotected. Some of the planes were flown by Italians and some by Germans, but a formation was usually led by a German. On arrival at the target they used to circle round and then dive out of the sun. At first they used to come very low, but later, owing to the accurate fire of the anti-aircraft guns, they got into the habit of diving only sufficiently to aim their bombs after which they disappeared in a hurry. They usually released a salvo of three bombs, one of 500 lbs carried under the fuselage and two of 100 lbs —one under each wing. They were never able to do much damage, since, in the desert, dispersion and slit trenches provided a fairly good measure of safety. Small-arms fire directed from trenches also proved a great deterrent. The rule for dispersion in the 4th Indian Division area required a distance of at least one hundred yards between the parked vehicles, preferably two hundred. Thus dispersed, the vehicles did not seem to attract the Stukas, the targets being too insignificant. The rule for the slit trenches required every man to dig his own trench at every halt of any length of time, the

---

[8] War Inf. Cir. No. 26-A, pp. 7-8.

trenches being just deep enough to permit a man to lie below ground-level. Shielded thus, men were known to escape harm from bombs falling five yards away in cases where surface objects two hundred yards distant were struck by fragments of the same missile. It was found that in the normal hard desert, a 500-lb bomb formed a crater some ten feet across and two feet deep, while the 100-lb bomb craters were about half that size. As a general routine, all slit trenches were filled before moving from a locality to avoid accidents among the vehicles following, especially during a night drive.

Thus, 13 December, the first day, passed off without the 4th Indian Division having made a deep enough impression on the Axis defences at Gazala. During the day's fighting it had collected some 371 prisoners including 21 officers; and the various artillery units under its command were responsible for 15 German tanks and 4 aircraft being put out of action in a single day. In addition, one of its infantry units, 1 Buffs, had secured a foothold on Pt. 204, which gain later proved to be more important than was at first supposed. Intelligence reports showed that Pt. 204 constituted a definite gap in the Gazala defences and that the Axis commanders were making strenuous efforts to fill that void.[7]

However, the Pt. 204 gap was not enough by itself to enable the Eighth Army to move onward. That same day, the 5th New Zealand Infantry Brigade had captured the Gazala landing ground, and was continuing its efforts to secure the rest of the Gazala line in other parts also. The most vital part was the Pts. 205-208 feature and once again the 5th Indian Infantry Brigade addressed itself to the task. But, for the second time, it was unable to overcome the defences of that hotly contested area. The attack came to a standstill soon after it had begun on 14 December, as its leading troops were effectively halted by heavy machine-gun fire.

On the afternoon of 14 December, there appeared the first signs of a disaster that later overtook 1 Buffs on Pt. 204. Groups of about fifteen Axis tanks at a time, accompanied by infantry, tried to attack the feature at midday and then again in the afternoon. On both the occasions the attacks were easily repulsed. But possibly these small attacks were in the nature of reconnaissance in force and, as such, preliminary to bigger attacks to come later on. In any case it was necessary to augment the tank strength of the 4th Indian Division as the situation was grave from other points of view besides. The most easily available reinforcement, at this time, was the 32nd Army Tank Brigade, which consisted of an assortment of thirty tanks of different kinds from Tobruk. It was moved

---

[7] 4 Indian Division's *Account of Operations in Cyrenaica*, p. 34. W/D. 5 Bde. W/D. HQ. 1 Div.

up and put under the command of the 4th Indian Division. In addition, the division also had about two dozen "I" tanks which were distributed equally between its two brigades. Thus strengthened, it began to lay fresh plans for breaking the Gazala defences.

Plan to break the Gazala defences

The new plan envisaged attacks on three different portions of the Gazala line during the following day, 15 December. Those portions were the area round Bir Halegh el Eleba, the Pts. 205-208 feature near Alam Hamza, and the Gazala locality on the west. Capture of Bir Halegh el Eleba was entrusted to the 7th Armoured Division which was to move round the southern flank of the Axis line and attack by 1100 hours. Starting at about the same time the 5th Indian Infantry Brigade was to secure the Pts. 205-208 feature by 1200 hours. It was expected that the move of the Armoured Division would relieve the pressure on this front. Finally, while the Armoured Division and the Indian brigade would be thus engaging the Axis troops, Gazala would be encircled by a joint move of the 5th New Zealand Brigade and a Polish brigade. Subsequently, the two Indian Brigades, the 5th and the 7th, would move to their originally fixed objectives, Tmimi and Bir Halegh el Eleba, mopping up the remnants of the Axis troops as they moved.

The operations began on 15 December according to plan but went wrong from the very start. The 7th Armoured Division was prevented from reaching its objective in time due to the roughness of the country it had to traverse. Its leading formation, the 4th Armoured Brigade, was late by four hours due to the bad going over the last twenty-five miles of its sixty-mile march.[8] In consequence the 5th Indian Infantry Brigade opposite Alam Hamza did not get the benefit that was expected from this move. There was no relaxation of resistance on its front and it had to attack the allotted feature against heavy odds. The attack went in, reinforced by an additional battalion, 3/1 Punjab, and some "I" tanks. The few tanks soon became casualties and no appreciable progress was made. Nor was much progress made in the coastal sector. Only half of the Gazala position was taken by the New Zealanders and the Poles in spite of a very spirited attack. But even that slight advantage was neutralised to a certain extent by a vicious onslaught which the Germans launched against the Pt. 204 feature on the same day.

Attack on Pt. 204

At about 1400 hours on that day, the Axis troops started an

---

[8] Gen. Auchinleck's *Despatch* in Supplement to *London Gazette*, 15 Jan. 1948, pp. 344-5. 4 Ind. Div's. *Acct. of Ops. in Cyrenaica*, p. 34.

intense artillery bombardment of Pt. 204 which was being held by 1 Buffs. The entire force on that point consisted of:

- 1 Buffs
- 31st Field Regiment
- One battery, 73rd Anti-Tank Regiment
- One troop, 57th Light AA Regiment
- One Squadron, Central India Horse (originally forward but driven into the sector by Axis tanks)
- Detachment of "I" tanks (ten)
- One Section, 18th Field Company SM.

It has not been found possible to compile a detailed story of the action that was fought at the end of the artillery bombardment, as the commander concerned and most of the officers had become casualties. But from the bits of information available it would appear that on the Axis side the attack had been prepared and executed with great care, whereas the defenders of Pt. 204 were unable to do anything equally good for their own defence, as they were in a very exposed salient, difficult to hold against a determined attack. The Axis forces consisted of some forty tanks with artillery and lorried infantry accompanying. They began with an intensive artillery preparation in which Mark IV tanks and field guns were used well forward, the range being 2000-3000 yards. Under the cover of that fire, the infantry began to infiltrate round the flanks and soon succeeded in bringing the Allied guns directly under their machine-gun fire. This lasted a considerable time during which the artillery had remained active. As soon as the bombardment ceased, a number of tanks rushed in and managed to penetrate certain localities. At the same time more tanks and armoured vehicles closed in from different directions on the gun positions which then became subject to close-range machine-gun fire.[9]

Caught in this position, the defenders of Pt. 204 hit back for all they were worth. They succeeded in disabling fourteen tanks and inflicted such heavy casualties on the German 115th Lorried Infantry Regiment that it was later heard to report on the wireless that it was in no condition to exploit its success. But in spite of their gallant and determined stand, 1 Buffs were finally overwhelmed. Their commanding officer, who was giving to the brigade head-quarters a running commentary of the action by radio-telephone, passed his last message at 1530 hours, reporting that his position was being overrun by tanks. Immediately after, the Indian operator announced that he was going to destroy his wireless set, ending the announcement with his last greetings. From this

---

[9] 4 Ind. Div's. *Acct. of Operations in Cyrenaica*, pp. 36-8.

holocaust, not more than one hundred men of the 1st Buffs managed to escape alive, while the 31st Field Regiment lost so many men that it had to be reorganised on a one-battery basis. Later, the Allied captives from this action were removed from Africa to Europe by the Axis High Command to avoid their falling back into the hands of the Eighth Army during its subsequent advance.

It may be mentioned here that the disaster which overwhelmed 1 Buffs was not entirely due to an unequal combat. There were certain weaknesses in defence which could have been avoided, and but for which the Axis attack might not have succeeded so completely. In the opinion of a General Staff Officer of the 4th Indian Division, the possible flaws in the defence of Pt. 204 were three. One of them was that properly dug gun positions had not been constructed. The second defect was that the disposition of other arms had failed to ensure the immunity of the field artillery from close-range small-arms and machine-gun fire. And finally, the few Allied tanks had wasted their ammunition by opening fire at an extreme range and by attempting a long-range duel during the period of artillery preparation of the Axis troops. Hence, when the Axis tanks actually arrived on the scene for close-quarter attack, the Allied tanks were nearing the end of their ammunition.

Thus, on the night of 15 December, the net result of the Allied gains and losses showed a rather disappointing balance. The Pts. 205-208 feature had not been taken; Pt. 204 had been lost; the Gazala locality had been only half taken, and the 7th Armoured Division had not even been able to begin its action. In short, after a whole day of hard fighting, the position had remained substantially unchanged, and the hurriedly-built Gazala line of the Germans seemed to stand as firm as ever. It now seemed necessary to reorganise and start the whole adventure over again as soon as might be practicable. Accordingly, the two Indian brigades were ordered to spend the whole of the following day, 16 December, in consolidating and securing their positions, while the 4th Indian Division drew in fresh reinforcements for the final struggle to break the Gazala defences. Those reinforcements were the 42nd Royal Tank Regiment which joined the 32nd Army Tank Brigade, and the 1st South African Infantry Brigade which thereafter came under the command of the Indian division.[10]

New Plans to break the Gazala Line

New plans were now devised for resuming the battle of the Gazala line on 17 December. The principal formation of the 7th

[10] 4 Ind. Div's. *Acct. of Ops. in Cyrenaica*, pp. 36-8.

Armoured Division, the 4th Armoured Brigade, had had enough time to get into the position originally intended for it—in the rear of the Axis troops defending the Alam Hamza area. Its role now was the same as before, namely, to draw off Axis armour from the 4th Indian Division's front. Simultaneously, the 1st South African Brigade, with the 42nd Royal Tank Regiment, was to attack the south flank of the Axis line and try to roll it northward or northwestward from that direction. For the rest, the whole of the original plan was left unaltered. A day before the plan was to be put into action, the 7th Armoured Division raided Tmimi in a hit-and-run fashion and returned to its line, while the Polish Brigade commenced its operations to encircle Gazala, which it was carrying out with remarkable success.

Further axis withdrawals

However, on the morning of 17 December, just as the 1st South African Brigade was about to begin reconnaissance for the attack, news arrived from the Corps Headquarters which made that reconnaissance unnecessary. The XIII Corps passed the information that the bulk of the Axis force had abandoned the Gazala line and withdrawn westwards leaving behind nothing more than some weak Italian rearguards. Patrols on the 4th Indian Division's front had already been reporting all through the preceding day that there were indications of a withdrawal since much noise of mechanical transport could be heard behind the Axis line. The news of withdrawal, therefore, did not come as a surprise to the 4th Indian Division which immediately changed its plan of attack into one of pursuit. It appeared that the threat produced by the 4th Armoured Brigade in his rear had induced General Rommel to withdraw rather than stay and risk destruction.

General Ritchie, it would appear, had foreseen that the Axis forces would thus make an effort to disengage suddenly and disappear in order to hold some other line further west, possibly between Derna and Mekili. He had therefore ordered a column of the Support Group to be sent to Carmusa to hold the cross-roads there, so as to make it difficult for General Rommel to establish himself at Derna. That column left early on 17 December and occupied Carmusa at midday on 18 December. In the meantime, the Eighth Army re-grouped for pursuing the withdrawing force. The pursuit lasted well over three weeks and took the Allied forces over the mountains known as Jebel Akhdar and across Cyrenaica to Benghazi and finally to El Agheila.[11] The story of that exciting chase cannot be made sufficiently intelligible without at least a brief

---

[11] Gen. Auchinleck's *Despatch* in Supplement to the *London Gazette*, p. 345.

description of the terrain and the road system of the country over which the pursued and the pursuing forces passed. It is therefore necessary to review briefly the topography of that part of Cyrenaica. Broadly, the region falls into two distinct physical groups: the green hills of Jebel Akhdar, and the featureless plains of the desert to their south.

CHAPTER XXV

Pursuit to Benghazi

Terrain and communications

The Jebel Akhdar, which means the Green Mountain, is the only part of Cyrenaica which the Italians found fit for large-scale colonisation. It is a hilly tableland stretching from Tmimi to Benghazi, some of the hills being as high as 200 feet. It stands out distinctly from the adjoining desert, in that, unlike that arid area, it is covered with green vegetation and is capable of sustaining life. In consequence, the whole countryside is dotted with patches of cultivation and with habitations, huts and houses, of the Italian settlers. The chief towns of the area are three: Derna in the east, Barce in the west and Benghazi in the extreme west. Derna is a modern town with a small port but a large aerodrome. The town with its bottle-neck approaches is situated at the foot of the escarpment and the aerodrome on the top. Barce, the centre of the Italian colonisation area, is an inland commercial town and a nodal point for the main road communications; and Benghazi is a coastal town on the main road with a large harbour but no natural defences.[1]

The principal artery of communication in the Jebel Akhdar area is the main coastal road running east to west. South-west of Derna this road divides into two branches both running roughly parallel to each other across the best part of Jebel Akhdar. The point where they divide lies somewhere near Martuba, the point of their reunion being at Barce. Thence a single road proceeds to Benghazi, Agedabia, El Agheila and beyond. The two parallel roads are, at places, linked by north-south arteries. Inevitably these links produce road-crossings, some of them of great importance in military operations. Road junctions of such importance, so far as the pursuit of the Axis force by the Eighth Army was concerned, were five. They were, from east to west, Martuba, Carmusa, Giovanni Berta, Lamluda and Barce.

South of Jebel Akhdar lies the vast expanse of barren desert, covered by a network of motorable desert tracks. At intervals those tracks converged on to certain localities forming desert junctions. The principal among them over which the Eighth Army passed were, again taking them from east to west, Mekili, Charruba, Zt. Msus, Antelat and Agedabia.

[1] Benghazi is not strictly in the Jebel Akhdar, but has been included here as being a part of the area colonised by the Italian settlers.

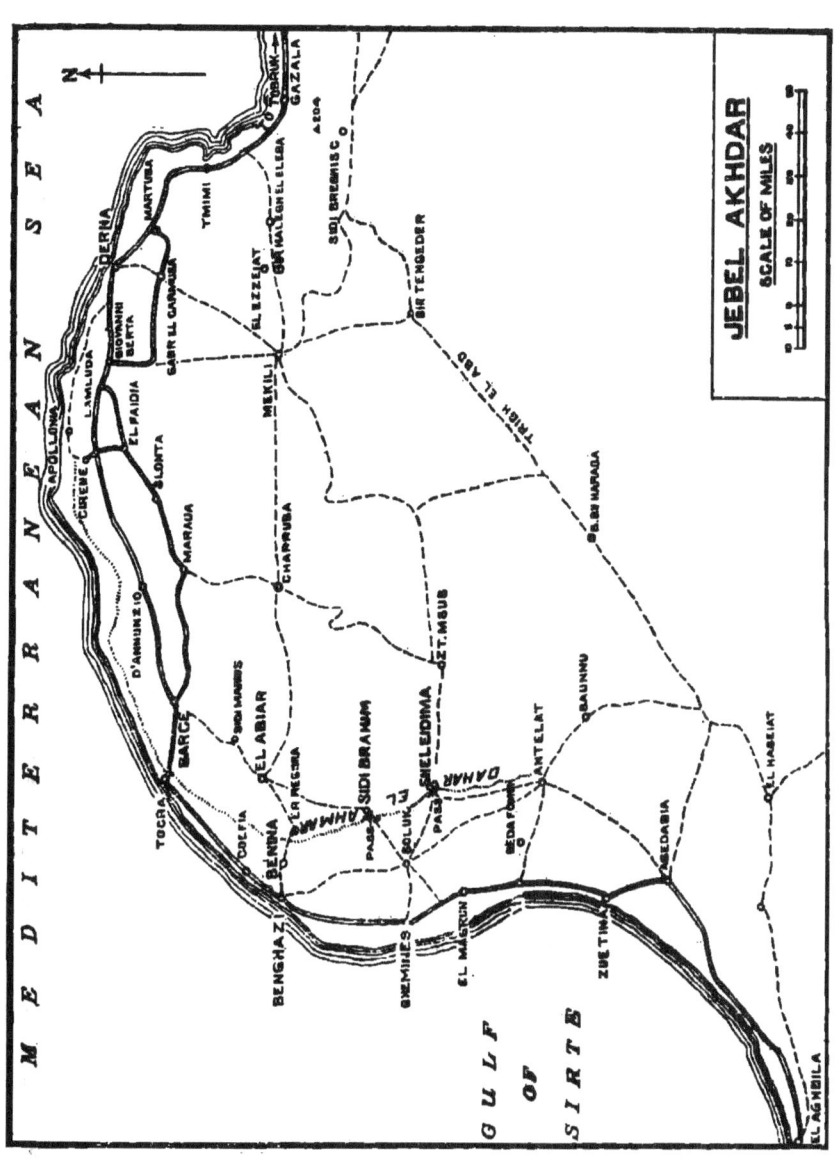

It will thus be seen that the country over which the Axis forces could retreat fell into two distinct regions, the Jebel Akhdar and the desert. Conforming to the topography, General Rommel's force divided itself, in retreat, into two groups. The German armoured divisions and the Italian Mobile Corps took the desert route through Mekili and Msus; while the Italian 21st Corps went along the main coastal road through Jebel Akhdar. Likewise, the troops of the XIII Corps also split themselves into two. The 4th Indian Division was sent over the Jebel Akhdar and the 7th Armoured Division across the desert.[2]

The 4th Indian Division resumes pursuit

The news of the withdrawal of the Axis from the Gazala line had reached the 4th Indian Division between 0800 and 0900 hours on 17 December; and the division had started out on the pursuit at 1000 hours, that is in a little over an hour. On the other hand, considerable delay occurred before the 7th Armoured Division could get started, the reason being that it was obliged to spend the whole day round Gazala trying to assemble transport and supplies for its advance. This was necessary on account of its having to move through the area of a desert. It was, however, able to compensate for the delay by harrying the departing Axis troops in and about its vicinity.[3]

The objectives allotted by the 4th Indian Division to its two brigades, the 5th and 7th, were Martuba and Gabr el Carmusa respectively. On reaching these localities, the two brigades were to exploit towards Derna. The Advanced Divisional Headquarters was to follow in their wake, at two hours' distance, keeping itself on an axis roughly in the centre of the two formations. It was to be accompanied by the 1st South African Brigade in reserve, one of whose battalions was to be left behind at Tmimi to protect the right flank of the advance. Another unit of the African Brigade, namely the 3rd South African Reconnaissance Unit, was to advance in front of the Division exploiting and doing as much damage as possible. The 32nd Army Tank Brigade which had been hitherto under the 4th Indian Division was ordered to revert to the command of the Eighth Army, except one of its units, the 42nd Royal Tank Regiment, which it left behind under divisional orders to accompany the Indian division in its advance.

For the first day of the pursuit, movements of the two brigades of the 4th Indian Division proceeded smoothly. At 1745 hours,

[2] Gen. Auchinleck's *Despatch* in Supplement to the *London Gazette*, p. 345. W/D. HQ 4 Div., 4 Ind. Div's. *Acct. of Ops. in Cyrenaica.*
[3] *Ibid.*

when the Indian division halted for the night, the 5th Indian Infantry Brigade was half way up to Martuba, having reached the track Tmimi—Bir Halegh el Eleba. The 7th Indian Infantry Brigade was likewise well on its way to Carmusa. It had been marching on an axis roughly parallel to the track Bir Halegh el Eleba—Gabr el Carmusa and was just west of El Ezzeiat when the halt was called. The Advanced Divisional Headquarters, with the 42nd RTR and the 1st South African Brigade in its rear, had placed itself for the night to the south-west of the 5th Brigade.

At this stage, the commander of the 4th Indian Division found it necessary to introduce a modification in the original plan to quicken the pace of the move. The 5th Indian Infantry Brigade had not advanced as fast as it had been expected to, as the ground over which it had to move was rough and rugged practically all the way. From the map this appeared likely to become worse with further progress. The divisional commander therefore issued certain orders that night, changing the brigade's objectives for the following day, i.e., 18 December. According to the new plan, the 7th Indian Infantry Brigade, and not the 5th, was to go to Martuba. This it was to do in addition to its own original task of reaching Carmusa. Having reached Gabr el Carmusa, it was to leave a detachment there and continue to Martuba, exploiting thence towards Derna. The 5th Brigade, on the other hand, was to change its axis of advance to one inclining westwards, where the going was better, and was to head for Carmusa. There it was to relieve the 7th Brigade and then proceed to exploit in a north-westerly direction.

Second day's advance

In conformity with this arrangement, the second day's advance started at 0630 hours on 18 December, the hour for first light being about 0645 hours. The 1st South African Brigade could not get started until midday due to the non-arrival of its petrol supply. The two brigades of the 4th Indian Division moved on, nevertheless, along their allotted axes. Owing to the difficult going, the axes of the two brigades, as also that of the Advanced Divisional Headquarters, converged more and more towards the track, Bir Halegh el Eleba—Gabr el Carmusa. The 7th Indian Infantry Brigade at last reached its objective, Carmusa, at 1100 hours. Leaving one of its battalions, 4/16 Punjab, to secure that area, it moved on with the two others towards Martuba and Derna. Martuba was reached by 1 Sussex some time in the afternoon and Derna by the 4th Sikh at about the same time.[4]

[4] 4 Ind. Div's. *Acct. of Ops. in Cyrenaica*, pp. 39-41. W/Ds. HQ 4 Div.; 5 & 7 Bdes.; 4/11 Sikh.

The 4th Indian Division gathers spoils

This advance proved quite fruitful. The 1st Sussex captured an Italian M-13 tank complete with crew, silenced a large gun and destroyed three aircraft on the landing ground of Martuba. But this was small booty compared to the windfall which fell to the 4th Sikh. Pushing on with speed, the Sikh battalion first came against a mass of Axis transport just then in the act of withdrawing westwards past the Derna landing ground. The transport was protected by four M-13 tanks and several guns. The 4th Sikh engaged the column and inflicted great damage on it, capturing in the action five 88-mm guns, three hundred prisoners and considerable transport. But yet more booty came to it in quite another manner. German troop-carrying planes were in the habit of using the Derna landing ground and they had no news of the arrival of the Sikh battalion in that vicinity. So, while the Sikhs were fighting the retreating column of the axis vehicles, twelve JU52s, which had probably flown from Greece, proceeded to land on the aerodrome unaware of the changed situation. Holding its fire, the battalion allowed the aircraft to touch the ground and then destroyed eight; the other four managing to escape, probably with inadequate petrol to complete their return journey.

After that incident the Sikhs began to mop up the Derna aerodrome which had fallen into their hands almost intact. The ground was strewn with one hundred and eighty-three damaged aeroplanes in various stages of disrepair—the result of the RAF's periodical bombing trips. In addition, there were enormous quantities of air force equipment and supplies which the retreating Axis troops had been unable to remove or destroy. It was from this landing ground that the Axis planes used to take off with supplies for Halfaya, where an isolated Axis garrison was still holding out. By nightfall, the capture of the Derna area as far as the coast had been completed and the 7th Indian Infantry Brigade was looking forward to new assignments.

The 5th Indian Infantry Brigade, on the other hand, had been less fortunate. Once again it had encountered rough roads and difficult terrain and its progress had become slow. As it seemed unlikely that it would reach its objective in time, the previous orders given to it were altered while it was still *en route*. It will be remembered that its original objective was Carmusa where it was to relieve the 7th Brigade so that the latter might occupy Martuba and Derna. The 7th Brigade had found itself able to attain all its objectives without the assistance of the 5th Brigade, which was now told not to proceed to Carmusa but to pass south of it and secure Giovanni Berta instead, as also the Lamluda cross-roads farther west.

It was hoped by this move to cut off such Axis troops as might be still remaining in Derna.

But this movement brought the 5th Brigade against the axis of advance of the 7th Brigade, which further delayed its progress, though unavoidably. Moreover, during its passage south of Martuba, it was dive-bombed by the Axis aircraft which were even then using that landing ground and which added not a little to the difficulties of the Indian brigade. In the circumstances, it took the 5th Brigade almost a whole day to clear the track Bir Halegh el Eleba—Gabr el Carmusa. At the end of that fatiguing advance it found further progress impossible due to darkness and still worse terrain, and halted for the night. Yet, however, it was not far from its objectives which it hoped to reach the following morning. In the meanwhile, during that day, the 1st South African Brigade had moved forward along a more southerly course and, making good progress, had reached Sidi el Meheigu in the evening. This movement eventually brought it on the southern flank of the 4th Indian Division's advance, enabling it to deal with such Axis troops as might manage to elude the Indian division and try to trickle through to the desert along the cross-mountain tracks or across the open country.

The Advanced Headquarters of the 4th Indian Division, together with the 42nd RTR, had managed to keep pace with the fast-moving 7th Brigade. Thus, in the evening of 18 December, it was established in a location just to the south of the Carmusa crossroads. The speed of the Indian division's advance appears to have completely surprised the Axis troops and upset some of their calculations. This was all the more difficult to understand as quite a few Italian aircraft had been overhead during that morning, who could not have missed seeing the unconcealed daylight movements. In any event, there was ample evidence all along the route of advance that the 21st Italian Corps was making a hurried, if not a disorderly, retreat. As already stated, no attempts were made by it to clear the landing grounds or destroy the equipment before leaving. There was, for instance, a large hutted camp near Martuba which bore particularly strong marks of a very hurried evacuation, so much so, that a meal lying prepared had not been eaten. The demolitions met with on the main road into and out of Derna, and on the escarpment, were so hastily carried out that they were ineffective and failed in their object of delaying the Allied advance to any appreciable extent. Similar other signs showed that it was safe to chase the hard-pressed Italian Corps with more speed than caution.

The night moves

Hence, it was not surprising that the same evening the 4th

Indian Division received orders to continue the pursuit during the night. Similar orders were also received by the 1st South African Brigade which was required to move a battalion by night to the Carmusa cross-roads, where it was to relieve the 4/16th Punjab and protect the left flank of the Indian division. The rest of the African brigade was to move up by daylight to the same area. The 4/16th Punjab, on being relieved, was to push a mobile night-column to Giovanni Berta along the main road in anticipation of the 5th Indian Infantry Brigade reaching that place in the morning. Moreover, one company of the 3rd South African Reconnaissance Unit was ordered to move at first light, again by the main road, to Giovanni Berta, whence it was to despatch patrols to Benghazi. Thus, by performing rapid night moves along the easily traversable main road, the divisional commander sought to accelerate the pace of his movement which was being slowed down by "bad going" such as the 5th Brigade had been experiencing during the two preceding days. Only light columns were being despatched in this manner, and their specific tasks were to hold certain important points for a few hours until the main bodies followed up after daylight and relieved them of their responsibilities.[5]

All the night moves were successfully accomplished, though not without some opposition. The mobile column of the 4/16th Punjab, particularly, encountered opposition on reaching the outskirts of Giovanni Berta. It remained halted in its position until it was relieved the next morning by the 5th Indian Infantry Brigade, after which that column as well as the remainder of the Punjab battalion reverted to the 7th Indian Infantry Brigade to support the latter's occupation of Derna. The 5th Brigade, having taken over the position, proceeded to make good the gain. It began by sending forward a mobile column, which started out before first light but which soon came to a stop on meeting a strong Axis position in the hills, about five miles south of Giovanni Berta. That position had to be cleared if progress was to be maintained. To that task, therefore, the 5th Brigade devoted all its energies for the rest of that day of 19 December.

Two of its battalions, the 1st and the 4th Rajputana Rifles (Raj Rif), became engaged in that action. The 1st Raj Rif moved across the country and attacked the position from the west. By evening, it had succeeded in ejecting most of the occupants of that position except for a small pocket of resistance in the north. Meanwhile, the 4th Raj Rif had made a profitable surprise movement. Going across the country which the Axis commanders had believed to be impassable for vehicles, this battalion suddenly appeared in the evening at Lamluda, six miles west of Giovanni Berta, where it intercepted

[5] W/Ds. 4 Div., 5 Bde., 4/16 Punjab.

the retreating and static Axis troops and seized about 500 prisoners as also a lot of material. This, however, was not enough to liquidate all the resistance south of Giovanni Berta; and it was, therefore, not until the 5th Brigade had hammered at it for another whole day, and taken some hundred more prisoners, that the way was at last cleared and Giovanni Berta occupied in the evening of 20 December.[6]

At this stage, the Headquarters of the Eighth Army appears to have reached the conclusion that it would not be difficult for the 4th Indian Division to clear the rest of the Jebel Akhdar single-handed, that is, without any extra-divisional unit under its command. Accordingly, on 20 December, the 1st South African Brigade was ordered to revert to the command of the Eighth Army; and a similar order was issued in regard to the 42nd RTR on the following day. Only the 3rd South African Reconnaissance Unit, less one company, was left under the divisional command. From then on the 4th Indian Division had no other extraneous unit under its command until it reached Benghazi a few days later.

Advance through the Desert

It may be recalled that the XIII Corps had divided itself into two groups for the pursuit of the Axis force. One group, the 4th Indian Division, was advancing across the Jebel Akhdar while the other, the 7th Armoured Division, was moving through the desert. The start of the Armoured Division had been delayed for about twenty-four hours due to its having had to assemble sufficient vehicles and supplies for a long cross-desert chase. But by the following day, 18 December, it had managed to put together enough to set two of its formations on the move—the Support Group and the 4th Armoured Brigade. The former was to engage Axis tank concentrations at Mekili; and the latter, swinging south, was to cut off their further retreat westwards.[7]

The Support Group moved swiftly to its destination, with the consequence that by nightfall all the Axis tanks had dispersed westward. The 4th Armoured Brigade then made a southward sweep to catch the fleeing armoured vehicles a little distance ahead. But that move brought it against a wide area of water-logged country, to avoid which it was obliged to make a long detour. This deviation took it very much out of its way and over extremely broken ground and not only retarded its progress but caused a comparatively greater expenditure of petrol. As a result, when it finally arrived

---

[6] 4 Ind. Div's. *Acct. of Ops. in Cyrenaica*, pp. 44-45. W/Ds. HQ 4 Div.; 1 & 4 Raj Rifs.

[7] Gen. Auchinleck's *Despatch* in Supplement to the *London Gazette* of 15 January 1948, pp. 345-6.

on the scene of its intended action, the Axis tanks had already disappeared and were safely out of its reach since it did not have enough petrol to follow up.

Acute Supply Difficulties

As a matter of fact, at that stage on 19 December, the Armoured Division was experiencing acute supply difficulties. It was unable to make any major move until a satisfactory field maintenance centre could first be established in the forward area. But that was not immediately possible and, till then, only a small force could be maintained ahead. It was, therefore, decided to employ no more than the Support Group plus two armoured car regiments for the next few days. As to the 4th Armoured Brigade, it was withheld at Mekili to await the arrival of petrol. In the meanwhile, the Support Group was ordered to advance to Benghazi (in the manner of the preceding year's successful advance to Beda Fomm) and intercept the 21st Italian Corps retreating along the coastal or lateral road. The two armoured car regiments, which were to accompany the Support Group, were despatched towards Msus and Charruba: one to keep touch with the retreating Axis troops passing Msus, and the other to watch the tracks leading out of the Jebel Akhdar.[8]

On the following day, 20 December, Allied aircraft, using the Mekili landing grounds, harried the Axis retreat and to some extent compensated for the inability of the Eighth Army to send out large land forces to catch and engage the main bodies of the withdrawing Axis troops.

The Support Group set out with a view to reaching the Benghazi area and there lying in wait for the 21st Italian Corps which was expected to pass thence in an attempt to reach Benghazi. But those hopes of interception were never realised. Many parts of the southern slopes of the Jebel, which it had to traverse, were lying under water as a result of the recent heavy rains. This not only hampered the progress of the tanks and armoured vehicles but made that of their supply echelons well-nigh impossible. As a result, the former began to suffer from shortage of petrol and finally came to a halt due to the non-receipt of fuel. The idea of reaching Benghazi had therefore to be abandoned, and on 21 December the Support Group was ordered to advance on Antelat instead, leaving only a small column to press on to Benghazi. Antelat was a vital road-junction to the south-east of Beda Fomm, from where an armoured force could control practically the entire stretch of the coastal road between Benghazi and El Agheila.

As to the 4th Indian Division, it had by this time, 21 December,

[8] *Ibid*

more than half completed its job of clearing the Jebel Akhdar. One of its brigades, the 5th, had occupied the general line Apollonia—Cirene—El Faidia and was engaged in sweeping the country to the west. Another of its units, the Central India Horse, with some armoured cars and anti-tank guns under its command, had extended the pursuit down the main road and was pressing fairly hard on the retreating Italians. By that time the hard-pressed 21st Italian Corps had almost ceased to exist as an efficient fighting formation. It was withdrawing in a disorganised condition and there seemed to be a chance to break it up further if it could be waylaid at Beda Fomm, or from Antelat, by the 7th Armoured Division.

But, as was discovered later, the Germans had not omitted to provide against that contingency. In fact, they had posted a force of about thirty tanks all around Beda Fomm to mask Antelat and cover their withdrawal down the coastal road. In the meantime, the 7th Armoured Division, which was striving to overcome its supply difficulties had at last managed to eke out enough to send forward a few units. They were the Support Group, the Guards Brigade and an armoured car regiment. The Guards Brigade reached Antelat on 22 December, gave battle to the German tanks and one of its battalions occupied Antelat. But the next day the German tanks returned to the attack, drove out the battalion and reoccupied the locality. At this, the Support Group, which was at first ordered to proceed to the small port town of Carcura in order to interfere with the supply and evacuation arrangements of the Axis, was asked to turn about and help the Guards Brigade instead. Seeing the two brigades assembled together for the attack, the Axis troops abandoned Antelat and began to withdraw towards Agedabia. They should have been pursued by the armoured car regiment which had arrived in the neighbourhood that very morning. But the latter was unable to give the chase as it had no fuel left after a brief but unavoidable engagement with some hostile tanks in the neighbourhood. Thus once again was the lesson rubbed in for the Allied commanders that the speed of movement of a force, at least in the desert, was conditioned by the speed with which the supplies could follow it.

In several instances, as the Axis troops withdrew from a locality, the local and neighbouring Arabs had begun to indulge in a wholesale looting and murder of the isolated Italian colonists. The task of preventing this fell to the lot of the 4th Indian Division whose two brigades soon became involved in restoring law and order. This slowed down the progress of the Indian division from 21 December onwards, from which date its two brigades were obliged to divert their energy increasingly to the internal security duties from their more important job of fighting.[9] There were other factors also that contributed towards the general slowing of the division's movements. In the first place the troop-carrying transport of one of its brigades was almost completely withdrawn and made to revert to the maintenance tasks owing to the necessity of speeding up the pursuit in the desert sector. Next, its allotment of petrol was reduced, being thereafter restricted to the essential needs only, although the division was able to use some out of the captured stocks. Many stragglers also remained to be rounded up; and of the salvage work to be done, there was enough to hold up the Indian brigades for several days. Among the salvage prizes, those worthy of mention were some thirty-five tanks in various stages of disrepair in the Derna workshop, and some twenty more Italian tanks abandoned on the road apparently through lack of fuel. In spite of these preoccupations, the 4th Indian Division was still able to send out some troops towards Barce, which place had not been evacuated by the 21st Italian Corps till then. The troops comprised two columns provided by the 5th Indian Infantry Brigade, which set out on 21 December along the two parallel roads converging on Barce, with armoured car patrols going in front of them.[10]

But the moves proved more than ordinarily difficult. There was heavy rainfall on that day and movement off the roads was not easy, since the ground on either side had become boggy and treacherous. The communications, too, had become complicated and unsatisfactory owing to long distances; and the hardships were further aggravated by the recent shortages in transport and petrol. Nevertheless, the column which was going by the north road had reached D'Annunzio on 22 December, while that moving by the south road got to within seven miles east of Barce, to reach which point it had to overcome a demolition obstacle and some further resistance on the way. As to the 7th Indian Infantry Brigade, it was all this time in the Derna area, attending to security duties, salvage work and tasks of civil administration. Units of the OETA (Occupied Enemy Territory Administration) had begun to arrive and were gradually taking over the civil administration from the hands of both the Indian brigades, and it seemed possible that at least one of the two brigades would be set free immediately for further operational tasks.[11]

On 22 December, the Advanced Divisional Headquarters was well ahead of its own troops, being established in Giovanni Berta,

---

[9] 4 Ind. Div's. *Acct. of Ops. in Cyrenaica*, pp. 45-6. W/Ds. HQ 4 Div., 5 Bde., 7 Bde., CIH.
[10] *Ibid.*
[11] W/Ds. HQ 4 Div., 5 Bde., 7 Bde.

with all its brigades in its rear and only the two columns of the 5th Brigade in front of it. On that day some Axis aircraft carried out bombing attacks on Giovanni Berta and Derna, and on the following day, 23 December, that column of the 5th Brigade which had been moving along the south road entered Barce, together with the Central India Horse, and occupied it at 1600 hours after overcoming the resistance offered by the Axis troops. On the preceding night an Allied patrol had raided the landing ground of Agedabia and succeeded in destroying some thirty-seven aircraft on the ground.

The Climax

The battle for Jebel Akhdar had by this time reached its climax. The Axis forces were known to be preparing to evacuate Benghazi; and to stop their getting away it was necessary to force the passes at Sidi Brahim, Sheleidima and further south, which the Axis had blocked with strong detachments to safeguard their exit from Benghazi. Their flank guard at Beda Fomm, too, was still strong and firm, and in fact had been strengthened even further by a tank force that had been lately withdrawn from Antelat and was now positioned a little to its west. To overcome these defences was the task of the 7th Armoured and the 4th Indian Divisions. But the Indian division had practically come to a standstill through lack of transport and fuel and through having to perform internal security duties in the Derna area; and as to the Armoured Division, it was still struggling with its supplies and maintenance difficulties, and could do no more than send out one column to take over the area El Abiar—Benina—Benghazi, whence entry into Benghazi might be possible.[12]

In the circumstances, it was not surprising that, on 24 December, the 4th Indian Division was ordered to send the Central India Horse to the area Al Abiar—Benina—Benghazi. There the CIH was to take over from the column of the 7th Armoured Division which had already reached that locality. The Indian division had nearly come to the end of its petrol and supply resources, nevertheless, it managed to collect enough for the Central India Horse who were sent off almost immediately. A few road-blocks and half-hearted rearguards were all that the CIH met on the way; and at 1800 hours on 24 December, their forward elements at last entered Benghazi, to find that the town had been evacuated by all Axis troops and even by most of the civilians. The harbour was empty except for some twenty-three ships lying sunk, as a result of the routine RAF bombings. Within a mile or so of the docks, the houses had also suffered from the bombing. Most of them had

[12] War Inf. Cir., p. 9. Gen. Auchinleck's *Despatch* in Supplement to the *London Gazette*, p. 346. W/Ds. HQ 4 Div., 5 & 7 Bdes.; CIH.

some sort of damage and nearly all showed signs of having been ransacked by the Arab looters. The town was indeed in a sorry state and its deserted appearance must have seemed all the more depressing to the new comers by contrast with the jollity associated with a Christmas eve.[13]

[13] *Ibid.*

CHAPTER XXVI

End of the Allied Advance

Benghazi was duly occupied. The bulk of the Axis forces had withdrawn to Agedabia, where they seemed to be hoping to make a temporary stand. If the port of Benghazi could now be opened and made to function normally, the supply problem would ease greatly and further pursuit of the Axis could be resumed with confidence. That was the object of the Eighth Army. But in the meanwhile it was also necessary to keep up the maximum possible pressure on the retreating forces. To that end it became essential to rearrange and redistribute the small body of the Allied troops in the forward area, and to that matter the XIII Corps directed its immediate attention.

Hence, on 25 December, the 7th Indian Infantry Brigade received orders to move forward and take over the Barce—Benghazi area. The Central India Horse, as well as other forward troops, were to pass under its command immediately on its arrival. The 5th Indian Infantry Brigade, shorn of all its troop-carrying transport, was asked to take charge of the rear area from Barce to Derna. The 4th Indian Division was warned to be prepared to give up its artillery, which was to pass under the command of the XIII Corps; and finally two battalions of the Libyan Arab Force were brought to the Barce area to relieve the Indian division of a major part of the internal security duties.[1]

Change in the Divisional Command

It took several days to complete these arrangements. The 7th Indian Brigade assumed command of the Barce—Benghazi area on 26 December. On the following day the 8th Field Regiment left the 4th Indian Division, followed on the 28th and 29th respectively, by the 1st Field Regiment and batteries of the 7th Medium and 65th Anti-tank Regiments. The Libyan Arab Force arrived in the divisional area on 30 December. At about the same time the Rear Headquarters of the 4th Indian Division moved to Barce and joined up with the Advanced Headquarters That was an event for a mild excitement in the divisional sphere as it was the first time since August 1940 that the two headquarters had come together again. Another noteworthy event, which followed on the same day, was the change of the divisional command. Major-General F. W.

[1] **W**/Ds. 4 Div.; 5 & 7 Bdes.; CIH.

Messervy, having been selected to command the 1st Indian Armoured Division,[2] left the 4th Indian Division on 30 December 1941, handing over the command to his successor, Major-General F.I.S. Tuker.

While the 4th Indian Division was thus adjusting itself to the prospects of a further pursuit, the 7th Armoured Division had got down to the business of making that pursuit possible. It may be recalled that to ensure a safe retreat the Axis Commander had placed a strong flankguard of tanks round Beda Fomm; and there was another similar force to the west of Antelat. For several days after the occupation of Benghazi, these forces remained rooted to their positions and could not be forced to quit. Frequent attempts were made by columns from the Guards Brigade to dislodge them, but they were strong in artillery and the attempts only resulted in severe losses to the Guards Brigade. At last on 26 December, the last of the Axis troops went past to Agedabia; and the flankguard, having completed its mission, followed in their wake. But this withdrawal did not make the pursuit any the easier. The halt of the Axis troops at Agedabia was only a temporary one to cover their preparation of a new defensive line in the rear on which they intended to make their final stand. This new line was being built in the marshes round Marsa Brega, about 20 miles from El Agheila; and the Axis commanders had deployed sufficient forces round about Agedabia to hold the Allied pursuit until those defences should be finally ready.

Axis stand at Agedabia

To penetrate the Axis screen protecting Agedabia was no easy matter. The country in that area is well suited for defence. The strip of land between the coast and the main road was swampy. The few dry paths to its east were composed of soft sand dunes not easily negotiable by the vehicles. Soft sand also covered the area further east and round the south; and the whole position was bounded, both on the east and south, by the Wadi el Fareg, which ran in a south-westerly direction from Gief el Matar to the Agheila marshes and formed a formidable obstacle. Bridging or otherwise crossing that wide and steep-banked wadi was not feasible for the small Allied force in the forward zone. Nor was it easy to outflank its south-eastern extremity, although it was possible, as a last resort, to turn the flank by a wide diversion over the difficult country much further east and south.[3]

---

[2] General Messervy, it appears, was to proceed to India to take command of the 1st Indian Armoured Division. But these orders were later cancelled and he was retained to command the 1st (British) Armoured Division.

[3] Gen. Auchinleck's *Despatch* in Supplement to the *London Gazette* of 13 Jan. 48, pp. 346-47.

Efforts to penetrate the Agedabia defences

For dealing with the Agedabia defences, therefore, there were only two courses open: a wide outflanking move or a frontal attack. The commander of the XIII Corps tried both. He ordered the Guards Brigade to make the frontal attack; while a simultaneous outflanking move was to be made by the 22nd Armoured Brigade, which was instructed to work round to the south towards Chor es Sufan.

The plan did not work as expected and both the brigades failed in their mission. The Guards Brigade, moving across the sand dunes, attacked on 26 December as arranged, but the attack miscarried owing to its having been made from a wrong direction. Next day, the 22nd Armoured Brigade, in the course of its wide outflanking movement, had the misfortune to stumble against a group of Axis tanks guarding the south-east approach to Agedabia. A fierce clash ensued in which the Armoured Brigade suffered a heavy reverse and, being obliged to fall back, withdrew to El Haseiat. One reason for this failure was that the German tanks were equipped with 6-pounder guns whereas the British tanks had nothing better than the 2-pounders. Another reason was that almost all the tanks of the 22nd Brigade had become worn out through a long march across the desert, starting from Gazala. Many of them had reached such a state of dilapidation that they became casualties on the way through mere mechanical breakdowns; and of the fourteen tanks with which the brigade at last attacked, eight were lost forthwith in the action.

Although the 22nd Armoured Brigade had thus failed in its object of getting behind the Axis defences round Agedabia, its efforts had not been completely wasted. It had inflicted heavy casualties on Axis tanks, having destroyed twenty of them and disabled a like number. All the same it was in no condition to parry further blows from the Axis armour. Therefore, when the Axis tanks attacked again on 30 December, the brigade was unable to hit back as before. It lost a number of tanks again, which drove the commander of the XIII Corps to the conclusion that it was not fit for further operations. It was accordingly withdrawn to the rear area, the 7th Support Group taking its place in relief.

End of the Campaign

Thus ended the year 1941. It had been a year of hard campaigning of which the last six weeks were filled with the fiercest tank battles yet fought by the Allied forces. The 4th Indian Division had played a notable part in the long advance from Matruh to Agedabia and had added to the high reputation which it had earned in East Africa. The advance had cost it 2,633 casualties in killed, wounded and missing, of which 150 were officers.[4] As to its hitting power, it was responsible for 51 German tanks (Marks III and IV) and 27 aircraft destroyed in action, and 6,000 prisoners taken in a little less than six weeks. It had further to its credit a large booty of abandoned aircraft and Italian tanks which it captured *en route*. In addition, it had inflicted considerable casualties on its opponents and caused some damage to the Axis armour, of which no proper record is available. It had, thus, more than justified its inclusion in the Eighth Army. Its contribution to this difficult campaign in Cyrenaica was acknowledged by General Auchinleck in a telegram to General Wavell, which said, "General Ritchie, in a letter to me just received says: 'The 4th Division have really done the most magnificent work. No praise can be high enough for their achievements.' I whole-heartedly endorse this praise."[5]

The dawn of the year 1942 found the two Corps of the Eighth Army engaged in actions at either end of Cyrenaica—the XIII corps in the extreme west trying to clear Agedabia and the XXX Corps in the extreme east endeavouring to clear the frontier. It will be recalled that some Axis troops, although cut off and completely isolated from the rest of the *Afrika Korps*, were still holding out in the frontier area. The main positions they were holding were Bardia and Halfaya. Bardia, being a port town, was supplied and maintained by the Axis ships from the sea. As to Halfaya, it was in a more difficult predicament. Its land communication with Bardia had been severed by the Allied troops, as also its water pipeline which carried water from Bardia to Halfaya. The two strongholds had however managed to retain a link by sea via Sollum, and the Sollum—Halfaya positions were thus continuing to receive supplies by launch from Bardia.[6]

Remnants of the Axis forces

The XXX Corps was charged with the task of eliminating these strongholds as quickly as possible, so as to restore direct land communication between Tobruk and Sollum. For carrying out its assignment it had under it the 2nd South African Division, a brigade of the 1st South African Division, a strong force of field and medium artillery, the 1st Army Tank Brigade, a bomber wing of the Royal Air Force and several other supporting and ancillary troops. The Corps Commander, General Norrie, was specially instructed to accomplish his task with the minimum of casualties,

---

[4] For details see Appendix R.
[5] 4 Ind. Div's. *Acct. of Ops. in Cyrenaica*, pp. 48-49.
[6] Gen. Auchinleck's *Despatch* in Supplement to the *London Gazette* of 13-1-1948, pp. 347-8.

as it was difficult to replace infantry wastages amongst the South African troops. He planned to attack Bardia first, hoping that the fall of that fortress would intensify the difficulties of the Halfaya garrison as to food and water and thereby reduce its capacity to resist.

The defences of Bardia at this date were much the same as a year ago when General Wavell had taken the place from the Italians. They were laid out in a number of self-contained and mutually supporting defensive localities. Each locality was covered by machine-gun and anti-tank posts. These posts were in turn protected by barbed wire entanglements and anti-tank minefields; and in one case by a concrete anti-tank ditch. The whole system was given depth by siting additional defended localities and machine-gun posts in the interior. The garrison was estimated to number about 4500 of whom about one-third were believed to be Germans; and it was thought that the defences included some twenty field guns and a few tanks. As Bardia had a long perimeter, it was calculated that the garrison could not have any large reserves. These speculations however proved to be somewhat optimistic. Bardia was actually holding almost double the estimated number of men and guns. This fact however had no serious effect upon the operations which commenced on 31 December 1941.

The operations were carried out by the 3rd South African Infantry Brigade with a regiment of the 1st Army Tank Brigade. Attacking from the south, his force broke through the Axis defences somewhere in the south-east corner of the perimeter on 31 December. The garrison of Bardia counter-attacked vigorously but the South African Brigade held its ground and attacked again on the night of 1 January 1942. This new-year-day attack appears to have convinced the Axis garrison of the futility of further resistance; for early on 2 January, the garrison commander, General Schmitt, announced his willingness to surrender unconditionally.[7]

All that now remained was to reduce Halfaya and Sollum, and it was hoped that the fall of Bardia would make this task comparatively easy. Sollum was attacked on 11 January by the Transvaal Scottish troops and captured the next day; and on the 13th the South African troops cut off the last source of Halfaya's water supply making its resistance impossible. However, there were no immediate overtures of surrender from the Halfaya garrison and it seemed necessary to mount a full-scale attack for the final elimination of this Axis pocket. Plans were under way for the attack to be launched in the near future when, on 17 January, the garrison commander, General de Giorgis, decided to surrender with his 5,500 men, of whom about 2,000 were Germans. This was the last

[7] *Ibid.*

victory of operation 'Crusader' which started on 18 November 1941. It removed the final lingering vestige of the Axis hold on eastern Cyrenaica and freed the Allied line of communication from all manner of impediments. From Cairo to Agedabia all land was now in the undisputed occupation of the Eighth Army.

Allied efforts to take El Aghelia

But the Eighth Army was by no means quite secure in its possession of these gains. The task of securing Cyrenaica could not be regarded as complete so long as the Axis forces remained in Agedabia. It was necessary, in order to hold it, to control the region round El Agheila. This was the area in which General Rommel seemed to be engaged in building a strong defensive line, while he held off the XIII Corps at Agedabia pending its completion. Were he to succeed in his object, he would be able to hold the Eighth Army at the gates of Tripolitania long enough for him to be reinforced and become sufficiently strong to launch a full-scale offensive in Cyrenaica. The Eighth Army, in that event, would have no alternative but to retire rapidly as it neither possessed a strong and manageable line of communication nor did it have a system of natural defences anywhere in its rear, up to and beyond Egypt.

Such was the situation that faced General Auchinleck early in January 1942. He had either to take El Agheila immediately or be prepared to withdraw his troops back to the Egyptian frontier. Tactically there was no via media. But to capture that natural fortress with the slender and ill-supplied force which he had pushed as far forward as Agedabia was not an easy matter.

The tract of country round El Agheila is one of the most easily defendable positions in Libya. It stretches southwards from the coast for about fifty miles. The whole belt is studded with small cliffs, sand dunes and salt pans, which are natural barriers to wheeled traffic. The southern extremity of this belt ends in an area adjacent to the Libyan Sand Sea, a vast expanse of shifting sand, which offered natural protection to the southern flank. This flank was particularly difficult to turn owing to the length of a barrier of salt pans which was contiguous with it and beyond which were precipitous hills extending the obstacle far to the rear. Only a few tracks crossed this inhospitable area, so that, by closing those roads, it was possible to hold the El Agheila area against heavy odds. General Rommel had still some thirty-five thousand troops left out of about one hundred thousand with which he had started. He set those troops to block the approaches to El Agheila —at Marsa Brega, Bir el Ginn, Bir es Suera, Bir el Cleibat and Marada. He withdrew his armour behind that line and put it on the job of refitting and re-equipping itself for still another struggle.

The defensive belt round El Agheila thus consisted of a series of natural obstacles such as the salt pans, sand dunes and cliffs. Between those several obstacles were gaps, being guarded by the Axis armoured and infantry troops, who were both German and Italian. The Italian forces were three armoured and motorised divisions, the Trieste, Ariete and Trento; and three infantry divisions, the Pavia, Sabrata and Brescia. The former guarded the gaps between Wadi el Fareg and Maaten Giofer. The latter were placed in El Agheila itself to guard its eastern approach. The German armour, the 15th and 21st Panzer Divisions, watched the gaps between the north bank of Wadi el Fareg and a position to its west, occupied by the 90th German Light Division. The latter formation, along with some infantry, patrolled the dangerous openings between Marsa Brega and Wadi el Fareg. With these dispositions and defences, General Rommel found it easy to check the further progress of the Eighth Army.

The Eight Army had only one of its Corps, the XIII, in the forward area. This formation was by no means in a position to attack immediately. Besides, it was not merely a question of attacking and dislodging the Axis from its position but that of invading Tripolitania thereafter. Such an undertaking called for concentration of sufficient troops and for the accumulation of reserves and improvement of the line of communication, as also for the reopening and organisation of the port of Benghazi. Anxious as General Auchinleck was to get all this through quickly, he saw that the work could not be completed before the middle of February. He was of the opinion that General Rommel would not be in a position to counter-attack before then. Till then he had to be satisfied with setting his light forces to watch the Axis moves.[8]

It was one of the responsibilities of General Auchinleck to foresee how soon Rommel would be ready to counter-attack. He had judged that the date would be somewhere in the latter half of February or the beginning of March; and his preparations were being based on that calculation. But as events transpired, the attack came about a month earlier, on 21 January 1942. Even had General Auchinleck correctly anticipated this earlier date, it is doubtful whether he would have succeeded in expediting his preparations or making other adjustments to an extent enough to meet that counter-offensive. Yet it is desirable in principle that the date of an expected attack should be estimated as correctly as possible. The point is important and it is therefore necessary to examine the grounds on which General Auchinleck based his belief about the probable date of attack.

[8] General Auchinleck's *Despatch in Supplement to the London Gazette* of 13-1-1948, pp. 347-8,

In the middle of January, General Rommel was known to have some 17,000 German and 18,000 Italian troops, with seventy medium tanks of which twenty-five were German. Safely ensconced as he was behind the Marsa Brega—Marada line, it was not to be expected that he would quit it or bring his small force out in the open for a trial of strength. It was, therefore, reasonable to assume that he would wait for reinforcements. An Italian armoured division with some hundred and forty tanks was expected to reach him within a month. But even that reinforcement, in General Auchinleck's opinion, would not enable the Axis to counter-attack, since General Rommel was believed to be having acute supply difficulties. A regular Axis offensive before the middle of February was therefore considered highly improbable.

The improbable, however, occurred on 21 January 1942, when the Axis forces began their advance, a month earlier than expected. This wide divergence between the estimated date and that of actual occurrence has been commented upon by General Auchinleck in his *Despatch*. He explains that the advance was probably only a reconnaissance in force sent out to locate Allied dispositions and impede preparations for a new Allied offensive; and that the unexpected success of this mission was skilfully exploited by General Rommel who turned it into a full-fledged campaign. In support of this view it is pointed out that the Axis troops appear to have started out with only three days' rations in hand; and that not more than about ninety tanks had been used throughout the operation. As to the acute supply difficulties which General Rommel was believed to be experiencing, it is explained that they were balanced by the "remarkable elasticity of his supply organisation."[9]

Whether it was only a reconnaissance in force or an actual advance, the Allied forces in the field were in no position to make a stand. The forward troops, on 21 January, were under General Messervy, commanding the 1st Armoured Division. They were the 201st Guards Motor Brigade and the Support Group of the 1st Armoured Division, and their main weakness was that their units were widely dispersed over a long front of about forty miles. The Guards Brigade was organised in four mobile columns (and a reserve), which were watching a front of some fifteen miles, running south from the coast and beginning at Marsa Brega. The Support Group was also organised in four mobile columns and a reserve. Taking over from the left of the Guards Brigade it carried the line up to Maaten Burruci, another 25 to 30 miles. The mobile columns consisted, each of a company of infantry, a field battery and some anti-tank and light anti-aircraft guns. The

---

[9] General Auchinleck's *Despatch* in Supplement to the *London Gazette*, dated 13-1-1948, pp. 347-8.

Support Group was inexperienced in desert driving and many of its vehicles were not desert-worthy. There was also a general lack of anti-tank weapons to deal with the heavy armour of the Axis.

General Messervy assessed that, all told, his troops were too weak and dispersed to resist even a local advance from General Rommel. He had therefore already drawn up plans for a withdrawal. In the event of an Axis counter-attack his troops were to fall back to the line Agedabia—El Haseiat, fighting a delaying action, if possible. Other troops from the rear area were to be brought up to this line which was to be held to the last. The troops available from the rear were the 2nd Armoured Brigade, the 4th Indian Division, some three field regiments and miscellaneous artillery. There was also the remnant of the Oases Force, some forty miles east of Agedabia, now reduced to a battalion and a field battery.

The state of the 4th Indian Division was none too compact on the eve of the Axis attack. Of its three brigades, the 7th Brigade was in Benghazi area, the 5th lay in the Barce sector and the 11th round about Tobruk. None of the brigades had any troop-carrying transport, and the division as a whole possessed no anti-tank weapons capable of dealing with the German tanks. The divisional artillery had been reduced to half its strength, consisting thereafter of only the 31st Field Regiment less one battery. The 1st Field Regiment and a medium anti-tank battery had been passed on to the 1st Armoured Division. All available field and anti-tank artillery of the 4th Indian Division was in the Benghazi area under the command of the 7th Brigade, while the Divisional Headquarters were at Barce.[10] The Indian division was, therefore, to all intents and purposes only equipped for a static defensive role and was wholly dependent on General Messervy's mobile troops for reconnaissance and flank protection. The reason for the division being so scattered and so deficient in transport and artillery was that all available transport was urgently needed to supply the forward troops and to build up the Corps dump; and no major operation was thought likely until the middle of February. The projected Allied advance towards Tripoli was not expected to begin till then. Preparations for this were in train and the 4th Indian Division had been marked out to take part in the attack, as a whole. The divisional reconnaissance for the operations had actually started and other relative preliminaries were in hand when, to the great surprise of the Eighth Army, General Rommel's forces sallied out of El Agheila in a vigorous all-out attack, heralding the beginning of a renewed drive towards Egypt.

---

[10] 4 Ind. Div's. *Acct. of Ops. in Cyrenaica*, pp. 51-52. W/Ds. HQ 4 Div.; 5, 7 & 11 Bdes.

CHAPTER XXVII

Allied Retreat Begins

Axis counter-offensive

A determined offensive against the Eighth Army was now on, which was the more difficult to deal with because it had come suddenly and without any pre-indication. A heavy shelling for a brief period was all the warning the Allied forward troops had of its inception. It was early morning of 21 January when shells began landing in the forward area, later increasing in concentration. Then the advance commenced somewhat abruptly, the attacking force moving forward in three columns. The left and right columns had about thirty to thirty-five tanks each and the centre column was motorised infantry. The Allied plan in the event of an Axis advance was to fight a delaying action while retiring to the line Agedabia—El Haseiat. But now it was neither possible nor necessary to make a stand on that line, as the reserves of supplies which that line was to cover as well as depend upon had not yet been placed in position. General Messervy, therefore, cancelled his previous order and called upon his commanders to fight a stiff delaying action instead.

But by then the Support Group, on the left flank, had already got into trouble. It had run into sand dunes to the south, chased by the Axis light tanks. The latter had caught upon some of its infantry and artillery, and were threatening the rest. On the right flank, the Guards Brigade tried to offer some resistance but had little success, and the Axis left column which was able to pass through its positions began a move towards Agedabia by the main road. During the whole of 21 January, Axis fighters and dive-bombers made intermittent attacks on the Allied troops, who could not get any support from their own aircraft as the recent rains had rendered the landing grounds marshy and unsafe.

The obvious remedy in such a situation was to bring up more troops from the rear area and free the forward mobile columns from the necessity of fighting an impossible delaying action. The XIII Corps took just those steps. It directed the 1st Armoured Division to move back and interpose itself between the Axis troops and Msus; at the same time it ordered the 2nd Armoured Brigade and the 4th Indian Division to move forward from the rear to the operational area. This was on 22 January, the second day of the Axis thrust. The Armoured Brigade was assigned the role of relieving pressure on the Support Group, while the 4th Indian Division, which had been reinforced by a battalion of heavy tanks, was to oppose the Axis advance on Benghazi. The Axis troops, by then, had reached Agedabia and were moving north and north-east towards Antelat.

The 4th Indian Division received the information of its intended role from the XIII Corps on 22 January. It was to operate over an area lying to the south of Benghazi and north of Antelat. Its particular tasks were, (a) to hold a position south of Benghazi, (b) to prevent any Axis move along the coastal road towards the north and (c) to patrol all east-west routes through the escarpment. From its position south of Benghazi, it was also to cover the evacuation of that town should that become necessary. Antelat was excluded from its operations but the division was responsible for all the area to its north.[1]

Efforts to halt the Axis advance

However, on the same evening, news reached the 4th Indian Division through its patrols that Axis troops could be seen round about Antelat. As a matter of fact, by that time, Antelat had already passed under the occupation of the Axis together with Saunnu, the next important locality in that area. This was a serious matter for the Eighth Army since it opened the way for an attack on Zt. Msus. A force which occupied Zt. Msus could, from there, establish an eastward control of the Desert up to Mekili and thus render the whole of the mountain region of Jebel Akhdar untenable by planting itself on the line Antelat—Saunnu—Msus—Mekili. Hence the tactical importance of Zt. Msus. It was the key to Jebel Akhdar through which ran the Allied line of communication as well as the possible line of retreat. It was also the key to the rest of the Western Desert, as there was hardly a desert track which did not pass through Antelat, Saunnu, Msus or Mekili. It was for this reason that the XIII Corps had ordered the 1st Armoured Division to interpose itself between the Axis troops and Zt. Msus. Were this not done, the two brigades of the 4th Indian Division in Benghazi and Barce, and the other Allied troops in that location, would be cut off from the rest of the Eighth Army, since the part of Cyrenaica over which they could withdraw would be in the hands of the Axis.

Accordingly, the 1st Armoured Division ordered its 2nd Brigade, then in reserve some twelve miles north of Saunnu, to send two of its regiments northwards, and the third towards Antelat. The former were to cover Msus against an Axis attack from Saunnu and the latter was to attack the Axis in Antelat. Each of the first

[1] 4 Ind. Div's. *Acct. of Ops. in Cyrenaica*, p. 52. W/Ds. HQ 4 Div.; 5 & 7 Bdes.

two regiments became engaged in separate actions with the Axis tanks and suffered heavily. This was not surprising since the German tanks were superior, both in armour and weapons, to the British machines, many of which were only light tanks mounting no better weapons than the ordinary machine-guns. The third regiment, however, managed to reach its appointed position north of Antelat without any incident but did nothing more. The net result of all these moves was that the 2nd Armoured Brigade had become reduced in strength to some eighty tanks, although it had succeeded in putting a temporary check on the Axis advance towards Msus. The Axis troops remained halted during the whole of 24 January.[2]

Proposed defence of Benghazi

In the meanwhile, the 4th Indian Division had begun its task of throwing a ring of defences round Benghazi. It planned to make a stand in Benghazi in such a manner as to achieve the double purpose of blocking the northward move of the Axis along the coast and preventing the Axis forces at the same time from gaining an access to Jebel Akhdar. The former aim required for its implementation the stationing of a considerable force south of Benghazi; and that task was entrusted to the 7th Indian Infantry Brigade. The latter aim of preventing an entry into Jebel Akhdar could, however, be secured with comparatively smaller forces, the object being to block only the two mountain passes of Sheleidima and Sidi Brahim. This job was assigned to the battalion of 1st Welch which had been recently transferred to the command of the 7th Brigade, from its parent formation, the 5th Indian Infantry Brigade, then at Barce. The 1st Welch was ordered to leave two companies to garrison Benghazi and to use the rest of the troops to secure the Sheleidima and Sidi Brahim passes.[3]

At the same time, the Advanced Divisional Headquarters moved to Benghazi and took up a location outside the town. The Divisional Commander, Major-General Tuker, held a conference on the same day, and explained the situation to all local commanders and service representatives. All possibilities were examined including that of the division being cut off, if the Axis succeeded in destroying the 1st Armoured Division and advanced east of Msus. In such an event, Benghazi would, undoubtedly, have to be evacuated, and outline plans for evacuation and demolitions were accordingly ordered to be kept ready. But this was only a routine precaution. The Indian division anticipated that its primary

---

[2] Gen. Auchinleck's *Despatch* in Supplement to the *London Gazette* of 13-1-48, p. 349.
[3] W/Ds. HQ 4 Div.; 5 & 7 Bdes.

role would be to hold Benghazi and to take the offensive in the Agedabia area, to assist the 1st Armoured Division in its battle about Msus. The XIII Corps was asked to permit the 7th Indian Infantry Brigade to move to the vicinity of Agedabia with this plan in view as soon as the troop-carrying transport would be available. But the Corps returned a discouraging reply, advising caution, since the 1st Armoured Division was not feeling equal to such an operation. Its instructions to the 4th Indian Division were to adopt a defensive-offensive attitude and be content for the time being with strengthening its defensive layout south of Benghazi.

Indecision and vacillation

Before the following morning, however, the Eighth Army appears to have abandoned the idea of holding Benghazi or defending to its south. That morning the Corps Commander, General Godwin-Austen, issued instructions that if the Axis troops again advanced in force and could not be held, there was to be a general withdrawal to the new line, Derna—Mekili.[4] The 1st Armoured Division in that case was to fall back to Mekili through Msus. The 4th Indian Division was to retire through the Jebel Akhdar. The withdrawal was to begin on the issue of a code-word by the 1st Armoured Division. As soon as the latter found it necessary to evacuate Msus, it would flash the code-signal to the Indian division, which would begin its withdrawal towards the area Derna—Martuba—Gabr el Carmusa. In order that the withdrawal might be carried out without congesting the main road, and that there might be enough time to demolish the base and administrative installations, the 4th Indian Division asked that a prior notice of 48 hours be given to it, if practicable.

In the meanwhile the RAF authorities had already received instructions from their own headquarters to evacuate Benghazi of all the RAF units and installations immediately, leaving behind only a small force of fighters to cover the withdrawal of the infantry. Taking its cue from these instructions, the Royal Navy also decided to clear the harbour of its shipping and installations that very night. To add to the seriousness of the situation, a report was received the same evening that the armoured fighting which had been going on in the Antelat—Saunnu area since the preceding day had gone against the 2nd Armoured Brigade and that the latter had suffered heavy losses in that prolonged struggle. The evacuation of Benghazi in the circumstances seemed to be a certainty, and the 4th Indian Division was expecting to receive the prearranged code-signal that very night or the following morning. Instead of the signal came the instructions on the evening of 24 January, cancelling

[4] W/D. HQ 4 Div.

all previous orders about the contemplated withdrawal and advising a return to the *status quo*.

Just what had caused the XIII Corps to change its plan was not clear from the brief instructions then received. Fuller instructions arrived the next morning (25 January) clarifying the situation. It appeared that the Eighth Army Command had reached the conclusion that the advance of the Axis troops to Antelat and Saunnu was by no means the beginning of a general counter-offensive, as was generally believed in the forward area. It was thought to be rather a big-sized raid, like the several ones General Rommel had carried out earlier in his efforts to stab the rear of the Eighth Army and interfere with its communications and supplies. In the opinion of the commander of the Eighth Army, General Rommel could not possibly be ready to launch an all-out offensive at such an early date. He was therefore believed to be merely trying to upset preparations of the Eighth Army to attack El Agheila, by distracting its attention with large-scale raids. It was only necessary, as on previous occasions, to stand fast and absorb the shock and the situation was bound to return to the normal. Benghazi was therefore safe and there was no danger of the two brigades of the 4th Indian Division being isolated.[5]

The Indian division was accordingly to remain in Benghazi and continue to block the main approaches to the town from the south. The Divisional Commander, Major-General Tuker was instructed to establish a series of defended areas on the general line Sidi Abd el Aati—Beda Fomm—Antelat—Saunnu. He was also to maintain contact with the Axis troops and harass them with his mobile columns. Finally, he was to form pivots on which mobile columns and armoured forces could later base their offensive operations against the El Agheila defences of General Rommel.

On receipt of these instructions, General Tuker despatched reconnaissance parties to select the areas of defence. But hardly had they moved out when they had to be recalled; for quite unexpectedly, at 1225 hours, the Indian division received the code-word from the 1st Armoured Division indicating that Zt. Msus was being evacuated. This meant that Benghazi was to be abandoned and withdrawal towards Derna was to begin. It also meant that the demolition scheme for Benghazi was to be put into force on receipt of another code-word.

General Tuker issued instructions for the base and administrative installations to begin evacuation immediately and be clear of the area by 0600 hours the following morning, 26 January. The fighting troops were to leave soon thereafter. Some slow-moving units, such as the medium artillery and 8 RTR, were also ordered

---

[5] 4 Ind. Div's. *Acct. of Ops. in Cyrenaica*, pp. 53-57. W/D. HQ 4 Div.

to move back to the divisional reserve at Barce during the night. The 1st Welch were withdrawn from the escarpment passes which they were guarding at Sheleidima and Sidi Brahim; and the 11th Indian Infantry Brigade, which was in the act of moving into Benghazi from Tobruk, was halted on the way. It was ordered to stop at Maraua, which it had just then reached, and from there to secure approaches into the Jebel from the south in order to ensure a safe passage for the 7th Indian Infantry Brigade, due to leave Benghazi in the morning.

General Tuker's instructions to his own troops for the evacuation of Benghazi had been issued late in the afternoon of 25 January. The same evening, the XIII Corps confirmed again that the withdrawal was to proceed and the division was to get ready to carry out the demolitions. Patrols of the Central India Horse reported at the same time that the Axis troops had already occupied Zt. Msus; and the information from the 1st Armoured Division was that it was re-rallying at Charruba. The Corps informed the Indian division that the south flank of its withdrawals would be protected by the 1st Armoured Division in the Maraua area.[6]

It will be recalled that earlier in the morning that day (25 January), the XIII Corps had issued instructions to the 4th Indian Division that it was to remain in Benghazi; yet within a few hours afterwards, the 1st Armoured Division had passed its previously appointed code-word for withdrawal. The reason for the sudden change of plan was that, after remaining quiescent for the whole of 24 January, the Axis troops had resumed their advance on the 25th in the direction of Msus. Two Axis columns had begun to converge on that locality, one from Antelat and the other from the east of Abd el Hafid. One of the arms of this pincer had been engaged by the 2nd Armoured Brigade, which suffered rather heavily, being reduced in that act to between thirty and forty tanks. The other arm of the pincer had moved so fast that its tanks could not be overtaken at all by the guns or transport of the pursuing column. The situation thereafter had worsened steadily. Parties of Allied troops had become surrounded and the whole of the Guards Brigade was in the danger of being cut off. Antelat too had become untenable and the 1st Armoured Division had decided to withdraw to Charruba, where it was later joined by the Guards Brigade who had finally managed to extricate themselves. It was in these circumstances that the 1st Armoured Division had passed to the 4th Indian Division its prearranged signal to withdraw.

The commander of the 4th Indian Division, however, saw that in the changed situation the withdrawal was not going to be without its attendant dangers. Should the Axis reach Mekili before the

[6] *Ibid.*

4th Indian Division could reach Derna, there was a danger of the withdrawal being intercepted and cut off at Gabr el Carmusa or to its west. The danger was brought to the notice of the Corps and it was requested to secure approaches to Carmusa, by placing either the 1st Armoured Division or some other forces in those positions. At this stage the Headquarters of the Eighth Army appears to have taken the matter out of the hands of the XIII Corps and got into direct communication with the HQ of the 4th Indian Division. The two headquarters exchanged several messages during the night of 25/26 January, the upshot of which was that the proposed withdrawal was once again cancelled, and the 4th Indian Division was ordered to stand firm in Benghazi.

This new decision had the support and encouragement of General Auchinleck himself, who had just then flown to the Eighth Army's Headquarters at Tmimi.[7] After examining the matter from all points of view, he and General Ritchie agreed that Rommel had perhaps intended, in the first instance, to make only a limited advance and was now skilfully exploiting an entirely unexpected success. If it be so, they thought, then it would be most unwise to play up to him. On the other hand, by offering stiff resistance, he could perhaps be induced to return to his lair. In any case, he did not appear to be heading for Benghazi. That seemed obvious from the fact that his main effort, so far, was in the direction of Agedabia—Antelat—Msus. Were Benghazi one of his objectives, he might have placed German troops in front of it—Italian troops not being considered enough for the job. But the Allied intelligence was certain that the troops in front of Benghazi were all Italian.

It was on these considerations that the Eighth Army got into direct touch with the 4th Indian Division and countermanded the order of the XIII Corps to withdraw. The Indian division was informed that it would pass under the direct command of the Eighth Army from 1000 hours the following day, 26 January. A new plan was now being evolved for taking offensive action at as early a date as possible. It was expected to take its shape from a proposal made by General Tuker for a converging attack on Msus to be carried out by the 7th Indian Infantry Brigade from the west and the 1st Armoured Division plus the 11th Indian Brigade from the north. Until then the Indian troops in the Benghazi area were to continue to delay the Axis advance and their mobile columns were to threaten General Rommel's line of communication running north-east from Agedabia. It was most vital to prevent the Axis forces moving north-eastward beyond Msus, as that would place

---

[7] Gen. Auchinleck's *Despatch* in Supplement to the *London Gazette* of 13-1-48, p. 350. W/D HQ 4 Div.

Mekili and Derna in danger. The 1st Armoured Division was to ensure that from its position in Charruba in co-operation with the other troops. The main and immediate role of the Armoured Division, however, was to deny to the hostile elements any access to the Jebel, between El Abiar and Charruba, and generally oppose any other northward move.

General Tuker accordingly took steps to oppose any Axis move northward or north-eastwards.[8] He ordered the 7th Brigade to organise columns for operating from the general line Ghemines—Soluk. At the same time he directed the 1st Welch to return to their former task of blocking the Sheleidima and Sidi Brahim passes. The 11th Brigade was likewise ordered to resume its move towards Benghazi. Pending its arrival, the 5th Brigade was made responsible for guarding the area between El Abiar and Maraua so as to be in a position to protect the left flank of the division, in case it had to withdraw across that region. The 5th Brigade was still without its troop-carrying transport ; but through luck it had become possible to remove that handicap, at least partially. A petrol convoy of the XIII Corps which was heading for Msus in ignorance of the place having been evacuated, had just about then been stopped by the Indian division and, pending disposal orders, its transport was made available to the 5th Brigade.

When the Eighth Army had issued its instructions to General Tuker on the night of 25/26 January, it had intimated that a staff officer was being despatched with fuller and more explicit instructions. The officer arrived in Benghazi on the following morning by air, with more detailed orders and information. The gist of these was that General Rommel's advance along the Antelat—Msus line need not cause any alarm. It was not a counter-offensive but only a powerful thrust. Rommel could not possibly have enough troops for pushing on indefinitely without becoming weak and sensitive on his line of communication ; and the intelligence appreciation was certain that he had already overreached himself. Further, there was nothing to indicate that he intended following up his advance in any strength, and at any rate he was paying no attention to the Jebel. He could therefore be repelled by energetic and bold action. Towards that end the 4th Indian Division was asked to take the maximum risk, to make the greatest show possible with as many mobile columns as possible, and to destroy or delay the Axis forces within its area of operation. Other troops in its adjacent areas would do the same. The XIII Corps, in particular, would protect the routes leading into the Jebel. The Polish Brigade would hold Mekili and the 150th Brigade would occupy Bir Hakeim. This, of course, meant that the 4th Indian Division would be

[8] W/Ds HQ 4 Div., 5 Bde., 7 Bde., 11 Bde.

deprived of the protection it had hitherto had of the Polish Brigade on its eastern flank; but the deficiency was to be made up by the 1st Armoured Division's deployment west of Charruba.⁹

General Tuker doubted if the 1st Armoured Division in its depleted condition was capable of stopping any Axis advance west of Charruba. He also could not agree with the Intelligence appreciation as to Rommel's line of communication or his intentions. The 4th Indian Division had only one brigade, the 7th, in fighting trim. The other two brigades were weak, tied up on the line of communication's protection, and very thin on the ground. One of them had no transport. Once the control of the desert was lost, the 4th Indian Division would be unable to look after its long line of communication, which extended from Benghazi to Derna and included elements of hostile population. Further, Benghazi had no natural defences and it could not therefore be held for very long.

Some alternative suggestions

General Tuker, therefore, feared that the role assigned to the 4th Indian Division would not, in the circumstances, produce the desired results. He had this view represented to General Ritchie, the Army Commander; and he advocated three alternative plans. The best course in his opinion was to withdraw to the Derna area, demolishing everything on the way. From there a counter-offensive could be prepared and launched under more favourable conditions for the recapture of Benghazi. If this course was not acceptable, his second suggestion was that he should be allowed to move his division at least as far back as Maraua. On any consideration Maraua was a better place from which to take the offensive than Benghazi which could not be easily defended. Finally, whether from Derna, Maraua or Benghazi, the only way to curb Rommel's aggressiveness quickly was to attack and capture Agedabia and the Agheila area. The 4th Indian Division was prepared to undertake this at once, if supported by an effective armoured division. But it was not strong enough then to do it alone. If, however, it was decided to adhere to the original plan of carrying out operations from Benghazi, General Tuker wished that the force at Mekili would be given a definite assignment of blocking all northward approaches in that area. He hoped that not too much reliance would be placed on the strength of the 1st Armoured Division. General Tuker did not then know in fact, how right he was; for, the same day it became known that the 2nd Armoured Brigade had already been reduced in strength to not more than

---

⁹ 4 Ind. Div's. *Acct. of Ops. in Cyrenaica*, pp. 59-61.

thirty-three tanks—from the eighty tanks it had had only three days before.[10]

It was arranged that the final decision of the Army Commander on General Tuker's views would be communicated to the latter by a prearranged code. The 4th Indian Division received that signal in the afternoon of 26 January, signifying that the operations were to continue from Benghazi. A message from the Eighth Army which confirmed this signal explained that the Axis forces were believed to be experiencing maintenance difficulties. It was not thought likely, therefore, that they would make any substantial effort in the direction of Jebel. Further, the 1st Armoured Division was considered adequate for guarding the 4th Indian Division's lines of communication, and the latter was therefore asked to carry out its previously assigned task without undue anxiety on that account. The role of the Indian division was, however, slightly altered and re-defined as being that of striking hard at the Axis forces and their maintenace in the area between Zt. Msus and Antelat, inclusive of both these places.[11]

The inadequacy of this plan was all too clear to General Tuker who did not hesitate to send a personal message to General Ritchie urging a more drastic remedy. He again suggested a co-ordinated converging move of the 1st Armoured and the 4th Indian Divisions on Zt. Msus, where the bulk of the Axis armour was concentrated. This led to a telephonic discussion between the two commanders, after which General Ritchie decided to visit Benghazi by air to settle the other details. The Army Commander reached Benghazi at midday on 27 January and was met by the Divisional Commander. The proposed operations were discussed and a plan was finalised on the basis of General Tuker's suggestions.

The Army Commander fixed 29 January as the D-1 day for the proposed operations. An earlier date was not feasible as the 1st Armoured Division needed time to get ready. The plan envisaged a converging move on Zt. Msus by the 11th Indian Infantry Brigade from Maraua, the 7th Indian Infantry Brigade from Benghazi and the 1st Armoured Division from Charruba. The Army Commander had ordered that the 11th Indian Infantry Brigade (less 1 Raj Rif) would move from Maraua on the night of 29/30 January and pass forthwith to the command of the 1st Armoured Division. The latter would then advance south to engage the Axis forces and attract their armour towards itself. The 7th Indian Infantry Brigade was to advance in the meanwhile through the Sheleidima pass. Its task was to attack Msus and at the same time operate a column south of the Sheleidima—Msus

[10] *Ibid.* W/D HQ 4 Div.
[11] *Ibid.* W/D HQ 4 Div.

track. The 5th Indian Infantry Brigade was to be responsible for the protection of the Indian division's line of communication. All the other details were satisfactorily settled and, at 1530 hours, General Tuker held a divisional conference and issued the necessary instructions.

CHAPTER XXVIII

Evacuation of Benghazi

Axis advance gathers strength

The basis of the impending operations was a co-ordinated movement by the 1st Armoured and the 4th Indian Divisions to envelop Msus. There were however weak spots in this bold plan of converging moves. Two factors were against it from the very start. They were the weather and the likelihood of unexpected moves by the Axis. Unluckily both turned out adversely and in full force.

As to the moves by the Axis troops, the intimation about the first of them came on 27 January at 1745 hours, that is soon after General Tuker had concluded his conference for settling the preliminaries. A report reached his headquarters at that hour, that a column of Axis troops was moving towards the Sheleidima pass from Msus. The track Msus—Sheleidima was described as being thick with Axis transport on the move. This development was nothing unforeseen but it had forestalled the action of the 4th Indian Division by more than 48 hours, and to that extent had placed it at a disadvantage. Thus, instead of the 7th Indian Infantry Brigade moving from Sheleidima to Msus as planned, the reverse was happening: an Axis force was moving from Msus to Sheleidima. At the same time rain had begun to fall in a heavy downpour. There was a chance of frustrating the Axis move, if the flank of the advancing column could be attacked during the night, after a wide detour. But the heavy rain and the consequent state of the ground made this impracticable.[1]

In the circumstances, the best that could be done was to reinforce the 1st Welch guarding the Sheleidima pass. This was done by the 7th Indian Brigade sending the required reinforcements. The Divisional Commander had at the same time ordered certain other troops to move to Benghazi from Barce, as further reinforcements. They were the 8th RTR, the 4th South African Field Regiment (which had joined the Indian division on 26 January), and a battery of the 7th Medium Regiment. The moves started at once but progress was slow due to the wet state of the ground. It was now a matter of speculation as to how soon

---

[1] W/D HQ 4 Div.

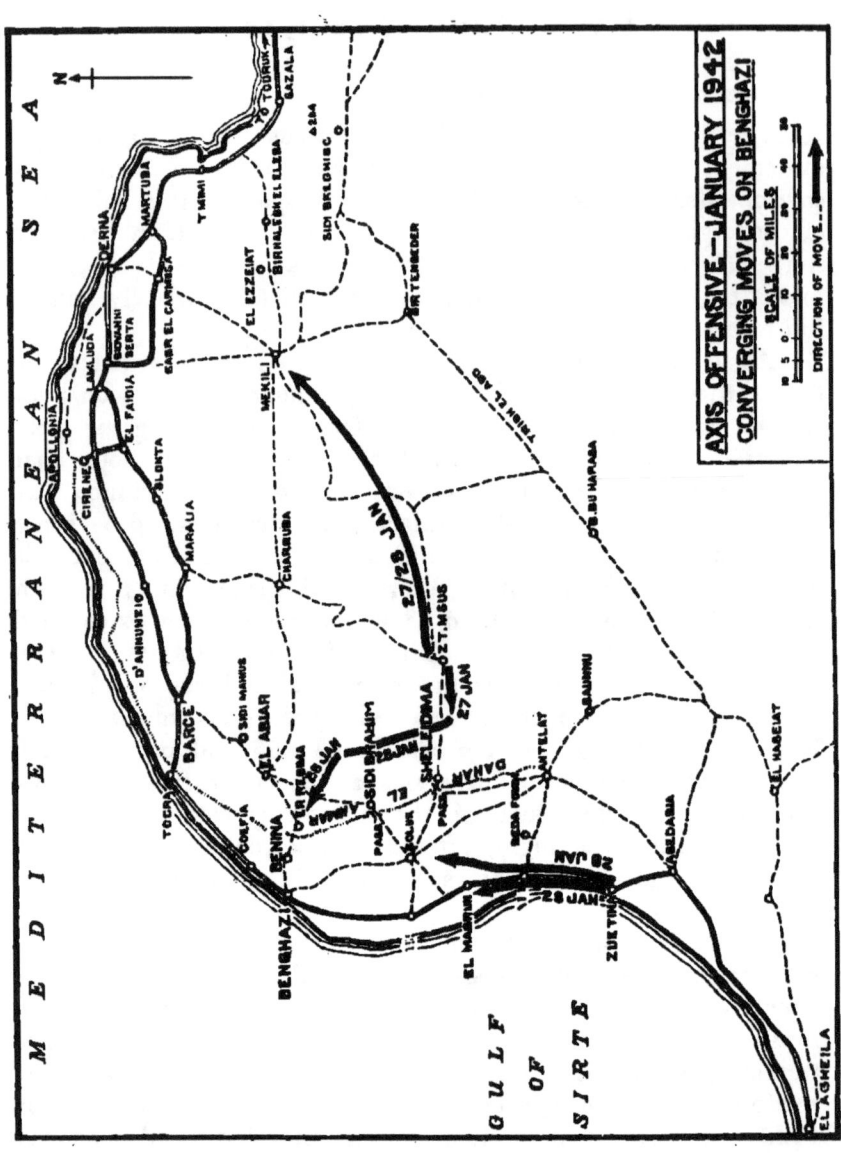

the Axis column would reach Sheleidima, Up to the sunset, patrols of the division had failed to contact any hostile elements within six miles east of Sheleidima.

The night of 27/28 January was undoubtedly a difficult one for the 4th Indian Division. During that night General Tuker addressed a personal message to General Ritchie acquainting him with the changed situation. He assured the Army Commander that his division would endeavour to halt and destroy the Axis troops; but he asked that the 1st Armoured Division should now commence its move earlier than originally intended. He suggested that it should get moving by the morning of 28 January, directed on Msus. Obviously, General Tuker was still adhering to the original plan of the converging moves, and only wanted the time schedule to be put ahead by about a day. A telephone conversation he had during the night with the Army Headquarters gave him to understand that his suggestion had been accepted and the 1st Armoured Division's offensive would take place more or less as he was hoping.

As a matter of fact General Tuker's personal message had crossed one from the Eighth Army containing divergent instructions. His telephone conversation had taken place before he received those instructions and, it appears, had led to a misunderstanding. At any rate the Eighth Army's communication revealed that the situation was more serious than had been supposed till then. Two Axis columns were reported as advancing, instead of the one known so far. Both were radiating from Zt. Msus. One seemed to be a thrust towards Mekili and the other towards Soluk or Benghazi. The former column was moving east and north-east, and the latter towards the west. Both forces seemed about equal in strength but the Mekili column included the bulk of the Axis armour and was therefore considered to be the greater effort.

Since the major part of the Axis armour was heading for Mekili, the Eighth Army naturally desired the 1st Armoured Division to pay greater attention to Mekili than to Msus. The Armoured Division was accordingly ordered to operate against the rear of the Mekili column by moving south or south-east. In the circumstances it was apparent that it would not be available to protect the south flank of the 4th Indian Division, and the latter was therefore asked to make its own arrangement to guard that flank. The Indian division was also informed that its new role now was to stop all Axis moves towards the west and to strike at the Axis flanks and communications. The message went on to add that the Axis forces, having split themselves into two, were now weaker than the Eighth Army's forces in both the areas. The

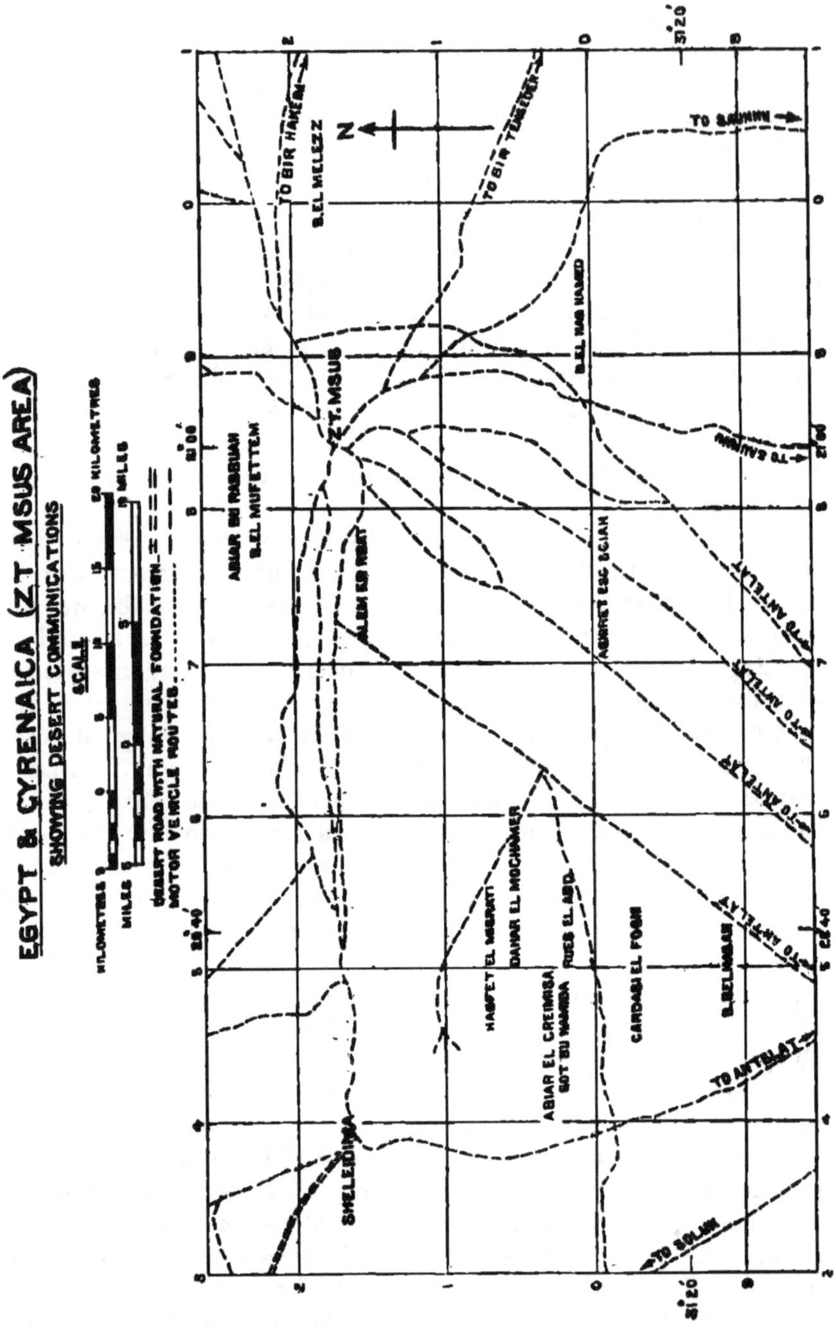
EGYPT & CYRENAICA (Z.T. MSUS AREA)
SHOWING DESERT COMMUNICATIONS
SCALE
KILOMETRES
MILES
DESERT ROAD WITH NATURAL FOUNDATION
MOTOR VEHICLE ROUTES
N
Z.T. MSUS
B.EL MUFETTEM
SHELEIDIMA
TO ANTELAT
TO SOLUK
ABIAR EL CREIMISA
CARDAB EL FOGM
DAHAR EL MOCHAMER
TO BIR HAKEIM
TO BIR TENGEDER

need of the hour, according to the message, was "offensive action everywhere". That was to be the keyword.[2]

The line Derna—Mekili was important to the Eighth Army in case it should be forced to withdraw. It was therefore natural for General Ritchie to be sensitive about any Axis thrust towards Mekili. Loss of Mekili would mean being taken in the rear by General Rommel's forces, and that would rule out all possibility of an orderly retirement, whether to the Derna—Mekili line or to any other line farther behind. It was logical therefore to think that the Axis would go for it; and when Rommel made a feint towards Mekili, General Ritchie fell for it and played up to Rommel's heart's desire by removing his armour to defend Mekili.

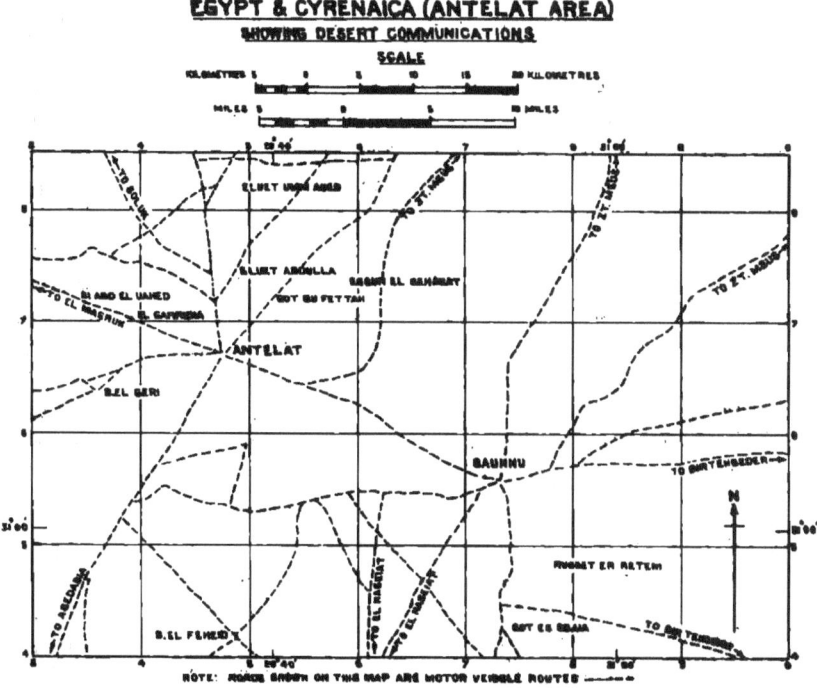

As a matter of fact that was exactly General Rommel's design. His objective was Benghazi but he made it appear as if it was Mekili. It has been seen that on 27 January two Axis columns had moved out from Msus, one heading for Benghazi or Soluk, and the other for Mekili, and the bulk of the Axis armour was with the latter force. This circumstance, combined with the

[2] Gen. Auchinleck's *Despatch* in Supplement to the *London Gazette* of 15-1-48, p. 350. 4 Ind. Div's. *Acct. of Ops. of Cyrenaica*, pp. 62-4. W/Ds HQ 4 Div.; 7 Bde.

importance of Mekili, had led General Ritchie to conclude that Mekili was the real objective and the thrust towards Benghazi was a demonstration. It later turned out to be the reverse. What was then neither known, nor suspected, was that the apparently weaker column heading for Benghazi might at a predetermined stage receive a sudden accession of strength and become strong enough to carry out a full-fledged attack. That was what happened on the morning of 28 January.[3]

The 4th Indian Division prepares to defend Benghazi

On this morning, the commander of the 4th Indian Division was obviously under the impression that the original plan of converging moves on Msus was still on the cards. He had disposed his troops accordingly. The 7th Indian Infantry Brigade was divided into three columns of which two were in the forward area and one in reserve. A portion of the reserve column had been sent off to reinforce the Sheleidima and Sidi Brahim passes as well as other gaps in the escarpment. An improvised force of two companies of the 1st Welch had been placed in Benghazi for local defence as well as for policing the town. This was reinforced by the Anti-tank Company of the 11th Indian Infantry Brigade, one troop of the 4th South African Field Regiment, and such elements of the 8th Royal Tank Regiment as had already arrived. Other dispositions would depend on the results of the air reconnaissances which had been already sent out to search the ground to the east of Sheleidima.[4]

The early morning reconnaissances returned rather soon with the information that there was a large Axis column moving north in the area of square S. 64, that is, about 18 miles north-east of Sheleidima. The column consisted of some 1500-2000 vehicles and was the same which on the previous day was reported as moving along the Msus—Sheleidima track. It had now deserted the track and turned north. It was no longer heading for Sheleidima but for El Abiar instead. Its final objective was not clear but could be Benghazi. There was still a chance to prevent its reaching El Abiar, were the 7th Indian Brigade to move speedily through the Sheleidima Pass and engage it on the way. The brigade was informed of this and began to make preparations forthwith for carrying out that task. But already there were signs of a growing complication: news had arrived at the Divisional Headquarters that another Axis column was approaching Benghazi from the south. It was now apparent that the immediate Axis objective was Benghazi, not Mekili; that the seemingly weaker Axis force

[3] *Ibid.*
[4] *Ibid.*

originally heading for Sheleidima was from the very first intended to be augmented in strength by collaboration from this second column.

At 0930 hours on the same morning, the commander of the 4th Indian Division telephoned the Eighth Army. At that moment he was concerned more about the Axis column approaching round the flank towards El Abiar than about the other one approaching frontally; and he asked that the 1st Armoured Division be moved west immediately to attack the El Abiar column. He was informed that that had been arranged, which was nowhere near the truth. All through that morning reports continued to reach the 4th Indian Division of the movements of the El Abiar column. It seemed to be making a slow progress due to the roughness of the ground, and had some tanks amongst its transport. The column was, however, attacked from the air with some measure of success.[5]

The 7th Indian Infantry Brigade, to the south of Benghazi, was to move east to engage that column. The move had begun but could not proceed as, just about that time, its forward patrols reported that two more Axis columns were approaching their front from the south. Each column was said to be consisting of about 400 vehicles and 40 tanks, and both were advancing from below the escarpment. The 7th Brigade could not leave these forces in its rear and turn eastward. It was therefore forced to remain in the same position and was unable to attack the El Abiar column. It was now clear that the Axis troops were converging on Benghazi from different directions. This was indeed the very reverse of the Eighth Army's plan to converge on Msus.

With the 7th Indian Brigade tied up in defending the southern approach to Benghazi, the commander of the 4th Indian Division had to find alternative means for engaging the El Abiar column. There was the improvised force in Benghazi itself, intended originally for the local defence of the town. It consisted of one company of the 1st Welch reinforced by the 8th Royal Tanks, 2/5th Mahrattas, 11th Brigade Anti-tank Company and one troop of the 4th South African Field Regiment. Of these, the 8th RTR, the Mahrattas and the Anti-tank Company were ordered to move out to engage the El Abiar column. This force was to proceed along the Er Regima—El Abiar road, contact the Axis column and try to delay its progress. It was also to establish contact with the detachments of the 5th Indian Infantry Brigade which were ordered to secure the area between Barce and El Abiar. It will be remembered that the 5th Brigade was then in the Barce area; not having its transport, it was unable to do anything more than send

[5] *Ibid.*

detachments forward. Finally, it was hoped that the 1st Armoured Division which was supposed to be on its way to attack the El Abiar column would turn up in time to save the situation.[6]

It was on this supposition that General Tuker based his plan for tiding over the crisis. He estimated that if the 1st Armoured Division could halt the El Abiar column, and the 7th Indian Infantry Brigade could stop the two columns in the south, then a stand in Benghazi itself would be justified. These were reasonable risks and General Tuker therefore decided to stand and fight in Benghazi. He moved his Advanced Divisional Headquarters into the town from its former location outside it. He further made arrangements for defending the town from a "keep defence", i.e. a self-sufficient defensive locality which included its own water supply and dumps of petrol, ammunition, rations, etc. This was the situation on the morning of 28 January.

That situation, however, changed for the worse before midday, rendering Benghazi untenable. Hitherto the two Axis columns to the south of Benghazi were advancing along the coast. It was noticed on the morning of 28 January, however, that one of those columns had turned north-east and was heading in a direction towards Soluk. At 1200 hours, the commander of the 7th Brigade reported that he was unable to disengage from the Axis troops in front of him to deal with those to his north-east. It seemed now that the 7th Brigade might be forced to fight a withdrawing action on to the town of Benghazi. In such a crisis, much depended on what the 1st Armoured Division might be able to achieve.[7]

General Tuker telephoned the Army Commander at 1230 hours and explained the situation. On asking for news of the 1st Armoured Division he got an answer that disillusioned him. He was told that it was operating to the east of Msus—a direction opposite to what he was hitherto waiting for. This was a deplorable situation. Free from the threat of the 1st Armoured Division, the El Abiar column of the Axis troops had now by-passed El Abiar and was in or near Er Regima, not more than about 15 miles east of Benghazi. The Soluk column was moving on unopposed as there was nothing available with which to stop it. Soon Benghazi would be surrounded and its small garrison driven in by Axis troops. There was perhaps just enough time to evacuate that town. General Tuker asked for permission to evacuate Benghazi that very night (28/29 January). He added that now it was going to be a very difficult operation. The permission was given; but the Army Commander at the same time emphasised that the Axis troops in the Benghazi area could only be Italian. This soon

---

[6] W/Ds HQ 4 Div.; 7 Bde, 5 Bde.
[7] 4 Ind. Div's. Acct. of Ops. in Cyrenaica, p. 65. W/Ds HQ 4 Div.; 7 Bde.

proved to be incorrect, as the improvised force which engaged the El Abiar column that afternoon, in an effort to stop its progress towards Er Regima, found that its opponents were Germans.[8]

Evacuation of Benghazi

After this, General Tuker ordered the evacuation of Benghazi. The necessary instructions were issued in the afternoon (28 January), and the work of demolition according to a prearranged plan was started at once. The plan of withdrawal required that the demolitions should be completed by 1800 hours, at which hour the improvised force was to commence withdrawing through Benghazi. That force was to be followed at 2000 hours by the 7th Brigade. The Advanced Divisional Headquarters was to move to Barce that same evening according to its own schedule; and it was hoped that all troops would be out of the danger zone before midnight. The limit of the danger zone could be roughly said to be the Escarpment line—Tocra—Sidi Mahius. The line was to be secured by the 5th Indian Brigade which was then in that area; and the 7th Indian Brigade was to pass through it in the course of its withdrawal. The 5th Brigade was to be joined by the 8th Royal Tank Regiment which was to move at dusk to Sidi Mahius. The general route of withdrawal was the main coastal road, known as Via Balbia, which runs from Egypt to Tunis. The 8th RTR was, however, to move across the escarpment; Sidi Mahius, its destination, being some twenty-odd miles from the coastal road.

The preliminary part of the withdrawal proceeded as ordered. Heavy equipment and administrative units poured out of Benghazi. Demolitions were carried out with a thoroughness which included the destruction of some 6000 tons of captured ammunition and extensive damage to the harbour. The 7th Indian Brigade commenced its fighting withdrawal on to Benghazi. Its administrative units and the 'B' echelon began to move through the town at 1730 hours, the road then being clear. On the outskirts of the town, however, some echelon units came across a team of German tanks and guns which had penetrated to the Benghazi by-pass road. A troop of light anti-aircraft guns and some captured Bredas belonging to the 'B' echelon engaged this group and knocked out four tanks, some guns and an ammunition vehicle. In the meanwhile, the improvised force about El Abiar had also commenced its move. One of its detachments, the 8th Royal Tank Regiment, moved on a wide circuit from Er Regima and, passing some eight miles south-west of El Abiar, successfully evaded all opposition. Nor did the Advanced Divisional Headquarters, moving towards

[8] *Ibid.*

Barce, meet any opposition. Thus, up to 1815 hours, the withdrawal seemed to be proceeding according to the plan.

The Indian Brigade cut off

However, within the next half an hour difficulties began to reveal themselves. At 1900 hours, some of the units which had already left Benghazi received the news that the 7th Brigade's line of retreat was no longer open. Some German armoured cars and anti-tank guns from the El Abiar column had moved north, across the country, and had cut the main road in the vicinity of Coefia. Nor were the escarpment passes at Sheleidima and Sidi Brahim any longer open. The Axis columns which had been pressing the 7th Brigade's withdrawal towards Benghazi, had afterwards moved on to those passes and captured them, assisted by troops from the top. The garrison of the 1st Welch guarding the passes had been attacked by overwhelming numbers and was obliged to give way.

The 'B' Echelon of the 7th Indian Brigade, which was withdrawing along the main road, came to a halt at about 1830 hours on reaching the Coefia road-block. The rest of the brigade which had also commenced withdrawing was following in its wake. When the brigade received the news of the road-block, which was reported to be fairly strong, it despatched one company of 4/16 Punjab, together with the local improvised force, to clear the road. The fight for the disputed passage appears to have gone heavily in favour of the Axis, as the troops sent out to liquidate the block did not return and had to be written off as missing. Only the 'B' echelons of the 25th and 31st Field Regiments managed to extricate themselves without any loss. They later rejoined their units, south of Benghazi.'

The Commander of the 7th Indian Infantry Brigade (Brig. H. R. Briggs) now found himself in a desperate situation. It was night and he was out of touch with the Divisional Headquarters. Benghazi was not only surrounded on all sides but would be entered by the Axis troops in a matter of hours. There was however a slender chance of breaking through with his brigade, as the area to the south-east of Benghazi had several unguarded tracks or gaps. The decision to take this chance required courage for accepting the grave risks inherent in a night desert march through Axis-held territory. Brigadier Briggs decided to take the risk. The brigade, therefore, turned about at 1945 hours and moved south into the desert in three columns. From this time on, wireless communication with the division was abandoned in the interests of security. A last message was however allowed to be sent out

---

' *Ibid.* W/D 4/16 Punjab.

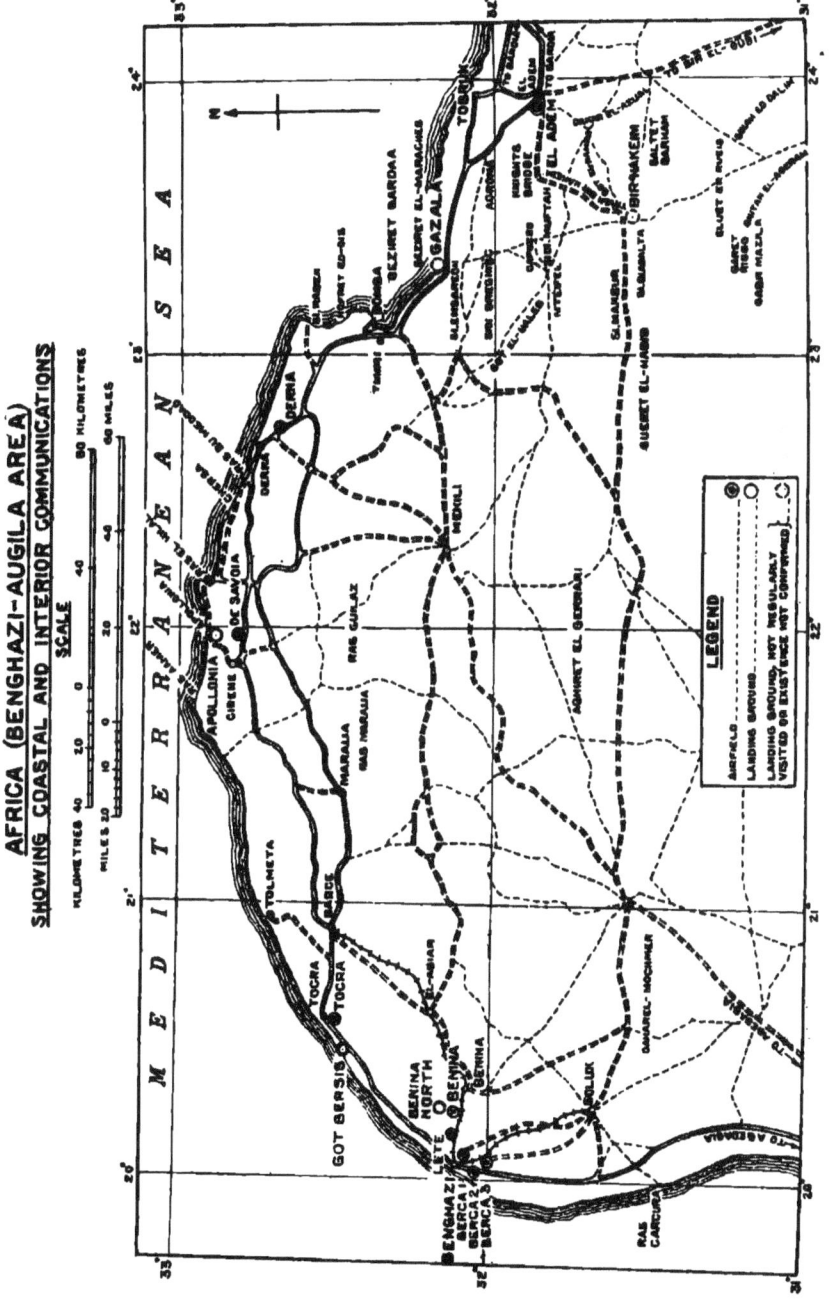

before the closing down of the wireless, announcing the brigade's decision to break out to the south. But it was not received at the Advanced Divisional Headquarters, then at Barce, due to distance and the effect of night conditions on radio communications. There was much anxiety and speculation that night (28 January) at the Divisional Headquarters as to the fate of this Indian brigade.

If the 4th Indian Division was in the dark as to what was happening in Benghazi, the Eighth Army was much more so. Even at this late hour, it was adhering to its original belief that Benghazi could and should be held. It was apparently quite convinced that the Axis troops in the vicinity of Benghazi were Italian forces and not in very great strength. There was nothing surprising, therefore, that at 2145 hours it should have suggested to the Commander 4th Indian Division that it might still be possible for the 7th Indian Brigade to leave a battalion group in Benghazi, should it find it necessary to withdraw from the town. The suggestion could not have seemed unreasonable to either of them, as just about that time a wireless message was picked up by the Divisional Headquarters, purporting to come from the 4/16th Punjab and reporting that efforts were being made to clear "a road-block".[10] It appears that the improvised force and the company of the 4/16th Punjab, who had been detailed to clear the Coefia road-block and had failed to return, had not been rounded up by the Germans to a man. There was apparently a small group still holding out and striving to clear the road, unaware of the fact that the 7th Brigade no longer needed it. Its belated message had produced a glimmer of hope which soon faded out as no further messages were received from that valiant band.

The idea of leaving a battalion group in Benghazi until an offensive could be launched, therefore, held ground for a while. It could not be immediately communicated to the 7th Brigade, as it was apparent that the brigade was observing wireless silence or was unable for some other reasons to answer wireless calls. The idea, however, had to be abandoned a little later, when an officer arrived at the Divisional Headquarters and reported that he had identified German armoured forces at Er Regima. The report was confirmed by a number of stragglers, who had escaped capture at the Coefia road-block and who arrived a little later. Their account left no doubt that the armoured troops near Benghazi were German, as Italians had not been seen at all. This evidence, along with other reports, pointed to the fact that the Axis were serious about their attack on Benghazi; and leaving a battalion group to garrison the town was therefore no longer considered to be a

---

[10] This message was sent by Brigadier S. S. Lavender DSO then in command of the battalion.

feasible proposition. Far from it, misgivings now began to be entertained as to the possible fate of the whole of the 7th Indian Brigade.[11]

Efforts to rescue the 7th Brigade

In view of the continued absence of communication from the 7th Brigade, it was decided to make an effort to locate its whereabouts by sending out reconnaissance parties for the purpose. The 5th Indian Brigade was ordered to operate fighting patrols from Tocra, towards Benghazi and also to demonstrate towards Er Regima, from the El Abiar direction, moving out at first light. At the same time it was suggested that the 1st Armoured Division should co-operate by moving on Benghazi, where, it was felt, the 7th Brigade might have been surrounded. The Armoured Division found it impossible to accede to this request, as its full armoured strength was not even equivalent to one regiment and the rough ground towards Benghazi might take a further toll of its vehicles. It however despatched patrols towards the west to try and establish touch with the 7th Brigade.

---

[11] 4 Ind. Div's. *Account of Ops. in Cyrenaica*; W/Ds HQ. 4 Div.

CHAPTER XXIX

Break-through of the 7th Brigade

The adventures of the 7th Indian Infantry Brigade, from the time it broke out to the south of Benghazi form an interesting episode. The task before the brigade was to find its way through the Axis-held parts of the desert and to rejoin the 4th Indian Division finally. Since a large body like a brigade cannot escape detection during a long march, it was decided to divide it into columns. Each column was to make its independent way through the desert and subsist on its own resources during the march.

Accordingly, the brigade was allowed to remain organised into the three groups in which it had been operating during the previous days. They were named the Headquarters Group, the Gold Group and the Silver Group. Each group was instructed to destroy such of its vehicles as were not mechanically fit for a prolonged desert move or for which sufficient petrol was not available. The three groups were then to find their separate ways through the Allied minefields which had been earlier laid by the 4th Indian Division to cover the southern approach to Benghazi. It was raining heavily and the moon had not risen when the moves commenced on the night of 28 January.[1]

The Headquarters Group

The rains, the darkness and the minefields made the progress slow and difficult for the first few hours. It was, therefore, not until 0230 hours that the Headquarters Group emerged out of the minefields and halted to adopt night formations. A little before this, it had been joined by about one and a half companies of the 1st Welch who, it will be remembered, were guarding the escarpment passes at Sheleidima and Sidi Brahim, where they had been attacked by Axis troops and forced to fall back. They had then withdrawn to Benghazi, and arriving there to find it being evacuated, had proceeded in the direction of the Headquarters Group and joined it finally.

After waiting a little for the moon to rise, the group resumed its march at 0310 hours, in the direction of Soluk, which was then in Axis occupation. Passing west of Soluk, from where the Axis light signals could be occasionally seen going up, the column moved south, and soon after dawn crossed the Axis-held track,

[1] 4 Ind. Div's. *Acct. of Ops. in Cyrenaica*, pp. 72-75. W/Ds HQ 4 Div.; 7 Bde.

Antelat—Beda Fomm, without attracting any attention. Thereafter it adopted the day formation and proceeded towards the track, Antelat—Agedabia.

As it was preparing to cross that track there appeared the first signs to show that the area was well and fully under Axis control. Two Stukas were noticed by the Group, flying parallel to it and on its eastern flank. On investigation it was found that they were covering the move of a large German convoy which was journeying south along the very track which the Group was about to cross. At this, the Group halted and took steps to prevent alarm being given by some German prisoners who formed a part of the Group. After that the convoy was watched in silence as it passed at a distance of not more than five hundred yards, followed by a Henschel flying slowly over it. Neither the convoy nor the accompanying aircraft suspected the presence of the Headquarters Group in that area.

When the convoy was well out of sight, the Headquarters Group proceeded to cross the track and met with a very bad mishap. There were in that area four stationary German tanks which had been seen but were thought to be derelict, as hitherto they had remained motionless and had given no indication of wanting to attack the HQ Group. However, as some of the last vehicles of the Group were getting clear of the track, they sprang to life and opened fire. As a result the Group lost one light anti-aircraft gun, two anti-tank guns and a whole platoon of the 4/16th Punjab. The rest of the column escaped unmolested and moved on rapidly in spite of the very rough ground.[2]

The journey now lay in the direction of Saunnu which was known to be under Axis occupation, the destination being Mekili, believed to be still in Allied hands. It was now decided to pass south of Saunnu, keeping at a safe distance from it, and then to take one of the many tracks going to Bir Tengeder or Mekili. With that aim, the Group changed its course to the north-east as it drew nearer to Saunnu. The move continued without incident till 0500 hours on 30 January, when the moon set and the consequent darkness slowed down the progress. Hitherto the Group had been continuously on the move with only five-minute halts every hour for rest and maintenance. It was therefore decided to make a long halt now for breakfast. Several vehicles had developed minor defects and were in tow.

Before resuming the march towards Mekili it was decided to ascertain whether that place was still in Allied hands. This was done at 0700 hours by opening the wireless and making inquiries from XIII Corps. The Corps replied in the affirmative and the

[2] *Ibid.*

journey was resumed. On the way the Group was joined by patrols of the 1st Royal Dragoons who had been shadowing it since dawn, suspecting it to be an Axis force. The Group finally reached Mekili at 1500 hours having completed some 300 miles in well under 48 hours.

The Gold Group

If the Headquarters Group had managed to reach the safety of the Allied lines, the Gold Group was no less successful. It was facing east on the night of 28 January when the breakout commenced and from that position it had to turn south for making its exit from Benghazi. The process was completed at 2300 hours after which the Group commenced its move along the main road between Benghazi and Ghemines. It gave up the main road just north of Ghemines and, having adopted the night formation, stepped into the desert for the rest of the journey.

The first hurdle of the desert was the Axis-dominated track Ghemines—Soluk. It proved easy to cross this without detection due to the darkness of the night, the moon being low at that hour. After that the journey was resumed in a south-easterly direction until a position was reached at 0600 hours in the morning, just to the south-east of El Magrun. This was a well-sheltered spot, being screened from Magrun by a high ground and was considered suitable for a day-time halt. The Group dispersed widely and remained halted for the rest of the day of 29 January. To avoid attracting attention, precaution was taken to minimise all kinds of tell-tale activities. Orders were issued, for example, that no slit trenches were to be dug, nor were fires to be lit, nor was any action to be taken against hostile aircraft flying about the area.

The precaution proved to be profitable, inasmuch as several Axis aircraft appeared over the area during the day and flew low enough to see but took no hostile action. It is possible that they failed to detect the existence of the Gold Group altogether due to its wide dispersal and absence of movement. The same may be said of another incident. An observation post reported at 1700 hours that an Axis column was advancing towards the Group's location. It was moving south along a desert track which joined the main road somewhere in the vicinity. Positions were ordered to be taken up in expectation of a clash. But the column turned off on to the main road and passed along the west of the Gold Group, apparently unaware of the latter's existence.

These two consecutive alarms had however shown that the camping-ground of the Gold Group, though comparatively a safe hiding place, was by no means an unfrequented spot. It was therefore considered prudent to quit it without much delay. The night's march was scheduled to commence at dusk, but the Gold Group decided to move off at once.

The march was resumed at 1730 hours, the column taking a south-easterly direction. There were two more hurdles to cross that night, the Axis-controlled tracks Agedabia—Antelat, and Antelat—Saunnu. It proved possible to cross both before dawn without any incident. Aided by a high moon the column moved on rapidly in spite of the roughness of the ground, and by 0400 hours was in a locality to the south-west of Zt. Msus. Msus was known to be under hostile occupation and it was necessary to proceed with caution after surveying the situation in daylight. The Gold Group therefore called a halt from 0400 to 0700 hours.

After three hours of rest, the Group changed the direction to the north-east and moved on again. At 0800 hours on 30 January, it found itself some 15 miles south of Zt. Msus, in the locality known as Balat Abd el Hafid (X. 88). It was deemed safe to open wireless communication from this spot. This was done and contact was quickly gained with the XIII Corps, who were informed that the Gold Group was proceeding to Mekili.

Hardly had this last phase of the journey commenced when the advanced guard gave the alarm that there was danger ahead. They reported having spotted an Axis column of about 800 vehicles and four tanks moving in the direction of the Gold Group and not very far from it at that moment. It was decided to attack this force, and the 31st Field Regiment and anti-tank guns were sent forward for the purpose. The rest of the Group was ordered to move six miles to the south so as to be out of the way. The anti-tank guns and the field guns of the 31st Field Regiment went into action, which made the Axis force withdraw to the north.

After that the Gold Group prepared to resume its march. But at this stage it was discovered that the stock of petrol which the Group was carrying was insufficient for completing the journey to Mekili with a safe margin. The destination of the Group was therefore changed from Mekili to Bir Tengeder, which was nearer and known to be in Allied hands.

At about this time, while the Group was still halted, there appeared a Henschel which flew over for the most part at a height of about fifty feet. It was not fired upon and it did not take any hostile action but remained over for about half an hour, possibly examining the strength and composition of the Group. It could not have failed to see everything. The consequences of this reconnaissance were felt soon after its departure when two Macchi G.-50 fighters appeared in the sky and made dive machine-gun attacks upon the column. They failed to cause any damage or casualties, but the attack was nevertheless a thoroughly unpleasant affair. Meanwhile the Group had started moving towards Bir Tengeder.

The march continued till late in the afternoon when the Group was met by the patrols of the 11th Hussars in the vicinity of Bir el Amia (Y. 66), where they went into a leaguer and rested for the night. The march was resumed at 0730 hours, the following morning, and Bir Tengeder was reached at 1200 hours the same day, 31 January. The travails of the Gold Group were at last at an end, and it settled down temporarily in the area of the 150th Infantry Brigade.

The Silver Group

The third group of the 7th Indian Infantry Brigade, the Silver Group, had no easy time. In fact, in terms of casualties and damage sustained on the way, it suffered more than the other two groups. Like the Gold Group, it was facing in the opposite direction on the night of 28 January when the decision was taken to break out to the south of Benghazi. It completed its about-turn to the south at 2300 hours that night and started moving parallel to the railway track linking Benghazi to Soluk. It was joined on the way by a squadron of the Central India Horse at En Nauaghia, a little after midnight, according to a predetermined arrangement. The whole column then began to move in a southward direction, two vehicles abreast, and kept moving for the rest of the night. Got es Saeti, a locality to the south-east of El Magrun, was reached at 0700 hours on 29 January, when the Group halted for rest and maintenance. The night march had proved very trying. All through the night the lights of Axis camps were visible at Sheleidima and Soluk; and during the period of darkness one platoon of 1 Royal Sussex became missing, possibly as a result of having lost the way.

The march from Got es Saeti was resumed at 0845 hours. At about 1000 hours, there occurred the first encounter with the Axis troops. A carrier of a platoon of 1 Royal Sussex, which was acting as the left flank guard of the Group, spotted a sizable Axis column of vehicles moving down the escarpment, some four miles north of Antelat. At that moment the column was half a mile away from the carriers and was preceded by two tanks. It was composed of about twenty lorries, two staff cars and three motor cyclists. On reaching the foot of the escarpment, it turned north and moved on, not suspecting the existence of the Silver Group in the vicinity.

1 Royal Sussex decided to engage this column in spite of the two tanks which were moving at its head. Two sections of carriers succeeded in getting between the tanks and the column and then attacking the latter. As soon as the attack started

the two tanks made off in a westerly direction as fast as they could, instead of going in the opposite direction to protect their charge. The rest of the column seeing their escort flee, did the same. They turned about and hurried back to the escarpment scattering in various directions. The carriers gave the chase and succeeded in destroying six lorries, one 50-mm. anti-tank gun, 800 gallons of diesel oil and eight motor cycles (five of them carried in lorries). They also took a toll of fourteen Italians killed, and captured another twenty-eight, including one officer. It was later learnt that these men belonged to the Italian Trieste Division. The carriers themselves suffered no damage or casualty during the action and rejoined the Group some three hours later.

This was an unqualified success but it was a short-lived one. Almost immediately afterwards, at about 1300 hours, four Axis aircraft, M.E.109Fs, appeared over the location of the Silver Group and started hovering around in an effort to inspect the ground. At this, contrary to orders, some guns of the Group opened fire and one plane was seen to be hit. The rest of the aircraft then machine-gunned the Group causing a number of casualties. An hour later, at 1400 hours, a further batch of six Italian aircraft came over and, dive-bombing the Group, took a toll of 12 killed and 16 wounded. Still further losses were suffered at 1500 hours when two M.E.109Fs appeared again and inflicted a few more casualties in low-flying attacks.

All this suffering the silver Group might have avoided had it been careful to conceal its location from the Axis troops. Had it, like the Gold Group, selected a sheltered spot and remained stationary during the daytime, it might have perhaps reached its destination with no more casualties than the missing platoon of Royal Sussex. It is worth speculating in this context whether the dashing attack on the small Axis convoy by the carriers of 1 Royal Sussex was at all justified, however praiseworthy it might have been from the point of view of courage and immediate results. At any rate, the Silver Group continued its march for the rest of the day and finally arrived at 1800 hours in the area Alam Bessanan, a locality very much in the interior of the desert but joined to Bir Tengeder by a motorable track.

The group halted for sometime at Alam Bessanan, for rest and maintenance. Here, it made the discovery that the petrol in hand was insufficient for the journey ahead and some vehicles would have to be left behind. The carriers of the Royal Sussex and some other vehicles were accordingly ordered to be destroyed and the march was resumed at 1945 hours. Moving all through the night, with only an hour's halt on the way from 0500 to 0600 hours, the Group at last reached its destination at 0815 hours on 30 January. This was Garet el Tartut, some 36 miles south of Bir Tengeder.

From here the Group tried to ascertain whether Tengeder was still in Allied hands. But its wireless set was not sufficiently powerful to span the distance and the matter remained in doubt. It was therefore considered safer to alter the final destination and move towards Giarabub instead. But this proved unnecessary, as just at this juncture there happened to arrive a patrol of the 150th Infantry Brigade who gave the information that Tengeder was in Allied occupation. Thereupon the Silver Group commenced moving north and soon completed the last lap of its adventurous journey.

All three columns of the 7th Indian Infantry Brigade had thus succeeded in extricating themselves from a desperate situation and rejoining the Eighth Army with much of their infantry and artillery. This satisfactory result was no doubt due to the bold decision of its commander, Brigadier H. R. Briggs, to break out of Benghazi. By 31 January, the whole Brigade was reunited and once again under a single command, with its troops partly at Mekili and partly at Tengeder. Later, it was sent to the frontier of Egypt to rest and re-equip in the rear area, while the Eighth Army strove to stem the tide of Axis advance and to attain stabilisation.

Eighth Army's efforts to stabilise

The plan of the Eighth Army was to return to the attack as soon as stabilisation was achieved and a measure of reorganisation carried out. The question was, where to stabilise? The answer depended upon the topography of the land. Roughly the country over which the Axis forces were advancing lay between Benghazi and Tobruk. It could be divided according to its physical configuration into three distinct parts: the coastal margin, the mountainous region of Jebel Akhdar, and the desert. The Axis could advance across any of the three regions; and if the advance was to be checked successfully, a line of positions had to be taken up blocking all the three routes.

However, for all practical purposes, the coastal margin could be ignored or left lightly defended, the reason being that at a little distance from Benghazi, that is at Tocra, the main road swerved inland on to the Jebel Akhdar, and the coastal strip ceased to exist for a distance of about 130 miles. In other words, there was no road or strip of the coast between Tocra and Derna which the Axis might have used for advancing towards Egypt.

The question of stabilising a position, therefore, resolved itself into taking up a line running across Jebel Akhdar and the desert. The line would necessarily consist of a series of positions guarding the nodal points of roads and tracks. In the desert there were only two such points, Mekili and Bir Tengeder. So long as these could be held firmly, the Axis would not be able to advance through the desert.

As to the possible Axis advance through the mountainous belt of Jebel Akhdar, the position, however, was different. Of the main trunk road which runs from Egypt to Tunisia, the portion that crosses Jebel Akhdar is that between Derna and Tocra. This stretch divides itself into two at Lamluda, whence both the arms run parallel until they reunite at Barce. West of Barce the two arms open out again to rejoin in Benghazi. Thus, between Lamluda and Benghazi, the Jebel has two roads practically all along its entire length. They have often been called the north and the south roads. Parallel to these two roads runs a motorable track. To defend Jebel Akhdar it was necessary to defend all these three routes.

The ten defensive lines

This could be best done by forming a defensive line running across the three routes and extending to Mekili or Tengeder. There were several points on the north and south roads which lent themselves to such a scheme, but there was only one such point on the track, namely a locality known as Charruba. The Eighth Army organised quite a number of defensive lines in these areas by selecting points opposite to one another on the north and south roads. There were ten such lines, one behind the other, which the 4th Indian Division took up and abandoned successively as the pressure of the advancing Axis troops increased. They were the lines: (1) Tocra—Sidi Mahius (2) Barce—Charruba (3) D'Annunzio—Maraua (4) Caf Tartagu—Slonta (5) Cirene—El Faidia (6) Lamluda—Tengeder (7) Derna—Tengeder (8) Tmimi—El Ezzeiat (9) Gazala—Bir Hakeim and (10) the Acroma and Hamra positions.[3]

Most of the above lines were extended across the desert by being linked to the desert line Mekili—Bir Tengeder, mentioned earlier; that is, they hinged on Mekili, pivoting on it from west to east. Not all these lines were of equal importance. From the point of view of the Eighth Army's plan for stabilisation, there were only two important ones, the Lamluda—Tengeder and the Gazala—Bir Hakeim lines. The rest were, however, good intermediate positions for delaying the advance of the Axis troops until the Lamluda and the Gazala lines in the rear could be strengthened and made ready for a more stable defence.[4]

---

[3] Obviously, the word 'lines' is used here in a loose sense.
[4] Gen. Auchinleck's *Despatch* in Supplement to the *London Gazette* of 15-1-48, pp. 350-51.

After the fall of Benghazi on the night of 28 January, General Ritchie decided that it was time to select an area in which to stabilise eventually. He chose the line Lamluda—Mekili—Bir Tengeder as the final limit of Eighth Army's withdrawal. But in order to have as much time as possible to prepare it and to assemble the necessary forces for a counter-offensive, he decided that the withdrawal through Jebel Akhdar should be slow and gradual. To that end he ordered the 4th Indian Division to fall back by stages, punctuating its withdrawal by occupation of the intermediate defensive positions.

At this time, the 4th Indian Division was greatly in need of reinforcements. It was out of touch with its 7th Indian Infantry Brigade. Its two other brigades, the 5th and the 11th, had only two battalions each. The former had lost 3/1 Punjab during the previous month when that battalion was withdrawn to Tobruk. The latter had likewise lost the 1st Rajputana Rifles a little later, owing to that unit having suffered heavy casualties in the fighting round Antelat and being subsequently sent to the rear to reorganise.[5]

Since the Indian division had to be strengthened for its difficult task of delaying General Rommel's advance, both these battalions were ordered to rejoin their division; so also the artillery which had been separated from it. The moves to the forward area started at once. The 1st Field Regiment reached Barce by the evening of 28 January, and the 144th arrived the following day. A battery of the 65th Anti-tank Regiment, now reduced to the strength of a troop through battle casualties, returned about the same time from the command of the 1st Armoured Division. All these were welcome reinforcements. But as the bulk of the 65th Anti-tank Regiment was with the 7th Indian Infantry Brigade, the Indian Division was still very much below par in tank artillery.

Such was the state of the 4th Indian Division on the night of 28 January. Its forwardmost elements were then to the north-east of Benghazi, trying to keep track of Axis movements. They were the troops of the 5th Indian Infantry Brigade, which was then in the Barce area, where was also located the Advanced Divisional Headquarters. The 11th Indian Infantry Brigade was around Maraua.

There were also other Allied forces in the vicinity whose dispositions closely affected those of the 4th Indian Division. They were the 1st Armoured Division, the 'E' Force, the 'L' Force and the 150th (British) Infantry Brigade. Of these the Armoured Division was at Charruba. Somewhere to its south was the 'E' Force, referred to earlier as the Oases Group; it consisted of HQ 29th Indian Infantry Brigade, 3/2 Punjab and some South African field-

[5] *Ibid.* W/Ds 5 Bde, 11 Bde.

guns and armoured cars. Finally there was the 150th (British) Infantry Brigade at Bir Tengeder, and the 'L' Force, consisting of the Free French and Poles, at Mekili.[6]

Until the morning of 29 January, it did not appear likely that the Axis troops would follow up the retirement of the 4th Indian Division through Jebel Akhdar, since the main Axis thrust so far had been directed on to Benghazi and no attempt had been made to move east from Zt. Msus. This fact also seemed to lend weight to the hypothesis hitherto favoured by the Eighth Army command that General Rommel was short of supplies and would not therefore be able to move very far east. Luckily, however, that dangerous belief did not persist for very long. A fresh assessment of General Rommel's supply situation revealed that it was much better than had been supposed earlier and was at least good enough to enable him to send out a whole armoured division, should he have chosen to do so.

Withdrawal to Line 3

It was therefore not surprising that at 1045 hours on 29 January, the 4th Indian Division received orders to commence its withdrawal. According to a prearranged plan it was to fall back through lines 1 and 2 (enumerated hereinbefore) to line 3, i.e. the line D'Annunzio—Maraua—Hagfet Gelgaf—Mekili—Bir Tengeder. To simplify matters, this was named line 'A' and it was to be occupied by the Indian division by 2359 hours on 30 January. Rear parties were to be left behind to dispute the advance of the Axis as far west as possible, without becoming seriously engaged. This could be best done by holding the intermediate line Barce-Charruba (line 2).[7]

The 4th Indian Division accordingly started preparations for moving to line 'A' as ordered. It planned to withdraw on a two-brigade front, the 5th Indian Infantry Brigade going by the north road and the 11th by the south. Instructions, in anticipation of this, had already been issued, the 5th Brigade being ordered to withdraw its forward elements to the line Tocra—Sidi Mahius (line 1). Prepared demolitions were to be blown up as necessary; but the maximum possible time was to be allowed before the roads were thus rendered unusable, so that, in case the 7th Indian Infantry Brigade was withdrawing along the same route, it might not be cut off.[8]

---

[6] Gen. Auchinleck's *Despatch* in Supplement to the *London Gazette* of 15-1-48, p. 351-52.
[7] 4 Ind. Div's. *Acct. of Ops. in Cyrenaica*, pp. 71-72. W/D HQ 4 Div.
[8] The 7th Indian Brigade had broken through to the south of Benghazi on the night of 28 January.

The Tocra—Sidi Mahius line (line 1) was taken up by the advanced elements of the 5th Indian Infantry Brigade during that same morning of 29 January, as ordered. But it could not be held for more than a few hours. The Axis armoured cars were there by midday. They were hovering round the Tocra village, below the escarpment, and seemed to be the precursors of a larger force already on the way. Since the task of the 4th Indian Division was to delay the Axis forces, but without actually engaging them, it was decided to withdraw. All hope of the 7th Indian Infantry Brigade being able to come through had to be abandoned, as the road in question was for all practical purposes in Axis hands. The Tocra demolition was accordingly blown up, at 1420 hours, and all troops retired to the Barce—Charruba line (line 2) to rejoin the 5th Indian Infantry Brigade.

But even this line was no longer safe, owing to the fluid state of affairs on the desert flank. The Axis advance was too rapid to permit a stay of more than twenty-four hours in that position. It became necessary, therefore, to retire to the main line D'Annunzio—Maraua, i.e. line 3. The Divisional Commander ordered the withdrawal to be completed during the night and the movement was carried out without any incident in spite of heavy rains. The Advanced Divisional Headquarters moved farther back than the rest of the Indian division, taking up its location at Luigi Razza (O.35) on the next succeeding defensive line. Meanwhile the Axis forces were following up rapidly.

Proposed withdrawal to Line 5

In its new location, the 4th Indian Division received a revised plan of action from the Eighth Army. According to this the line Barce—Charruba (line 2) was to be denied to the Axis at least up to 1200 hours on 30 January. After that the next stand was to be on the line Cirene—El Faidia—Mekili—Bir Tengeder (line 5), which was to be occupied by 2359 hours on 1 February and was named line "B". On arrival there the 4th Indian Division was to revert to the XIII Corps, at a time to be notified later. At the same time some other units were to pass under the command of the 4th Indian Division. They were the whole of the 'E' Force and the King's Dragoon Guards with the 7th South African Reconnaissance Unit and the 4th Libyan Arab Force Battalion. Of these the Reconnaissance Unit had about forty armoured cars, which was a valuable accession to the Indian division's strength and a great help in its task of having to protect its desert flank. But the Libyan Arab Battalion was not of much military value, as it was poorly equipped at that time and had hardly any transport at all. Nor was the 'E' Force able to make any material contribution to the division's transport, its vehicles being in a dilapidated condition after three months of strenuous service in the desert.

During the rest of the day on 30 January, the 4th Indian Division had no contact with the Axis troops. But air reports indicated that some movements were in progress and the direction was towards Maraua. Instructions were therefore issued that the two brigades should be ready to quit the line 'A' (D'Annunzio—Maraua) and withdraw to the line 'B' (Cirene—El Faidia—Mekili—Bir Tengeder). The Advanced Divisional Headquarters moved to Giovanni Berta as control of communications and operations on the two roads was easier from that locality.

As the expected reinforcements of troops arrived, they were taken under the division's command and assigned to various units. Thus the 'E' Force was initially placed under the 11th Brigade and the King's Dragoon Guards under the Advanced Divisional Headquarters. The divisional boundary to the south was the road Maraua—Slonta, thence 30 Northing Grid (later changed to 20). South-east of this line was the 'L' Force, with which contact had been established by patrols of the Dragoon Guards. Thus strengthened and disposed, the 4th Indian Division stood guard on line 'A', ready to fall back on line 'B' at the first effective impact of the advancing Axis troops on its forward elements.[9]

[9] W/Ds HQ 4 Div; 11 Bde.

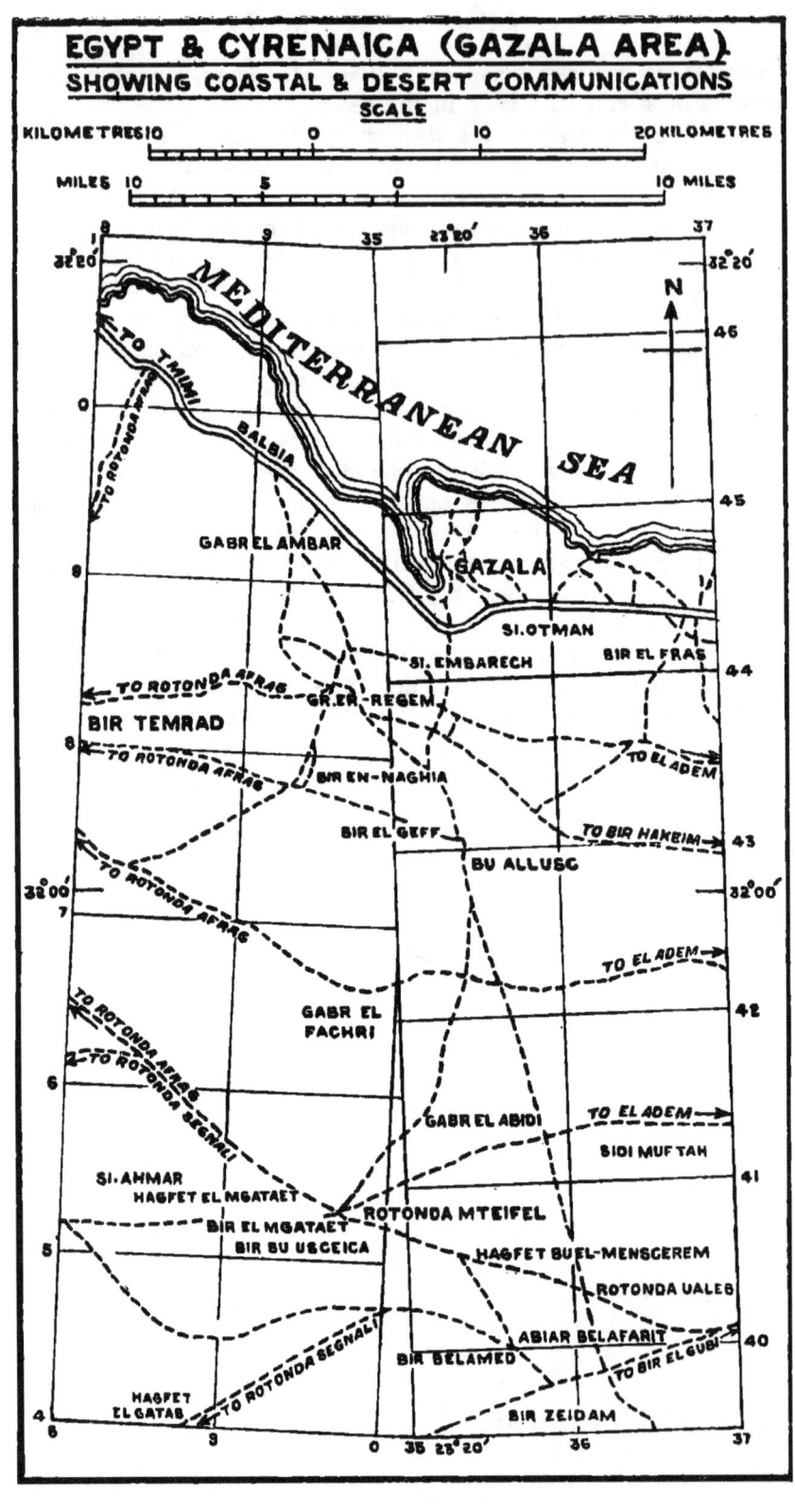

CHAPTER XXX

Withdrawal to Gazala

The 4th Division on Line 3

The forward elements of the 4th Indian Division reported contact with the hostile forces late in the morning of 31 January. There was activity all along the front, from D'Annunzio in the north to Maraua in the south. The Axis troops appeared to be attempting infiltration round the north and south flanks and in-between the two positions. Their lorried infantry attacked the 2nd Camerons at Maraua, in the 5th Indian Infantry Brigade sector, other troops trying to infiltrate past the flank. At the same time two armoured cars approached the positions of 4/6 Raj Rifs, at D'Annunzio, in the 11th Indian Infantry Brigade sector, and made attempts to get through. Simultaneous endeavours were also made to filter through the centre of the line.[1]

All endeavours were, however, defeated in the initial stages. The 2nd Camerons successfully repulsed the lorried infantry's attack on themselves, inflicting considerable losses on the assailants; while the Raj Rifs destroyed both the armoured cars in their sector and quashed the infiltrating moves with a firm hand.

Thus the morning of 31 January was spent in minor clashes all along the line 'A', after which the front became agreeably quiescent. But the quietude was broken in the afternoon when another Axis column approached Maraua and appeared to settle down as if in preparation for a major assault. Inasmuch as the line 'A' was to be held temporarily only and for the mere purpose of delaying the progress of the Axis, the commander of the 4th Indian Division felt that there was no point in holding it any longer. There was the risk of the forward troops being cut off, were the line to be held merely for the sake of adhering to a time schedule. He, therefore, made a representation to the Eighth Army and secured permission to withdraw ahead of the schedule. He did not desire to fall back at once to line 'B', but only to the next intermediate position, the line Caf Tartagu—Slonta, i.e. line 4, which had better natural defence than the position intended to be abandoned.[2]

---

[1] 4 Ind. Div's. *Account of Ops. in Cyrenaica*, pp. 77-8. W/Ds 4 Div., 5 Bde., 11 Bde, 4 Raj Rifs.

[2] Lines 'A', 'B' and 'C' were respectively lines 3, 5 and 7.

Withdrawal to Line 4

The Eighth Army having agreed to the proposal to withdraw, orders were issued accordingly and arrangements made to complete the move during the night of 31 January. It was somewhat difficult to disengage from the Axis troops in the forward area; for no sooner had the withdrawal commenced than they launched an attack against 4/6 Raj Rifs at D'Annunzio. The attackers were, however, driven back with losses, a German tank being destroyed in the action, after which the Raj Rifs were permitted to retire unmolested. On the other hand, the 2nd Camerons, at the other extreme of line 'A' managed to break contact with ease and fell back in their own time, blowing up demolitions and mining the roads in their rear.

The evening of the withdrawal was crowded with several instances of major and minor importance. The outstanding one among them took place at 1630 hours when the Divisional Commander, dissatisfied with the way the withdrawal was proceeding, took it upon himself to send a personal message to General Ritchie, in which he pressed certain matters to the attention of the Army Commander and urged a reconsideration of the whole plan of withdrawal. In particular, he deprecated the method of slow withdrawals over short distances which, he protested, could only lead to the most serious consequences. He, therefore, stressed the need for a complete and rapid retreat to an area east of the Jebel. His reasons for thinking so were that the 1st Armoured and the 4th Indian Divisions were too weak to prevent infiltration, and that the XIII Corps was unduly tied up in protecting approaches to the south. Such preoccupations might prevent vital demolitions from being carried out in time and the Eighth Army might find itself outstripped by the Axis troops, with its many miles of administrative transport falling a prey to them. It was better, he argued, to retire in one's own time to a more distant line of defence than wait to be driven there ultimately, with the Axis troops always on one's heels and in a position to prevent one's returning to the offensive.[3]

As if to lend a point to this representation, the Divisional Headquarters received an air report, almost immediately afterwards, stating that an Axis column had been seen in the vicinity of line 'B'. The report placed the column somewhere south of El Faidia, the southern terminal of the said line. The presence of hostile forces, so far east, indicated that the Axis troops were moving faster than the Indian division. The inevitable result of this would be that while the 4th Indian Division continued to waste time holding line after line, the Axis troops would by-pass it along its desert

---

[3] *Ibid.*

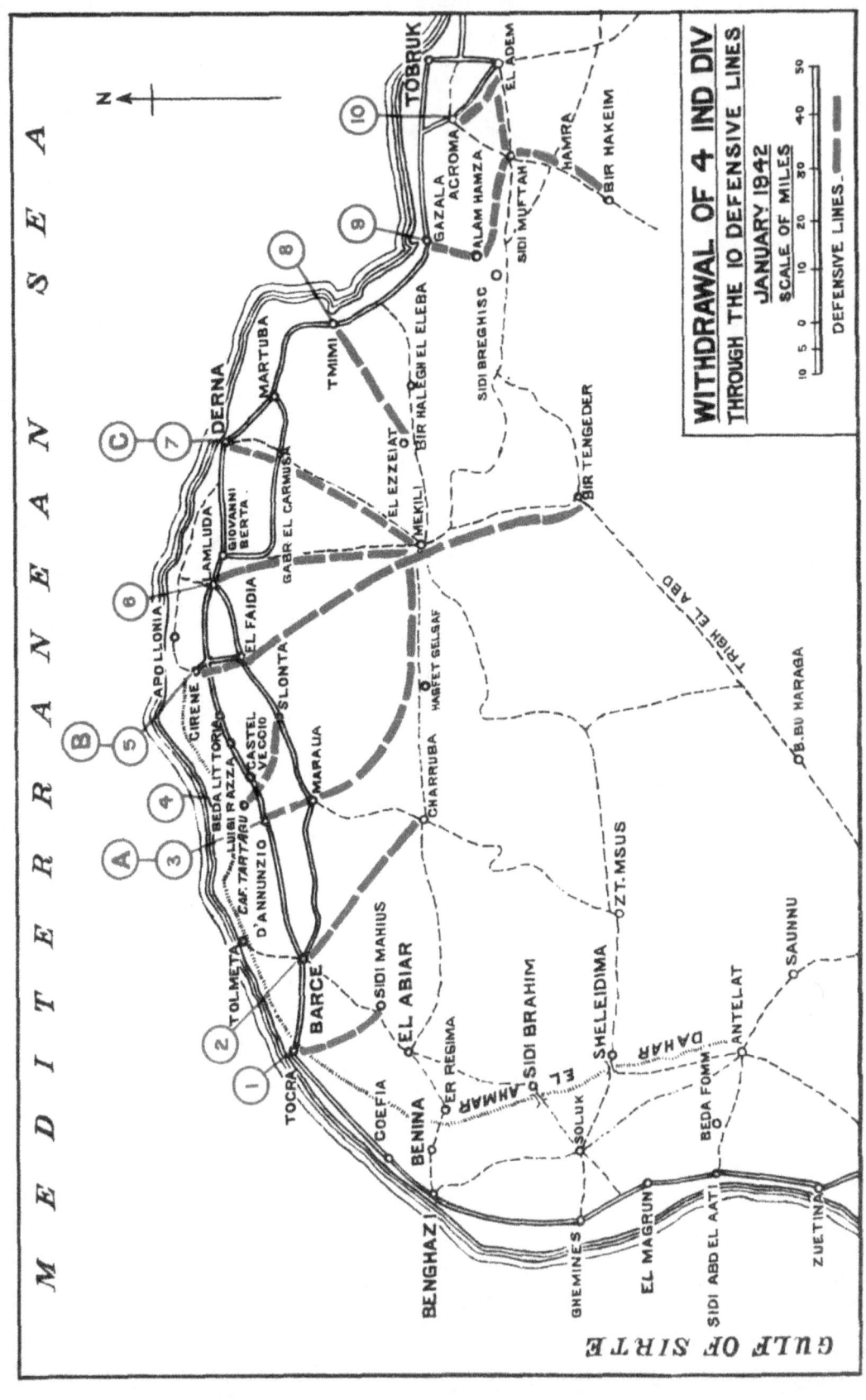

flanks and appear in its rear. They would then be able to cut the main road and isolate the Jebel or raid the Martuba landing ground and eliminate an important means of air support. In either case the consequences would be serious.

On receiving the news of the presence of an Axis column near line 'B', the Divisional Commander ordered the 'E' Force to proceed east and block the main road against any advance towards Martuba. The 'E' Force was to take up a suitable position south of Giovanni Berta and dispute the Axis column's progress. Meanwhile, more troops were to be moved to Martuba to protect the landing ground. The nearest unit was 1/6 Raj Rifs then stationed at Tmimi. It may be recalled that the 5th and 11th Indian Infantry Brigades were deficient by one battalion each and that 3/1 Punjab and 1/6 Raj Rifs had been ordered to rejoin their respective brigades. That order was now slightly modified: 1/6 Raj Rifs were ordered to proceed to Martuba, instead of rejoining the 11th Brigade; and 3/1 Punjab were made to join the 11th instead of the 5th Indian Infantry Brigade to which they had formerly belonged. Almost the only other troops who were moved east, at this stage, were the 8th Royal Tank Regiment and a detachment from the 'L' force. The former were withdrawn from the division and despatched to Tobruk and the latter were moved out northward to intercept the threatening Axis column, if possible.

This Axis column which threatened Martuba was not a force of any considerable strength. But its appearance so far east was a pointer to the direction from which worse dangers would appear at no distant time. It was not surprising therefore, that the headquarters of the Eighth Army lent a ready ear to the representation of the commander of the 4th Indian Division to alter the existing plans of withdrawal and to make a rapid retreat to the east of the Jebel. The Army plan was altered accordingly, and the XIII Corps was ordered, in the event of an attack in force, to quit the line Lamluda—Mekili—Tengeder (line 6) and retire to the last two defence lines, namely the Gazala and the Acroma lines, or to put it numerically, lines 9 and 10. The withdrawals were to begin on receipt of a code-word which was also to indicate the D-1 day.[4]

As to the 4th Indian Division it was to conform to that plan. It was to withdraw, during the night D-1/D-2, to the area between the Derna landing ground and Gabr el Carmusa. On the succeeding night it was to move further back to the area Tmimi—Gabr el Aleima; and from there it was to continue the withdrawal to the Acroma position during the D-3 day and thereafter. The Acroma position was defined as the area Acroma—Hagiag Batruna—Baten Umm el Hatian; the area between Gabr el Amber and Alem

[4] W/D HQ 4 Div.

Hamza being designated the Gazala position. All these movements were to begin on the receipt of the code-word indicating the D-1 day. Before then, as a measure of immediate adjustments, the Indian division was ordered to revert to the XIII Corps from 2359 hours on 1 February.[5]

Like lines 'A' and 'B,' there was also a line 'C'. This was originally the Derna—Mekili—Tengeder line, i.e., line 7 in the series of ten. It was now slightly modified and redefined as the positions: Escarpment (P.2256)[6]-Road junction 0.9935—Mekili—Bir Tengeder.

The situation on the night of 31 January was that the 4th Indian Division, heavily cluttered up with the forward and base units it had brought back from Benghazi, was just leaving line 'A' and taking up the intermediate position between lines 'A' and 'B.' In view of the altered programme, the XIII Corps authorised the division to continue the withdrawal to line 'B' (Cirene—El Faidia), if found necessary. The intermediate position which the 4th Indian Division did subsequently occupy, however, before the morning of 1 February, was the area between Caf Tartagu and Slonta. But there was no question of holding it for any specified length of time. The Axis troops were following fast; and 2 Mahrattas, who had just arrived at Slonta, found themselves engaged in fighting within a few hours of their arrival. Bodies of hostile forces tried to infiltrate round both the flanks of the Mahrattas and, although they were successfully stopped, it had become necessary to expedite the withdrawal towards remoter backward positions.[7]

Withdrawal to Line 7

The two Indian Brigades were therefore ordered to fall back to line 'B' (Cirene—El Faidia), the 11th Indian Infantry Brigade leading. This was accomplished rapidly and successfully but the new line proved no haven of safety. The Axis troops were again there soon after midday (1 February). The 2nd Camerons were heavily attacked at 1400 hours, near El Faidia; and the 11th Brigade reported constant Axis endeavours to get round its south flank. An hour later, several Axis vehicles appeared in the 5th Indian Infantry Brigade sector and groups of them moved towards the left flank. Once again there were attempts at infiltration all along the front, which were difficult to stop, and once again was a long retreat called for. This time there was no question of holding any intermediate position. A withdrawal directly to line 'C' (Derna—Mekili—Tengeder) was ordered at 1600 hours. The 11th Brigade was to lead and the 5th was to conform. The intermediate position,

---

[5] W/D HQ 4 Div.
[6] The map references are to GSGS maps, 1/250,000, Egypt and Cyrenaica.
[7] W/Ds 4 Div., 5 Bde, 11 Bde, 2 Mahrattas.

Lamluda—Mekili—Tengeder (line 6), was to be skipped and the next halt was to be in the Derna—Mekili area (line 7). Before disengaging for this withdrawal, the Camerons inflicted heavy losses on the German lorried infantry at El Faidia. After that the two brigades began an orderly retirement during the night toward the line 'C.'[8]

It would seem that the premonitions of General Tuker, commander of the 4th Indian Division, as to the consequences of a piecemeal withdrawal were coming true; and yet there was no move from the headquarters of the Eighth Army to carry out the earlier promise to permit rapid retreat, in a few bounds, to the Gazala or Acroma positions. It will be remembered that such a plan was agreed to and its operation was made dependent on a code-word to be issued by the Eighth Army. That code was to indicate the D-1 day and was to be the signal for the swift and total removal of the 4th Indian Division from all contact with the Axis. The idea was to give the division some time in which to stabilise in a rear position, without being badgered by hostile pressure. The division had now reached the last line immediately before the Gazala position but there was no trace of the code-word yet. It is true that events had moved too fast to permit much benefit being got out of the arrangement. Still it cannot be gainsaid that the decision could have been taken a little earlier. As it was, the delay of a few hours in issuing the code involved the widely dispersed Indian division in much aimless fighting and left it exhausted at the end of the withdrawal. Be that as it may, the word was at last issued by the XIII Corps, late on 1 February, giving 2 February as the D-1 day.

At the same time the original plan was modified slightly. The line Derna—Mekili—Tengeder was now not to be abandoned totally but only partially; that is, the outposts at those three localities were to be retained as long as might be possible. With that aim the 4th Indian Division was instructed to drop a column *en route*, in the Derna—Martuba area, as it withdrew towards Acroma. The task of that column was to harass and delay the advancing Axis troops. Similar columns were to be left by Force 'L' at Mekili and by the 1st Armoured Division at Bir Tengeder. All these detachments were given the discretion to withdraw if they felt themselves in the danger of being cut off.

The decision to retire to the Gazala—Acroma area had not come a moment too soon. Axis troops reached the line 'C' on 2 February and made contact with the forward elements of the 4th Indian Division. The pressure increased considerably during the morning in the 11th Brigade's sector, later threatening the safety of the 5th Brigade also. The latter was on the south road, to the

[8] *Ibid.*

west of Gabr el Carmusa, and had to cross the Carmusa road-junction in order to reach Gazala. Precautions had been taken to protect these vital cross-roads by posting two companies of 3/1 Punjab, with field and anti-tank guns in support, to cover that position.[9]

But the precaution proved useless, as the Axis troops had already destroyed that valuable post. Their infantry had approached it in the afternoon, mounted in captured 3-ton lorries and accompanied by tanks. The captured vehicles were escorted by the tanks only up to a certain point, after which the latter disappeared round the north flank in order not to give their identity away. The rest of the infantry-bearing vehicles moved on and, being mistaken for friendly troops, were not challenged until they had got between the Allied infantry and artillery and rushed the gun positions. The crew were surprised and so were the two companies of 3/1 Punjab. Their positions were overrun one by one and, by 1500 hours, the Axis troops had secured control of the vital road-junction of Gabr el Carmusa.

While occupation of Gabr el Carmusa was thus proceeding on the 5th Brigade's front, there was some confused fighting going on simultaneously in the 11th Brigade sector. Axis troops attacked the 2nd Camerons and 2 Mahrattas in an effort to exploit eastwards. Their progress was stopped by the two battalions who, supported by the 1st and 14th Field Regiments, fought out a stubborn action, inflicting heavy losses on the attackers. One battery of the 1st Field Regiment was particularly successful in imposing the maximum delay on their progress by fighting determined rearguard actions, retiring troop by troop over a considerable distance.[10]

It was now apparent that due to the Axis hold on the Carmusa road-junction, the 5th Indian Brigade was at a great disadvantage as to its movements. Its line of withdrawal by road had been cut, both towards the south and east. If it did not withdraw in good time across the country, it stood in the danger of becoming completely isolated. The Indian brigade was therefore instructed to commence moving towards Derna, with Martuba as its ultimate destination. At about the same time, a report was received from the 11th Indian Infantry Brigade too, that it was being pressed hard with continual outflanking attempts on both of its sides. In fact, it was surrounded and General Tuker ordered that formation also to break out towards Martuba. The report of these happenings was passed on to the XIII Corps and its permission sought for the retreat of the division as a whole over a distance long enough to shake off the pursuit. The Corps was anxious to avoid the risk of the troops

---

[9] W/Ds HQ 4 Div., 5 Bde, 11 Bde, 3/1 Punjab.
[10] W/Ds 4 Div., 3/1 Punjab, 5 Bde, 11 Bde, 2 Mahrattas.

being cut off and gave the permission readily. The Indian division was to "withdraw at discretion."[11]

There was only one line left before the Gazala position, on which a temporary stand might be possible. That was the line Tmimi—El Ezzeiat (line 8). The Advanced Divisional Headquarters was already in Tmimi, having moved there during the afternoon of 2 February. Orders were now issued, at 1800 hours, that the 5th Indian Infantry Brigade was to fall back on Tmimi and the 11th on El Ezzeiat. If the 11th Indian Infantry Brigade found El Ezzeiat difficult to reach or to hold, it had the permission to move to Tmimi also. 'E' Force was to conform to and protect the left flank of the 11th Brigade; while 'L' Force was to stage an attack, north-west from El Ezzeiat, to relieve pressure on the Indian brigade from that direction.

Withdrawal to Line 8

The night of 2/3 February was an anxious one for the 4th Indian Division. Its two brigades had to disengage themselves and give a slip to the Axis troops who were otherwise in a position not only to carry out a close pursuit but also to outstrip them and cut in on their line of retreat. After the disengagement, the brigades were to find their way to the line Tmimi—El Ezzeiat, the 11th Brigade having to move cross-country. The moves were however carried out successfully. By 2300 hours on 2 February, the 5th Brigade had begun to arrive at Tmimi and news was also available of the 11th Brigade having successfully broken contact and being on the move. In the circumstances, there was no longer any need of a demonstration by the 'L' Force and its orders to counter-attack were cancelled. The following morning (3 February), the division was at last concentrated at Tmimi, in a wide perimeter, with the 5th Brigade on its western and north-western faces, the 11th on the south-west, 'E' Force on the south-east and 'L' Force conforming generally. An important feature of the perimeter was that it enclosed, among other things, large numbers of army administrative units which had been shepherded into it for protection.[12]

The Axis troops were not slow in following up the retirement of the 4th Indian Division at Tmimi. They started out in pursuit soon after daylight and, at 1140 hours, were reported to be moving down the main road, being engaged intermittently by Allied tanks and artillery. By 1500 hours, they had reached the positions held by the Indian division and were preparing to attack the 5th Indian Infantry Brigade, the artillery registration for which had already been going on for some time. The actual attack was launched

---

[11] 4 Ind. Div's. *Acct. of Ops. in Cyrenaica*, pp. 80-82.
[12] *Ibid.* W/D's 4 Div.; 5 Bde, 11 Bde; 1/1 Punjab.

at 1615 hours and was directed against the position held by 1/1 Punjab. It appears to have been mounted in haste, with insufficient tanks, and was easily beaten off, the Axis troops suffering rather heavy casualties. But it was not the last of the Axis efforts. Several of their tanks were now reported moving up and there were indications of preparations for yet another attack. As the final destination of the 4th Indian Division was the Acroma position, there was no justification for tarrying in the Tmimi position, engaging in fruitless combats and at the same time taking risks with a long administrative tail which it was the division's duty to protect. The Divisional Commander, therefore, sought permission to retire that night (3/4 February), to the very last defensive line. This was agreed to by the XIII Corps at 1545 hours and the necessary orders were issued immediately.

As a preliminary to the move all unnecessary transport and units were evacuated during daylight and the work of destroying the dumps of the RAF bombs was taken in hand and carried out energetically. The 5th and 11th Brigades were instructed to be ready to break contact at 1830 hours and get clear by 2030 hours when the moon would rise. After putting the Axis troops off their scent in these two hours of darkness, they were to halt for one hour to reorganise and then withdraw in brigade groups across the desert. The main road was to be used by the Advanced Divisional Headquarters which was to be followed by 'E' Force acting as rearguard. This latter force was to be dropped at Gazala, where it was to pass under the command of the 1st South African Division, then guarding the Gazala position. From there, with some armoured cars, it was to cover the Gazala area, its chief task being to harass and delay the Axis troops until the 4th Indian Division had passed through to Acroma.[13]

Withdrawal to Acroma

The withdrawal began at dusk. To divert the attention of the Axis as well as to facilitate the breaking of contact, 1/1 Punjab staged a small counter-attack which succeeded in its aims. The two brigade groups then disengaged under the cover of night and moved off before their opponents could guess their intention. Some tanks attempted to follow but were easily shaken off in the darkness. Once the contact was broken the withdrawal proceeded smoothly. By 1200 hours the next day, the Acroma position had been reached and the 4th Indian Division found itself on the last defence line from which there was to be no further withdrawal. Before reaching this ultimate position, the division had passed through nine

---

[13] 4 Ind. Div's, *Account of Ops.* op. cit.

successive defence lines of which it had held seven for brief periods. It had been attacked several times and had suffered some five hundred casualties, although possibly it had inflicted the same number on its opponents. The morale of the fighting troops was high but they were suffering from fatigue and lack of sleep. They were at last able to settle down and relax, as the Gazala line, which was intended to form a permanent defence, was expected to hold up the hostile advance at least long enough for them to recover and reorganise.

In its new location, the Indian division was allotted the task of preparing a two-brigade position to cover Acroma. The work began immediately, with the 5th Indian Brigade operating at Pt. 209 and the 11th strengthening the locality about Eluet et Tamar. During this time, the 7th Indian Brigade was reorganising at the railhead near Tobruk, and the Advanced Divisional Headquarters was located on the escarpment, about six miles west of El Adem. A certain amount of hostile air activity was taking place in the general area of El Adem but there was no active contact with Axis troops east of Gazala. Maintenance difficulties appeared to have affected the speed of advance of the Axis troops since their arrival at Tmimi.

The Eighth Army at Gazala

Thus by the night of 4 February, all Allied forces had fallen back to the Gazala line and the task of effecting that withdrawal had been brought to a successful end. But it had proved a costly withdrawal inasmuch as the 1st Armoured Division had lost over one hundred tanks, out of an original total of about one hundred and fifty. The loss to the artillery units of the Eighth Army, at the same time, was thirty field guns, the same number of two-pounder anti-tank guns and twenty-five Bofors light anti-aircraft pieces. As compared to this, the tank and artillery losses of the Axis were by no means heavy. About thirty tanks was the maximum number that could safely be taken as 'destroyed or probably destroyed', out of about one hundred including light tanks, while the damage done to the artillery of the Axis could not have been more than negligible.[14]

The Gazala Line

The Gazala line was hardly ready when the withdrawal of the Eighth Army came to an end. It was then no more than a series of defendable points, extending from Gazala on the coast to Bir Hakeim in the desert, with the strong point of Alam Hamza in the centre. The area round Gazala was being guarded by the 1st South

---

[14] Gen. Auchinleck's *Despatch* in Supplement to the *London Gazette* of 15-1-48, p. 351. W/Ds HQ 4 Div.; 5 Bde, 11 Bde.

African Brigade, later reinforced by the Polish Brigade Group. Alam Hamza was held by the Free French Brigade Group which was a part of the 'L' Force; and Bir Hakeim was in charge of the 150th Infantry Brigade Group acting alongside the Guards Brigade. The role of the 1st Armoured Division was to watch the gap between Alam Hamza and Bir Hakeim; and that of the 4th Indian Division to give depth to the Gazala line by building defences along Acroma—Pt. 209—Eluet et Tamar—Er Rigel and thence southward.

It was General Ritchie's intention to make a stand on the Gazala line and from there return to the offensive. At first General Auchinleck was doubtful as to the Eighth Army's ability to hold that line in view of the weakened state of its armour. He had in fact given orders for preparing positions on the frontier, to which he thought the Army might be ultimately obliged to retire. But he changed his mind the next day on reviewing the situation in the light of fresh prospects of reinforcements of tanks. He, therefore, ordered General Ritchie on 2 February to stand at Gazala, so as to preserve Tobruk as a forward supply base for the eventual resumption of counter-offensive.[15]

This decision removed any hesitation that General Ritchie might have felt on the subject. No sooner did he receive the orders than he threw himself into the task of constructing a number of defensive positions in the triangle between Gazala, Tobruk and Bir Hakeim. The general idea was to bar the eastward access to Tobruk, El Adem and Bir el Gubi, three points which might make another defence line to fall back upon. In any case these were the points, all or any of which the Axis forces must capture before they would think it safe to venture farther east. To deny them these, was one of the functions of the Gazala line. The most important object of course was to stop the Axis dead at this point.

For achieving that aim, the Gazala area seemed to General Ritchie to be the proper choice and indeed later came to be considered so by several other military authorities also. It had been described by General Wavell as "just about the natural balance in the desert."[16] A force that crossed this point from either side would find the balance going against it, in that it would begin to feel the strain of lengthened communications and supply difficulties. Outflanking this line was not an easy proposition as that would produce maintenance problems of formidable size, and from that point of view the position of the line was ideal. There was also the further advantage that the line could be given a depth without

---

[15] *Ibid.*
[16] Alan Moorehead, *African Trilogy*, p. 314.

The Halfaya Pass, Egypt, February 1942

The 4th Indian Division's troops in Western Desert

Subedar (later Sub-Major) Lalbahadur Thapa
of 1/2nd Gurkha Rifles, V.C.

Laying the railway track in the desert, March 1942

unduly dispersing forces or withdrawing them from lines of communication or training areas.[17]

General Ritchie selected a number of points which he wished to fortify initially. These were Gazala, Alam Hamza, Sidi Muftah and Bir Hakeim. He decided to plant the area between Gazala and Alam Hamza with a series of strong points, and to raise two detached fortified positions at Sidi Muftah and Bir Hakeim respectively. By this arrangement, he intended to block all routes to the east and the vital points beyond. The area Gazala—Alam Hamza, for instance, would cover the approach to Tobruk as also the tracks leading out from Bir Temrad. The Sidi Muftah position would shield El Adem and Bir el Gubi by dominating the Trigh-Capuzzo and Trigh el Abd routes ; and Bir Hakeim would perform a similar role by denying the roads to Gubi and Tengeder.[18]

Structure and design of the Gazala Line

Such was the shape of the Gazala line in the early stages. As time passed it underwent alterations by additions of further defensive constructions. For instance, strong points were built in the rear of the line, at Acroma, El Adem, El Mrassas and Knightsbridge. These gave depth to the Gazala line along with the Tobruk defences which were then still considered to be satisfactory although somewhat dilapidated and outworn and lacking in suitable obstacles. To these were later added the defences prepared on the frontier, so as to provide an additional depth. These later comprised the defended areas around Sollum, Halfaya and Hamra, besides a number of other subsidiary protective points at different places. All defence works were so connected up as to give a strong back to the Gazala line and eliminate the risk of its being isolated from the rear.

The structure and design of the Gazala line was something unique in the tactics of defensive warfare. It was so unorthodox in conception that officers from distant fronts went there to see and study it on the spot. The central idea was of course to establish a line which was defendable. But it was always difficult to build one in a desert. Of the two terminals of such a line, one might be securely planted on the coast ; but the other had invariably to stand in the empty desert where it could be outflanked—that is, there was almost always enough space beyond the farthest end of the line for by-passing it and attacking the line from the rear. This was the situation that General Ritchie and his two Corps

---

[17] In spite of this possibility, there did exist a certain amount of dispersal all along the line.

[18] Gen. Auchinleck's *Despatch*, in Supplement to *London Gazette* of 15-1-48, pp. 351-52.

commanders planned to avoid. They decided to drop the time-worn idea of a continuous chain of defences and to evolve a pattern which might be better able to satisfy the needs of the situation.

The result was a curious system of minefields forming enclosures, which came to be known as "boxes". A solid bed of mines, thirty-five to forty miles long, was first laid down along a line running out from the sea southward into the desert. This was intended as protection against a frontal attack. At certain spots the continuity of the minefield could not be maintained and there were, inevitably, weak links in the long chain. These were danger points at which the mined zone might be pierced and a flank turned. Troops entrenched behind the mines would, in such cases, find themselves being attacked on either flank as well as from the front and rear. To meet such four-sided attacks it was necessary to enclose those spots in a defensive perimeter facing all sides. Thus arose the idea of "boxes". Each box was completely surrounded on all sides by a broad belt of landmines and barbed wire. Inside that enclosure were troops as they would be inside a fort.

These boxes stood four-square, ready to meet attack from any side, the guns facing outward in all directions. A War Correspondent has described it as "the old idea of the British square at Waterloo, adapted to modern fast armoured fighting."[19] Each box was a mile or two square and had narrow lanes of unmined and unwired passages which served as entrances and exits. Like so many fortresses, the boxes were garrisoned by troops and provided with food, water and ammunition to withstand a siege. The ample space within these unwalled fortresses provided enough scope for movements and dispositions and yet produced no difficult problems of supply and communications.

Outside the boxes were empty spaces. These were patrolled by British tanks which were kept in a fluid condition and which had the task of guarding the intervening space between the boxes. The tanks were in a position not only to attack hostile troops in the open, if any penetrated the lines, but also to go to the rescue of a box that might appear to be staggering under a particularly severe onslaught. There were more than half a dozen boxes situated tactically along the main line and to its rear. The principal ones were located at Gazala, Knightsbridge, Bir Hakeim, El Adem and at other points between Gazala and Alam Hamza. Roaming the intervening spaces were three British tank brigades of the 1st and 7th Armoured Divisions under the command of General Messervy, which included the newly received American 'Grant' tanks with 75-millimetre guns, a weapon powerful enough to match the one carried by German armour. Incidentally, this was a secret of

[19] Alan Moorehead: *African Trilogy*, pp. 314-15.

General Ritchie of which the Germans then had no knowledge. Another such secret was the recently produced British six-pounder anti-tank guns, as compared to the two-pounders hitherto in use.

The tanks constituted the mobile part of the Gazala defences; otherwise the defence line was essentially static, judged by its composition and functions. The boxes were not intended to go into action unless attacked. But attacking the boxes was no easy matter. The attackers would not be able to get at them unless they first out-flanked or pierced the main line of minefields which stretched from Gazala to Bir Hakeim over a distance of forty miles. A big-scale frontal attack would be necessary to break that line. Should the Axis succeed in that, they would be free to roam all the desert immediately behind the line, except for the spaces enclosed by the boxes. But the freedom of the empty desert would not be of much use to them. For one thing, their lines of communication would always be threatened by Allied tanks; and if they tried to push ahead, the garrisons of the boxes might sally out of their strongholds and take them in the rear or on the flanks.[20]

Such was the Gazala line, a strange creation of the needs of the time. It was not constructed in a day or a week but was the result of a gradual growth. The line as described above did not exist until early in May 1942, that is three months after the Allied troops had arrived in Gazala. But it had by then fulfilled the two major aims it was designed to serve: it had shielded Tobruk during that time and halted General Rommel's lightning advance through the desert.[21]

---

[20] For this, it was necessary to have adequate transport in the boxes, which however was not there.

[21] With all this, the Gazala line was not without its defects, for which a penalty had to be paid in the end when it had to be abandoned. This aspect has been very well brought out by Gen. Tuker in his *Pattern of War*, Chapter X.

CHAPTER XXXI

The Stand at Gazala

The withdrawal of the 4th Indian Division, it will be remembered, had ended at Acroma. On its arrival there, the division had been placed on the job of preparing a two-brigade position which was to serve as a delaying line of defence immediately behind what was later to be known as the Gazala line. However, the division had hardly been at work for four days when it received orders, on 8 February, to quit Acroma and move forward to the Gazala area to relieve one of the formations manning the defences there.

At this date, the Gazala defences were sited along the general line, west of Gazala—Alam Hamza—Gabr el Abidi—Bir Hakeim. The troops manning them were, from right to left: the 1st South African Brigade, the Polish Independent Brigade Group, Force 'L', the 1st Support Group, the 202nd (late 22nd) Guards Brigade and the 150th Brigade. Of these, it was the 1st Support Group which was to be relieved by the Indian division on the latter's arrival at Gazala.

But the Indian formations ordered to move forward were only the 5th and the 11th Brigades, the 7th being required to remain behind to prepare a defensive position on the Egyptian side of the frontier. While doing so, this latter brigade was at the same time to refit and recuperate from the strain of its recent breakthrough operations, after the fall of Benghazi. The position it was to prepare was near Hamra, on the escarpment, about 36 miles south-east of Sollum.[1]

The other two brigades moved to the front line during the night of 11/12 February and relieved the 1st Support Group. The Advanced Divisional Headquarters opened at Bu Alluse the next morning, and assumed command of the left sector of the Gazala position. Two days later 'L' Force moved to Bir Hakeim, its place being taken by the 150th Brigade which passed under the Indian division's command and took charge of its right sub-sector.

Forward of these front-line troops were the Allied armoured car patrols; and farther beyond were the Axis outposts along the line Tmimi—Mekili. The extensive Allied minefields, which later covered the front area, had not yet been laid, and if the Axis chose to attack, the tanks would have to fight it out. There was no

---

[1] 4 Ind. Div's. *Acct. of Ops. in Cyrenaica*, pp. 83-4.

doubt at this date (13 February) that after a brief halt to reorganise, the Axis would try to press forward again. This the Axis did as early as 14 February when, from 1545 hours that day, reports began to be received of movements of some Axis columns towards the Allied positions. The force on the move, in the sector directly opposite to the 4th Indian Division, was estimated to consist of some 50 tanks and 60 other vehicles which the division prepared to meet, if attacked.

However, for the whole of the next day, the Axis columns showed no activity and made no efforts to contact Allied positions. All that they did, in fact, was to carry out some vague movements in the distance which an officer on the divisional staff described as something in the nature of a "swan around". Two Allied columns, one from the 2nd Camerons and the other from 'L' Force, then moved out to test the strength of this force. But no contact could be established and next day (16 February) that force was reported to have withdrawn altogether. As a counter-blast to this, the Indian division extended its patrolling operations as far west as the track Tmimi—Bir Halegh el Eleba. No encounters with Axis troops resulted from this, except that about ten tanks were seen on the 19th, which withdrew on being engaged. The division then continued its patrolling activity, making it thereafter more aggressive from day to day.

Thus, one of the patrols undertook the audacious task of raiding an aerodrome behind the Axis lines, which action was particularly remarkable for the cold courage and confidence with which it was carried out. This was a detachment of 2/5 Mahrattas who set out in two trucks on the night of 22nd February to raid the Martuba airfields, sixty miles inside the hostile territory. The party consisted of ten riflemen and two sappers under the command of a British officer. Driving through the desert during the night, they arrived the next day within a few miles of their objective and commenced spying. They remained in hiding for the first night. On the second night they found only a single plane occupying the landing strip, and took no action as the booty was not considered good enough. On the third night they found three more fighter aircraft settled on the ground and decided to strike the blow. Fixing charges of explosives in the proper places, they dynamited the planes and an adjacent dump of bombs, and returned to their unit without any loss. At first two men were found missing but these, too, turned up ten days later after having traversed the distance on foot.[2]

The 4th Division at Hamra

Although the 4th Indian Division seemed well suited to hold

[2] Lt.-Col. Stevens: *Fourth Indian Division*, pp. 160-61.

a sector of the Gazala line, it was nevertheless not destined to remain there very long. Orders for its withdrawal were received within a week of its occupying the new position. It was to be relieved by the 50th Northumbrian Division and the commander of that division arrived on 16 February, his advanced headquarters following up on the 19th. The relief started on the 21st and was completed by 1 March. At the end of this period, the 4th Indian Division found itself once again in the rear area, this time at Hamra. The 7th Indian Infantry Brigade, which was already there, moved farther back to the Delta. The division, less the 7th Brigade, then came under the command of the XXX Corps and addressed itself to the new task of finishing that still incomplete defensive position on the frontier.

The Hamra position was intended to be a two-brigade front, covering the southern routes into Egypt. The defences being built there consisted of two strongholds, named the Playgrounds and the Kennels. They were sited so as to enclose certain sections of a large area of raised ground commanding the routes to Egypt, and they consisted of defended localities, surrounded by a belt of mines and wire-fencing with gun positions and strong points in support. The 4th Indian Division worked there until 15 March, by which time the task was nearly completed, after which it received orders to move to Sollum. On arriving there, it relieved the 2nd South African Division in the Sollum Box where, with the Royal Yugoslav Guards under its command, it carried out the normal line-of-communication duties, such as organising traffic control, guarding stores and minding salvage and local administration, for a little over two weeks.

Early in April, while it was still at this job, the call came for it to disperse. The 7th Indian Brigade was ordered to Cyprus against the possible danger of a German invasion; the 5th Indian Infantry was transferred to Palestine for normal garrison duties; and the 11th Indian Infantry was sent to the Canal Zone to train in combined operations. Simultaneously, the division's order of battle was slightly modified and a number of its important units passed to other commands. Thus the 1st Field Regiment, the 57th Light Anti-aircraft Regiment and the 65th Anti-tank Regiment, all of which had strong ties of comradeship with the division, now parted company. So did its cavalry, the Central India Horse, which was posted to an armoured formation for training. So also did some of its infantry units which changed places with other battalions. By the middle of April the 4th Indian Division was fully dispersed and was no longer in the Western Desert, having been relieved there by the 5th Indian Division.[3]

[3] W/D's HQ 4 Div., 5 Div.

Company Havildar-Major Chhelu Ram
of 4/6th Rajputana Rifles, V.C.

Moving through the Desert, 4th Indian Division

The 4th Indian Division in action, March 1942

Indian troops advancing—Western Desert

The Indian Division leaves Western Desert

And so ended the second campaign of the 4th Indian Division in the Western Desert. During that period of fighting, from 18 November 1941 to 28 February 1942, it had acquitted itself creditably. It had suffered casualties totalling 4,385, of which 2,197 were Indian personnel and the rest British.[4] As the division was withdrawing from the forward area, a special Order of the Day was issued by Lt.-Gen. Gott, Commanding the XIII Corps, which ran as follows:—

> "On the departure of the 4th Indian Division from the 13th Corps, I wish to congratulate all ranks on the splendid fighting spirit the Division has shown during six months' continuous active operations in the Western Desert. During the great battles of this winter you have proved that you can achieve, against German troops and tanks, the same successes you had already won against the Italians. In good times and in bad, the Division has maintained its high standard and has well earned the great reputation for determination and aggression which it now holds amongst all who fought with you."

Axis advance comes to a stop

It has been seen that the Axis troops first approached the Gazala positions on 14 February but evaded contact and finally withdrew on the 16th. Thereafter they kept themselves at a distance. The bulk of their forces remained in the neighbourhood of Martuba and Msus, being screened by outposts on the general line Tmimi—Bir Temrad—Mekili. General Rommel was apparently unable to make a move in force. A captured document revealed that he considered the seizure of Tobruk an essential preliminary to an advance on Egypt. He had other difficulties also, the principal among them being absence of supplies to sustain a prolonged struggle and the inadequacy of armour. All these factors combined to bring his advances to a halt in front of Gazala; although, had he ignored the handicaps and attacked the yet incomplete Gazala line, he might, in all likelihood, have succeeded. In any case, as the events turned out, General Rommel preferred to engage in a battle of supplies and reinforcements rather than in one of movement and speed. With that purpose he called his force to a halt and settled down to a policy of making gradual advances over small distances, while at the same time building up for the coming conflict. This kept him occupied during February, March, April and a large part of May, and

---

[4] For further details see Appendix S.

incidentally provided the Eighth Army with the much needed time for stabilizing a position.[5]

During this period, the Eighth Army was by no means inactive. First it had to build and fortify the Gazala line. Then it had to turn into a secure base from which to launch a fresh offensive. Finally, it had to prepare for the offensive itself. Concurrently with these activities, it had to undertake many an incidental task, such as extending the railway line, sending out offensive patrols or staging minor attacks to gain information, and last but not the least, raiding Axis airfields to divert attention from the Allied convoys sailing to Malta from the east. The last was a major item in the operational programme of the Eighth Army during those hectic days of the uneasy pause in the fighting in Western Desert. Malta was resisting a ruthless bombardment from air and was badly in need of supplies, and a convoy carrying food and equipment was to sail from Alexandria in the middle of March. The Axis bombers were so active during that period that no Allied ship was safe in that part of the Mediterranean. It was, therefore, vitally necessary to do something towards helping the convoy's passage. General Auchinleck instructed the Eighth Army to create a diversion so as to tie up or draw away the Axis aircraft during the period of the convoy's sailing. With that object, the Eighth Army raided the landing grounds of Barce, Benina, Benghazi, Tmimi and Martuba on 20 March and other positions on the following day. The mission was successful and had the intended effect of mitigating the blow that fell upon the convoy nevertheless.

Allied preparations for counter-offensive

Other activities of the Eighth Army concerned administrative arrangements for the forthcoming offensive. Three forward bases were established at Tobruk, Belhamed and Giarabub respectively. The extension of the railway track to Capuzzo, from its last terminus at Bir Misheifa, was undertaken and completed by 13 March; and a further extension from Capuzzo to Belhamed was taken in hand as from 3 April.

The greatest of all administrative tasks, however, was the provision of adequate water in the forward area. The general water ration at this period was three quarters of a gallon a day per head, the same quantity being allowed for every vehicle when stationary and half a gallon more when on the move. But even this limited scale of ration could not be maintained and it was frequently

---

[5] Gen. Auchinleck's *Despatch* in Supplement to the *London Gazette* of 15-1-48, p. 353.

necessary to draw on the water-reserves of Tobruk, which had to be replenished in turn by bringing shiploads of water across the sea. It was therefore very necessary to increase the water supply in the forward area. The existing pipeline could not be extended due to the shortage of material. The best that could be done in the circumstances was to increase the storing capacities, and that course was adopted. The sources at Buq Buq and Bardia were developed and linked together and reservoirs were constructed to supply the defensive positions on the frontier.

Equally important improvements were also carried out on the equipment side, the most far-reaching among them being the one relating to the system of delivery of tanks to the forward areas. A tank delivery regiment was created for the Eighth Army, in which scheme each corps had its tank delivery squadron and each brigade its delivery troop. Simultaneously, improvements were made in the recovery and repair systems with a view to ensuring quicker replacement of the tank casualties. Many tank transporters had also arrived which aided this process and the system worked smoothly and efficiently in the subsequent operations.

It had been decided earlier that the Eighth Army's preparations should be completed by 15 May. This date had been fixed on two assumptions. First, that a tank superiority of 3:2 plus 50% reserve, which was desirable at the start of the operations, would not be available before that date; and second, that the new Belhamed railhead and base could not be made ready any earlier. Actually however the railhead could not be completed even by 15 May and the date of the offensive had therefore to be shifted to 1 June. This was rather unfortunate as it enabled General Rommel to anticipate the Allied offensive by about four days. It happened by a curious coincidence that the railhead opened exactly on the day he struck, 26 May, and came in handy for delivering the tanks, though it could not be used for stocking the forward areas before the start of operations, which indeed was the primary aim.[6]

In the race for collecting reinforcements and supplies, the Eighth Army had started with certain handicaps. It had to get its men and equipment along a twelve thousand mile detour round the Cape of Good Hope, and then through a bottle-neck at Suez, where docking and railroad facilities were meagre and labour untrained. On the other hand, the Axis ships had to do only a short run from Naples or Sicily to Tripoli. Thus, whereas the Germans and Italians could bring a tank into the desert within a month of its leaving a workshop in Europe, the Allies had to wait three or four months to get the same weight of armour from

---

[6] Gen. Auchinleck's *Despatch, op. cit.*

England or America. Then again, while the Axis air force was able to interfere with the Allied convoys on a considerable scale, the Allies lacked any comparable means for dealing effectively with the Axis shipping. In due course this produced a difference in the fighting potentials; and early in April, General Rommel seemed to think that his supply position had eased enough to justify a few minor advances.

These advances were apparently intended by him to be small but they had a far-reaching significance in that they aimed at clearing the way for the ultimate major offensive. With that object, General Rommel began a gradual concentration of his troops in the forward area, using Italian formation to cover the front and mask his preparations. Then he steadily closed up on the Gazala line, occupying Segnali, Bir Temrad, Sidi Breghisc and other points, in a series of well-planned moves.

To test the strength and reactions of the occupying troops, General Ritchie made a small but sharp attack on Segnali on 12 April. Segnali was a tactically important locality, as indeed it proved to be a little later. It could be used by General Rommel as a jumping-off ground in a major offensive against the Eighth Army, and General Ritchie was therefore anxious to dislodge the Axis from that position if possible. The attack was planned and carried out with great care but produced no worthwhile result; so also a subsequent operation further south carried out early in May.[7]

By this time it had become painfully clear that General Rommel had won the supply race. The shortage of shipping, the long voyage around the Cape of Good Hope and diversions of material to Russia handicapped the Allies. The Axis troops had been reinforced by a number of mobile Italian formations and by the 164th Infantry Division from Crete. Benghazi was landing 2000 tons of war material daily as against 500 tons a day until two months back. The *Afrika Korps* had in fact attained the magnitude of two corps. Intelligence reports indicated that General Rommel was ready to strike. A drunken German officer in a Balkan town is said to have divulged the exact date. The offensive was to open on 27 May.[8]

Some tactical appreciations

At the General Headquarters, in Cairo, it was regarded as almost certain that the main objective of Rommel would be Tobruk and that his best efforts would be directed to that end. The belief was based on two facts. Firstly, that General Rommel considered the capture of Tobruk necessary for an advance on Egypt; and

---
[7] Gen. Auchinleck's *Despatch*.
[8] Lt.-Col. Stevens: *Fourth Indian Division*.

secondly, the Allied main supply bases were located in and around Tobruk. It was easy therefore to see where the blow would ultimately fall, irrespectively of the direction it would be coming from. General Ritchie drew the attention of his two Corps Commanders to this possibility and took steps to strengthen his defences accordingly.[9]

There were three possible ways of reaching Tobruk which was well sheltered and covered by the Gazala line: one was to break through in the north and take the coast road; the second was to smash across the minefields in the centre and follow the Trigh-Capuzzo road to El Adem; and the third course was to by-pass Bir Hakeim from the south, and then turn north towards El Adem. Thus an assault on Tobruk would be inevitably preceded by an attack on the Gazala line. It could be expected to come from the north, south or centre.

An attack in the northern or central sector would mean a direct endeavour to smash through the Gazala line and would lead to heavy fighting. An approach from the south, on the other hand, would mean leaving the Gazala line alone and turning the flank. But this would lead to serious supply difficulties for the Axis, as there would be no satisfactory line of communication. Thus the advantages and handicaps were so balanced that the attack might come from almost any direction; and the dispositions of the Eighth Army had to be such as to be capable of meeting all possible contingencies.[10]

The Eighth Army had the following troops at its disposal on the eve of the attack on the Gazala line:—

XIII Corps
(Lieutenant-General W. H. E. Gott)
    50th British Division
        (Major-General W. H. C. Ramsden)
    1st South African Division
        (Major-General D. H. Pienaar)
    2nd South African Division
        (Major-General H. B. Klopper)
    1st Army Tank Brigade
        (Brigadier H. R. B. Watkins)
    9th Indian Infantry Brigade
        (Brigadier B. C. Fletcher)

---

[9] Gen. Auchinleck's *Despatch* in Supplement to the *London Gazette* of 15-1-48, p. 353.

[10] Nevertheless, the HQ Eighth Army were firm in their belief that the attack would come via Bir Hakeim. This was not the view of GHQ Cairo, who, a short while before the attack, had put forward a proposition that the most likely line of attack would be direct on Tobruk. In fact, after the attack had taken place, Gen. Ritchie received a signal from the Commander-in-Chief acknowledging that the Eighth Army had been correct.

XXX Corps
(Lieutenant-General C. W. M. Norrie)
    1st British Armoured Division
        (Major-General H. Lumsden)
            2nd Armoured Brigade
                (Brigadier R. Briggs)
            22nd Armoured Brigade
                (Brigadier W. G. Carr)
            201st Guards (Motor) Brigade
                (Brigadier J. C. O. Marriott)
    7th British Armoured Division
        (Major- General F. W. Messervy)
            4th Armoured Brigade
                (Brigadier G. W. Richards)
            7th Motor Brigade
                (Brigadier J. M. G. Renton)
    3rd Indian Motor Brigade Group
        (Brigadier A. E. Filose)
    29th Indian Infantry Brigade Group
        (Brigadier D. Reid)
    1st Free French Brigade Group
        (Brigadier-General J. P. F. Koenig)

In addition to the above, some more troops were on the move to join the Eighth Army or to assist its operations generally. They were the 10th Indian Division from Iraq; the Guides Cavalry from Syria; and the 11th Indian Infantry Brigade from Cyprus. In the Western Desert itself, there were two more brigades outside the operational area. They were the 2nd Free French Brigade Group and the 10th Indian Infantry Brigade. The latter had the important task of guarding the Advanced Headquarters of the Eighth Army then situated at Gambut. It had also to guard the Headquarters of the Air Officer Commanding Western Desert, which were in the same location; and the Allied fighter base, which was just across the main road at a little distance from the Army Headquarters.[11]

Allied dispositions

General Ritchie, commanding the Eighth Army, had so to dispose his infantry and armour as to be able to meet an attack, whether it came from the north, south or centre; or from more than one direction simultaneously. With that object he divided his forces amongst three principal areas. They were: (1) the Gazala line proper (2) the Tobruk area and (3) the triangle Knightsbridge—Bir el Gubi—Bir Hakeim. This last area was the concentration ground for practically all the armoured divisions and motor brigades which

---

[11] W/Ds 10 Ind. Div., 4 Ind. Div., 5 Ind. Div., 11 Bde.

the Eighth Army possessed. Curious as it might seem, the armour in this case defended the rear of the fighting troops instead of operating independently to the flank or front. But this arrangement had been specially decided upon to conform to the peculiar structure of the Gazala line. The wide belts of minefields were considered to be adequate as frontal defences. The armour was to perform the triple function of shielding the rear of the Gazala positions, protecting the flanks of the Tobruk perimeter, and generally denying access to the coast or to the frontier of Egypt.

The dispositions in the triangle Knightsbridge—Bir el Gubi—Bir Hakeim were as follows:—The units of the 1st Armoured Division were deployed round Knightsbridge. The 7th Armoured Division lay to its south. The 3rd Indian Motor Brigade was two miles to the south-east of Bir Hakeim. The 7th Motor Brigade held a defensive locality between the 3rd Indian Motor Brigade and Bir el Gubi; and the locality of Bir el Gubi itself was held by the 29th Indian Infantry Brigade of the 5th Indian Division.[12]

The vital Tobruk area was garrisoned by the 2nd South African Division and the 9th Indian Infantry Brigade. The former occupied the western part of the perimeter and some strong points below the escarpment in the direction of Gazala. The Indian Brigade held the eastern half of the Tobruk defences.[13]

As to the Gazala line proper, its infantry and other arms were disposed in "boxes", from the Gazala inlet in the north to Bir Hakeim in the south. The 1st South African Division held the northern sector of this line from the west of the inlet up to Alam Hamza, with its units astride the Via Balbia and on parallel tracks going towards Tobruk. From Alam Hamza the line was prolonged eastwards by the 151st and the 69th Infantry Brigades of the 50th Division, who carried it up to the point where it again turned southward. Here the 150th Infantry Brigade manned the detached strong post of Sidi Muftah, while the Free French Brigade Group held Bir Hakeim. The 1st Army Tank Brigade, with its heavy tanks, was divided for the supporting tasks between the 1st South African and the 50th (British) Divisions.

The arrangement of infantry and armour as described above was perhaps the best that could be achieved in the circumstances. The idea governing the dispositions was preparedness for meeting attack from any direction whatsoever. Whether the Axis broke through the centre, or passed south of Bir Hakeim, the broad outline of the defence plan was to remain unaffected while permitting small adjustments within that framework. The basis of the plan was that if the opponents could be stopped, the right place to stop them was

[12] W/Ds 4 Div., 3 Ind. Motor Brigade, 5 Div., 29 Bde.
[13] W/D 9 Bde.

in front of the Gazala line ; but if they had to be fought the proper place to fight them in was behind that line, and with all the available armour thrown into the fight. Should such a fight ensue, care was to be taken to place the Axis at a disadvantage for their supplies, by forcing them to depend on the long and exposed line of communication via the southern route. This was to be achieved by keeping the minefields intact at all costs. If the Aixs troops made a wide detour round the desert flank, then the mine-belt would remain undisturbed. But if they penetrated it at any point, the breach was to be closed at once.[14]

Extent of Eighth Army's preparedness

An analysis of the forces manning the Gazala line would show that General Ritchie had enough infantry to deal with any likely situation. More, in the opinion of General Auchinleck, might have been an encumbrance. As for the armour, the three brigades under the XXX Corps were fully trained and equipped. They were the 2nd, 4th and 22nd Armoured Brigades, of which the 2nd had, however, just finished training and therefore lacked battle experience. To this trio, General Auchinleck proposed to add the 1st Armoured Brigade. That formation had received its tanks only a little while ago and was still on the job of learning to handle them. But it was decided to send it forward nevertheless and permit it to complete the training in the Eighth Army area, not far from the battle front. Thus, sufficient armour was concentrated in the probable battle area to give a solid backing to the Gazala line. To leave no room for doubt, General Auchinleck arranged to send forward also the 32nd Army Tank Brigade with its two regiments of infantry tanks. That brigade began to arrive as the battle opened and was placed under the command of the XIII Corps.

Numerically, the Eighth Army was thus, undoubtedly, superior to the Axis in tank strength ; and in quality there was a great improvement over the previous armour. There were, for instance, a considerable number of the American 'General-Grant' medium tanks, equipped with 75-millimeter guns. They were a match for the German tanks in speed, and their principal weapon, the 75-mm gun, was a great advance in firepower over the previous equipments of the kind. But the gun had its limitations also, in that its arc of traverse was very narrow and it was mounted so low that it could not be fired without the whole turret being exposed during the action. As to the infantry tanks of the Army Tank Brigades, they were much too slow to be put into battle against the medium tanks of the Axis, a fact which restricted their use very greatly. In spite

[14] Gen. Auchinleck's *Despatch* in Supplement to the *London Gazette* of 15-1-48, pp. 353-55.

of these handicaps, the Eighth Army could not be said to have been badly off in armour and, indeed, had a much larger reserve of tanks to draw on than the Axis.

With quite enough of infantry and about nearly enough of armour, all that the Eighth Army needed for completing its effective strength was sufficient artillery. In the fighting during the preceding winter, the Allied tanks had suffered acutely from the German 88-millimeter dual-purpose guns, and the Eighth Army had no weapon of any comparable strength with which to retaliate. The crying need of the hour therefore was of course the anti-tank guns—of better calibre and in large numbers—though the need for more field guns was almost equally pressing. Until Gazala, the Eighth Army had only a small quantity of 2-pounder anti-tank guns and had to rely mostly on the solid shot from the 25-pounders for dealing with the Axis tanks. This had made both defence and offence difficult for the infantry. Now, at last, things were changing and the Eighth Army had started receiving anti-tank weapons of sufficient power to oppose the thick armour of General Rommel's tanks. They were the new six-pounder guns. These were being issued to the motorised brigades just as fast as they were coming in. But they were nevertheless so late in arriving that the men who were to handle them had no chance to get familiar with them. Nor did the infantry, who took over the old two-pounder guns from the motor brigades, have any time to train with their new weapons before the battle started.

As to the field guns, the Middle East had always suffered from a chronic shortage of this class of artillery. There was never enough of it, until August or September 1942, to give the infantry divisions their full complement of this supremely important arm. On the eve of General Rommel's offensive, neither General Ritchie nor his two Corps commanders had any reserve of field guns with which to reinforce divisions whose fire-power might need bolstering up during critical periods of a battle. Often this resulted in a lack of balance in the striking power and a general unsteadiness in defence—a characteristic partly responsible for some of the worst misfortunes of the Eighth Army.[15]

Such was the general state of the Eighth Army towards the end of May 1942, when General Rommel struck his blow, forestalling the Allied offensive by about a week. Apparently General Auchinleck was not prepared to consider this as a bad surprise. He rather welcomed it as "the opportunity we had been seeking." The plan

---

[15] There were, however, also instances of unjustifiable dispersal of field guns over vast fronts, according to a military authority, who says, "We had enough at Alamein in Oct. 42. We had enough at Gazala. The trouble always was that they were dispersed on those huge fronts."

of the Eighth Army depended upon inducing General Rommel to attack in an area favourable to the Allies. Here the Axis were doing it of their own accord. There was no longer any need to weaken the Gazala position by sending out a part of the armoured force on a provoking expedition. The Axis had obliged by opening the offensive. The task of the Eighth Army now was to throw back the initial thrust and then pass on to the counter-offensive.

CHAPTER XXXII

Axis Attack on the Gazala Line

The attack on the Gazala line was preceded by no heavy shelling or mass movement of vehicles. It started without noise or display as if the idea was to take its defenders by surprise. General Rommel's plan, as we now know, was to get behind the Gazala line by rushing its southern flank and from there to press its isolated garrisons back on to their own vast minefields.

The first report of the Axis force being on the move reached the Army Headquarters on 26 May. It gave the warning that a column of vehicles was seen that afternoon moving out from Segnali, the concentration area of the *Afrika Korps*. Whether this was a prelude to an attack on the Gazala defences or only a demonstration or reconnaissance in force, it was yet too early to say.[1]

Subsequent observations revealed that the column was headed in a south-easterly direction as if Bir Hakeim was its objective. Bir Hakeim being the southern terminal of the Gazala line, this movement was significant. In the evening the same column was reported to be in a position about 15 miles south-east of Bir Hakeim, where it was leaguering for the night. When it resumed its advance at sunrise on the following day, there was no mistaking its intention. It was already forming up for an attack round the southern flank—the Panzer Divisions on the left and the 90th Light Tank battle-group on the right.

To realise the significance of this flank attack, it is necessary to assess the importance of Bir Hakeim in the context of its value to the Gazala line. As described earlier, the Gazala line consisted of a number of irregularly placed strong points or "boxes", linked by deep minefields. The boxes were not confined to any one alignment. Those in the forward area were held by infantry garrisons; while those farther back served not only for holding static reserves but also as areas from and round which the armour could operate.

This irregular line of "boxes" and mined positions started out from the coast and ended in an area of a sprawling salt marsh. The end touching the salt marsh was Bir Hakeim, and the marsh itself was some four thousand yards long. To turn the southern flank of the Gazala line, therefore, it was necessary to make a wide detour round the salt marsh.

---

[1] Gen. Auchinleck's *Despatch* in Supplement to the *London Gazette* of 15-1-48, p. 355.

The 'box' at Bir Hakeim was in the shape of a triangle, with its base facing the north and all three sides surrounded by wide minefields. The northern face was about two and a half miles long, the eastern and western faces being three and four miles respectively. The garrison inside the triangle consisted of Free French troops under General Koenig. About 30 miles east of the triangle stood Bir el Gubi, with the 29th Indian Infantry Brigade in occupation. In an area, roughly 25 miles to the north of Bir el Gubi, lay the 7th Armoured Division, with its three brigades, the 4th, 7th and 22nd, spread out between Eluet et Tamar and Bir et Tamar.[2]

The Indian Motor Brigade at Pt. 171

Some four miles south-east of Bir Hakeim was a hill feature, named Point 171. It was held by an Indian unit, the 3rd Indian Motor Brigade. The precise role which this brigade was expected to perform is not clear and was probably never defined due to the haste with which it was committed to battle. But there is some slight evidence to show that it was to serve as a pivot for the British armoured forces. The evidence occurs in a popular account written not long after the battle of Point 171, and seems a plausible explanation.[3] Otherwise one can only surmise that the brigade was located on that particular feature, either as an additional defence for Bir Hakeim or merely as an obstacle to break the force of the first impact of the Axis onslaught.

The 3rd Indian Motor Brigade was by no means a new formation. A little over a year ago it had fought a gallant action at Mekili and had successfully blunted the point of General Rommel's attack on Tobruk. It seemed destined to stand once again between Rommel and his objective, Tobruk, though with less effective result this time. In each case it served the purpose of an unintended rearguard; and in each case it paid the supreme price of self-disintegration for its devotion to duty. The fighting at Mekili had nearly cost it its existence. After that action, it had fallen to pieces and two of its regiments were unable to muster more than a squadron and a half between themselves, while the third regiment had been besieged in Tobruk. The brigade had thereafter been sent out of the battlefield to reinforce and re-equip; and by the time it had re-formed and returned to the Western Desert it had undergone so many changes that it was an old formation only in name.

One such change was that it was without its 1941-veterans. Those old warriors had been withdrawn to India as instructors for the cavalry training centres where new cavalry units were being

---
[2] W/Ds 29 Bde., 3 Mot. Bde.
[3] *The Tiger Kills*, 1944, p. 172.

raised. The 3rd Indian Motor Brigade was therefore minus their experience. Another change was that its artillery, now all Indian, had not seen action before; while as a compensating factor, the brigade was equipped with a group of anti-tank battery and more powerful anti-tank guns. But this last factor did not have a chance of becoming fully operative, as the brigade became involved in a disastrous action before it had had time to take delivery of its full complement of the anti-tank guns.

The rush and hurry with which the 3rd Indian Motor Brigade was moved to the battle area had something to do with its being caught unprepared in the action that followed. On 21 May, the brigade was at Matruh, employed in a coast defence role. By this date it had become clear to the Eighth Army Command that General Rommel was about to launch his attack and it was not considered unlikely that the main blow would fall on the southern end of the Gazala line. One of the last-hour steps taken by the Eighth Army to meet this threat was to post the 3rd Indian Motor Brigade near the southern tip of the Gazala line, under command of the 7th Armoured Division.[4] The brigade was accordingly directed, on 21 May, to move to Point 171, a locality some four miles south-east of Bir Hakeim. The move commenced almost immediately and by the evening of 25 May, the leading elements of the brigade had arrived on Point 171.

But delays dogged the movement of the rest of its units from the very beginning. The distance from the brigade's starting point to Pt. 171 was long, and the time at its disposal too short. Its carriers had therefore to be lifted by transporters and brought up by stages, the transporters being provided by "Q Movements" of the various line of communication areas. The brigade's anti-tank guns and its field artillery were equally handicapped through lack of means for swift movement. But the move was pressed with all urgency; and batches of infantry, artillery and carriers were being received and allotted positions at Point 171 throughout the night of 25/26 May and the whole of the following day.[5]

On 26 May at 1500 hours, General Messervy, commanding the 7th Armoured Division, visited the Brigade Headquarters, when he warned the Brigade Commander that a heavy attack on the Allied positions was not considered unlikely by the high command and might, indeed, be regarded as impending. To enable the formation to better withstand the blow, should one fall in its sector, he ordered that the Indian brigade should be reinforced by two squadrons of Valentine tanks and six British Bofors. The latter arrived the same afternoon. But the promised tanks failed to show

[4] Gen. Auchinleck's *Despatch*.
[5] *Ibid*. W/Ds 3 Ind. Mot. Bde, 2 RL, 11 Cav., 18 Cav.

up altogether; so also some of the carriers and anti-tank guns which, in spite of their all-night forced marches, failed to reach Point 171 in time.

How this happened is worth describing, since the lack of these essential items of equipment not only handicapped the Indian Motor Brigade in its defence and, to that extent, contributed towards its annihilation a few hours later, but it also shows that somebody in authority had erred in calculation and that better care and judgement in planning might have produced different results. To make this point more clear, it is necessary to inquire into the composition and movements of this formation a few days before it was attacked. This must take us back to Khatatba, on the Cairo—Alexandria road, where the brigade was in training early in May.

Composition and equipment

At Khatatba the 3rd Indian Motor Brigade consisted of three cavalry regiments and a number of units of artillery and other arms. These were:

    2nd Royal Lancers
    PAVO Cavalry (11th Frontier Force)
    18th King Edward VII's Own Cavalry
    Motor Brigade Group Anti-tank Battery
    2nd Indian Field Regiment RIA
    31st Field Squadron IE
    Brigade Group Signal Section
    13 & 27 Workshop Companies IAOC
    Brigade Field Ambulance
    A and B sections, Motor Brigade Provost Unit
    One Transport Company RIASC
    3rd Security Intelligence Section

Each of the above mentioned three cavalry regiments had on its establishment an anti-tank squadron of sixteen 2-pounder guns, the squadron being divided into four troops of four guns each. In addition, the brigade's anti-tank battery had 16 guns by itself. Thus the total authorised strength of anti-tank guns was sixty-four for the whole brigade. Similarly each regiment had on its strength two squadrons of Bren-carriers, totalling thirty carriers per regiment, each squadron consisting of three troops of five carriers each.

This was the composition of the 3rd Indian Motor Brigade when it was pulled out of its training towards the middle of May and ordered to proceed to Matruh. It reached Matruh on the 15th and was allotted the task of defending the coast. At this time, according to General Auchinleck, it was clear that an attack by the Axis was impending and it seemed to him almost certain "that our own offensive would be anticipated".[6] Both he and General Ritchie believed that one of the possibilities was that Rommel would open his offensive by launching an attack on the south of the Gazala line. The Eighth Army thereupon decided to move the 3rd Indian Motor Brigade from Matruh to Point 171. The order was issued on 21 May and the brigade began a hurried move which lasted several days. The march was complicated by the difficulty of transporting the carriers and the anti-tank guns.

In the meanwhile General Rommel's force was on the move for the attack. Axis columns had started out from Segnali on the evening of 26 May, taking a south-easterly direction. The columns might reach the Indian Motor Brigade's position any time during the night, and yet the brigade was without its full complement of artillery, carriers and tanks. The two squadrons of Valentine tanks which was promised by General Messervy had been despatched but had not arrived and a Liaison Officer was sent out at 1900 hours to meet them and guide them in. He failed to contact these tanks and the brigade remained without this valuable support to the end.[7]

As to the artillery, it arrived at dusk on 26 May and, though exhausted, completed the registration of its targets at a late hour. Among other late comers were the anti-tank battery, the regimental carriers and the 31st Field Squadron of Indian Engineers. The last named unit arrived too late to lay the mines, with the result that several portions of the defensive perimeter had wide gaps in them, which could not be closed.[8]

The carriers and anti-tank guns continued to arrive in small batches throughout the night of 26/27 May. Some of the last entries made in the war diaries of different units give a graphic account of the difficulties encountered in conveying them to the front line. For that fateful night of 26/27 May, for instance, the entries run as follow: "26 May, 1500 hours: Regimental carriers, B and C squadrons, arrived on transporters at El Adem. 2000 hours: Remaining carriers arrived at eight miles away; all carriers were short of petrol. 27 May, 0100 hours: Carriers did a night-march passing 'B' echelon area. 0700 hours: Battle with German Panzer Division and Italian Ariete Division started. 0845 hours: ....positions completely overrun with enemy tanks in the box. Regimental carriers did not arrive on our position".

As to the defensive layout, the Indian Brigade was not able to

---

[6] Gen. Auchinleck's *Despatch*, in Supplement to the *London Gazette of 15-1-48*, p. 353.
[7] According to one authority the Valentines, being slow and equipped only with the 2-pounder guns, would not have helped much.
[8] The infantry usually laid their own mines but in this case the task was assigned to the Indian Engineers, presumably because the infantry would be too busy digging in after their hurried arrival.

secure its perimeter even till the final hour of battle, due to the late arrival of the sappers and insufficiency of mines. Each regiment was allotted a stretch of 1700 to 2000 yards to defend. But of the mines necessary for this only a fraction had arrived. Writing of this period, a British officer of the 2nd Royal Lancers, who was present in the action, has remarked that until the last moment they were working on "an assumption that our defensive layout could be based on our having sixteen guns" and a sufficient number of mines. The result was that when the attack came in, a whole 2000-yards part of their sector was empty. This emptiness, it is to be presumed, was felt all the more keenly because of the grave lack of anti-tank guns in the brigade. Another such instance was given by Lt.-Col. McConnell, who in his report after the action said, "in effect, regiments had only two A.-Tk. Troops, two Lorried Troops and some personnel of other two A.-Tk. Troops armed with small arms, besides their HQ Squadron and HQ Squadron personnel. Not much for a 2000-yards front with no mines..........'. The Indian Artillery and the six Bofors guns had been placed at the centre of the Brigade's position and were, naturally enough, not able to cover all the points of the brigade's front.

This was the condition of the 3rd Indian Motor Brigade when the alarm that the Axis forces were on the move was sounded in the evening of 26 May. The first report of this was made by a tactical reconnaissance aircraft of No. 40 Squadron RAF and the information reached the brigade via the 7th Armoured Division. Later, at 2000 hours, an officers' patrol from the 2nd Royal Lancers reported the approach of a wide Axis column bearing down on Bir Hakeim. Independent reports from Bir Hakeim to the XXX Corps stated that the Axis armour was advancing east-south-east on a thirty mile front and that it appeared to be moving at a considerable speed.

The 3rd Indian Motor Brigade overwhelmed

The advancing column appeared to turn south during the night of 26 May, and it became clear that it was attempting to get round the Bir Hakeim box. The rest of its movements during that night was performed in the darkness and, probably, also in complete ignorance of the fact that the 3rd Indian Motor Brigade was lying astride the direction of its march. The result of this was that after wheeling north and north-east, the Axis armoured column stumbled on the brigade at dawn and found itself in full view of the latter's southern and north-eastern perimeter. The sight that confronted the brigade, on the other hand, was that of the entire *Afrika Korps* lined up within close range of its "box", with the Italian Ariete Division nearest to it.[9]

[9] W/Ds 3 Ind. Mot. Bde., 2 RL, 11 Cav., 18 Cav.

This was a surprise for the 3rd Indian Motor Brigade and must have been the same for the *Afrika Korps* too. As the dawn gave way to the morning light, the Indian brigade prepared for the battle. At 0630 hours, the 2nd Field Regiment RIA picked out concentrations of soft-skinned Axis vehicles and lorried infantry and subjected them to heavy short-range fire. The Italian Ariete Division which was the nearest was caught in so badly and so unexpectedly that all its transports, but the tanks, fled or at least temporarily dispersed. But that was about the best that the brigade could do. In actual fact, this effort to stop the advance of practically the whole of the *Afrika Korps* was an audacious and forlorn affair from the very start; and it was clear that now the Indian brigade was in for heavy punishment.

The Axis armour counter-attacked almost immediately. By 0730 hours on 27 May, the 15th Panzer Division was moving up the eastern ridge, like a steam-roller, shelling briskly as it moved. It crossed the valley that was lately occupied by the Brigade Headquarters and by the 31st Field Squadron of the Indian Engineers. This was but the first wave of the Axis tanks. The second wave, it would seem, was to be provided by the Ariete Division. This armoured division could be seen forming up for an attack on the Indian brigade's box. To hinder this preparation, and later to check the advance, every weapon, including the small arms, was fired directly at the Ariete column which, in the first batch, consisted of some sixty tanks. Working diagonally from south-west to north-east, the Italian division went straight into and across the 18th Cavalry positions, emerging on the other side to link up with the fast moving *Afrika Korps* proceeding north and north-east.

Following the Ariete Division came another wave, this time of the German Mark III and Mark IV tanks. There were about two hundred of them. The wave rolled straight in and across the positions held by the 2nd Royal Lancers, swamping the forward guns by sheer weight of metal and taking a heavy toll in human casualties. Chaos reigned in the entire brigade area for about forty-five minutes. The Indian 25-pounders and the regimental anti-tank guns worked to the maximum capacity during the engagement, crews of the anti-tank guns suffering heavy casualties. The carriers of the 18th King Edward's Own Cavalry, meeting the Ariete Division as it emerged at the north-east corner of the box, charged to what was for them certain death. But the action proved as unavailing as it was gallant and foredoomed. The Indian brigade found itself alone and unassisted, as no help from outside seemed to be forthcoming. By 0800 hours all organised resistance was at an end.[10]

[10] *Ibid.*

But there was no mass surrender. At 0830 hours, the Brigade Commander, Brigadier Filose, ordered everything out of the box and gave a rallying point at 376378,[11] four and a half miles east of Point 171. An hour later, those who reached there were despatched to Bir Scerrara (376386), where they formed up for moving off again. But by 1000 hours, roads towards the north had become blocked by large numbers of Axis transport. The survivors of the brigade thereupon changed their direction to the south, and then to the east, towards Bir el Gubi. In the course of this move they had to break through an Axis column, which opened machine-gun and artillery fire upon them and gave chase to their vehicles. The pursuers were however driven off by columns from the 29th Indian Infantry Brigade, which had come out of Bir el Gubi to meet and assist this surviving band of the gallant 3rd Indian Motor Brigade.

The casualties of this engagement were by no means slight. The losses in killed and wounded for three regiments and the Indian artillery were 41 officers, including three commanding officers, and 453 men, including VCOs. The number lost as prisoners was about 600 and there were possibly other casualties in the brigade area outside the fighting units, which do not occur in the regimental war diaries. The analysis of the list of killed and wounded is as follows: 2nd Royal Lancers——Officers 3, VCOs and men 175; 11th Cavalry Regiment——Officers including CO 6, VCOs and men 28; 18th Cavalry Regiment——Officers including CO 10, VCOs and men 17; 2nd Field Regiment RIA——Officers including CO 22, VCOs and men 233. The six hundred prisoners underwent a brief but peculiar treatment in the Axis camps. It appears that the Axis command did not want to be burdened with so many prisoners at a time when speed of movement was of paramount importance and rations and water were running out fast. The prisoners, except the officers, were therefore made to march to and fro for several hours without food and water so as to tire them out, and were then released to go where they pleased. Most of them made their way to Bir Hakeim and rejoined their units later.

When the Indian Motor Brigade was being pressed hard by the Axis advance, it should, in the normal course, have received assistance from its neighbouring formations. There were the Free French on its left, the 29th Indian Infantry Brigade on the right, and the 7th Support Group to its north. But neither the war diaries of the Indian Motor Brigade nor those of its regiments make any mention of such aid having been asked for or received. It is likely that at least the artillery within the Free French box of Bir Hakeim exerted itself in the defence of Point 171 and that other boxes considered sending aid but failed to do so in time. If,

---

[11] The references are to the GSGS map, 1/250,000, Egypt & Cyrenaica, Sheet 3.

however, none of the neighbouring formations really bestirred themselves to despatch assistance to the Indian Motor Brigade, it would be fair to surmise that it was a case of poor co-ordination, for which the brigade had to pay a very heavy penalty.[12]

It is not surprising that after this action the brigade got a mention in the British Parliament. On 2 June 1942, the Prime Minister of the United Kingdom included the 3rd Indian Motor Brigade in a statement to the House of Commons when reporting on the progress of the war in Libya. He commended the Indian brigade for its gallantry at a time when it was overpowered by sheer weight of metal during the initial advance of the Axis armour. The brigade also received telegrams of congratulations from the Commander-in-Chief, Middle East Forces, and Headquarters Eighth Army. There is no doubt that the officers and men who composed the brigade were imbued with the highest sense of duty. An evidence of this can be found in a routine entry in the war diary of the 2nd Royal Lancers. The item is dated 28 May, when the brigade had just emerged from action in a shattered condition, and was reorganising somewhere between El Gubi and Capuzzo. It runs thus: "The Brigadier forms a column with what is left of us to go back as a nuisance force. 8th Army do not agree. Orders received to move to Buq Buq". Thereupon the brigade made its exit from the area of combat.

Appreciation of stand at Point 171

It may be asked in conclusion: what was the precise achievement of the 3rd Indian Motor Brigade? In terms of damage and casualties inflicted on a hostile force, not much, though infinitely more than might be expected from a poorly-equipped formation of this type. The number of Axis tanks actually stopped on the position is uncertain. But a war diary records a statement from a reliable VCO, who visited the site of action on 29 May after the Axis forces had passed over. The VCO reported having counted 25 crippled Axis tanks of which 22 were burned out. The figures proved to be rather an underestimate, since General Tuker himself counted upwards of 50 destroyed tanks on this position when he went there in December 1942 to examine the area. If so, this certainly made a big dent in the Axis armour. In addition, the Indian brigade made the Axis forces disgorge their ammunition, which could not be readily replaced due to a long line of communication round the south of Bir Hakeim. Further, although the brigade did not delay the Axis advance for more than about half an hour, it created enough noise and scuffle to give alarm to the neighbouring formations, while it took the first shock of the

[12] W/Ds 29 Bde, 3 Ind. Mot. Bde., 2 RL, 11 Cav., 18 Cav.

impact on itself and cushioned the blow for the next formation. But what is more important than all this, is that it might have certainly done much better, had it not been moved to the prospective battle area in extreme haste and left there to rough it out without the full complement of its anti-tank guns, carriers and land mines and without the support of a single tank.[13]

A question of calculation

Could this state of affairs have been avoided? With reasonable forethought and care, perhaps the story might have been different. This brings us to the point mentioned earlier, namely, whether somebody had erred in calculation in moving the brigade so far forward without proper equipment. When the brigade was attacked it had only 30 anti-tank guns out of its authorised establishment of 64; no tanks at all, although two squadrons of Valentines had been allotted to it; only a portion of its full strength of carriers; no more than a fraction of the mines requisitioned by it; and an artillery that had no time to get dug-in before the action. All this happened because the brigade was made to move in small batches. It was ushered into the battle position piecemeal, in driblets. It was thereby robbed of a chance of exerting itself as a full and complete formation.

Such a state of affairs could have been foreseen and avoided, because the factors involved were simple and easy to calculate. The approximate date when General Rommel might strike was known with a fair amount of accuracy. It was also known that the distance over which the brigade had to move was long, and that due to disparity in speeds of travelling of different types of its transports, the brigade would be naturally moving in small groups. From this, it should be easy to infer that a definite risk existed of only a portion of the brigade being in position, and that too without its full strength of weapons, should the attack mature as expected. Such a risk has no doubt to be taken in the field. But it was perhaps possible to minimise it in this case by moving the brigade by stages, that is, the whole formation waiting at each successive stage to complete itself before moving on to the next. In such an event it is possible that the progress of the brigade might have been much too slow for it to reach Point 171 when that feature was attacked. But there is reason to believe that it might have given a better account of itself by strengthening the defence in depth from whatever stage it might have then reached, against an adversary weakened or divided by preliminary tank battles with masses of Allied armour waiting in their proper places for doing that job.

[13] *Ibid.*

A much bigger mistake, according to an eminent military authority, was to have used mobile formations like the 3rd Indian Motor Brigade and the 7th Support Group in static roles. In fact, the orders to both were to stand and fight where they were. That could be one reason why the Support Group did not go to the assistance of the Indian Motor Brigade when the latter was overwhelmed by the *Afrika Korps*.

CHAPTER XXXIII

Battle of Bridgeheads and 'Cauldron' Offensive

In the preceding chapter an account has been given of how the 3rd Indian Motor Brigade was overrun by the *Afrika Korps* on 27 May. This was not, however, the only formation to meet that fate. Another such body was a British motorised formation, the 7th Motor Brigade, which was then guarding a portion of the Trigh el Abd under the 7th Armoured Division. The *Afrika Korps* was advancing on a thirty-mile front, with the Panzer Divisions on the left and the 90th Light Division's battle groups on the right. In the course of that advance the 90th Division hit the 7th Motor Brigade and simply swept over it. It then captured the headquarters of the 7th Armoured Division and inflicted some casualties on the 4th Armoured Brigade when the latter tried to engage it.[1]

This led to a disorganisation which, however, did not last long. The survivors of the 7th Motor Brigade rallied at Bir el Gubi. They were joined by some two hundred more personnel who had been captured but had managed to escape, and the brigade was ready to fight again the next day. The headquarters of the 7th Armoured Division also was soon functioning again. Last but not the least, the 4th Armoured Brigade, which had permitted the 90th Light Division to penetrate as far north as El Adem, recovered from its shock on the following day and drove the latter back, well away to the south. Thus the effects of the initial surprise had been practically overcome.

Tobruk, El Adem and Knightsbridge

However, this surprise produced one important consequence. It revealed a weakness in the Allied dispositions. The lightning dash of the German 90th Light Division to El Adem showed that Tobruk was not well shielded from the south. General Ritchie was particularly sensitive about any weakness in this area. The reason was that the Eighth Army had its main supply dumps at Tobruk, sufficient to sustain the Army for three months and to keep the Tobruk garrison going for a like period. The success or failure of

---

[1] Gen. Auchinleck's *Despatch* in Supplement to the *London Gazette*, 15 Jan. 1948, p. 355.

the operations of the Eighth Army, therefore, depended on the safety of those dumps.

But Tobruk could not stand if El Adem fell. The two were linked together by a short by-pass road, so that the occupation of the latter would lead, almost immediately, to the former being isolated and besieged.[2] It was, therefore, necessary to strengthen the El Adem locality; and General Ritchie accordingly moved the 29th Indian Infantry Brigade to that place from Bir el Gubi where it was performing a less vital role. This transfer took place on 29 May. At the same time he ordered that the 21st Indian Infantry Brigade be brought over to occupy the Sidi Rezegh ridge, from where the valley surrounding El Adem could be watched and controlled. Pending the brigade's arrival the ridge was to be held by the 7th Support Group.[3]

On 28 May, the first day of the German offensive, when the 3rd Indian Motor Brigade was overwhelmed and the 7th (British) Motor Brigade was pushed back to El Adem, equally important events were taking place in other parts of the front. The Panzer Divisions were racing towards Knightsbridge; the Ariete Division was attacking Bir Hakeim; the Trieste Division was trying to penetrate the minefield in the centre; and other Axis units were demonstrating in the north. Knightsbridge was a vital road junction giving access to Acroma, Gazala and Tobruk, and ranked next to El Adem in importance. The area was guarded by the 1st Armoured Division. Its formations, the 22nd Armoured Brigade and the Guards Brigade, tried to oppose the advance of the Panzer Divisions, in which task they were joined by the 1st Army Tank Brigade. The Panzers nevertheless succeeded in reaching Knightsbridge. They were attacked there once again by the 1st Armoured Division, but without conclusive results.

As to the fighting opposite the Gazala line, the Axis troops were not so fortunate. The Ariete Division's attack on Bir Hakeim was unsuccessful. The Trieste Division had failed to penetrate the minefield; while the demonstrations against the northern positions achieved nothing and cost the Axis twenty tanks. Worst of all, the reserve of supplies and rations carried by the Axis troops was coming to an end and they were out of touch with their supply line. This was going to produce an awkward situation for the Axis. In fact, it was precisely going to be the situation which General Ritchie had anticipated and worked for, and it did at last come to pass. The Axis forces were soon stranded without supplies. The alternatives before

---

[2] With a different type of defensive layout, however, this need not have been the case. A treatment of this other aspect of the defence of Tobruk will be found in *The Pattern of War* by Lt.-Gen. Sir Francis Tuker.
[3] W/Ds 29 Bde., 21 Bde.

them were to abandon their attack and withdraw, or procure supplies somehow.

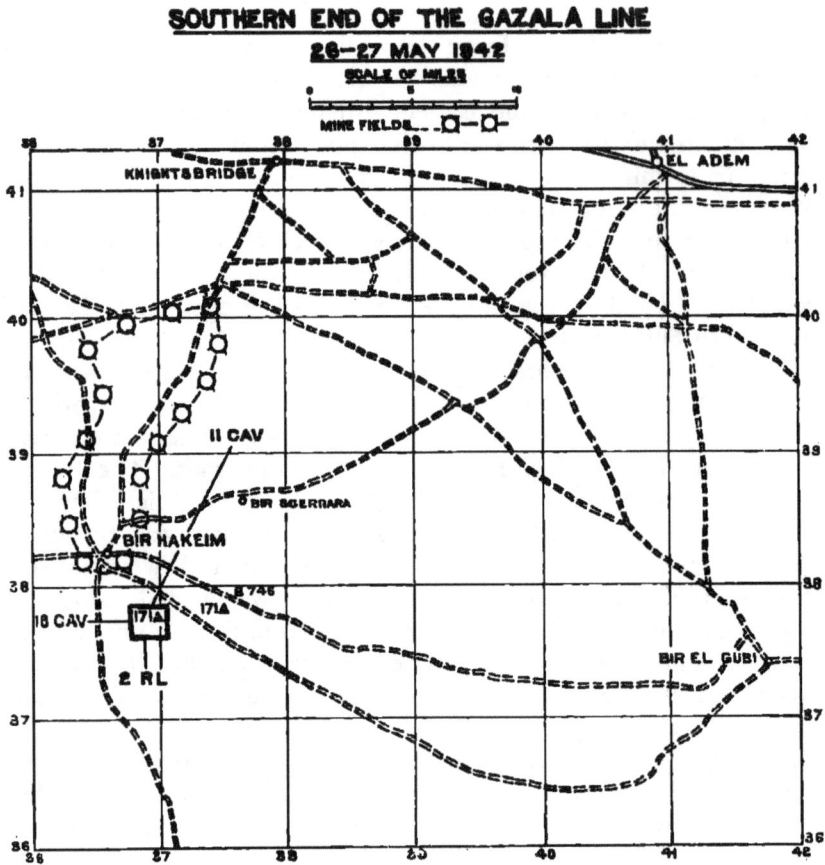

Fighting for communications

If General Ritchie had foreseen this state of affairs, General Rommel had not been unmindful of it either. He, too, had taken steps to avert such a situation. He had planned for two supply convoys to be kept ready, one at the northern end of the Gazala line and the other at the southern. It was arranged that after the main battle the Axis forces would divide themselves into two groups one of which would proceed northwards to contact the northern convoy and the other would turn south to meet the southern one. This last, which was coming round Bir Hakeim, was the main supply column; and it was this that General Ritchie was anxious to destroy or put off. He had devised sufficiently strong measures for the purpose.[4]

[4] Gen. Auchinleck's *Despatch*, p 356.

Thus on 28 May, after demonstrating towards Acroma, the German tanks dispersed into small parties. The Italian Ariete Division did likewise and moved north to contact the maintenance convoy. At the same time the rest of the Axis force, which formed the main bulk, made a general move southwards. But here the Eighth Army had its plans ready for preventing the supplies reaching this stranded force. At a given moment, the Royal Air Force descended upon the Axis supply column coming round Bir Hakeim and played havoc with it; while the two armoured brigades of the 1st Armoured Division, plus the 1st Army Tank Brigade, hurled themselves on the scattered groups of German tanks and subjected them to a gruelling attack. The battle, which may be called the battle for communications, raged furiously for some time; and although the issue was more than once precariously balanced, the Eighth Army seemed to be coming out on the top at last. But just then an unfortunate incident occurred. Taking advantage of the Eighth Army's preoccupation in the south, the Italian Trieste Division attacked the centre of the Gazala line and succeeded in making a breach in the minefields.

This was a matter of grave concern to the Eighth Army. The minefield had been breached where it was crossed by two desert highways—the Trigh-Capuzzo and the Trigh el Abd. This had produced a pair of dangerous gaps in the Gazala perimeter; and the gaps were along two important tracks which led straight to the frontier of Egypt. Axis vehicles poured through these openings and were evidently moving to the east of the Gazala line to build a bridgehead at the far end of the gaps. They were shelled heavily by the 150th Brigade and the Free French in an attempt to obstruct their movement. But the attempt was only partially successful; and General Rommel now bent all his energies on securing his newly-won positions and establishing the necessary bridgeheads for a further move.[5]

These bridgeheads, it may be pointed out, were intended to serve two purposes simultaneously: firstly, to keep the Gazala line broken and divided; and secondly, to enable the supply lines to be shortened. The shortening of the supply lines would result from their being connected directly to the gaps instead of their going round Bir Hakeim. This would eliminate all problems of exposed and dubious lines of communication for the Axis troops. All that now remained for them was to make the bridgeheads secure and extend their communications as far as the gaps. The fight for the lines of communication had thus been half won by the Axis; to complete the victory it was necessary for them to fight and win another battle, the battle for the bridgeheads.

[5] *Ibid.*

The Battle of the Bridgeheads

This battle, which took place on the following day (30 May), was paradoxically enough started by the Allies themselves, since the latter wanted to prevent the consolidation of the bridgeheads. That morning the main Axis force was still lying on the scene of the previous day's fighting, when three British armoured brigades approached the position and engaged it in a battle. The fighting started at daybreak and lasted till noon. At the end of that period the Axis troops appeared to have had enough of it and seemed to be abandoning their bridgeheads and withdrawing westwards through the gaps.

The British armour decided to intercept the withdrawal by placing itself between the Axis troops and the mouths of the two gaps. But the task was by no means easy. The Axis forces covered their retirement with a powerful anti-tank screen which could neither be penetrated nor outflanked.

The screen was established in a wide arc on the high ground on both sides of the Trigh-Capuzzo road. Its southern flank rested on the Allied minefields and was therefore inaccessible; while the northern flank was well protected. The only Allied formation which could possibly undertake an outflanking operation was the 1st Army Tank Brigade, which was located nearer to the southern flank than the rest of the brigades. But it did not have the necessary speed and mobility to cover the eighteen or twenty miles in the limited time that would be available for rounding the northern flank and closing the gaps in the minefield. It was, therefore, decided to give up the idea of closing the gaps from the other side. Instead, the multitude of Axis vehicles that was passing through them was subjected to a heavy aerial and artillery fire. But, although a number of vehicles were thus knocked out, most of them succeeded in getting through.

This withdrawal, it appears, was interpreted by General Ritchie as the end of the battle of bridgeheads.[6] He therefore decided that the time had come for the Eighth Army to pass on to the offensive. But he soon discovered that the withdrawal was by no means a rout as he had thought, but merely a move on the part of the Axis command for reorganising and redistributing their forces to better advantage. The Axis had not given up their bridgeheads. All that they had done was to exchange them for a strong consolidated position to the east of the Gazala line, which had a direct route of supply from the west. Nor had they abandoned the gaps in the minefield. Rather they had fortified them and had infantry and tanks at both ends of the gaps as well as inside them. In actual

---

[6] *Ibid.*

effect, therefore, they could be said to be sitting astride the Gazala minefield.

Apparently, General Ritchie was unaware of this precise situation when he decided that the time had come for starting his counter-offensive. He proposed to attack in the north with his infantry and in the south with his armour. The 1st South African and the 50th Divisions, aided by some heavy tanks, were to attack and secure Tmimi and Afrag in the north, after which the 5th Indian Division was to pass through and penetrate the Jebel Akhdar. At the same time the armoured divisions were to move south towards Mekili, attacking the Axis armour as opportunity offered itself, and generally operating against the southern flank of the Axis. The attack was to commence on the night of 31 May. The whole plan was based on the assumption that the Axis forces had been routed and were engaged in carrying out a general withdrawal.[7]

General Auchinleck was anxious that no time be lost in developing the proposed counter-offensive and so was General Ritchie. But the latter's two corps commanders asked for a twenty-four hours' extension for assembling their forces. The date was therefore put off to 1 June, and preparations proceeded apace. It was just then that the discovery was made that the Axis troops had not withdrawn and that the greater part of them were still lying astride the minefield with a large tank force in their midst. These facts could not be ignored. Reviewing his plan in the light of this new situation, General Ritchie had no difficulty in seeing that the proposed counter-offensive was much too full of hazards to be allowed to go in at all. Against the two hundred and odd medium tanks with which he proposed to attack, the Axis could certainly produce no fewer; and with a tank force of that size, it could take Tobruk and play havoc in the rear of the Eighth Army, were the projected offensive set into motion. General Ritchie therefore decided that it was very essential, as an important preliminary, to attack and reduce this main body of the Axis armour first so as to make conditions safe for a general offensive.

Efforts to destroy Axis armour

The original plan of the counter-offensive was therefore cancelled and substituted by a new plan for attacking the concentrations of the Axis armour. The date for the attack was the same—1 June, and it was hoped that the Eighth Army would be able to pass on to the originally contemplated general offensive as soon as the Axis armour was sufficiently liquidated. The battle was planned to take place in the area of the anti-tank screen. The aim was to push back

[7] W/D, 5 Div.

the screen, and establish two brigade-group positions within it, which might be used as safe harbours by the artillery for shelling concentrations of the Axis tanks. A third brigade was already well within that area and was to be the mainstay of the contemplated battle. This formation was the 150th British Brigade which was then situated at Sidi Muftah.

The battle however never started. The operations were to begin on 1 June, but many hours before that the 150th British Brigade had ceased to exist. It had been attacked heavily by an Axis force early in the afternoon of 31 May; and although the 1st Armoured Division and the 1st Army Tank Brigade hastened to its assistance, it was finally overpowered in the morning of 1 June and succumbed after a valiant defence. Undeterred by this mishap, General Ritchie decided to persist in his objective with a slightly altered plan. He aimed at capturing a ridge, Sghifet es Sidra, which would offer a vantage point for shelling Axis concentrations. At the same time he planned a double thrust, from north and east, at the area of the anti-tank screen. The 69th Infantry Brigade was ordered to advance from the north with Sghifet es Sidra as its objective; and the 10th Indian Infantry Brigade was directed to attack from the east, from somewhere near Bir el Harmat.[8]

But this plan, too, failed like the one before. The attack commenced to schedule but soon came to a standstill. The Axis resistance proved more stubborn than expected. The 69th Infantry Brigade was held up a little short of its objective; while the 10th Indian Infantry Brigade could not even get started, as a raging sand-storm made it impossible to carry out the preliminary reconnaissances, which were thought to be very essential. The whole operation was a disappointing failure and left the Axis in secure posssession of the dangerous salient in the centre of the Gazala line.

General Auchinleck now began to feel concerned at the way the things were moving. The Eighth Army was in a fix. It could not risk the destruction of its armour by ordering its tanks to battle their way through the anti-tank screen. Nor could it safely split the armoured strength for containing a hostile force in one sector while defeating it in another. For that matter, it could not attack Bir Temrad or Alam Hamza in the north as suggested by General Auchinleck; or send the 5th Indian Division, as contemplated by General Ritchie, round the south of Bir Hakeim, to the rear of the Axis lines. On the other hand, the Axis were continuing to consolidate their deep wedge in the centre of the Gazala line; and

---

[8] Gen. Auchinleck's *Despatch* in Supplement to the *London Gazette*, 15 Jan. 1948, p. 357.
W/Ds. 1 Div., 10 Bde.

there were reports that they were moving more tanks into the salient. If this continued, the Gazala line, and particularly Bir Hakeim, would become untenable. That would confront the Eighth Army with the necessity of abandoning the planned offensive and retiring to the frontier. It was clear that the Eighth Army was on the verge of a major defeat, and some way out had to be found quickly if the danger was to be averted. In the circumstances, General Ritchie decided that the only practicable course was to use infantry and make a direct assault on the Axis salient.

The 'Cauldron' offensive

This salient, it will be remembered, had resulted from the gaps made in the Gazala minefield at two points where the roads Trigh el Abd and Trigh-Capuzzo crossed the minebelt. Both these gaps, and all the area to the east of them, as far as Knightsbridge, came to be known as the 'Cauldron'. It is easy to see that the most vital area of the Gazala defences was now the 'Cauldron'; and the most menacing points in the 'Cauldron' were the spurs made by the two gaps. To counter this threat, General Ritchie too had formed two strong points, one facing each gap. The troops used for this purpose were under the command of the 7th Armoured Division, and included the 9th and 10th Indian Infantry Brigades, as well as one British battalion of the 10th Indian Division. They were intended to take the offensive against the Axis bridgehead position as soon as possible. The 10th Indian Division, it may be mentioned, had been ordered from Iraq to Libya and was just arriving.[9]

General Ritchie decided that his assault on the salient should be in the form of a pincer movement. One arm of the pincer was to come out from the north and the other from the east. The attack from the north was to be made by the 69th Infantry Brigade, supported by the 32nd Army Tank Brigade, both under the command of the XIII Corps. That from the east was to be made by the 9th and 10th Indian Infantry Brigades of the 5th Indian Division, operating under the XXX Corps. The northern objective was limited and was, as before, the capture of the ridge Sghifet es Sidra. The eastern thrust, on the other hand, was to be the main thrust and its objective was the vital ground around Got el Scarab, by seizing which the Indian Brigades would be able to open a corridor through the anti-tank screen. On this being done, the 22nd Armoured Brigade was to pass through and close the minefield gaps behind the Axis salient, after which the Eighth Army was to return to the general offensive, putting forward its right shoulder, i.e. striking first in the northern sector. Briefly the

---

[9] W/Ds. 5 Div., 10 Div.; 9 Bde., 10 Bde.

operations aimed at crushing the Axis in the 'Cauldron' and then passing on to conquer the rest of Cyrenaica.[10]

These important operations, however, could not get started until the night of 5 June, due, presumably, to the need for reconnaissance and administrative preparations. Had they commenced on 1 June they might have possibly gone as planned. But by now, during the interval of about four days, the Axis commander had taken steps to fortify the ridge strongly and had obtained tanks for supporting its garrison. As a result, the 69th Brigade met with a stiff resistance when it started its operations at 0250 hours on 5 June. While it was trying to overcome this, Axis tanks attacked the 32nd Army Tank Brigade on its right flank. The Tank Brigade moved about swiftly to adjust its position for a battle, but in trying to do so ran on an uncharted Axis minefield and lost no less than fifty out of its original seventy tanks.

This was an unmitigated disaster for the XIII Corps, since the 32nd Army Tank Brigade was the supporting armour of the 69th Infantry Brigade and that support had now practically vanished. No sooner did the Axis tanks realise that this was the plight of the infantry than they turned about and placed themselves between the 69th Brigade and its objective—Sghifet es Sidra. As a result, the brigade's progress came to a complete standstill. It stood pinned down short of its objective and was attacked and harassed by the Axis tanks until at last it was obliged to give up the effort. The operation of the XIII Corps had thus failed, and about half of the 'Cauldron' battle had been lost by the Allies.

The failure of the XIII Corps made the task of the XXX Corps no easier. The operations of the two Corps had been interlinked to the extent that the former was to support the attack of the latter with flanking fire from Sghifet es Sidra. The absence of that support increased the difficulty of the XXX Corps, when its striking arm, the 10th Indian Infantry Brigade, attacked the Aslagh ridge. However, the operation was still successful; the ridge was captured and a way opened for the 22nd Armoured Brigade to pass through. Four regiments of field artillery then moved up to the Aslagh ridge to defend this corridor during the passage of the Armoured Brigade; and the 9th Indian Infantry Brigade stood ready to follow the armour through this gap to attack and secure the important Axis position of Sidi Muftah. The Axis anti-tank screen had been pierced at last.[11]

At this moment, there seemed no doubt that the XXX Corps would succeed in its aim of working its way to the rear of the Axis

---

[10] Gen. Auchinleck's *Despatch* in Supplement to the *London Gazette*, 15 Jan. 1948, pp. 357-58.
[11] W/Ds. 5 Div., 10 Bde., 9 Bde.

salient and closing the minefield gaps from behind. But before long, the 22nd Armoured Brigade came up against an insurmountable obstacle. It was a second anti-tank screen which the Axis had thrown round Sidi Muftah. There was no point in trying to force a way through it as that would entail enormous losses in tanks. So the Armoured Brigade wheeled north. It was attacked on the way by Axis troops who caused it considerable damage. Nevertheless, it at last managed to reach a leaguer just before dawn on 6 June.

As to the infantry, there was the 10th Indian Infantry Brigade on its recently won ridge, Dahar el Aslagh. On the southern flank of the ridge was the single British battalion of the 10th Indian Division, which it will be remembered was also assigned for the operation. In addition there was one battalion of the 9th Indian Infantry Brigade, which had pushed its way through the corridor in the wake of the 22nd Armoured Brigade. All these were attacked by the Axis tanks and troops. The 22nd Armoured Brigade did not intervene to protect them as it had been informed that it had no responsibility for the infantry. The infantry had however the four field regiments and a motor battalion of the 22nd Armoured Brigade to help them in defending the ridge. All those troops were under the 5th Indian Division which at this period consisted of the following:

 Commander—Maj-Gen Briggs
  9 Bde (Brig Fletcher)
   2 W Yorks
   3 RFFR
   3 Jats
   4 Fd Regt RA
   20 Fd Coy IE
  10 Bde (Brig Boucher)
   2 HLI
   4 Baluch
   2/4 GR
   28 Fd Regt RA
   2 Fd Coy IE
  29 Bde (Brig Reid)
   1 Worc R
   3/2 Punjab
   1 Mahrattas
   3 Fd Regt RA
   21 Fd Coy IE

The aim of the Axis attacks was the recapture of the ridge, Dahar el Aslagh. After much desultory fighting, which lasted all day on 6 June, a strong Axis detachment worked round the southern flank of the ridge. It attacked and overcame the British battalion defending that flank. Further Axis attacks inflicted heavy casualties on the 10th Indian Infantry Brigade. The tactical headquarters of the 5th Indian Division and the headquarters of the 10th Brigade were also overrun and one battalion of the 9th Indian Infantry Brigade found itself in great difficulties. The result of all this was that the 9th Brigade was withdrawn to cut down losses to the minimum and arrangements were made to send help to the hard-pressed garrison on Dahar el Aslagh.[12]

Failure of the 'Cauldron' offensive

The 22nd Armoured Brigade, however, was not in a fit condition to undertake this mission of taking succour to Dahar el Aslagh. Other formations available for the task were the 4th and the 2nd Armoured Brigades and these had been despatched immediately. But the progress of the 4th Armoured Brigade was rather slow due, it is said, to its being too full of new and untrained personnel; and the 2nd Brigade, through some misunderstanding of orders, deviated too far to the north, thus finding itself against an impassable escarpment. In the meanwhile, the Axis troops had attacked Dahar el Aslagh position and overwhelmed the 10th Indian Infantry Brigade as well as the four artillery regiments. The 10th Brigade virtually ceased to exist, some scattered elements escaping on their own. The two armoured brigades sent out on the rescuing mission did put in counter-attacks at last but these were ineffectual and attained nothing. The battle of the 'Cauldron' was by that time over and had been won by the Axis.

The failure of the 'Cauldron' offensive was not a serious matter in itself. Nor did it alter General Ritchie's determination to return to the offensive. His tank force was still equal in size to that of General Rommel's, and his prospects of obtaining reinforcements just as good. But he needed a few days for reorganising before he could seriously consider mounting a sizable offensive. In the meanwhile, he decided to carry out intensified attacks against General Rommel's supply lines. The 50th British Division was doing this from the north and it was necessary to find a unit to do the same from the south also.

The unit selected for the purpose was the 7th Motor Brigade which was then operating in support of the Free French garrison at Bir Hakeim, and General Ritchie decided to withdraw it and send it to Mteifel to obstruct the Axis line of supply from the south. Realising, however, that the Free French might not be able to hold Bir Hakeim if deprived of this support, he warned them to be ready for a withdrawal. This was on 6 June.

The removal of the 7th Motor Brigade from the vicinity of Bir

[12] W/Ds 5 Div., 10 Div., 9 Bde., 10 Bde.

Hakeim produced a change in the tactical balance, the significance of which General Rommel could not have failed to appreciate. Whether by design or coincidence, the Axis forces were just about then engaged in taking up new dispositions, and this happened to place them in the right position for making the most of the altered situation. Moving the bulk of his armour north-eastwards, towards Knightsbridge, Rommel quickly took up a pivotal position from where he could threaten Tobruk as well as Bir Hakeim. His intention no doubt was to attack the one while he contained the other; and from his subsequent dispositions it could be seen that he was planning to reduce Bir Hakeim first, while he held out a threat to Tobruk at the same time. The threats thus poised by him to Bir Hakeim and Tobruk were considered so serious that it was decided to send out the Allied armour to challenge his tanks to a battle at once, that is without waiting to reorganise for a proper full-fledged offensive as was originally intended. This resulted in an armoured battle round Knightsbridge, on 6 June, in which both the Panzer Divisions and all the three British Armoured Brigades tried to decide the issue by hard fighting. Neither side gained any advantage and the tank fighting died down soon after. Meanwhile, the Axis had already started its attack on Bir Hakeim.

Axis attacks on Bir Hakeim

The first assault on Bir Hakeim had come on 6 June, the day of the armoured battle at Knightsbridge, and had been repelled by the Free French garrison. But the Axis persisted and carried out several more attacks during the following two days. At last on 8 June, the Free French commander, General Koenig, was obliged to report that the situation had become extremely serious and his stronghold might even collapse unless the garrison was given support from outside. The support asked for was some action to relieve pressure on Bir Hakeim and a quick replenishment of the garrison's supplies.

The problem of supplying Bir Hakeim, however, was becoming increasingly difficult. This difficulty had been growing over the last many days because the 90th Light Division had been surrounding the position methodically, with a series of entrenched posts. The cordon had been tightening progressively since the withdrawal of the 7th Motor Brigade, and the eastern face of the Bir Hakeim position had become completely masked already.

Although it was the intention of General Ritchie to withdraw the Free French garrison from Bir Hakeim if the position became untenable, he was nevertheless willing to make one more effort to hold it. There were several reasons why such an effort was justified. Firstly, the Free French were putting up a spirited stand which held forth hopes of their ultimate success if given moderate support. Secondly, if Bir Hakeim were lost, a new front would have to be formed which would be more extended than the existing one, and would be facing southwards instead of being opposite to the Axis line. Such a front would have the added disadvantage in that the Allied force would be hemmed in, with a narrow space behind and little scope for manoeuvre. Thirdly, the threat to the rear of the Eighth Army would increase, since there would be no continuous line to hold the advance of the Axis frontally; and finally, since the need to strike at the supply line of the Axis was now greater than ever, Bir Hakeim was the most suitable position for performing that task.

Looking at the problem in this light, General Ritchie decided to send help to the 1st Free French Brigade which had so valiantly repelled repeated thrusts of the Axis since 6 June. Orders were accordingly issued for an attack to be made on the German 90th Light Division, taking advantage of which a supply convoy was to be passed through, while aircraft were to drop in additional supplies. The force earmarked for this operation was an armoured regimental group from the 4th Armoured Brigade, plus two columns supplied by the 29th Indian Infantry and the 7th British Motor Brigades. The attack was to be made on 9 June, in the rear of the 90th Light Division, and the attacking force on completion of its job was to join up with that at Mteifel.[13]

Fall of Bir Hakeim

Meanwhile, on 8 June, the Axis delivered one more of its several assaults on Bir Hakeim, and this last one achieved more than the previous ones. One of the Free French positions was overrun; and on the following day (9 June), the garrison was heavily dive-bombed and shelled and attacked again from the north, where the relief force could not reach as it was positioned for striking from east or south. However, the Free French succeeded in repelling the attack single-handed, after a full day's fighting. In the meantime the relief force set to work to relieve pressure in the south. But the effort was not as successful as was expected. The French garrison, too, was by now worn out and there seemed little hope of saving this southern terminal of the Gazala line. Accordingly on 10 June, General Ritchie ordered the evacuation of Bir Hakeim which took place during the night, the withdrawing force being escorted by the 7th Armoured Division. By the next morning, about 2000 men had been withdrawn safely and more were coming in.

The fall of Bir Hakeim solved the problem of supplies and communication for the Axis. It also freed the 90th Light Division

[13] W/Ds, 5 Div.; 29 Bde.

which had been tied up in trying to surround Bir Hakeim and in masking it from east and south. It is not surprising therefore that the reaction of the Axis to the Allied evacuation was now quick and decisive. The 90th Light Division swiftly moved north-east and by the midnight of 11 June was leaguering some nine miles south of El Adem. Two Axis divisions, the 15th Panzer and the Trieste, followed up and took up positions to the left and rear respectively. Two more Axis armoured divisions, the 21st Panzer and the Ariete, which were already lying to the west of Bir el Harmat, would also be available for being thrown into the fight in that locality. It was now obvious that the objective of the Axis was El Adem and the ridges round about.

At this stage El Adem was being guarded by the 29th Indian Infantry Brigade which was holding a defensive locality on the ridge to the south. Immediately to its west lay the 2nd and 4th British Armoured Brigades, with orders to engage the Axis armoured force at an opportune moment. Still farther to the west, at Knightsbridge, was the 22nd Armoured Brigade, which was instructed to keep a watch over the movements of the Axis armour at Bir el Harmat. To the south of the 29th Indian Infantry Brigade were the 11th Indian Infantry Brigade and the 7th British Motor Brigade. Their tasks were to drive for the southern and eastern flanks of the Axis troops engaged in attacking the El Adem locality.[14]

Thus the stage had been set for the final battle of the Gazala line. It will be the purpose of the succeeding chapter to discuss the events that marked the course of this furious fighting and culminated in the Allied withdrawal from Gazala and the eventual fall of Tobruk.

---

[14] W/Ds. 5 Div., 29 Bde., 11 Bde.

CHAPTER XXXIV

Battle of Gazala Line

After the fall of Bir Hakeim, what remained of the Gazala line was very little indeed. Its southern terminal had been lopped off and it had been broken into at two places in the centre. Whether it would continue to hold or not, depended hereafter upon whether the Eighth Army would be able to retain its grip on the two vital places behind it, namely El Adem and El Gubi. Given either, the Axis could isolate the garrisons, both of Tobruk and the Gazala line, by cutting their eastward communications. General Rommel appeared to have fixed upon El Adem as his immediate objective; and his attempt to take that place resulted in one of the fiercest armoured battles yet fought in North Africa.

The events that led to that battle began on 12 June. That morning the German 90th Light Division was preparing to attack El Adem; and to its left was the 15th Panzer Division which was to protect the 90th Division's left flank as well as to join the battle at a crucial moment. To interfere with this project it was necessary to bring the Panzers to an immediate battle, and the 2nd and 4th Armoured Brigades were sent out for that purpose. But the attempt did not succeed as the Germans put up an impenetrable anti-tank screen and successfully held off the armoured brigades.

At the same time, the 90th Light Division commenced its action with an assault on a part of the El Adem ridge that was being held by the 29th Indian Infantry Brigade. The Indian brigade fought back vigorously and repulsed the onslaught. But in the melee some Axis troops got round and seized the landing ground to its north. This loss, however regrettable, did not materially affect the general situation and, a little later, the 90th Light Division, having failed in its object, withdrew from the battle area.[1]

As the fighting in the 29th Indian Infantry Brigade area was dying down, the 15th Panzer Division came into action, and swinging north-west went out to meet the 2nd and 4th Armoured Brigades, whose efforts to come to grips it had been evading since the morning. As a result a fierce armoured battle ensued which lasted till nightfall, and in the course of that hard fighting, the two brigades got gradually pushed back to an area some four miles north of the Batruna ridge. Meanwhile, the 90th Light Division,

---

[1] Gen. Auchinleck's *Despatch* in Supplement to the *London Gazette*, 15 Jan. 1948, p. 359.

taking advantage of their preoccupation, consolidated and extended its defensive positions against the 29th Brigade's area, evidently with a view to containing this Indian formation during the next day's operations and attacking it again at a more convenient opportunity.[2] The next day's operations, it would seem, had become necessary because the armoured battle of the preceding day had failed to secure conclusion, and even the stalemate resulting from it was so precarious that it was dangerous for either of the contestants to let it remain so for very long. It was therefore not surprising that, on the following day, the 15th Panzer Division returned to the field in an effort to complete the unfinished job. It attacked after a quiet morning (13 June) and the fighting flared up once again. As the combat grew in intensity and the decision hung in the balance, both the Allies and the Germans decided to throw their all into the battle. The Germans brought in their 21st Panzer Division and the Allies despatched the 22nd Armoured Brigade. Soon all the three armoured brigades of the Allies and the two Panzer Divisions of the Axis were irrevocably committed to a combat which was the culmination of the battle of the Gazala line.

The battle lasted till dusk and most of it was fought in the area of the ridges Maabus es Rigel and Hagiag er Raml. When the evening came it was found that the Axis had gained possession of both those ridges and the Allied armour had been forced off the battlefield. The net result of the battle was that the Allied tank force had become reduced to the ridiculous number of thirty cruiser and twenty infantry tanks and the German armour to about double that figure. But the Axis had an additional advantage in that they were in possession of the battlefield and could recover the damaged tanks from the area of fighting, for being put back into service again.

Decision to withdraw

The stage had now been reached when General Auchinleck was forced to take a decision whether or not to hold on to the Gazala line. Since the fall of Bir Hakeim, the line had been practically reduced to the Gazala—Alam Hamza position and its southward extensions, while the rest of it had ceased to exist more or less completely. The problem pressing for an immediate solution was, therefore, whether the Gazala—Alam Hamza position might or might not be abandoned wholly in view of the changed situation.

General Auchinleck was reluctant to abandon it. The position had a great tactical value in that it blocked the coastal road and thus denied to the Axis an easy access to their supplies while making their reinforcements slow at the same time. It would prove still more valuable at a future date when the Allies would be in a position to

[2] W/D. 29 Bde.

return to the offensive once more. But retaining this position meant defending the twenty-four-mile long southern flank between Gazala and Tobruk. The safety of this flank depended upon a strong armoured backing which no longer existed, and it would be some time before the armoured strength would be restored sufficiently for the purpose. But meanwhile some positions constituting the former Gazala line had become dangerously exposed and could not be left in that condition; while on the other hand there was a definite risk of at least two forward divisions being cut off their supply lines unless withdrawn promptly.

These forward divisions were the 1st South African and the 50th British Divisions. They were in the Gazala—Alam Hamza position. Were their supply line to be cut, their reserves would not last them beyond a week; and in that short period there was no chance of the Allied armoured strength being restored to the extent of being able to drive the Axis out of that area. Thus General Auchinleck had no choice but to agree with General Ritchie when the latter asked if he might withdraw the two threatened divisions immediately. Having received the permission, General Ritchie gave orders on 14 June for the 1st South African and the 50th British Divisions to be withdrawn from the Gazala—Alam Hamza area into reserve. The previous night, he had similarly ordered the 201st Guards Brigade, which had been garrisoning Knightsbridge and whose position had then become gravely exposed, to retire to Acroma. These steps meant the total abandonment and evacuation of the Gazala line.[3]

If the decision to withdraw from Gazala was difficult to take, the actual withdrawal was by no means any the easier. The 1st South African Division began the retirement at dusk on 14 June by taking the coastal road to the frontier via Tobruk. But the Axis decided to intercept the retreat and began a northward drive on the following day with a view to cutting the coastal road ahead of that South African Division. This move, however, was vigorously opposed by the few remaining Allied tanks as well as by the garrisons of Acroma and its satellite localities. In the seven hours of furious fighting which followed, these troops repulsed Axis tanks three times as many as theirs, with the loss of but one position. The 50th British Division also helped to cover the withdrawal and, with whatever help it was possible to give, the South African Division was at last enabled to reach the frontier in safety. But it was different with the 50th Division. This formation, which had already lost its 150th Infantry Brigade a fortnight earlier, had stayed behind to cover the withdrawal of the South Africans; and when

[3] Gen. Auchinleck's *Despatch* in Supplement to the *London Gazette*, 15 Jan. 1948, pp. 359-60.

it was time for it to leave, it could no longer use the coastal road but was obliged to cut across the desert south-eastwards, through the Axis-occupied territory. Nevertheless, a large proportion of its troops managed to reach the frontier safely before the midnight of 15 June, and that was the end of the Gazala line.

Next line of defence

The fall of Gazala brought two questions to the forefront. What was to be the fate of Tobruk and where was the next line of defence to be located? General Auchinleck was determined that the Eighth Army should not yield more ground than was absolutely necessary and it was on this basis that he took the decision regarding these two matters. He ordered General Ritchie not to let Tobruk become besieged, but to that end to hold a line through Acroma and El Adem and thence southwards, so as to fence off Tobruk. General Ritchie had taken steps to this effect even before receiving that order. He had decided to make a stand on the western perimeter of Tobruk through Acroma, El Adem and Belhamed, and to extend the line further south with a mobile force. The eastern perimeter was to be protected by the high ground near Gambut. Thus, not only was Tobruk to have a defence line to its west but it was to be virtually surrounded by a defensive ring, starting from Acroma, passing through El Adem and Belhamed, and terminating in the east on the high ground near Gambut, in the vicinity of which stood the headquarters of the Eighth Army.

Although the Eighth army had suffered heavy losses in the fighting on the Gazala line, it had not become quite incapable of defending Tobruk. The losses were chiefly among the armoured brigades; the infantry had fared better. Three infantry divisions and a brigade group had come out practically intact out of the original five divisions and two brigade groups. In addition there were several detached groups and units which could be organised into bigger groups or formations as might appear necessary.

Thus there were the 1st and 2nd South African Divisions; the 10th Indian Division which had lost only a field regiment and an infantry battalion; and the 11th Indian Infantry Brigade. Among the fragments of formations were the two brigade groups of the 50th Division and one of the 5th Indian Division. Of the motorised brigades, the 201st Guards and the 7th Motor Brigade were in fighting trim, and these were to be joined by the 3rd Indian Motor Brigade which was being reorganised for the purpose. Finally, a complete infantry division was due to arrive shortly, namely, the New Zealand Division which was moving down from Syria. Obviously, therefore, there was enough infantry available for providing a strong garrison for Tobruk and for maintaining a large enough force outside it to prevent its being besieged.[4]

The great desideratum, however, was the armour. The 1st Armoured Division had only about thirty runners left; and the 32nd Army Tank Brigade had no more than twenty-four. The only comparatively strong formation which remained, therefore, was the 4th Armoured Brigade which, after recoveries and repairs, could still count about sixty tanks. Thus the three formations together totalled over a hundred tanks which was hardly enough. But there were definite prospects of improvement in the number in the near future. A complete new formation was due to reach the front shortly. It was the 10th Armoured Division which, though still under training, was likely to add about ninety tanks to the Eighth Army's armoured force when ready. While this would give General Ritchie a slight superiority over General Rommel's armour, which too had become greatly depleted in the preceding battles, there was yet another source of possible reinforcement. There were about a hundred and fifty tanks of various types undergoing repairs in the Eighth Army's workshops, of which some at least could be put back into action in the immediate, foreseeable period.

Defence of Tobruk

But all this would take time, at least a few days if not weeks; and in the meantime it was vital that the Axis forces should be held. Tobruk might hold out but it was doubtful if it could be prevented from being besieged. Hitherto General Auchinleck had held the view that it was better to give up Tobruk and withdraw its garrison than permit a large bulk of troops to be isolated and immobilised by a siege. In arriving at this view he was not unappreciative of the part played by Tobruk the year before, but he believed that the changed situation called for a different approach. Now, however, he was willing to revise his view and accept a brief investment of Tobruk to gain a little time. He therefore telegraphed to General Ritchie on 16 June, that he did not mind taking the risk of a temporary isolation of Tobruk and that General Ritchie could therefore organise the garrison as he thought best.[5]

Already the garrison was being organised by General Gott who, the day before, had appointed Major-General Klopper to command the fortress. General Klopper, who was commanding the 2nd South African Division, was to defend Tobruk at all costs and to be prepared to hold it for some time. The troops assigned to him for the purpose consisted of three infantry brigades and a motor

---

[4] W/Ds. 10 Div., 5 Div., 11 Bde., 29 Bde., 3 Mot. Bde.
[5] Gen. Auchinleck's *Despatch* in Supplement to the *London Gazette*, 15 Jan. 1948, pp. 360-61.

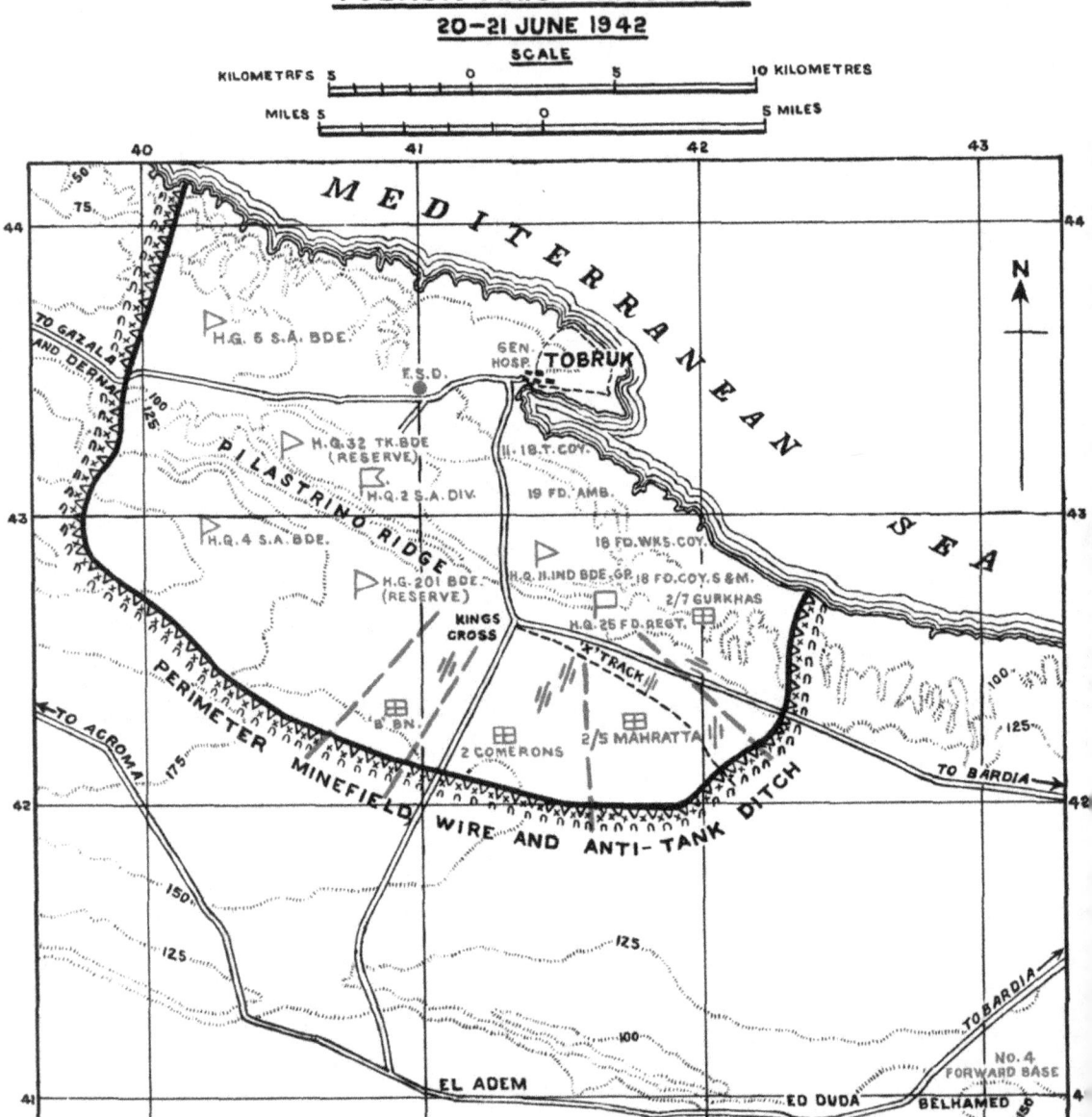

and an army tank brigade besides some anti-aircraft regiments. In all the forces were:—
- HQ 2nd South African Division
    - 4th South African Infantry Brigade
    - 6th South African Infantry Brigade
- HQ 201st Guards Brigade
    - 2 Coldstream Guards
    - 1 Sherwood Foresters, and elements of 1 Worcesters,
    - 11th Indian Infantry Brigade
    - 32nd Army Tank Brigade
    - 4th Anti-Aircraft Brigade
        - (less 18 guns), and
    - 83rd Sub-area Headquarters.

Of the above formations and units, the last three had been in Tobruk during the earlier siege and could therefore bring valuable experience to bear upon their task.

Tobruk was the responsibility of the XIII Corps and therefore of General Gott. During the Gazala fighting, the defence of the fortress and of the coastal area between the fort and the rear of the Gazala position had been assigned by him to General Klopper who had been commanding the 2nd South African Division since 15 May and had his headquarters in Tobruk. General Gott remained for two days in Tobruk, (15-16 June), to help organise the defences. Before he left, he gave a series of instructions to General Klopper which threw no light burden on the latter.

According to those instructions General Klopper was to hold Tobruk for as long as might be required. In addition, he was to offer vigorous opposition to the Axis outside the defences of the fortress also. Next, he was to take care of his own landward communications and keep them open by co-operating with the mobile columns to the south; and finally, if Belhamed fell, he was to provide a force of all arms to recapture it in conjunction with the XXX Corps. He had the discretion to withdraw from Tobruk if he found the situation too critical, but it was hoped that such a step would never become necessary.

Prior to the evacuation of Gazala, it had suffered to defend Tobruk with defences sited only on the western and south-western faces of the perimeter. Now all sections of the perimeter had to be guarded equally and the defences had to be readjusted accordingly. The perimeter of Tobruk consisted of a series of mutually supporting posts, each mined and wired, and was divided into three sectors, the western, southern and eastern. Of these the first two sectors were held by the 6th and 4th African Brigades respectively and the third, viz the eastern sector, by the 11th Indian Infantry Brigade. All the three sectors were allotted roughly equal proportions of the available field artillery, as also of the anti-tank guns which were mostly sited close to the perimeter. The 32nd Army Tank Brigade and the 201st Guards Brigade formed the fortress reserve. Of the tank forces which consisted of the 4th and the 7th Royal Tank Regiments, the former was located at the junction of the Bardia and El Adem roads, known as Kings Cross, and the latter near Pilastrino, with one squadron north of the Derna road.

The 11th Brigade in Tobruk

The eastern sector occupied by the 11th Indian Infantry Brigade extended from the El Adem road to the coast and covered a frontage of approximately 13 miles, exclusive of the coastline. The brigade, commanded by Brigadier A. Anderson, took charge of this sector on 6 June, when it consisted of the following principal units:—

Brigade HQ
K Signal Section (Indian)
2 Cameron Highlanders
2/5 Mahratta Light Infantry
2/7 Gurkha Rifles
25th Field Regiment RA
18th Field Company S & M
18th Field Workshop Company IAOC
11th Infantry Brigade Transport Company RIASC
19th Field Ambulance (Indian)
11th Brigade Anti-tank Company (Bofors)
11th Brigade Medium-Machine-Gun Company (Indian), and
a Composite Infantry Battalion (3 South African Companies).

The Composite Battalion in this order of battle, was named the "B" Battalion. It consisted of three rifle companies from the 1st South African Division and was commanded by Lieut-Col. De Beer. It came under the command of the 11th Brigade on 8 June and the original idea was to turn it into a brigade reserve. But the battalion was unable to fulfil that role as it had no transport and was almost completely immobile. It was therefore given a portion of the perimeter defences to the west of the El Adem road, between 2 Camerons and the 4th South African Brigade, which stretch of the front it was to defend in a static role.[6]

The state of defences in the eastern sector was far from satisfactory when the 11th Indian Infantry Brigade took over on 6 June. Portions of the minefields were non-existent, because some time earlier large quantities of mines had been removed and taken forward to strengthen Gazala line, and these had never been

[6] *Diary of Events in Tobruk* by 11 Bde., pp. 6-10; W/Ds. 11 Bde., 2/5 Mahrattas, 2/7 GR.

replaced. Even the mines that were there were mostly of the Egyptian pattern. They had been laid there a year previously and during that period many of them had become defective. As was proved later they were hardly any obstacle to the attacking troops. This state of affairs was the result not so much of negligence on the part of troops as of what might be called the vacillation of the high command. At first it had been given out emphatically that Tobruk was not to be held in the event of a withdrawal from the Gazala line; then the decision was suddenly reversed. The consequence was that the defences, which were not actually occupied by troops, were hardly given any attention. However, now it was the task of the 11th Indian Infantry Brigade to bring back the defences into their proper shape. It was estimated that 20,000 mines would be required to put the inner and outer perimeters into a reasonable state of defence; but only 4,000 were actually available. The best that could be done with them was done, that is, they were laid on the perimeter, giving a greater measure of protection to the infantry posts and anti-tank guns than to the other units or locations.

From 6 to 13 June, the 11th Indian Brigade occupied itself with repairing and improving defences, training on 2-pounder anti-tank guns and spigot mortars, and sending out mobile columns or patrols to help in the defence of Bir Hakeim. Then on the night of 13/14 June began the evacuation of the Gazala line; and the danger of isolation and attack drew ever nearer. Soon after, troops of the Indian Brigade witnessed the withdrawal of the 1st South African and the 50th British Divisions through Tobruk, and the departure of the rear headquarters of the XIII Corps the same night, which could have left them in little doubt as to the seriousness of the situation.

On the following day, 14 June, the commander of the 2nd South African Division, the principal formation constituting the garrison of Tobruk, held a conference at his headquarters, which was followed by an administrative conference. Some of the facts made known at these meetings were that there were dumps of supplies in Tobruk capable of lasting for three months, but that there would be no shipping to and from Tobruk; and that there was a great shortage of ammunition in the perimeter but that efforts were being made to remedy this by opening a new line of communication between Maddalena and El Gubi. It was expected that an armoured force would be able to achieve this by operating from El Gubi to the perimeter of Tobruk. After this the garrison set itself to adjust its defences to the existing supply situation. The supply dumps were redistributed so as to spread them over the three brigade sectors, and the artillery was rationed to a daily minimum of ammunition, the 4.5 guns for instance being allotted no more than three rounds per gun per day. The situation however improved a little later, when a convoy of ammunition arrived in "A" Lighters.[7]

On the same day, 14 June, the Tobruk garrison received an unexpected reinforcement of about 250 personnel. A German convoy, carrying Allied prisoners of war, was driving past Acroma towards the Derna road. It was fired on and stopped by the South African garrison of Acroma, and about 250 prisoners were released who were sent to Tobruk. The Indian personnel of the rescued party were handed over to the 11th Indian Infantry Brigade who organised them into platoons, armed them with rifles and put them on the coast-watching duties. As these duties were hitherto being performed by parties from the 2/7th Gurkha Battalion, this had the salutary effect of releasing the Gurkha personnel for the more important duties of defending the perimeter.

Attacks on El Adem, Acroma and Sidi Rezegh

Defence of the perimeter was hereafter the all-important job in Tobruk, since the encirclement of that fortress had already begun. The Axis forces were in a position to strike at Acroma, El Adem or Belhamed as they wished, any of which could give them an easy access to Tobruk. Leaving Acroma in peace for the time being, they turned their attention to El Adem on 15 June, projecting strong feeler-patrols at the same time towards Belhamed and Sidi Rezegh. El Adem was attacked three times that day by the 90th Light Division, supported by tanks. But all the attacks were repulsed by the 29th Indian Infantry Brigade with the help of the 7th (British) Motor Brigade from the south and the 11th Indian Infantry Brigade from the north, and with generous and effective support from the air force.[8]

Thus frustrated, the Axis commander tried another move the next day. He split his armour into two, and on 16 June sent one part to attack Acroma and the other to take Sidi Rezegh. The group that went to Acroma was the 15th Panzer Division and the other one was the 21st Panzer Division. At this time Sidi Rezegh was being guarded by a single battalion of the 20th Indian Infantry Brigade and the way to it was through the valley surrounding El Adem. The whole of the 21st Panzer Division could not traverse this valley without being detected and engaged by the Allied troops *en route*. The Panzer Division therefore sent out only a detachment. This little force slipped through successfully and was about

---

[7] *Diary of Events in Tobruk* by 11 Bde.
[8] Gen. Auchinleck's *Despatch* in Supplement to the *London Gazette*, 15 Jan. 1948, p. 360,

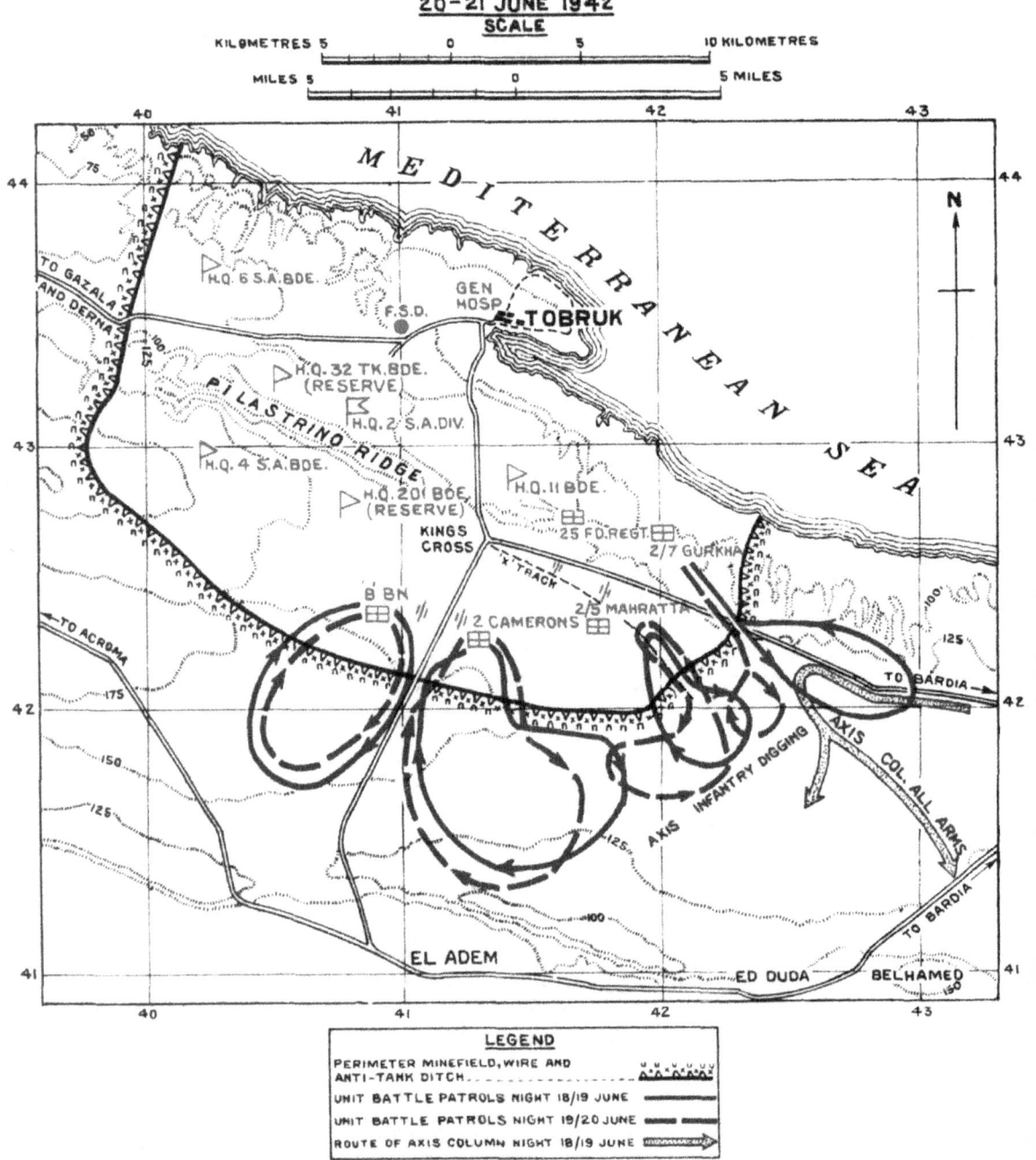

to attack the single battalion at Sidi Rezegh when it was dispersed by bombing and artillery fire as it was forming up.[9]

Threat to Tobruk increases

But this was only a minor setback and did not influence the Axis plans. The main body of the 21st Panzer Division now began to move down the valley towards Sidi Rezegh, while, to divert attention from this move, the 90th Light Division made a feint towards El Adem. In spite of this latter distraction, the main columns from Tobruk and tanks of the 4h Armoured Brigade succeeded in keeping their attacks concentrated on the Panzers moving through the valley. But they were too few and weak to be able to achieve much and it soon became obvious that Sidi Rezegh would not be able to withstand an attack from the armour that had managed to get through in considerable bulk in spite of those fierce attacks. As the safety of El Adem was dependent upon that of Sidi Rezegh, and as it too was being menaced by the 90th Light Division, General Ritchie reluctantly decided to give up El Adem. Accordingly, the 29th Indian Infantry Brigade was withdrawn on the night of 16 June, except for one battalion and a battery of artillery both of which fought their way into Tobruk. Sidi Rezegh fell the next day, leaving a big gap in the defensive ring round Tobruk.[10]

Tobruk was now in greater danger of isolation than ever before. But so long as Belhamed held out, and the high ground near Gambut was in Allied hands, it would continue to have a link with the Eighth Army through the Bardia road. Belhamed, at this time, was being guarded by the 20th Indian Infantry Brigade less the single battalion that had been defeated at Sidi Rezegh. The high ground near Gambut was occupied by the 21st Indian and the 2nd Free French Brigades. The only tank force available for support to these infantry formations was the 4th Armoured Brigade with sixty tanks and one more squadron operating with the 7th (British) Motor Brigade. Of the remaining tanks of the Eighth army, some were tied up on the frontier, while the rest were in the workshops or in the course of delivery. All therefore depended on whether, and how far, the sixty tanks of the 4th Armoured Brigade would be able to hold back the 21st Panzer Division.

At this distance of time the result would seem a foregone conclusion, but it was perhaps not so obvious to those who were then too near the events and were observing them from the edge of the battlefield. The Panzer Division with a force of about one hundred

---

[9] W/Ds. 10 Div., 5 Div., 20 Bde.
[10] W/Ds. 10 Div., 5 Div., 29 Bde.

and twenty tanks struck on 17 June. The 4th Armoured Brigade reeled under the blow and staggered back to Gambut, having lost all but twenty of its tanks. Momentarily at least, the Eighth Army was now without a tank force and Belhamed was in worse danger than before.[11]

It will be recalled that the commander of the Tobruk fortress, General Klopper, had earlier received instructions that if Belhamed fell, he was to provide a force of all arms to recapture it in conjunction with the XXX Corps. But the Eighth Army now decided to evacuate Belhamed which relieved the Tobruk garrison of its obligation. The 20th Indian Infanty Brigade withdrew on the night of 17 June and the danger to Tobruk drew one step nearer. Worse still, Gambut too had to be evacuated the same night due to lack of armour to defend it, which was another great blow for Tobruk, as it involved the loss of the landing ground from where fighter aircraft could support its garrison.[12]

The Axis forces arrived at Gambut the following day, 18 June, and cut off a battalion of the 20th Indian Infantry Brigade which was acting as a rearguard. It was a question now, whether General Rommel would return west to reduce Tobruk or proceed east to invade Egypt. At the headquarters of the Eighth Army it was felt that he would not risk invading Egypt so long as Tobruk held out. The prophecy proved correct, for after occupying Gambut, the Axis forces turned back on 19 June and proceeded towards Tobruk. The expected attack on that fortress began on 20 June.[13]

Meanwhile, inside the Tobruk fortress preparations had been going apace to meet the inevitable assault. The garrison had continued to receive some scattered reinforcements between 15 and 20 June. First, on the fall of El Adem, a detached battalion of the 29th Indian Infantry Brigade had found its way into Tobruk with a battery of field artillery. Next, two mobile columns which had been sent out of the perimeter on aggressive patrolling had returned intact, which had added greatly to the anti-tank and artillery defences. Finally, on 18 June, the garrison of what was known as the 'Acroma Keep' had been withdrawn into Tobruk, which released a proportion of medium artillery for other tasks. On the other hand some unwanted troops were evacuated; and from 17 June onwards, all the gaps in the perimeter minefields had been closed with G. S. mines, but were opened daily to allow the patrols in and out. All the bits of reinforcements mentioned above had been placed in the 11th Indian Infantry Brigade sector. At the same

---

[11] W/Ds. 5 Div., 10 Div., 20 Bde., 21 Bde.
[12] *Diary of Events in Tobruk* by 11 Bde., p. 10.
[13] Gen. Auchinleck's *Despatch* in Supplement to the *London Gazette*, 15 Jan. 1948, pp. 361.

time all medium artillery had been withdrawn from this sector, leaving the brigade with one South African field battery and two 25-pounder batteries of the 25th Field Regiment.[14]

The main activity of the 11th Indian Infantry Brigade during this period was sending out battle-patrols every night, that being the only way of keeping an effective vigil on the outer edge of the perimeter. The task of these patrols was to prevent the massing of the Axis forces within a fighting distance of the perimeter. The battle-patrols harassed and dispersed such concentrations themselves, or called for artillery fire. In any event they were unable to detect any pronounced concentration until the night of 18/19 June. That night, Axis activity seemed to have increased considerably in the sector of 2/5th Mahrattas. Sounds of tracked vehicles moving towards Tobruk, from the Belhamed direction, were heard and digging was reported on a broader front. The usual harassing battle was offered, and sporadic fighting went on throughout the night but failed to check the Axis activities.[15]

During the day of 19 June, further efforts were made by the 11th Indian Infantry Brigade to prevent the hostile force from forming up. Armoured observation posts of the artillery moved out at first light and directed the fire of the 25-pounders on groups of Axis troops, while a battery from the Divisional Reserve also moved up to assist. Whether due to this effort, or whether for reasons of their own convenience, the Axis force made no move whatever during that day. But the commander of the 11th Brigade realised that it would certainly make an effort to assemble more troops during the night and that it was necessary to prevent this. He, therefore, decided to send out strong patrols that night from the 2/5th Mahrattas and the 2/7th Gurkhas, while the 2nd Camerons and the "Beer" Battalion undertook to send similar patrols to the south to keep the Axis off the El Adem road. The plans for this crucial night were co-ordinated and finalised at a conference of the unit and patrol commanders, which met at the Brigade Headquarters during the day.

After the evening "stand to", the patrols moved out and returned at first light on 20 June. The 2nd Camerons and the "Beer" Battalion reported complete absence of Axis troops in their respective areas. But the 2/5th Mahrattas and the 2/7th Gurkhas had a different story to tell. They had located Axis troops in the same position as on the previous night, that is about one mile from the centre of the Mahratta's position, towards the south-east; and they confirmed the preceding night's reports, namely further digging on a broad front and more sounds of tracked vehicles moving towards

[14] *Diary of Events in Tobruk* by 11 Bde., pp. 9 & 10.
[15] W/Ds. 11 Bde., 2/5 Mahrattas, 2/7 GR.

Tobruk. Once again there had been an all-night intermittent fighting as the Indian patrols engaged the Axis troops in harassing clashes.

The same day an early morning message was received from the Divisional Commander giving the garrison the general warning that an attack on Tobruk during the day was considered highly probable. The message gave no indication as to where the attack was most likely to develop; but from the defensive preparations made, it would appear that it was to be expected to come from the south-west. Whatever the Divisional Commander's reasons for thinking so, the commander of the 11th Indian Infantry Brigade could not overlook the fact that signs were not wanting of a possible thrust towards his side of the perimeter. Axis troops had been perseveringly concentrating, for the last two nights, to the south-east of the 2/5th Mahrattas and there were no anti-tank ditches between the Mahrattas and the 2nd Camerons. It was therefore to be expected that some attack, if not the main one, would be launched against the 11th Indian Infantry Brigade. The anticipation proved well founded. The main attack did after all fall on the Mahratta sector, that is, it came from the south-east of the Tobruk perimeter and not from the south-west where the maximum defensive preparations were being made.

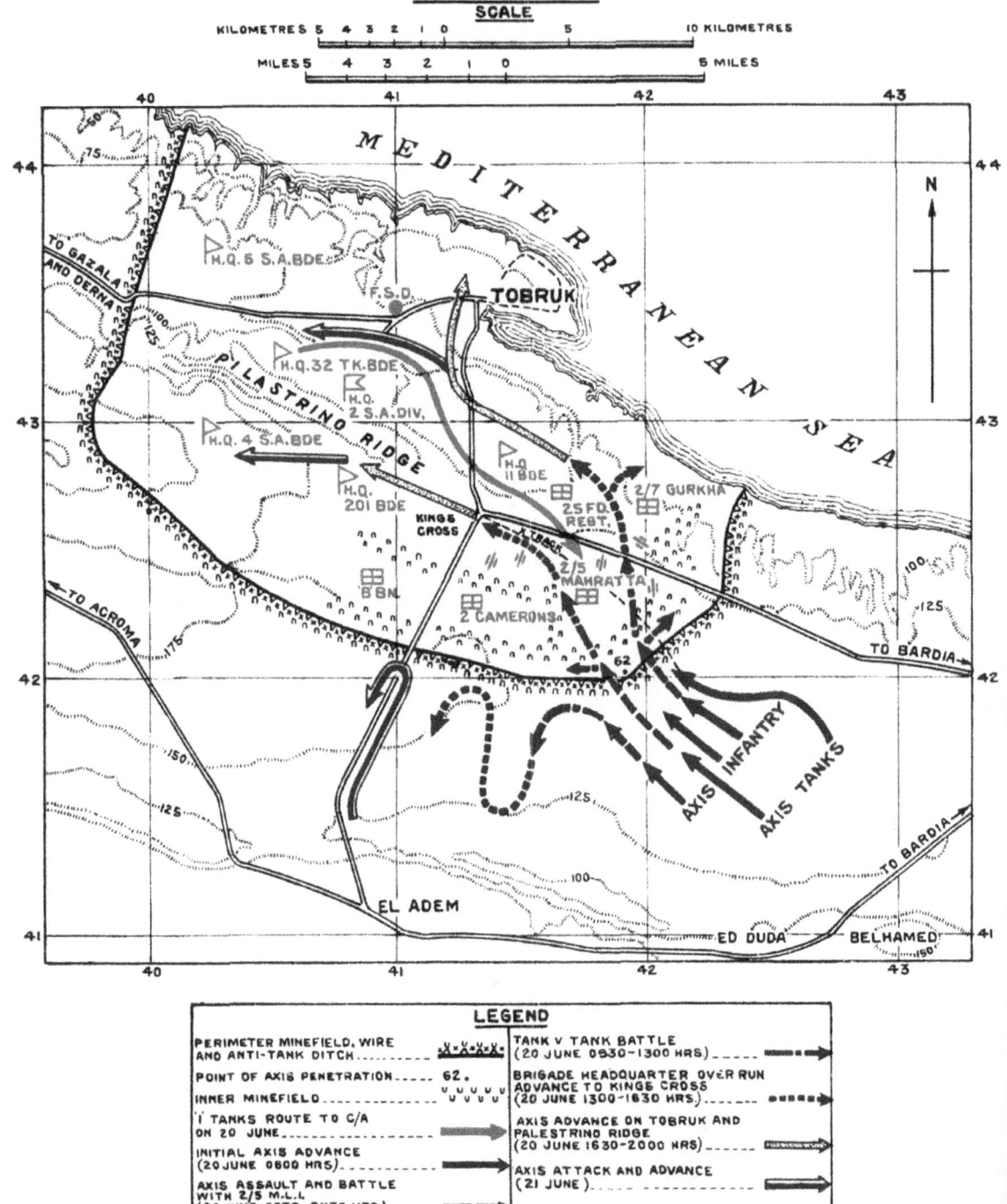

CHAPTER XXXV

Attack on Tobruk

The attack on Tobruk opened at 0600 hours on 20 June with a heavy dive-bombing and artillery assault in the sector of the 11th Indian Infantry Brigade. Stukas bombed the front of 2 Camerons and of 2/5th Mahrattas, the bombing being closely followed up by an artillery concentration of high explosive and smoke shells in both those areas. At first the air attacks were confined to the forward posts and the gun positions in their immediate rear. But later the action was extended to cover the whole fortress. The Axis aircraft had the mastery of the area, since the Allied aircraft, which had been withdrawn from the Gambut airfield, were in the process of occupying the new landing grounds, and were therefore not in a position to intervene just then. However, the anti-aircraft artillery and the small arms of the various units went into action immediately and succeeded in bringing three aircraft down during the day.[1]

From 0600 to 0630 hours, the Axis troops continued to draw nearer to the perimeter of the Indian brigade's sector, covered by air and artillery bombardment and an excellent smoke screen. At 0630 hours they attacked the outer perimeter, the attacking troops being the 21st Panzer Division, the 90th Light Division and a new special German infantry brigade, known as *Sonderverbund*. It was the *Sonderverbund* who first began the operations by edging up to the perimeter and making gaps in the minefield; after which came the 21st Panzers with Mark III and Mark IV tanks, followed last of all by the motorised 90th Division whose function it seemed was to clear the battlefield of the isolated points of resistance. The initial break-through had taken place on the front of the 2/5th Mahrattas at defence post No. 62 in the outer perimeter. Later an offshoot of this penetrating force proceeded towards the left flank of 2 Camerons, where no anti-tank ditch existed. Having done this, it extended itself further towards the El Adem road which brought it right opposite to the Cameron's sector.

As to the Mahrattas, the first half hour's artillery concentration on their forward posts had cut the communications between their advanced companies and their battalion headquarters. This had happened at 0640 hours, just as the German infantry had begun to attack. At this, the battalion commander, not being able to communicate with his forward units, engaged the attacking troops with

[1] W/Ds. 11 Bde., 2/5 Mahrattas, 2/7 GR

his own reserve company and carrier platoon, being assisted from his left by the carrier platoon of the 2/7th Gurkhas. This bold counter-attack actually achieved more than was hoped for and did finally succeed in stopping the German infantry, which had by then advanced to within 400 yards of the battalion headquarters. But this had been possible more or less because until then no Axis tank had entered the perimeter.

At this stage the Divisional Commander, struck by the gravity of the situation in his eastern sector, decided to intervene with his divisional reserve. He personally rang up the 11th Indian Infantry Brigade and informed its commander that he was despatching a force of infantry, tanks and guns to assist him in restoring the situation. The force thus ordered to proceed consisted of two infantry companies of the Coldstream Guards, the 4th Battalion "I" tanks and a platoon of anti-tank guns. The commander of the "I" tanks who had been appointed to command the whole force, had been ordered to take his instructions from the brigade commander, after contacting the Indian brigade. At the same time on the 11th Brigade side, arrangements had been made to send a party of liaison officers or guides, to meet the advancing force halfway and to guide it to a specific rendezvous, which was fixed to be just behind the headquarters of the 2/5th Mahrattas. Immediately on the arrival of the force at this spot, the officer-commanding of the Mahrattas was to acquaint the commander of the new force with the situation on the ground and tell him of the plan of action for restoring the situation.

This plan was simple. The Axis armour had not arrived on the spot so far, and only the infantry had penetrated the perimeter by opening a gap in the minefield with their own hands. The plan therefore aimed simply at driving the Axis infantry back through the gap and then closing the breach with the mines once again. This was to be done by the tank battalion pushing the Axis infantry through the opening, after which the anti-tank platoon, assisted by the infantry detachment of the Coldstream Guards, was to 'plug' the gap, that is to hold the German infantry outside it by its fire. The gap was then to be re-mined during that period by the sappers and miners of the 18th Field Company, who were being held in readiness for the task.[2]

Had the detachment of the divisional reserve arrived in time, or even an hour earlier than it did, the gap would have been closed in all probability as intended. But that force did not commence arriving until 2½ hours after it had been ordered out of the divisional area; and then only the tanks made their appearance. The two companies of the Coldstream Guards and the anti-tank

[2] W/Ds. 11 Bde., 2/5 Mahrattas, 18 Fd Coy

platoon failed to arrive altogether. According to a brigade officer, who later compiled a diary of these events, these units "escaped from Tobruk" when they ought to be making their way to the area of fighting. The tanks, too, had not come in full strength, but began to dribble in from 0930 onwards in small batches. Worse still, the tank commander did not present himself personally or even send his representative to the headquarters of the 11th Indian Infantry Brigade, as had been aranged, with the result that he could not be acquainted with the general situation or the plan of action.

2/5 Mahrattas versus Sonderverbund

All through this time, from 0700 hours to 0930 hours, the Mahrattas continued to fight a gruelling battle against the *Sonderverbund* troops. In this they had the stout comradeship and help of the 25th Field Regiment RA. An additional South African 25-pounder battery and a troop of anti-tank guns also arrived to offer support, and were sited north of the Bardia road to stop any northward penetration. The situation did not look very gloomy at 0930 hours, as the "I" tanks were arriving in increasing numbers and soon they would be rolling back the *Sonderverbunds*. But just at that point a piece of bad news reached the Mahratta headquarters. The observation post of the 25th Field Regiment reported that 40 German tanks, Mark III and Mark IV, had entered the gap in the perimeter. Ten were moving east, ten west and twenty north towards the headquarters of the Mahratta battalion. This meant that the situation had changed radically and the old plan would not work. It was no longer a matter of "I" tanks fighting it out with the German infantry. The battle would now be one of tanks versus tanks.

The German tanks, equipped with heavier guns than those of the Allies, at once picked out the few "I" tanks and engaged them in action. That probably was the reason why the tank commander had not been able to report at the headquarters of the 11th Indian Infantry Brigade or send his officer. At the same time the officer-commanding the 2/5th Mahrattas reported to his brigade that his headquarters was about to be overrun by the German tanks and that he was destroying his wireless set. This was the last communication received from this unit. No message was ever received from the commander of the "I" tank battalion; but another tank unit, the 7th Infantry Tank Battalion, which was in divisional reserve, reported that most of the 4th Battalion's tanks were already in the forward-most area, having taken up "hull down" position on the line, where it was intended to stop the Axis tanks. At that moment, the 25-pounders and anti-tank guns had been trying hard to check the advance of the Axis tanks towards that line.

While this artillery versus tanks battle was in progress, the 7th "I" Tank Battalion proceeded to King's Cross, where it took up a position intended to block all Axis moves towards the Tobruk harbour or towards the west. One of its squadrons was posted to the rear of the Camerons to prevent any possible westward advance from the south of King's Cross. At the same time the artillery observation post reported that another batch of 20 Axis tanks had entered the gap, making a total of 60 inside the perimeter. These new entrants were moving northwards against the 31st Battery of the 25th Field Regiment and in the direction of the "I" tanks stationed a little beyond.[3]

So far, the Axis tanks had left the eastern sector of the perimeter alone. This sector was being held by the 2/7th Gurkhas, and through the centre of it ran the Bardia road, which proceeded to King's Cross and thence north to Tobruk. Prior to the German attack, the Bardia road used to be opened and closed daily for inward and outward traffic by lifting the mines and replacing them. But this process applied only to the outer minefield. The inner minefield had a permanently open gap in front of the position of the 2/7th Gurkhas. Now, to avoid the danger of the German tanks using the gap for making a short cut to the Tobruk harbour, or to King's Cross, the gap was ordered to be closed up. Up to this time, that is 1200 hours on 20 June, no ground attack had been made either on the 2/7th Gurkhas or on the "Beer" Battalion.

Resistance by 2/7 Gurkhas

At about the same time, however, the artillery observation post reported that most of the "I" tanks appeared to be withdrawing northwards, chased by the Axis tanks. This proved to be the last report from this post which was now cut off by the advancing Axis force. The loss of that post was a great blow to the division as it had been the division's main source of information during the battle. Soon after this, the greater part of the 25th Field Regiment was overrun by a further advance, and its headquarters ceased to function at about 1345 hours. In the meantime, German infantry and tanks had started a general move towards the Bardia road and had entered the sector of the 2/7th Gurkhas from the rear of that battalion. As a result, the Gurkhas and the 18th Field Company Sappers and Miners were cut off from the rest of the Tobruk garrison. Nevertheless the Gurkha battalion reacted fiercely and a battle followed which lasted for several hours. The Gurkhas fought to the last and had to be rooted out platoon by platoon, while the 18th Field Company set fire to all its vehicles

[3] W/Ds. 11 Bde., 2/7 GR, 18 Fd Coy

with its own anti-tank mines and then surrendered to the overwhelming force. The only units left thereafter in the Indian brigade's sector were the Camerons, the "Beer" Battalion and the Brigade Headquarters.[4]

It was not long, however, before the Brigade Headquarters too was overrun. By 1400 hours the Indian brigade had lost its communication links by line telegraphy with all its units. But the wireless link had continued to function to the last, except with the 2/5th Mahrattas; and it was through that link that a message was received soon after 1400 hours warning the Indian brigade that the Axis tanks were moving directly towards its headquarters. It appears that the German tanks had split themselves into two parties after finishing the battle astride the Bardia road and both groups had moved north-west, one keeping to the south of the Bardia road and the other to its north. The Headquarters of the 11th Indian Infantry Brigade, which lay in the path of the latter, moved into a wadi in its rear, to avoid being captured, leaving its Protective Platoon in battle positions and hoping to return to its former location as soon as the Axis tanks had passed on. Care was taken, however, before doing so, to burn all documents and destroy as much equipment as possible including the wireless set.

The Axis tanks reached the Indian brigade's location a little after 1400 hours and occupied the ground. The brigade's personnel who had moved to the wadi could see no hope of being able to return to their former location and the Brigade Commander therefore decided to establish new headquarters to the south of Tobruk. All personnel were organised into parties and told to make their way to a given point, while the Brigade Commander himself, with one staff officer, proceeded to the divisional headquarters to meet the Divisional Commander and acquaint him with the situation. As a result of this conference the brigade's tactical headquarters was made to move to the escarpment, near to the site of the divisional headquarters, so that the former might be able to make use of the latter's means of communication, although the only units with which the brigade would now need any communication were the Camerons and the "Beer" Battalion. Both these units had already moved their headquarters nearer the edge of their perimeters in order to be in a better position to evacuate, should the Tobruk garrison be obliged to capitulate.

Having conferred with the Divisional Commander, the Brigade Commander returned to his main headquarters, making a reconnaissance of the forward area on the way. He found that a large number of German tanks were operating in the area of King's Cross, which was not far from the Tobruk harbour. Yet he did

[4] *Ibid.*

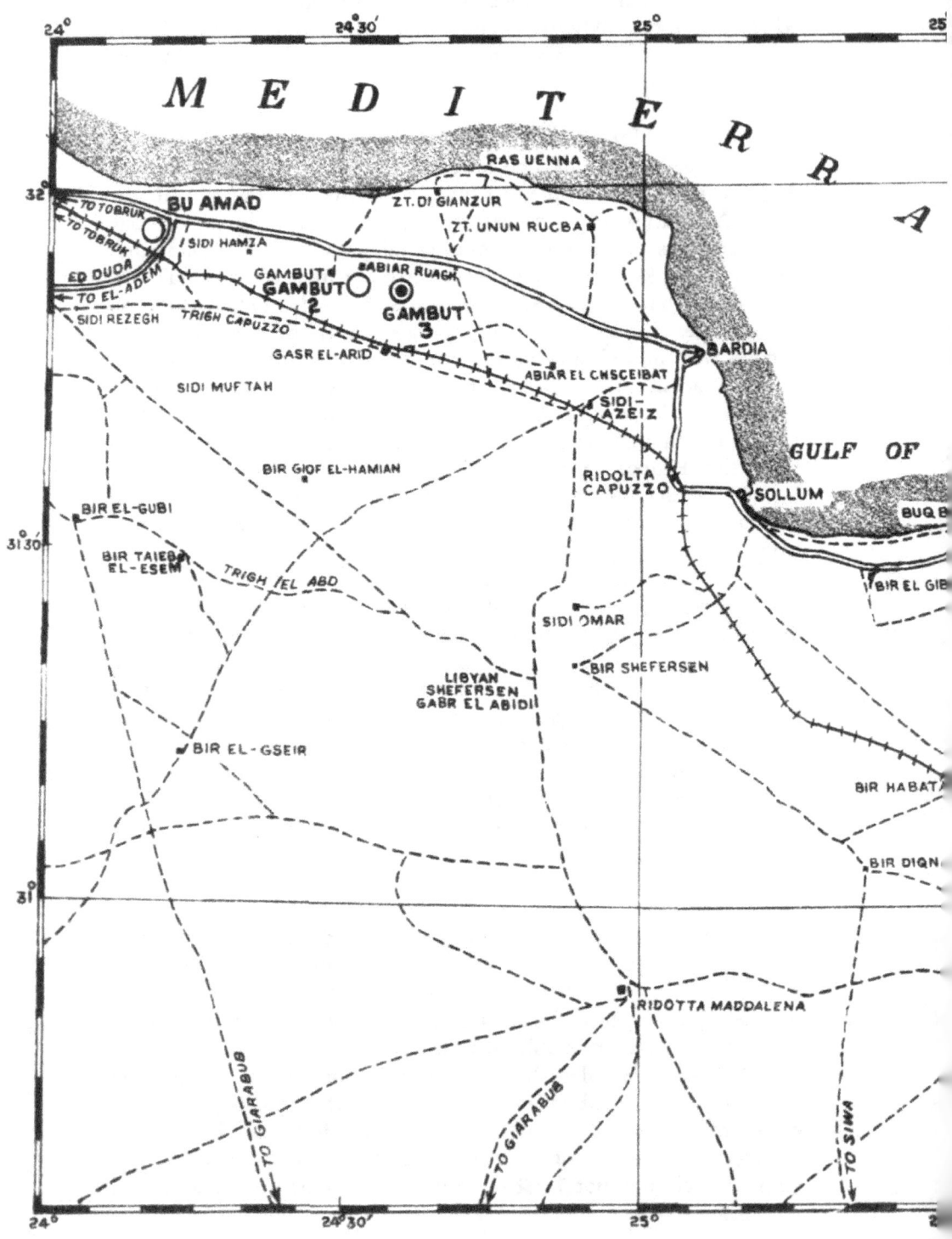

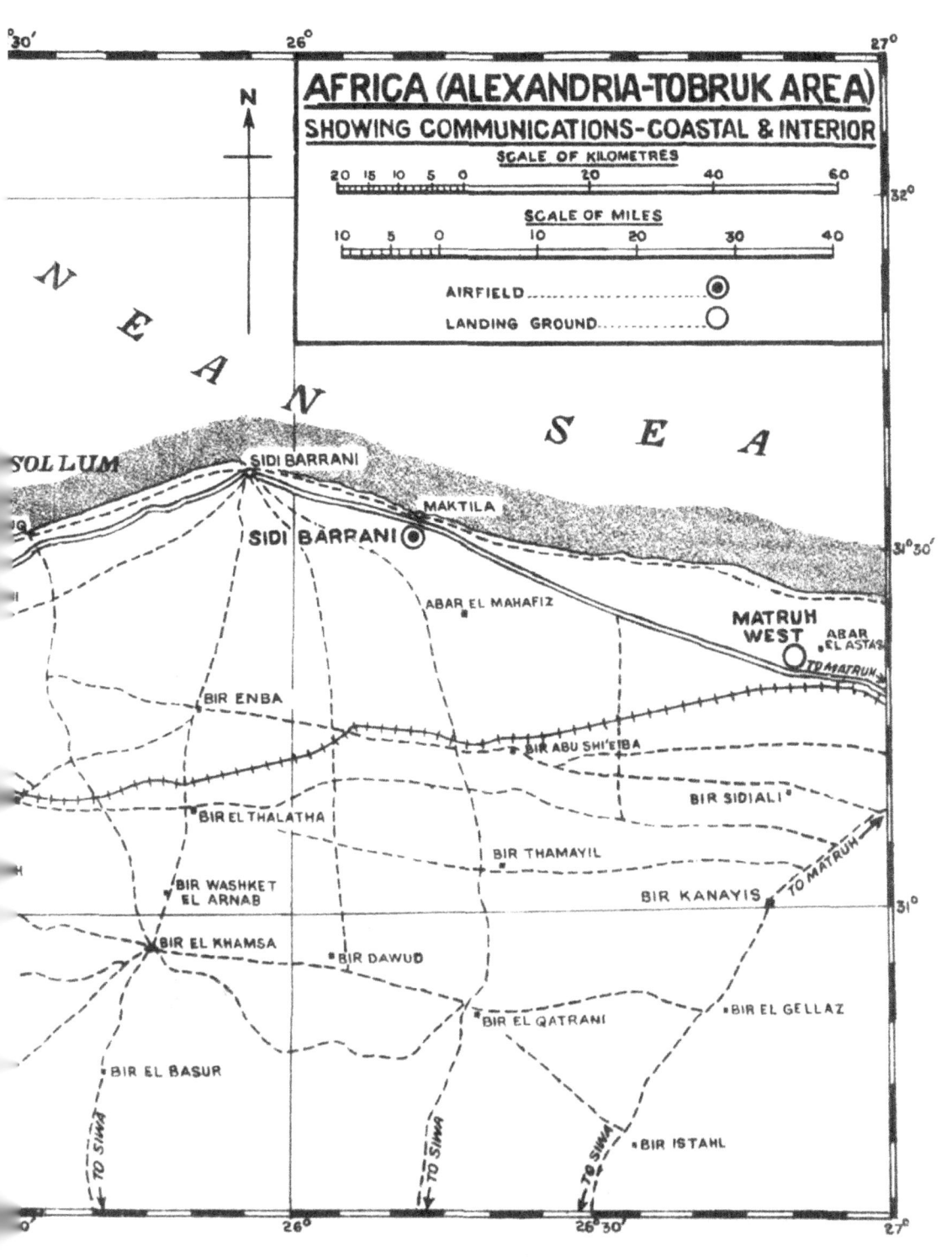

not see any sign of giving in on the part of the Allied troops. Fighting units did not withdraw on the approach of large numbers of tanks or infantry, but remained in their positions to the last. On the contrary, many riflemen from various unit headquarters, and some of the 25-pounder guns, were seen moving deliberately towards the area of the fighting near King's Cross.

The battle at King's Cross continued until 1800 hours. It will be recalled that earlier the German tanks had split themselves into two roughly parallel columns, one of which had begun moving along the north of the Bardia road and the other along its south. The fighting at King's Cross was done mostly by this southern column. Taking advantage of this, the northern column had started heading for the Tobruk harbour. In its anxiety to reach the harbour before the night, the column, it appears, tried to take the Gubi landing-ground in its stride and paid dearly for the attempt. For, the heavy anti-aircraft guns of this landing strip, lowering their barrels and attacking in an anti-tank role, caused great damage to the advancing armour. Nevertheless a large number of tanks were able to dodge the guns and proceed northward, and these reached and occupied the Tobruk harbour at 2000 hours in the evening of 20 June.

While the harbour of Tobruk was being thus threatened by the northern column of the German tanks, the Divisional Headquarters which was to the south-west of the harbour, and not very far from it, appeared to be in the double danger of being caught between both the northern and the southern columns. It therefore moved to the comparatively safer area of the 6th South African Brigade, in the north-west corner of the perimeter, where it reopened at 1830 hours, being joined there an hour later by the tactical headquarters of the 11th Indian Infantry Brigade.

Re-appreciation of the situation

After reaching the town of Tobruk, the Germans halted for the night, which provided General Klopper with a valuable opportunity for analysing the situation and re-grouping his remaining force. The situation was not altogether desperate; the loss of the town and harbour of Tobruk was not a serious matter in itself, as there had never been an intention of using the harbour to supply the garrison. The fortress had within it dumps of supplies capable of lasting it for three months, many of which were still intact, including the main Field Supply Depot. The Germans had so far overrun only the eastern sector of the perimeter. The western and southern sectors, as well as a small part of the eastern sector, had not even been touched. In those last named sectors, the following troops still remained in action:—

HQ 2nd South African Division
    4th South African Brigade Group
    6th South African Brigade Group
    Sherwood Foresters ⎱ 201 Brigade
    Worcestershire Regiment ⎰
    2 Camerons ⎱ 11 Brigade
    'B' Battalion ⎰
    11th Indian Brigade MT Coy
    11th Indian Brigade Tac HQ
HQ 32nd Army Tank Brigade, and
    About 50% Divisional artillery.

The principal losses so far had been the infantry battalions of the 2/5th Mahrattas and 2/7th Gurkhas, the 25th Field Regiment RA, and the 4th and 7th Infantry Tank Battalions. Thus, while there still existed a remote possibility of saving Tobruk, the scales were nevertheless weighed heavily in favour of the Germans; and the Eighth Army found itself faced with the grave necessity of choosing between the alternatives of saving the remaining garrison of Tobruk by withdrawing them during the night, or advising them to hold on, thus risking their complete destruction.

On that fateful night, General Klopper got into wireless communication with the Army Commander and after reporting the situation sought his instructions. There was a discussion over the W/T on the relative chances of breaking out or fighting on, and the decision eventually taken was to fight on, forming a new front line. The new line was to be roughly: west of Tobruk—west of King's Cross—east of the area of 2 Camerons. This was just about the course followed by the El Adem—Tobruk road, which had the effect of dividing the Tobruk perimeter into approximately equal halves, the eastern half now being under German occupation and the western half in Allied hands.[5]

The inevitable decision

In not opposing the decision to fight on, General Klopper was probably influenced by the fact that breaking out was no easy proposition. Practically all his transport had been cut off in the Tobruk harbour and there was a great shortage of the lifting vehicles that would be necessary for a break-out. Besides, the Army Commander had ordered the 7th Armoured Division to advance on Tobruk and there was some reason for hoping that this might compel the Germans to withdraw from the perimeter. But the progress of the Armoured Division was slow and the resolution to hold out weakened during the night, both at the Army and Divisional Headquarters. At 0430 hours on 21 June, therefore, when the

[5] *Ibid.*

Brigade Major of the 11th Indian Brigade visited the Divisional Headquarters for the latest information, he was told that the Divisional Commander had decided to capitulate. The reason given was that certain information had been received during the night, which, in the opinion of the Divisional Commander, made it impracticable to hold out. This information was probably nothing more than a false report received at the headquarters that the 2nd Camerons had been overrun.[6]

Before this decision had been taken, the Army Commander had authorised General Klopper to break out if he could, and had informed him that an attempt would be made to hold open a gap between El Adem and Knightsbridge. But General Klopper found breaking out impossible in view of the shortage of transport. He informed the Army Headquarters that he had caused all petrol and water to be destroyed and had advised the units to destroy all their vehicles, equipment and arms. The Army Commander, however, suggested that as many officers and other ranks as possible should be got away. This was communicated to all formations and units, along with the information about capitulation. As a result certain detachments which possessed transport elected to break out and some of them actually succeeded in rejoining the Eighth Army.

The Camerons hold out

The decision to capitulate did not, however, put an immediate end to the fighting inside the perimeter. Two units, the 2nd Camerons and the "Beer" Battalion, decided to hold out in spite of the instructions to surrender. These units had been given the capitulation orders on the wireless through the headquarters of the 4th South African Brigade. But the orders appeared so unreliable that they decided not to act upon them until a satisfactory confirmation was available. No confirmation was available all through the following day; so that when the Germans tried to enter their area by the El Adem road to receive their surrender, they were attacked and thrown back by the Camerons and the "Beer" Battalion, whose 2-pounder detachments and tank-hunting squads destroyed no less than seven German tanks. This naturally infuriated the German commander who sent his representative with a white flag to the Camerons to demand a surrender. The representative informed the officer commanding the Camerons that the rest of the Tobruk garrison had by then capitulated, and that if he did not do so himself, all guns would be turned on his battalion. The threatening envoy was sent back with the reply that no surrender would be made until confirmation was received; a promise was however given

[6] W/D. 11 Bde.

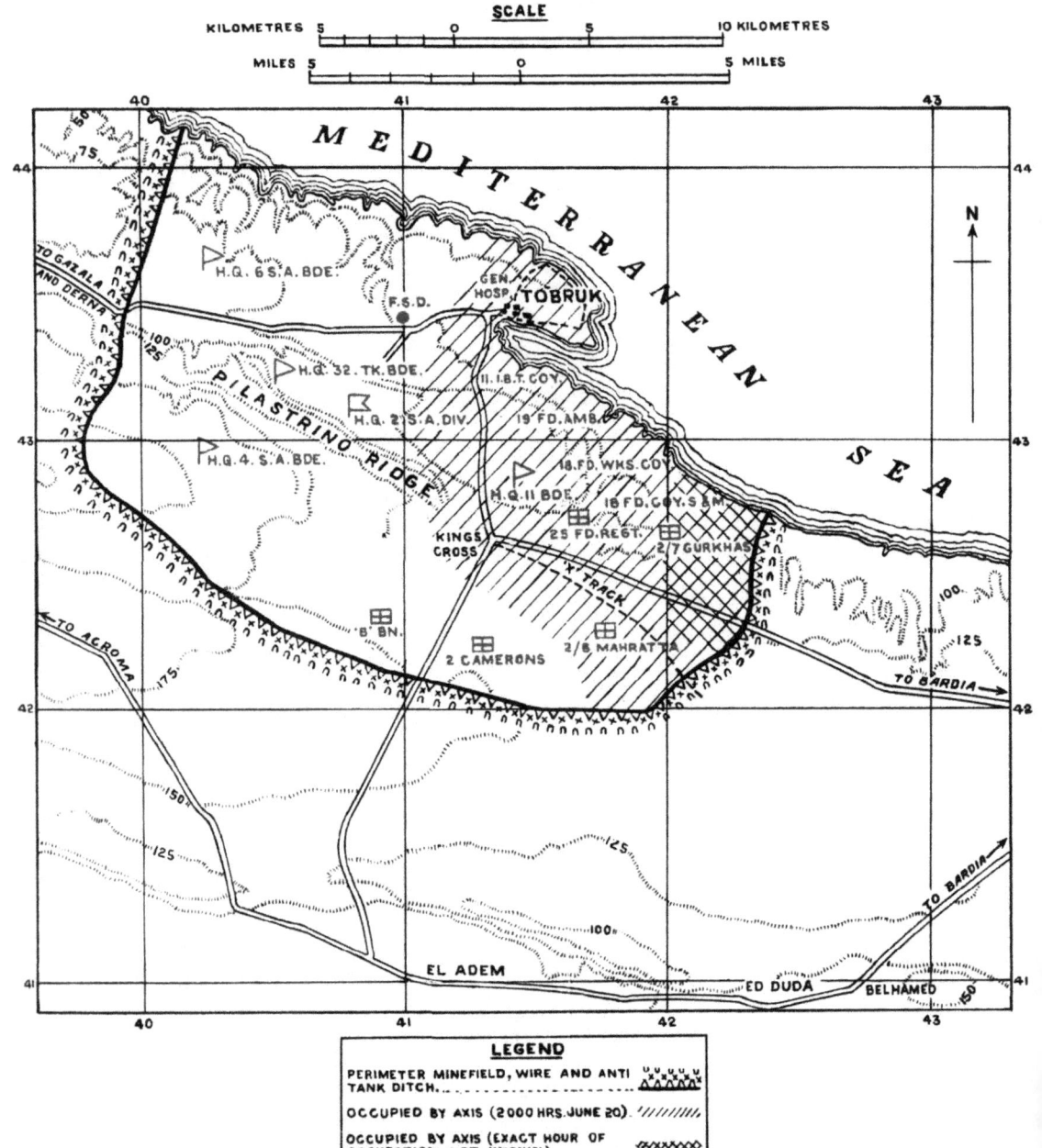

that the battalion would refrain from attacking the Germans until 0500 hours.

End of resistance in Tobruk

Long before that stipulated hour the units received a second message confirming the capitulation. All equipment was now destroyed and it was decided that those who were able to break out might do so. Approximately 15 officers and 200 other ranks of 2 Camerons in vehicles, and the whole of the "Beer" Battalion on foot, made a break-out towards El Adem. But the majority of these were soon intercepted and captured by the Germans.

Just at about this time, the Brigade Commander of the 11th Indian Infantry Brigade held a conference of his headquarters personnel and took a similar decision to escape. The personnel were divided into small parties and advised to make a break-through using transport as far as might be available. Attempts were made but hardly anybody succeeded; and all were eventually rounded up and made prisoners within the next 48 hours. Those who did manage to reach Egypt were very few and belonged mainly to the 25th Field Regiment RA and to the battalion of 2 Camerons.[7]

---

[7] W/D. 11 Bde.

CHAPTER XXXVI

Withdrawal to El Alamein

Ordinarily the next defensive position after Tobruk would be the frontier of Egypt. But a successful defence of the frontier would require a strong backing of armour, which was no longer available. General Ritchie therefore wished to retire further back, to Matruh, in order to gain time to recruit his armoured strength. Just as Tobruk was about to fall, he had telegraphed to General Auchinleck to sound him on the point. The reply brought him no comfort. General Auchinleck was himself undecided; and he therefore left the final decision in the hands of General Ritchie after merely indicating that in his opinion Matruh was even more vulnerable than the frontier.[1]

Having sent this reply, General Auchinleck proceeded to consult the Middle East Defence Committee on the question. The latter approved the proposal to fall back on Matruh. Orders were accordingly issued to the Eighth Army to prepare to fight a decisive action round Matruh, while at the same time delaying the Axis advance as far west as possible with a covering force.

This meant that General Ritchie had to find two forces, one for delaying the advance of the Axis and another for constructing a defensive position at Matruh. The former task was entrusted to the XIII Corps and the latter to the XXX Corps. Still another Corps —the X Corps—was then on its way to Egypt from Syria and it was arranged that on arrival it would relieve the XXX Corps, which would then move back to El Alamein, a hundred and twenty miles further east, where also some defences were being built and occupied. There, the XXX Corps was to devote itself exclusively to completing that work, as a precaution, in case the Matruh defence should prove untenable or collapse like its ante-types.

According to this arrangement, the main burden of defence fell on the XIII Corps, as its role was to delay the Axis until such time as the Matruh defences were ready. At this moment this Corps had under its command, the 7th Armoured Division and three infantry divisions. The Armoured Division consisted of the 4th and 22nd Armoured Brigade Groups with seventy and twenty-two tanks respectively, plus the 7th Motor Brigade Group of four battalions, and the 3rd Indian Motor Brigade Group, just

---

[1] Gen. Auchinleck's *Despatch* in Supplement to the *London Gazette*, 15 Jan. 1948, pp. 362-64.

reorganised but still below strength. The infantry consisted of the 50th (British), the 10th Indian and the 1st South African Divisions. It was decided to organise the three infantry divisions into one block of forces and the four armoured brigade groups into another. The infantry block was then named the holding force and assigned a static defensive role, while the armoured block became the mobile striking force. Thus the XIII Corps came to be split into two elements and it was hoped that this division would permit it to develop its maximum delaying strength.[2]

As to the XXX Corps, it could be given very few troops for occupying Matruh. The troops placed under its command were the New Zealand Division and the 5th Indian Division, the latter having one brigade group only. At a later stage, however, the 151st Infantry Brigade (from the 50th Division) was to pass to the XXX Corps, on being released by the XIII Corps. The New Zealand Division was incomplete, in that it was then just arriving from Syria and most of its units were still *en route*.

After capturing Tobruk, the Axis troops spent two more days in organising for the next stage of advance. They began to move forward again on 22 June. Their light forces appeared the same day on the northern end of the Egyptian frontier and occupied Bardia. The same night General Ritchie authorised a partial withdrawal of the XIII Corps from the frontier. Accordingly, the 10th Indian Division, the 151st Infantry Brigade and the 2nd South African Brigade began a gradual retirement by units. At the same time, the 7th Armoured Division mustered strong on the frontier to prevent Axis tanks and vehicles from crossing the border.

The situation continued to grow worse and on the following day some significant Axis movements were noticed farther south. These made it appear that the Axis divisions were gathering for a thrust round the south of Sidi Omar, in an effort to get behind the XIII Corps. General Ritchie was somewhat alarmed at the prospect of the rest of the Corps being cut off on the frontier and he authorised a further withdrawal of more troops. By the evening of 23 June, the entire infantry of the XIII Corps, except the 69th Infantry Brigade, and all the armoured formations, except the two motor brigade groups, had moved well to the east of the frontier and were on the way to Matruh. The delaying action of the Corps was virtually at an end and it was now merely a question of organising the Maruh defences as quickly as possible with as many additional troops as could be rapidly got away from the XIII Corps area.[3]

[2] *Ibid.* W/Ds. 5 Div., 10 Div., 3 Mot. Bde.
[3] *Ibid.*

The Battle Groups

The distance from the frontier to Matruh is about 140 miles, which meant that there was still some scope for fighting a delaying action. This task was assigned to the 69th Infantry Brigade, and the 7th (British) and 3rd Indian Motor Brigades, who were at the time the only Allied formations in actual contact with the Axis troops.

Meanwhile, feverish preparations were going on about a hundred miles behind for fighting a decisive battle round Matruh. It was found in the course of these activities that there was a great shortage of field artillery compared to the infantry which was available for such a battle. The great significance of such a situation was that there was a surplus of infantry for which field artillery support could not be provided, and which was therefore useless for the battle. Such infantry, with the large number of vehicles necessary for its movements, would, it was felt, rather prove an encumbrance and tend to decrease the mobility in a battle. To get over this difficulty it was decided to reorganise the defence of Matruh on a different basis. All surplus infantry was sent to the rear area to help in preparing the El Alamein position. The remainder was then organised into what were called "battle groups". Explaining this innovation in his *Despatch* General Auchinleck writes: "These battle groups had as their foundation the maximum number of field guns that could be provided for each, and only just as many infantry as were needed to protect them. The idea was that in this way the defence could be kept mobile, the battle groups being moved rapidly to that part of the front where the danger was the greatest".[4]

This rather unconventional method of fighting in battle groups has been severely criticised in certain quarters or has been referred to derisively as if it was a sign of bankruptcy of generalship. It is true that the system involved the breaking up of the fighting force into small bodies, and that divisions and brigades, not being allowed to fight as a whole, could not develop their maximum fighting strength as full-fledged formations; and it is perhaps also true that this method was hardly different from the tactics of guerrilla fighting which is the last resource of a defeated army. Further, the results achieved were also so meagre, as will be seen presently, that the criticism would seem justified. Yet, it is doubtful whether it might not have led to a much bigger disaster to have let the divisions and brigades fight as full formations in spite of a great deficiency of artillery. One thing at least seems certain, that the surplus infantry transferred to Alamein at an early stage was largely instrumental in making the Alamein position

[4] *Ibid.*

Around El Alamein

Attacking in the desert, July 1942

Indian Light Armoured Squadron patrolling the desert, July 1942

General Alexander inspecting Indian troops, Egypt, September 1942

reasonably ready in the nick of time; but for which, the army of the Axis might have swept through Alamein and overrun the rest of Egypt.

In fact, according to one military authority, the battle groups were the only solution to General Auchinleck's fatal lack of anti-tank artillery, a lack which simply meant that about three quarters of his infantry were unfit to take part in mobile operations against armour. One alternative, that some critics of the battle-group method appear to favour, is that the infantry divisions, cumbersome though they would be, should have been used as mobile formations to fight it out with the German Panzers—a course which could most assuredly have ended in a total rout of the Eighth Army. That the battle groups did not succeed in stopping Rommel for good may perhaps be attributed, among other things, to their not being as well co-ordinated as they might have been, had the circumstances been different and more favourable.

At the time the battle groups were being organised, the Axis forces were on the frontier. They began advancing again on 24 June, at dawn, the move being in three columns, of which two struck north from Shefersen, towards Halfaya, while the third proceeded on a more easterly axis from Maddalena. This advance met no more resistance than could be offered by light columns from the 7th (British) and 3rd Indian Motor Brigades and the 69th Infantry Brigade. Brushing this opposition aside, the Axis columns made rapid strides forward while the Allied light columns retired with equal precipitation. By evening the Allied columns were level with Sidi Barrani and on the following day well into Matruh. During the same time two of the three Axis columns had reached points on the railway and the main road, some forty miles from Matruh, while their vanguards had penetrated farther east and were being engaged by the British tanks.

Change of Command

At this stage General Auchinleck decided to take over direct control of the Eighth Army from General Ritchie. He did so on the evening of 25 June near Baqqush, where the Army Headquarters was then located. No changes were made in regard to the other commanders and staff officers of the Eighth Army, except that General Auchinleck's Deputy Chief of General Staff accompanied him as his principal staff officer. There is no doubt that General Auchinleck considered the situation serious enough to warrant his taking such a drastic step. He was evidently afraid that, unless decisions were taken rapidly and energetic measures adopted to implement them, the 69th Infantry Brigade might be cut off in its retreat, or a great part of the Eighth Army be shut up in Matruh, since, owing to the configuration of the coast, Matruh could be easily isolated by a movement past its southern flank.[5]

Defence of Matruh

Two corps were engaged on the task of defending Matruh, the X and the XIII. The former was garrisoning the town and strengthening its defences; the latter, organised in battle groups, was to fight mobile actions with a view to preventing Axis troops from reaching Matruh. Since the New Zealand Division was considered better equipped for mobile warfare than the 10th Indian Division, the latter changed place with the former. Thus the X Corps had under its command the 10th Indian Division and the 151st Infantry Brigade, while the XIII Corps had the New Zealand Division and the 1st and 7th Armoured Divisions. The 69th Infantry Brigade was withdrawing from Sidi Barrani to Matruh in contact with the advancing Axis forces; while the 3rd Indian and 7th British Motor Brigades, both of the 7th Armoured Division, were also fighting similar delaying actions to the west of El Kanayis.

The Matruh position consisted of a forfeited perimeter round the town itself. The perimeter was reinforced by an additional covering position to the west of the town from which direction the threat was the greatest. This external position was further protected by a deep minefield, which ran south from the coast, then in front of it, then to Charing Cross and thence eastward. Twenty miles to the south of Matruh was another protective position, a detached strong point on the high ground near Minqar Sidi Hamza el Gharbi. Two more minefields started out from there, running northwards and sealing up the area behind. There was however a gap of six miles between these two separate groups of minefields and it was necessary to close this opening with infantry. The 29th Indian Infantry Brigade was put on that job, thus completing the defensive ring round Matruh.[6]

The Axis forces were to the west of this ring, from where they could drive in to its south. The ring was therefore more vulnerable from the west and south than from the north or east. The western flank had been strengthened by an additional covering position as described, but the southern flank presented a more difficult problem. There was the main escarpment on the southern flank which formed a natural obstacle; and between this escarpment and the defensive ring enclosing Matruh was a wide corridor of fairly level country, which would require vast numbers of tanks and infantry to defend adequately. A strong fighting group provided by the New Zealand Division was placed in this passage, round Minqar Qaim, about

[5] *Ibid.*
[6] W/Ds. 10 Div., 29 Bde.

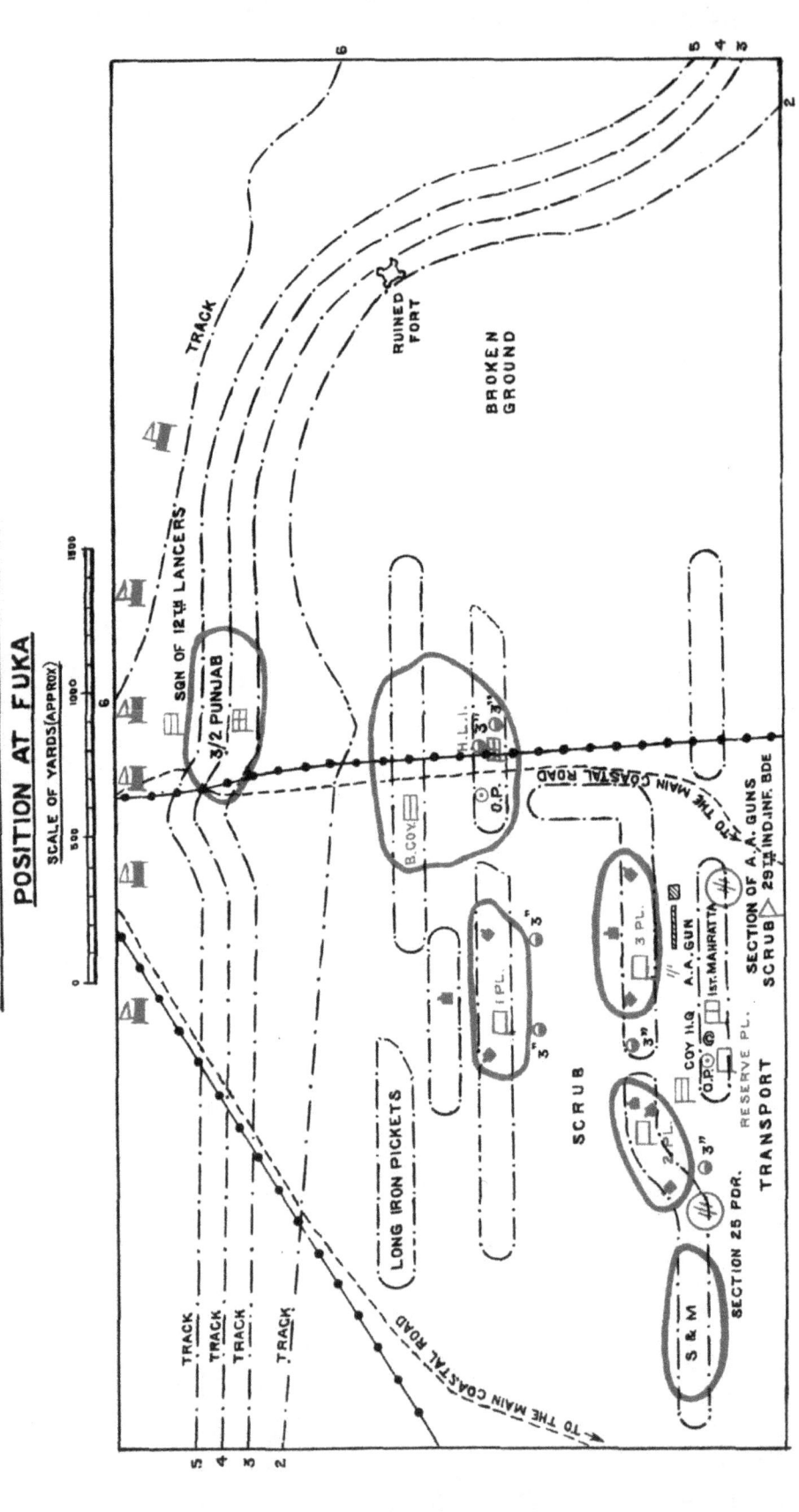

25 miles south of Matruh, where it was to act in a mobile role under the XIII Corps. Further south, between Minqar Qaim and the escarpment, were disposed the 4th and 2nd Armoured Brigades of the 1st Armoured Division, also under the XIII Corps. Thus the gap between the Matruh perimeter and the escarpment was blocked, as well as could be, with the two armoured brigades, the New Zealand group and the detached strong point at Minqar Sidi Hamza.

All these forces were, however, too inadequate to ward off the threatened thrust from the Axis. Given sufficient infantry and armour, Matruh was certainly defendable. But there was a great shortage of armour and artillery and, as mentioned earlier, the infantry thus rendered superfluous had been sent away to Alamein. Consequently, it was doubtful whether the existing forces would suffice to perform the double function of keeping a close watch not only on the long stretches of minefields but also on the gap in the southern flank. There was the undeniable risk that the Axis troops might find it possible to pierce the one or the other almost overnight.

On assuming personal command of the Eighth Army, General Auchinleck reconsidered the matter and finally decided to evacuate Matruh. He planned instead to turn the X and XIII Corps into fully mobile forces and to bring the Axis advance to a halt in the area between Matruh, Alamein and the Qattara Depression. In his opinion this arrangement would obviate the possibility of the X Corps being isolated in Matruh or the XIII Corps being overwhelmed. While these two corps would be battling to hold or defeat the Axis, the XXX Corps was to complete the defences of El Alamein.[7]

Hardly had this course of action been decided upon when the Axis made a move which forestalled the evacuation of Matruh. Axis tanks broke through the gap held by the 29th Indian Brigade, on the evening of 26 June. The brigade—consisting, as it then did, of only battered and depleted columns—was too weak to obstruct this move; and next day the Axis tanks were swarming round Minqar Qaim, engaging the 1st Armoured and the New Zealand Divisions. Before the end of the day they had succeeded in driving a wedge between the X Corps and XIII Corps; and in addition the X Corps in Matruh was also being engaged. The situation was fraught with the risk of the XIII Corps being cut off or overwhelmed, and General Gott therefore ordered his Corps to withdraw to Fuka. The X Corps was simultaneously ordered by General Auchinleck to conform to that withdrawal.

[7] Gen. Auchinleck's *Despatch* in Supplement to the *London Gazette*, 15 Jan. 1948, pp. 362-65.

The Indian Division isolated

At this critical stage, it was discovered that the X Corps was in no position to make a withdrawal at such short notice. It had given up most of its transport to the New Zealand Division to make its battle group fully mobile, and the best it could do in the circumstances was to leave behind or destroy large stocks of stores and equipment, and retire at its own pace. But as the Axis forces could move much faster, the inevitable happened. The road of retreat of the X Corps was cut at a point twenty miles east of Matruh, resulting in the 10th Indian Division and 151st Brigade being isolated and placed in the imminent danger of being captured or destroyed.

These formations had therefore no alternative but to try and fight their way out, which they began to do during the night of 28 June. To assist their passage down towards Alamein, the XIII Corps ordered the 29th Indian Brigade to hold the passes near Fuka. But just before dark on 28 June, the brigade was attacked and overwhelmed by the Axis troops and the passage through Fuka was no longer available to the X Corps. Giving up the coastal road, therefore, the Corps decided on the following day to break out southwards and complete its withdrawal by way of the desert. The break-out commenced the same day, covered by the 7th Motor Brigade which kept attacking northwards against the flank of the advancing Axis troops so as to screen the withdrawal of the X Corps. The withdrawal proved a success and the Corps reached the Alamein position before the next morning. But it was so disorganised that its two main formations, the 151st Brigade and the 10th Indian Division, had to be sent farther back, to the Delta, to reorganise and refit. While this was happening, the XIII Corps was fighting a delaying action west of Alamein.

The danger to the Alamein position, however, was drawing ever closer, in spite of whatever opposition the XIII Corps could offer. So rapid was the progress of the Axis troops, that their forward elements were at Sidi Abd el Rahman, only fifteen miles from El Alamein, on the evening of 29 June. On the other hand, the Allied armoured and motor brigades were still operating far to the west; and, in consequence, were well behind the farthest line reached by the Axis. It was imperative that they should be withdrawn without any delay; and this was done the next day, after which they were placed in the army reserve.

The El Alamein Line

Long before this, General Auchinleck had decided to hold a line of positions at Alamein, which later became well-known as the Alamein Line. El Alamein, after which the line is named, is only a minor station on the Desert Railway which runs along the coast. However, it was important from the defence point of view, in that it was the northernmost strong point of the Alamein Line. The southernmost point was formed by the Qattara Depression, a vast expanse of quicksand and salt marshes and therefore a perfect obstacle to vehicle traffic. To the south of the Depression lay the great Sand Sea, equally impenetrable.

Thus the Alamein Line was flanked on the north by the sea, at Arabs Gulf; and on the south, by the sandy wastes of Qattara Depression and the Sand Sea. The only piece of land, suitable for the passage of an army, was therefore the area between these two extreme obstacles. This stretch measured about forty miles across its narrowest, which can by no means be regarded as too long a line in desert warfare. The great strength of the line lay in the fact that it was open only to a frontal attack over this narrow distance, since it could not be outflanked from either side. Further, this stretch of forty miles was covered by ridges and hillocks in the centre, which could be made into strong defensive positions; while scattered about were other high features, capable of being put to a similar use.[8]

Construction of the Alamein Line had been first taken in hand in 1941, though it is doubtful whether the potentialities of this great defensive position had been fully understood at that early period of the fighting in the desert. It should not therefore be surprising that when its construction was first taken in hand in 1941, it was done in an indifferent frame of mind, that is, more in the style of a routine defensive position to fall back upon than as an ideal bastion for the last-ditch defence of Alexandria and the rest of Egypt. Even then, work on it was stopped as soon as the emergency disappeared, and was resumed only intermittently as convenience permitted or necessity dictated.

As a result, the Alamein Line was hardly ready for use when General Auchinleck assumed command of the Eighth Army and ordered the evacuation from Matruh. It was then no more than a chain of scattered positions, weak in troops, disconnected and lacking in depth. The only prepared positions were three: the semi-permanent fortification in the north, round El Alamein itself; the defences in the centre, round Bab el Qattara; and those in the extreme south, round Naqb Abu Dweiss. The troops available for manning those positions were neither sufficient nor well organised. They were the New Zealand and the 5th Indian Divisions under the XIII Corps; and the 50th (British) and the 1st South African Divisions under the XXX Corps. The New Zealand Division had suffered about 650 casualties at Minqar Qaim only two days before,

[8] *Ibid.* W/Ds. 5 Div., 10 Div., 29 Bde.

and the 50th Division, by this time, was only a little more than a very weak brigade group.

On withdrawing his troops to the Alamein—Qattara Depression line on 29 June, General Auchinleck had to re-group and redistribute them to the best advantage. With the Axis forces pressing on relentlessly, he hurriedly allotted the southern half of the line to the XIII Corps, and the northern sector to the XXX Corps. As to the wide gaps between the positions of these two Corps, he hoped to fill them with what remained of his armour, supplemented by the mobile battle groups. This was by no means an ideal arrangement for defending the most vital line, on which depended the fate of Egypt and the Middle East. But the shortage of armour and artillery was so great that nothing more ambitious could be attempted. It was natural in this condition for General Auchinleck not to place too great a reliance on the impregnability of the Alamein Line but rather to be prepared against the possibility of its collapse. Such, indeed, seems to have been the trend of his thought, for behind the Alamein Line, at this stage, was being prepared yet another position for defending the final approaches to Alexandria and Cairo.[9]

This work was being handled by the Delta Force. Not needing a third corps headquarters in Alamein, General Auchinleck despatched the headquarters and staff of the X Corps to Alexandria, to take command of the Delta Force and to supervise preparations of what may be called the threshold-defence of the Nile Delta.

Attack on the Alamein Line

Hardly had the XXX and XIII Corps taken up their positions in the northern and southern sectors of the Alamein—Qattara Depression line, when the Axis troops closed up and attacked in the areas of both the Corps. That was on the morning of 1 July. The 1st South African Division was then holding the El Alamein fortification in the north; and the 18th Indian Infantry Brigade group of the 5th Indian Division was holding the Deir el Shein feature in the centre.[10]

On the eventful morning of 1 July, Axis forces launched simultaneous attacks against the South African and Indian positions. The more powerful of the two attacks seemed to be aimed at the Indian position. It was an infantry attack, with strong artillery support, and was launched with great dash and vigour. The 18th Indian Brigade was new to such experience, having just arrived from Iraq and having had to take up positions at very short notice.

---

[9] Gen. Auchinleck's *Despatch* in Supplement to the *London Gazette*, 15 Jan. 1948, pp. 363-65.
[10] W/Ds. 5 Div., 18 Bde.

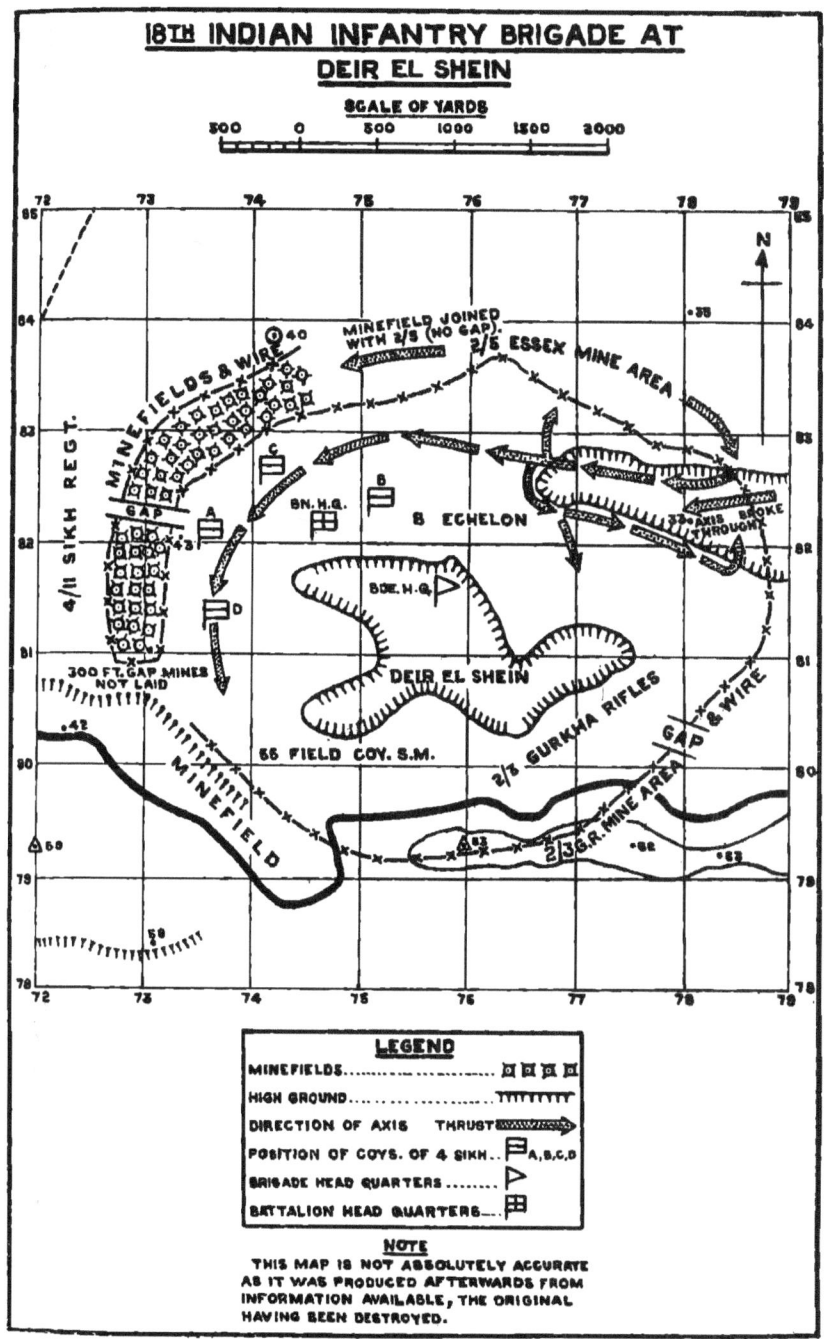

Still it held the ground, retaliated stoutly, and finally succeeded in repelling the attackers.

But that was by no means the end of that action. The Axis forces returned in the afternoon, this time with a strong support of tanks. They attacked under cover of a heavy dust storm, which undoubtedly favoured the attackers; and there developed a battle which lasted for about five hours. The brigade was eventually overrun, only a fraction of a battalion surviving. But the five-hour stand it made produced far-reaching results. It broke the shock of the first attack, robbed the Axis of a precious initiative and generally gained time for the organisation of the rest of the Alamein Line.[11]

First Allied counter-attack

It was now to be expected that, having disposed of the Indian brigade, the Axis would turn its attention to the south African Division which was holding the El Alamein railway-station fortress. A concentrated blow on this strong point would open the coastal road to the Axis for a drive to Alexandria, and it was essential to prevent this. General Auchinleck decided that the best way to help the South African Division was to launch a fierce counter-attack against the Axis and thus create a major diversion. He accordingly ordered the XIII Corps to wheel north and strike at the flank and rear of the Axis disposition; while the XXX Corps would hold the ground in the north and check all attempts to advance eastwards.[12]

The XIII Corps started its attack in the afternoon of 2 July, employing the New Zealand and the 5th Indian Divisions. The attack received ample support from the air force and progressed very rapidly at first. On 3 July the Corps took several prisoners and guns and destroyed a number of tanks. During the 4th and 5th it occupied El Mreir and approached Deir el Shein, where the 1th Indian Brigade had been annihilated only a few days ago. But from then on, resistance began to stiffen as the Corps reached a line of Axis positions extending westward from Deir el Shein.

After their capture of Deir el Shein, the Axis troops had consolidated that locality and converted it into a point of strong resistance, from where they had laid out a series of strong points in a westerly direction so as to safeguard their line of communication with Daba. It was on coming up against this collection of strong points that the XIII Corps slackened in its progress and finally came to a standstill.

The net result of the XIII Corps' offensive was that a thrust against El Alamein fortification, if such had been the intention of

---

[11] A special sketch narrative of the fighting at Deir el Shein will be found in App. T.
[12] W/D. 5 Div.

the Axis, was not allowed to take shape; and some more time was gained for strengthening the northern and central sectors of the Alamein line. The steps taken to strengthen those vital sectors included the moving up of the 9th Australian Division to a position just behind the Alamein fortress and despatching one of its brigades to the Ruweisat Ridge to buttress up that key-position in the centre.

After this there were some more minor moves, both on the part of the Axis as well as on that of the XIII Corps, mainly for securing tactically advantageous ground. The XIII Corps ordered the three New Zealand Brigades, then withdrawing eastward, to occupy the ground about Deir el Hima, so as to close up a gap which existed between the left flank of the XXX Corps and the right flank of the XIII Corps. To counteract this, the Axis troops occupied Deir el Qattara on 9 July, so as to keep a gap open in the extreme south. Eventually the Axis troops settled down along a line running through Qaret el Khadim and the El Taqa plateau, which put them on the left flank of the XIII Corps and made it unsafe for the Corps to engage in any operation lest its flank be attacked in the meanwhile.

Second counter-attack

The Axis had thus succeeded in forcing a standstill on the XIII Corps front. As to the XXX Corps, it was already inactive, being positioned to contain merely a frontal assault. Were the Axis to start an offensive now, at a point of its own selection, the Eighth Army would be obliged to play to that move and thus lose the initiative. But General Auchinleck was not willing to give up that advantage. In order, therefore, to keep the Axis perpetually conforming to moves of his own choice, he ordered the XXX Corps to open a fresh offensive in the coastal area.[13]

The Corps was to attack the Tel el Eisa feature, which consisted of a group of mounds on the railway, to the west of El Alamein. These heights were of certain tactical importance, in that they overlooked the Axis positions to the south. The attack was launched early on 10 July by the 9th Australian Division, supported by the 1st South African Division and infantry tanks. It made quick progress and was successful and the Australians entrenched themselves on the Tel el Eisa mounds. The Axis forces counterattacked immediately, with tanks and infantry, supported by artillery, but the Australians held fast to their gains. The fighting cost the Axis a number of tanks and fifteen guns captured, besides over a thousand prisoners, mostly Italians.

It was, however, not possible to keep up the momentum of the

---

[13] Gen. Auchinleck's *Despatch* in Supplement to the *London Gazette*, 15 Jan. 1948, pp. 364-65.

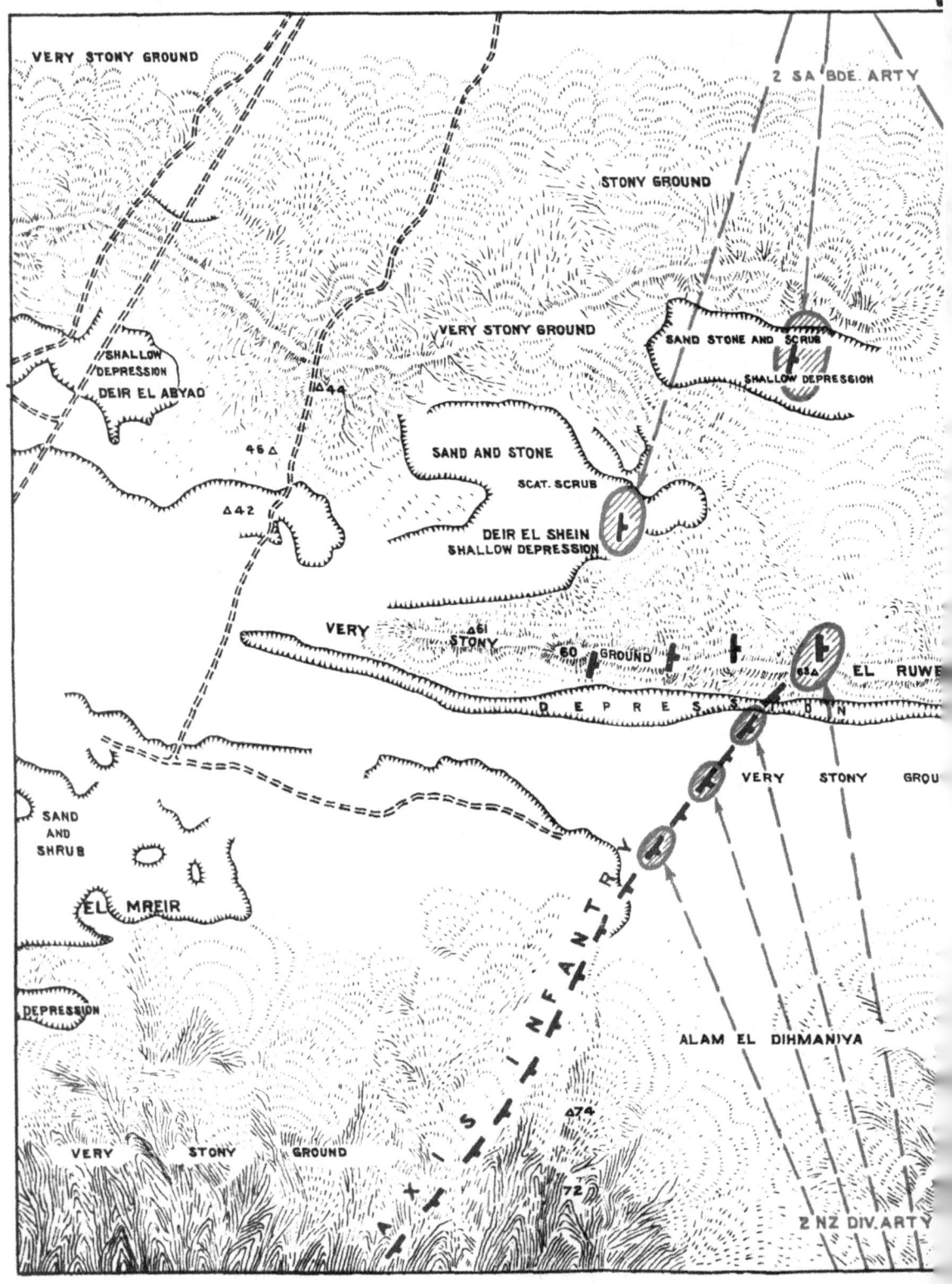

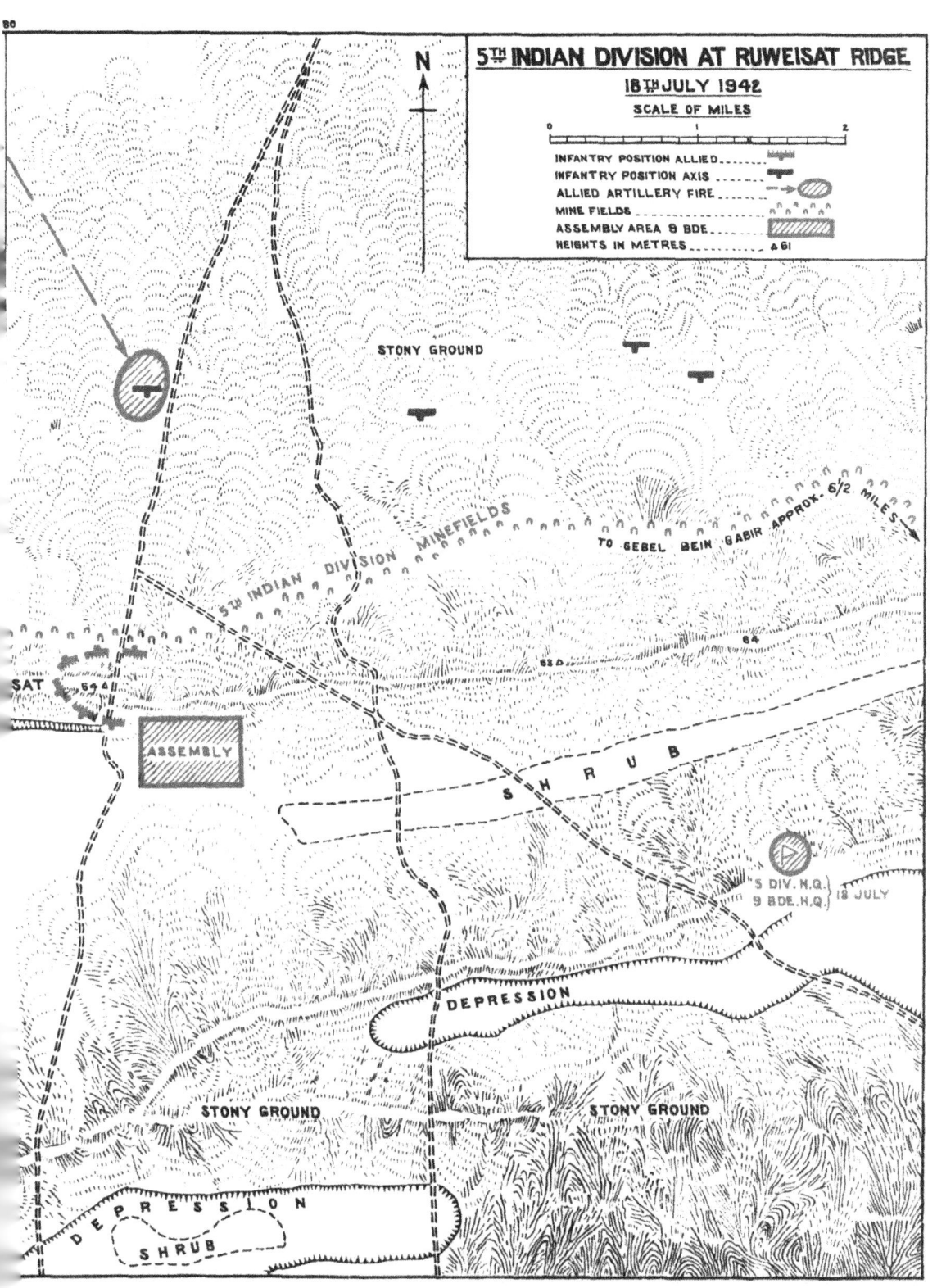

attack. It had been originally planned that the success should be exploited south and west, if and as weakness might be discovered in the dispositions of the Axis. But no such weakness existed and in fact resistance had increased. Further, there were no reserves with which to reinforce the attack. The Australians therefore contented themselves with retaining a firm base on the Tel el Eisa feature, from where they continued to threaten the western and southern positions of the Axis. Sensitive to this threat, the Axis troops launched several counter-attacks to retake the feature all of which were successfully repulsed.

Third counter-attack

The attack of the XXX Corps having come to an end, General Auchinleck planned to start a fresh offensive in another part of the front, in keeping with his resolve to give no chance to the Axis to wrest the initiative. As a result, on the night of 14 July, the New Zealand Division and the 5th Indian Infantry Brigade attacked in the centre, along a feature of great tactical importance, namely the Ruweisat Ridge. This was one of the most important of a series of parallel ridges in the Alamein Line. Running from east to west, those ridges were at right angles to the front, which made them the most desirable salients; and of these, the Ruweisat salient dominated the northern sector and was therefore considered a very important objective.[14]

The attack was successful and the 5th Indian Brigade consolidated its position around Pt. 64, while the New Zealanders occupied a position to its west. Together, those two formations had gained considerable ground, including valuable observation posts on the ridge itself, overlooking the Deir el Shein area and the country to the north. But the New Zealand positions were unfortunately overrun by Axis tanks in the afternoon of 16 July, and the 5th Indian Brigade thereafter became the most exposed of the Allied formations in the Alamein Line. It was thereupon attacked for two days by Axis artillery and aircraft, in the course of which the German 8th Tank Regiment and 155th Lorried Infantry Regiment put in a full-fledged assault on it at 1805 hours on 16 July. There was heavy fighting in that engagement for about three hours, but the 2nd Armoured Brigade, assisted by artillery, came to the rescue of the Indian brigade, which ultimately managed to retain its foothold on the Ruweisat Ridge. About 2000 Axis prisoners were taken in these operations, most of them Italian.

Fourth counter-attack

With a view to relieving pressure on the Ruweisat sector, General

[14] W/Ds. 5 Div., 5 Bde., 9 Bde.

Auchinleck had arranged for a two-corps offensive to take place on the rest of the front. The idea was to press the Axis back simultaneously on the northern and southern flanks. The attack commenced on the night of 16 July. The 9th Ausralian Division in the northern sector, which was the first to strike, captured Tell el Makh Khad, a low ridge about eight miles west of the Alamein railway station ; and in doing so took about 500 prisoners. Two days later, the 7th Armoured Division struck in the south sector, with light tanks and motorised units, and tried to exert pressure against the Axis positions on Jebel Kalakh and the Taqa plateau. Neither of the two Corps achieved any notable success. Nor were they together able even to relieve the pressure against the Ruweisat Ridge, since the Axis continued to attack the ridge intermittently during 18 and 19 July. All those attacks were repulsed by the 5th Indian Brigade. However, the primary aim of the offensive can be said to have been achieved, in that the Axis troops were kept busy fighting all along the front and were given no time in which they could take the initiative in opening an offensive of their own choice.[15]

Fifth counter-attack

This set-back did not discourage General Auchinleck whose determination to throw back the Axis never flagged. Hardly had his last effort failed when he was ready with yet another. This time he planned to strike at the centre of the Axis line with a view to dividing it into two and then rolling up the northern half. The main central thrust was to be made in the areas Deir el Abyad and El Mreir and was to be assisted by simultaneous supporting and diversionary attacks on either flanks. The attack was to be preceded and supported by heavy artillery and aerial bombardment, while infantry, in the central sector, was to open the way through minefields for armoured forces to break through.

The advance in the central sector began from the Ruweisat Ridge, just before dusk on 21 July. The 161st Indian Brigade attacked towards Deir el Abyad and the 6th New Zealand Brigade towards El Mreir. At the same time the 9th Australian and 1st South African Divisions opened an offensive in the north, while the 69th Infantry Brigade did the same in the south. The aim of the northern offensive was to support the main central thrust, and at the same time to further exploit the success gained earlier at Tel el Eisa. The object of the operations on the southern flank was to capture the Taqa plateau and by that attempt to divert the attention from the operations proceeding in the central sector.

The initial advance in the centre went well and the infantry

[15] A special sketch narrative of the fighting at Ruweisat Ridge will be found in Appx. U.

gained most of their objectives before dawn on the 22nd. However, as they were proceeding to clear the gaps in the minefields for the passage of tanks, the Axis troops counter-attacked. They overran the positions of the 6th New Zealand Brigade, taking a large number of prisoners; while at the same time they attacked and practically destroyed a whole battalion of the 161st Indian Brigade which had then just occupied the Deir el Shein locality. In spite of these interruptions, however, the infantry went on with its task. The 23rd Armoured Brigade then passed through the gaps in the minefields and made considerable progress towards its objective. But soon it lost its effectiveness and cohesion, through lack of control due to a breakdown of wireless communications, and finally its progress came to a halt. It was then attacked and defeated by the Axis armour before it had had time to make a safe withdrawal.

The loss in tanks thus suffered by the 23rd Armoured Brigade was so heavy that it was in no position to stage a counter-attack. Its place was therefore taken by the 2nd Armoured Brigade which had been held up all this time by the Axis minefields but had at last managed to cross through to the battle area. This new formation attacked the same evening (22 July), in support of the main central thrust, which made fresh progress and gained some important ground. But the advance had involved a heavy loss in men and tanks, and the attack finally failed in its main object of breaking through the centre of the Axis line and dividing it into two.[16]

If this was the situation in the centre, it was hardly any better on the northern and southern flanks. In the north of the Alamein Line, the 9th Australian and the 1st South African Divisions did manage to reach their objective, but subsequently the Ausralians were counter-attacked and forced out of some of their gains, rendering the whole position precarious. In the south, the 69th Infantry Brigade, which had secured a footing on the Taqa Plateau, was likewise expelled from its position by a successful Axis attack. The plan to break through the Axis line and roll up its northern wing had thus failed. The failure was no doubt due, as General Auchinleck very rightly points out in his *Despatch*, to the lack of reserves with which to maintain the momentum of the attack.

Sixth counter-attack

Firm in his intention to go on attacking the Axis forces without respite, General Auchinleck, in spite of his rapidly dwindling resources, planned yet another offensive. Owing to the losses suffered so far, his reserves were next to nothing and to that extent the new operation was a desperate essay. But the alternative to it was a

[16] Gen. Auchinleck's *Despatch* in Supplement to the *London Gazette*, 15 Jan. 1948, pp. 365-8.

standstill defence which the Axis might have overcome with very little difficulty. General Auchinleck aimed at giving no such chance to the Axis and to that end was ready for yet another counter-offensive. The basis of the plan of this sixth one was an attack in the northern sector of the Alamein Line, the idea being to make the most of Tel el Eisa salient which had been captured earlier. The XXX Corps was to break through and get into a position in the rear of the Axis troops from where it might be possible to roll down the coastal wing of the Axis towards the latter's centre. As the infantry of the XXX Corps had been fighting continuously and was feeling the effects of exhaustion, the Corps was reinforced by the 69th Brigade which was withdrawn from the southern flank for the purpose. This, no doubt, weakened the XIII Corps front. But the risk had to be accepted as unavoidable. However, the XIII Corps was instructed to try and conceal its weakness by aggressive patrols and feint attacks so as to mislead the Axis as to its strength and prevent it from reinforcing its northern sector.

The operations commenced on the night of 26 July with an attack along the south of the Tel el Eisa salient. The intention was to pierce the minefields and then pass the armoured and motorised formations through. The 9th Australian Division quickly secured Sanyet el Miteiriya and the 1st South African Division began to clear mines to the south of that point for giving passage to the 69th Brigade and its supporting armour. At this stage, the Axis troops counter-attacked the Australians and forced them to vacate their positions at Miteiriya. In addition, they also attacked the South Africans and attempted to hinder the clearing of the minefields. But by then the South Africans had managed to open a way for the 69th Brigade which passed through to the other side, expecting its armour to follow. It turned out, however, that the lane through the minefields was too narrow and unsafe for the passage of tanks and needed widening. The South Africans tried to do this but were thwarted in the attempt, with the result that the 69th Brigade found itself to the west of the Axis minefields without the protection of the tanks. While in this condition, it was set upon by Axis troops, at noon on 27 July, and its leading battalions were cut off. Thereupon, the 1st Armoured Division moved forward to extricate it from the situation and finally succeeded in fetching it back to the east of the minefields. But the losses suffered by the brigade were so heavy that it became unfit for further operational tasks and had to be taken out of the Line.

This failure convinced General Auchinleck that the Eighth Army was incapable of undertaking a successful offensive in its existing condition. Its great drawback was a continued lack of armour and artillery and, considering the long front it had to hold

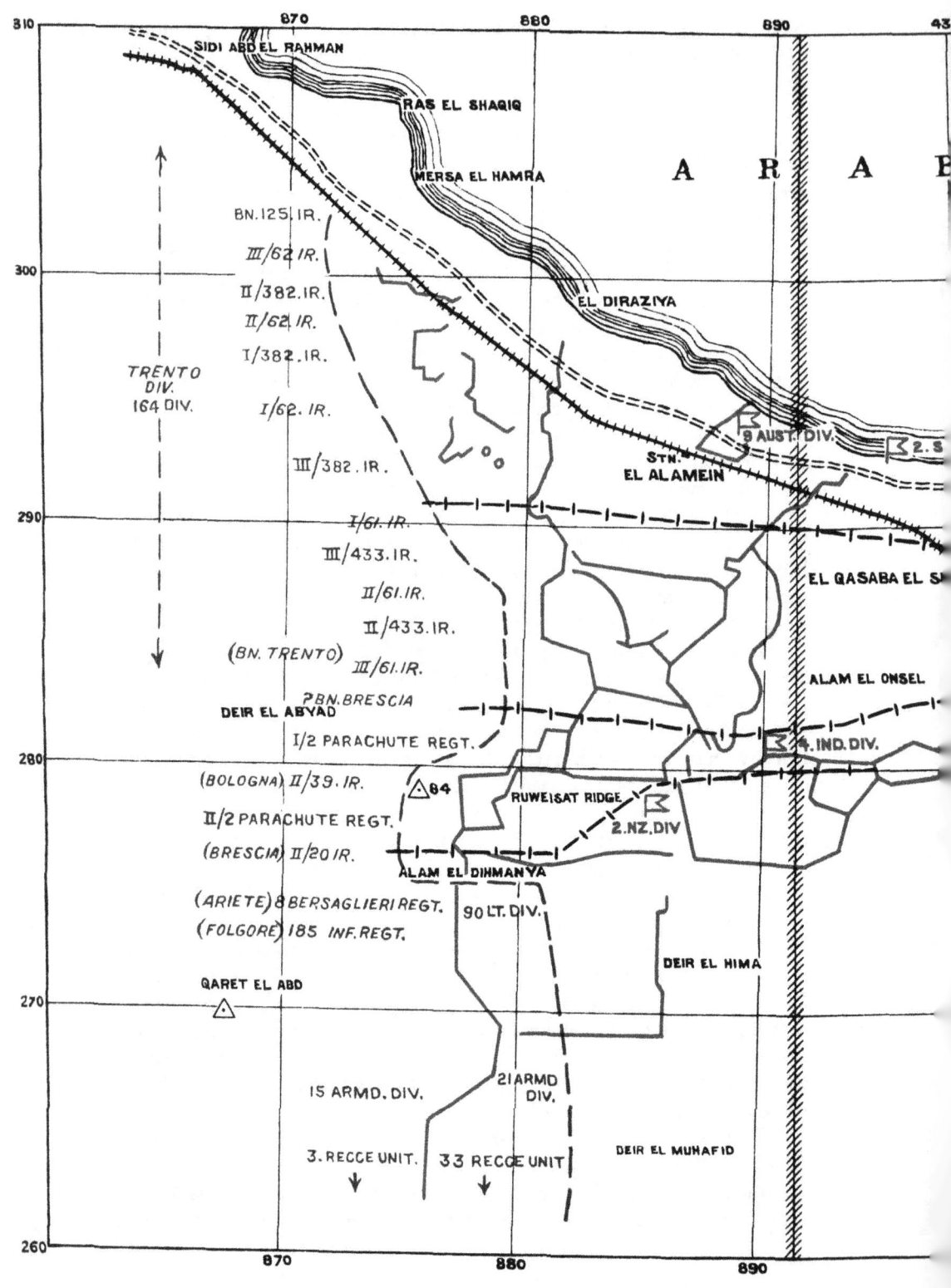

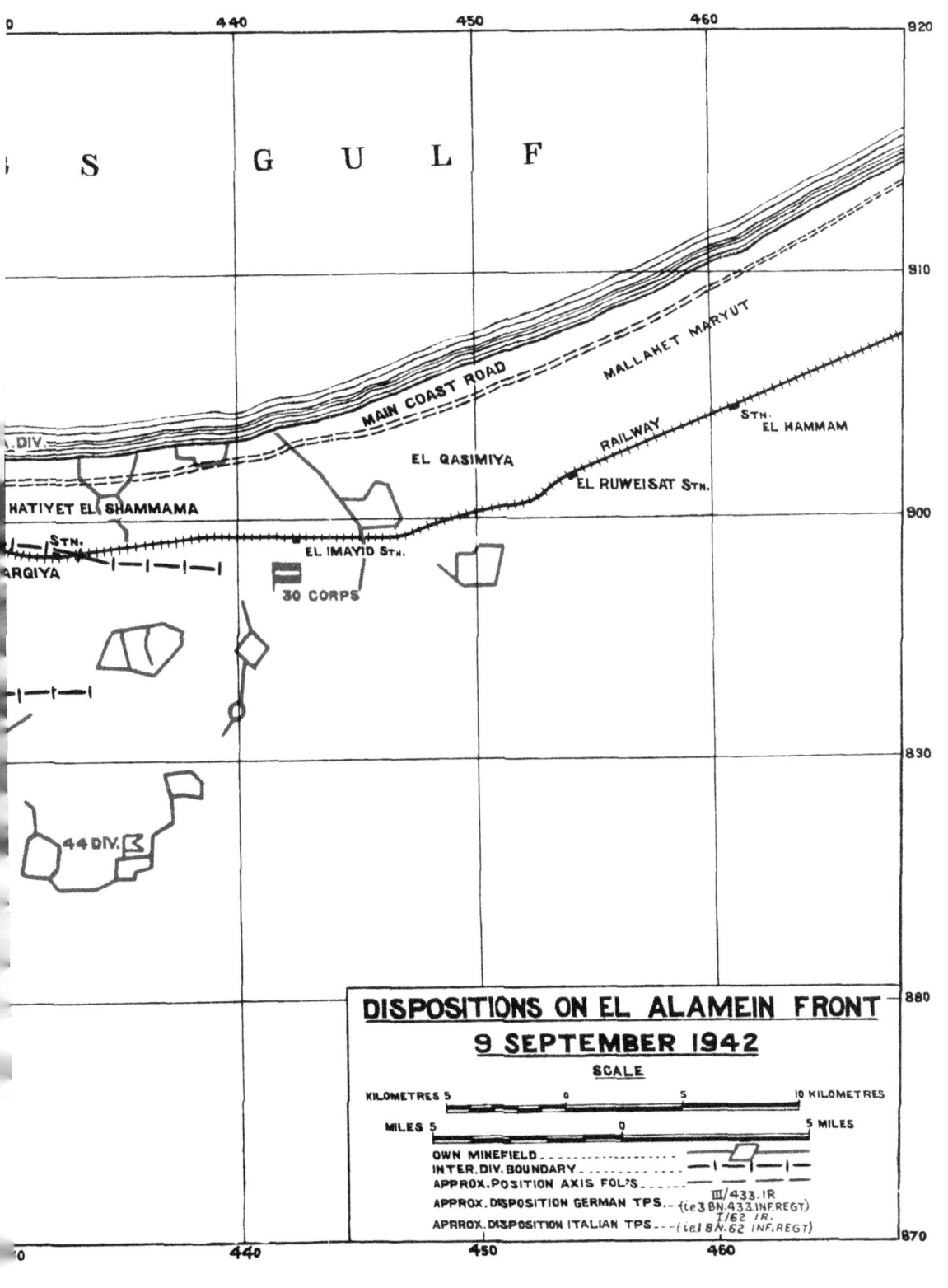

and watch, it was also deficient in infantry. This prevented the formation of an effective reserve with which to sway decisions at critical moments of a battle, and also restricted the chances of troops being sent to the rear to rest, re-form and train for fresh tasks. While the Allied troops were thus feeling the effects of exhaustion, Axis troops were being steadily reinforced and were growing in strength. The prospects of immediate Allied reinforcements were comparatively meagre. There was, for instance, the 44th Division which had just arrived from the United Kingdom and was training near Cairo but which could not be expected to be ready in less than a month. Similarly, there were the 8th and 10th Armoured Divisions, still under training and occupied in rearming themselves with American medium tanks or other equipment, but unlikely to be ready for action for another month and a half.

Considering everything, and having discussed the situation with his two Corps commanders, General Auchinleck at last reached the conclusion that further offensive operations were not feasible for the time being. He decided, therefore, to remain on the defensive until he should be ready for a fresh and final drive. That event did not seem to be likely before the middle of September, till which time he would have to be content with defending his frontline and recruiting his armed strength simultaneously.[17]

During the preceding month (July 1942), the Eighth Army had made six well-organised counter-attacks and many offensive sallies, and suffered great losses. Its casualties for that month were 750 officers and 12,500 men, of which more than 3000 were sustained by the 5th Indian Division. Moreover, during the same month it had improved the El Alamein position enormously. Defences were constructed to give depth to the Alamein Line, which had at last turned out to be a stabilising factor of immense value in bringing a long-drawn retreat to a halt. The Alamein Line had been the means of saving Egypt, and by consolidating it the Eighth Army had laid the foundation for the ultimate victory in North Africa.

Particular attention was paid, during consolidation, to the key defensive zone contained in the triangle El Alamein, El Hammam and the Qattara Depression. The most vital positions in this zone, and for that matter in the whole of the Alamein Line, were three prominent ridges running east and west. Of these, the northern ridge lay roughly along the coast, the central one was the well-known Ruweisat Ridge, and a southerly one was the Alam el Halfa Ridge. Strong points were sited on these ridges so as to have them within the artillery range of one another and to deny observation to the Axis. Each strong point was designed to take a garrison of

[17] *Ibid.*

two infantry battalions and one artillery regiment of 25-pounder guns. The rest of the field artillery was kept mobile. Escorted by motorised infantry and in combination with the armour, the mobile artillery was to attack the Axis troops with fire, wherever they might be seen, using the strong points as pivots of manoeuvre and observation.

Apart from the area of those strong points, there were other tactical spots that needed watching. The main defensive zone was about thirty miles deep and there were tactical areas to its north and south which had to be manned. For instance, in the north, light armoured troops guarded the passage towards Burg el Arab and in the south the Sudan Defence Force kept a watch on the road from Siwa, leading to Cairo through the Bahariya Oasis, that is, along the southern edge of the Qattara Depression. Another similar road, known as the Barrel Track, directly linking the south of the Alamein Line to Cairo, was left practically unguarded, as it lay across vast patches of soft sand and was considered unfit for use by heavy vehicles.

From 1 August onward, activities of the Eighth Army were confined to patrolling, exchanges of artillery fire and preparations for the renewal of the offensive. The XXX Corps was ordered to begin an intensive planning for a frontal attack south of the Tel el Eisa salient; and the XIII Corps was instructed to explore the possibilities of a break-through in the south and a movement round the southern flank of the Axis.[18]

While these preparations were going on, the Prime Minister of the United Kingdom, Mr. Churchill, accompanied by the Chief of the Imperial General Staff, General Sir Alan Brooke, paid a visit to Cairo, to study the Middle East situation on the spot. General Auchinleck was summoned to meet them on 6 August. Later there was a conference at which Field Marshal Smuts, General Wavell and the three Commanders-in-Chief were among those present. This was followed by a tour of the front-line for a study of the tactical situation in the areas of the XXX Corps and the XIII Corps. The final upshot of all those inspections and discussions was that on 8 August, General Auchinleck received a letter from the Prime Minister, informing him that in the opinion of the War Cabinet the moment had come to make a change in the Middle East Command and that it had been decided that he should be relieved of his responsibilities by General Sir Harold Alexander. The letter further stated that it was proposed to form Iraq and Persia into a new independent command, outside the Middle East Command. General Auchinleck was offered this new appointment; but this he declined after some days of careful consideration.

[18] *Ibid.*

Handing over the command of the Eighth Army temporarily to General Ramsden, General Auchinleck went to Cairo on 9 August, where he met General Montgomery, the Commander-designate of the Eighth Army, to whom he explained the existing situation and his future plans. After that, in accordance with the instructions received from Mr. Churchill, he handed over his command to General Alexander on 15 August 1942, thus bringing to a close one more chapter in the hard fighting in North Africa.[19]

[19] *Ibid.* Also *Operation Victory.*

CHAPTER XXXVII

The Battle of Alam el Halfa

The new Middle East Command

General Alexander assumed command of the Middle East Forces on 15 August 1942. The area of his command was smaller than that under his predecessor, General Auchinleck. It embraced Egypt, Syria, Palestine, Transjordan and Cyprus, but not Persia or Iraq. The latter two had been simultaneously constituted into a separate command, to be known as Persia and Iraq Force (better known by the abbreviation Paiforce) for which General Alexander carried no responsibility.[1]

At this particular period of time, the Middle East was being threatened from two directions, north and west. From west the German-Italian forces were advancing towards the Nile Delta and to stem that advance was going to be the main preoccupation of the Middle East Command. In the north, the menacing regions were Anatolia and Caucasus from either of which the Germans could burst into the Middle East group of countries, unless opposed by strong forces. Hitherto both the northern and western frontiers had been the responsibility of General Auchinleck who, not infrequently, found his attention divided by simultaneous threats from two different directions. This appears to have produced a belief in the War Office that General Auchinleck might have succeeded better in his operations in the west had he not been constantly worried by threats from the north.

The obvious remedy was to split the Middle East Command and divorce the northern from the western front. Mr. Churchill took this step during his visit to Cairo, and the result was the independent Persia and Iraq Command whose prime task it was to fend off the dangers from the north.

As already stated, these northern dangers threatened the Middle East from two regions of Anatolia and Caucasus. But only from Caucasus was the threat immediate and pressing. That from Anatolia was considered comparatively remote, as it was estimated that the Germans would not be ready to invade Turkey before the spring of 1943. It was therefore decided that Paiforce needed not concern itself with the probable break-through across Anatolia but should concentrate all its efforts against the menace from Caucasus.

[1] General Alexander's *Despatch*, pp. 840-44; *Alamein to Sangro*, pp. 1-10 and *Operation Victory*, pp. 142-150.

The Anatolian frontiers therefore remained the responsibility of the Middle East Command as not needing immediate attention. Freed from the anxiety of watching the Caucasian frontier, it was hoped General Alexander would be able to direct all his resources towards removing the Axis menace from Egypt and Libya before the spring. After that he would be in a position to oppose an advance through Turkey, should one materialise at all.

Thus on assuming command General Alexander found that he had one, single, all-important commitment—to clear the Axis out of Libya. The Directive given to him by Mr. Churchill stated: "Your prime and main duty will be to take or destroy at the earliest opportunity, the German-Italian Army commanded by Field Marshal Rommel together with all its supplies and establishments in Egypt and Libya." Tunisia was not mentioned at this stage as that field was then marked off for a separate expedition. It was reserved for a combined Anglo-American force which was to make a landing on the Algerian and Moroccan shores of North Africa some time later.

The new Army Commander

On taking his appointment General Alexander established an advanced tactical headquarters at Burg el Arab, adjoining the headquarters of the Eighth Army. His own headquarters continued to be located at Cairo. The command of the Eighth Army was to be given to Lieut.-General Gott, until then General Officer Commanding XIII Corps. But General Gott was killed a few days before, in an air-raid over the airfield from which he was to fly to Cairo for a brief rest. The next choice for this important command was General, later Field Marshal, Viscount Montgomery of Alamein, KG, GCB, DSO. General Montgomery was an old comrade-in-arms of General Alexander and had served under him in 1941. His experience and capacities were therefore well known to the latter.

It was natural that both, Generals, Alexander and Montgomery, should commence their tasks by reviewing the Alamein Line. It was here that the Axis advance had been stopped and it was through this line that the Axis forces would have to pass to reach Alexandria and Cairo. The line, as mentioned earlier, was a narrow waist of land between the sea and the Qattara Depression—the latter, a vast area of quicksands and salt-marshes reputed to be unsuited even for camel traffic. At its narrowest, the waist was about forty miles, and this width was initially covered by prepared defences which were based on four main defended localities. These latter were, from north to south, El Alamein, Deir el Shein, Qaret el Abd and the Taqa Plateau.

However, when General Alexander took command of the Middle East, he found that three out of these four defended localities had

General Sir Harold Alexander

Major-General F. I. S. Tuker

On Ruweisat Ridge

Indian troops re-enter Mersa Matruh

already been lost to the Axis. The only one that remained was what used to be called the Alamein "box". The line, therefore, on which the Axis troops were finally halted was not the Alamein Line as it originally existed but rather a revised version of it. Its left flank no longer rested on the Qattara Depression but on a peak called Qaret el Himeimat.

This shifting of the southern terminal of the Alamein Line from the Qattara Depression to Qaret el Himeimat, however, was not so great a disadvantage as might seem at first. The value of the Qattara Depression lay in its being able to stop an Axis advance towards the Nile. In the then existing state of the Alamein Line some such advance from its south flank was possible but only along one single road, namely the Barrel Track. This track, it will be remembered, was the one used by the 4th Indian Division, sometime earlier, for making its very first entry into the Western Desert and it led straight to Cairo. However, at this juncture it was not in a fit condition for being used for a full-scale advance as it had been worn out by the heavy traffic of the preceding operations. In addition, there was the further handicap that it was overlooked from Qaret el Himeimat. There was, therefore, little risk of the Axis troops attempting to use that route to reach the Nile Delta; and from that point of view it made little difference whether the left flank of the new line rested on the Qattara Depression or not.

Similarly it did not seem to make a vital difference whether the defended localities of Deir el Shein, Qaret el Abd and Taqa Plateau were in Allied hands or not. This was due to several reasons. Firstly, the country between the sea and the Barrel Track was forbidding. It was what might be described as a confusion of ridges, depressions and patches of soft sand such as no army would light-heartedly attempt to cross. Secondly, if the Eighth Army had lost those defended localities, it had, by way of compensation, scored some valuable gains in other directions. For instance, a month earlier it had captured two small but tactically useful ridges of Tel el Eisa and Tell el Makh Khad; and later it built defensive positions on another two very important key ridges of El Ruweisat and Alam el Halfa. All of these more than balanced the loss of defended localities constituting the original Alamein Line.

The Alamein Line

The new Alamein Line was therefore substantially different from that which barred the way of General Rommel early in July. Briefly it consisted of the El Alamein "box," the Tel el Eisa and Tell el Makh Khad features and the Ruweisat and Alam el Halfa ridges. The line started from the railway station of El Alamein which was closed in by a semi-circle of mines, wires and weapon pits. The south-east portion of that perimeter was joined by another line of defences commencing from Tel el Eisa and passing through Makh Khad. About twelve miles from this junction, down south, stood the Ruweisat Ridge, a long narrow cliff, about 200 feet high. The line from Tel el Eisa can be said to have continued up to this point, from where it ran roughly southward, over flat ground interspersed by depressions, of which the most important depression was the Deir el Munassib. South of Munassib at a distance of about eight miles stood Qaret el Himeimat, the most southerly strong point of the Alamein Line; and behind this chain of strong points, extending from Alamein to Himeimat, was situated the key position of the Alamein defences, the Alam el Halfa ridge.

Alam el Halfa stood in the rear of the Alamein—Himeimat line, roughly 15 miles from its centre. This ridge, more than 400 feet at its highest point, lay in a north-easterly direction overlooking the country to the south. It was the key post of the whole defensive system and ultimately proved to be a formidable barrier in the path of General Rommel. Its strength lay in its location in relation to the topography of the area over which General Rommel's forces should pass to reach the Nile Delta.

The topography of the land permitted an advance along the south of Alam el Halfa and the Ruweisat ridges but hardly from any other place. Were the Axis to occupy those two ridges, both of them would offer it a corridor of easy passage by which to outflank all defences to the north and drive straight on to Alexandria. But so long as those ridges remained Allied possessions, this was impracticable.

Such was the new Alamein Line which General Alexander inherited from General Auchinleck. It was by no means a weak structure. Tactically, the defences were well sited though militarily they were poor, having been prepared in haste and without enough troops or reserves. The Alam el Halfa ridge was particularly found to be poorly defended as if its paramount importance had not been fully realised.

Allied and Axis dispositions

When General Montgomery took over the Eighth Army, the Allied dispositions were, from north to south, the 9th Australian, the 1st South African and the 5th Indian Divisions. All of them were under XXX Corps. The front of the XXX Corps extended from the coast to the Ruweisat Ridge; that of the XIII Corps from that point to Himeimat. A little later, another division, the 50th (British), was added to this group of the above-mentioned dispositions. There were also other formations elsewhere, so that on the whole the Eighth army could be said to have at this date a strength of eight infantry divisions and four armoured divisions plus four independent brigades of which three were armoured formations.[2]

Facing this force of twelve divisions and four brigades was the Axis force comprising an equivalent of four German and nine Italian divisions, plus one German Para Brigade. The command of this force was nominally in the hands of Signor Mussolini who acted through his representative Marshal Bastico. Actual command in the field, however, was exercised by the Germans through General Rommel, whose immediate chief was Field Marshal Albert Kesselring. General Rommel's headquarters bore the name: *"Deutsch— Italienich Panzer Armee Africa"*, the Italian equivalent for it being *"Armata-Corazzata Italo-Tedesca"*. Both these designations meant the same thing: "The German-Italian Armoured Army of Africa".

This Army comprised four Corps, three Italian and one German. The German Corps was the well-known *Afrika Korps*; the other three were the X, XX and XXI Italian Corps. The German Corps comprised the 15th and 21st Panzer Divisions, the 90th Light (Motorised) Division, the 164th Infantry Division and what was known as the Ramcke Brigade of parachutists. In addition there was the 288 Special Force which was a heavily armed motorised group. The Italian force had two armoured and seven infantry divisions besides some odd groups. The Italian armoured formations were the Ariete and Littorio divisions; their infantry, which included the mobile or motorised groups, were the Trieste, Trento, Bologna, Brescia, Folgore, Pavia and Pistoia Divisions. Finally, there was, just then in the Siwa Oasis, another newly arrived formation known as the Young Fascists Division.

All German formations except the 164th Division were fully motorised.[3] The Italian divisions on the other hand were foot infantry except the three formations under XX (Mobile) Corps; namely the Ariete and Littorio armoured divisions and the Trieste motorised division. The 164th German Division had seen service in Crete. And in the African theatre of war its function was to stiffen the Italian infantry. For that reason, it used to remain nominally under the command of XXI Italian Corps while being administered directly by the *Panzer Armee*.

The XXI Corps thus consisted of the Trento and Bologna Divisions and the German 164th Division. Similarly the X Italian Corps, too, had a stiffening of German troops. It consisted of the Brescia and Folgore Divisions with two Battalions from the Ramcke Parachute Brigade. This last named was a body of four battalions

---
[2] For a detailed list of Allied and Axis forces, see Appendix V, p. 555.
[3] General Alexander's *Despatch*, pp. 842-43.

consisting of specially trained men, which had been organised in the first instance for an assault on Malta but was later used as infantry when the Malta attack was cancelled. The other three Italian Divisions, Pavia, Pistoia and Young Fascists, were outside the Corps.

This German-Italian force of four Corps, as described above, seemed to be well and suitably equipped for desert warfare. The German armoured divisions had Mark III and Mark IV tanks. Of the latter, some were mounting high-velocity guns of 75-millimetre calibre and were of the latest model. The Italian armoured divisions, too, were tolerably well off in the matter of arms and equipment. They were equipped with M-13 tanks—the thirteen-ton class —which were served by 47-millimetre guns. They were however poorly armoured and mechanically untrustworthy.

The greatest asset of Field-Marshal Rommel's army, however, was not tanks so much as anti-tank guns. Both German and Italian infantry divisions had a generous allotment of this weapon. They were usually 50-millimetre calibre, though captured Russian 3-inch, i.e. 7.62-mm. pieces, were also noticeable. The anti-tank guns were decentralised down to infantry companies, each company having from three to six pieces. This had the effect of turning infantry into strong anti-armour units which could produce good anti-tank screens at short notice, a method of defence which became a characteristic feature of German tactics during 1942-43. Infantry companies, thus equipped, were at times combined into special groups, when they were called *"Rampfgruppen"* or *"Raggruppamenti"* which were something like "columns of all arms" or "task forces" created for specific jobs.

New defensive arrangements

Such were Allied and Axis armies in the matter of their strength and composition in August 1942 when Generals Alexander and Montgomery arrived on the scene. The Eighth Army however was not the only body of Allied Troops in the Middle East. There was the British X Corps in the rear and some more troops under HQ, BTE, i.e. Headquarters, British Troops in Egypt. The latter were responsible for the administration and defence of Cairo and the Nile valley while the British X Corps had the task of defending Alexandria and the Delta.

The employment of the X Corps so far behind the operational area was more in the nature of a precaution against a possible collapse of the Alamein Line than anything else. The idea was that in such an emergency the Corps should defend the Nile Delta by holding the western edge of its cultivated area. The troops to be used were those which could not be used operationally due to lack of equipment or training. They were the 1st and 10th Armoured Divisions and the 44th, 50th and the 51st (British) Infantry Divisions. All of these were unfit for operations due to various reasons. The two armoured divisions, for instance, were re-equipping themselves; the 50th Division had had very heavy losses in recent actions at Gazala and Matruh; while the 51st Division had only just disembarked and was not even fully mobilized, much less trained. Only the 44th Division was somewhat ready for action.

General Alexander, as also General Montgomery, held the view that precautions against possible failures could be carried too far at times.[4] In their opinion keeping prepared positions ready to fall back upon in emergency was not always a sound policy; and if overdone it could breed diffidence, defeatism or a spirit of indifference in the army. They did not therefore look with favour upon all the defensive preparations going on behind the Alamein Line, particularly the Eighth Army's plan to withdraw in the last resort in two directions, namely eastward to Palestine and southward towards the Sudan. In fact, according to General Montgomery, the morale and determination of troops had been already undermined by plans for further withdrawals.[5] Referring to this state of affairs in his despatch, General Alexander said: "My first step in restoring morale, therefore, was to lay down the firm principle, to be made known to all ranks, that no further withdrawal was contemplated and that we would fight the coming battle on the ground on which we stood. General Montgomery, on his arrival, fully concurred in this policy and expressed his confidence in being able to fight a successful defensive battle in our present positions."

Having thus pinned his faith to the defence of the Alamein Line, General Alexander proceeded to curtail defensive preparations in the rear so as to release more troops for the operational area. He made the commander of the British Troops in Egypt responsible for the whole of the Delta and made the X Corps Headquarters available for the Eighth Army.

The task of the Eighth Army, briefly, was to hold its present position and to prepare, at the same time, for a general offensive. This was laid down in a Directive which General Alexander issued to General Montgomery on 19 August. Confirming previous verbal instructions, the Directive went on to say: "Your prime and immediate task is to prepare for offensive action against the German—Italian forces with a view to destroying them at the earliest possible moment. Whilst preparing this attack you must hold your present positions and on no account allow the enemy to penetrate east of

[4] General Alexander's *Despatch*, pp. 842-43.
[5] Gen. Montgomery: *Alamein to Sangro*, pp. 1-10.

them." The Eighth Army commander was further directed to make these decisions known to all troops.

Creating a new outlook

General Montgomery proceeded to give effect to the Directive by redisposing his troops and by taking steps to bring his army into full accord with his views as to what an army should be like. He had clear-cut ideas and strong views in these matters and not infrequently these were different from prevalent practices or orthodox teachings, and sometimes were even brand-new innovations. An important one amongst these, touching the disposition of troops, was his theory of tactical and strategic balance in the matter of proper distribution of the fighting forces. "Balance on the field," he wrote, "implies the disposal of available forces in such a way that it is never necessary to react to the enemy's thrusts and moves; a balanced army proceeds relentlessly with its plans in spite of what the enemy may do."

Even before taking command of the Eighth Army, General Montgomery had decided that the Eighth Army lacked such a 'balance' and needed a reserve corps for supplying the deficit. Such a corps would consist primarily of armoured divisions, would have to be well equipped and highly trained, and would never be used to hold static fronts. It would have to be specially trained to act as a spearhead in offensives, and would be generally held in reserve to be unleashed at a suitable moment in a battle so as to tip the scales at a critical juncture, or force the battle to conform to a predetermined pattern, or to neutralise surprises and maintain, so to say, a steady keel. The idea of holding such 'reserves' was not new by any means. But such reserves seldom consisted of highly trained and powerfully equipped troops in as large a formation as a corps. General Montgomery decided to use the X Corps in such a role. He ordered its equipping and training to begin at once as a matter of priority.

Among other military doctrines of General Montgomery were the ideas, enunciated so clearly for the first time then, that the morale of the troops was of paramount importance; that the men should have confidence in their leaders; they should be explained the overall plan so that they may know how they fit into it; that their living should be comfortable yet tough; that they should not be asked to perform jobs beyond their capacities or training; that they should not be broken up into groups of independent units but should be allowed to fight as whole and integrated divisions; that the armour and artillery should be employed in mass; that the three services should co-operate closely in any important action; that the worn-out commanders should be replaced by fresh minds; that the enthusiasm of men must be kept at a high pitch; that the atmosphere about them must be free from distractions; and finally, that the Eighth Army should be re-formed on a foundation of leadership, equipment and training.

These conceptions of managing an army may appear trite at this date. Nor were they new even then, as every one of them could be found in any standard military text-book. But their forceful implementation by General Montgomery was something novel and roused a tremendous enthusiasm amongst the men of the Eighth Army. That was one of General Montgomery's most remarkable contributions to victory in North Africa. He personally toured his command, met his officers and talked or lectured to them, explained his plans, views and methods of working, and took them into confidence without reserve. The Eighth Army proved highly receptive to his tonic suggestions and responded with enthusiasm. It felt new and rejuvenated; its self-confidence and morale returned. It was in that state of fitness when, towards the end of August, it looked as if General Rommel was preparing to launch an allout attack against it during the coming full moon.

The Alam el Halfa Ridge

Preparations against such an attack were already under way but by no means complete. Since all plans for withdrawal were cancelled, the old defence arrangements required major alterations. Defences now needed additional depth; and stocks of ammunition, rations and water had to be increased in the forward area. These matters were expedited as also the garrisoning of the Alam el Halfa Ridge.

Alam el Halfa Ridge as already explained was a feature of vital tactical importance. It had been spotted by General Montgomery, early during his tour of the battle zone. The ridge commanded a wide area of the desert and was so positioned that it could serve as a base from which to block the progress of the Axis to the north, i.e. towards Ruweisat Ridge which was the central bastion of Alamein defences. Alternatively, an Axis attempt to drive east or north-east could also be quashed from this same hill. Further, unless the Axis first secured this ridge it could not go past it in the southern sector either. The Alam el Halfa Ridge was thus one of the keys of the entire defensive system and General Montgomery decided to garrison it with a whole division. He asked for the 44th Division to be sent up from the Delta at once and entrusted it with the task of holding and strengthening the Alam el Halfa defences.

It may be mentioned here that while these preparations were going on, the Allied air force was waging a relentless war against the line of communication of the Axis. The Axis supply line had become considerably stretched and part of it lay across the sea from Italy to Africa. Fuel was then a great headache of General Rommel's QMG (Quarter Master General) who was receiving it across the Mediterranean in tankers. The submarines of the Royal Navy and aircraft of the Royal Air Force attacked these tankers as a first priority and more of them were sunk than were allowed to reach the Axis shores. As a result the already existing shortage of petrol must have become acute which, it is believed, had a vital effect on subsequent warfare.[6]

The Axis attack

The expected attack of General Romel came just after midnight on 30/31 August; and with that began a crucial battle, the Battle of Alam el Halfa, loss of which by the Allies might well have resulted in their final exit from North Africa. General Rommel was certain that the battle would accomplish the annihilation of the Allied army and actually announced to his troops that in two or three days they would be in Alexandria.

On the night of the attack the dispositions of the Allied forces were, from north to south, 9th Australian, 1st South African, 5th Indian and 2nd New Zealand Divisions. Behind them were disposed the 44th Infantry Division, the 22nd Armoured Brigade (of 7 Armed Div) and the 10th and 7th Armoured Divisions. Amongst these, as events proved, the important dispositions were the 5th Indian Division on the Ruweisat Ridge and the 44th British Division on the Alam el Halfa Ridge. The Alamein Line was held by two corps: from the coast to the Ruweisat Ridge inclusive, was the XXX Corps with Australian, African and Indian Divisions; from that point to the southern end was the XIII Corps front with the rest of the above named forces.

German-Italian dispositions opposing the Allied forces were, from north to south, the 164th German Division, the Italian Trento Division, the German Parachute Battalion, the Italian Bologna Division, another German Parachute Battalion and the Italian Brescia, Trieste, Ariete and Littorio Divisions. In the rear of this line, somewhat in the centre, was the German *Afrika Korps*.

The Battle of Alam el Halfa

The attack came in three thrusts—in north, centre and south. The main thrust was one in the south. It came in between the left flank of the New Zealand Division and the isolated hill, Himeimat.

---

[6] There was also a week-long pre-battle air offensive against Axis concentrations in the southern sector, during this period of preparations. About 430 tons of bombs were dropped and a direct hit was scored on the Afrika Korps HQ. Rommel attributed his failure in a large measure to this pre-battle "softening-up."

Here General Rommel employed the whole of his *Afrika Korps* and the 20th Italian (Mobile) Corps which included the Ariete and Littorio Armoured Divisions. All told, the southern thrust was a formidable affair. In comparison, the one in the north was a pretty weak effort and was easily repulsed by the Australians, being no more than a raid, while that in the centre was a medium-sized advance which hit the right of the 5th Indian Division and scored some successes on the Ruweisat Ridge. The western end of the Ruweisat Ridge was at this time being held by the Axis, and they therefore found it easy to press their advance. However, a strong counter-attack was put in by the Allies at first light on 31 August, and the whole of that hill was cleared successfully.

On superficial observation it was clear that the plan of the Axis was to break through the lightly-held southern sector of the Allies, and then, turning north, to drive towards the sea, behind the XXX Corps, thus rolling up the Allied line or encircling the Allied centre and right. But it was necessary for the Allies to wait and ascertain that there was no ruse or surprise involved in these apparent moves.[7]

General Montgomery says that his main preoccupation during 31 August was to determine exactly the direction of the Axis thrust line, and that on the morning of 1 September he was satisfied that the advance was directed on the Alam el Halfa Ridge and thence north towards the Ruweisat Ridge. Not until then did he move the bulk of his armour which he was holding to the south of Alam el Halfa for fear lest the Axis might attempt to strike east or north-east in a straight drive to the Delta.

Having convinced himself that the drive was not directed towards east or north-east, General Montgomery switched all that armour, which was under Headquarters 10th Armoured Division, to the area between the Alam el Halfa Ridge and the New Zealand Division's position. By the middle of the day (1 Sep.) nearly 400 tanks had been concentrated in that vital area. They were so disposed as to block the northward move of the Axis troops towards Ruweisat. At the same time the Ruweisat Ridge was strengthened by the addition of one brigade which was withdrawn from the South African Division. In order to preserve balance, a brigade of the 50th Division was brought from the rear area and posted in the area vacated by the 10th Armoured Division. Re-grouping of the forces was also taken in hand simultaneously as it was necessary to form new reserves to take place of the original ones moving into action.

It is necessary here to review all the successive Axis moves up to this stage. By 1000 hours on the first day of the attack (31 Aug.), strong Axis tank columns had penetrated the Allied minefields in

---

[7] General Alexander's *Despatch*, pp. 845-46; *Alamein to Sangro*, pp. 5-10.

the southern sector. They were moving eastward, while the troops of the 7th Armoured Division, whose task it was to oppose them, fell back in accordance with the orders that they should avoid becoming pinned to the ground. Late in the afternoon that day the Axis armour began to move north-east, i.e. directly towards the area favourable to the Eighth Army. It is believed that in doing so, General Rommel's troops walked into a trap carefully laid out for them. This is how it happened. General Montgomery was hoping that the Axis advance would proceed north in a "tight wheel" towards Alam el Halfa and not in a wide curve towards El Hammam. To induce the Axis to adopt the former course a false map was made purporting to show the desert surface in so far as movements of vehicles were concerned.

Eighth Army was accustomed to produce such maps showing terrain, some of which had been captured by the Germans who were known to be making use of them. It was now decided to make a similar "going" map wherein the area of "rough going" was to be shown as "good going" so as to induce the Axis troops to move in a narrow arc towards Alam el Halfa. The fake map was put through an ageing process by covering it with tea stains etc. and was "stuffed away in a haversack". A scout car, containing this haversack and sundry soldiers' kits, was then sent into the forward area and was got deliberately blown up on a mine during patrolling hours of the night. Next day the car was found to have been ransacked and the map was missing.

How far the Germans let themselves be deceived by this map is difficult to say. But their subsequent movements showed as if they had swallowed the bait. They moved over the sandy terrain, got "bogged down" badly, used up more petrol than anticipated and generally found themselves in a "fix". They still kept moving towards south of Alam el Halfa in a narrow arc.[8] At 1700 hours they made contact with 22nd Armoured Brigade which was well in a position to receive the impact. The Axis tanks suffered heavy casualties and withdrew to reorganise. During reorganisation their concentrations were bombed throughout the night.

The next morning, 1 September, they renewed their attack against the 22nd Brigade. Once again they suffered heavy casualties and withdrew to reorganise. By this time the 10th Armoured Division, with about 400 tanks, was firmly established in its new position. The German armour renewed its charge on the 22nd Brigade during the afternoon but meeting the 10th Armoured Division disengaged with a heavy loss.

Now the tide had turned and General Montgomery began planning a counter-stroke, while the relentless bombing of Axis con-

[8] Major-General De Guingand: *Operation Victory*, p. 149.

centrations continued throughout the day, 1 September. He decided to close the gaps in the minefield through which the Axis tanks had come in. This would bottle up the Axis armour. The XIII Corps formations began to move southward for closing the gaps, on the night of 3/4 September. The Axis forces fought back fiercely and withdrew successfully during 4 and 5 September. Thereafter fighting continued on the edge of the minefield until 0700 hours on 7 September when General Montgomery called off the battle. He was not prepared to waste the Army's strength in shoving the Axis off the western edge. Nor was he prepared to pursue the Axis if they started retreating, as he was determined to proceed methodically in his own time, i.e. only after all preparations for the big offensive were completed. Besides, he saw certain advantages in keeping some of the Axis troops tied up on his southern flank while he was preparing for the major offensive.

Thus ended the Battle of Alam el Halfa, an engagement of great significance. It was the Eighth Army's first major action under its new commander, and General Rommel's second major reverse since his arrival in Africa. Military critics are mostly agreed that it was a model defensive engagement in that the battle was fought with the automatism of a machine. All contingencies were foreseen and provided against. The units and individuals had their roles well defined and the battle virtually fought itself, everything moving smoothly like the parts of a well-oiled machine.

A few more characteristics of this battle are worth mentioning here. At a certain stage of fighting, about 3/4 September, General Montgomery directed that the fighting troops should pay greater attention to destroying the soft-skinned vehicles of the Axis. He laid stress on the need for knocking out as many supply lorries as possible so as to increase General Rommel's difficulties of administration. The Axis were known to be short of fuel; General Rommel himself declared later that his offensive had failed due to shortage of petrol. It would seem therefore that the destruction of vehicles, normally not a worthwhile objective in itself, was a proper, timely move. To further aggravate the shortage a night-bomber raid was directed on the Tobruk harbour which proved quite effective.[9] There were, besides, heavy and continual bombing attacks against the Axis L of C directed by the Headquarters of General Alexander in Cairo.

In this battle the Eighth Army fought as a single, united body

---

[9] It is claimed that by far the greatest destruction of soft-skinned vehicles, in the battle of Alam el Halfa, was the result of the RAF policy of "round-the-clock" bombing (by light and fighter-bombers during the day and medium bombers by night) against Axis concentrations in the Ragil Depression.

The highly debatable question of whether the destruction of soft-skinned vehicles is normally "a worthwhile object in itself" or not is best left to the judgment of each student of military tactics to decide as he thinks best. This military dictum is not intended to be taken in a final or decisive sense.

under the direct control of the Army Headquarters. Artillery and armour were used in concentrations. Defensive positions were so sited that the Allied armour never had to quit a ground once it had chosen it for making a stand. Tactical balance was maintained throughout the combat by re-grouping and continually drawing in reserves. The layout of the defence was such that the Axis troops met a dead wall in whatever direction they tried to go. The Air Force worked to the tactical plan of the Army and played the Army's game which it did for the first time on so large a scale as on this occasion. The battle fulfilled, it would appear, practically all the expectations of General Montgomery and prepared the way for the subsequent historic battle of El Alamein.

CHAPTER XXXVIII

Preparations for Counter-offensive

The Battle of Alam el Halfa delayed the final major offensive by about a fortnight. This was a disappointment to those who wanted an earlier offensive for political reasons. Mr. Churchill, whose legitimate function it was to balance the political against the military results, had sounded General Auchinleck on this point during his visit to the Eighth Army in August 1942. The latter however would not promise an early date and even refused to be drawn into a discussion on the point. Mr. Churchill was then on his way to Moscow and probably wanted to be in a position to promise something concrete to the Russian allies. But neither General Auchinleck nor his successor, General Alexander, nor for that matter General Montgomery, was willing to be hustled into an offensive without adequate preparations.[1]

Fixing the D-day

General Alexander estimated that the earliest date for opening the offensive would be some day during the last few days of September 1942. General Montgomery's estimate was nearly the same and Mr. Churchill had reluctantly agreed. But in the meanwhile, as already narrated, the German-Italian force attacked the Alamein Line during the last week of August which caused a set-back to that plan. About a whole week had been lost in actual fighting and subsequent reorganisation; and yet another week had to be allowed to go through for reaching the period of the full moon since moonlight was necessary for infantry attacks and for the operation of lifting mines. The next full moon was on 24 October and therefore 23 October was fixed as the D-day.

This revised date was accepted by Mr. Churchill but not without some dissatisfaction. Perhaps one of Mr. Churchill's anxieties was to so time the Eighth Army's offensive that it would fit smoothly into yet another and grander strategy of the African theatre of war which was then being prepared in great secrecy. That strategy concerned the landing of an Anglo-American force at certain selected points on the shores of North Africa. The landing

---

[1] General Alexander has since given the information that Mr. Churchill had told him that "Torch" would land in North Africa on 8 Nov. 1942 and that he wanted a big victory in the Western Desert, early enough to influence French opinion in North Africa, favourably to the Allies.

was in fact to be an invasion of North Africa from the west, while the Eighth Army would be driving on from the east. The invasion was scheduled for 8 November and understandably enough Mr. Churchill might have wanted to see an Eighth Army's offensive half way through before that date. The landing operation was code-named 'Torch' of which the final object was the occupation of the whole of Tunisia. But a factor to be reckoned with was the French Army in Tunisia which might resist with fatal consequences to 'Torch'. There was also a remote chance that Spain might admit Germans into the Spanish Morocco and thus jeopardise the success of the invasion project. Steps were being taken to win over the French through secret negotiations before making the landing, and Mr. Churchill no doubt felt that a successful offensive by the Eighth Army would favourably influence the attitude of the French. The date for D-day, 23 October, though rather late, still left about a fortnight for achieving such a result.

Ensuring secrecy and surprise

After the victory of Alam el Halfa, the Eighth Army threw itself heartily into the task of preparing for the offensive. A striking feature of these preparations was a deception scheme calculated to mislead the Axis commanders as to the actual date and the direction of the attack. General Montgomery calls it a 'cover plan' which is perhaps a more appropriate name as the aim of the scheme was to put an impenetrable cover on all preparations. The means adopted to attain this end were simply elaborate camouflage and at this stage of time there is nothing in them that is new. But when first produced, the cover plan was novel and original and some of the items are worth enumerating even today.

The basis of the camouflage was the maintenance of a constant density of vehicles throughout the entire zone of operations and in the rear area. The idea was to preserve an unchanging pattern of vehicle concentration on the ground so as to defeat the Axis air reconnaissances which necessarily relied on such clues for anticipating the moves and intentions of the Eighth Army. General Montgomery had already decided on making the main attack from the north while staging a feint in the south; and the deception scheme was accordingly aimed at suggesting a contrary intention on his part, i.e. a major offensive from the south and a diversion in the north. Care was also taken to suggest through the same means a possible date of attack which was about a fortnight behind the actual D-day.

The vehicle density was maintained by constructing a large number of dummy lorries, and by pooling all divisional transport. The layout of vehicles required for the main assault in the north was established on the ground as early as 1 October. This was not allowed to be disturbed except that during the period of concentrating troops in the forward areas the dummy transport was gradually replaced by real operational transport. This was done night after night during hours of darkness. All other reinforcements, including artillery, were dealt with in the same manner. Care was taken to preserve a uniform density even in the rear areas. As units and formations moved out from the rear, steps were taken to substitute dummies instantly so as to display the same unvarying pattern to an observer from the air. Dumps in the forward zone were concealed by stocking them so as to resemble vehicles. Similarly, dummy dumps were also made and located in a highly suggestive manner. Most important of all, a deliberate construction of a dummy pipeline was taken in hand ostensibly and started late in September, the progress of work being so timed as to suggest its completion by the first week in November. The pipeline was made of old petrol tins with fake pumping stations and reservoirs. It started from the real pipeline and lay in the direction of the southern sector whence only a diversionary attack was intended. Further, a large mock dump was started in the southern sector on 7 October and it was made to increase at a rate that would point to its completion by 5 November. Finally, the wireless network of the 8th Armoured Division was used to exchange sham internal messages purporting to be about preparation for an offensive from the south in early November.

Concentrations of artillery on the XIII Corps front were first shown by dummy guns; later they were replaced by real ones. The principal difficulty in all sectors was that vehicle tracks were impossible to conceal and yet they were the most revealing indications of movements and concentrations since they could be seen clearly in aerial photographs. The only solution that proved practicable was to refrain from making tracks beyond a certain point until a very late hour, and conversely to make purposeless tracks in other directions that could mislead.

Difficulty was also experienced in concealing the forward movement of X Corps. This formation was training about fifty miles behind the line from where it had to move forward to two separate staging areas and thence to the assembly areas. The moves could be carried out openly, as training moves, up to the staging areas only. Any progress beyond, towards the assembly areas, had to be carefully camouflaged. This was done by filling the two staging areas with about 2000 vehicles each, as early as 6 August. The vehicles also included about 700 dummy vehicle-bodies to be placed over the tanks of X Corps. The final moves to the assembly areas commenced on 19 October after the hour of darkness. All tanks and guns moved entirely by night and exchanged places with their dummy opposite numbers which, in turn, went back to fill the vacancies in the staging areas.

Supplies and equipment

Amongst other items of preparation not the least important were those relating to supplies and equipment and their delivery. The Middle East already possessed a highly developed administrative machinery and the staffs were well experienced in desert problems. The railway transport, too, was enough and the distances were short. There was, therefore, no difficulty initially in laying up stores and reserves. But it would be different in case of a pursuit of retreating Axis troops over long distances and preparations were necessary to meet such a situation. The problem was solved by raising a sufficient number of transport companies.

In previous campaigns pursuits were limited by the bulk of transport available. Third-line transport was never enough in the past. Now, since 23 August, the situation had changed favourably due to the arrival of enough personnel and equipment to create more than fifty General Transport Companies.[2] The function of a general transport company was to carry ammunition, petrol, water, etc. to the forward troops and normally one such company sufficed to keep a division well-supplied over a distance of fifty miles on good roads. As there were very few good roads in the desert, sometimes as many as six companies were required to do the work of one. The task of carrying provisions to the fighting troops was further simplified by the arrival, in the Middle East, of about 300 Carriers.

There had also arrived at about the same time, 13 September, nearly one thousand tanks which included nearly three hundred "Shermans" received from the United States.[3] These latter were equal in armament, armour and performance to the best that the Germans had yet brought to Africa. To these were being added daily a large number of repaired tanks and lorries from the workshops of the Eighth Army. Finally, as many as forty-nine pioneer companies were assembled and equipped to carry out the various manual tasks which indirectly eased the general supply and transport problems.[4] The vastness of those problems may be gauged from the fact that at about this period the Middle East ports were handling something like 460,000 tons of military stores per month; and the number of men employed in those operations amounted to about

---

[2] Gen. Alexander's *Despatch*, p. 848.
[3] To give precise figures, 1348 tanks had arrived by the third week of October, of which 285 were Shermans.
[4] According to a U.K. version, however, only 23 Pioneer Companies were available till 23 Oct. 1942.

three-hundred-thousand troops, half a million civilians and a million and a half of contracted labour.

Training and acclimatisation

Side by side with the administrative preparation the operational preparations went ahead, especially after 6 September. Training of the troops received a high priority since General Montgomery was building his campaign on the three basic principles of leadership, equipment and training. The first two essentials were satisfactorily available but the standard of training left much to be desired. The general rule adopted, after 6 September, was that all troops, whether in the line or in the rear, were to undergo a course of intensive instructions in which the characteristics of terrain and the conditions of fighting were to be anticipated and reproduced as far as possible. All arms were trained together and taught to co-ordinate. Troops were drilled in the special characteristics of desert warfare, such as maintaining direction by compass, controlling movement of convoys, lifting mines, using wireless, and above all keeping healthy. A rapid exchange of units and formations between the forward and the rear areas started from 8 September, so as to give to the troops deployed in the Delta a chance to get acclimatised to life in the desert.

One of the most important training jobs was to prepare the X Corps for the important role it was to fulfil, namely that of an armoured force which was intended to be the decisive factor in the coming battle. The three hundred Sherman tanks received from the USA were utilised to equip some three armoured brigades and all tank crews were given a chance to see and study their new equipment.

It may be mentioned here that the overall plan for the forthcoming offensive was to employ all the three corps headquarters available, namely XXX, XIII and X, the first two of which were infantry corps with some armour, while the last, the X, was to be entirely armoured. It was hoped to include three armoured divisions in the X Corps, the 1st, 8th and 10th. But there was shortage of infantry which must go with an armoured division. It was therefore decided to disband the 8th Armoured Division and put its brigades under the command of such infantry or armoured formations as would be best able to employ them.

First plan

While his staff were busy with administrative problems, General Montgomery was finalising his plan for the main offensive. The first plan which he submitted to General Alexander was more or less on the accepted orthodox lines. In that General Montgomery outlined his intention to make the main thrust in the north, with a secondary attack in the south to pin down in that place as much of the Axis strength as possible. The XXX Corps, under General Leese, was to open a way through the northern defences. This was to be done by clearing two corridors through the minefields along both of which was to pass the X Corps under General Lumsden. At the same time the XIII Corps, commanded by General Horrocks, was to carry out two operations in the south, one against the Himeimat—Taqa features and the other in the areas round Gebel Kalakh and Qaret el Khadim. The X Corps, after passing through the gaps in the northern defences, was to sit astride the supply line of the Axis and thus force the latter's armour to come out for clearing that line. The hostile armour was then to be engaged and destroyed, after which the unarmoured infantry was to be dealt with in the normal traditional manner. This plan was evolved in September.

The modified plan

Early in October, however, it became evident to General Montgomery that the standard of training achieved by the Eighth Army was not enough to push through such an ambitious project. In his view a modification was necessary to balance this weakness. Accordingly, while retaining his original plan intact, he introduced one simple innovation which changed the entire aspect of the fighting. Instead of adhering to the prevailing practice of first destroying an opponent's armour and then dealing with his helpless unarmoured troops, General Montgomery decided to do the reverse. The infantry was to be destroyed first while the hostile armour would be merely held off at a distance. No armoured force can function successfully unless there is enough infantry to ensure for it firm and safe bases from which to operate and manoeuvre. Without such bases, which are held and protected by infantry, units of an armoured force would be completely at sea. They would not know where to go for re-fuelling and for drawing supplies or ammunition. Nor would they be sure of their line of communication or of the area vital for their movements and action. Placed in such a predicament, an armoured force has to withdraw or perish. Therefore the decision of General Montgomery to upset the normal sequence of attack was a brilliant stroke and a bold departure from the text-book standards.

The new plan, including this prior attack on Axis infantry, was given out by General Montgomery on 6 October. The process of destroying the infantry as a first task has been designated by General Montgomery himself as the "crumbling" process, i.e. a methodical grinding down of the unarmoured troops. It was to be expected that the Axis armour would not permit this and would attack the Allied forces carrying out this grinding process. In anticipation of that General Montgomery decided that the "crumbling" operation would start only after the 10th Armoured Division had been passed through the Axis defences, and positioned on a ground of its own choosing. Should the Axis tanks attack it there, the 10th Division would be fighting them from entrenched positions and would be in a position to inflict heavy casualties. Were the Axis, on the other hand, to refuse to take that risk, the effect would be that of their armour being held off at a distance while their infantry were being subjected to a systematic "grinding."

Except for this notion of the "crumbling" process, the final plan of the Eighth Army's offensive was substantially the same as the previous one. Six simultaneous operations were intended: two in the north for forcing two corridors in the XXX Corps sector and two more in the south to keep the Axis troops tied up in the XIII Corps sector, while one operation was to take place in the coastal area and another one on the Ruweisat Ridge.[5]

All these operations related only to the first phase of the offensive which later started from the Alamein Line. That offensive, it may be explained here, was eventually carried out in three distinct phases. The first of these was the stage of blasting an opening in the Axis defences and has been named by General Montgomery as the "break-in" attack. The second has been called by him the "dog-fights" which was expected to be a period of hard and prolonged fighting for breaking right through those defences. This was the period for the "crumbling" operations. And the last was the "break-out" stage leading on to advance towards Benghazi. The six operations enumerated above related only to the "break-in" stage and the plan setting forth the manner of their development went under the code-name of operation 'Lightfoot'.

A few more points only remain to be mentioned in this connection. First, although the primary task of the X Corps was to hold off or engage the Axis armour, it was also expected to assist the XXX Corps in the latter's operations against the German-Italian infantry whenever possible. Secondly, again, although the main job of the XIII Corps was to make a feint attack, it was also expected to perform a secondary task if possible, that is, to open a lane through the minefields in its own sector and to send out the 7th Armoured Division through it to exploit northward towards Daba, which was the rear of the Axis troops. However, since this Armoured Division was a part of the general reserve for maintaining the tactical balance on the front, it was not to be risked in an obviously rash venture.

Air Plan

The general plan of attack by the three corps was closely interlinked with air, navy and artillery plans. The air plan, under Air

---

[5] *Alamein to Sangro*, pp. 18-26; Gen. Alexander's *Despatch*, p. 852.

Marshal Tedder and directed from General Alexander's Headquarters at Cairo, rested on about 500 fighters and 250 bombers then available.[6] This force, by no means very large by present-day standards, was to fight and win the air battle before the land fighting could commence. It was first to win an ascendancy over the Axis air force, and then turn its whole effort to assisting intimately in the land battle. In between, it was to undertake attacks against the Axis gun positions, aid the counter-battery war of artillery and keep a watch on hostile armoured divisions. The pre-battle air offensive against Axis airfields was to commence about five days before the land offensive.

Navy's plan

The plan of the navy was to distract the attention of the Axis Commanders during the battle by making a feint landing behind their lines. The landing was timed to take place about three hours after the commencement of the land battle. It was hoped that this would tie down some Axis reserves. The operation was deliberately designed to create a scare, and so the assault ships were loaded openly in the hope that they would be seen by the Axis agents and duly reported. The convoy sailed west from Alexandria at about 4 p.m. on D-day. Shelling of the Axis coast started after dark and much noise and show was made with mortars, machine-guns and light signals. Nothing substantial resulted but it is possible that it helped the land battle by creating confusion behind the fighting lines of the Axis.

Artillery's plan

By far the best, however, was the artillery plan. It was something never seen before in the Eighth Army. A formidable number of guns was collected for the opening phase of the offensive. The number of field, medium and anti-tank guns available for D-day, excluding the replacement was 2182. There were 832 25-pounder (Field), 849 6-pounder (anti-tank) and 554 2-pounder (infantry anti-tank) guns. Besides there were guns of other calibres, of which twenty-four were 105-mm (Field) guns. The artillery's was not the only fire-power available to the Eighth Army. There were tanks with 6-pounder and 2-pounder guns, Shermans, Grants, Stewarts, Crusaders and Valentines. They totalled 1348 as on D-day, excluding replacements.[7] The plan of using the artillery was to start with a heavy bombardment of located Axis batteries and then to switch

---

[6] Another 60 torpedo bombers were concentrated against the Axis lines of communication across the Mediterranean.

[7] In addition, there were available, in an anti-tank role, there 18-pdrs of 1 SA Div., sixty-five 75-mm captured guns in possession of the Free French and 7 more captured guns of the 50-mm type.

on to forward position with intense concentrations and barrages. The guns kept in readiness for the H-hour were over a thousand and in a particular six-mile sector they averaged to one gun for every twenty-three yards.

Axis dispositions

If the Allied preparations for the coming offensive were proceeding apace, those of the Axis were not far behind. After their defeat at Alam el Halfa, the Axis commanders were in no mood to be self-complacent. They had been most energetic during the two months thereafter, strengthening and deepening their defences. In the northern sector they had fortified their positions with three belts of minefields and defended localities. These were at places linked up by transverse minefields. The whole layout was contrived to entice the attackers into certain easy-going channels and then lure them on to areas, seemingly clear but actually encircled by mines, where they would be brought under fire from all sides. The defences in the southern sector were not so intricate or thorough but the general idea behind their build-up seemed to be to canalise any possible Allied advance into narrow lanes. As a rule, the minefields were from 5000 to 9000 yards in depth and were well protected by infantry.

Entrenched behind and inside the minefields were the Italian and German infantry and armour. The infantry, mostly Italian, were in the front line. Behind them stood the armour and the light motorised divisions. The infantry, counting them from north to south, were the Bersaglieri, the 164th German Division, some detached German units, the Italian Trento and Bologna Divisions, two German para battalions, the Brescia Division, another German para battalion, the Folgore and Pavia Divisions and the German Kiel and Recce groups. Echeloned behind in depth were the four Axis armoured divisions, two facing the northern sector and the other two the southern sector. The former were the 15th Panzer and Littorio Divisions and the latter 21st Panzer and the Ariete Divisions. Still further behind, right in the north, were the 90th Light and the Trieste Divisions.

A careful study of these dispositions would reveal three interesting facts, namely that the Italian troops were sandwiched between German troops on either side, to hold them in place; that the whole of the *Afrika Korps* was held in reserve, and that the German infantry were kept nearer the coast to protect the vital coastal road.

Allied dispositions

Facing the Axis line stood the Allied forces, disposed, from north to south, in this order: the 9th Australian, the 51st British, the 2nd New Zealand, the 1st South African and the 4th Indian Divisions, the Greek Brigade, the 50th and 44th British Divisions,[8] and the Free French. Between the 4th Indian Division and the Greek Brigade was the Corps boundary line, the southern boundary of the XXX Corps being the Ruweisat Ridge inclusive. Behind the line of infantry, and in depth, were held the reserves of Eighth Army which were intended to preserve the tactical balance during the fighting. They were the X Armoured Corps in the north and the 7th Armoured Division in the south. The formations under the X Corps were the 1st and 10th Armoured Divisions.

As D-day drew nearer, General Montgomery toured the Eighth Army and addressed its officers, down to the rank of Lieutenant-Colonel. He explained to them the manner of fighting the battle and the issues depending on it and took them into confidence on every pertinent detail. The officers were thus enabled to visualise the pattern of the coming battle and to conform to it. They likewise explained the battle to their own troops on 21 and 22 October and the result was that the Eighth Army went into action with every man aware of what was expected of him.

By now, (21 Oct.), the Allied air force which had been preparing the ground for the Eighth Army's offensive by continual raids on Axis airfields, was getting into swing. It stepped up its heavy air attacks against Axis airfields and communications.[9] The climax was reached on 22 October.

Eve of the battle

D-day was 23 October and on the night of 22/23 the fighting troops settled down in their forward assembly areas. By first light all were dug in and well camouflaged. They spent 23 October in their slit trenches, unobserved and waiting for the moment of crisis. Absence of shelling told them that the Germans and Italians in front of them were unaware of their presence. It was a happy augury for they would have all the advantage of a tactical surprise.

---

[8] 133 Inf. Bde. of 44 British Div., it would appear, was out of the line at this date and attached to X Corps.

[9] Ample testimony is available in captured German documents as well as in papers of General Rommel of the great work done by the air force in completely cutting off the Panzer Army from its seaborne supplies of fuel and ammunition. In fact, it would be hardly any exaggeration to say that without it the Cover Plan of General Montgomery would not have succeeded as well as it did.

CHAPTER XXXIX

The Battle of El Alamein

The battle of El Alamein opened at 2140 hours on 23 October 1942. Dead on the minute, nearly a thousand field and medium guns went off with a crash, all of them firing against previously located Axis batteries. The fire lasted fifteen minutes. A counter-battery fusillade on so massive a scale cannot but produce impressive results and the noise and spectacle at the firing end have been described by witnesses as terrific. At the Axis end nearly all the guns were silenced before 2155 hours, after which there was a 5-minute pause to induce Axis troops to emerge from cover. The fire reopened at 2200 hours against the forward positions facing the Alamein Line, and almost simultaneously the infantry of the XIII and XXX Corps advanced to attack.[1]

Four divisions of the XXX Corps, moving in a line, attacked in the northern sector between the Tel el Eisa feature and the Miteiriya Ridge. It was a narrow front of 6 to 7 miles and the attacking troops (from north to south) were the 9th Australian, the 51st Highland, the 2nd New Zealand and the 1st South African Divisions. The New Zealand Division, in addition to its own infantry formations, had the 9th Armoured Brigade under its command. The task of the attackers was to force two corridors on their front through the minefields. Two divisions, the 9th Australian and the 51st British attacking due west, were to make the northern corridor, just north of the Miteiriya Ridge, New Zealanders and South Africans were responsible for the southern corridor.

The diversionary moves, relative to this XXX Corps front, were a feint attack in its extreme north and a vigorous raid in the south. The former was to be carried out by an Australian brigade; the latter, which was to be a strong attack on the Ruweisat Ridge, was entrusted to the 4th Indian Division. A minor landing in the rear, as already mentioned, was calculated to produce distraction in the Axis camp.[2]

Breaking in

The XXX Corps made satisfactory progress for the first few

---

[1] Gen. Alexander's *Despatch*, p. 583; *Alamein to Sangro*, pp. 18-20 and *Operation Victory*, pp. 195-200. War Diaries 4 Division, 1 R. Sussex, 7 Rajput, 2 Gurkhas.
[2] W/Ds 4 Division, 5 Brigade, 1/4 Essex, 4/6 Raj Rif., MG Bn., 6 Raj Rif., 3/10 Baluch.

hours after the attack. It captured most of the forward defences in two hours and carried forward the attack to the main Axis positions after a brief halt for reorganisation. Soon after, leading elements of the 1st and 10th Armoured Divisions (X Corps) crossed the start-line as planned. But stiffer resistance began to be encountered thereafter, as Axis troops recovered from the shock of the initial attack. Heavy fighting continued all night and it was not until 0530 hours that the XXX Corps was in possession of most of its final objectives. The two corridors through the minefields had been made as intended and the armour was moving forward to pass through. In the southern corridor, the 9th Armoured Brigade had already managed to get across the first belt of mines.

While the infantry of the XXX Corps found it comparatively easy to push the two corridors through the first belt of minefields, its task grew more difficult as it penetrated deeper. In consequence, the armour that was to follow through got behind schedule. The 1st Armoured Division slowed down and stopped, as the 51st Division which was to pave the way for it was itself held up in front of a strong Axis locality. The 10th Armoured Division was likewise checked in its progress by a strong anti-tank screen and artillery fire; and even the 9th Armoured Brigade which had started off well came to a halt a little forward of the Miteiriya Ridge on meeting further minefields and heavy anti-tank fire. The situation at daybreak on 24 October was that the infantry had gained most of its tactical objectives but the engineers were unable to clear gaps in the minefields for the X Corps to pass through.

In the southern sector of the Alamein Line where the XIII Corps was operating, the situation was no more gratifying. The operating divisions there were the 50th and 44th Infantry and the 7th Armoured. The role of the XIII Corps was secondary to the main attack in the northern sector. It was merely to tie up the Axis troops, especially the 21st Panzer Division. It tried to achieve this object by forcing two gaps in the minefields, north of Himeimat. The attempt was unsuccessful and the XIII Corps found itself held up by some scattered patches of mines between two major minebelts. An attempt by the Free French to take Hunter's Plateau was also unsuccessful.

Whether the XIII Corps made a headway or not was actually not important so long as it achieved its primary aim of containing the Axis troops on its sector. But progress of the XXX Corps was very vital to the success of General Montgomery's offensive, since on it depended the progress of the X Corps. On the morning of 24 October, General Montgomery studied the situation as far as it had developed and reached the conclusion that it would be fatal to lose any more time in pushing the X Corps through the minefields. He accordingly left the XXX Corps to carry on with its efforts to carve out the required corridors while, to aid it, he instructed the XIII Corps to commence "crumbling" operations in the southern sector.

Following up those instructions, the XIII Corps spent the day in "crumbling" actions and achieved some valuable results. During the same day and the following night, the XXX Corps made vigorous efforts to get the X Corps out into the open. It launched two fresh attacks for opening the north and south corridors respectively. The attack for the north corridor started at 1500 hours. It was made by the 51st and the 1st Armoured Divisions and was pressed with determination. After three hours of fighting a brigade of the 1st Armoured Division broke through the minefields and took up positions beyond. As to the southern corridor, the offensive was resumed at 2200 hours, the 10th Armoured Division attacking with the support of the XXX Corps artillery.

It soon became evident that the attack towards the southern corridor was making no worthwhile progress and was in fact in the danger of an imminent collapse. Should it fail, it would cancel much of the advantage of whatever little success was achieved in the sector of the northern corridor. That would mean a complete failure of the XXX Corps' operations and therefore of the whole of General Montgomery's offensive which was based on the assumption that the XXX Corps would be able to open the corridors necessary for the passage of the X Corps. General Montgomery certainly had other plans ready to meet such a breakdown. But the failure of the initial effort would mean delay in fulfilling a laid down programme and might perhaps result in a loss of morale and initiative.

Therefore, when reports reached the Army Headquarters during the night of a lack of progress in the sector of the southern corridor, the Army Commander took the matters in hand and after reviewing the situation issued firm orders at 0400 hours that the 10th Armoured Division could, and would, get forward. His peremptory and uncompromising orders were fully justified when at 0800 hours the leading brigade of that division reported itself as being 2000 yards beyond the minefield. A regiment of the second brigade also broke through at about the same time. The 9th Armoured Brigade in the New Zealand sector had in the meanwhile crossed over in its own area. Thus on the morning of 25 October the situation stood completely transformed. The objective of getting the armour across had been achieved and the "break-in" phase of the offensive was over. The "dog-fight" stage began almost at once.

The Dog-Fight

The "dog-fight", as predicted by General Montgomery proved to be a ten-day spell of the fiercest struggle. The first day was marked by several counter-attacks from the 15th Panzer Division, including one near the Kidney Hill in which about 100 tanks were used by the Axis. But the Eighth Army's armour was now firmly placed and was able to repulse all attacks with heavy casualties to the Axis.

While the tank clashes were going on near Kidney Hill, the XIII Corps was carrying out "crumbling" operations, particularly in the New Zealand Division's sector. At that stage, General Montgomery took two important decisions which greatly enhanced the speed of Eighth Army's drive. His first decision was to switch the "crumbling" process from the New Zealand sector to the 9th Australian Division's sector in the north; and the second decision was to stop XIII Corps' advance altogether and instead to push the 1st Armoured Division north-westwards, towards the Rahman track, to cut the main supply line of the Axis. The 1st Armoured Division, it will be recalled, was in XXX Corps sector as also the 9th Australian Division; so the effect of the change-over was to transfer the weight of the attack almost completely to the XXX Corps front. Thus the XIII Corps would be saved from incurring heavy casualties as its operations were proving expensive, and the 7th Armoured Division would be kept intact for preserving the tactical balance of the Eighth Army's front.[3]

The Australian operations went very well, considering that the defences opposite to them were strong and were manned by Germans. The area saw some of the fiercest fighting of the campaign. About three hundred casualties were suffered by the Germans who also yielded some ground to the Australians. But the most fruitful consequence of the operation was that General Rommel began to suspect, much to his own detriment, that the Eighth Army's main attack was going to be made from that sector; he therefore began withdrawing troops from XIII Corps area and massing them opposite to the Australians.

While the Australians were thus engaging the Germans, the 1st Armoured Division was trying to penetrate westwards. The object of that move was to pass an armoured brigade on to the Rahman track which was the main supply route of the Axis. In doing so the armour would not only cut General Rommel's supply line but could also pave the way for getting behind the Axis defences of the coastal salient. The Rahman area was the key to the Axis supply routes in their rear and capture of that area was sure to

---

[3] *Alamein to Sangro*, pp. 22-26; *Operation Victory*, pp. 202-207. General Alexander's *Despatch*, pp. 853-55.

complicate supply problems of General Rommel and accentuate his shortage of petrol. It was natural for Germans to be sensitive to such a threat and they therefore offered a very strong resistance. As a result, the 1st Armoured Division failed to make appreciable progress until the night of 26/27 October when at last one of its formations, the 7th Motor Brigade, reached the area of the Kidney Hill. As it turned out ultimately, General Montgomery's action in stopping the operations in the XIII Corps area had had a profound effect on the course of the campaign in the next few days. For one thing, General Rommel was led to pin his faith to his appreciation that the Eighth Army's drive was coming from the Australian sector; and he lost that gamble. For another, it enabled General Montgomery to pull out formations from the XIII Corps front and to start re-grouping for the final phase of the offensive. The idea behind re-grouping, it may be presumed, was to create a large reserve for launching a drive in a direction different to that to which General Rommel might be irretrievably committed, or failing that to exploit otherwise according to the opportunities of the situation.

The first stage in re-grouping was to withdraw the 2nd New Zealand Division into reserve. The gap was filled by the 4th Indian and the 1st South African Divisions spreading themselves out, towards the right, so as to cover all New Zealand positions. As a result the 4th Indian Division passed under the command of the XIII Corps.[4]

On this day, 26 October, the situation was by no means so clear as to warrant an optimistic outlook. Therefore General Montgomery's foresight in starting to re-group at this stage must be regarded as something very remarkable. The X Corps had broken out into the open country but only to find that its "break-in" area was ringed by a strong wall of anti-tank guns and infantry. The Axis had withdrawn these in time and had rearranged them in a greater depth so that X Corps lacked space for a free manoeuvre, in spite of its having broken out into the open. As to infantry, the assaulting divisions among them had suffered rather heavy casualties and the XXX Corps needed a short pause to reorganise. There was also a lack of replacements for the New Zealand and South African Divisions. The only bright spots were that the Eighth Army's armour still consisted of about 800 runners and the ammunition situation was quite satisfactory.

As the XIII Corps front relapsed into quiescence, the Germans made bold to withdraw their 21st Panzer Division from that area and to move it northwards. This they did during the night of 26/27 October. In the morning, the Allied wireless direction finding team located it as being opposite the Kidney Hill.

---

[4] W/D's 4 Div, 5 Bde, 1/4 Essex, 4/6 Raj Rif., 3/10 Baluch.

The same day, 27 October, General Montgomery asked the XIII Corps to make arrangements for moving the 7th Armoured Division and other troops to the northern sector. This was the second stage of re-grouping. The other troops were some three brigades, namely a brigade each of the 44th and 50th Divisions and the Greek Brigade. All these formations were to be sent to the northern front to assist the Australians, by reliefs and otherwise, in developing a vigorous drive in that sector. General Montgomery had been earlier impressed with the results of the Australian attack on the night of 25/26 October and he now decided to intensify their drive. He also decided to persist in his original plan of establishing armour in the Rahman track area and eventually getting behind the Axis troops holding the coastal salient. That, at the moment, appeared to be the proper course for opening the coastal route for an advance towards Benghazi.

The position on 27 October was that the whole of the *Afrika Korps*, i.e. the 15th and 21st Panzer Divisions, was ranged against the northern corridor. Throughout that day these two German divisions made heavy counter-attacks against the Kidney Hill. In all cases they were repulsed with considerable losses to themselves. The 1st Armoured Division alone took a toll of fifty Axis tanks knocked out. The RAF must have played a similar havoc with their constant bombing of Axis tanks as they were forming up for attack. On the whole, enough German armour had been knocked out in one day to prevent the Axis from mounting further attacks in that sector. General Montgomery therefore put that sector on to the defensive and withdrew the 1st Armoured Division, along with the 24th Armoured Brigade, into reserve.

The Break-out

All was now ready for a vigorous drive to the west. That was to be the final break-out stage. The New Zealand Division was selected to lead the thrust. But since that formation was below strength, it was arranged that the three brigades that had been moved up from the XIII Corps area were to work with it and keep it at operational strength during the attack.

It would appear that the plan of attack which General Montgomery had in his mind at this stage was not the one which finally succeeded. The other plan which did succeed was no doubt also present in his mind as one of the many possibilities, but it was not the one which appealed to him in the situation then existing. As late as 27 October he was firm in his belief that the best course for a safe and speedy advance was a vigorous attack by the 9th Australian Division northwards for reaching the coastal road and wiping off the coastal salient of the Axis; this being combined with a westward drive by the XXX Corps along the coast—the New Zealand Division leading. The armour in that case was to be used to protect the southern flank of the XXX Corps and generally to hold off the Axis tanks. The XXX Corps, progressing along the road and railway route, was to capture Sidi Abd el Rahman which was a vital point on the line of communication of the Axis. On the basis of this plan, General Montgomery gave orders on 27 October for the 9th Australian Division to launch its attack on the night of 28/29 October.

This in essence was the "break-out" plan. It was christened 'Supercharge', a code-name which General Montgomery used repeatedly hereafter to designate some of his most important battles. The attack by the 9th Australian Division was to prepare the ground for launching the 'Supercharge'. Therefore it was not a part of the "break-out" operations proper.[5]

The Australians attacked on the night of 28/29 October as ordered. They succeeded in driving a wedge into Axis positions and reaching out to within half a mile of the coast road. It was a strong effort to wipe off the coastal salient of the Axis and much opposition was encountered round Thompson's Post which was the bastion of that salient. Axis forces made several counter-attacks, that and the following day, to destroy the Australian wedge. But all those attacks, made with tank and infantry, were held and repulsed.

It was after the Australian attacks had gone in that 'Supercharge' came into being. While it was being discussed and given its shape on the morning of 29 October, an alternative plan was suggested by some concerned in the discussion. These latter thought that it would be better to shift the axis of advance a little more to the south, since there were more German troops and mines on the coastal axis already selected. General Montgomery did not agree with this view and the line of advance remained as already decided. It is, however, possible that even then the Army Commander was actively considering contingencies in which he might have to revise his view and adopt the suggestion made to him.

Such a contingency arose within a few hours. Late that morning, 29 October, the Army Commander received information which showed that the 90th Light Division had moved into Sidi Abd el Rahman area. That was an important piece of information. It showed that General Rommel had reached the conclusion that the main attack of the Eighth Army would emerge from the extreme north and proceed along the rail and road axis. Such indeed was the plan of General Montgomery, and General Rommel

---

[5] War Diaries 4 Div, 5 Bde, 1/4 Essex, 3/10 Baluch, 4/6 Raj Rif.

had guessed it correctly. No doubt the vigorous Australian attack was the most important factor in leading the Axis Commander to that conclusion.

As a result General Montgomery modified his breakout plan. He moved the axis of his westward drive further to the south. The new line of advance meant that the blow would fall mainly on the Italians at a point where the Italian and German troops formed a junction. There was however to be no slackening in the drive of the Australians northwards to the sea, lest a hint should reach General Rommel of the change in the Allied plan. On the contrary, the drive was to be intensified and General Rommel's suspicions were to be strengthened so that the 90th Light Division might remain tied up in the Sidi Abd el Rahman area.

Accordingly the 9th Australian Division resumed its northward thrust on the night of 30/31 October. After crossing the coast road, the Australians turned east to hem in the Germans in the Axis salient. The German troops thus threatened were the Panzer Grenadiers of the 164th Division; and it looked at one time as if they had been trapped. Axis troops outside the salient made several counter-attacks to rescue them and towards evening managed to send them a reinforcement of tanks, after which the Grenadiers forced their way out, suffering considerable casualties in the process.

This coastward thrust proved very profitable. It finally convinced General Rommel that the major battles in the coming struggle would be fought along the road and railway axis; and he proceeded to cover these strongly. On 1 November General Montgomery learned that the 21st Panzer Division, too, had moved north to join the 90th Light Division. This suited him admirably. It meant that the bulk of the German force was now concentrated on the coast, away from the new line of advance adopted by him. The way had been cleared for 'Supercharge', i.e. the final 'break-out' attack.

'Supercharge'

'Supercharge' began at 0100 hours on 2 November. The assaulting infantry advanced behind a creeping barrage. They were the 151st and 152nd Infantry Brigades under command of the 2nd New Zealand Division. The frontage of their attack was 4000 yards and their depth of advance 6000 yards. The attack was supported by three hundred 25-pounders and the Corps' medium artillery, and was intended to blow a new gap through Axis positions about two miles south of the German flank.

After the gaps had been successfully made, the X Corps was to be passed through and brought out into the open. It was to consist of the 1st, 7th and 10th Armoured Divisions and two armoured car regiments. Should infantry fail to penetrate, the armoured divisions of the X Corps were to fight their way through. On reaching the other end, they were to bring the German armour to battle and cut the lines of communication of the Axis. Thus was the final break-out to be consummated.

The first part of the operation went very well. The infantry fought through during the night and established the corridor. It had then to get the armour out, which was to be done in two stages. In the first stage, only the 9th Armoured Brigade was to pass through and establish a bridgehead. Through that bridgehead, next, were to debouch the 1st, 7th (and later 10th) Armoured Divisions together with the armoured car regiments. The armoured divisions were to engage the Axis tanks; the regiments were to make deep raids in the Axis rear.

The 9th Armoured Brigade did its part. It passed through and formed a bridgehead before first light on 2 November, a little beyond the track running south from Sidi Abd el Rahman. It was followed by two armoured car regiments who turned south-west and reached the open country. But as daylight appeared, the Axis troops rallied and the progress slowed down. As a result the 9th Armoured Brigade found itself in front of a tough anti-tank gun screen, and in trying to force it, suffered 75 per cent casualties. However, it held on to its gains, until the 1st Armoured Division came through to assist. The latter appeared near Tel el Aqqaqir where a big armoured battle was fought and both sides suffered heavy losses.

The situation that afternoon, 2 November, was that the corridor made by the infantry, and the armoured bridgehead beyond, were intact, but the anti-tank gun screens had stopped all further progress. Two steps now appeared essential for completing the break-out: first, to extend the width of the corridor, and next, to get through the anti-tank screen. The former was successfully accomplished the same afternoon, the 51st Division enlarging the salient at its southern edge, and Maoris (New Zealand Division) doing the same in the north. But forcing the anti-tank screen was a different matter. The 1st Armoured Division was altogether unable to pierce it.

In the situation, General Montgomery decided to outflank the screen if possible. He ordered an infantry attack to be made south of Tel el Aqqaqir, in the direction of the Rahman track. Accordingly, the 51st Division and the 5th Indian Brigade mounted a speedily prepared attack and quickly reached the Rahman track on a four-mile front, piercing the softer part of the screen to the south and thus outflanking the stronger resistance in the north.

The attack had gone in on the night of 3/4 November and by the morning of 4 November the screen had been forced back just sufficiently for the armoured divisions to pass through. Soon the rest of the armour and infantry of XXX Corps were on the move. The break-out was accomplished at last. The battle of Alamein was over and an Indian Brigade—the 5th—had had the privilege of delivering some of the last winning strokes of that world-renowned combat. On completing that task the brigade received a message of congratulation from the Commander of the XXX Corps, stating that it was the extraordinary deep penetration made by the brigade that enabled the armoured divisions to be passed through with such success.[6]

The anti-tank gun screen which had held up the 1st Armoured Division proved to be merely a sort of rearguard, for behind it the Axis troops had already started withdrawing. Twenty-four hours before the screen was pierced, i.e. 3 November, the Desert Air Force had reported movement of Axis troops westwards; and after the screen collapsed the movement became a general retreat. Although all Axis units must have been anxious to make a get-away, not all were able to do so. The transport was insufficient for the purpose and the fuel was even scarcer. In the circumstances, the Germans had to decide as to who should have the priority over transport and who may be left out. The choice naturally favoured the German troops and a few Italian formations that might be of use. The transport of the rest of the Italians was taken away and they were left behind to shift for themselves with very little food or water. Amongst them were four complete Italian divisions in the XIII Corps area.

Extent of Success

In the battle of El Alamein, the Axis had suffered a severe blow. Before 6 November, the Allied forces had collected some 30,000 prisoners including nine Generals, among whom was General von Thoma, Commander of the *Afrika Korps*.[7] Casualties in killed and wounded were about 12,000 more. Nearly one-third of the total casualties, including prisoners, were Germans. The Littorio and Trieste Divisions were practically destroyed and only a fraction of the Ariete escaped. The 15th and 21st Panzer Divisions had become shadows of their former selves having lost all but eighty tanks between the two. The 90th Light Division was reduced to the size of a regimental group as also the 164th Division. On the whole, the

---

[6] W/D 4 Div., 5 Bde, 1/4 Essex, 3/10 Baluch, 4/6 Raj Rif, MG Bn. 6 Raj Rif.
[7] This figure includes those reported 'missing' also. The precise personnel casualties, i.e. those killed, wounded, missing or prisoners, were, Germans 13,085 and Italians 29,301. These include all casualties up to 30 November 1942.

strength of the Italian-German Army had suffered a diminution by about two-thirds, that is, an equivalent of about eight divisions had been crippled, disabled or destroyed. Losses in tanks, guns and stores were also immense. Of the 600 tanks with which General Rommel had started, 450 were left behind for lack of fuel or as casualties; and 75 more were given up during the retreat. A large number of vehicles and over a thousand artillery pieces were captured or destroyed by the Eighth Army; while enormous quantities of stores, weapons and ammunition were left behind by the fleeing troops who could not carry them away.

Considering these results, the Allied casualties were not very heavy. The losses in killed, wounded and missing were 13,500. About a hundred guns had to be written off as destroyed, and as to tanks, about five hundred became unserviceable during the battle, of which only a hundred and fifty were found to be beyond repair.

It took the Eighth Army 'eleven days of hard fighting to win the Battle of Alamein, i.e. 'to break in, break through and break out' as its three phases have been popularly named. The battle ended just four days before the Anglo-American Expeditionary Force under General Eisenhower landed in French North Africa.

CHAPTER XL

Pursuit of Axis Forces

With Axis forces in full retreat the question of pursuit assumed an immediate importance. The coast road was seething with retreating transports, and columns of vehicles were moving head to tail. The congestion seemed to present an easy target from air, and the full weight of the Allied air force was therefore turned on to strafe the long line of fleeing transports. But the results were far from what were expected, since the technique of low-flying strafing was then in its infancy and the standard of aiming was necessarily poor. More than that, the air force was allotted only a subsidiary role and the objective set to it was only to provide air cover for the Eighth Army's light armoured forces engaged in the pursuit, and to harass the withdrawing Axis force.

The main burden therefore of doing the maximum damage to the retreating troops fell on the infantry and armour of the Eighth Army. Plans were ready for sending out a specially organised pursuit force as soon as the need arose. But the situation did not develop along clear-cut lines as had been assumed, and, instead of the special force going out on a well-organised pursuit, the X and XXX Corps found themselves trying to overtake the fleeing Germans and Italians without any particular plan.[1]

Flanking moves for interception

This was just as well, for, as events turned out, the immediate question was not so much of pursuing a retreating force over a long distance but of cutting off that retreat near at hand by blocking the bottle-necks through which that force would have to pass. Such bottle-necks existed near Fuka and Matruh and provided a good chance of intercepting the retreat and annihilating the retreaters so that the need for a prolonged pursuit might disappear altogether. General Montgomery had no desire to let slip such an opportunity and he therefore made some quick changes in the previously worked out plans: the specially prepared pursuit force was scrapped and its role assigned to the X Corps.

The X Corps was ordered to proceed to Fuka and the XXX Corps was directed on to Matruh, while the XIII Corps was instructed to stay behind and clear up the battlefield which was in a state of disorganisation from armed Italian troops roaming about in

[1] W/Ds 4 Div, 5 Bde, 4 Raj Rif, 3 Baluch.

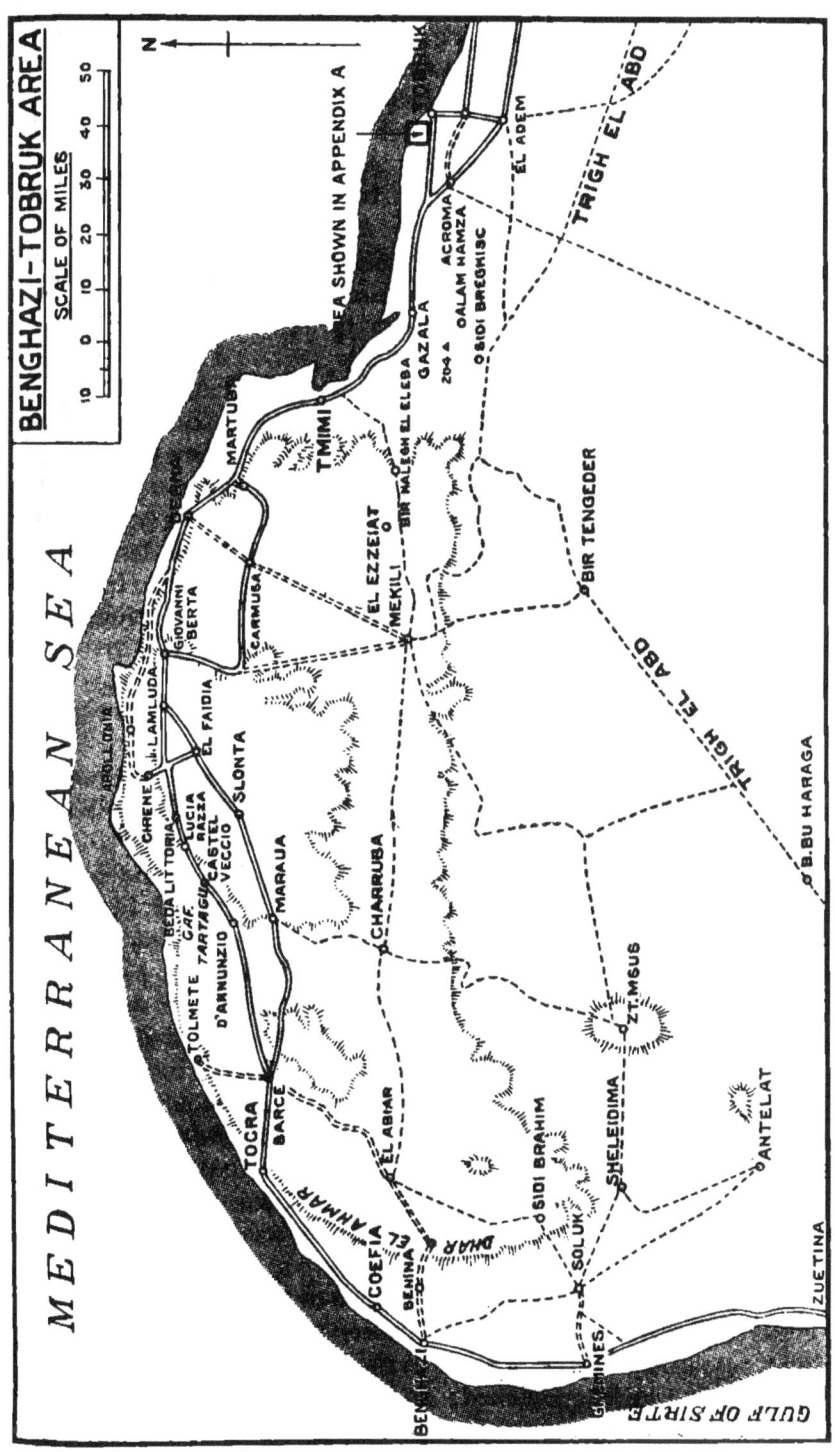

search of food and water, or trying to retreat on foot. Masses of abandoned stores were also lying about in a state of confusion, awaiting collection, sorting and disposal.

In conformity with the orders received by it, the XIII Corps formed mobile columns and despatched them to overtake the Italian units trying to escape westwards. At the same time, it set itself to the task of salvaging the vast booty and rounding up other wandering bands of Italian troops who had to be disarmed, fed and evacuated to the Delta. While this was being done, the X Corps and a New Zealand formation from the XXX Corps were speeding towards Fuka and Matruh in an effort to intercept the Axis retreat.

The X Corps was the first to hit the Axis rearguard which it did south of Ghazal on 4 November. The New Zealand Division bypassed it to the south and continued to move westward. Neither of these moves were successful due to a reason to be explained presently and, as a result, what started out to be an intercepting move of a brief duration became in fact a long pursuit which lasted fifteen days, covered over 700 miles and ended at El Agheila. In view of the importance and the prolonged character of the pursuit, it will be useful to compare at this stage the relative strengths of the pursuers and the pursued.

Allied and Axis Strength

The retreating Axis force was little more than one composite division. Its chief components were the 90th Light and the 164th Divisions each of whom had been reduced to the size of a brigade group, and the 15th and 21st Panzer Divisions who could count no more than eighty tanks between themselves. The Axis had had to leave their heavy weapons behind and their artillery was therefore deficient. Due to lack of petrol their mobility, too, had become less, and for the same as well as other reasons their air strength was on the decline. They however had two complete divisions in the rear—Pistoia on the frontier and the 80th Spezia in Tripolitania. But both were inexperienced and probably under-equipped.

The fighting power of the Eighth Army on the other hand had remained practically unimpaired. Its tank strength stood at 600 runners and was backed by an efficient tank recovery-and-repairs organisation. Its loss of a hundred guns or so was more than balanced by the capture and destruction of nearly a thousand Axis guns; while its casualties in men, amounting to only 8 per cent of the force engaged in fighting, were negligible compared to more than 60 per cent casualties suffered by the Axis. In the air, too, the Allied superiority was unquestioned; and in the matter of supplies, the Axis had to work a much longer line of communication than the

Allies. Indeed, the disparity between the respective strengths of the pursuers and the pursued was so great that it may be asked how at all were the Germans able to reach El Agheila. The answer is that they were helped at the critical moment by a spell of bad weather as we shall see presently.

Progress of the flanking moves

Apparently, General Montgomery was very clear in his mind at this stage, that it would be easier to capture or destroy the Axis remnants at the near-end of a line of communication rather than at the far-end after a long pursuit involving administrative and tactical risks. He had therefore planned to halt the Axis retreat at the bottle-necks of Fuka and Mersa Matruh ; and the X Corps and the 2nd New Zealand Division had been accordingly set in motion on 4 November. The same day the X Corps encountered an armoured rearguard at Ghazal and the New Zealanders by-passed it on their way to Fuka. The road at Fuka passes over a three-hundred-feet escarpment which is difficult to cross except along the coast road and the railway line. By moving quickly across the desert and blocking this narrow lane a great many of the Axis troops could be prevented from escaping ; another such outflanking move near Matruh and the rest would be trapped in the area between Charing Cross and Mersa Matruh.

The outflanking moves, as we have seen, were being made by the X Corps and the New Zealand Division. The latter, which also had the 4th Light Armoured Brigade under command, was transferred to X Corps on 5 November. Other formations of X Corps were the 1st, 7th and 10th Armoured Divisions. The pursuits to Fuka and Matruh were carried out along three separate lines of advance. Along the coastal route went the 1st Armoured Division followed by the 10th, both heading for Matruh. Much to the south, and across the desert, went the 7th Armoured Division directed on Charing Cross, while in between the two axes of advance was the 2nd New Zealand Division, moving towards Fuka. The first obstacle, as already mentioned, was met at Ghazal where an armoured rearguard tried to delay the pursuit in order to gain time for the Axis forces about to pass through Fuka.

The rearguard withdrew during the night of 4/5 November. On the following day the 1st Armoured Division entered Deba and was now directed to quit the coastal axis and move across the desert to Matruh. The 10th Armoured Division which was following up, continued to advance along the coastal route and soon came upon another Axis rearguard. It was the German armoured force which had taken up a defensive position at Galal, twelve miles east of Fuka. A brief engagement followed in which the Axis lost forty-four more of their remaining eighty tanks. After that the division pressed on towards Fuka.

The next rearguard was met at the entrance to the Fuka escarpment itself. It was the third Axis effort in two days to delay the pursuit until Axis troops had cleared the Fuka bottle-necks. The rearguard succeeded in holding up the New Zealand Division which came upon it from the south. The 4th Light Armoured Brigade, however, managed to force its way past and the New Zealand Division moved on without entering Fuka. The task of capturing Fuka was now assigned to the 10th Armoured Division and the New Zealand Division was directed on Matruh. Fuka was captured the same day, after the 8th Armoured Brigade had cleared the Axis rearguard and taken over a thousand more prisoners in the process. No prisoners or equipment were found inside the town as it had been successfully evacuated by the Axis troops. Meanwhile the New Zealand Division was making good progress. It reached Baqqush at midday on 6 November, thirty miles from Mersa Matruh. The 10th Armoured Division was made to halt at Fuka for administrative reasons. The formations, therefore, speeding towards the Charing Cross—Matruh area were only the 1st and 7th Armoured Divisions and the 2nd New Zealand Division.

It was a close race with the Axis as to who would reach the Charing Cross area first. So far the pursuit had gone much as the Army Commander had anticipated. Although the Axis escaped being caught at the first bottle-neck, it still had sustained severe losses—first at Galal, then at the Fuka escarpment and finally at Sidi Haneish, just west of Baqqush. At Sidi Haneish, the 7th Armoured Division had stumbled upon a large party of retreating troops. The party was attacked, fifteen more tanks and seven guns were knocked out and about two thousand prisoners taken. The Axis tank strength was now down to thirty or so and its infantry strength a little more than two brigade groups.

It was this force that General Montgomery was trying to intercept at the Charing Cross—Matruh bottle-neck. The 1st and 7th Armoured Divisions and the 2nd New Zealand Division were racing ahead to reach there before the retreating force might go through. At this stage the Axis suffered yet another blow. The 4/6th South African Armoured Car Regiment, operating on the road west of Matruh took two thousand more prisoners. There was now, 6 November, every prospect of finishing off what remained of the German-Italian Army in Egypt.

Towards nightfall on 6 November, the 1st Armoured Division approached the Charing Cross area and drew level with Matruh to the south. It was well on the way to snapping the trap from behind and it looked as if General Rommel's fate was sealed. But at this

Field Marshal Viscount Montgomery of Alamein, Commander Eighth Army

"We enter Benghazi again"

The 4th Indian Division moving into Mersa Matruh

Berta—Cyrenaica, March 1943

stage, the weather gave a break to the Germans. A heavy rainstorm occurred on the night of 6 November which flooded the desert and turned it into a morass. Tanks could move only with difficulty and wheeled transport not at all. The New Zealand Division, which was lorry-borne, thus came to a halt and remained immobile for thirty-six hours. The supply echelons of the 1st and 7th Armoured Divisions could not function at all nor could their motor brigades. The pursuit was bogged. The only usable thoroughfare was the main coastal road over which the Axis troops were moving fast while three Allied divisions stood helplessly at a distance. It might have been possible to send on the 4th Light Armoured Brigade and the South African Armoured Cars as these were on hard ground and within an easy reach of the road. But they were considered too weak to overcome the strong rearguard that might be covering the evacuation of Matruh.

The long pursuit to El Agheila

Since the coast road was the only navigable thoroughfare, General Montgomery ordered the 10th Armoured Division, which was then at Fuka, to move by that road and attack the Axis at Matruh. The move commenced on the morning of 7 November and Matruh was reached just before nightfall. One attack was put in which was unsuccessful. A second one was launched the following morning and Matruh was entered after a brief engagement. But the Axis troops had evacuated the town and the opportunity of intercepting their retreat had gone. The weather had robbed the Eighth Army of a brilliant victory. From next day began the long and difficult pursuit over Jebel Akhdar which was not to end till El Agheila, there being no other position nearer than Agheila where General Rommel could possibly have made a successful stand.

Failure to encircle the Axis at Matruh produced a difficult situation for the Eighth Army. There was now little chance of repeating the outflanking tactics until El Agheila was reached. The pursuit hereafter would therefore be nothing more than a following-up movement in which a series of delaying rearguards would have to be overcome. That would give General Rommel enough time to fortify the natural stronghold at El Agheila and to receive reinforcements. The Pistoia and Spezia Divisions were intact and further additions would not be long in coming. Rapid reinforcements for General Rommel were not at all unlikely since the Axis still dominated the Central Mediterranean from its airfields in Cyrenaica, and had all Libyan ports at its disposal. Further, due to the gradual shortening of its line of communication its administrative difficulties would disappear progressively while those of the Eighth Army would start coming into existence.

Worse still, repercussions of this situation would be felt most acutely in Malta. The garrison and the people there were on the verge of starvation, since no large convoy of provisions had reached them during the preceding three months. So long as the Axis held the coastal landing grounds of Cyrenaica, there was no way of providing air protection to any such convoy and it was for the Eighth Army to capture that vital group of landing grounds, especially before 16 November as, on that day, a convoy was due to sail from Alexandria in a desperate effort to reach that island.

Finally, as the pursuit progressed the supply difficulties would increase and a point would be reached beyond which all advance would come to a halt. The size of the advancing force would have to be progressively reduced as distance increased; but previous experience had proved that it was futile to follow up with a small force. Nothing would suit General Rommel better and it would therefore be wiser to stop the advance altogether rather than carry it on with a small force.

Such was the situation on 8 November when the Eighth Army forces entered Matruh. The situation, however, was not without its relieving feature. For, news had arrived just about then that the Anglo-American expeditionary forces, which were scheduled to invade North Africa from the side of Gibraltar, had made successful landings on the shores of French North Africa. But that was 2000 miles away and would not immediately lighten the Eighth Army's burden.

In the circumstances, it was essential that the pursuit should proceed as expeditiously as possible and should not have to stop for want of supplies. To provide against the latter possibility, it was necessary to seize and quickly reopen the ports of Tobruk and Benghazi. Forward aerodromes in Egypt, too, were to be captured without any loss of time so that air cover might be made possible for Tobruk, and those in Cyrenaica were to be occupied before 16 November so that a suitably strong escort might be available for the convoy for Malta. This in brief was the plan of General Montgomery. The Army was going to have its hands full carrying out this programme, and would not be in a position to strike hard at the retreating Axis troops. That task therefore became almost exclusively a job for the air force which, in keeping with its traditions, rose to the occasion and operated successfully, sometimes even from landing strips ahead of the ground troops and protected only by armoured cars.

Liberation of Egypt

Accordingly, the second stage of the pursuit began at dawn on 8 November. The pursuit force consisted of the 7th Armoured and the 2nd New Zealand Divisions under X Corps. The New Zealand Division included the 5th New Zealand Infantry Brigade, the 9th Armoured Brigade and the 4th Light Armoured Brigade. The first major objective of this force was the frontier of Egypt. Tobruk was the second. Incidentally, at about this time the men of the Eighth Army heard a news that must have added to their elation from recent successes. Their Army Commander was promoted to the rank of a full General.[2]

In the advance to the frontier the first oposition was encountered at Sidi Barrani on 9 November. It was one of the several rearguards which tried to delay the New Zealand Division. However, the 4th Light Armoured Brigade had no difficulty in overcoming this opposition and the advance continued during the night of 9/10 November. Other rearguards were met during the day following, but were swiftly knocked out by virtue of superior numbers. Halfaya Pass was captured during the night of 10/11 November by a company of infantry which made a surprise attack and took 600 prisoners from the Pistoia Division. Next day, Capuzzo, Sollum and Bardia yielded without resistance and Egypt was finally freed of Axis occupation.

After that, the New Zealand Division remained in the frontier area to reorganise, while the 1st and 7th Armoured Divisions continued the pursuit. The air force had a busy day at the same time, 11 November, attacking Axis aircraft on the frontier and even reaching out to the landing grounds of Gambut and El Adem, then in Axis occupation. The forward aerodromes of Egypt were now available for giving cover to Tobruk.

It was while the 7th Armoured Division was moving towards Tobruk that the rains interfered for a second time and deprived General Montgomery of another big chance of cutting short the Axis retreat. The Armoured Division was then crossing the frontier between Sollum and Fort Maddalena, with a view to reaching the escarpment bottle-neck of Sollum before the Axis troops got clear of it. It had got within a few miles of its objective on 10 November, but had to wait for further supplies of petrol which were following up. All seemed to be going well and it looked as if the job of closing the bottle-neck was within an inch of accomplishment. But just then the rains came down in torrents and imposed a delay on all movements, giving enough time to the Axis troops to clear the vital bottle-neck. Foiled in its mission, the 7th Armoured Division then swung north-west and joined the New Zealanders at Capuzzo.

---

[2] W/D's 4 Div, 5 Bde, 7Bds.

Help for Malta

So far the advance had proceeded at a hot pace. It was essential that there should be no slackening now, when there remained only five days in which to capture airfields necessary for assisting convoys to Malta. Therefore, while the New Zealand Division stayed behind on the frontier, the rest of the troops resumed advance the next day. The advancing force now consisted of the 7th Armoured Division, with the 4th Light Armoured Brigade and 131st Lorried Infantry Brigade. Starting out on 12 November, the Light Armoured Brigade captured Gambut and El Adem the same day; while the Lorried Brigade followed by the Armoured Division entered Tobruk without opposition, at 0900 hours on 13 November.

The next objective now was the group of airfields and their satellites in the triangle Derna— Tmimi—Mekili. They were called the Martuba group from the name of the locality where the principal airfield was situated. Since they had to be taken without delay, the advance from Tobruk continued with a halt. But the supply line had become so stretched, that only a small force could now be risked forward. So far, the X Corps had advanced 360 miles in eight days and that had been made possible only by the energy of those who had repaired and reopened the harbours of Matruh and Bardia within two days of their capture. Sollum was also brought into use for landing supplies. But these were small harbours and it was very important that the major harbour of Tobruk should be opened without delay, if advance to El Agheila was to proceed without a long pause. The matter was taken in hand and work was started immediately.

Meanwhile, elements of the X Corps were on their way to the Martuba area. They moved out in two columns during 13/14 November, one column consisting of the 4th Light Armoured Brigade, and the other of light forces from the 7th Armoured Division. The former advanced along the road; the latter across the desert, via Bir Hakeim and Rotonda Segnali, so as to outflank any possible opposition on the road. Tmimi was captured by the Light Armoured Brigade on 14 November and the other force occupied Martuba on the following day. Derna was reported clear on the 16th while the Gazala airfield was brought into use at the same time. The whole of the Martuba group was thus in hand just about the time that the convoy for Malta set sail from Alexandria. It was a fine achievement to schedule and was instrumental in ending the siege of Malta for good.

Pursuit towards Agedabia

From Martuba, the coast road climbs the big mountain bulge of Jebel Akhdar on the way to Benghazi. It was along this route that General Rommel's forces were now retreating. It is possible to by-pass this bulge by a short-cut drive through the desert, although the journey would be over rough ground and not without risks. A force using that route could appear at or near Agedabia before the retreating Axis troops could arrive there, and thus be in a position to cut the retreat. Such an experiment had been tried successfully, earlier in February 1941, and General Montgomery was urged to repeat the tactics. He was however quick to see that the two situations bore only a partial resemblance and that the Axis Commander was now wiser by the experience of the past. Were a large force to be sent, administrative arrangements would break down. If a small force were despatched instead, it would be in a weak position from having no bottle-neck to hold, and General Rommel would be able to defeat it or manoeuvre round it. Finally, at that particular time of the year there was a definite risk of the rains spoiling the operation.

The Army Commander therefore turned down the suggestion for a cross-desert dash of Agedabia but not altogether. He decided to send a small force of armoured cars only, which he later enlarged hopefully. But there being no firm go-ahead decision in the matter, the flanking move produced no dramatic result. It however had the merit of being free of risks, as will be seen in the succeeding chapter.

Thus by 16 November forward elements of the X Corps had covered nearly five hundred miles from El Alamein and had been twelve days on the move. The port of Tobruk had not yet been restored to use and it would not be working to full capacity for another two weeks. Yet the supply system had somehow worked satisfactorily.[3] General Montgomery decided to stop the X Corps at Tmimi, partly to ease the strain on supplies and partly to shield and defend Tobruk in case General Rommel turned back and made a dash for Egypt. At the same time he ordered the XXX Corps to be brought forward for an attack on the El Agheila position, since it was fairly certain that the Axis would try and make a decisive stand there, if not at Agedabia.

---

[3] The supply system, apart from road and rail transport, was assisted by the ships of the Inshore squadron and merchant ships, and by naval clearing parties at the ports of Mersa Matruh, Bardia, Sollum and Tobruk.

CHAPTER XLI

Operations in Tripoli

Advance to Benghazi

As the Eighth Army drew nearer to Benghazi, its supply difficulties increased. Its line of communication was growing long and problems of maintenance had begun to limit the pace and size of its advance. General Montgomery found that it was not possible to send out any large-sized force in pursuit of the retreating Axis troops and that it was necessary to wait until supplies had been built up sufficiently for undertaking a major move.

At the same time he was unwilling to relax pressure on the retreating force in front of him. He was also anxious to reach Benghazi quickly so as to prevent destruction of that port through heavy demolitions and to round up stores, material and prisoners before they could be got away from there. It was known that General Rommel did not have enough petrol and transport to carry through a rapid evacuation; and consequently there was a fair chance of catching him in pincers or intercepting his retreat. If thus caught, he could be attacked again in his still disorganised condition which would reduce his capacity to make a fresh stand beyond Benghazi.

Acting on these considerations, General Montgomery ordered the X Corps to send out two columns of light forces immediately. One of these was to threaten Benghazi from the north; the other was to cut the main coastal road south of it, at the same time. The former consisted of the 4th Light Armoured Brigade which proceeded to operate northwardly and found it possible to reach Maraua on 18 November, in spite of the roads being blocked by demolitions and mines. During the same time, the other force consisting of armoured cars and tanks was moving across the desert to gain access to the coastal road on the south. This body consisted of 11th Hussars and the Royals, with supporting arms. It operated under the command of the 7th Armoured Division and was directed towards Msus and Antelat in the first instance. Thence, it was eventually to reach the coastal road and block the southern exit from Benghazi.

But this plan unfortunately did not work. It was interfered with by heavy rains which started on 16 November and turned the desert into a quagmire. It took the Hussars and Royals twenty-four hours to struggle through sixty miles of boggy and water-logged ground; and therefore it was not until 18 November that they reached the escarpment where the Axis rearguards were holding ground to cover the evacuation of Benghazi. These covering troops were guarding the vital passes of Sheleidima and the track-junction at Antelat, and were engaged by the Hussars and Royals on the same day. But the latter were unable to force their way through.

During the night, however, the Axis troops completed their evacuation of Benghazi and the passes were abandoned. The Allied coulmns resumed their advance but the progress was slow for the whole of 19 November due to the wet and difficult desert surface. Benghazi was at last reached on 20 November and entered by the 11th Hussars who found the town and its neighbourhood clear of all Axis troops. Incidentally, 11th Hussars were the first British troops to enter Benghazi on its earlier capture in February 1941 also. Later they had the privilege of being the first in Tripoli and among the first in Tunis.

Approach to El Agheila

After Benghazi, the Axis had the choice of making a stand at Agedabia or El Agheila. The latter was by far the stronger of the two positions and more easy to hold. But Agedabia was the key to the approaches to El Agheila and, therefore, a good delaying position. It was obvious that General Rommel would try and hold both these positions if he could. But, as it turned out, he did not have sufficient forces for manning the two defences simultaneously, and he therefore appears to have decided to hold Agedabia for a brief duration only, that is, just enough to cover the preparation of the El Agheila defences. Therefore he offered resistance initially when the Royals attacked his rearguard at Agedabia on 21 November, but quickly withdrew to El Agheila two days later when the 22nd Armoured Brigade (7th Armoured Division) appeared to his south and began to turn his flank. The Armoured Brigade followed up that withdrawal although its progress was greatly impeded by thick minefields. Finally, on 25 November, its patrols gained contact with the El Agheila position, the last Axis bastion in Cyrenaica.

The next task of the Eighth Army was to dislodge the Axis from that formidable position. El Agheila is a natural fortress. It is a bottle-neck between the coast and an untraversable area of salt marshes and is the main gateway into Tripolitania.[1] Twice before, the tide of Allied advance had touched this high-water mark but had rolled back almost immediately. Now for the third time the Axis was standing entrenched in the same position. It was going to be the acid test of General Montgomery's genius to throw it out of that position. So far, his undoubtedly brilliant victories were over the

[1] This bottle-neck is actually slightly east of El Agheila, at Marsa Brega.

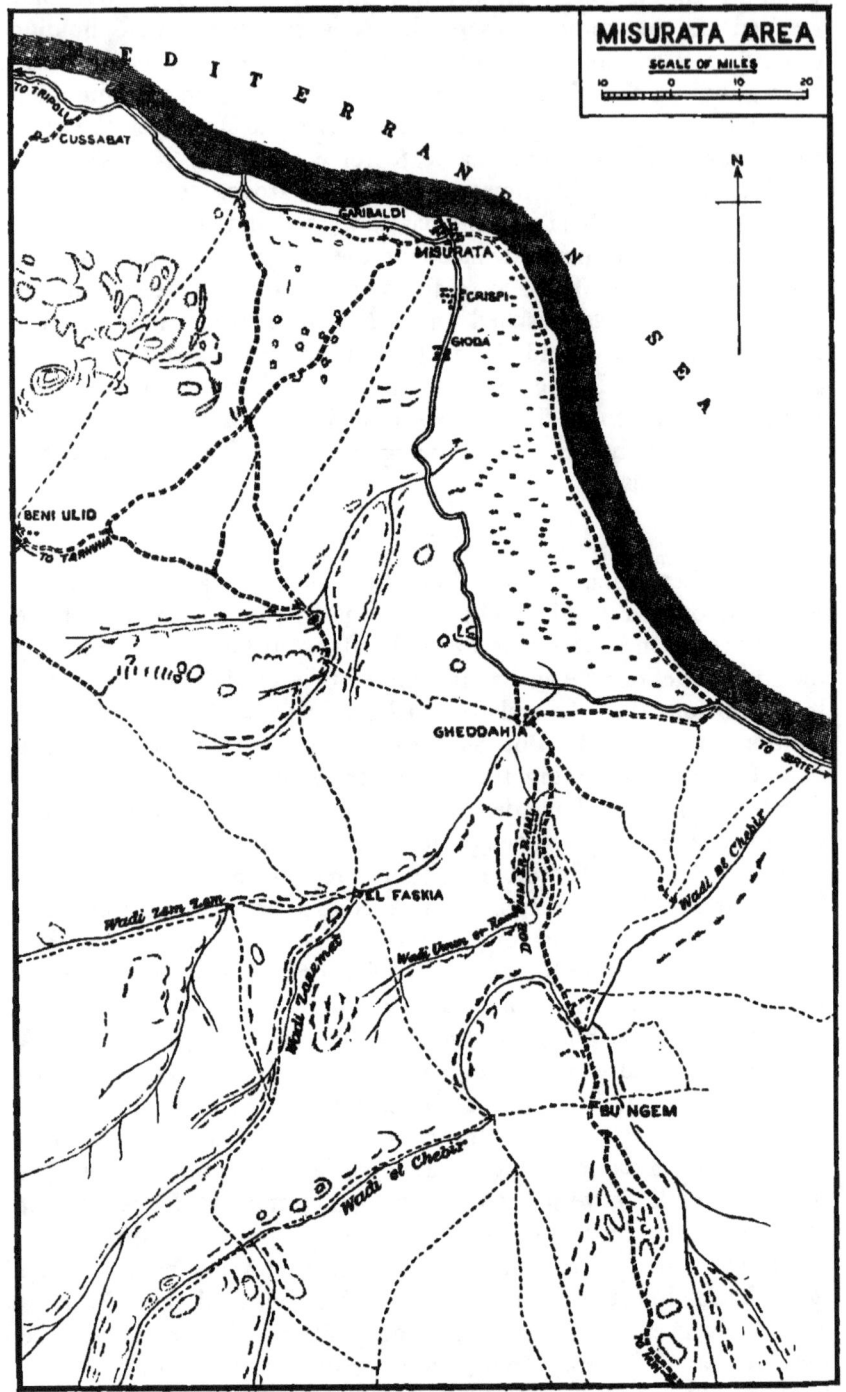

ground already covered twice before by his predecessors, who had far less of resources and experience to back their efforts than he now commanded. By taking El Agheila General Montgomery could start a new chapter in the history of World War II. By failing to do so he would only be re-writing the old history of the shuttle-cock journeys between Alamein and El Agheila.

General Montgomery now toured the forward areas, reconnoitred and got down to making his plans. At the same time, he brought forward the Headquarters of the XXX Corps, placed the 7th Armoured Division under its command and began to build up administratively. He considered and rejected a plan of frightening General Rommel out of his position by bluff and manoeuvre on his desert flank. He decided finally that since bluff would not suffice, substantial operations were necessary. Later events proved however that not only might the deception have worked but perhaps General Rommel would have abandoned El Agheila anyhow, i.e. without being forced to do so. It appears, from some statements in the Italian diaries of Count Ciano now available, that a decision to evacuate Cyrenaica generally had been taken as early as 8 December. And in any case the Italian infantry had started withdrawing westward some days before the actual attack was launched by the Eighth Army. The withdrawal of the Italians ahead of the Germans, in such a case, is understandable, since the Italian troops had no transport worth the name, and if they were not to be left behind, as at Alamein, to be mopped up by the Allies, they had to leave El Agheila in advance.

Operations against El Agheila

However, the facts of the situation were not known with this clarity at the time when General Montgomery was considering an attack on the El Agheila position. He therefore formed a plan resting on the assumptions that the Axis were still working hard on El Agheila defences; that the port of Tripoli was still functioning and handling heavy traffic; and that General Rommel was showing no sign of wanting to give up the position.

Considering all factors, General Montgomery decided upon a plan of making a triple thrust at the Axis defence. One of these thrusts was to be an outflanking move, to be carried out by the 2nd New Zealand Division. This was the major move of the operation and was to take the shape of a wide detour round the desert terminal of the El Agheila line, ending up astride the coast road in the rear of the defenders. The other two thrusts were intended to help the outflanking move indirectly as well as to prod for a possible weak spot.

Of these two subsidiary thrusts, one was to be at the coastal terminal of the El Agheila line and the other was to pierce the centre.

The central thrust was to be carried out by the 7th Armoured Division, with a lorried infantry brigade leading, and the armour positioned in the rear. The coastal thrust was entrusted to the 51st Division which was to attack astride the coast road and was to develop, if possible, an enveloping move in conjunction with the 2nd New Zealand Division.

Obviously enough this plan depended upon finding a suitable route for the 2nd New Zealand Division. The El Agheila position occupied the desert area between the sea and the Wadi el Fareg. This latter was a deep and difficult obstacle running east and west, starting a little to the west of Marsa Brega on the sea. The approaches to this position were covered by stretches of salt marshes, sand dunes and soft sand, and constituted a very 'rough going'. The ground was unsuitable for movements not only in the region of approaches to the Wadi el Fareg but also for some distance to the south of it. As a result, a very wide detour would be necessary for outflanking the defences, and this would have to be carried out in secrecy. The 2nd New Zealand Division was accordingly ordered to make a wide circuit of some 40 miles radius, round the Axis position, starting from El Haseiat and finishing on the coast, about sixty miles behind El Agheila.

It had been the intention of General Montgomery to launch the attack on 16 December. But as news of the Italian withdrawal arrived, the date was advanced to the 14th so as not to let the Axis forces escape intact. The attack was to be preceded by heavy artillery and air bombardments lasting for over two days. General Montgomery decided that the air attacks, which were planned to be on a large scale, should now commence on 11 December and the New Zealand Division should set out on the following day.

Two days of heavy air bombardment left no doubt in the mind of General Rommel as to what the Allied intention was; and presumably because a withdrawal had been already decided upon, he began to pull out of the Agheila position in the early hours of 13 December. He relied principally on mines, booby-traps and demolitions to cover his retreat. Nevertheless, he was followed up fairly closely. The 51st Division penetrated the coastal sector the same day. The 7th Armoured Division reached just east of Agheila on the following day (14 December) and the New Zealand Division arrived on the line of Wadi Regel-Merduma within another twenty-four hours.

The situation on 15 December therefore was an uncomfortable one for the Germans. They were caught between the 7th Armoured Division advancing from the east and the 2nd New Zealand Division approaching from the west. Intense fighting followed when the retreating troops met the New Zealand Division. But the Germans had one advantage. The New Zealand troops had taken up positions during the night in a previous unknown country which they had no time to reconnoitre and for which they had insufficient troops. Consequently there were some gaps in their deployment. The Germans broke into small groups and began to escape through those gaps. This led to a whole day of skirmishes and confused fighting on 16 December, as the New Zealanders tried to stop their sallies. In this the Germans lost about twenty tanks, some guns and 500 prisoners. But they succeeded in getting the main body away.

Towards Tripoli

A pursuit was organised, as far as the administrative situation permitted it, to follow the retreating troops into Tripolitania. The 4th Light Armoured Brigade was sent out on a special harassing chase. The New Zealanders were already on the same job. But the progress of both these formations was hampered by mines and demolitions. Almost every one of the bridges and culverts over the several wadis had been blown up. The wadis were sown with mines and so were portions of the main road. On either side of the road the country was extremely rough and the armoured cars found difficulty in moving.

In spite of this, the advanced guard of the Armoured Brigade reached Nofilia on the evening of 16 December. The brigade engaged in skirmishes round Nofilia for the next two days, being joined on the 18th by the New Zealanders. That same day, the New Zealand troops fought a sharp engagement with the Axis rearguards, who began to retire on the 19th towards Sirte. Meanwhile the main body of the Axis troops had reached their next defensive position—El Buerat. The German 90th Light Division and the 21st Panzer Division joined this body on 22 December, and all of them began constructing the Buerat defences. The 15th Panzar Division remained at Sirte to cover these preparations.

The next step for the Allies was to clear the village of Sirte and then contact the El Buerat position. But administrative considerations intervened again to retard the pace of progress. The last post of supply was the Benghazi harbour and it had not yet been repaired sufficiently to make it work at its normal strength. Therefore about 800 tons a day were still being delivered from Tobruk by road. Sirte is 360 miles from Benghazi and about 630 miles from Tobruk and any advance in force, with such a long line of communication, would be a hazardous undertaking.

The situation had become all the more difficult because, in addition to the routine supplies, the Royal Air Force required a specially heavy tonnage of supplies to be delivered to them west of El Agheila. The needs of the RAF had arisen out of the necessity for building all-weather runways in the forward area. Tripoli was

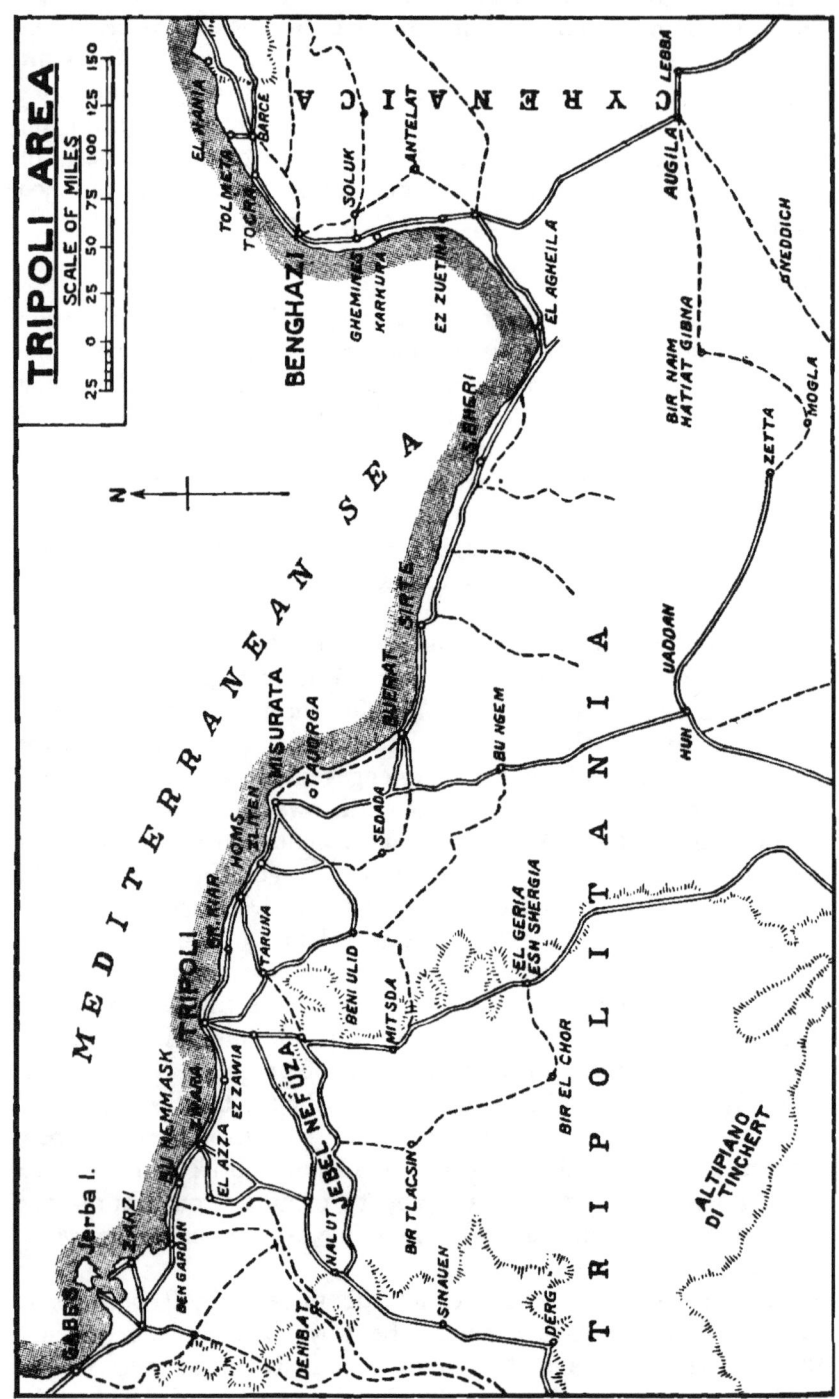

deficient in the airfields for heavy bombers; and further advance was conditional on these being available. The RAF was therefore required to move forward and establish itself at Marble Arch and Merduma with advanced squadrons at Nofilia. Later it was to build airfields at Sirte, so that the Desert Air Force might be able to support the attack on the Buerat position. All this could not be achieved without straining the supply and transport resources of the Eighth Army.[2]

An immediate attack on Buerat was therefore not a feasible proposition. As a first step General Montgomery had to build up stocks in the forward area. He had decided to plan for the Buerat battle on the basis of ten days' heavy fighting, using four divisions. It was calculated that the dumping necessary for maintaining this force would take some three weeks to complete. General Montgomery therefore decided that he could not resume the offensive until mid-January.

Meanwhile there were various preliminaries to be gone through—particularly the redistribution of forces in the rear areas and re-achieving of the correct balance amongst the attacking troops. For restoring the balance, General Montgomery decided to bring forward the X Corps to occupy the El Agheila position. The XXX Corps which was already there was to move further west. During the interval between the departure of the XXX Corps and the arrival of the X Corps, that position was to be held and cleared by the 51st Division. As to redistribution of the forces it was decided that the 7th Armoured Division should remain at Marble Arch, the 2nd New Zealand Division at Nofilia and the 4th Light Armoured Brigade between Nofilia and Sirte. On Sirte being reached, a forward base was to be established there for maintaining contact with Axis troops through armoured car patrols.

Sirte was being occupied by the Germans merely to prevent the Eighth Army from gaining contact with the Buerat position. It was therefore a delaying spot and not a holding line. As such it would not be held against heavy risks and there was reason for hoping that it might yield to a pressure on the flank. An armoured car regiment with artillery was accordingly sent to outflank it from the south. The manoeuvre succeeded completely. Fearful of losing some of its previous tanks, the 15th Panzer Division withdrew at once. Sirte was entered without opposition on 25 December.

Two days later the Allied patrols had crossed the Wadi Tamet. On 28 December they were overlooking the Wadi el Chebir. This

---

[2] It is claimed now, however, that the Western Desert Air Force actually had no need for all-weather airfields and had often worked successfully from improvised landing grounds, the clearance of the site for which used to be effected with the help of the Eighth Army troops.

meant that the Axis troops had withdrawn to their main defensive position—the Buerat line, which was reported to be running from Maaten Giaber on the coast, to the south-west, so as to cover Gheddahia, and thence along Wadi Umm er Raml towards Bu Ngem. The village of Buerat stood a little to the east of Maaten Giaber. On 29 December the Allied patrols found both the Buerat village and Bu Ngem clear of the Axis troops, and thereupon the general patrol line was shifted further west so as to be opposite to what might be called the Buerat line proper.

The Buerat defences

The Buerat position was not particularly strong. Its defences consisted of two natural obstacles, the Wadi Umm er Raml and Wadi Zem Zem. An additional obstacle, outside the defence zone, was provided by Wadi el Chebir. The whole defensive system was so laid out that the English Army, approaching from the east, would first encounter Wadi el Chebir, then the Wadi Umm er Raml and finally the Wadi Zem Zem. The last was the biggest of all the three obstacles, and it was on this that General Rommel sited his main defensive position, which was nearly 25 miles long from the coast to its southern terminal. The coastal or northern end of this defensive system lay astride the main road to Tripoli. The southern end finished up in the desert. It was this southern end that constituted the chief weakness of General Rommel's defences, for it rested on no natural obstacle and could therefore be easily outflanked by a detour through the desert.

General Montgomery fixed 15 January as the earliest date for resuming the offensive. This interval, as already mentioned, was necessary for improving the supply and maintenance system of the Eighth Army. An earlier start than this would not have answered his chief aim, which was to drive straight through to Tripoli once the offensive began. For this reason he wished to have an administrative build-up, so secure that there would be no need for major halts on the way to await supplies or reinforcement. He estimated that he would not be thus ready before 15 January 1943 and he had no intention of being hustled. He therefore hoped that General Rommel would stand fast till then on his comparatively weaker Buerat defences and not withdraw to the much stronger Homs—Tarhuna natural line, which was not far behind him and from which it would be difficult to dislodge him.

It was in fact a matter of constant speculation at the Eighth Army's headquarters as to why General Remmel had at all chosen the Buerat position. The Homs—Tarhuna position was a naturally stronger one. Homs, which stood on the coast, was protected by a northern abutment of the main escarpment, on the edge of which stood Tarhuna. To the south-west of Tarhuna was another strong position, Garian, which also bordered the escarpment and which could have been easily included in the main defensive system. These three positions together might have proved a formidable barrier in the path of the Eighth Army which had to move past them to enter the plains of Tripoli.

Why then did General Rommel choose to expend time and energy on the Buerat position which he might have more profitably applied to Homs—Tarhuna line? One conjecture is that he might have been ordered to do so by his nominal Supremo, Sgr. Mussolini, and had no choice left. Another conjecture, which is however more plausible, is that before he could take up the Homs line, the Axis high command had decided to evacuate the whole of Tripolitania and concentrate their entire available strength on the defence of Tunisia. Such a plan would be strategically sound, since the Axis could, after occupying Tunisia, continue to block the Mediterranean sea at the Sicilian narrows, keep the Eighth Army from joining up with the Allied Expeditionary Force and prepare for a counter-attack both towards east and west.

In any case the longer General Rommel remained on the Buerat position the less time he would have to fortify the Homs—Trahuna line. General Montgomery, having fixed 15 January as the earliest date for starting the offensive, was determined to stick to his time-table. He had therefore decided not to follow up the Axis forces even if they abandoned the Buerat position and commenced work on the Homs—Tarhuna line. On the other hand, he did not intend to scare them off their position by a show of preparation for the offensive. With that idea he arranged to keep his main attacking force in the back area and confronted General Rommel with only a light screen of armoured cars from the 4th Light Armoured Brigade.

Planning for attack

The plan for breaking through the Buerat line was fixed on this basis. Two corps were to be used, the XXX and the X. The XXX Corps was to carry out the attack; the X Corps was to garrison El Agheila and turn it into a firm and secure base for the offensive. On reaching Tripoli the XXX Corps was to take its turn at garrisoning, while the X Corps would leap-frog through it for operations to the west of Tripoli. In each case, the garrisoning corps was intended to serve also as a sort of reserve for preserving the overall balance during the attacks.

For attacking the Buerat position the XXX Corps was to use four divisions. Three of these were infantry divisions, the 50th and 51st British and the 2nd New Zealand. The fourth was the

7th Armoured Division. An additional formation, the 22nd Armoured Brigade, was to be held in Army reserve, to be thrown into the battle as the changing contingencies might demand. All these forces were kept well to the rear so as not to scare the Axis off their present line prematurely. Thus, for instance, the 7th Armoured Division was stationed some 45 miles behind the front; the New Zealand Division was about a hundred miles away and the 51st Division, except for one brigade, some two hundred miles. The idea was to bring up these bodies to the battle area just before the beginning of the attack. This arrangement had the double advantage of concealing the preparations for the offensive and easing the maintenance problem in the meanwhile.

The plan of the battle was to make two simultaneous attacks at either end of the Buerat line. Thus the 50th and 51st Divisions were to attack up the coastal road in a straight thrust towards Tripoli. At the same time, the 7th Armoured and the 2nd New Zealand Divisions were to make a wide outflanking move through the desert and stab towards Beni Ulid and Tarhuna. The 22nd Armoured Brigade, which was in reserve, was to remain between the lines of these two thrusts, ready for being switched to either flank as required. The attack was to be preceded by the customary bombing of the ground defences and by an air combat to obtain air superiority over the battlefield.

While the preparations for the contemplated offensive were going ahead two important incidents occurred. First, reports were received at the headquarters of the Eighth Army which indicated that an Axis withdrawal from the Buerat line had almost begun. Intelligence sources announced on 4 January that Italian formations were withdrawing from the Buerat position. The Pistoia and Spezia Divisions had already left and the Young Fascists were following up. General Montgomery did not regard this as a prelude to a complete withdrawal but rather as a repetition of events at El Agheila, namely removal of the Italians from the battle area in advance, lest they should have to be left behind in the event of a forced withdrawal through lack of transport. The Eighth Army Commander therefore continued his policy of sitting well back and preparing for the offensive.

The second incident was of a more serious nature and was due to the caprice of the weather. A heavy gale broke out on 4 January and lasted till the 6th. It created havoc in the Benghazi port. Ships broke their moorings and drifted dangerously about the harbour. Heavy waves breached the breakwaters and deluged the inner harbour. Four ships sank outright, one of which contained 2,000 tons of ammunition. Several other tugs and lighters were damaged and the capacity of the port was generally reduced to one-third of its former intake. This raised the question as to whether the date of attack on the Buerat line should or should not be postponed by a few more days.

General Montgomery decided to adhere to the date already fixed—15 January. To overcome the difficulty of shortage of supplies, he resolved to reduce the size of his attacking force. He also decided to reduce his garrisoning troops which he had intended to maintain at El Agheila. Accordingly he cancelled the projected move of the X Corps to the Agheila position and instead took away all its transport and tanks. The transport was put to the work of ferrying stores and supplies from the Tobruk harbour so as to compensate for the reduced output of Benghazi. The tanks were used to augment the striking power of the assault force which had now been reduced from four divisions to three, the 50th Division being left out. This last mentioned formation was moved to the Agheila position to fill the gap created by the elimination of the X Corps.

For all practical purposes, the X Corps was now out of the picture. This spoiled the overall balance which General Montgomery was always anxious to preserve. But that sacrifice seemed worth making and the risk accepted was by no means very great. The Italian infantry had already evacuated the Buerat position, and by stripping the X Corps of all its tanks, General Montgomery was able to concentrate something like 450 tanks for the battle. Besides, he still had the 22nd Armoured Brigade in reserve with which he could control the battle situation to no small extent.

To complete the arrangements for the attack there remained only one more point to be settled—that about command of the assault forces. The plan of attack involved two widely separated thrusts, one at each end of the Buerat line, with an armoured brigade moving between them. General Montgomery believed that it would not be possible for one corps commander to handle both the thrusts effectively, due to the distance between them. He therefore decided to take over the command of the coastal thrust himself. This part of the attack was going to be made with one division only and would therefore need to be handled with great discretion and energy. At the same time there was an obvious advantage in thus leaving the Commander of the XXX Corps free to concentrate all his attention on the outflanking operation.

The Battle

The battle of Buerat commenced on 15 January. The outflanking column, i.e. 7th Armoured and 2nd New Zealand Divisions, moved off at 0715 hours. The column soon contacted the 15th Panzer Division at Dor Umm er Raml and went into action almost straight from the approach march. About 15 German tanks were knocked out and the Panzer Division was pushed back to the Wadi Zem Zem, as a result of a cautious manoeuvre on its flank. The outflanking column now seized the main crossing at El Faskia, while the Germans began a full-scale withdrawal on the whole front. The Wadi was crossed on the following morning, 16 January, and the battle of Buerat was practically over.

As to the 51st Division on the coast, it did not have much opposition as its principal opponent, the 90th Light Division, had started withdrawing before it could be attacked. The coastal column was therefore through the Buerat line bofore the morning of 16 January and was advancing on Gheddahia, while the 22nd Armoured Brigade was moving towards Bir Duffan. The Buerat line had been completely crossed and the Eighth Army was now, 16 January, advancing towards the Homs—Tarhuna position.

On 17 January General Montgomery directed the southern column on towards Garian with a view to developing another outflanking move. From Garian a thrust was to be made towards Tripoli from the south, so as to play on the sensitiveness of the Axis to any move on its unprotected flank. It was hoped by this device to induce General Rommel to weaken the Homs area in order to strengthen the Tarhuna sector where the pressure would be greater than on the coast. If this happened and the Homs area was weakened, the coastal column would drive through Homs and release the 22nd Armoured Brigade into the plains of Tripoli.

The southern column moved on steadily during 17 January. Meanwhile the Germans were manoeuvring for an unmolested withdrawal to the Homs—Tarhuna line. The withdrawal had proved a complicated affair for them since their fighting line could not be pulled back with equal speed in all its sectors. First the southern end of their line moved faster than the coastal end, so that the former reached Beni Ulid while the latter was still at Misurata. This was due to tactical circumstances and the general layout of the country. From Beni Ulid their southern column would have to move next to Tarhuna; but their coastal column would not be able to reach Homs in the same duration, as it had to move through a greater distance. The Beni Ulid end had therefore to remain stationary while the whole of the Axis fighting line pivoted on it, moving radially from Misurata to Homs. Unless this was done, the Axis could not present a continual north-south front to the Allied troops. On Homs being reached, the Beni Ulid end could be rapidly pulled back to Tarhuna.

The Axis were naturally anxious to avoid any engagement during this complicated withdrawal; and therefore wished to keep the Allied troops at as great a distance as possible. They laid mines in the coastal region to cover their withdrawal and blocked the road with skilful demolitions. In the desert area they relied more on the roughness of the ground to slow down their progress. Nevertheless, the two Allied columns moved on steadily during 17 January. By the evening the southern column had reached Beni Ulid and the coastal column was only ten miles from Misurata.

The axis troops continued to withdraw during the whole of the following day, 18 January. The Allied advance however could not be kept up at the same speed. The rough ground and the heavy demolitions proved difficult to negotiate and on both flanks the Allied columns lost contact with the Axis troops. However, the progress improved the next day, 19 January. Homs was entered by the 51st Division ; Tarhuna came under pressure of the southern column ; and the 22nd Armoured Brigade, which was still in reserve, moved to Zliten without attracting much attention of the Axis command. If the Axis had any intention of making a stand on the Homs—Tarhuna position, that object was frustrated. The Eighth Army crossed Homs—Tarhuna region on 20 January and continued to move towards Tripoli.

News was received at this stage that the Germans had transferred the Ramcke Parachute Brigade from the north to the south. It will be recalled that this was what General Montgomery was trying to bring about. He had been steadily increasing pressure on the desert flank of the Axis line to induce the Germans to reinforce it by withdrawing troops from the coastal sector. General Montgomery now decided that the moment had come for carrying out his plan of breaking through the weakened coastal sector with the help of his reserve—the 22nd Armoured Brigade.

This did not prove as easy as anticipated. Skilfully placed road demolition, and a hilly terrain full of ravines, had more than made up for the weakness in the coastal sector. In addition, the German rearguards were now beginning to offer opposition. A rapid advance was impossible under such conditions. However, by the evening of 21 January the 51st Division had managed to struggle through to Corradini, followed by the 22nd Armoured Brigade. After overcoming the prepared defences of Corradini, it emerged into the plain of Tripoli and captured Castelverde on the following morning. There were thirty miles more to go before reaching the town of Tripoli.

The level country between Castelverde and Tripoli was suitable for the employment of the armour and therefore the 22n Armoured Brigade was in a better position to lead the advance than the 51st Division. The armoured brigade was accordingly passed through Castelverde and brought into the open. It advanced to within fifteen miles of Tripoli and came to a halt on meeting German rearguard from the 90th Light Division, who were covering a demolished causeway leading to the town. Darkness fell as tanks vainly cruised about trying to find a way round the demolition. It soon became apparent that the way lay through an area of deep, soft sand on the flank, and it was therefore more a job for the infantry than for the tanks.

Fall of Tripoli

But there was only one company of infantry available. More had not been sent owing to traffic blocks. General Montgomery now ordered a whole battalion from the 51st Division to be sent forward at once. The troops of the battalion were to ride to the front on Valentine tanks and attack in the moonlight immediately on arrival. The attack was successful and the infantry and tanks pressed on through the night, down the main road to Tripoli. Meanwhile, the southern column had reached a point within 17 miles of the town, after slowly and painfully pushing back the Axis rearguards through a difficult country. Shortly after midnight the last of the Axis troops evacuated the town and Tripoli fell to the Allies in the early hours of 23 January. It was entered at 0050 hours from the east and south simultaneously; and at 0900 hours General Montgomery received the formal surrender of the town from the Italian civil authorities who met him for the purpose outside the town.

CHAPTER XLII

The Mareth Line

Following the fall of Tripoli, the Axis forces continued their withdrawal westward. But the lengthening line of communications had once again begun to restrict the size of the force that could be sent in pursuit. Caution was necessary in committing tired troops too far forward without ensuring a steady flow of supplies. The Eighth Army had already advanced 1400 miles from Alamein in just exactly three months; and now it was more than 600 miles from Benghazi, its nearest port of supply.

The port of Tripoli could not be used immediately on occupation. It had been wrecked by the Germans before they evacuated that city. Quays, wharves and installations had been destroyed or damaged and the harbour entrance was blocked by sunken ships. Two to three weeks were necesssary before the port could be got working again.[1]

Towards Tunisia

General Montgomery therefore decided to send forward only the 7th Armoured Division. The rest of his troops he held back in the Tripoli area for re-equipping and reorganising until the port of Tripoli should start functioning again. In actual fact, Tripoli was ready to receive its first complete convoy by 6 February; and from 10 February onwards it was handling a cargo-load of some 2000 tons per day. During this interval of about three weeks, General Montgomery proceeded to clear the rest of Tripolitania by small and cautious advances.

The 7th Armoured Division moved forward on 23 January and began to exert pressure on the retreating Axis troops. By 25 January it had pushed back the retreaters to Zavia; and two days later it was near Zuara, less than 50 miles from the Tunisian border. Zuara proved difficult to take as the German rearguard from the 90th Light and the 164th Divisions put up a strong resistance, while the wet weather and bad ground hampered the movements of armoured cars and other vehicles. However, chiefly as a result of the decision of the Axis to withdraw into Tunisia, the rearguard abandoned Zuara on 31 January which was entered the same day; while Nalut was reported clear almost simultaneously. A little more

---

[1] *Alamein to Sangro*, pp. 51-4. General Alexander's *Despatch*, pp. 863-64. W/D 4 Div.

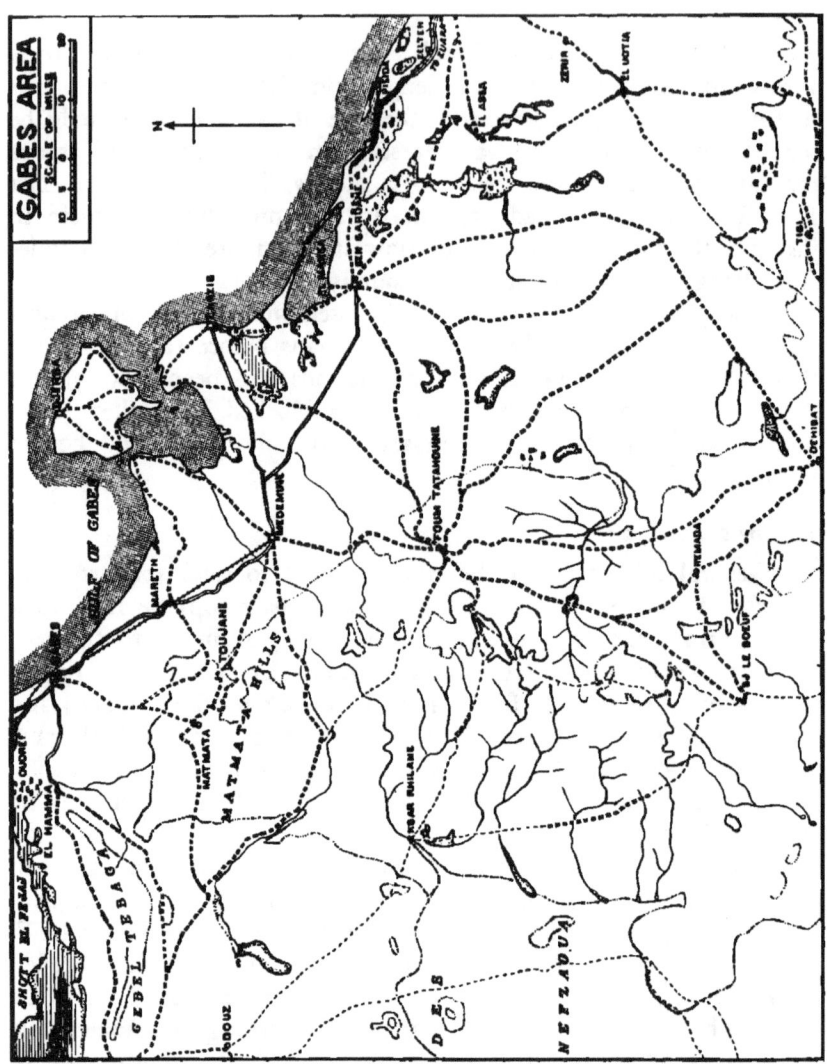

pressure during the next three or four days sufficed to push the remaining Axis troops beyond the border. By 4 February the whole of Tripolitania was in Allied hands and the Italian colonial empire in Africa had ceased to exist. The Eighth Army had entered Tunisia.

Tunisia was the last bastion of German defence and the last hope of the Axis in Africa. It was therefore natural for the Axis to resist to their utmost any further Allied advance into that country. The strongest defensive position in Tunisia was what later came to be known as the Mareth Line. It was a region of natural obstacles, built-up defences and hilly terrain and was almost as strong as the Alamein Line or the El Agheila position. It was obvious that General Rommel would make his most determined stand in this part of the country and intelligence reports confirmed that the Mareth defences were being improved and strengthened with great haste, much activity being noticeable in that region. It was to be expected that, in order to gain the maximum time for these preparations, the Germans would try to delay the Allied approach to this position; and this was the apparent explanation of the increased resistance which the Eighth Army began to experience after crossing the border of Tripolitania.

The first main Axis outpost in Tunisia was Ben Gardane. It was a fortified village, to the south-west of which was located the 15th Panzer Division. It was essentially a delaying position and it appears that the Axis intended to hold up the Eighth Army here for no more than a week or ten days. The 7th Armoured Division approached this position on or about 5 February and proceeded to tackle it from the south-east. To give the Armoured Division some confidence as well as to provide the requisite tactical balance, General Montgomery moved the 22nd Armoured Brigade close behind the front line. Unfortunately the attack could not be put in as planned, as a spell of heavy rain upset the programme. The weather did not clear for quite a few days and, after 10 February, the operations became completely impossible as the rains had turned the desert into quagmire. This state of affairs lasted till 25 February by which time the Germans had probably completed their preparations on the Mareth Line and made ready to withdraw from Ben Gardane. Ben Gardane was attacked the next day and taken without great difficulty.

General Montgomery's next step was to secure the main approaches to the Mareth Line. This required the taking of the important road centres of Medenine and Foum Tatahouine. Medenine was specially important in that it had an airfield which would be an asset in an attack on the Mareth Line. It was also the nearest point to Mareth Line where the assault troops could assemble in case the line was to be attacked from the front. In view of such importance of that place the Axis were expected to offer strong resistance and General Montgomery therefore brought the 51st Division forward as a precaution. Medenine was then attacked by the 7th Armoured Division and fell on 17 February. Foum Tatahouine was taken the next day. The way was cleared for an attack on the Mareth Line.[2]

The attack against the Mareth defences was going to be a major operation and was not intended to commence until 20 March. This late date had been fixed by General Montgomery with the specific purpose of giving sufficient time to the Eighth Army to get ready for that difficult task. Planning had been taken in hand and the necessary reconnaissances were being made locally as well as through the Long Range Penetration Group. Reinforcements and supplies were also coming in satisfactorily. The port of Tripoli was working at its fullest capacity and was discharging some 3500 tons of cargo per day. Tanks were arriving in sufficient numbers to enable the tank replacement programme to be carried out without a hitch. It was intended to concentrate the assault troops in the Tripoli area by 16 March and to start the operations on the 20th.

Axis Offensive Against Anglo-U.S. Force

Hardly had these preparations commenced when a new circumstance arose which created a major diversion from the scheduled programme. There was a great upset in another part of the Tunisian front which altered the balance in the Allied fighting line; and the Eighth Army was called upon to undertake immediate extempore operations to redress that balance.

It will be recalled that as early as 8 November 1942 an Allied expeditionary force had landed in North-West Africa. It consisted of the British and American troops who were joined by the French troops within a few days of their landing. These three forces had, together, advanced into Tunisia from the west and had taken up a line running from the coast to Shott el Djerid. The southern portion of that line was being held by the American troops whose IInd Corps was concentrated in and around Gafsa.

On 15 February, General Rommel launched a strong attack against the Gafsa sector and forced the IInd U.S. Corps to withdraw to Tebessa. That withdrawal created a grave situation for the Allies as it placed the Axis troops in a position to outflank the Anglo-French-American line from the south, with the result that the whole line, or at least its northern end, would have to fall back precipitately, giving up much ground that might be difficult to retake afterwards.

That was the situation with which General Alexander found

[2] 4 Div, 5 Bde, 7 Bde.

himself confronted as he was in the act of assuming command as the Deputy of General Eisenhower. He immediately decided to use the Eighth Army for relieving the situation. In driving towards Tebessa the Axis had had its back to the Eighth Army. General Alexander directed the Eighth Army to exert all possible pressure on its own front so as to draw General Rommel off his Tebessa drive.

The Eighth Army was not administratively ready for such a move. There were grave risks inherent in a premature attack; for, were General Rommel to quit the Tebessa drive and turn back to counter-attack the Eighth Army, the latter would be caught in an awkward situation. Besides, answering this sudden call for help was sure to upset the carefully worked out plan of General Montgomery to attack the Mareth line in his own time. Nevertheless General Montgomery accepted both, the risks as well as the inconvenience involved in responding to the needs of the moment, and decided to proceed against the Mareth line at once. He saw that General Rommel had weakened his Mareth front in order to strengthen his thrust towards Tebessa and that he could perhaps be dislodged from the former position by a dashing and energetic attack. General Montgomery accordingly launched a drive along the coastal road and supplemented it with another drive along the escarpment in the interior.

The advance along the coastal road was to be carried out by the 7th Armoured and the 51st Divisions; that along the escarpment was entrusted to a French formation under General Leclerc. This remarkable little force had joined the Eighth Army only recently. It consisted of Frenchmen and native soldiers, equipped with a mixed assortment of odd types of artillery, machine-guns, multifarious transport and an armoured car or two. General Leclerc had led these troops from Lake Chad to Tripoli across the desert and had placed himself under the command of the Eighth Army. He was now directed to take his force along the escarpment to Ksar Rhilane and then operate north towards the coast.

Thus on 26 February, while the French force was advancing along the escarpment, the other two divisions had moved up to the Mareth defences. They were the 51st, now located on the north of the main road with all three brigades up, and the 7th Armoured Division astride and to the south of the road. These began to operate against the outer defences of the Mareth line and soon succeeded in drawing General Rommel's attention to the drawing danger in the Mareth sector. General Rommel reacted exactly as had been anticipated. He halted his drive towards Tebessa and began to re-group for an attack on the Eighth Army. Reports reached the Headquarters of the Eighth Army, on 27 February, that the 21st Panzer Division was moving south again. The 15th Panzer was already located in the Mareth region having been absent from the Tebessa drive; and as was learnt later, a new German armoured formation, the 10th Panzer Division which had recently arrived in Tunisia, was also brought up to that sector.

It was clear that General Rommel intended to strike hard at the Eighth Army, taking advantage of its overstretched communications. His tank strength had improved since his entry into Tunisia and he had at his disposal the new German "Tiger" tanks which had proved very effective in some operations against the First Army. If now he could deal a strong blow to the Eighth Army in its existing weak state, he would gain some valuable time in which to turn and deal with other sectors of the Allied front in Tunisia. That obviously was his plan.

General Montgomery lost no time in preparing to meet that threat. He ordered the 2nd New Zealand Division to move at once from Tripoli, where it was then located, to Medenine. The move was executed with speed and secrecy and the division was concentrated to the south of Medenine on 2 March. His next step was to provide himself with sufficient armour. Tanks were then arriving in Tripoli for equipping the 2nd Armoured Brigade; so he handed over those tanks to the 8th Armoured Brigade, which was then resting near that town, having been earlier divested of its equipment to furnish other units, and thus completed an armoured formation. He aimed at getting the 8th Armoured Brigade ready for action by 4 March, by which time he hoped to have about 400 tanks for the battle, since he already had the 22nd Armoured Brigade at his disposal besides about eighty Valentines from the 23rd Brigade. In addition, he had a strong artillery force of about 500 anti-tank guns. He thus expected to have sufficient infantry, armour and artillery for fighting a defensive battle in front of Medenine. As to the local defence of the administrative area, he arranged for a nucleus of the X Corps headquarters to be brought up to Ben Gardane.

Battle of Medenine

All these hurried preparations had one drawback: they could not be completed until 4 March which was the earliest date by which the Eighth Army could be ready for the battle. Were the Axis to attack it before that date, its forward formations would be overwhelmed. As it turned out, the Axis did not launch its major attack until 6 March. General Rommel began on 3 March with a minor probing attack against the 51st Division, which was quickly repulsed. During 4 and 5 March his infantry and tanks were reported to be on the move in the mountains west of Medenine. It was easy to infer his intentions from the air observation reports. He was planning to launch his main attack from the mountains, coming down approximately at the centre of the Allied dispositions.

These dispositions were, from north to south, the 51st Division, the 7th Armoured Division and the 2nd New Zealand Division. The New Zealanders were disposed round Medenine so as to be astride all roads and tracks leading into it. The Armoured Division covered the Medenine—Gabes road as well as the overlooking feature known as Tadjera; and the 51st Division was deployed in the gap between the coast and the Tadjera feature. The 500 or so anti-tank guns were positioned round about Medenine. A noteworthy feature of their deployment was that they were not disposed with a view to protecting the infantry, as might be ordinarily done, but with a view to shooting down tanks at short range. This innovation was necessary as there was no time to lay minefields or erect wires. Reliance had therefore to be placed on the skilful positioning of the anti-tank guns to do that job.

As the Axis forces drew nearer, there was no doubt left that the main thrust was being aimed at Medenine. The capture of that important road junction would cut the communications of the Eighth Army with Tripoli, and at the same time encircle a part of the Allied forces to the north. The key to Medenine was the Tadjera feature, a hill to the north-west of that town; and it was towards that hill that the Axis tanks poured out of the mountains, in the early morning of 6 March, in an attempt to attack Medenine from the north. All the three Panzer Divisions (10th, 15th and 21st) seemed to be converging on the same spot.

The first clash occurred at 0800 hours in front of the anti-tank gun screen round north of Medenine. That attack was repulsed and so were several other minor ones, resulting in a loss of 21 tanks to the Axis. The next major attack came at 1430 hours, with infantry supporting the 15th, 21st and part of the 10th Panzer Divisions. This too was held. The Allied line remained firm and stable and could not be pierced at any point. There were two more attacks during the same day which met a similar fate. The Axis lost 52 tanks before the end of that day. After dark it disengaged and withdrew and the battle of Medenine was over.

It was General Rommel's last battle in Africa after which he returned to Germany. His command was taken over by General von Arnim on or about 19 March. General Rommel was suffering from desert sores on the day the battle was fought and it is probable that his return to Germany was due to the aggravation of that illness. According to some other reports, however, he was also ill with malaria and was evacuated to Munich towards the end of March, General von Arnim not taking over from him until 1 or 2 April.

If so, then General Rommel was in command during the Battle of Mareth which took place from 20 to 28 March.

The preparation for attacking the Mareth Line continued after the brief interruption caused by the Medenine flare-up. The date originally fixed for this was 20 March. It was decided to adhere to this date in spite of the upset suffered as a result of that temporary dislocation.

General Montgomery had decided that once the Eighth Army got moving, it should drive straight on Sfax. To reach that objective the Army would have to go across a stretch of level plain lying between Medenine and Gabes. On one side of that plain was the sea, on the other a mountain range known as the Matmata Hills; and in between was a gap which narrowed down to about 22 miles somewhere near Mareth. Years ago, the French had sought to close that gap by constructing a system of defensive positions across it. Gradually that system acquired the name Mareth Line. The original idea behind the line was merely a routine precaution against a possible Italian invasion of Tunisia from Libya. But after the Franco-German armistice, the Axis took possession of it and converted it into a bulwark against any allied advance from the east.

Mareth defences

In the strength of its natural defences, the Mareth Line was next only to Alamein. It ran from Zarat on the coast to Toujane on the Matmata Hills. The coast-line in this part is almost north to south, and the Mareth Line, being roughly perpendicular to it, lay in an east-west direction. Two formidable natural obstacles gave strength to this line. One was the Wadi Zigzaou and the other the Matmata Hills. The hills are jagged and rough, and form a complete barrier to wheeled transport except along a few tracks running through narrow passes. The wadi too, being deep and wide, could not be crossed by vehicles in any part of it. The wadi commenced where the hills terminated and extended right up to the sea, so that together, the Matmata Hills and Wadi Zigzaou barred any approach to upper Tunisia from the east. Nor was it considered possible to outflank the Matmata Hills by moving along their southern and western periphery, as that would involve a journey of 150 miles over waterless desert and then a ground would be reached which was too ragged to permit movement of vehicles. The French were said to have tested this satisfactorily by sending a small transport column in an outflanking exercise and it was said that all but two lorries broke down during the manoeuvre. Even in case a column did manage to survive the rough journey it would come up against another obstacle at the other end—a narrow pass between the two hills of Djebel Melab and Djebel Tebaga traversed by a deep wadi, the Wadi Merteba. The Axis had fortified this position and had constructed a switch-line along the Wadi Merteba.

Thus the western end of the Mareth Line was considered impenetrable, both by the French as well as the Germans. As to the eastern end, the basis of defence there was the Wadi Zigzaou. The Axis had left nothing undone in turning it into a strong defensive position. The banks of the wadi had been widened and deepened and made steep so as to form a difficult tank obstacle, and were covered along their whole length by a complicated system of concrete and steel pill-boxes, gun emplacements, anti-tank ditches, protective wires and minefields. The covering positions had been sited skilfully in order to mislead the attacker and make it difficult for him to contact the main position. On the whole it was a formidable array of built and natural defences.

Operation 'Pugilist'

General Montgomery had two courses open to him for overcoming the Mareth defences—to break through by a frontal attack or to get round it by an outflanking move. As a matter of fact, to begin with, he could pursue both the courses simultaneously and then transfer the weight of the main attack to whichever seemed the more promising. This in fact was the gist of his plan which was named 'Pugilist' and of which he sent an advance copy to General Alexander on 27 February.

A noteworthy feature of that plan was that it did not rule out the outflanking move round the south of the Matmata Hills as impossible, in spite of the considered opinion of the French to that effect. General Montgomery took the view that his vehicles were superior in performance to those which the French could have sent out in their experimental manoeuvre. He therefore decided that it was worth reconnoitring the ground again and re-assessing the chances. The reconnaissance was entrusted to the Long Range Desert Group which was then at his disposal. The Group set out on its mission in December 1942 as General Montgomery had begun to apply his mind to the Mareth problem as early as that. The full report of the reconnaissance was received in January 1943. It confirmed his belief that a way round the Mareth Line was not impossible to find; hence the inclusion of the outflanking move in the 'Pugilist'.

For operation 'Pugilist', the Eighth Army was to be organised into two corps, the XXX and X, with an additional outflanking force loosely called the New Zealand Corps. The XXX Corps was to have under it the 50th and 51st British and 4th Indian Divisions plus the 201st Guards Brigade. The X Corps was to have the 1st and 7th Armoured Divisions and the 4th Light Armoured Brigade, and was to be an Army reserve. The frontal attack was to be made by the XXX Corps after which the X Corps was to pass through and exploit the success. Meanwhile the New Zealand Corps was to carry out the outflanking move. For this purpose, it was to consist of the 2nd New Zealand Division, the 8th Armoured Brigade and General Leclerc's L Force.

Among other things, the plan 'Pugilist' provided for two external aids to the Eighth Army in the Mareth battles. Firstly, the combined air forces from both sides of Tunisia were to give a powerful striking support to the ground troops. Secondly, the American IInd Corps was to co-operate by recapturing Gafsa so as to draw away a part of the Axis strength towards its own sector. Later it was to establish a supply line from Gafsa to assist the advance of the Eighth Army beyond Mareth.

Anglo-U.S. Offensive

It has been seen how the Axis had launched a sharp and sudden attack on Gafsa (through the Kasserine Pass) and driven the American troops in. The same tactics were repeated on 10 March, against the French troops. It will be remembered that a French force under General Leclerc had been sent to Ksar Rhilane to threaten the western flank of the Axis defences from there. The Axis were naturally not happy to have a hostile column operating towards the weak side of their defences and decided to liquidate it. Accordingly they launched a heavy attack on that column on 10 March, with armoured cars, artillery and aircraft, apparently intending to destroy it. But the French force stood firm and drove off the attack with the help of the Desert Air Force, inflicting some slight loss on the attackers. After that it was left unmolested and continued to remain at Ksar Rhilane, where it later served as a useful screen to conceal the outflanking move of the New Zealand Corps.

The Mareth attack was timed to commence on 20 March and General Montgomery began clearing the way for it a few days earlier. He started certain operations on 16/17 March with the aim of destroying the last covering positions of the Axis. These were successful except in one case. One of those covering positions was a hill feature known as the "Horseshoe" from its shape. It was situated at the south-west end of the Mareth defences, dominating the main road to Mareth and it was to be cleared by 201st Guards Brigade. This formation however had the misfortune to strike an unusually heavy minefield which its carriers and other transport were unable to negotiate. After that a heavy hand-to-hand fighting ensued during a night attack and the brigade had to withdraw on account of the severe casualties suffered by it.

Except for the "Horseshoe" feature all obstacles covering the main defences had been removed by the morning of 18 March. By that time the IInd United States Corps, too, had carried out the part assigned to it. It had attacked and captured Gafsa on 17 March and had thus drawn towards itself the 10th Panzer Division as well as some other Italian formations, which was a welcome relief on the Mareth front.

There were no operations on the front line during the two days preceding the opening of the Mareth offensive. General Montgomery was satisfied that the conditions were shaping themselves favourably for the attack; and he therefore decided to let the front relapse into a quiescence so as to avoid disturbing the existing state. His plan for opening the offensive was at this stage substantially the same as in 'Pugilist'. Briefly, the XXX Corps was to deliver the coastal attack using the 50th and 51st Divisions and the 23rd Armoured Brigade. The New Zealand Corps was to move towards Nalut with the Gabes area as its ultimate objective. It was to fight its way to that destination via the Wilder's Gap, Ksar Rhilane and the El Hamma switch-line. The X Corps, entirely armoured, was to be in the Army reserve and was intended to reinforce either the XXX Corps or the New Zealand Corps according to Tactical necessities. A very heavy weight of air support was to be made available to the fighting troops.[3]

The Allied dispositions opposite the Mareth line were in keeping with this plan. At the coastal end of the line was the 50th Division. At its Toujane end (on the Matmata Hills) was the 7th Armoured Division, and between the two was the 51st. The 4th Indian Division which was not intended to go into action until at a later stage was held to the north-east of Medenine; while the New Zealand Corps stood to the west of Foum Tatahouine, ready to move out on its outflanking expedition on receiving the word to go. The corresponding Axis dispositions were as follows: At the coastal end of the Mareth Line was the XX Corps, with under command the Young Fascists, the Trieste Division and the German 90th Light Division. The stretch of front occupied by these three formations was roughly the same as that occupied by the 50th and 51st British Divisions on the Allied side of the Mareth Line. The rest of the front was occupied by the XXI Corps commanding the Spezia and Pistoia Divisions and the 164th German Light Division. Opposite to these was the sector of the 7th Armoured Division. In Axis reserve were the 15th and 21st

---

[3] The RAF helped also in the opening stages of the battle of Mareth, with its 162 heavy and medium bombers attacking Axis concentrations on 20 March, followed by an attack of 180 light bombers on the 21st, and 63 more bombing attacks on the night of 21/22 March.

Panzer Divisions, both of which eventually found their battle ground on the El Hamma switch-line.[4]

The battle

The New Zealand Corps commenced its outflanking move on the night 19/20 March, thus heralding the opening of the Mareth offensive. The actual offensive started at 2230 hours the next day. Protected by the cover of a tremendous barrage of artillery, the 50th Division crossed Wadi Zigzaou and attacked three previously selected strong points on its opposite bank. The idea was to capture those points and turn them into bridgeheads, after which crossings could be built across the wadi for tanks, guns and carriers to pass on to the other side.

The wadi proved as difficult an obstacle as was feared. The banks were steep and wide apart and the bottom was muddy and in some parts covered by standing water. General Alexander, in his *Despatch*, compares this obstacle to the fosse of an old-fashioned fortress and adds that the Allied troops advanced to the assault carrying fascines and scaling-ladders as though at the storm of Badajoz. The wadi was crossed on foot by the assaulting infantrymen in spite of an accurate frontal and flanking fire put down by the Axis on the parts of the banks sought to be crossed. The three selected points on the opposite banks were captured and the required bridgeheads were firmly established.

The taking of the strong points had involved the 50th Division in a rather heavy fighting as those spots had been thickly wired and were protected by minefields and weapons of all descriptions. After a whole night of fighting, there still remained some pockets of resistance in the locality of the bridgeheads at dawn on 21 March. The resisters did their best to harass the sappers who were trying to construct crossings to the other side. That contest lasted all through that day and at last a few Valentines did manage to get across, but they were not enough and the tank losses were somewhat heavy. The anti-tank guns and other transports were unable to follow up and in consequence the troops on the bridgeheads found themselves at a disadvantage. The situation on the night of 21 March was that a foothold had been gained on the opposite bank of Wadi Zigzaou and fighting was in progress; but the odds were almost balanced and the result was in doubt.

The crying need of the moment was suitable crossings to carry heavy weapons and transport across. The attempts of sappers to build bridges were not successful, since their working parties were being constantly dispersed and harassed by intense fire from the Axis side. The only remedy seemed to be to expand the bridge-

[4] W/D's 4 Div, 7 Bde, 4/16 Punjab, 4 & 12 Fd. Coys SM.

heads both laterally and in depth so as to put more distance between the Axis firearms and their targets. To achieve that the XXX Corps put a heavy artillery barrage on the night of 21 March, under the cover of which the areas of the bridgeheads were enlarged. That effort however failed to produce the benefit expected of it. For, on the following morning a heavy rainfall flooded the Wadi and washed out or spoiled the work so far done by the sappers towards constructing a crossing. In consequence the Allied troops on the far bank were in a worse plight than before; to add to their troubles, German reinforcements began to arrive and fighting increased in intensity.

Axis counter-attack

Seeing the 50th Division in such difficulties, the Germans decided that the moment had come for putting in a strong counter-attack. On the morning of 22 March, their 15th Panzer Division was reported to be forming up for such an attack. Ordinarily the light bombers of the Desert Air Force might have struck hard at the troops concentrating for the battle and perhaps succeeded in dispersing them. But owing to the rains the aircraft were unable to take off. The expected counter-attack came that very afternoon and the Allied troops had to fight it out without the support of tanks, artillery or aircraft. The maximum resistance possible was offered in the hope that the weather might change and the Desert Air Force be able to throw its weight into the balance. But the Germans had reinforced their front heavily and were making rapid progress; and the 50th Division seemed to be unable to resist much longer. Accordingly, on the night of 22/23 March, General Montgomery decided that the attack on Wadi Zigzaou had failed and that his real hope lay in the western sector of the Mareth Line, that is in what the New Zealand Corps might be able to achieve. The 50th Division was withdrawn the next night under the cover of a well-placed artillery fire.

The outflanking move

The New Zealand Corps which consisted of 27,000 men and 200 tanks under General Freyberg was at this juncture carrying out its flanking move. It had started out on its operation on the night of 19/20 March and hoped to take the Germans unawares by confining its movements to the hours of darkness. But its efforts to maintain secrecy were unsuccessful. The Germans appeared to have detected its existence on their flank before the morning of 20 March after which there was no sense in limiting the advance to the hours of night. General Montgomery therefore directed the Corps Commander to speed up his advance by moving during the day time also.

All through that day the corps pressed on making a steady progress over difficult ground. General Leclerc's French force helped its passage through Ksar Rhilane by pushing the Axis troops off a difficult wadi and making a crossing possible. The march continued till the last light of 20 March, when the El Hamma switch-line was reached. This was a narrow defile leading to El Hamma, between two high features known as Djebel Tebaga and Djebel Melab. It was a prize worth fighting for, as its possession would open the way to Gabes in the rear of the Mareth Line. The Eighth Army called it the Plum defile.

The success of the New Zealand Corps in reaching the Plum defile, and the failure of the 50th Division's attack on Wadi Zigzaou, left no doubt in General Montgomery's mind as to which of the two thrusts needed backing up. He took a final decision on the morning of 23 March to withdraw the 50th Division and to throw the bulk of his resources in the outflanking movement instead. He planned to pin down the Germans in the coastal sector by giving the impression that he was organising for another attack. The idea was to keep their forces tied up at Wadi Zigzaou in such a way as to prevent the transfer of their reserves to the El Hamma switch-line. Meanwhile he would send the HQ X Corps and the 1st Armoured Division to the New Zealand sector and strike a decisive blow before the Germans had time to move their reinforcements.

It was however possible that the Germans would anticipate this plan and strengthen the switch-line in time. But that could only be done by weakening the Wadi Zigzaou sector. In such an event the XXX Corps could resume its coastal thrust and fight through to Gabes along the main road. There was a reasonable chance of achieving such a result as the Germans had already removed their 164th Division to the switch-line and a further depletion of the Zigzaou sector would make the task easier.

Accordingly, the XXX Corps was ordered to prepare for making a fresh attack in the centre of Wadi Zigzaou. It was to have the 7th Armoured and the 50th and 51st Divisions for the purpose. Its primary role was to contain and tie up the Axis troops on its own front by making it appear through raids and artillery fire that the major attack would be made from that direction. If it could thus delay the switching of Axis troops by about 36 hours, the outflanking move stood a fair chance of success.

One handicap however of the outflanking move was its long line of communication over a very difficult ground. It was therefore necessary to find a shorter route, preferably through the centre of the Matmata Hills. There was now a better opportunity for securing such a shorter line of advance since the Axis troops were preoccupied to resist an advance over the mountains. The road

Medenine—Halluf—Bir Soltane was accordingly selected as an ideal short-cut. It would reduce the line of communication to about half its length and provide a good alternative route of supply. It would also serve as an excellent middle axis between the two thrust lines, thus facilitating the switching of forces from one line to the other; and it might enable an additional thrust to be made towards Toujane and Zelten and thence to the rear of the Mareth Line. The opening of this new road was entrusted to the 4th Indian Division which set out on its mission on the evening of 23 March.

Operation 'Supercharge'

This new plan was not very different from the original plan 'Pugilist.' However the latter name was given up and the second plan was christened 'Supercharge', thus bringing in the associations of successes at Alamein. 'Supercharge' catered for a lightening attack and a break-through into the open tank-country on the other side of the Plum defile. The attack was to take place on 26 March. It was to be preceded by a heavy night-long bombing so as to make the defenders sleepless and overwrought. The bombing was to continue on the following day and reach its climax at 1500 hours. From that point the artillery was to take over and carry on for another hour. The attack was then to commence at 1600 hours with the sun behind the back, an old stratagem of Rommel. The infantry was to aim at pushing the armour through on a narrow front and the fighter-bombers were to maintain continuous operations overhead.

It was essential that all troops should be in position before the launching of the 'Supercharge'. Accordingly, the 7th Armoured Division, on the Wadi Zigzaou sector, moved up as close to the Mareth Line as possible so as to demonstrate an intention to attack. To heighten the effect, aircraft were kept active over the front. Meanwhile the 4th Indian Division was making good progress towards Halluf although the progress of the X Corps Headquarters and the 1st Armoured Division was causing a certain amount of anxiety. The route taken by the X Corps for reaching the Plum defile was the same as that traversed by the New Zealand Corps. But as it involved very rough and difficult going, the last vehicles of the Armoured Division were just able to struggle in some half an hour before the starting of the attack.

The day of attack was characterised by heavy dust storms from early morning. This upset the bombing programme in that the aircraft could not begin their work until after midday; but it helped to conceal the forming up of X Corps and the New Zealanders. The storm subsided in the afternoon and the Desert Air Force went into action. Its light and fighter bombers machine-gunned and bombed their targets for two and half hours causing great destruction amongst Axis guns and transport.[5] Then the New Zealand Division moved to attack, the 8th Armoured Brigade leading. It soon broke into the defensive system of the Germans and was followed up by the 1st Armoured Division which penetrated to a depth of about four miles before being halted by darkness.

The advance was resumed with the rising of the moon. It was necessary to get through the bottle-neck before dawn since the heights on both sides would give an excellent observation to the Axis during day-time. The advance was therefore speeded up and turned out to be a magnificent success. There must have been a great confusion both amongst the Allied and Axis troops, since the 1st Armoured Division drove straight through the Axis-held country past the bulk of the hostile armour, including the 21st Panzer Division, without, as it would seem, either suspecting the presence of the other. At daybreak the leading Allied tanks were only two miles from El Hamma, where they were stopped by a strong screen of anti-tank guns.

The Germans needed to hold El Hamma a little while longer in order to provide a safe corridor for the withdrawal of their troops from the Mareth Line; hence the anti-tank screen. The main Axis formations at Mareth were the 15th Panzer, the 90th Light and the 164th German Divisions, besides the Italian Divisions of Trieste, Spezia nad Pistoia. The Italian troops had started thinning out as early as 25 March and simultaneously the 15th Panzer Division had moved out to reinforce the Plum defences. The 164th Division, too, had started withdrawing towards El Hamma on the night of the 26th leaving the 90th Light Division behind to act as rearguard. The withdrawing troops were moving along the main road to take up their next defensive position to the north of Gabes; and it was essential for their safe passage that El Hamma should be held until they were well beyond that town.

As a result of all these moves, the respective positions of Allied and Axis troops had by now become somewhat complicated. The 21st Panzer Division found itself sandwiched between the New Zealand Corps on the left and the 1st Armoured Division on the right. The latter similarly found itself squeezed between the 21st Panzer and 15th Panzer Divisions from its left and right respectively. Thus cornered, the 21st put up a fierce struggle to extricate itself; but the 15th Panzer Division had only just arrived and had no time to deliver a well-organised counter-attack. The New Zealand Corps effectively kept down the 21st Panzer Division.

[5] This was one of the best examples of close air support in the whole of the North African campaign. 26 squadrons carried out intensive bombing and low level attacks in the space of 2¼ hours.

Jawans of the 16th Punjab Regiment during the battle of Wadi Akarit, April 1943

Indian troops attacking Wadi Akarit area, April 1943

The 4th Indian Division advancing through a Tunisian town, April 1943

Indian Sappers clearing mines in Tunisia, May 1943

Elements of the 15th Panzer who tried to intervene were quickly dealt with by the 1st Armoured Division; so that 164th Division was the only Axis formation that could engage the vanguard of the X Corps.

However, the three German Divisions successfully managed to keep the three Allied corps well occupied until the Axis were able to leave Gabes and take up their next defensive position on Wadi Akarit. The New Zealand Corps remained engaged in a very stiff 'mopping up' operation on the plum features until 27/28 March after which it started moving towards Gabes. The XXX Corps was hampered in following up the German withdrawal by an excess of mines, demolitions and booby-traps which littered their way; and the X Corps was unable to enter El Hamma until after it was evacuated by the Germans on 28 March.

Thus the battle of Mareth Line was finally won by an outflanking move which was completed on the evening of 27 March. Gabes was occupied by the New Zealand Corps on the 29th. All three Axis divisions who tried to delay the advance to Gabes received tremendous knocks and lost about 7000 men as prisoners.

CHAPTER XLIII

Fall of Tunis

The objective of the Eighth Army after the Mareth Line was Sfax. But access to Sfax was through a bottle-neck then known as the Gabes Gap. Tunisia is divided horizontally into two halves by a system of lakes and salt marshes running across it from east to west. The eastern portion of this system is known as Shott el Fejaj; and between Shott el Fejaj and the sea is a narrow neck of coastal plain, 12 to 15 miles wide, which the Eighth Army called the Gabes Gap.

Gabes defences

On being dislodged from the Mareth Line, the Axis forces withdrew to the far end of this gap. There they endeavoured to make a new stand. The greater portion of this gap is covered by a deep wadi known as Wadi Akarit which formed a serious obstacle to wheeled traffic and almost completely blocked the 12-mile passage to the Tunisian plains. Formidable as Wadi Akarit was in itself, it was rendered more so by having on its northern bank two hills from which it was overlooked and from where accurate fire would be directed on to its banks and environments. The two hills dominating the wadi were Gebel Fatnassa on the west and Gebel er Roumana on the east.[1]

The Axis were not slow in taking advantage of this strong natural position. They based their defences on that steep-banked obstacle which they extended westwards by adding an anti-tank ditch so as to block the whole gap between the sea and Shott el Fejaj. That gave them a line, about 12 to 15 miles long to defend. It was obvious that, given sufficient time, the Germans could turn it into a position of great strength, requiring immense efforts to overcome. The task before the Eighth Army therefore was to attack as quickly as possible so as to give no time to the Axis to get settled in its new location.

That task involved two distinct operations, namely occupying the two hills— Fatnassa and Roumana—and crossing Wadi Akarit. Occupation of these hills was essential also for the additional reason that between them these heights commanded a low col across which lay another comparatively easier passage into the plains of Tunisia.

[1] W/D's 4 Div, 5 Bde, 7 Bde.

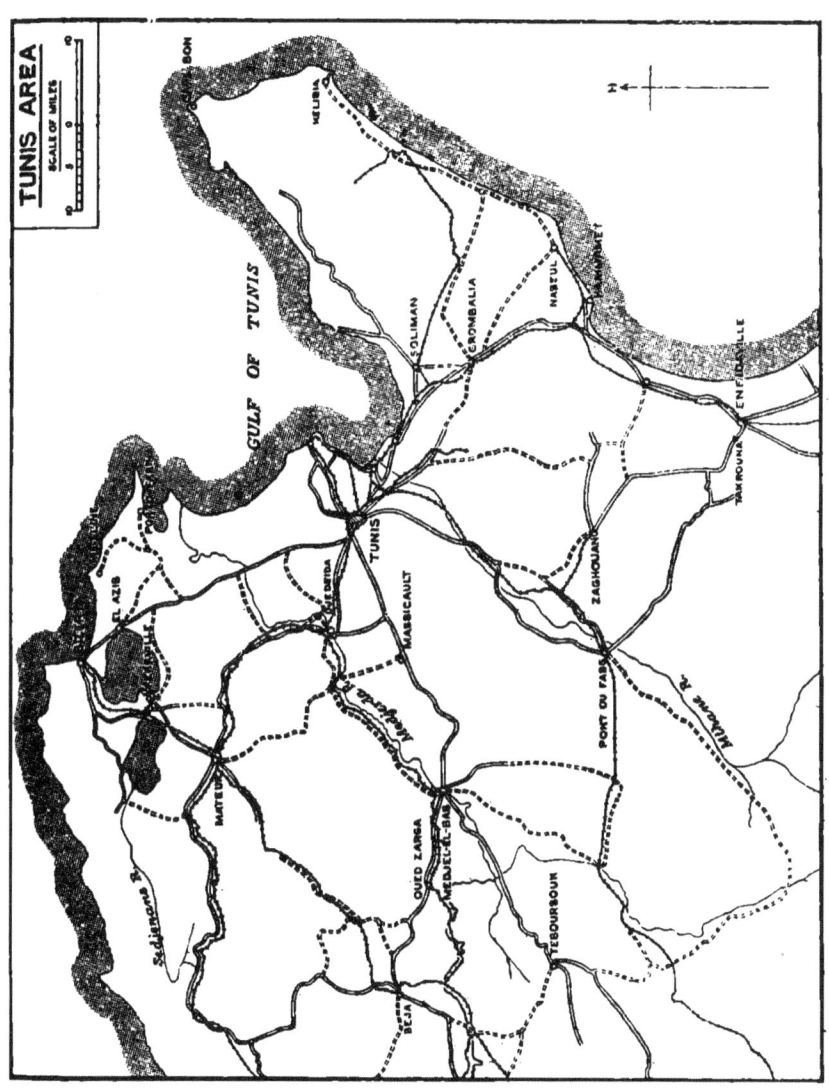

The operation for forcing the Gabes Gap began on 29 March, i.e. on the day, as mentioned earlier, on which the New Zealanders occupied the town of Gabes, as distinct from the Gabes Gap. The same day the New Zealanders also occupied another town to its north-west, called Oudref. Oudref was located on the road Gabes—Gafsa which passed through a defile between Fatnassa and the salt marshes, round the western end of Wadi Akarit.

The 1st Armoured Division pushed along that road and soon contacted the western portion of the Akarit defences, while the 2nd New Zealand Division did the same at the eastern end. These two divisions now consituted the X Corps. The XXX Corps was a little to the rear, between Mareth and Gabes. The temporarily created New Zealand Corps, which was no longer needed, was abolished and its units were reorganised.[2]

Crossing the Wadi

Thus the position on 29 March was that the X Corps had contacted Wadi Akarit and had begun to reconnoitre that region to see if the wadi could be forced, and if so, with what resources. The actual task of crossing the wadi was assigned to the XXX Corps which had already started making preparations to that end.

The general plan was to attack the wadi and make a bridgehead across. The XXX Corps was to be moved forward for the purpose and was to take over temporary command of the 2nd New Zealand Division which was to remain in a holding role. It was then to attack Akarit with the 50th, 51st and the 4th Indian Divisions and secure a bridgehead. The X Corps was then to pass through, taking the New Zealand Division along with it. After crossing the wadi, the two corps were to proceed on a broad front towards the area Mahares—Mezzouna, that is, the XXX Corps was to direct its 51st Division to Mahares along the main road, and the X Corps was to send the New Zealand and the 1st Armoured Divisions towards the Mezzouna airfields. The region between the axes of the two corps was to be cleared by the 7th Armoured Division.

It will be seen from the above that the basis of the plan was an infantry assault on Wadi Akarit with three divisions—the 4th Indian Division opposite to Gebel Fatnassa, the 51st Division against Gebel er Roumana and the 50th Division in the centre. The attack was to be carried out without the aid of moonlight as the next moon would be ten days hence and there was no time to wait. It had been decided to turn the handicap of moonless night into an advan-

---

[2] W/D's 4 Div, 5 Bde, 7 Bde, 4/16 Punjab, 4 Raj Rif, 1/9 GR.

tage by making a silent attack in darkness, unheralded by artillery preparation, so as to take the defenders by surprise.

The attack started at 0400 hours on 6 April. The stratagem of a noiseless advance in darkness produced excellent results for the 4th Indian Division. The role of this division was to capture the Fatnassa feature and thus help in preparing the way for the major break-through by the X Corps. The Indian Division moved forward against great difficulties of terrain with its two brigades, the 5th and the 7th. The 7th Indian Brigade, led by Royal Sussex and 2nd Gurkhas, captured all their objectives by dawn. Then the 5th Indian Brigade passed through and cleared the surroundings, after which it advanced further and placed itself in a position to attack Akarit defences from the rear, so as to ease up the progress of 50th and 51st Divisions who were meeting with stiff resistance in their respective sectors. By 0845 hours the Indian troops had penetrated the Axis defences to a distance of more than three miles and had loosened up the resistance so much that General Montgomery considered the situation ripe for a major break-through.

Accordingly at 1200 hours General Montgomery put in the X Corps with instructions to smash its way through to the open ground before nightfall. That led to very fierce fighting as the Germans and Italians resisted and counter-attacked with great determination. For a time it looked as if the break-through was going to fail and General Montgomery actually began preparations for another attempt to be made the next day with full-scale artillery and air support. But it soon became evident that the Axis strength had after all been broken and it was in no position to offer further resistance. That very night the Axis troops began a withdrawal towards Enfidaville, their next defensive position. By dawn they were in full retreat.

Contact with the First Army

The X and XXX Corps set out in pursuit, the former along an inland route, the latter along the coastal margin. The pursuit continued during the following day, 7 April, when at 1600 hours, a patrol of the 4th Indian Division met an American patrol, thus establishing what appears to be the first effective contact between the two Allied forces approaching from opposite directions.

At this stage the Royal Air Force was engaged in an intensive operation against Axis transport and armoured concentrations, and its great achievement was that it successfully smashed up a number of armoured counter-attacks which were in the forming-up stage and which might have proved fairly formidable had they been allowed to develop. About 188 bomber aircraft attacked such concentrations in the early afternoon of 6 April, while a further 150 fighter-bomber and "tankbuster" aircraft were at the same time in operation against the Axis transport left out in the rear. The intensive bombing continued on 7 and 8 April with 675 more bombers attacking the retreating forces during these two days. The end of the battle, if at all in doubt, was now finally sealed by the air force on 8 April, which day has been described in a War Diary as "the biggest day since El Alamein."

The battle of Wadi Akarit cost the Axis some 7000 prisoners, most of whom were Italians. According to General Alexander, the major credit for the victory goes to the 4th Indian Division. It broke through successfully on the left of the wadi, while the 51st Division on the right was thrown back by a counter-attack and the 50th Division in the centre was seriously delayed by an insurmountable resistance. Had it not been for the 5th Indian Brigade going round and threatening the rear of these resistances, the crossing of Wadi Akarit might have proved a tougher proposition than it did.

The position on 7 April was that the leading elements of the Eighth Army were lined up in the area between Cekhira and Sebkhret er Noual. The XXX Corps was pressing along the coastal margin and the X Corps was doing the same to its west. But the Axis troops seemed to be in no mood to yield further ground and intense fighting occurred in some areas. Progress remained slow until 9 April when the situation improved a little, partly as a result of an operation on the First Army's front.

On that other front, the IX Corps had commenced a move against the Fondouk Gap and had directed the 6th Armoured Division towards Kairouan. That armoured formation broke through successfully to the east on the afternoon of 9 April, which undoubtedly caused the Axis to speed up their programme of withdrawal.

At the same time a chance victory fell to the 7th Armoured Division on the Eighth Army's front. Here, the 22nd Brigade caught the 15th Panzer Division at a disadvantage. The latter was in the act of withdrawing, which it was doing piecemeal, one part of it being embussed for the move and the other part actually moving. The 22nd Brigade engaged a number of those units near Agareb on 9 April, and had a very successful action after which it pushed on to within a few miles of Sfax.

It was now evident that Sfax would yield to a well directed pressure. The X Corps, which was operating inland, was already to the west of Sfax trying to secure the airfields of Triaga and Fauconnerie. General Montgomery ordered it to alter its course and swing east so as to appear on the more vulnerable side of Sfax at some point near La Hencha. This alteration in the direction of the thrust had the effect of weakening resistance to the XXX Corps which immediately resumed its move along the coast and entered Sfax on 10 April.

Enfidaville defences

There was no natural defensive position available to the Axis after Sfax, except at Enfidaville. That was about a hundred miles further north. It was therefore to be expected that the Eighth Army would meet with no serious opposition until that place was reached. Accordingly, on 11 April, General Montgomery directed the X Corps to move on towards Enfidaville. It was to capture Sousse on the way and join up with the First Army at Kairouan. Sousse fell on 12 April and next day the leading troops of the X Corps were up against the Enfidaville position.

The country round Enfidaville was well situated for defence. A high ground north of that town forms a barrier to the maritime plain behind it. It reaches out almost to the sea, narrowing the coastal margin down to a thin strip. At the foot of this hilly barrier and all around is an expanse of broken ground unsuitable for movements of tanks and armoured vehicles. Even on the narrow coastal strip, water channels and other obstacles would make deployment of the armour difficult. The mountainous barrier and the rough ground surrounding it extend westwards up to Gebel Fkirine massif and together they present a continuous wall to any advance from the south.

This wall was pierced by three roads which started from Enfidaville and converged on Tunis after traversing the intervening plains. One of those roads was the coastal road and it was the only good one available in spite of the fact that long stretches of it passed along a narrow neck of coast with salt marshes to its right and mountains on its left. The other two roads ran due north and north-west through a series of narrow passes which made them unsuitable for any advance in strength.

The Enfidaville position was more like a line of defences than a single, impregnable position. Strictly speaking, it was a chain of widely separated defensive localities placed along the line Enfidaville—Pont du Fahs—Medjez el Bab—Sedjennane. Only a small portion of this 120-mile front faced the Eighth Army. The rest of it faced the First Army and the IInd U.S. Corps.

It has been seen that there were three roads going out of Enfidaville and converging on Tunis. That was as from the Eighth Army front. Three more roads similarly led towards the latter city from the First Army area also; and Axis defences along the

Enfidaville—Sedjennane line were so sited as to block all these accesses to the capital of Tunisia. There was one material difference between the Eighth Army front and the First Army front facing this line. While the Eighth Army front was unsuitable for deployment of armour and was overlooked from the high ground to its north, the latter was free from either handicap. In fact, the First Army front had one road which offered particularly good scope for the use of tanks. It was the Medjez—Massicault road, the most direct route to Tunis from the west.[3]

This difference meant that the First Army was in a better position to reach Tunis than the Eighth Army. The Eighteenth Army Group Commander, General Alexander, therefore decided, that the main effort in this final battle of North Africa should be made by the First Army and not the Eighth. The Eighth Army was, during the course of the operations, to pin down as much of the Axis strength as possible by exerting pressure from the south of Enfidaville. This decision was conveyed to General Montgomery on 12 April and he was required to transfer an armoured division and an armoured car regiment to the First Army. General Montgomery divested himself of the 1st Armoured Division and King's Dragoon Guards, both of whom joined the First Army in due course.

To Tunis

At the same time, 12 April, there started the high-level planning for the capture of Tunis and Bizerta and for the final liquidation of the Axis in Africa. It was to be the largest full-scale offensive in which the Eighteenth Army Group was to employ all its resources. Tunis was to be the objective of the First Army and Bizerta that of the IInd U.S. Corps; and 22 April was fixed as the target date for the capture of Tunis. The operations were to be initiated by the Eighth Army on its own front on the night of 19/20 April. The First Army was to attack on 22 April and the IInd U.S. Corps the next day. Yet another formation, the XIX (French) Corps, was to fix its own time of attack; but it was not to take to the field until the First Army had made considerable progress in its own offensive. The main thrust of the offensive was to be made by the First Army and was to be directed towards the Medjez el Bab portion of the Enfidaville—Sedjennane line.

The Eighth Army's role

The reason for requiring the Eighth Army to initiate operations was to pin down as much of the Axis strength as possible in that part of the front, before the First Army launched its final thrust.

---

[3] W/D's 4 Div, 5 Bde, 7 Bde.

The battle of Enfidaville, 4th Indian Division, May 1943

Benghazi

The King Emperor with Indian troops in Tunisia, 1943

Capture of General von Arnim, Tunisia, May 1943

Much therefore depended upon the success with which General Montgomery would tie up the Axis on his own front, and from that point of view the Eighth Army's operations were very important.[4]

General Montgomery attacked at 2130 hours on the night of 19/20 April as scheduled, directing his assault from the centre of his front towards the Enfidaville sector. The attacking force consisted of the 7th Armoured, the 2nd New Zealand, the 4th Indian and the 50th Divisions. The New Zealanders and Indians were to make the main thrust astride the village of Takrouna while the 50th Division was to make a subsidiary move against the town of Enfidaville along the coast road axis. The 7th Armoured Division was to guard the west flank and eventually link up with the XIX (French) Corps.

The fighting that followed the opening of the attack was hard and fierce but failed to produce the desired result. The 50th Division captured Enfidaville. The New Zealanders advanced to a point three miles west of that town. The 4th Indian Division took Gebel Garci after a fierce struggle and held it against several counter-attacks and in spite of heavy casualties. A sanguinary combat took place the next day on the Takrouna heights in which the New Zealand Division captured the vital ground necessary for having a foothold. The Germans too, on their part, suffered many casualties and lost about 800 prisoners to the Allies during 20 and 21 April. Yet all told the results were not satisfactory. It soon became evident that, notwithstanding the gains, the progress was slow and expensive, and was not achieving its aim of pinning down a large number of Axis troops.

General Montgomery therefore decided, late on 21 April, to call off the attack and switch the main thrust from the centre to the coast. This required re-grouping in order to pull out the 4th Indian and the 2nd New Zealand Divisions from the centre and transfer them to the coastal sector. There were also some other adjustments to be made. The 50th Division, for instance, had to be withdrawn for training as it was selected for taking part in the projected invasion of Sicily. The necessary 'reliefs' were provided by bringing forward the 51st and 56th Divisions, neither of whom was in fighting trim, though still capable of serving in a holding role, while the main divisions were being transferred from one sector to another.

The attack in the new sector was to be made by three divisions—the 56th, the 4th Indian and the 2nd New Zealand. The object was to establish all three divisions in the Hammamet area at the

---

[4] W/D's 4 Div, 5 Bde, 7 Bde, 4/16 Punjab, 1/9 GR, 1/2 GR, 4 Raj Rif, 6 Raj Rif.

base of the Cape Bon peninsula. The operations were to commence on 29 April.

This second attack by the Eighth Army, like the first one, was to be a part of the bigger plan of the Eighteenth Army Group to liquidate all Axis resistance in Africa. But the progress achieved this time was even less satisfactory than that achieved on the earlier occasion. Just as the 56th Division was taking up positions for the battle, on the high ground which flanked the attack-area of the 4th Indian Division, it came under a heavy artillery fire and suffered several casualties. Crippled from the very start, it was unable to take its objective. As a result General Montgomery became doubtful about the possibilities of success. He signalled to General Alexander, apprising him of the situation. There was a meeting between the two Generals the next day and the Eighth Army was authorised to abandon the attack.

General Montgomery was however ordered to divest himself of more troops in order to strengthen the First Army front from where the final finishing assault was to be launched. He had already transferred the 1st Armoured Division and the King's Dragoon Guards to the First Army. Now he sent to the First Army a further quota of the 7th Armoured and the 4th Indian Divisions besides the 201st Guards Brigade and some medium artillery. That left to the Eighth Army the 2nd New Zealand and the 51st and 56th Divisions plus two armoured brigades, and a French Division—the 12th—then newly placed under its command. With these the Eighth Army was to hold its own sector while the final assault went in from the First Army's front.

The First Army launched its offensive in great strength on 6 May from the Medjez el Bab sector, directing it on Tunis. It was a complete success. Both Tunis and Bizerta fell the next day. Within another twenty-four hours the German High Command issued a statement that Africa would be abandoned and that the remaining Axis troops would be withdrawn by sea.

But the Royal Navy had laid down an effective blockade at sea and the RAF was alert. Very few of the Axis troops were therefore able to get away.

Mass surrenders started from 12 May. General von Arnim, the German Army Group Commander, surrendered to the Commanding Officer of 2 Gurkhas. He appeared dazed by the suddenness of the defeat. The Italians in the more inaccessible hills held out a little longer and General Messe did not give himself up until the morning of the 13th. About a quarter of a million of Axis troops in all laid down their arms, and surrendered with immense stocks of weapons, ammunition and supplies of all kind. It is said that only about six hundred and odd managed to make good their escape.

The campaign in Tunisia during April and May 1943 had witnessed some very hard and bitter fighting between the Allied and Axis troops. The Indian troops had covered themselves with glory and had won many awards for gallantry and courage including two Victoria Crosses. The first of these was won by Subedar (later Sub-Major) Lalbahadur Thapa of the 1/2nd Gurkha Rifles in the fighting near Fatnassa in the first week of April. In command of two sections, he was ordered to attack and secure the only passage by which a vital commanding feature could be secured. Fighting every inch of the way, Lalbahadur cut his way into a small arena into which the defenders poured a sleet of fire. Undaunted, he led his men on and fought his way up a narrow gully, overcoming all opposition with his *kukri* or revolver. He eventually reached the summit with only two riflemen. Meanwhile other Gurkha companies rushed up to capture the dominating peaks and ridges from which the defenders fled. Lalbahadur Thapa thus won a brilliant victory for the 4th Indian Division almost single-handed. Later, when the King Emperor came to Tripoli, he personally pinned the Victoria Cross upon Subedar Lalbahadur Thapa.[5]

The second Indian VC of this campaign was Company Havildar-Major Chhelu Ram of the 4/6th Rajputana Rifles who won the award during the fighting on 19 April at the Gebel Garci. Armed with only a tommy-gun, CHM Chhelu Ram dashed through a hail of fire and captured a German post. He then rushed to an exposed place where his Company Commander was lying wounded and, while attending to him, was himself wounded. Seeing all officers down, he took command, reorganised his company and led the assault with great skill, rushing from one post to another and encouraging his men. Inspired by his example, his men met the surge of desperate Germans with bayonets and stones. CHM Chhelu Ram was wounded again and laid down his life on the battlefield;[6] but the Germans were driven away from the contested feature.

These and many other brave deeds were performed during the campaign in Tunisia by the victorious Indian and Allied troops. With the capture of General von Arnim in May the victory was as complete as might be desired. The climax was reached on 13 May when General Alexander sent the following telegram to the British Prime Minister:

"Sir, it is my duty to report that the Tunisian campaign is over. All enemy resistance has ceased. We are masters of the North African shores."

---

[5] See *Red Eagle: the story of the 4th Indian Division*; and *India's VCs in the two World Wars*. See also photographs facing pp. 347 and 352.
[6] *Ibid.*

Appendices

APPENDIX A

ORDER OF BATTLE—FORCE 'HERON' (EGYPT) AUGUST 1939.

STAFFS	Indian Army Liaison Staff.
	HQ 11th Indian Infantry Brigade.
ARTILLERY	4th Field Regiment RA.
ENGINEERS	No. 18 Field Coy. Royal Bombay S & M.
SIGNALS	4th Field Regiment RA Signal Section.
	11th Indian Infantry Brigade Signal Section, 4th Division Signals.
INFANTRY	2nd Battalion Cameron Highlanders.
	1/6 Rajputana Rifles.
	4/7 Rajput Regiment.
MISCELLANEOUS	Mixed Reinforcement Camp.
	2nd Echelon.
	Field Accounts Office.
	No. 19 Field Post Office.

SERVICES

SUPPLY & TRANSPORT	No. 15 Supply Issue Section.
	No. 62 Depot Section, Supply Personnel Coy.
	No. 16 Cattle Supply Section Class II.
	Nos. 9 & 10 Cattle Supply Sections Class III.
	Composite MT Coy.
MEDICAL	No. 19 Field Ambulance.
	No. 15 Field Hygiene Section (less two sub-sections).
	No. 11 Indian General Hospital (HQ and 400 beds).
ORDNANCE	Ordnance Field Company.
	Ordnance Workshop Company.
	HQ Nos. 18, 19 & 29 Workshop Sections.

ORDER OF BATTLE—FORCE 'HAWK' (ADEN)

2/5 Mahratta Light Infantry.
Detachment RIASC (MT drivers).
17 Indian Staging Section.

NOTE:—One Company 2/5 Mahratta LI and the detachment RIASC (MT) were in Aden since 30 April 1939.

APPENDIX B

INFANTRY BATTALIONS IN MIDDLE EAST COMMAND ON 3rd SEPTEMBER 1939.

A. *Egypt*

    (i)   1 KRRC   Mot. Bn. in Armd. Division.

    (ii) 2 Camerons
          1/6 Rajput   11 Ind. Inf. Bde.
         4/7 Rajput

    (iii) 2 Scots Guards
          1 NF (MG)   Cairo Brigade.
         1 Buffs

         1 R Sussex
         1 Essex   Canal Brigade.

         1 Bedfs Herts   18 Inf. Bde.
         3 Coldstream Guards   in Alexandria.
         1 Hampshire   in Western Desert.

B. *Palestine*

    (i)   2 Rifle Brigade
         1 A and SH   14 Inf. Bde.
         2 Queens

         2 Leicesters
         1 S Stafford   16 Inf. Bde.
         1 Welch

         1 Foresters   less one Coy. in Cyprus.

         2 Black Watch
         2 HLI   under Jerusalem Area.
         2 King's Own

         2 W Yorks   under Lydda Area.

C. *Sudan*

         1 Cheshire
         2 Y & L
         1 Worc R

APPENDIX C

ARMY COUNCIL INSTRUCTIONS TO THE GENERAL OFFICER COMMANDING-IN-CHIEF IN THE MIDDLE EAST.

1. You are appointed General Officer Commanding-in-Chief in the Middle East.

2. The area over which your command extends, in peace, comprises:—

>   Egypt
>   The Sudan
>   Palestine and Transjordan
>   Cyprus

3. In these areas you will exercise general control over all British land forces in matters of high policy in peace and will, in particular, be responsible for the review and co-ordination of war plans for reinforcements in emergency, including the distribution of available land forces and material between these areas.

4. In addition you will be responsible for the preparation of all war plans, in co-operation with the local military or air force commanders, for the employment of land forces in British Somaliland, Aden, Iraq, and the shores of the Persian Gulf.

5. In carrying out these tasks you will where appropriate consult and co-operate with the Naval Commander-in-Chief, Mediterranean, the Naval Commander-in-Chief, East Indies Station, the Commander-in-Chief in India, the Inspector General, African Colonial Forces, and the Air Officer Commanding-in-Chief in the Middle East.

6. You will maintain close touch with His Majesty's Ambassador in Egypt; His Majesty's Ambassador in Iraq; the Governor General in the Sudan; the High Commissioner for Palestine and Transjordan; the Governors of Cyprus, Aden and British Somaliland; and the Political Resident in the Persian Gulf.

7. The policy of His Majesty's Government with regard to the Egyptian Forces is that they shall be developed into efficient modern forces capable of co-operating with the British forces in the defence of Egypt. You will maintain close touch with His Majesty's Ambassador in Egypt, the Head of the British Military Mission, and the Egyptian General Staff in all matters of High policy affecting the development and employment in war of the Egyptian Army, with due regard to the existing responsibilities of the General Officer Commanding-in-Chief, Egypt, in such matters as local defence, co-operation between British and Egyptian troops, and training. You will delegate to the General Officer Commanding-in-Chief, the British Troops in Egypt, such matters as are, in your opinion, best arranged by him direct with the appropriate Egyptian authorities and, subject to the agreement of the Egyptian Government at the time, command of the Egyptian Army in war.

The agreement of the Egyptian Government to place the Egyptian Army under the command of the General Officer Commanding-in-Chief in Egypt will be obtained by His Majesty's Ambassador through whose intermediation all requests to the Egyptian Government will be made.

8. You should bear in mind that His Majesty's Ambassador must retain in all circumstances his existing position *vis-a-vis* the Egyptian Government. This does not exclude direct communication between the General Officer Commanding-in-Chief, British Troops in Egypt, and the Egyptian authorities on routine matters agreed by His Majesty's Ambassador.

The same considerations will apply as regards your relations with His Majesty's Diplomatic Representatives in the other countries included in the area over which your command will extend in war. In the case of Iraq, this will not preclude direct communication with the Inspector General of the Iraq Army on such matters as may be agreed by His Majesty's Ambassador to Iraq.

9. You will visit all areas which are included in war in your Command (*vide* paragraph 14 below) to study local situations and inform yourself of local problems.

10. Subject to the direction of the Chiefs of Staff and of the War Office in respect of the land forces, you are responsible, in conjunction with the Naval Commander-in-Chief, Mediterranean, the Naval Commander-in-Chief, East Indies Station, and the Air Officer Commanding-in-Chief, Middle East, for co-ordinating the British war plans with the war plans of Allies of His Majesty's Government in the Near and Middle East and North Africa.

This will involve at present co-ordination with the French military authorities in North Africa, Syria and French Somaliland; the Turkish General Staff; and possibly ultimately the Greek and Rumanian General Staffs.

You will arrange to exchange visits with these authorities as may be required.

11. To assist you in these tasks you will be provided with a staff for your own use. Of this Staff, the Senior General Staff Officer will also be a member of the Joint Planning Staff for the Middle East, which will include the Chief Staff Officers of the Commander-in-Chief, Mediterranean, and the Air Officer Commanding-in-Chief, Middle East.

The Joint Planning Staff will be responsible for the inter-service co-operation of all war plans as may be directed by the Commanders concerned, namely the Commander-in-Chief, Mediterranean, the Commander-in-Chief, East Indies, the Air Officer Commanding-in-Chief, Middle East and yourself.

12. Your requirements as regards intelligence will be provided by the Middle East Intelligence Centre, which is being established in Cairo.

13. Your headquarters will be located at Cairo.

14. Should war break out the area of your Command will be extended to include all military forces in British Somaliland, Aden, Iraq and shores of the Persian Gulf, with the exception of those which are normally under the control of the Royal Air Force.

15. Your tasks in war are to co-ordinate (in consultation with the Air Officer Commanding-in-Chief, Middle East, for matters affecting Iraq and Aden) the action of the land forces in the areas under your command and the distribution of available resources between them. You will be guided by the policy for the conduct of operations which will be communicated to you from time to time.

You will co-ordinate the operations of the forces under your command with the operations of the various allied forces in the areas mentioned in paragraph 10.

For this purpose you will work in direct co-operation with allied military commanders concerned.

By Command of the Army Council
H. J. Creedy

The War Office,
24th July, 1939.

APPENDIX D

ITALIAN MEDIUM TANK M 11/39 (11 TONNER).

Length	15′ 6″.
Breadth	7′ 2″.
Clearance	1′ 2″.
Weight with full load	11 tons (approx.)
Engine	2 cylinder 135 h.p. Water cooled.
Fuel	Diesel oil.
Capacity main fuel tank	32 gallons.
Capacity of reserve tank	8 gallons.
Maximum gradient	45 degrees.
Vertical obstacle	2′ 8″.
Trench crossing	6′ 7″.
Maximum fording depth	3′ 3″.
Maximum speed on roads	21 m.p.h.
Maximum speed across country	9 m.p.h.
Armament	One 37/A.P. semi-automatic cannon in fixed turret on right hand side. Two 8mm Breda machine guns in revolving turret.
Crew	Three (1 driver, 2 gunners of which one is commander and wireless operator).

SPECIFICATIONS OF THE ITALIAN LIGHT TANK L 33/35 (CARRO VELOCE 3 TONNER—C.V.3).*

Length	10′ 4″.
Breadth	4′ 7″.
Height	4′ 3″.
Width of track	7½″.
Weight with full load	3.4 tons.
Max. speed on roads	26 m.p.h.
Max. gradient	45 degrees.
Vertical obstacle	2′ 2″.
Trench crossing (max. width)	4′ 9″.
Fording depth	2′ 2″ to 2′ 4″.
Armament	Two MGs, Fiat Model 35, or one MG Fiat Model 35 and one flamethrower (flamethrower tank tows a trailer).
Ammunition	Normally 2,400 rounds in 30 metallic drums each containing 80 rounds. 10 extra drums can be carried if required, making total 3,200 rounds. The flamethrower tank never carries more than 2,400 rounds.

*See diagram, p. 523.

Arcs of fire.
 (*a*) Horizontal   40 degrees (20 degrees each side).
 (*b*) Vertical   40 degrees (20 degrees elevation and 20 dgs. depression).

Fire discipline   Only one MG is fired at a time, the other is kept in reserve in case of stoppage or overheating. Owing to limited visibility, fire at long range is inaccurate.

           Tanks approach the target as near as possible, halt for a few seconds and fire, then go on again.

           Owing to limited traverse on the guns, close co-operation between driver and gunner is necessary, the driver pointing the tank approximately at the target before halting.

Engine   4 vertical cylinders, "monoblock" 43 h.p.

Crew   2 (gunner-commander and driver).

Armour   Front plates 16 mm
           remainder 4—8 mm

Range   Cross country about 5 hrs. running. Road 100 km. (60 mih)

NOTES. (1) The portholes and louvres are very susceptible to "splash" from SA fire.
   (2) Petrol tank is inside just behind the driver's head.
   (3) Observation is extremely bad. When the tank is closed the driver only has a narrow slit in front of his eyes to enable him to steer. The gunner has a small aperture about ½" sq. to his front to enable him to sight his guns on either side; at eye level, are small portholes about 5" × 2" which can be closed if required.

LIGHT TANK L 33/35 (CARRO VELOCE 3 TONNER)

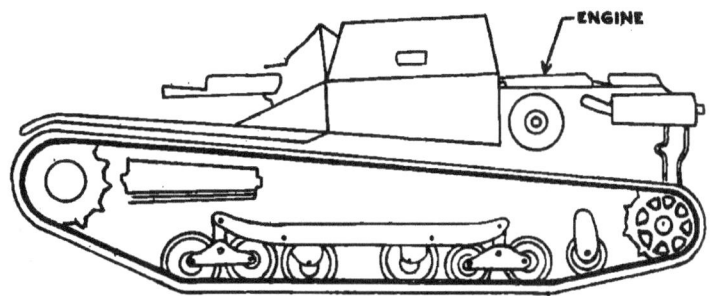

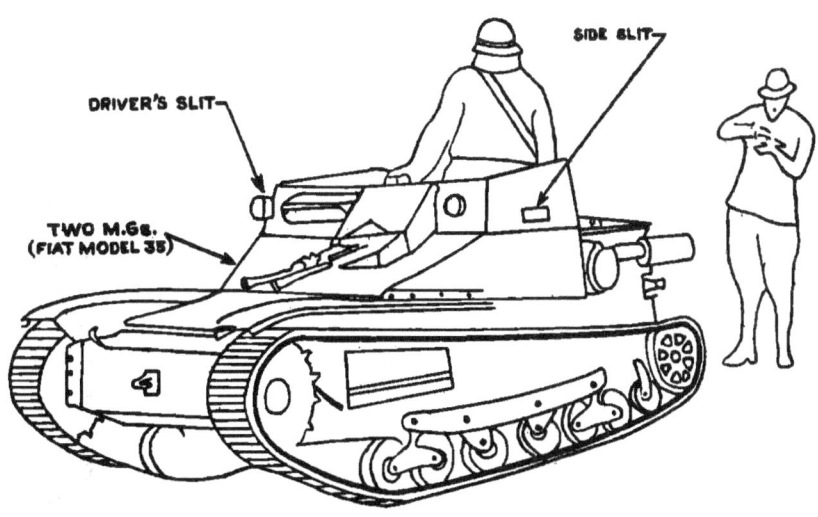

APPENDIX E

SOME AXIS BOMBS

ITALIAN 'THERMOS' BOMB*

(Extract from Supplement to 4 Ind. Div. Intelligence Summary No. 27)

1. DESCRIPTION

    The bomb consists of two main parts.

    (i) *The Firing Mechanism*
    A heavy piece of brass, with a black bakelite dust cover, which screws into the HE container. Usually the bomb is on its side looking like a khaki thermos flask with a black and brass top with spiral spring round it. Sometimes however the top may have an aluminium cap over it in which case the bomb is probably safe, but this cannot be relied upon.

    (ii) *The explosive Container*
    A steel cylinder $2\frac{1}{4}''$ diameter and $7''$ long painted brown and containing about 6 lbs. of HE.

2. ACTION OF THE BOMB

    Before released from the aeroplane the firing mechanism is covered over with an aluminium cap held on by a small screw to which is attached an aluminium propeller.

    Before releasing the bomb a locking pin is withdrawn from the propeller and the rush of air causes both propeller and aluminium cap to come off. The shock of hitting the ground will put the bomb into a highly sensitive and dangerous state. Sensitivity varies but the slightest movement may release the striker, particularly if the bomb is lifted upright. It is emphasised that this is *not* a delay action bomb. It can remain dangerous for an indefinite period until disturbed.

3. FIRING MECHANISM

    The bomb is made sensitive by a piston slowly forcing its way against a resistance of oil within a container. This action takes approximately 10 seconds and allows the bomb to settle, after which it is likely to explode at the slightest movement. In certain cases vibration may be sufficient to explode the bomb.

4. METHOD OF DESTRUCTION

    The cap and detonator of this bomb are both very powerful and can severely injure personnel. The charge of HE makes the bomb dangerous at 100 yds. and heavy pieces from the head can fly up to 300 yds. No attempt should be made to disarm complete bombs. A noose on the end of a 100 yards rope should be placed round the bomb without touching or disturbing it in any way and the bomb should then be towed from behind cover or a vehicle. Sandbags round the bomb localise its effect. Unexploded bombs should be towed into a heap, the site marked and protected and the RE informed, who will arrange for their destruction by explosive.

*See diagram opposite

ITALIAN 'THERMOS' BOMB

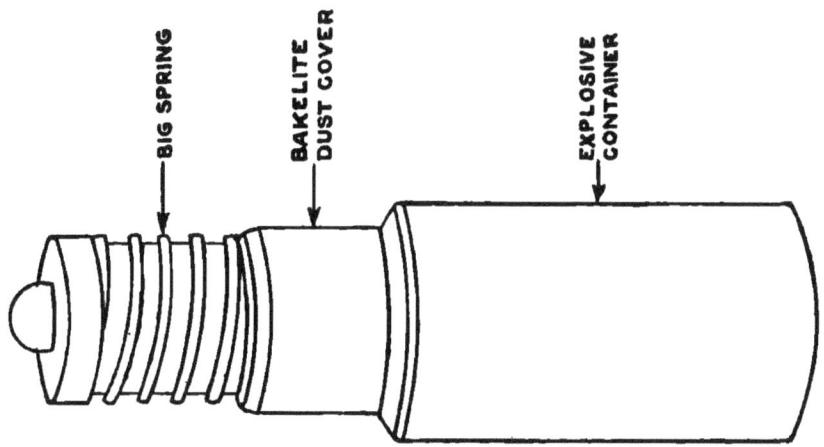

BOMB IN 'LIVE' CONDITION

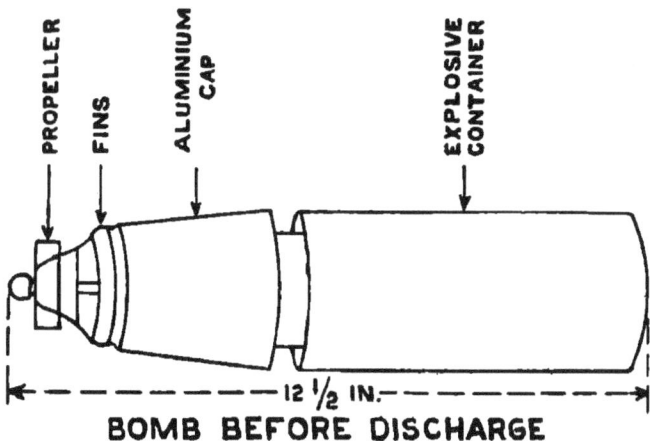

BOMB BEFORE DISCHARGE

ITALIAN H.E. BOMB (250 lbs) S.A.F.

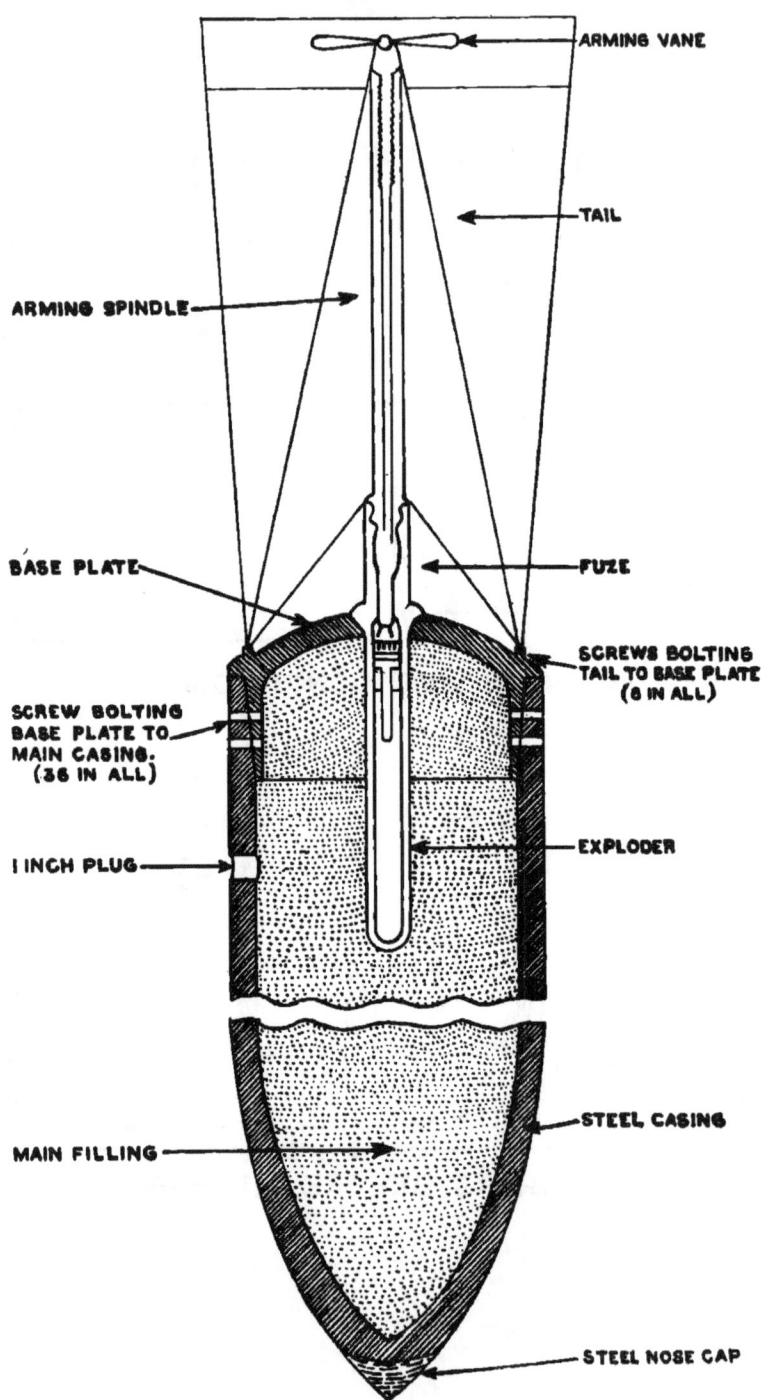

APPENDIX E

*ITALIAN HE BOMB (250 lbs.) SAF.
(Extract from Supplement to 4 Ind. Div. Intelligence Summary No. 47)

1. DESCRIPTION

   Dimensions:

Weight (complete with tail)	250 lbs.
Length (complete with tail)	4 ft.
Length of tail	1 ft. 8 in.
Diameter	10 in.

   The body of the bomb is in two pieces—the main casing and the base plate, which are bolted together. Both are made of steel. The tail is screwed to the base plate, and is made of tin.

   The main filling is presumed to be Amatol.

   The tail is painted grey. The main casing is naturally grey, with traces of red and grey paint. The base plate is always painted red.

   The purpose of the 1-inch plug in the side of the bomb is not apparent.

2. ACTION OF THE BOMB

   The bomb becomes armed by the withdrawal of the arming-vane and spindle during flight. The needle pellet is then held off the detonators by the creep spring only. On striking the ground, the needle pellet in the fuse compresses the spring and the needles pierce the twin detonators, which detonate the exploder and main filling.

   Detonation is invariably complete, and very violent. Average size of fragments 6 x 2 sq. inches.

3. METHOD OF DEALING WITH DUD BOMBS

   This depends on the position of the needles. If their situation cannot be ascertained, the bomb is dangerous to handle and should be blown up by demolition explosives.

   If, as it happens in the majority of cases, the tail is torn off, and it can be seen that there is no obstruction to the detonators, then the bomb is safe to handle or transport, if done carefully.

   If the base-plate is missing, the bomb is safe, but the base plate must be considered dangerous.

4. PENETRATION

   The bomb will burst after the nose has penetrated to a depth of 2-5 ft., according to the hardness of the ground. An unexploded bomb may penetrate soft ground to a depth of 10 ft. and, if it strikes hard rock under the surface may run horizontally, or turn up.

   On digging for duds, the possibility of the exposed condition of the detonators must be borne in mind.

   NOTE: The Italian HE Bomb (130 lbs.) is similar in most respects; works, and can be dealt with, in the same way. Its penetration is less.

*See diagram opposite

ITALIAN INCENDIARY BOMB (43 lbs)

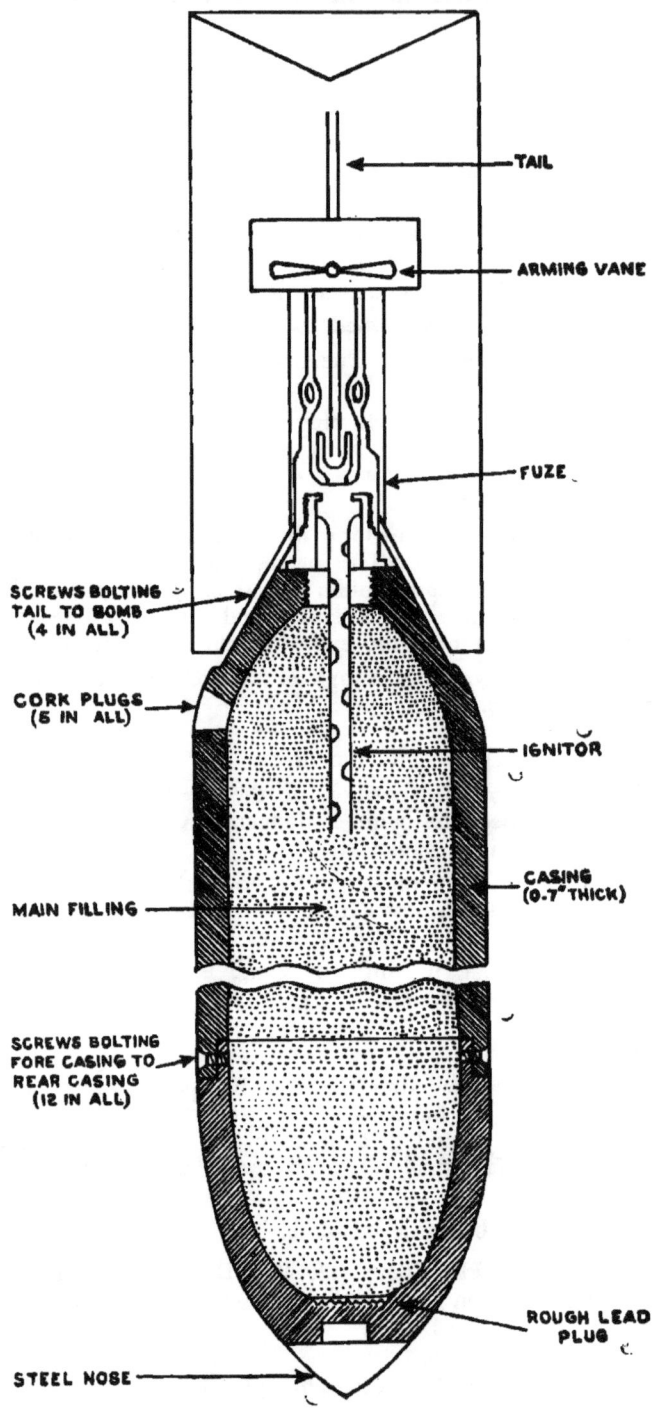

APPENDIX E

*ITALIAN INCENDIARY BOMB (43 lbs.)

(Extract from Supplement to 4 Ind. Div. Intelligence)
Summary No. 48)

1. DESCRIPTION

Dimensions :

Weight (complete with tail)	43 lbs.
Length „	2 ft. 9½"
Length of tail	1 ft. 3"
Diameter	6½"

The bomb consists of a casing of brittle material normally painted bluish-grey,—material probably electron. It is fitted with a steel nose-cap. The tail is made of tin, painted grey, or of the same material as casing.

The base of the bomb is fitted with an adapter, which carries the igniter consisting of a perforated aluminium tube, corked at fore-end and encased in paper. It contains a light grey powder.

The main filling is presumed to be thermit.

2. ACTION OF THE BOMB

The action is the same as for the 250 and 130 lb. bombs. The detonator, which makes a crack when fired, sets off the igniter which fires the main filling. After a few seconds the corks are blown out and then, for 2 or 3 minutes, there is a violent spluttering and sparks are thrown out to a distance of 10 yards, which is the minimum safety distance. For the next 10 minutes, the spluttering ceases and the bomb burns with a white heat. It can be approached to within one yard.

3. METHOD OF DEALING WITH DUD BOMBS

Unscrew the 4 screws attaching the tail to the body—a piastre can be used for this—and withdraw the tail. It may be necessary to unscrew the arming vane. Unscrew the rear half of the fuze and remove the detonator. It is now quite safe.

4. PENETRATION

On hard ground the bomb often breaks up, the tail and fuze breaking, otherwise, it goes in about half its length. In soft ground, the point may bury itself to a depth varying up to five feet.

*See diagram opposite

50 Kg. GERMAN BOMB WITH RHEINMETAL

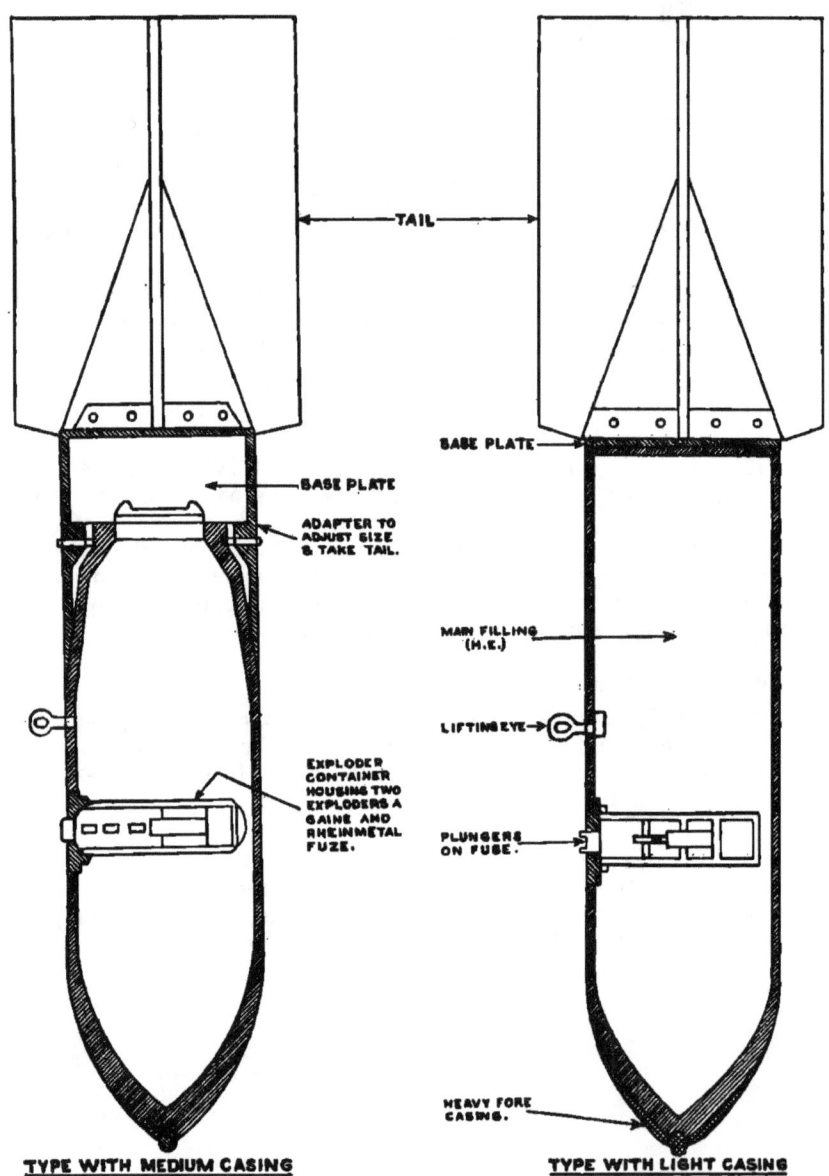

TYPE WITH MEDIUM CASING

TYPE WITH LIGHT CASING

APPENDIX E

SOME GERMAN BOMBS

*Description of some of the German Bombs in use at about the same period as the Italian Bombs, as given in a Supplement to 4 Ind. Div. Intelligence Summary No. 62

GERMAN BOMB FUZES.

The Germans are now using three new types of aerial bomb fuze:—
Rheinmetal type EIAZ (17) (figures 17 in a circle).
Fuze 50—(no other letters or figures beyond 50).
Fuze EIAZ (38) (figures 38 in a circle).

The Rheinmetal type EIAZ (17) fuze can be identified by the external marking EIAZ 17. The number in the ring is *most important*. It has been established by trial and examination that the mechanism is designed to give a maximum delay of 80 hours. While it is not possible to give a definite figure for the minimum delay, there are sound reasons for suggesting that it is $2\frac{1}{2}$ hours. From the results of examination up to the present, there is no evidence of the use of any anti-handling device or booby trap. It should be, perhaps, noted that the construction of the clockwork is such that it enables the time disc and its driving wheel to be readily replaceable by another combination which would give a different ratio and hence different times for maximum and minimum delays. This would probably be, in simple arithmetical ratios of say $\frac{1}{3}$, $\frac{1}{2}$, 1, 2, 3. It is recommended that after the fuze has been removed from the bomb no attempt should be made to unscrew the gaine and the whole unit should be set aside in a safe place for a minimum of ten days.

There has been a later report to the effect that the clockwork mechanism of a fuze of this type was still working after 136 hours. This and the following fuze 50 are usually used together in 250 kg. bombs with two fuze pockets.

Fuze 50. Similar to the Rheinmetal type, but painted green, is believed to be the delay type with a booby trap incorporated, so that if a fuze discharger is attached to the fuze within a certain period, the electrical firing circuit is completed. Therefore, when extracting this fuze only dischargers with the two contacts removed should be used. Preliminary investigation points to a delay of $\frac{1}{4}$ to 12 hrs. This fuze and fuze EIAZ (17) are usually used together in 250 kg. bombs with two fuze pockets.

Fuze EIAZ (38). Painted black with the marking on the rim of the fuze. A superficial examination indicates that the fuze is charged in the same way as EIAZ (15) but it is believed to be a long delay acid type. This fuze has only appeared in 50 kg. bombs up to date.

German Incendiary Bombs. One kilogram German incendiary bomb usually explodes from three to five minutes after incendiary process has commenced to function. Burning fragments of magnesium are thrown to a considerable distance though explosive effect is not great. Protection to persons dealing with these bombs is afforded by wet blankets folded double and hanging over the left arm, i.e. four thicknesses held as a shield. The explosive is held in a container one inch in diameter and one and a quarter inches long screwed into the tapered end just below tail or fins in sockets normally occupied by filling screws.

* See diagram

APPENDIX F

ORDER OF BATTLE—TENTH ITALIAN ARMY—SEP. 1940

HQ 10TH ARMY

   HQ XXI Corps[1]
      62 Metropolitan Div.
      63 Metropolitan Div.

   HQ Group of Libyan Divs.
      1 Libyan Div.
      2 Libyan Div.

   Tank Group "Libya"
      Consisted of Lt. and Medium Tanks. Possibly formed by withdrawing Lt. Tank Bns. from Divs. and Medium Tank Bns. from Corps to form a species of Armd. Bde. to operate independently.

   Maletti Coln.
      1 (23 March) Blackshirt Div.
      Libyan Tps.
      Arty.
      Tanks.

---

1. In Marshal Graziani's book *"African Settentriona 1940-41"*, 62 and 63 Metropolitan Divisions have been shown as being under XXIII Corps instead of XXI Corps. Obviously there had been some changes in the allocation of the Corps at a later period. The order of battles given by Marshal Graziani is as follows:—

   10TH ARMY (HQ Tobruk)
      1st Libyan Division   ...⎫ One group.
      2nd Libyan Division   ...⎭

      Maletti Mobile Column   ...⎫ One motorised group.

   XXIII CORPS (HQ Bardia)
      62 Metropolitan Div.
      63 Metropolitan Div.
      1 Blackshirt Div.

   XXII CORPS (guarding L of C)
      Cantanzaro Div.
      4th Blackshirt Div.

APPENDIX G

ITALIAN DISPOSITIONS WITH LOCATIONS AS KNOWN BY HQ, WDF BEFORE OPERATIONS BEGAN

	Place		Estimated Strength
(a)	MAKTILA	621373	5,000 Libyans.
	SIDI BARRANI	598379	15,000 Italians, 12 Medium and 24 Field Guns.
(b)	TUMMAR WEST	598366	6,000 Libyans.
	TUMMAR EAST and Pt. 90	606364	1,000 Italians, 48 Field Guns.
(c)	NIBEIWA	594356	Maletti Raggruppamento, 2,500 Libyans, 12 Field Guns (M.II. Tanks).
(d)	SOFAFI	570335	Portion of 63rd Metropolitan Division. One Infantry Regiment (3 Battalions).
(e)	RABIA	574337	2 Field Artillery Regiments, Three Tank Battalions (of which two probably MH Tanks), 7,000 Italians, 12 Medium and 76 Field or Light Guns, 72 Medium and 30 Light Tanks.

ITALIAN REAR AREA

(a) Coast from Sidi Barrani to Buq Buq 560369 and probably in support of Libyan Division at Maktila.   Blackshirt Division (10,000 men, 24 Field Guns, 20 Anti-Tank Guns, Mixed Tank Force of 72 Medium and 30 Light Tanks.

(b) Remainder of 63rd Division dispersed along escarpment up to Halfaya 526366.

APPENDIX H

ADVANCE TO EL AGHEILA

(February 1941)

Prisoners and Equipment Captured

GHQ 10 Army.
HQ XX Corps.
60 Inf. Div. (Two Bde. Gps.)
Armd. Gp. (Babini).
Guns	110
Tanks	120
Personnel	20,000 (Approx.)

HQ XXII Corps.
61 Inf. Div. (Two Bde. Gps.)
Two Gps. GAF (7000).
Guns Fld.	140
Guns Med.	68
Tanks Med.	23
Tanks Lt.	64
Personnel	30,000 (Approx.)

HQ XXI & XXIII Corps.
62 Div.
63 Div.
1 CCNN Div.
2 CCNN Div. (less one legion).
GAF (7,600).
Guns Fld.	217
„ Med.	7
„ AA (Hy.)	27
Tanks Med.	13
„ Lt.	115
Personnel	45,000 (Approx.)

HQ (Libyan Corps)
1 Libyan Div.
2 Libyan Div.
64 Div.
One Legion 2 CCNN Div.
4 CCNN Div.
Guns Fld.	200 (Approx.)
„ AA	55 „
Tanks Med.	28
„ Lt.	45
Personnel	40,000 (Approx.)

APPENDIX J

ORDER OF BATTLE—'CYRCOM'
(31 March 1941)

At 0500 hrs. 31 March 'Cyrcom' contained the following formations and units:

HQ CYRCOM	Barce.
1st French Motor Bn. less 1 Coy.	Msus.
HQ 2 ARMD. Division	Mersa Brega.
1st KDGs	Position.
3rd Armd. Bde.	
3 Hussars	
5 RTR	
6 RTR	
1 Regt. RHA	
2 Support Gp.	
1 Tower Hamlet Rifles	
C. Coy. 1 RNF (MG)	
1 Coy. French Motor Bn.	
J Bty. RHA (A/Tk.)	
104 RHA	
HQ 9 AUSTRALIAN DIVISION	Barce.
51 Army Fd. Regt. RA	
20 Australian Inf. Bde.	Derna.
2/13 Aust. Inf. Bn.	
2/15 ,, ,, ,,	
2/17 ,, ,, ,,	
26 Australian Inf. Bde.	Barce.
2/24 Aust. Inf. Bn.	
2/48 ,, ,, ,,	
24 Australian Inf. Bde.	Tobruk.
2/28 Aust. Inf. Bn.	
2/43	
2/32 (detached)	
TOBRUK GARRISON	Tobruk.
HQ 3 Indian Mortar Brigade	
2 Royal Lancers	
11 PAVO Cavalry	
18 KEO Cavalry	
3 RHA less 'J' Bty.	
HQ 26 Australian Inf. Bde.	
NOTE. AA Units	Not shown.
RE Units	,,
RAF Units	

APPENDIX K

ORDER OF BATTLE—FORCE 'ASSURANCE'

Serial No.	Unit	Mobilization Station	Remarks
1	HQ 3 Motor Brigade	Sialkot.	
2	3 Motor Brigade Employment Section	Sialkot.	
	CAVALRY		
3	2nd Royal Lancers (Gardner's Horse)	Sialkot.	
4	PAVO Cavalry (11th FF)	Sialkot.	
5	18th KE VII's O Cavalry	Rawalpindi.	
	ENGINEERS		
6	35 Field Squadron S & M	Sialkot.	
	SIGNALS		
7	3 Motor Brigade Signal Squadron	Sialkot.	
	RIASC		
8	3 Motor Brigade Transport Company	Sialkot.	
	MEDICAL		
9	3 Motor Brigade Field Ambulance	Sialkot.	
10	"A" Det. Field Hygiene Section	Sialkot.	
	ORDNANCE		
11	13 IAOC Mobile Workshop Coy.	Meerut.	
12	27 IAOC Mobile Workshop Coy.	Sialkot.	
	PROVOST		
13	3 Motor Brigade "A" Indian Provost Section	Sialkot.	
14	3 Motor Brigade "B" Indian Provost Section	Sialkot.	
	POSTAL		
15	28 Field Post Office	Sialkot.	
	REINFORCEMENT CAMP		
16	101 and 102 Sections Mixed Reinforcements Camp	Sialkot.	
	MESS UNITS		
17	23 Mess Units (officers)	Sialkot.	For Serial 18.
18	24 Mess Units (officers)	Sialkot.	—do—

APPENDIX L

DIAGRAM OF FORMATION OF THE ADVANCE OF ESCARPMENT FORCE FROM SOFAFI TO ALAM BATTUMA,

(14/15 June 41)

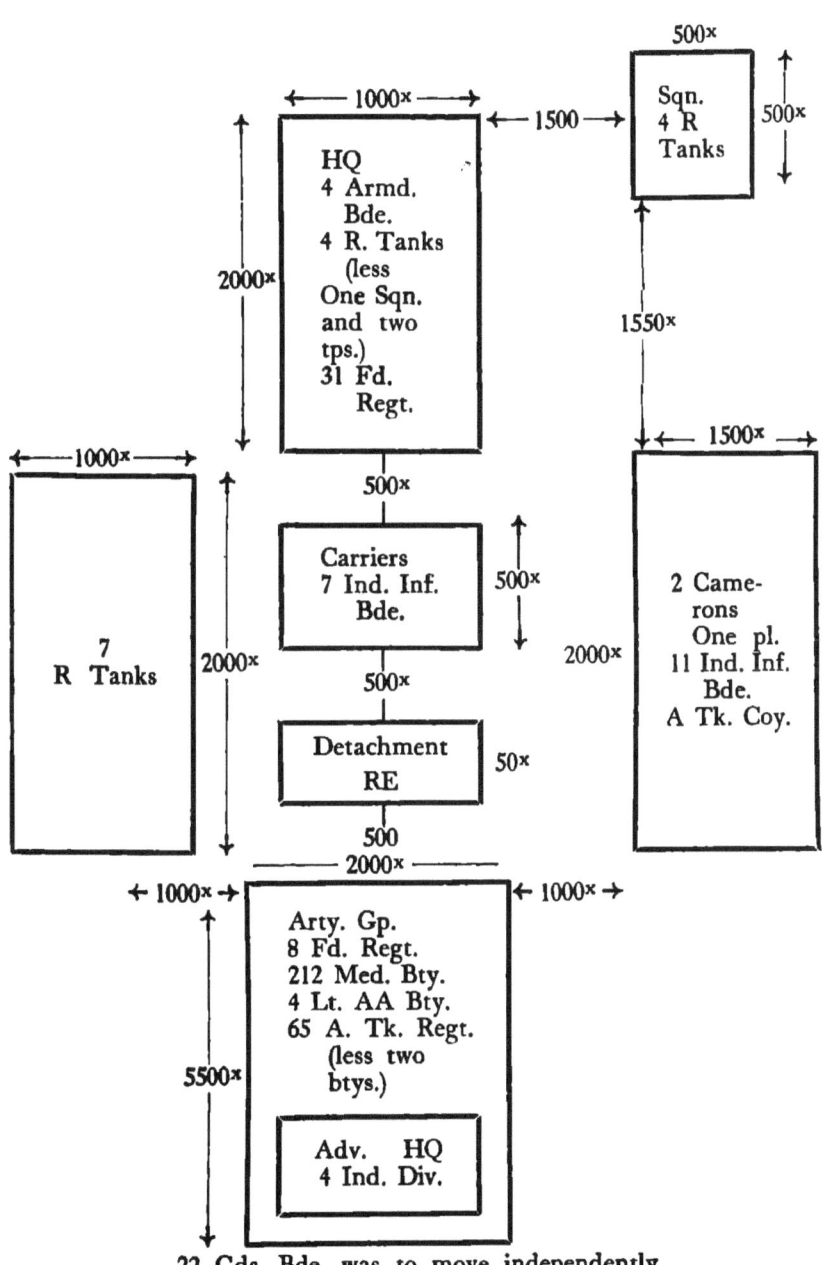

22 Gds. Bde. was to move independently.

APPENDIX M

THE FOURTEEN ALLIED LANDING GROUNDS IN CHARGE OF 4 IND. DIV.

(April-May 1941)

No.		
05.	SIDI BARRANI (606354) ...	⎫ Guard was to be a
06.	Rd. SIDI BARRANI (663354) ...	⎬ squadron of Armd.
07.	Rd. SIDI BARRANI (685351) ...	⎭ Cars less on troop.
060.	25-30 miles S. of BAQQUSH (752278)	One troop Armd. Cars.
010.	GARAWLA (734333)	One troop Armd. Cars.
011.	QASABA (744332)	(One Coy. of Infantry)
012.	SIDI HANEISH, North (753326)	(One Coy. of Infantry).
013.	SIDI HANEISH, South (749321)	(One Coy. of Infantry).
014.	BAQQUSH MAIN (762329)	(One Coy. of Infantry).
015.	BAQQUSH SATELLITE (769324)	(One Coy. of Infantry).
016.	FUKA SATELLITE (777321)	(One Coy. of Infantry).
017.	FUKA (788319)	(One Coy. of Infantry).
09.	South of GALAL (812308)	(One Coy. of Infantry).
021.	12 miles SW of D383 (823308)	(One Coy. of Infantry).

APPENDIX N

ORDER OF BATTLE AND ORGANISATION OF THE ESCARPMENT & COAST FORCES

Ser. No.	Group	Formation or Unit	Remarks
A—Escarpment Force			
1	HQ Gp.	Adv. HQ 4 Ind. Div.	
2		HQ RA, 4 Ind. Div. ...	...
3		One Tp. Royals (Three Armd. Cs.)	
4	Armd. Gp.	(Comd.: Brig. A. H. Gatehouse, MC, RTR)	
5		One sqn. 3 H	...
6		4 Armd. Bde. (less one sqn. and two tps.)	...4 R Tanks. 7 R Tanks.
7		31 Fd. Regt. ...	...
8		One coy. 2 RB	...To guard B. Ech.
9		Carriers, 7 Ind. Inf. Bde.	
10		Det. 12 Fd. Coy. RE (Bangalore Torpedo party in carriers)	
11	Halfaya Gp.	(Comd.: Major T. P. Saunders, MC 2 Camerons)	
12		One sqn. 4 R. Tanks	
13		2 Camerons ...	...
14		One pl. 11 Ind. Inf. Bde. A Tk. Coy.	
15	Arty. Gp.	(Comd.: Lt. Col. S. Attemborough, RA)	...
16		8 Fd. Regt. (16 guns) ...	
17		212 Med. Bty. (8 6" hows.)	
18		4 Lt. AA Bty. (12 guns)	...
19		One bty. 65 A Tk. Regt. (12 guns)	
20		DAC	
21	Gds. Bde. Gp.	(Comd.: Brig. I. D. Erskine)	
22		22 Gds. Bde.	...3 Coldm. 2 SG 1 Buffs.
23		65 A Tk. Regt. less one bty. and one bty. (32 guns)	
24		9 Aust. Lt. AA Bty. less one Sec. (8 guns) ...	
25		One sqn. PAVO	...
26		Sec. 12 Fd. Coy. RE less det.	...
27		Det. 11 Fd. Pk. Coy. SM (Div. reserve A Tk. mines)	
28		Det. 14 Fd. Amb.	

Ser. No.	Group Formation or Unit	Remarks

B—Coast Force

(Comd.: Brig. R. A. Savory, MC)

29	11 Ind. Inf. Bde. (less 2 Camerons and one A Tk. pl.)	(a) 2 Mahrattas and 1 Raj Rif. (b) 2 Camerons and A Tk. pl. revert to comd. 11 Bde. at Halfaya.
30	HQ RE 4 Ind. Div.	
31	CIH	
32	Two tps. 4 R. Tanks (6 tanks)	
33	25 Fd. Regt. (16 guns)	
34	27/28 Med. Bty., 7 Med. Regt. (8 6" hows.) ...	
35	4 Fd. Coy. SM ...	
36	7 Ind. Inf. Bde. A Tk. Coy.	
37	One coy. 19 Ind Fd. Amb.	

C—Area Sidi Barrani

38	Rear HQ, 4 Ind. Div.	
39	One sqn., 2 R.L.	Guarding LGs.
40	Two coys. 4/16 Punjab	Guarding FSDs at Sidi Barrani and Rabia.
41	12 Fd. Coy. SM ...	⎫ Allotted work in coastal sector under orders CRF
42	Det. 11 Fd. Pk. Coy. SM ...	⎭
43	Div. RIASC less dets. ...	
44	19 Ind. Fd. Amb. less det. ...	
45	18 Ord. Wkshop. Coy. and 18 LRS	
46	19 LRS	
47	20 LRS	

D—Area Halfway House (B. Ech. tpt.)

48	PAVO less two sqns.	
49	One tp. 65 A Tk. Regt.	
50	One sec., 9 Aust. Lt. AA Bty.	
51	B. ech. tpt. of Escarpment Force	

APPENDIX P

LOCATION OF PRINCIPAL UNITS IN THE BAQQUSH BOX
(18th—30th June 1941)

The Advanced and Rear HQs of 4th Indian Division were in the Baqqush Box at 76083308. Its two Brigades along with 22 Guards Brigade were protecting the South, East and West faces as follows:—

South face:	HQ 7 Ind. Inf. Bde.	75903276
	1 R Sussex	76363265
	4 Sikh	75993276
	4/16 Punjab	75593290
East Face:	HQ 11 Ind. Inf. Bde.	76753315
	2 Camerons	76873297
	2 Mahrattas	765327
	1 Raj. Rif.	76343277
West Face:	HQ 22 Guards Brigade	75593318
	3 Coldstream Gds.	75493307

Of the other units of 22 Guards Brigade, 2 Scots Guards were at Daba and 1 Buffs. in the forward area.

APPENDIX Q

4TH INDIAN DIVISION

ORDER OF BATTLE AND GROUPING—18 NOVEMBER 1941

5TH INDIAN INFANTRY BRIGADE

HQ 5th Ind. Inf. Bde.
    1st Buffs.
    3rd/1st Punjab.
    4th Raj. Rif.
A Tk. Coy., 5th Ind. Inf. Bde.
Carrier Pls.:
    3rd/1st Punjab.
    4th Raj. Rif.
1st R Sussex.
1st Fd. Regt., RA, less 52nd Bty.
169th Lt. AA Bty., RA
One Sec. 18th Fd. Coy., SM
2nd SA Div. A Tk. Regt.

7TH INDIAN INFANTRY BRIGADE

HQ 7th Ind. Inf. Bde.
A Tk. Coy., 7th Ind. Inf. Bde.
4th Sikh.
4th/16th Punjab.
25th Fd. Regt., RA
65th (NY) A Tk. Regt.:
    HQ
    257th Bty.
    259th Bty.
171st Lt. AA Bty., RA
42nd RTR
One sec. 4th Fd. Coy., SM
One coy., 17th Fd. Amb.

11TH INDIAN INFANTRY BRIGADE

HQ 11th Ind. Inf. Bde.
A Tk. Coy., 11th Ind. Inf. Bde.
2nd Camerons.
2nd Mahrattas.
1st Raj. Rif.
105th Bty., 31st Fd. Regt., RA
68th Med. Regt. RA
    less 234th Bty.
    (4.5), less one tp.
12th Fd. Coy., SM

CIH

CIH, less carrier sqn.
One sqn. 6th SA Armd., C. Regt.

APPENDIX Q

    31st Fd. Regt., RA, less 105th Bty.
    258th (NY) A Tk. Bty.
    170th Lt. AA Bty., RA, less two tps.
    One sqn. 44th RTR

1st Army Tk. Bde.
    HQ, 1st Army Tk. Bde.
    8th RTR
    44th RTR
    8th Fd. Regt., RA
    Units of 4th Ind. Div. under comd.
    Carrier sqn. CIH
    One tp. 170th Lt. AA Bty., RA

CRA
    HQ, RA, 4th Ind. Div.
    HQ 57th Lt. AA Regt., RA
    52nd Fd. Bty., RA
    234th Med. Bty., RA (4.5), less one tp.
    260th (NY) A Tk. Bty., less one tp.

CRE
    HQ, RE, 4th Ind. Div.
    11th Fd. Pk. Coy., SM
    4th Fd. Coy., SM, less one sec.
    18th Fd. Coy., SM, less one sec.

Adv. Div. HQ
    Adv. Div. HQ
    One tp. 260th (NY) A Tk. Bty.
    One tp. 170th Lt. AA Bty., RA
    Det. 4th Raj. Rif.
    4th Ind. Div. Signals.

Rear Div. HQ
    Rear Div. HQ
    Det. 4th Raj. Rif.

A/Q CRIASC
    HQ, RIASC, 4th Ind. Div.
    Div. HQ MT Sec.
    Div. Tps. Tpt. Coy.
    5th Ind. Inf. Bde. Tpt. Coy.
    7th Ind. Inf. Bde. Tpt. Coy.
    11th Ind. Inf. Bde. Tpt. Coy.
    52nd Coy., RASC

Ordnance
    HQ, Ord., 4th Ind. Div.
    17th Mob. Wkshop. Coy.
    18th Mob. Wkshop. Coy.
    19th Mob. Wkshop. Coy.
    20th Mob. Wkshop. Coy.
    Ord. Fd. Pk.

MEDICAL

    HQ, Med., 4th Ind. Div.
    14th Fd. Amb.
    17th Fd. Amb., less one coy.
    19th Fd. Amb.
    15th Fd. Hyg. Sec.

PROVOST

    4th Ind. Div. Pro. Unit.
    384th FS Sec.

POSTAL

    13th FPO
    17th FPO
    19th FPO
    25th FPO

APPENDIX R

SUMMARY OF CASUALTIES IN THE 4TH INDIAN DIVISION

(November—December 1941)

	British		Indian		
	Officers	Other Ranks	Officers	Other Ranks	Total
Killed	27	164	6	112	309
Wounded	83	374	13	658	1,128
Missing	40	841	9	306	1,196
Total	150	1,379	28	1,076	2,633

APPENDIX S

SUMMARY OF TOTAL CASUALTIES OF 4TH INDIAN DIVISION

(18 November 1941—28 February 1942)

	British		Indian			
	Officers	Other Ranks	Viceroy's Commissioned Officers	Other Ranks	Followers	Total
Killed	27	182	7	125	1	342
Wounded	83	495	13	697	2	1,290
Missing	81	1,320	33	1,280	39	2,753
Total	191	1,997	53	2,102	42	4,385

APPENDIX T

THE 18TH INDIAN INFANTRY BRIGADE AT DEIR EL SHEIN

(28 June 1942—2 July 1942)

Opening Phase

General Auchinleck records that he took over direct control of the Eighth Army from General Ritchie at his headquarters near Bagush on the evening of the 26 June 1942, and that the Army was then falling back on Matruh (Tobruk having been overrun) but that he decided that Matruh as a position was less defensible with his few troops and lack of armour than that of El Alamein and he issued orders that the Army would be kept fully mobile and would bring the Axis advance to a halt in the area between Matruh, El Alamein and the Qattara Depression. X and XIII Corps were to provide the mobile element of the Army. XXX Corps was to occupy the El Alamein position.

XXX Corps had under its command 50th British Division and 1st South African Division. The El Alamein defences at that period were broken up into a series of defended localities known, for convenience, as "boxes" with mobile columns filling the gaps between them. To the south of El Alamein railway station, and about eight miles from it is the beginning of a depression in the desert known as Deir el Shein.

This narrative is concerned with the "box" being built at Deir el Shein.[1] It lay between a properly concreted "box" held by 1 SA Div[2] at the station itself known as the "station" or "Alamein box" and one ten miles south along the Deir el Shein depression held by the remnants of the New Zealand Division. Inclusive of the NZ "box" the defended area southwards was under command of XIII Corps.

The 18th Indian Infantry Brigade at Deir el Shein was commanded by Lt. Col. C. E. Gray of the 2nd/3rd Gurkha Rifles. The Brigade moved by air from Iraq to Palestine; its transport was to meet the Brigade in Palestine where the men were to halt for a week to receive it.

The 18th Brigade consisted of:
    2/5 Essex Regiment
    4/11 Sikh Regiment
    2/3 Gurkha Rifles.

The units' MT did not all arrive in time and, as the call for troops was pressing, the Gurkhas travelled to Egypt by road, the two other battalions by train; the train party suffered from air activity of the Axis which caused some casualties among them. The Brigade assembled outside the El Alamein station "box" by first light of 28 June, but again there was insufficient transport for all. It reached the position assigned to it by dawn of 29 June where it had to prepare the "box" around the Deir el Shein depression.

The terrain is marked on the map as "very stony" and "sand and stone", with palms and scrub scattered to the immediate west of it. Water was difficult to get, it having to be transported from El Hammam forty miles away.

The "box" was approximately 4000 yards by 2000 yards defended by 4/11 Sikh Regiment on the north-west and the Essex on the

[1] See map on p. 419.
[2] First South African Division.

north-east; the south-west was held by 66 Field Company, Sappers & Miners and the south-east by the Gurkhas. The Brigade, tired from lack of sleep for several days and cramped from its long journey, set to work on arrival and dug intensively, the men averaging 18 to 20 hours work out of 24 hrs., during which occasional enemy planes visited them and hindered progress. By evening 30 June section posts were completed and a double dannert wire fence had been laid on the enemy side of the minefields which the Brigade had hastily laid around the "box". There was no lack of wire but there was difficulty over mines, three different types being supplied and often arriving without fuses as there was no RE officer in charge of the issuing. Moreover, they were not supplied as fast as they could be laid and much valuable time was wasted. Colonel Bamfield's personally written story says: "Guns did not exist when we first arrived but there were rumours of some coming from various sources. Eventually the Commander, 121 Field Regiment RA arrived and after a reconnaissance sited the guns we expected. These were eighteen 25-pounders, sixteen 6-pounders and twenty 2-pounders A.-tk. There was little time to dig them in and they later suffered accordingly."

The Gurkhas had a semi-circular front of about 6000 yards running from north to south-west and they placed their Companies as follows: "D coy. right, B Coy., A Coy. and C Coy. left. No. 3 (Mortar) Platoon was distributed amongst the rifle companies to thicken up their fire. Battalion HQ and the rest of HQ Coy. were situated behind B Coy. in the depression. D & B Companies' positions were along a small ridge, while A & C Companies were on more or less flat ground above the lip of the depression. A-tk Guns of various calibres were distributed in Company areas."

There were considerable gaps in the perimeter, particularly at battalion, and even company, junctions and it was impossible to close these for lack of mines.

Within the "box", besides the three battalions and Sappers and Miners, there were four medium machine guns manned by men from the Cheshire Regiment, seven Matlida tanks manned by scratch crews from 42 RTR and the artillery already listed with gun crews drawn from 121 Field Regiment RA and 79 Field Regiment RA. The 2-pounder A-tank guns were manned by South African units helped by men of the Welch Regiment. The 6-pounder A-tank guns had scratch crews drawn from various units. There was an Advanced Dressing Station from 32nd Field Ambulance and a few South African sappers with compressors.

Colonel Bampfield writes:—

"*30 June*: the A-tk guns were only drawn during the afternoon and arrived during the night. Positions, however, had been dug in our area. The 25-pounders arrived late in the day and they could not all be dug down. The 6-pounder A-tk guns were a complete gift from the blue but were completely in the open. Although we had plenty of guns they were not all dug down and, as a result, half their effectiveness was lost. The whole show was, of course, against time, improvising the A-tk defence fire plan as the stuff arrived. Men dug and mined to about 1000 hrs. and then had to halt as no more mines were available."

*Commanding 4/11th Sikh Regiment.

Before the Brigade began forming this "box" forward elements of the Eighth Army that had been dropping back in this direction had been using every available track across this ground. With the encircling by wire and mines of this area further incoming troops found the halt at this "box" welcome but the garrison suffered the inconvenience of having them drift through in "bunches" as it strained their own water and ration reserves to a considerable extent.

The western front of the "box" was screened by patrols from the Guides Cavalry.

On the evening 30 June, the Axis troops reached the South African "box" at El Alamein astride the main Alexandria—Mersa Matruh road, but were driven back. They then turned south and 1 SA Division warned 18th Indian Infantry Brigade to expect an attack in force from the north-west.

All efforts within the "box" were doubled to get the guns dug down, the wire fixed and the position made as secure as possible. The battle outside the El Alamein "box" could be heard and through the night it sounded as though it was ominously nearing their own position. At 0545 hrs., 1 July, Guides patrols reported Axis tanks and infantry moving towards the "box". At 0900 hours two shells fell on the southern edge of the "box" followed by two in the Brigade Headquarters position. The Axis artillery then ranged methodically for about half an hour though where its observation posts were concealed could not be discovered. It used a considerable amount of air burst HE for this purpose.

At about 1000 hrs. the Axis artillery concentrated on the Essex (holding the north-east perimeter) and pounded them heavily. The Battalion sat tight in their trenches through an hour of heavy shelling during which they received surprisingly few casualties. From 1100 hrs. onwards, while still keeping heavy fire on the Essex, Axis artillery searched the rest of the "box" pretty thoroughly.

At 1115 hrs. two British prisoners under a white flag were then sent forward by the Axis and were admitted; they had a message that the defenders were to surrender or suffer attack. The prisoners were able to leave some valuable information with the Brigade (which was relayed to 1 SA Div.) before returning with a message "to stick it up and be damned."

At about 1300 hrs., aided by a dust storm and the dust raised by their shelling, the Axis troops lifted the mines between the Essex right and Gurkha left and pushed in some infantry and machine-guns. The infantry were immediately engaged by mortar and other fire and most of them hurriedly left but the machine-guns were established and later caused a considerable amount of trouble.

About 30-40 German MK IV tanks now appeared. Twelve of them and a few light tanks were pushed through the gap in the minefield and formed up behind the Essex and the Gurkhas. The Essex A-tk guns and 25-pounders engaged the tanks and knocked out two, but they and their artillery opened fire with such accuracy that most of the guns of that battalion were knocked out. After silencing the guns the German tanks closed in on the Essex and forced its surrender.

The tanks now turned their attention to the Sikhs, though losing a few more of their number, worked their way round and captured most of the Battalion, although the Battalion Headquarters was not spotted and escaped unhurt. During the tank attack within the "box", they shelled Brigade Headquarters and the Gurkhas intensely. At the same time an attack was put in on the Gurkhas' position in the south-east perimeter but was repulsed. The German tanks still outside then tried every Company gap in turn but the unit's A-tk fire was too much for them.

Then an Allied force of tanks loomed up from the east, outside 'A' Company (Gurkhas) minefield, but withdrew when engaged by the Axis.

The Brigade had sent out appeals for aid at about 1500 hrs. but it was either too late to ask or the help was too far away to arrive in time. It later transpired that the 1st Armoured Division had been despatched by XXX Corps to assist and though they reached within three miles, owing to a hitch, they never put in an attack.

When the Axis tanks first came through the gap in the north-east, between the Essex and the Gurkhas, some had turned left (i.e. south-east) behind the (Gurkhas) 'C' Company while others had pressed close from outside the wire. Both, the tanks inside and those outside, poured a devastating fire on 'C' and 'D' Companies of the Gurkhas, whose disposition, however, saved them from annihilation.

The Brigade Headquarters was overrun by five MK IV tanks supported by Infantry guns. A brisk hand-to-hand fight took place during which the Brigade Commander was wounded. All at Headquarters were captured but some escaped later when an aerial bombardment occurred.

At about 1900 hrs., 2/3 GR Bn HQ considered the position untenable and as the other units were evacuating the area, the Battalion Commander issued an order for all 'keymen' to leave immediately (in trucks where possible). The order could not reach 'A' and 'C' Companies who were cut off. Under cover of darkness and dust the remnants of the Gurkha battalion broke through a gap which, though not held by the enemy, was effectively covered by fire to a depth of two miles.

Most of the Brigade that did escape also had to use this gap and the loss in vehicles sustained here was considerable, most men having to get away on foot. An Allied aerial bombardment at 2230 hrs. fortunately created a diversion and enabled others who had been captured to get away in the confusion; those who could, made for the El Alamein "box", while others drifted about and joined units and small groups of the Eighth Army moving east.

Lt. Colonel Bampfield of 4/11 Sikh Regiment assumed command of the remnants of the Brigade at Amiriya and reports that the final tally of those who got back was:—

Bde HQ	1 Officer, 30 Other Ranks.
2/5 Essex	12 Other Ranks.
2/3 Gurkha Rifles	12 Officers including VCOs and 580 Gurkha Other Ranks (The CO was captured).
4/11 Sikh Regiment:	3 Officers & 370 Other Ranks. The MO was captured and escaped after this count.
66 Fd. Coy. SM	: Practically complete.
18 IBT Coy.	: Practically complete.
33 Fd. Amb.	: One Section missing.
121 Fd. Regt. RA	: A few got away.
Wkshp. Section	: The CO and most of his vehicles safe.

Lt. Colonel Bampfield's narrative concludes with two statements. One is to the effect that, had the enemy attacked twenty-four hours later, the results would have been different. The guns did not arrive till the afternoon of 30 June and "a 6-pounder A-tk on a portee is a very conspicuous object." The other is that, in the opinion of General Norrie (Commanding 1 Armd. Div.) whom he met on the way back from Deir el Shein, the resistance put up by 18 Ind. Inf. Brigade and the delay caused to the Axis enabled the Eighth Army to complete further concentration of troops to stem the Axis advance. General Auchinleck on page 92 of his Despatch No. 2, 1st November 1941 to 15 August 1942, says of this action: "Only one infantry battalion survived the attack but the stand made by the brigade certainly gained valuable time for the organisation of the El Alamein line generally."

APPENDIX U

THE 5TH INDIAN DIVISION AT RUWEISAT RIDGE

(18 July 1942)

In the EL ALAMEIN line, the RUWEISAT RIDGE was the most important of a series of parallel ridges which, running east and west, that is, at right angles to the front, dominated the northern sector. During the establishment of the EL ALAMEIN line after the long withdrawal from TOBRUK, the RUWEISAT RIDGE became a major objective for the Eighth Army.

The 5th Indian Division moved up to the eastern end of the Ridge on 12 July 1942 under the command of 30 Corps. Later 1300 hrs. 17th July, the Division was placed under the command of 15 Corps.

There were during this phase, only two infantry brigade groups under command of 5 Ind. Div. There was, firstly, the 9th Indian Infantry Brigade, one of the original brigades of the Division. The two Indian battalions of this Brigade, 3 Jats and 3 RFFR, had been disorganised in the fighting near TOBRUK and were in the DELTA refitting. Its third battalion, 2 West Yorks, had been reduced to about half strength.

10 and 29 Ind. Inf. Bdes., the second and third of the Division had been overrun at El ADEM and FUKA respectively and were not present at RUWEISAT RIDGE.

As part replacement, the 5th Indian Infantry Brigade (of 4 Ind. Div.) was temporarily posted to 5 Ind. Div.

In the early hours of 15 July, 5 Ind. Inf. Bde., together with 2 NZ Div., had attacked along the Ridge with the object of clearing the western end and thereby denying the Axis the use of the Ridge for observation purposes. The attack had been successful and 5 Ind. Inf. Bde. had consolidated around pt. 64. Unfortunately the following night 15/16 July, the New Zealanders' positions west of pt. 64 were overrun by enemy tanks. 5 Ind. Inf. Bde., was therefore the most westerly of Allied formations on RUWEISAT RIDGE (*see* map opposite).

9 Ind. Inf. Bde. was at this time on the GEBEL BEIN GABIR (432892) where it had relieved 5 Ind. Inf. Bde. on 14 July.

For two days, 5 Ind. Inf. Bde. around pt. 64 was subjected to shelling and air attacks. At 1805 hrs. 16 July, an attack on 5 Ind. Inf. Bde. by the German 8 Tank Regt. and 155 Lor. Inf. Regt. was beaten back after three hours' fighting with heavy losses to the Axis. The following evening, one company of 4 Raj Rif scouted forward to a point approximately one mile west of pt. 64 and ultimately took up a position (88052792) half a mile west of pt. 64.

With the object of exploiting this situation 9 Ind. Inf. Bde. was ordered to capture pt. 63 (878279) on 18 July. It must be remembered that the Brigade still had only the one weak battalion—2 West Yorks.

The battalion was provided for this operation with the following under its command:—

One tp., 1 Lt. AA Regt.
One Bty., (6 pdr.) 149 A/TK. Regt.
One MG Coy. 6 Raj Rif.

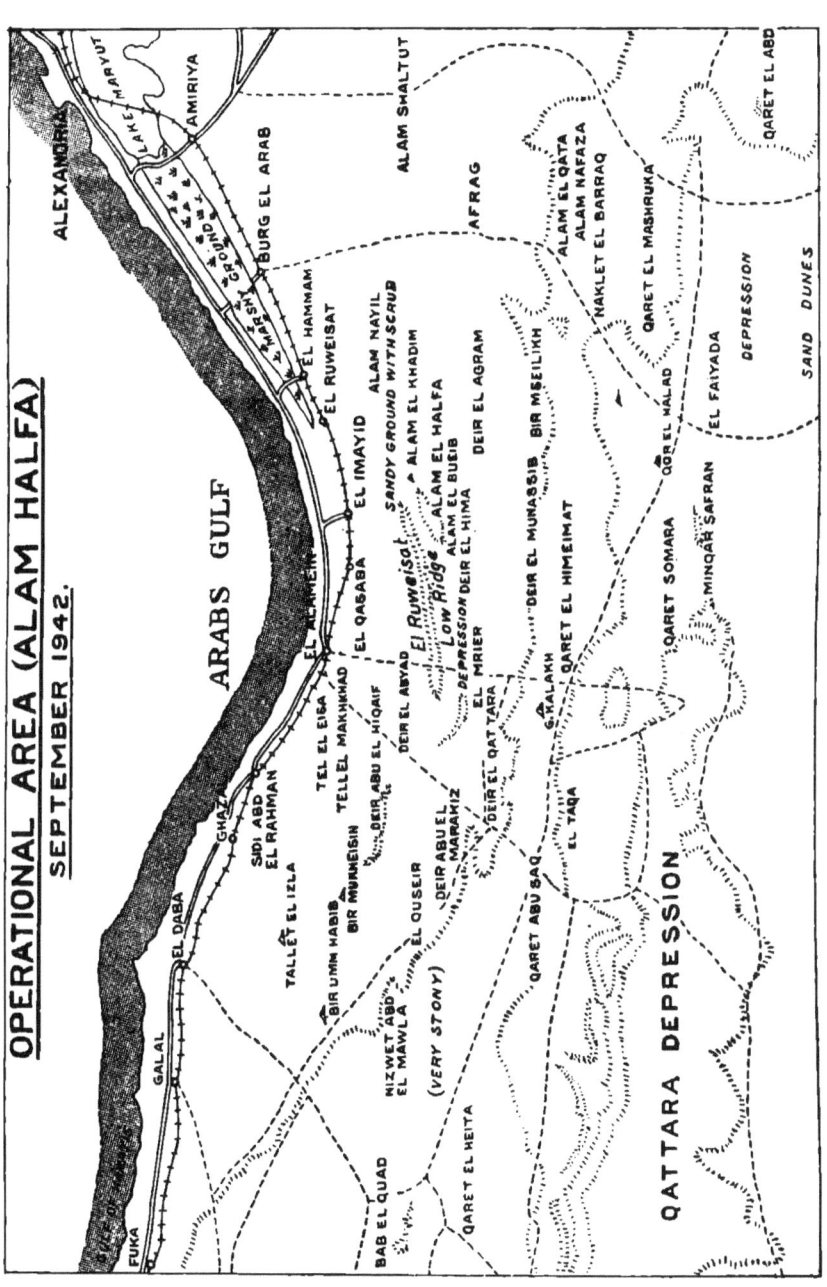

By 1500 hrs. its MG Coy. (less one platoon) was put into position in the low scrub 2500 yards south-west of pt. 64 from where it could support the attack on the south flank.

By about 1630 hrs. 2 West Yorks was forming up on its start line. Although the Axis should have been able to observe this it took no action and everything remained very quiet. 4 Raj Rif (5 Indian Infantry Brigade Group) still held the post half a mile west of pt. 64, where there was a Gunner OP.

At about 1715 hrs. 2 West Yorks were formed and moved 500 yards forward on to the start line where they halted. Still all remained quiet.

At 1730 hrs. the Divisional artillery opened its barrage two hundred yards west of the start line on a front of 1500 yds. and centered on the crest of the Ridge, to which heavy hostile shelling all along the ridge came in reply. The advance of 2 West Yorks and supporting arms went forward quickly being limited only by the barrage, 100 yds. in two minutes.

The Axis infantry broke up in disorder as soon as the barrage and 2 West Yorks approached. The Battalion went past its objective in an attempt to come to grips with the fast retreating Axis troops and it was some time before it could be brought back and reassembled.

The Axis troops attempted to counter-attack with ten tanks in support but were driven back.

The West Yorks remained at pt. 63 though continuously shelled by artillery and dive-bombed by aircraft.

Thereafter the RUWEISAT RIDGE remained in Allied hands.

APPENDIX V

ALLIED AND AXIS FORCES—AUGUST 1942

On 8 August 1942, the Eighth Army comprised:

In the El Alamein Position 9 Aust. Div. ⎫
                                       1 SA Div. ⎬ XXX Corps
                                       5 Ind. Div.
                                     23 Armd. Bde. ⎭

                                   2 NZ Div. ⎫ XIII Corps
                                   7 Armd. Div. ⎭

In Reserve and refitting   1 Armd. Div.
                                 10 Ind. Div.
                                 50 UK Div.
                                 4 NZ Inf. Bde.

Total: 2 Armd. Divs.—6 Inf. Divs.—2 Inf. Bdes.

In addition the following were 8 Armd. Div.
under orders to join 8th Army— 10 Armd. Div.
                                   44 Inf. Div.
                                   51 Inf. Div.
                                   1 Army Tk. Bde.
                                   9 Armd. Bde.

Grand Total ⎧ Four Armd. Divs.
                ⎨ Eight Inf. Divs.
                ⎩   plus 4 additional Bdes, 3 of which were Armoured.

The Axis Forces facing the Eighth Army on 8 August were:

German   15 Pz. Div. ⎫ DAK
                   21 Pz. Div.
                     90 Light Div.
                     164 Inf. Div.
                     Ramcke's Para Bde. ⎭

Italian   Ariete Armd. Div. ⎫
                     Littorio Armd. Div. ⎬ XX AK
                     Trieste Motor Div. ⎭

                     Trento Inf. Div. ⎫
                     Bologna Inf. Div. ⎬ XXI AK
                     Pistoia Inf. Div. ⎭

                     Brescia Inf. Div. ⎫
                     Folgore Inf. Div. ⎬ X AK
                     Pavia Inf. Div. ⎭

    Total   13 Divisions of all sorts plus one Para Bde.

BIBLIOGRAPHY

This volume is based primarily on official records possessed by the C.I.S. Historical Section. Of these the most important are the war diaries of the various units which took part in the campaign in North Africa. The Historical Section has an almost complete set of these diaries, particularly of the Indian forces.

In addition, there are a number of 'appreciations' written during the course of the war by military officers and men at the top. The contents of these appreciations must have formed the basis for strategy in North Africa and a study of these is therefore not only valuable but essential.

The 'despatches' written by the different commanders soon after the completion of operations form another useful source for an understanding not only of higher policy but also of the administrative and logistical difficulties inherent in the conduct of a modern military campaign. It is not possible to give a complete list of all the diaries, appreciations and despatches consulted in the writing of this narrative but some of these are listed below.

Since ample documentary sources of a primary nature were available, much use has not been made of the secondary published sources or accounts, except perhaps for describing Allied strategy and diplomacy at the highest level. However, a list of these secondary sources which have been consulted is also given below:—

War Diaries

War Diaries of all units that took part in the North African Campaign, and particularly of the following:—

4th, 5th, 9th and 10th Indian Divisions; 3rd Indian Motor Brigade; 5th, 7th, 9th, 10th, 11th, 18th, 20th, 21st, and 29th Indian Infantry Brigades; 1st, 4th, 6th and 7th Rajputana Rifles; 2 Royal Lancers; 2 Mahrattas; 1st, 3rd and 4th Punjab Regiments; 11th and 18th Cavalry; 1st Gurkha Rifles; 4th Sikh Regiment; 1 R. Sussex; 1 Essex; 3rd Baluch Regiment; Central India Horse; and various Field Companies of Sappers and Miners.

Despatches and Reports

General Sir Archibald Wavell's despatch on Operations in the Middle East from August 1939 to November 1940 and February-July 1941.

General Auchinleck's despatches on Operations in the Middle East, 5th July 1941 to 31st October 1941 and 1st November 1941 to 15th August 1942, published in the London Gazette of 21st August 1946 and 15th January 1948.

General Sir Harold Alexander's Despatch, African Campaign from El Alamein to Tunis—10th August 1942 to 13th May 1943.

Report on Western Desert Move of the 4th Indian Division by Commandant, 4th Indian Division, June 1941.

Report of Brigadier E.W.D. Vaughan.

Other Official Documents
  Commitments of the Army in India, West of India, Historical Section—File No. 7422.
  Diary of events in Tobruk by 11th Indian Infantry Brigade.
  Middle East Training Pamphlet No. 10.
  Operation Instructions (4th Indian Division) April 1941-October 1941.
  Scheme "Assurance", File No. F/1002.
  War Information Circular No. 26-A.
  4th Indian Division's Account of Operations in Cyrenaica by C.I.S. Historical Section (India and Pakistan).

Secondary Sources
  Africa, Walter Fitzgerald.
  Africa Settentrimale, Marshal Graziani.
  African Trilogy, Alan Moorehead.
  Alamein to Sangro, General Montgomery.
  Australian Account of Operations in Cyrenaica.
  British Survey, Vol. VII, No. 8 (Egypt), and No. 14 (Italian North Africa).
  Chronology of the Second World War, Royal Institute of International Affairs.
  Conquest of North Africa, Burke Publishing Co., Ltd.
  Conquest of North Africa, HMSO Pamphlet.
  Defence of India: Policy and Planning, Historical Section, (to be published).
  Encyclopaedia Britannica, Vols. I, VII, IX, XXVI and XXVII.
  Fourth Indian Division, Lt.-Col. G. R. Stevens.
  Imperial Geography, 10th edition, Brigadier D.H. Cole.
  Operation Victory, Major General De Guingand.
  Our Armoured Forces, Lt.-General G. Le Q. Martel.
  Pattern of War, General F.I.S. Tuker.
  Playing with Strife, P. Neame.
  Recalled to Service, General Weygand.
  Rommel, D. Young.
  Statesman's Year books 1939 and 1946.
  The Grand Alliance, Sir Winston S. Churchill.
  The Tiger Kills, The Tiger Strikes, Director of Public Relations, India Command.
  Tobruk, Chester Wilmot, Angus and Rovertson.
  War in Outline, 1939-44, USA's Fighting Forces Series.

INDEX

Abar Ailet Idris, 192
Abar Abu Safafi, 172-3
Abd el Hafid, 305
Abdulla, Emir, 41
Abyssinia, 199
Acroma, 258, 64-5, 331, 339, 341, 346-7, 350, 375-6, 390-1, 396; withdrawal to, 344-5
Aden, 28, 41; military situation in, 45
Afrag, 379
African Division, 12th, 125
Afrika Korps, 123, 125, 127-8, 132-3, 160-1, 167, 191, 193, 195, 214, 237, 262, 294, 356, 363, 368-9, 372, 374, 433, 439; advance of, 144-55; pursuit of, 267
Agareb, 510
Agedabia, 10, 102, 117-9, 121, 140-1, 144, 162, 278, 287, 289, 291, 299-301, 303, 306, 308, 325-6; Axis stand at, 292-6; pursuit towards, 472-3, 475
Agha Jari, 26
Agheila, *see* El Agheila
Ahmad Pasha Caramanli, 18
Ain Melfa, 196-7
Air Squadron, 5th, 129
Aix la Chapelle, 19
Alam Battuma, 174
Alam Bessanan, 329
Alam el Fakhri, 228
Alam el Halfa, 426, 451; Battle of, 429-42
Alamein, *see* El Alamein
Alam el Idris, 172-3
Alam Hamid, 187-8
Alam Hamza, 273, 275, 339-40, 345-6, 348, 350, 359, 380, 389-90; battle of, 267-9
Alexandar, General Sir Harold, 427-30, 432, 435, 492-3, 497, 500, 510, 512, 514-5
Alexandria, 2, 5, 14-17, 29, 31, 41-2, 51, 55, 74, 161, 163, 189, 210, 213, 238, 354, 417-18, 420, 432, 450, 470, 472
Algeria, 10, 19, 25; its population, 6
Algiers, 25
Allied Desert Force, 190, 193
Amiriya, 55
Anatolia, 429
Anderson, Brigadier A., 394
Anglo-American Expeditionary Force, 463, 483, 492
Antelat, 118-19, 140, 278, 286-7, 289, 292, 301-2, 304-7, 309, 325, 327-8, 332, 474-5
Anti-aircraft Brigade, 4th, 393
Anti-tank Battery, 73rd, 274
Anti-tank Regiment, 65th, 177, 181, 191, 291, 332, 352
Appolonia, 287
Arabs Gulf, 417
Argyll and Sutherland Highlanders, 88, 94-5 (*see also under* British Forces)
Armoured Division, 1st, 299-309, 311, 313, 317-18, 323, 332, 338, 341, 344, 346, 348, 358-9, 375, 377, 380, 392, 414-15, 425, 435, 454-8, 461-2, 467-9, 471, 497, 503-5, 508, 512, 514

2nd, 125-6, 136-8, 140-1, 146, 148, 150-3, 155, 163, 165, 205, 422
6th, 510
7th, 39, 44, 59, 69, 76-8, 80-1, 84-9, 95-7, 100-1, 106-7, 109, 113, 116-19, 121, 125-6, 131, 165, 168-9, 171, 175, 177-8, 180-1, 183-5, 187-8, 190-3, 201, 205, 217, 222, 231-2, 237, 255, 257, 265, 273, 276, 280, 285, 287, 292, 348, 358-9, 364-5, 368, 374, 381, 407, 410-11, 423, 438, 440, 449, 452, 456, 458, 461, 467-72, 477-8, 481, 483, 485, 489, 491-3, 497, 499, 502-3, 508, 510, 513 (*see also* Support Group)
8th, 426, 445, 447
10th, 392, 426, 435, 438-9, 448-9, 452, 454-5, 461, 467-9
Armoured Brigade, 1st, 126, 156, 360
2nd, 299-300, 302, 305, 308, 358, 360, 384, 387-8, 415, 424, 494
3rd, 126, 136-8, 140-2, 144, 147-8
4th, 44, 87-9, 94, 100-2, 118-20, 170-1, 174-6, 183-6, 215, 217, 222-3, 225, 237-8, 257, 273, 276, 285-6, 358, 360, 364, 374, 384, 386-8, 392, 397-8, 410, 414
7th, 44, 87, 89, 91, 98, 101-2, 118, 120, 172, 175-7, 184, 223, 225, 258, 289, 364, 386
8th, 494, 498, 504
9th, 453-5, 461, 471
22nd, 223, 225, 237, 293, 358, 360, 364, 375, 381-2, 387, 410, 438, 475, 484-7, 491, 494-5, 510
23rd, 424, 494, 499
24th, 458
Armoured Car Regiments, 257
Armoured Cars, S.A., 226
Army Co-operation Group, 85 (*see also* Royal Air Force)
Army Group, 18th, 512, 514
Army Tank Brigade, 1st, 215, 226, 231, 258, 294-5, 357, 359, 375, 377-8, 380
32nd, 205, 215, 257, 261, 272, 275, 280, 360, 381-2, 389, 392-4, 407
Army Tank Regiment, 1st, 205, 229, 236
Arnim, General von, 495, 514
Aslagh, 382
Assab, 42
Auchinleck, General Sir Claude J. E., 198-203, 208, 210-11, 219, 238, 246-7, 253, 257, 294, 296-8, 306, 346, 354, 360-1, 366-7, 379-80, 389-92, 410, 412-13, 413-18, 420-5, 427-8, 432, 443

Australian Forces:
Australian Division, 6th. 45, 99, 106, 109, 111, 116, 118, 120, 125-6, 135, 165-6
7th, 125-6
9th, 125-6, 135-8, 140, 142-4, 146, 155, 161, 163, 166, 181, 191, 195, 209, 421, 423-5, 432, 438, 451, 453, 456, 458-60
Australian Brigade, 3rd, 106
6th, 44, 106

16th, 44, 106, 109, 112-13, 117
17th, 107, 109, 112, 117, 134
18th, 135, 209
19th, 109, 112-13, 117
20th, 135-8, 142
24th, 137
26th, 135, 137
Australian Anti-tank Regiment, 2nd, 150
Australian Cavalry Regiment, 112
Australian Infantry Battalion, 2/1st, 109
   2/13th, 258

Azeiz, *see* Sidi Azeiz
Bab el Qattara, 417
Bab el Qaud, 201
Babini, General, 115
Babini Force, 115-6
Bahariya Oasis, 9, 427
Bahig, 55, 203
Bahrein, 27
Balat Abd el Hafid, 327
Balearic Isles, 25
Baluch Regiment, 4th, 383
Baqqush, 65, 68, 74, 76, 82, 88, 90, 165-6, 188-91, 193, 195, 197, 199-201, 413, 468; withdrawal to, 72-3
Barce, 10, 12, 115, 117-18, 120, 138, 143, 146-7, 163, 278, 288-9, 291, 299, 301-2, 305, 311, 317, 319, 322, 331-4, 354
Bardia, Advance to, 101-8; Fall of, 109; *see also* 60, 62, 66, 100, 110-12, 114, 166, 169, 193, 197, 212, 214, 221-2, 229, 236-7, 239, 244-5, 250, 252, 257, 259-60, 265, 294-5, 355, 394, 397, 403-6, 411, 471-2
Barka plateau, 3
Basra, 33-4
Bastico, Marshal, 198, 433
Baten Umm el Hatian, 339
Batruna ridge, 388
Beda Fomm, 136, 286-7, 289, 292, 304, 325; battle of, 119-21
'Beer' Battalion, 404-5, 408-9 (*see also* De Beer)
Belhamed, 250, 254-7, 354-5, 391, 393, 396-9
Ben Gardane, 491, 494
Benghazi, 3, 10, 12, 20, 115-18, 133-4, 136-8, 140, 144, 162, 210, 212-13, 226, 253, 265, 276, 284, 286, 289, 291-2, 297, 299, 301-3, 305-9, 313, 322, 324, 326, 328, 330, 332, 340, 350, 354, 356, 449, 458, 470, 472, 484-5, 498; fall of, 121; pursuit to, 278; evacuation of, 311 sq; advance to, 474-5
Beni Ulid, 486-7
Beni Yusef, 37
Beresford Peirse, Major General, N. M. de la P., 49, 99, 166, 168, 200
Bergonzoli, General, Italian Force Commander, 121
Bir Bu Deheua, 229; capture of, 230-2
Bir Duedar, 260
Bir Duffan, 486
Bir el Afarit, 79

Bir el Amia, 328
Bir el Cleibat, 296
Bir el Ginn, 296
Bir el Gubi, 60, 63, 215, 217, 221-2, 226, 230, 258, 260-5, 346-7, 358-9, 364, 370-1, 374
Bir el Harmat, 264, 380, 387
Bir el Hurush, 243
Bir el Khireigat, 185
Bir el Mahafiz, 96
Bir el Miluz, 118
Bir Enba, 83-4, 91
Bir es Suera, 296
Bir et Tamar, 364
Bir ez Zibli, 265
Bir Ghirba, 232, 236, 265
Bir Gibni, 216-17, 230
Bir Hafid, 172
Bir Hakeim, 63, 215, 221-2, 264, 331, 345-50, 358-9, 363-4, 368, 370, 375-7, 380-1, 384-8, 395, 472
Bir Halegh el Eleba, 267-9, 273, 281, 283, 351
Bir Kanayis, 91
Bir Khalda, 51
Bir Misheifa, 204, 213
Bir Musaid, 172, 177
Bir Nuh, 172, 183-4, 186
Bir Scerrara, 370
Bir Shefersen, 68-9, 230, 239, 413
Bir Sidi Hamza, 91
Bir Soltane, 503
Bir Temrad, 347, 353, 356, 380
Bir Tengeder, 325, 327-8, 330-5, 339-40
Bir Ucheida, 268
Bir Wair, 168, 170-2, 175, 177, 180, 187
Bizerta, 4, 25, 512, 514
Blamey, General Sir Thomas, Commanding, Australian Imperial Forces, 208
Bomba, 118; seaplane base at, 67
Bona, 25
Border Regiment, 4th, 167
Boucher, Brigadier, 383
Brigade (composite), 23rd, 167, 169
Briggs, Brigadier H. R., 320, 330, 358, 383
Brindisi, 25
Brink, Major-General G. E., 215

British troops:
   Infantry Division, 6th, 125
      8th, 39
      44th, 426, 435, 437-8, 452, 454, 458
      50th, 357, 359, 379, 384, 390-1, 395, 411, 417-18, 435, 452, 454, 458, 483-5, 497, 499, 500-2, 508-9, 513
      51st, 435, 451, 453-5, 461, 478, 481, 483-4, 486-8, 492-5, 497, 499, 502, 508-10, 513-14
      56th, 513-14
      70th, 209, 215, 221, 236, 253, 255, 257, 267
      150th, 380
   Infantry Brigade, 16th, 73, 88-9, 91, 93-5, 102
      23rd, 263-4

British Somaliland, 39, 59, military situation in, 45
Brooke, General Sir Alan, Chief of the Imperial General Staff, 427
BTE (British Troops in Egypt), 201
Bu Allusc, 350
Bu Amad, 10
Bulgaria, 126
Bu Ngem, 482
Buq Buq, 69, 84-7, 94-9, 187-9, 217, 222, 355, 371
Buerat, 479, 481-6
Burg el Arab, 55-6, 427, 430
Caf Tartagu, 331, 337, 340
Cagliari, 25
Cairo, 2, 5, 15-17, 31, 38, 49, 140, 161, 165, 167, 203, 238, 247, 256, 418, 426-8, 430, 450
Canal Zone, 352
Cantanzaro Division, 71-2 (see also Italian Troops)
Cape Bon, 12, 24, 514
Cape Horn, 24
Cape of Good Hope, 24, 26, 42, 46, 355-6
Capuzzo, 60, 62, 66, 68, 100, 107, 167-73, 175, 178-85, 187, 193, 212, 214, 221-2, 236, 239, 244-5, 248, 251, 354, 371, 471; attack on, 176-7
Carr, Brigadier W. G., 358
Carcura, 287
Carmusa, 276, 278, 281-2, 284
Cartagena, 25
Castelverde, 487
Cavalry Division, 1st, 44-5
Cavalry Regiment, 2nd, 157
11th, 182, 370
18th, 137, 150, 152-4, 157, 165-6, 209, 366, 269-70
Cekhira, 510
Central India Horse (21st KGO Horse), 49, 65, 73, 77, 157, 170, 187, 226, 229, 231, 235, 241, 251-2, 263-4, 268, 274, 287, 289, 291, 305, 328, 352 (See also under Indian Forces)
Ceuta harbour, 25
Chamberlain, Mr. Neville, 31
Charing Cross, 192, 414, 467-8
Charruba, 141, 278, 286, 305-6, 308-9, 331-4
Chatfield Committee and its report, 32-3
Cheshire Regiment, 1st Battalion, 111
Chhelu Ram, Company Havildar-Major, V.C., 515 (See also photo facing page 352)
Chor es Sufan, 293
Churchill, Sir Winston S., 126, 134, 427-8, 443-4
Cirene, 287, 331, 334, 340
Coast Force, 170-2, 175, 178-9, 182, 187, 190
Coefia, 320, 322
Cologne, 127
Corradini, 487
Corps IX, 510
Corps X, 201, 410, 414-5, 418, 445, 447-8, 452, 454-5, 457, 460-1, 464, 466-7, 471-4, 481, 483, 485, 494, 497-9, 502-5, 508-10
Corps XIII, 106, 115, 121, 123, 127-8, 132, 215-7, 222, 225-7, 229, 231, 236, 239, 248, 250, 256-8, 262-3, 265-7, 276, 291, 293-7, 300-1, 303-7, 325, 327, 334, 339-41, 344, 360, 381-2, 393, 395, 410-11, 414-18, 420-1, 425, 427, 432, 438, 440, 445, 447-9, 453-8, 462, 464, 466
Corps XX (Axis), 499
Corps XXX, 215-18, 222-3, 225, 229-31, 236-41, 246, 257-8, 260, 262, 265-6, 294, 352, 358, 360, 368, 382, 393, 398, 410-11, 415, 417-18, 420-2, 425, 427, 432, 438-9, 447-9, 452-7, 459, 462, 464, 466, 473, 477, 481, 483, 485, 497-9, 501-2, 505, 508-11
Ciano, Count, 477
Cova, 232, 265
Crete, 25, 27, 125, 356
Cunningham, Sir Alan, Commander XIII Corps, 198, 203, 210-11, 223, 226, 237-8, 246-7, 253
Cyprus, 25, 27, 39, 352; military situation in, 45
Cyrenaica, 3, 4, 7, 17, 21, 76, 80, 100, 115, 117, 121, 126, 129, 133-4, 136, 144, 166, 196, 202, 210, 226, 277, 294, 296; advance into, 101-14
Czechoslovak Battalion, 11th, 258
Czechoslovak Force, 167
Daba, see El Daba
Dahar el Aslagh, 383-4
Dakar, 29.
Dakhla Oasis, 7, 9, 10
Daladier M., meets Hitler, 31
Dardanelles, 40
D'Annunzio, 288, 331, 333-5, 337
De Beer, Lt. Colonel, 394
Delta Force, 418
Deir el Abyad, 423
Deir el Hima, 421
Deir el Munassib, 432
Deir el Qattara, 421
Deir el Shein, 418, 420, 422, 424, 430-1
Derna, 20, 63, 67, 102, 111, 113, 115-17, 142, 146-7, 150, 163, 169, 267, 276, 278, 280-3, 288-9, 291, 303, 306-8, 315, 330, 339-42, 396, 472
Djebel Melab, 496, 502
Djebel Tebaga, 496, 502
Dodecanese islands, 25, 42
Dor Umm er Raml, 485
Durham Light Infantry, 2nd Battalion, 43
East African Brigades in Kenya, 45.
Ed Duda, 214, 216, 218, 221-2, 224, 232, 236, 253-5, 263
Eden, Mr. Anthony, 76
Egypt, area and population, 2; historical and political background, 20-1; military situation in, 44-5; invasion of, 65-73; Italian advance to, 65-9; liberation of, 99-100 and 471
Eighth Army, 239, 265, 278, 285, 291, 294-7, 300-1, 303-4, 306, 308, 313, 315, 317, 322, 330-3, 338, 341, 345-6, 353,

INDEX

355-62, 365, 367, 374, 377, 379-81, 386, 391-2, 397-8, 407, 413, 417, 421, 425-8, 444, 448-50, 452, 456-7, 462, 464, 469, 471, 474-5, 477, 481-4, 486, 491-8, 502, 506, 510-14; change in Command, 247-8
Eisenhower, General Dwight, Commander, Anglo-American Expeditionary Force, 463, 493
El Abiar, 141, 289, 307, 316-20, 323
El Adem, 10, 111-12, 151, 154, 158, 163, 169, 214, 217, 221-2, 226, 256-8, 260, 262-5, 345-8, 357, 367, 374-5, 387-8, 391, 394, 397, 399, 401, 407-10, 471-2
El Agheila, 10, 121, 123, 131-3, 134, 136-8, 144, 158-9, 276, 286, 292, 296-7, 304, 308, 466-7, 472-3, 477-9, 481, 483, 485, 491; advance to, 115; long pursuit to, 469; approach to, 475
El Alamein, 156, 160-1, 163, 189, 193-4, 197, 202, 430-1, 438, 449, 454, 473-4, 491, 496, 503, 510; withdrawal to, 410-28; battle of, 453 sq., 473, 510
El Buerat, see Buerat
El Daba, 10, 49, 55, 165, 167, 201, 420, 449
El Ezzeiat, 331, 343
El Faidia, 287, 331, 334, 338, 340-1
El Faskia, 486
El Hamma, 499-500, 502, 504-5
El Hammam, 426, 440
El Haseiat, 293, 299-300, 478
El Kanayis, 414
El Magrun, 326, 328
El Mrassas, 347
El Mreir, 420, 423
El Ruweisat ridge, see Ruweisat ridge
El Tahag, 158, 194
El Taqa, 421, 423-4, 430, 448
Eluet et Tamar, 345-6, 364
Enfidaville, 10, 509, 511-13
En Nauaghia, 328
Eritrea, 124, 199
Er Regima, 137-8, 142, 146, 317, 319, 322-3
Er Rigel, 346
Escarpment Force, 170-4, 177-8, 180-2, 187, 190; operations of, 175
Escarpment Line, 319
Farafra Oasis, 7, 9
Fayid, 35
Fezzan, 3
Field Battery, 11th, 243
Field Battery, 52nd, 243-4
Field Company I.E., 2nd, 383
   18th, 56, 65, 274
   20th, 383
   21st, 383
Field Company RASC 232nd, 56
Field Company Sappers & Miners, 4th, 65
   18th 78, 94, 402, 404
   Field Hygiene Section, 15th, 56
Field Post Office, 17th, 56
Field Regiment RIA, 2nd, 369
   3rd, 85
   14th, 342
   25th, 170, 179, 188, 226, 270-1, 320, 394, 399, 403-4, 407, 409
   31st, 39, 45, 56, 174, 177, 180, 186, 188, 191, 226, 241, 251-2, 259, 263, 274-5, 299, 320, 327
   51st, 137, 332
   149th, 206
Field Regt. Royal Artillery,
   1st, 37, 52, 56, 226, 243-4, 291, 299, 342, 352
   4th, 31, 35, 39, 383
   8th, 183-4, 186, 231, 291
   28th, 383
Field Regt. New Zealand Artillery, 44
Field Regt. Supply Depot, 50th, 241
Field Regt. Workshop Company IAOC, 18th, 394
First Army, 511-12 514
Fletcher, Brigadier B. C., 357, 383
Folgore Division, 433, 451 (see also Italian Troops)
Fondouk Gap, 510
Force 'Assurance', 158
Force 'E', 334-5, 339, 343-4
Force 'L', 335, 339, 341, 343, 346, 350-1, 498
Fort Maddalena, 471
Foum Tatahouine, 491-2, 499
France, collapse of, 41; fall of, 59
Free French Brigade Group, 1st, 346, 358-9, 370, 377, 384-6
   2nd, 358, 397
French Corps, IXX, 512-13
French Division, 12th, 514
French Motor Battalion, 137
Freyberg, Major-General B., 215, 254, 501
Fuka, 10, 51, 55, 90, 415-16, 464, 466-9
Gabes, 4, 12, 495-6, 499, 502, 504-5; defences of, 506 sq
Gabr Abu Milha, 51, 223
Gabr el Abidi, 269, 350
Gabr el Aleima, 339
Gabr el Amber, 339
Gabr el Carmusa, 280-1, 283, 303, 306, 339, 342
Gabr Saleh, 60, 62-3, 225, 231
Gabr Taieb el Essom (see Taieb el Essom)
Gach Saran, 26
Gadd el Ahmar, 150
Gafsa, 492, 498-9, 508
Galal, 467-8
Gallabat, 59
Gambier-Parry, Major-General, 137, 147-8, 153
Gambut, 214, 237, 259, 358, 391, 397-8, 401, 471-2
Garawla, 51
Garet el Tartut, 330
Garian, 483, 486
Garibaldi, General, Commander Italian Fifth Army, 72, 123, 198
Gatehouse, Brigadier A. H., 215
Gazala, 10, 67, 137, 162-3, 226, 263, 265, 267-9, 272-3, 275-6, 280, 293, 331, 375, 377-81, 386, 435, 472; withdrawal to, 337; the stand at, 350-62; Axis attack on, 363-73; battle of, 388-400
German Forces: (see also Panzer Divisions)

Armoured Division, 15th, 133, 144
Division, 164th, 356, 433, 438, 462, 466, 489, 499, 502, 504-5
Kiel Group, 451
Light Motorized Division, 5th, 133, 144
Light Division 90th, 214, 222, 297, 374, 385-6, 388, 396-7, 401, 433, 451, 459-60, 462, 466, 479, 486, 488-9, 499, 504
German Parachute Battalion, 438
German Recce Group, 451
German Tank Regiment 5th, 244
8th, 422

Gebel er Roumana, 506, 508
Gebel Fatnassa, 506, 508-9
Gebel Fkirine, 511
Gebel Garci, 513
Gebel Kalakh, 448
Germain, General (French), 59
Ghazal, 466-7
Gheddahia, 482, 486
Ghemines, 119, 121, 307, 326
Ghot Adhidiba, 232, 239
Giarabub Oasis, 18, 63, 195-7, 210-11, 218-19, 229-30, 354 ; capture of, 127
Gief el Matar, 292
Giorgis, General de, 295
Giovanni Berta, 278, 282, 284-5, 288-9, 335, 339
Godwin-Austen, Lt. General A. R., 215, 257, 303
Gold Group, 324-8
Got Derva, 115, 147, 153.
Got el Scarab, 381
Got es Saeti, 328
Gott, Major-General W. H. E., 215, 353, 357, 392-3, 415, 430
Graziani, Marshal, Supreme Commander, Italian Forces in North Africa, 72, 74, 80, 82-3, 99-100, 123-4
Greece, 40, 125-6 ; Allied troops in, 124
Greek Brigade, 452
Guards Brigade, 22nd, 170, 173, 176-8, 183-5, 187-8, 190-1, 215, 222, 261-5, 287, 292-3, 300, 305, 346, 350, 375
Guards Motor Brigade, 201st, 298, 358, 390-1, 393-4, 497-8, 514
Guides Cavalry, 358
Guidi, General, Commander Italian Tenth Army, 72
Gurkha Rifles, 2/7th, 394, 396, 399, 402, 404, 407, 514
Habbaniya, 34
Haditha, 27
Hafid Ridge, 175-8, 180
Haft Khel, 26
Hagfet Gelgaf, 333
Hagiag Batruna, 339
Hagiag er Raml, 263-4, 389
Haile Selassie, the Emperor of Abyssinia, 47
Halfaya, 98-9, 168-72, 174, 178-80, 182-4, 187, 193, 197, 214, 221-3, 227, 229, 231, 235, 252, 265, 282, 294-5, 347, 413, 471
Halfaya Group, 170-2, 174-5, 178-9, 244

Halfway House, 173-4, 185-7, 227
Halluf, 503
Hammamet, 12, 513
Hamra, 331, 347, 350-2
Hareifet en Nibeidat, 237
Highland Division, 51st, 453
Highland Light Infantry, 2nd, 383
Himeimat, 438, 448, 454
Hitler, Adolf, 31
Homs, 482-3, 486-7
Horrocks, General, 448
Hunter's Plateau, 454
Hussars, 3rd (King's Own), 137-8
Hussars, 11th (Prince Albert's Own), 101, 118, 328, 474-5
Ilwet el Naas, 172-3, 187

Indian Forces:
Indian Armoured Division, 1st, 292
Indian Division, 4th, 31, 37, 39, 44, 49, 56, 58-9, 63, 65-8, 72-4, 76-7, 79, 81, 84-5, 88-9, 91-2, 94-6, 98-9, 101, 125, 128, 165-6, 168-70, 177-8, 184, 188, 190-3, 196, 205, 215, 217, 225-6, 228-31, 235-6, 239-42, 248, 250-2, 257, 260-5, 267-73, 275-6, 280-3, 285-9, 291-4, 299-309, 311, 313, 316-19, 321, 323-4, 331-5, 337-41, 343-5, 350-3, 430, 452-3, 497, 499, 503, 508-10, 513-14 ; Royal Engineers of, 69
5th, 194, 197, 201, 352, 379-80, 383-4, 391, 411, 417, 420, 422, 426, 432, 438-9
10th, 358, 381, 391, 411, 414, 416
44th, (air-borne), 260
Indian Field Ambulance, 14th, 37, 56, 157
17th, 241, 244
19th, 394
Indian Field Regiment, 2nd. R.I.A., 366
Indian Infantry Brigade, 5th, 37, 43-4, 52, 72-3, 76, 88, 91-3, 125, 165, 190-1, 217, 226-7, 239, 248, 251, 257, 259-60, 263-4, 268-70, 272-3, 280-5, 287-9, 291, 299, 302, 310, 317, 319, 322, 332-4, 337, 339-45, 350, 352, 423, 461-2, 509-10
7th, 88, 174, 191, 196-7, 217-18, 222, 226, 228-32, 242, 251, 257, 260, 263-5, 268, 270, 273, 280-4, 288, 291, 299, 302, 305-7, 309, 311, 316-20, 322-3, 345, 350, 352, 509 ; breakthrough of, 324-35
9th, 32, 357, 381-4
10th, 31, 380-4
11th, 31, 35, 37, 39, 44, 58, 72-3, 76, 88, 91-2, 95, 170, 172-3, 178, 187-8, 191, 217-18, 222, 226, 228, 251, 257-8, 260-5, 267-8, 299, 306-7, 309, 316, 332-3, 335, 337, 339-45, 350, 352, 358, 387, 391, 394-6, 399, 401-3, 405-9
18th, 418, 420, 460
20th, 396-8
21st, 375, 397
29th, 197, 215, 229, 232, 358-9, 364, 370, 375, 383, 386-9, 396-8, 414-16

38th, formed, 257-8
69th, 359, 380-2, 411-14, 423-5
161st, 423-4
Indian Motor Brigade, 3rd, 137-8, 143, 146, 148, 150, 152, 154-8, 161, 165, 182, 358-9, 364-72, 374-5, 391, 410, 412-14
Infantry Brigade 151st, 411, 414, 416, 460
152nd, 460
Transport Company 11th, RIASC, 394
Infantry Tank Battalion, 4th, 407
7th, 403-4, 407
Ionian islands, 25
Iraq Petroleum Co., 194
Ismail, ruler of Egypt, 15
Ismailia, 16, 204

Italian troops:
Army fifth, 72
Tenth, 115, 121, 129
Corps X, 72
XV, 72
XXI, 71-2, 214, 280, 283, 286-8, 433, 499
XXII, 71-2, 111
XXIII, 72
Mobile, 214
Ariete Division, 133, 214, 222-3, 230, 237, 297, 367-9, 375-6, 387, 433, 438-9, 451
Blackshirt Division, 1st, 71, 82, 87, 98
4th, 71, 87, 94-5, 97
Bologna Division, 214, 221, 262, 433, 438, 451
Brescia Division, 214, 221, 297, 433, 438, 451
Cantanzaro Division, 71
Infantry Division, 60th, 111, 115
61st, 111
Libyan Division, 1st, 71, 87, 96-8
2nd, 71, 87
Littorio Division, 433, 438-9, 451, 462
Metropolitan Division, 62nd, 71, 82, 87
63rd, 71, 82, 87
Young Fascists Division, 433, 499
Maletti Mobile Group, 71-2, 87, 262, 280, 439
Jalo, 201, 210, 219
Jats 3rd Regt., 383
Jebel Akhdar, 3, 5, 6, 115, 142, 159, 276-8, 280, 285-7, 289, 301-3, 306, 308, 330, 332-3, 338-9, 379, 469
Jebel Kalakh, 194, 423, 472
Kabrit, 204
Kairouan, 510-11
Kantara East, 204
Kassala, 50
Kasserine Pass, 498
Kenya, 44, 47, 59; military situation in, 45
Kesselring, Field Marshal, 433
Keren, 127
Key, Lt. Colonel, 35
Khatatba, 366
Kidney Hill, 456-8

King's African Rifles, battalion of, in Somaliland, 45
King's Dragoon Guards, 334-5, 512, 514
Kirkuk, 27, 41, 194
Klopper, Major-General H. B., 357, 392-3, 398, 406-8
Knightsbridge, 263, 347-8, 358-9, 374-5, 381, 385, 387, 390, 408
Koenig, General J.P.F., 358, 364, 385
Kopanski, Major-General S., 215
Ksar Rhilane, 493, 498-9, 502
Kufra Oasis, 9, 10, 18; capture of, 128
Kurmuk, 59
Kuwait, 27
La Hencha, 511
Lake Chad, 129, 493
Lalbahadur Thapa, Subedar (later Sub-Major), V.C., 516 (*see also* photo facing page 347)
Lamluda, 278, 282, 284, 331-2, 339, 341
Landing Ground Group, 190-1
Lavender Brig. S. S., 322
Lease-lend Bill, 127
Lebanon, 25, 28
Leclerc, General, 493, 498, 502
Leese, General Sir Oliver, 448
Legentilhomme, General, holds out in French Somaliland, 59
Leicesters, 2nd Battalion, 88, 94
Leros, 25
Libya, 28, 40; topography, 3; population, 6; historical background, 17-19; fighting strength in, 125
Libyan Air Force, 291
Libyan Arab Force Battalion, 4th, 334
Libyan Omar, 226-9, 232-3, 239, 242, 246, 248, 250-2; attack on, 234-5
Libyan Plateau, 2, 4, 90
Libyan Sand Sea, 3-4, 296
Light Anti-aircraft Battery, 4th, 181
Light Anti-aircraft Regiment, 57th, 274, 352
Light Armoured Brigade, 4th, 467-9, 471-2, 474, 479, 481, 483, 497
Tank Group, 90th, 363
Long Range Desert Group, 213, 219, 492, 497
Lorried Infantry Brigade, 131st, 472
Lorried Infantry Regiment, 115th, 274
155th, 422
Luftwaffe, 131-4
Luigi Razza, 334
Lumsden, Major-General H., 358, 448
Maabus es Rigel, 389
Maadi, 73
Maaten Burruci, 298
Maaten Giaber, 482
Maaten Giofer, 297
Maddalena Fort, 59, 63, 222, 244, 257, 395, 413
Mafraq, 34
Mahares, 508
Mahratta Regiment, 1st 383
2nd, 173, 178-9, 182, 191, 226, 317, 340, 342
5th, 2nd Battalion, 351, 395, 399-403, 405, 407
Maktila, 83-5, 87, 89, 94, 96-7, 99

Maletti, General Pietro, 72, 83
Malta, 25, 27-8, 334, 470; help for, 472
Marada, 298
Maraua, 305, 308-9, 331-3, 335, 337, 474
Marble Arch, 7th Armoured Division at, 481
Mareth Line, 389 sq, 508
Marriott, Brigadier J. C. O., 215, 358
Marsa Brega, 133, 138, 158, 192, 196-8, 292, 475, 478
Martuba, 278, 280-3, 303, 339, 341-2, 351, 353-4, 472
Masjid-i-Sulaiman, 26
Massawa, 42
Massiet, General, replaces General Weygand, 48
Matapan, Battle of, 127
Matmata Hills, 486-7, 499, 502
Matruh, 10, 46, 63, 67, 74, 77, 79-82, 84, 88, 90, 96, 106, 165, 172, 189-92, 197, 199-201, 212-13, 216, 293, 365-7, 410-13; 416-17, 435, 464, 466, 469, 472; defence of, 414-15
McConnel, Lt. Colonel, 368
McPherson, Brigadier A. B., 35
Medenine, 10, 491, 499, 503; battle of, 494-6
Medium Battery, 212th, 180
Medium Regiment, 6th, 31
  7th, 39, 45, 58, 291, 311
  73rd, 206
Mediterranean High Command, restrains Rommel, 167, 189
Medjez el Bab, 511-12, 514
Meduar, 195
Mekili, 102, 111, 115-17, 136, 138, 140, 146-8, 150, 156, 162-3, 165, 265, 267, 276, 278, 280, 285-6, 301, 303, 305, 307-8, 313, 315-16, 325, 327, 330-5, 339-41, 350, 353, 364, 379, 472; attack on 151-5
Mena, 25, 37, 49, 55, 76, 165
Menastir, 169, 239, 251
Mersa Matruh, 51, 88, 106, 124, 158, 190, 467-8
Messe, General, Italian Commander, 541
Messervy, Major-General F. W., 166, 215, 267-8, 291-2, 298-300, 348, 358, 365, 367
Meteiriya Ridge, 453-4
Mezzouna, 508
Middle East, war approaches to, 40-8
Middle East Command, 37, 47, 106, 208, 210, 427, 429
Middle East Defence Committee, 199, 410
Minqar Qaim, 190, 414-15, 417
Minqar Sidi Hamza el Gharbi, 190, 192, 414-15
Misurata, 20, 486-7
Mittlehauser, General, French Commander in Syria, obeys Vichy Government, 59
Modernisation Committee (India), report of, 32-3
Mogadishu Port, 42
Mohamed el Habib Bey, King of Tunisia, 21

Montgomery, Field-Marshal Sir Bernard (Viscount), 428, 430, 436, 439, 448-9, 454-61, 467-8, 471, 474-5, 477-8, 482-3, 485-9, 491-5, 497-9, 501-2, 509-14; issue of a directive to, 435; proceeds to give effect to the directive, 436; estimates D-Day, 443; outlines his intention to make the main thrust in the North, 447; tours the Eighth Army, 452; plan of, 470; decides to stop X Corps at Tmimi, 473; decides to bring forward the X Corps to occupy El Agheila, 481
Morocco, 25; its population, 6
Morshead, Major-General L. J., 135-6, 140, 209
Mosul Airfield, 40
Motor Brigade, 7th, 358-9, 374, 384-7, 391, 396-7, 410, 412-14, 416, 457
Mountain Regiment, 1st, allotted to Force 'EMU', 32
Moyale, 59
Msus, 118, 120-1, 140-1, 144, 146, 162-3, 280, 286, 300, 302, 306, 309, 311, 313, 315-17, 353, 474
Mteifel, 384, 386
Muhammed Ali, ruler of Egypt, 15
Munich, 32; conference at, 31
Musaid, 68-70, 168, 171-2, 175, 177-8, 180-3, 236, 239, 244
Mussolini, Benito, 29, 31, 42, 129, 433, 483
Naduret el Chesceuasc, 264
Neame, Major-General, Commander 4th Indian Division, 49, 134, 138, 140, 144, 146, 158, 163-4
Naghamish, 49, 51, 55, 58-9, 65, 72-4, 76-8
Nalut, 489-99
Naqb Abu Dweiss, 194, 417
Nazarain, 69
New Zealand Anti-tank Battery, 73
New Zealand Corps. 498-501, 503-5, 508
New Zealand Division, 2nd, 44, 125-6, 205-6, 215, 222, 226, 229-30, 236-7, 239, 246, 250, 253, 256, 391, 411, 414-17, 420, 422, 438, 452-3, 457, 467-8, 470-2, 477-9, 481, 483-5, 494-5, 498, 508, 513-14
New Zealand Infantry Brigade, 4th, 44, 254, 258
  5th, 239, 245, 248, 251-2, 258-9, 267-9, 272-3, 471
  6th, 237, 255, 258, 423-4
New Zealand Brigade Group, 73
New Zealand Cavalry Regiment, 250-2
New Zealand Infantry Battalion, 18th, 258
  19th, 258
  22nd, 250-1
Nezuet Ghirba, 175-6
Nibeiwa, 83-5, 87-8, 93-4, 96; attack on 91-2
Nile Delta, 72, 197, 200, 353, 416, 418, 429, 431-2, 434, 466
Nofilia, 479, 481
Nogues, General, French Commander, 59

Norrie, Lt. General C.W.M., 215, 257, 262, 294, 358
North Africa, topography, 1-4; area and climate, 5; population, 6; communications, 9; historical and political background, 14-21; strategic background, 22-7; strategic importance, 27-9; Indian troops in, 30-9; British strength in, 38; military situation on Italy's entry into war in, 44; cleared of Axis troops, 515
Northumbrian Division, 50th, 352
Oases Force, 196-7, 215, 218-19, 299
O'Connor, Lt. General Sir Richard Commander XIII Corps, 80, 82, 115, 117, 120, 142, 163
Omar Nuovo, 226-32, 234-5, 239, 241-2, attack on, 232-3
Operation "Battleaxe", 175-88
Operation "Crusader", 210-20, 296; beginning of, 221-35; in progress, 236-52; its success, 253-66
Operation "Lightfoot", 449
Operation "Pugilist", 497-9, 503
Operation "Supercharge", 460, 503
Oran, 25, 29
Oudref, 508
Paiforce, 429.
Palestine, 25, 31, 33, 35-6, 39, 203, 352; military situation in, 45
Panzer Divisions (*see also* German Forces):
    10th, 494-5, 499
    15th, 214, 222-4, 297, 363, 369, 374-5, 385, 387-9, 396, 433, 451, 456, 458, 462, 466, 479, 481, 485-6, 491, 494-5, 499, 501, 504-5, 510
    21st, 214-15, 222-4, 297, 363, 374-5, 385, 387, 389, 396-7, 401, 433, 451, 454, 457-8, 460, 462, 466, 479, 494-5, 499, 504
Panzer Grenadiers of 164th Division, 460
Panzer Gruppe, Afrika, 214
Pavia Division, 214, 221, 297, 433-4, 451 (*see also* Italian Troops)
PAVO (Prince Albert Victor's Own), 137, 147-8, 151-2, 157, 165, 182, 188, 366
Philipville, 25
Pilastrino, 111, 113, 394
Pistoia Division, 433-4, 466, 469, 471, 484, 499, 504 (*see also* Italian Troops)
Plum Defile, 502-4
Point 90 (south of Sidi Barrani), 83, 85, 87, 97
Point 171—3rd Indian Brigade at 364 *et seq.*
Point 206, Fighting at, 177
Polish Brigade Group, 125-6, 273, 276, 307, 345
Polish Carpathian Brigade, 47, 180, 215, 257-8
Polish Independent Brigade, 209, 350
Polish Infantry Brigade, 221, 308
Port Said, 24, 28, 204
Pownall Committee, 32-3
Punjab Regiment, 1st, 3rd Battalion, 37, 79-80, 226, 251, 264, 273, 332, 339, 342, 344
    2nd, 332, 383
    16th, 32, 196-7, 226-7, 232-5, 239, 248, 252, 281, 284, 320, 322, 325
Qabr Husri, 229
Qaret Abu Faris, 172, 175
Qaret Agnes, 201
Qaret el Abad, 430-1
Qaret el Himeimat, 431-2
Qaret el Khadim, 421, 448
Qaret el Ruweibat, 229
Qattara Depression, 2-3, 9-10, 193-4, 200, 415, 417-18, 426, 430
Quassasin, 194
Queen's Own Cameron Highlanders, 2nd Battalion, 35, 58, 65, 76-7, 88, 92, 95-6, 170, 174, 178-9, 182, 191, 226, 261, 337-8, 340-2, 351, 394, 399-401, 404, 407-8
Queen's Royal Regiment, 2nd Battalion, 88, 95, 99
Queen Victoria's Own Madras Sappers & Miners, 12th Field Company, 37
Rabia, 83, 87, 91, 97-8
Radley Report, 33
Radley, H. P., Lt. Colonel, 33-4
Rahman track, 456
Rajendrasinhji, Major M. K. (Later General Rajendrasinhji and Commander-in-Chief of the Indian Army), 147, 154
Rajput Regiment, 4th, 58, 80
    7th, 4th Battalion, 35, 91
Rajputana Rifles, 6th, 1st Battalion, 35, 58, 79-80, 88, 178, 182, 191, 226, 267-8, 284, 332, 339
    4th Battalion, 37, 65, 79, 88, 93, 95, 226, 269, 284, 337-8
Ramadi, 35
Ramcke Brigade of Parachutists, 433, 487
Ramla, 68
Ramsden, Major-General W. H. C., 357, 428
Rayat, French air force at, 41
Reid, Brigadier D. W., 215, 358
Renton, Brigadier J. M. G., 358
Richards, Brigadier G. W., 358
Rifle Brigade, 2nd, 69
Ritchie, Major-General N. M., 247, 256-7, 260, 263, 265, 276, 294, 306, 308-9, 313, 316, 332, 338, 346-8, 356-8, 360, 367, 374-6, 378-81, 384-6, 390-2, 397, 410-11, 413
Rommel, General, 123, 127, 132, 140, 150-1, 154-6, 161-2, 164, 166-8, 188-9, 192-3, 195, 197-8, 200, 214-15, 219, 238-9, 244-5, 260, 265, 276, 280, 296-9, 304, 306-8, 315, 332-3, 349, 353, 355-6, 361-5, 367, 372, 376-7, 384-5, 388, 392, 398, 413, 430, 432-4, 438-9, 452, 456-7, 459-60, 463, 468-70, 473-4, 477-8, 482-3, 486, 491-6, 503
Rotonda Segnali, 472
Royal Air Force, 46, 67; armoured cars, 101; No. 40 squadron, 368; No. 202 group, 67, 70

Royal Army Medical Corps, 207
Royal Army Ordnance Corps, 207
Royal Army Service Corps, 207
Royal Artillery Group, 39
Royal Australian Air Force, 134
Royal Buffs, 1st, 167, 177, 181-2, 185-6, 190, 226, 269, 272-5
Royal Dragoons, 1st, 326
Royal Engineers, 58
Royal Frontier Force Rifles, 3rd, 383
Royal Horse Artillery, 69-70, 78, 101, 118, 137, 148
Royal Horse Artillery Anti-tank Regiment, 3rd, 39, 44, 76
Royal Horse Artillery Regiment, 4th, 39, 44
    104th, 137
Royal Horse Artillery 'J' Battery, 137
Royal Lancers, 2nd, 137, 147-8, 150-4, 157, 165, 366, 368-71
Royal Northumberland Fusiliers, 1st Battalion, 58, 65, 88, 93, 112, 137
Royal Sussex, 1st, 191, 197, 226-33, 235, 281-2, 328-9, 509
Royal Tanks 2nd, 95
    4th, 174-6, 178-9, 184-5, 194
    5th, 137-8
    6th, 137-8
    7th, 81, 84, 88-9, 91, 101, 106, 109, 111, 174-5, 177, 184, 194
    8th, 268, 270, 311, 316-17, 319, 339
    42nd, 231, 275-6, 280, 283
    44th, 231
Royal Yugoslav Guards, 352
Rumania, 40
Rutba, 34
Ruweisat Ridge, 421-3, 425, 431-2, 438-9, 449, 452-3
Sabrata Division, 297
Safaga, 204
Sahara desert, 4, 5, 7
Salonika, 25
Sanyet el Miteiriya, 425
Sappers & Miners, Field Squadron, 35th, 157
Sardinia, 25, 27, 42
Saseno, 25
Saunnu, 301, 304, 325, 327
Scarlet, Major-General, P. G., 37
Schmitt, General, 295
Scobie, Major-General R. Mack., 209, 215
Scots Guards, 2nd, 176-7, 180, 190
Sebkhret er Noual, 510
Security Intelligence Section, 3rd, 366
Sedjennane, 511-12
Segnali, 356, 367
Selby Force, 84-5, 88-9, 96-9
Sfax, 4, 12, 496, 506, 510-11
Sgifet es Sidra, 380-2
Sheleidima, 118, 289, 302, 305, 307, 309, 311, 313, 316-17, 320, 324, 328, 475
Sherwood Foresters, 393, 407
Shott el Djerid, 492
Shott el Fejaj, 506
Signal Section K (Indian), 394
Sicily, 25, 27, 42, 132, 355, 513
Sidi Abd el Aati, 304
Sidi Abd el Rahman, 416, 459-61

Sidi Azeiz, 66, 68-9, 169, 178, 239, 245, 249, 259
Sidi Brahim, 289, 302, 305, 307, 316, 320, 324
Sidi Barrani, 10, 46, 65-6, 68-70, 72, 74, 76-7, 80-1, 83-6, 94, 97-9, 106, 114, 121, 124, 165, 167, 169, 172-3 187-8, 191, 233, 413-14; 471; battle of, 87-91; capture of, 95-6
Sidi Breghisc, 269-70, 356
Sidi el Meheigu, 283
Sidi Haneish, 165, 468
Sidi Mahmoud, 111-13
Sidi Mahius, 319, 331, 333-4
Sidi Muftah, 217, 231, 347, 359, 380, 382-3
Sidi Omar, 68-9, 99-100, 169, 181, 183, 212, 214, 217, 221-2, 229, 411
Sidi Rezegh, 214, 216, 218, 221-5, 229, 231-2, 236-9, 245-7, 250-1, 253-6, 260, 375; attack on, 396-7
Sidi Suleiman, 168, 185, 187
Sikh Regiment, 11th, 4th Battalion, 181, 197, 235, 243-4, 270, 281-2
    5th Battalion, 31-2
Silver Group, 324, 328-30
Sirte, 134, 479, 481
Sitra, 201
Siwa Oasis, 9, 67, 128, 195-7, 201, 218, 427, 433
Slonta, 116, 331, 335, 337, 340
Smith, Lt. General Sir Arthur, 80
Smuts, Field Marshal, 427
Sofafi, 83-7, 89-91, 97-9, 167, 174, 189
Solaro, 111, 113
Sollum, 10, 59, 62, 68-70, 85, 90, 98-100, 102, 106, 109, 115, 165-6, 168-72, 177-8, 180, 182-4, 187, 195, 214, 218, 221-2, 228-9, 236-7, 239, 244, 248, 294-5, 347, 350, 352, 471-2
Soluk, 12, 118, 120, 307, 313, 315, 318, 324, 326, 328
Somaliland Camel Corps, 45
Sonderverbund, 401, 403
South African Air Force, 46
South African Division 1st, 125, 191-3, 196, 205, 215, 223, 225, 256, 275-6, 280-1, 283-5, 294, 344-6, 350, 357, 359, 379, 390-1, 394-5, 399, 407, 411, 417-18, 421, 423-5, 432, 438, 452-3, 457
    2nd, 201, 215, 250-1, 257-8, 260, 265, 294, 352, 357, 359, 391-3
    Armoured Car Regiment, 6th, 215, 229, 241, 468-9
    Anti-tank Regiment, 2nd, 243
    Field Regiment, 4th, 311, 316
South African Infantry Brigade, 1st, 256-7
    2nd, 258
    3rd 258, 295
    4th, 393, 407-8
    5th, 224-5, 237, 240, 258
South African Reconnaissance Unit, 3rd, 280, 284-5
    7th, 334
South Staffords, 1st Battalion, 98
Sousse, 12, 511
Special Force, 288th, 433

Spezia, 25
Spezia Division 80th, 466, 469, 484, 499, 504 (see also Italian troops)
Sudan, 16, 99, 101, 166; military situation in, 45
Sudan Defence Force, 39, 45, 427
Suez Canal, 15, 27-8, 31, 35, 46, 166, 194, 204, 355; its importance, 26
Support Group (of 7th British, Armoured Division), 44, 59, 77, 87-8; 100, 137-8, 165, 190, 224-5, 260, 264, 270, 276, 285-7, 293, 298-301, 370, 372, 375
Syria, 28, 42
Tadjera, 495
Taieb el Essom, 225, 230
Takrouna, 513
Tangier Port, 25, 28
Taqa (see El Taqa)
Taranto, 25
Tarhuna, 482-3, 486-7
Tebaga gap, 4
Tebessa, 492-4
Tedder, Air Marshal, 450
Tel el Aqqaqir, 461
Tel el Eisa, 421-3, 425, 427, 431, 453
Tel el Kebir, 16
Tell el Makh Khad, 423, 431-2
Thoma, General von, Commander, *Afrika Korps*, 462
Tilly, Major-General J. C., 126
Tmimi, 67, 147, 153, 267-9, 273, 276, 278, 280-1, 306, 331, 339, 343-5, 350-1, 353-4, 379, 472-3
Tobruk, 3, 10, 67, 100, 115, 137-8, 143, 150, 155-6, 161-9, 171, 180-1, 188-9, 191, 195, 197, 199-200, 202, 208-9, 211-16, 218-19, 221-3, 227, 232, 236, 239, 245-6, 251-2, 256, 259, 265, 267-8, 272, 294, 299, 305, 330, 332, 339, 345-7, 349, 353, 355-7, 359, 364, 374-5, 379, 385, 387-8, 390-3, 395-400, 410-11, 470-2, 479, 485; advance to, 109-13; fall of, 113-14; operations in, 250; Axis attack on, 261; attack on, 401-9
Tobruk Garrison, 215
Tocra, 137, 140, 323, 330-1, 333-4
Toujane, 496, 499, 503
Toulon, 25, 29
Transjordan, 25, 27, 33, 36, 203
Transport Company RIASC, 366
Transvaal Scottish troops, 295
Treaty between Great Britain, France & Turkey, 40
Trento Division, 214, 221, 297, 433, 451 (see also Italian Troops)
Triaga, 510
Trieste, 25
Trigh el Abd, 213, 216-17, 222-3, 225, 230, 269, 347, 374, 377, 381
Trigh Capuzzo, 214, 216, 218, 221-2, 231, 239, 252, 259-60, 347, 357, 377-8, 381
Tripoli (Libya), 3, 5, 10, 12, 17, 20, 119, 130-4, 210, 213, 216, 299, 355, 489, 492-5; operations in, 474-88; fall of, 488

Tripoli (Mediterranean Port), 27
Tripolitania, 3, 4, 6-7, 17, 21, 121, 123, 133-4, 202, 210, 296-7, 475, 479, 483, 489, 491
Tuker, Major-General F. I. S., 292, 302, 305-8, 310-11, 313, 318-19, 341-2, 371
Tummar East, 83, 85, 87, 93-4
Tummar West, 83-8, 96; attack on, 92-4
Tunis, 4, 10, 12, 25, 28, 475; fall of, 506-15
Tunisia, 4, 5, 21, 40, 134, 483, 489, 491-2, 494, 498; rainfall and population, 6-7; historical and political background, 19-20
United States Corps, IInd, 492, 498-9, 511-12
Vaughan, Brigadier E. W. D., 147-8.
Via Balbia, 319, 359
Vichy, 59
Villiers, Major-General I. P. de, 215
Wadi Akarit, 505-6, 508-10
Wadi el Chebir, 481-2
Wadi el Fareg, 292, 297, 478
Wadi Harun, 34
Wadi Maatered, 104
Wadi Majid, 192
Wadi Merteba, 497
Wadi Regel, 478
Wadi Umm er Raml, 482
Wadi Zem Zem, 482, 486
Wadi Zigzaou, 496-7, 500-3
Watkins, Brigadier H. R. B., 215, 357
Wavell, General Sir Archibald P., 38, 40, 42-4, 46, 48, 74, 80, 99-101, 115, 121, 124-9, 131-6, 138, 140-2, 144, 158, 161, 191, 196-7, 200, 202, 294-5, 346, 427
Welch, 1st, 302, 304, 307, 311, 316-17, 320, 324
Western Desert, 2, 31, 49, 125, 159, 200, 203, 301, 352-3, 358, 364
Western Desert Force, 73, 76-7, 80-1, 86-8, 99-100, 102, 106, 187, 189, 191, 201, 462, 481, 498, 501, 503; conference between commanders, 81
Western Desert Railway, 204
Weygand, General, 38, 43, 48
Wilder's Gap, 499
Willison, Brigadier A. C., 215
Wilson, General Sir Henry Maitland, Commander, Allied Forces in Greece, 125, 135, 198, 203
Worcestershire Regiment, 1st, 383, 393, 407
Workshop Company, 13th, 157, 366
27th, 157, 366
West Yorkshire Regt., 2nd, 383
Yugoslavia, 126
Zafraan, 254, 256
Zarat, 496
Zavia, 489
Zelten, 503
Zliten, 487
Zt. Msus, 278, 301, 304-5, 309, 313, 327, 333
Zuara, 12, 489

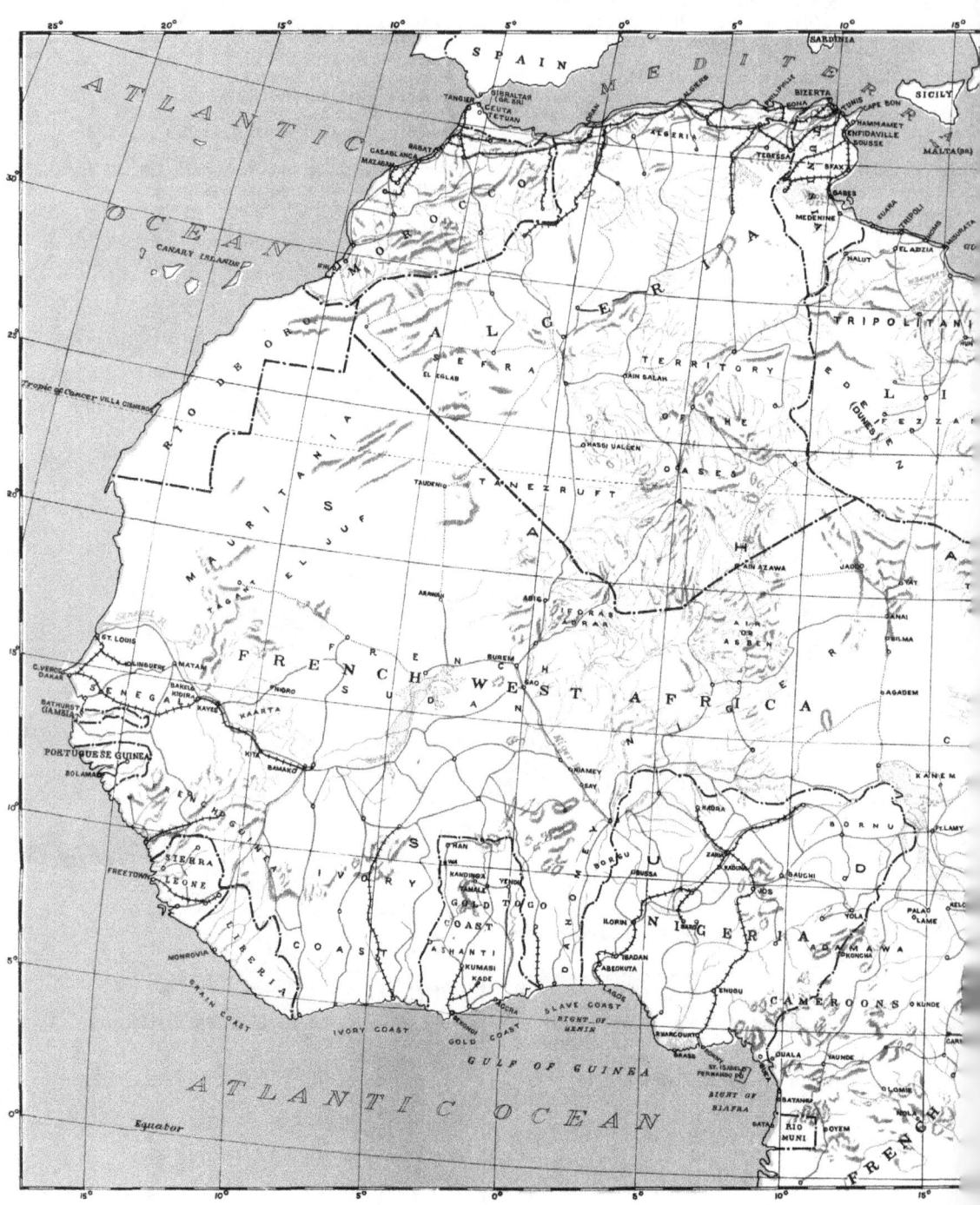

INDIAN DIVISIONS WON A FINE REPUTATION IN WORLD WAR TWO

Field Marshal Auchinleck, Commander-in-Chief of the British Indian Army from 1942, asserted that the British *"couldn't have come through both wars (World War I and II) if they hadn't had the British Indian Army"*.
British Prime Minister Winston Churchill also paid tribute to *"the unsurpassed bravery of Indian soldiers and officers"*.

Between 1945 and 1947, the Director of Public Relations, War Department, Government of India, published a series of short publications covering the individual histories of the WWII Indian Divisions. They followed a consistent format, having between 44 and 48 pages within illustrated soft card covers. They have an average of 50 monochrome photographic illustrations, and each has a full colour centrespread depicting a scene from the Division's wartime operations (drawn by official war artists). They were printed at various presses in Bombay and New Delhi, and each contains at least one map.

As condensed histories they are useful – particularly those which relate to Divisions for which no other record was ever produced.

The British Indian Army during World War II began the war, in 1939, numbering just under 200,000 men. By the end of the war, it had become the largest volunteer army in history, rising to over 2.5 million men in August 1945. Serving in divisions of infantry, armour and a fledgling airborne force, they fought on three continents: in Africa, Europe and Asia.

This Army fought in Ethiopia against the Italian Army, in Egypt, Libya, Tunisia and Algeria against both the Italian and German Army and, after the Italian surrender, against the German Army in Italy. However, the bulk of the British Indian Army was committed to fighting the Japanese Army, first during the British defeats in Malaya and the retreat from Burma to the Indian border; later, after resting and refitting for the victorious advance back into Burma, as part of the largest British Empire army ever formed. These campaigns cost the lives of over 87,000 Indian service- men, while another 34,354 were wounded, and 67,340 became prisoners of war. Their valour was recognised with the award of some 4,000 decorations, and 18 members of the British Indian Army were awarded the Victoria Cross or the George Cross.

RED EAGLES
The Story of the 4th Indian Division
9781474537520

During the Second World War, the 4th Indian Division was in the vanguard of nine campaigns in the Mediterranean theatre, Egypt, Eritrea, Syria, Tunisia, Italy and Greece. The 4th Division captured 150,000 prisoners and suffered 25,000 casualties, more than the strength of a whole division. It won over 1,000 honours and awards, which included four Victoria Crosses and three George Crosses. Field Marshal Lord Wavell wrote: "The fame of this Division will surely go down as one of the greatest fighting formations in military history."

THE FIGHTING FIFTH
History of the 5th Indian Division
9781474537513

As described in much greater detail in Anthony Brett James's book 'The Ball of Fire', the division saw active service in East Africa, North Africa and Burma.

GOLDEN ARROW
The Story of the 7th Indian Division
9781474537506

The role of this division is also duplicated by a much larger work the book by Brig. M. R. Roberts. However, this booklet gives a good account of Kohima and Imphal and the crossing of the Irrawaddy. In 1945, the division was flown into Siam, so becoming the first Allied formation to re-enter South East Asia.

BLACK CAT DIVISION
17th Indian Division
9781474537483

This formation was committed to Burma from the early days when the British were in full flight from the invading Japanese. It remained in Burma right through to the end, when the starving remnants of the Japanese Army were making their own desperate retreat.

ONE MORE RIVER
The Story of the 8th Indian Division
Biferno, Trigno, Sangro, Moro, Rapido, Arno, Senio, Santerno, Po, Adige
9781474537490

The 8th Indian Division started its overseas service in the Middle East in the garrisoning of Iraq and then the invasion of Persia to secure the oil fields of the area for the Allies, before moving to Italy in 1943. Landing at Taranto, it pushed up the length of the peninsula in a series of major battles: breaking the Sangro Line, forcing the Rapido and turning the defences at Cassino, breaking the stubborn German resistance at Monte Grande and, finally, forcing the Po River. It won four VCs, 26 DSOs and 149 MCs along the way. During the war the 8th Indian Division sustained casualties totalling 2,012 dead, 8,189 wounded and 749 missing.

TIGER HEAD
The Story of the 26th Indian Division
Arakan, Ragoon
9781474537452

This is a history of the division said later by the Japanese to have been the opponent which they most feared. The 26th held the Allied monsoon line in the Arakan during two such seasons, repulsing every attack launched against it. Later it made a series of leap-frog landings down the coast to clinch the issue in the Arakan. It was the first division to enter Ragoon, invading the city from the sea.

THE TWENTY THIRD INDIAN DIVISION
"The Fighting Cock Division"
Burma, Malaya, Java
9781474537469

The Fighting Cock Division is well recorded in the book by Doulton. This book gives coverage of the heavy fighting at the Kohima Battle, the capture of Tamu, the reoccupation of Malaya in August 1945, and then its strange role on the island of Java – concurrently disarming the Japanese garrison, fighting the insurgent Indonesian nationalists, and caring for 65,000 former internees pending the arrival of a new Dutch administration.

A HAPPY FAMILY
The Story of the Twentieth Indian Division,
9781474537476

One of the few Indian divisions in the 14th Army trained specifically for the war in Burma. Raised in Bangalore in 1942, it commenced active operations in late 1943 and served from Imphal through to the end. It established the 14th Army's first brigade-head across the Chindwin and its second such brigade-head across the Irrawaddy. Its final task was to round up the Japanese in French Indochina.

TEHERAN TO TRIESTE
The Story of the Tenth Indian Division
9781783317028

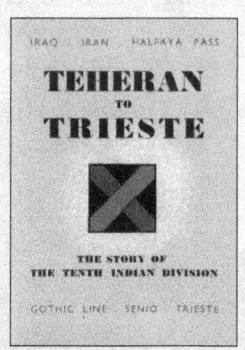

This History deals with the 10th Indian Div's exploits in Iraq (under Maj Gen "Bill" Slim) its role in the Libyan battles leading up to El Alamein, the following two years of garrison duties in Cyprus and Syria, and finally, its fighting services in the Italian campaign (from Ortona onwards).

THE STORY OF THE 25th INDIAN DIVSION
The Arakan Campaign
9781783317585

Formed in Southern India in August 1942 for defence of that area in case of Japanese invasion, the "Ace of Spades" Division had its baptism of fire in Arakan in February 1944. It served throughout the remainder of that campaign the climax being the battle of Tamandu. Its victorious fight for the Kangaw roadblock was considered by many to have been the fiercest battle of the entire Burma war, while its liberation of Akyab was the first convincing proof to the rest of the world that the tide had turned against the Japanese.

DAGGER DIVISION
The Story of the 19th Indian Division
9781783317035

Raised in the late 1941, the 19th was the first "standard" Indian Division. Its troops were the first to breach the Japanese defence line in Burma and to raise the flag at Fort Dufferin. It crossed the Chindwin in November 1944, driving on to Mandalay and Ragoon during seven months of continuous fighting. The 19th's exploits are graphically described also in John Masters' personal memoir, *The Road Past Mandalay*.

www.ingramcontent.com/pod-product-compliance
Lightning Source LLC
Chambersburg PA
CBHW060407300426
44111CB00018B/2852